TEXAS RANGERS, RANCHERS, AND REALTORS

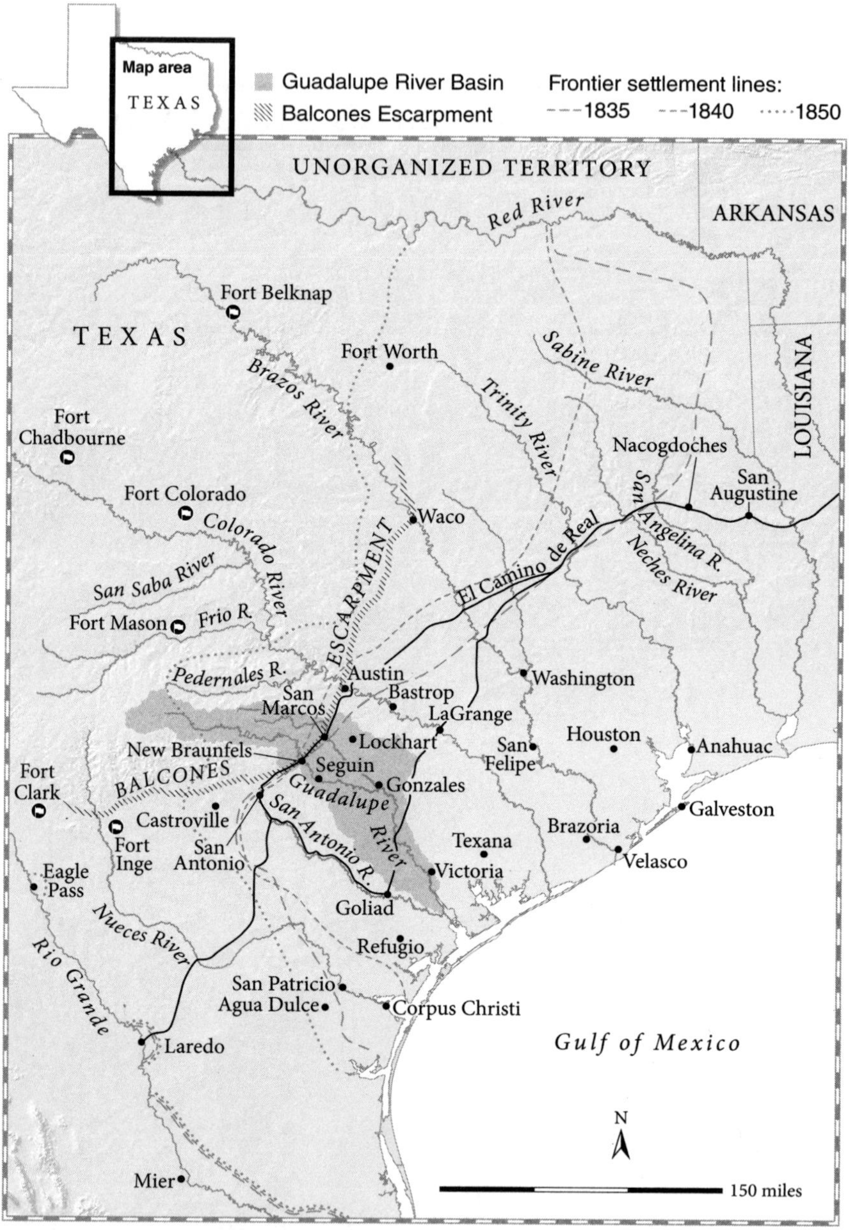

frontispiece. Texas map showing major roads in the 1830s; frontier settlement lines in 1835, 1840, and 1850; and key towns 1830–1860. Map by Carol Zuber-Mallison.

TEXAS RANGERS, RANCHERS, AND REALTORS

James Hughes Callahan and the Day Family in the Guadalupe River Basin

THOMAS O. McDONALD

UNIVERSITY OF OKLAHOMA PRESS : NORMAN

Library of Congress Cataloging-in-Publication Data

Names: McDonald, Thomas O., 1942– author.
Title: Texas rangers, ranchers, and realtors : James Hughes Callahan and the Day family in the Guadalupe River basin / Thomas O. McDonald.
Description: Norman : University of Oklahoma Press, [2021] | Includes bibliographical references and index. | Summary: "The lives of James Hughes Callahan, Sarah Medissa Day, and their extended families become a social history of nineteenth-century Texas during the days of the Revolution, the Republic, and early statehood"—Provided by publisher.
Identifiers: LCCN 2020041735 | ISBN 978-0-8061-6855-5 (hardcover)
Subjects: LCSH: Callahan, James (James Hughes), 1812–1856. | Day, Sarah Medissa, 1822–1857. | Day family. | Guadalupe River Watershed (Tex.)—History—19th century.
Classification: LCC F392.G863 M33 2021 | DDC 976.46—dc23
LC record available at https://lccn.loc.gov/2020041735

The paper in this book meets the guidelines for permanence and durability of the Committee on Production Guidelines for Book Longevity of the Council on Library Resources, Inc. ∞

10 9 8 7 6 5 4 3 2 1

Contents

Preface

"Your great-great-great-great-grandfather, was James Clinton Neill, spelled N-E-I-L-L and pronounced *Nail,* and he came to Texas in the 1820s." This was my grandfather's preamble to his saga about James Hughes Callahan, my great-great-great-grandfather, his wife, Sarah Medissa Day, and the Day family. From my boyhood until his death in 1979, O. B. Phillips, known to his family as Papa, regaled me with his colorful accounts of people, places, and adventures, and I began to seek confirmation of his oral history, my own family history. Thus, I embarked upon a journey that has spanned four decades, and has been a consistent feature of my adult life.[1]

The lives of James Hughes Callahan and Sarah Medissa Day form the central thread of this narrative, but it is more than a history of two individuals: it is a story about people, places, politics, cultures, and society. Sarah Medissa's mother, Sarah Hembree Day, and her brother and five sisters, along with their spouses, constitute a unique opportunity to explore an extended family's odyssey and their impact on a space in Texas. Individuals cannot be separated from the influences of their ancestors, family, or the people with whom they interact. They are also shaped by their physical and political environment and, in turn, they exert their own influence. These factors and stimuli transform an individual from a flat and two-dimensional character into a complex person who learns from experience, adjusts in attitude, and matures with age and responsibility. Myriads of people intersect during a lifetime, and the mainly plain folk with whom the Callahans and Days lived and worked left an indelible imprint on their lives and vice versa. As you read their story, remember this is a chronicle of people.

Fig. 0.1. Sarah Medissa Day Callahan. Author's collection.

It is also a narrative of a transforming Texas landscape, focused on the Guadalupe River Basin, which came to be punctuated with towns whose names reflected the cultural identity of the people living there, names like Victoria, Gonzales, Seguin, New Braunfels, Prairie Lea, Curry's Creek, Lockhart, San Marcos, and Pittsburg. At the eastern edge of the basin lies fertile black land ideal for growing cotton, sugarcane, hay, and vegetable crops. In the center, the rolling prairies sprout huge grasslands, divided by strips of oak forests, seemingly designed to support vast herds of cattle and horses. On the western edge looms the Balcones Escarpment, a succession of rocky hills and ridges that extend from Austin southward to San Antonio, then westward toward Eagle Pass on the Rio Grande, ultimately rising to form the Edwards Plateau. To the south an inhospitable chaparral stretches from the coastline north of Brownsville westward to the Pecos River. The various groups of people that lived in central and south Texas in the early 1800s were constantly challenged by the geography of the region, but their desire for land ownership or dominance was an incessant force driving the ambitions and determination of those who chose to settle there.

In controlling their natural environment, the Callahans, Days, and settlers like them were forced to compete against or cooperate with groups of people from other cultures, making this also a chronicle about Texas cultures. The Guadalupe River Basin is the specific region where the main narrative takes place. In the formative four decades before the American Civil War, it was a point of intersection for peoples of eight cultures—Texan, Texian, American Anglo (mainly from the South), European (mostly German), Tejano, Mexican, American Indian (principally Lipans, Tonkawas, and Comanches), and enslaved Africans. To clarify terminology, "Tejanos" were people of Hispanic heritage who were living in Texas and "Texians" were non-Hispanics residing in Texas prior to the annexation of Texas by the United States. This cultural milieu has been explored in various studies, though generally analyzed at a structural level and often through the lens of only one culture. However, an examination of interactions between members of the various groups on a local and personal level facilitates a different understanding of attitudes, prejudices, alliances, and aspirations. The unfolding lives of the Callahans and Days provide a canvas on which to explore the people and the communities of south-central Texas during the formative decades of the mid-nineteenth century.

Between 1820 and 1860, the inhabitants of the region, irrespective of their culture group, were rocked by events occurring on a wider plane. Political and social movements in Mexico and the United States shaped their experiences and viewpoints. The mores and attitudes of American Anglos who migrated to Texas melded in a cauldron that was tempered by the British colonial and American revolutionary periods, as well as a massive westward migration and the associated land distribution policies that saw the displacement of native Indians. Economic crises and, in the South, the establishment of the cotton industry and the expansion of slavery, reverberated through the relatively distant communities of south and central Texas as local politics weighed in on the debates over states' rights. The loss of Texas in 1836 became a national disgrace for Mexico, and the aftermath created a turbulent political scene for decades. Fear of invasion was a constant feature in the hearts and minds of Texians, particularly those closest to the Rio Grande border. The annexation of Texas by the United States and the subsequent war with Mexico in 1846 put Texas on the front pages of newspapers across America, and headlines touting the untold possibilities of the California gold rush enticed many Texans, including James Hughes Callahan. Events occurring at the national level in the United States and Mexico were also intertwined with local transformations. South and central Texas saw the growth of the region's cattle industry, the temperance and religious movement prompted a new style of moralism that included an antigambling attitude, and a wave of immigration from Germany gave rise to a nativist sentiment that intensified ethnic prejudice, particularly toward Tejanos and Mexicans. All of these factors affected the lives and perspectives of the Callahans, Days, and their neighbors in the valleys of the Guadalupe River Basin.

In my nearly forty-year journey through Texas history, five books in particular have influenced the scope and structure of my narrative. The eminent Texas historian Joseph Milton Nance set my standard for research in his two celebrated classics, *After San Jacinto* and *Attack and Counter-Attack.* I admire his depth of descriptive detail and wealth of sources. Three books focusing on families and a confined local area in south Texas provided a structural framework for my narrative: Ana Carolina Castillo Crimm's *DeLeón: A Tejano Family History;* Mary Margaret McAllen Amberson, John A. McAllen, and Margaret H. McAllen's *I Would Rather Sleep in Texas;* and Jane Clements Monday and Francis Brannen Vick's *Petra's Legacy.* My work here, to one extent or another, follows the approach laid out so elegantly by these accomplished authors. I do not claim to have met the standards set by these acclaimed narratives, but I do believe my effort makes a valuable and unique contribution to Texas history.

Besides being chronological, many chapters of my narrative are thematic, as the examination of individual lives exposes broader topics, such as land distribution in Texas, divorce, probate law, and the plight of orphans. The early chapters bring the Callahan and Day families from the colonies of British North America to Texas via the Carolinas and Georgia. The hardships and experiences of the young James Hughes and Sarah Medissa are reflected in their attitudes and prejudices as adults as they establish their lives in the newly independent nation of Texas. James Hughes's introduction to Texas was as a member of the Georgia Battalion, and it was his carpentry skills that saved him from the Goliad massacre. Settling in Gonzales and then Seguin, Sarah Medissa and her mother and siblings faced the everyday hazards of frontier life, and James Hughes's exploits with the Texas Rangers against invading Mexicans and Indian raids illustrate the response of the frontier communities to the threats they faced. The resolution of Sarah Medissa's complicated marital circumstances finally leads to her marriage to James Hughes Callahan. Meanwhile, the Guadalupe River Basin evolves from a primitive frontier to a more settled state with churches, towns, schools, and other markers of transition. Like many early Texans, the extended Day family members were also occupied by land acquisition and disposition and they and others seeking land moved the central and south Texas frontier westward in the 1840s and 1850s. During this time, the Callahans and their in-laws focused on cattle rather than cotton and Callahan himself took advantage of a financial opportunity to lead a cattle drive to California.

Back in Texas, the creation of the Callahans' land development plan along the Rio Blanco that led to the sensational 1855 Callahan Expedition is extensively explored. Using newly discovered primary sources, I present an updated interpretation of the motives and consequences of the expedition. While starting auspiciously, the expedition ended as a fiasco, adding to the existing tension between the U.S. and Mexican governments. Returning to his Rio Blanco farm and ranch, Callahan, sullen and disillusioned, was assassinated by a neighbor, resulting in a chain of events that began with an arrest and lynching and culminated in the prolonged prosecution of almost two dozen men. Sarah Medissa died only a few months after her husband, leaving five orphans and a complicated probate that persisted until 1870. In following the orphans until their deaths, their personal experiences illustrate a broader theme—the plight of Texas orphans. Lastly, the fate of the Sarah Hembree Day extended family is summarized.

I am confident my narrative brings a greater depth and clarity to our understanding of south and central Texas. I am sure Papa Phillips would have been proud to see his family history used in such a way. As I began my quest to confirm Papa Phillips's stories, I feared my education—a PhD in cell biology—had ill prepared me for historical research and writing. However, since much of my career had been spent as an executive in the research and development division of a pharmaceutical company, I was adept at collecting, organizing, and interpreting data. These skills served me well as I carried out my exhaustive research. The fabric of the Guadalupe River Basin and the lives of the Callahans and the Days are woven from hundreds of threads found in public records in county, state, and national archives, district courts, tax rolls, muster rolls, and land documents. These lives and events are given geographic and historical context using a wide range of sources including local and national newspapers, private letters, government reports from the United States and Mexico, a prayer journal, and Native American oral and scholarly histories. Each source is meticulously cited in the notes.

The result of this conscientious and painstaking approach is not trivial, but rather a comprehensive, complete, and balanced narrative of an extended family's odyssey in Texas. Examining their successes and failures, their hopes and dreams, their friendships and prejudices, creates a robust and nuanced impression of the development of the Guadalupe River Basin in mid-nineteenth-century Texas.

Acknowledgments

This exploration of James Hughes Callahan and the Day family is grounded in extensive research and the reader will find detailed citations in the notes to guide any further study they wish to undertake. Thousands of documents were accessed from sources as diverse as county deed and court records to personal correspondence held by a family in Hamburg, Germany, and a collection of work on Black Seminoles found in New York City and records kept in archives in Mexico. A work of this depth has not been completed singlehandedly and over the decades numerous individuals have assisted me in a multitude of ways, but they broadly fall into two categories: those who helped to collect the scattered and somewhat hidden source material and those who helped to interpret and organize it.

I owe an exceptional debt of gratitude to the researchers and archivists at many facilities including the Texas State Library and Archivcs, thc Dolph Briscoe Center for American History at the University of Texas in Austin, the Hargrett Rare Book and Manuscript Collection at the University of Georgia, the Beinecke Rare Book and Manuscript Library at Yale University, the Austin History Center, the state archives in Georgia and South Carolina, the Secretaría de la Defensa Nacional in Mexico City, and the state archives for Nuevo León and Coahuila in Mexico. Additionally, I am indebted to numerous individuals in various county offices who retrieved and sent me records, especially those in Gonzales, Caldwell, Comal, Guadalupe, and Blanco Counties. Special recognition goes to those researchers who unearthed crucial documents that filled gaps in the historical record. I must particularly recognize for their assistance and advice Ralph Elder, John Chapman, Joan Smalley, Lahnice Hollister, Terry Moore, Sue Cooper, William Hallmark, Kate Skinner-Klee, Caitlin Donnelly, Donaly Brice,

Bart Wales, Mike Miller, Linda Dieter, Beverly Wigley, Julia Cowart, Alice Adamczyk, Luis García, Miguel Muñoz Borrego, and José Medina González Dávila. To all those who diligently searched for and copied thousands of documents, I am immeasurably grateful.

I would be remiss not to recognize my good fortune to write this narrative at the time when a plethora of archived documents were digitized and placed in a readily accessible format by libraries, archives, and even in various commercial sources. Written words are inadequate to express my indebtedness to all of those who have the vision and skills to see that precious, friable historic documents are being digitally preserved and made accessible to the general public and historians.

The value of family history cannot be overlooked and I must acknowledge those who allowed me access to personal diaries, prayer journals, letters, and photographs. I particularly recognize JoBeth Gerrard, who possesses the rare documents of Sarah Hembree Day and her family; Billie Jo Nichols Bennett, who kindly offered information on the Nichols and Day families; Michael Gonzales, who lent records on the James Milford Day family; Robert Lundy, who gave copies of the Wuppermann diary and letters; Candice Ducoin, who possesses the William Early Jones family records; and José Medina González Dávila, who shared his ongoing oral history study of the Lipans living today in northern Coahuila, Mexico.

I am indebted to those who assisted me in interpreting my findings and organizing my thoughts. I sourced hundreds of pages of foreign languages and I thank Asta McCarthy for translating German documents, and José Medina González Dávila, Luis García, and Virginia Dias for their translation of Spanish records.

Several recognized historians read portions of the manuscript and I was rewarded by the critiques of Robert Davis, Craig Roell, Sam W. Haynes, Michael Collins, Rebecca Sharpless, Byron Price, James David Nichols, Luis García, Miguel Ángel González-Quiroga, and Ron Tyler. Some also spent hours listening to my musings and correcting me when I veered off course. Randolph Campbell, and later Andrew Torget, were always available when I needed to discuss perspectives on slavery in Texas. I would be remiss not to thank Laurie Jasinski and John Loffler, who helped me through the early stages of the writing process. As my manuscript matured, I was immensely fortunate to have the editorial oversight of Jenny Luke, Bonnie Lovell, and Susan Walters Schmid, who read and edited every page. It is impossible to express my gratitude to you all! Maps form an integral feature of my narrative and I depended upon the cartography expertise of Carol Zuber-Mallison. I had the good fortune to engage talented individuals to assist in tabulating and organizing data. My gratitude goes beyond just saying thanks to Shane Teveris, Iris Serinken, Erin Nishimura, and Alby Sack. I am enormously grateful to too many people to list by name, but to anyone who advised, searched, read, or assisted in any way, I give you credit. It has been too large an endeavor to undertake without assistance. However, any errors of fact or interpretation are mine alone.

I am a novice in writing and publishing a historical narrative. In my search for a publisher, my manuscript ended up on Kent Calder's desk. This fortunate event cannot be overstated. Kent was a rock-solid supporter with the most prudent advice as I struggled with my revision process. He also placed me in contact with Rick McCaslin, whose counsel kept encouraging my inquisitive exploration. In the inevitable revision process, Rick gave sage advice on condensation and composition. Kent and Rick, thanks ever so much!

One of my objectives in writing this detailed narrative based on thorough research is to be accurate and transparent in my citations. This forty-year mission has seen the advent of a technological revolution that has enormously increased the access and availability of documents and information. My substantial collection of sources and records will be placed in an archive so as to facilitate further research. In large part due to my scientific background, I have been frustrated by the neglect of some published historians to adequately cite their sources. Such would have been an extraordinary omission in the heavily regulated pharmaceutical industry in which I spent my professional career. With my records in a public archive, succeeding generations of historians may delve into the documents and form their own conclusions as to the validity of mine. This is the essence of the scientific principle, a process that applies to historical research just as well.

CHAPTER I

The Callahan Family in North Carolina and Georgia, 1760–1836

The stonecutter set aside the sandblasting nozzle and removed his goggles and mask. Sweeping the granite dust from the carved surface, he scrutinized the monument. At five and one-half feet, the tombstone as tall as he stood. Running his hands over the surface, he read:

JAS. HUGHES CALLAHAN
BORN NEAR MARION GA. SEPT. 10, 1814
DIED AT BLANCO, TEXAS APRIL 7, 1857
HIS WIFE, SARAH MEDISA
BORN DECEMBER 18, 1822
DIED SEPTEMBER 25, 1857
THEIR SON, WILLIAM MILFORD
BORN FEBRUARY 18, 1852
DIED SEPTEMBER 6, 1855

The craftsman was unaware the inscription contained errors. Callahan was neither born near Marion, Georgia, nor did he die on April 7, 1857. Moreover, his wife's death occurred in 1856, her middle name is misspelled, and it is almost certain that two sons, not one, are buried there. Similar mistakes, and myths, about Callahan and his family persisted after his death and have been cultivated by historians ever since.[1]

The inaccuracies on James and Sarah's tombstone in the Texas State Cemetery are difficult to explain. Mid-1850s newspaper accounts in Georgia and Texas confirm his birthplace as Jackson County, Georgia, and in 1907 Catherine Callahan, their oldest daughter, wrote to historian James T. DeShields that her father was born in Jefferson, Jackson County, Georgia, on September 10, 1814. Moreover, Sarah's date of death was also recorded in Texas newspapers.[2]

People are selected for burial in the Texas State Cemetery because they have contributed to Texas history. Callahan fought in the Texas Revolution, escaped the Goliad massacre, and led ranger patrols against Indian and Mexican incursions. Facts about Sarah are more obscure, yet as a fifteen-year-old she helped her mother, Sarah Hembree Day, and others establish the town of Seguin, despite having been abandoned by her first husband. As a married couple, the Callahans started two towns, helped establish churches and schools, and embarked on a land development project in south-central Texas.[3]

Any attempt to understand the Callahans must be rooted in the times in which they lived. Born and raised in Georgia and South Carolina during the early 1800s, their adult outlooks and attitudes were shaped by the turbulent times of their youth. Their mores were reinforced by what they learned from their parents and uncles and aunts, and what had been passed down from their ancestors, who had lived through the colonial, revolutionary, and formative periods of the United States.[4]

Callahan's Irish great-grandfather, John Callahan, was born in 1696 and by the 1740s he was in Pennsylvania. About 1760, he and his family settled in Rowan County, North Carolina, where he died in 1766. Two years later his son, Edward Callahan, James Hughes's grandfather, moved to Old Tryon County, later renamed Rutherford County, where he developed a homestead on 340 acres. Edward and his wife, Mary, led a simple life of subsistence farming, living in a log cabin and making do with handmade tools and furniture. Edward and his brother, William, sat out the Revolutionary War, though they became constables. An attempt to deliver a summons to a traitorous neighbor resulted in a bloody public fracas and indictments that were later dismissed. Seeking a more agreeable place, Edward sold his place in January 1783 and moved to Georgia, settling in Wilkes County on two headrights totaling 400 acres. Soon the families of his brothers William and John Jr. joined him. In 1796, the legislature designated part of Franklin County as Jackson County, and Edward moved his family north seventy-five miles to settle there. In April at a sheriff's sale he purchased 187½ acres on the North Fork of the Oconee River. During these years Mary gave birth to four boys and one daughter. She died in 1816, and Edward married again and moved to Maury County, Tennessee, where he died on January 21, 1821.[5]

Edward lived a simple life and seemingly avoided confrontation. Other than serving as a juror and constable, he never ventured far beyond his farm. However, he was well known and respected by neighbors and witnessed countless deed transactions. He did not engage in land speculation, but he did constantly move west in search of better opportunities, behavior that would surface again in his grandson, James Hughes Callahan.

Growing up, Edward's third son, James, learned the value of the hard work required of a frontier farmer. These first pioneers were simple men and women who survived many hazards and isolation, but they also congregated, gossiped, danced, raced horses, wagered, and drank whiskey. Community bonds were reinforced when Methodism entered Wilkes County during the late 1780s and attracted many converts. Religion played an important role in the lives of future Callahans, so it is worth noting that James, his parents, and his siblings made their first religious commitments to an itinerant Methodist missionary about this time.[6]

James, father of James Hughes Callahan, first appeared in the records of Jackson County on May 3, 1799, when he witnessed a land transaction, the first of many such documents he signed for neighbors and family members. Unlike many of his relatives, James never migrated or speculated in land. Nonetheless, he never missed a chance to enter Georgia's land lotteries. He did not win in the 1805 raffle, but in 1820 and 1821 he acquired parcels of land in neighboring Walton and Monroe Counties. He sold the Walton property, 250 acres, for $1,000 on April 2, 1825, and three months later sold the second tract for $200. In 1840, at the age of sixty-four and after thirty-five years as a subsistence farmer, James sold his 100-acre homestead in Jackson County for $500. One month later, he signed a $450 promissory note to his son John, pledging his horses, cattle, oxen, pigs, corn, bacon, and household furniture as collateral. James never explained these transactions; either he needed cash, or he had decided to retire.[7]

James and his wife, Mary, had at least thirteen children; their first, Margaret, was born November 20, 1805, and James Hughes Callahan arrived on September 10, 1814. It is worthwhile to explore the lives of James Hughes' siblings as some played an influential role in his life and those of his children. Seven of Mary and James's children never left Jackson County. John, their oldest son, married Nancy Lay, who delivered five children and died by 1846. John then wed Abrilla Sharpe, and she gave birth to one daughter in 1851. John did not speculate in land—he bought a fifty-acre farm in 1835 and sold it in 1844. He abandoned farming and established a successful wagon manufacture and repair business in Jefferson, where he died on May 24, 1874. The fourth daughter, Elizabeth, married William L. Street; they also resided in Jefferson until their deaths. A blacksmith, Street helped John in the wagon business. Fifth son Asbury Hill died at the age of twenty-two on August 20, 1845, and his twenty-year-old sister, Martha Caroline, died just one month later. Another daughter, Amanda, married Carlos Williams in Jackson County. Carlos worked as a laborer and had a personal estate of only fifty dollars by 1860, after which he and Amanda vanished from official records. The Callahans' second youngest daughter, Mary, wed a farmer, James Roberts, in Jackson County and she died in 1870. The youngest daughter, Sarah, never married, and is believed to have also died in Jackson County. Two Callahan daughters moved elsewhere in Georgia. The firstborn, Margaret, married Josiah Rounsavall in Jackson County. The couple moved to DeKalb County by 1830, then to Walton County before 1840, where Josiah farmed, finally settling in Walker County, in Georgia's northwest corner. Josiah died in 1850 and Margaret married Marcus Napoleon Bonaparte Jonathan Hampton Alley, a Walker County farmer and lawyer. Margaret died before 1863. James and Mary's second child, Nancy, married Alexander C. Hamilton. They first lived in Walton County, but by 1850, they had moved to Walker County and lived next door to Margaret.[8]

Three of James and Mary's sons, who engaged in the wagon manufacturing business, left Georgia for Chambers County, Alabama, and after the Civil War one migrated to north Texas. William, the second son, used his carpentry skills to establish a wagon shop. Complications from a fever cut his life short on January 16, 1860, but not before he named his first son James Hughes. James and Mary's fourth son, Josiah, followed his older sibling William to Chambers County and joined the wagon manufacturing venture; he died in 1851. Wesley, the youngest son, followed his brothers to Chambers County and became a partner in their wagon-making business. In April 1862, he joined the Forty-Seventh Alabama Infantry and went to Virginia, where he was debilitated by diarrhea and bronchitis. He received a medical discharge and returned to the family business. After his first wife died, he wed again and had four daughters. In the early 1870s, Wesley and his family moved to Collin County, Texas, where he died on July 12, 1892.[9]

It is germane that no male child of James and Mary Callahan chose farming as his livelihood. Instead, each, including James Hughes Callahan, became a wagon builder. Land was scarce by the time the Callahan sons reached manhood, and the only means of acquiring it was by purchase, lottery, or inheritance. Moreover, having witnessed their parents' constant struggle to eke out a living, they found farming tedious and unrewarding and looked for other options. As road networks expanded in the 1820s and 1830s, the demand for wheeled vehicles was high and their repair a constant necessity, so the Callahan brothers were fortunate in their choice of a craft. By 1860, almost 6,700 blacksmiths, carpenters, and mechanics worked in Georgia.[10]

James was a hardworking farmer who subsisted on his small homestead. His name never appeared in Jackson County court records except as a juror, and he paid his debts on time. His experience on the frontier shaped the outlook of his children, especially his sons. His first son, John, was described in his obituary as "a man of strong will, industrious habits, very frank in his disposition, a zealous Mason, a warm supporter of the temperance cause, an honest citizen, and for thirty-five years a member of the Methodist Church." All of John's siblings exhibited similar traits.[11]

While a child's habits, personality, and character are often shaped by his family, outside influences such as the political, social, and economic circumstances of the time also contribute. James Hughes Callahan was a literate man, so he must have been influenced by articles he read in the area's newspapers as well as by conversations with neighbors at militia training sessions, church meetings, and social gatherings. It was on the Georgia frontier that his character developed. Broadly speaking, this area was dominated by land acquisition and settlements, disputes with Indians, and slavery. On the personal level, civic duties, social events, religion, and education defined communities and shaped people's viewpoints. Understanding this context provides a more nuanced perspective on the attitudes and outlooks that James Hughes carried with him to Texas.

In the late 1700s, white settlements in Georgia were confined to the eastern and coastal areas of the state by the Creek and Cherokee homelands, but by 1838 most of the Indians had left. Both Edward's and James's families experienced firsthand the events surrounding the Indian departure, and James Hughes's views, like those of many other future Texans, were shaped by that experience. Despite repeated concessions from Indians, Anglo Georgians still insisted upon their right to confiscate territory occupied by Creeks and Cherokees. After twenty years of skirmishes with Georgia frontiersmen and federal troops, the Creeks capitulated in 1826 and began relocating west of the Mississippi River. Meanwhile, the Cherokees steadily assimilated into Anglo culture, becoming farmers and traders and maintaining peaceful relations with intruding whites. Many Cherokees intermarried with Anglos, attended schools in the eastern United States, and owned slaves. By the mid-1820s, the Cherokees had schools, a constitution, a legislature, and courts, many were Christians, and only a few raided Anglo settlements. But the invention of the cotton gin led to an explosion in cotton production across the South, and the valleys inhabited by the Cherokees became more desirable. When gold was discovered on tribal land in 1829, the final Cherokee exodus of 1838 was set in motion, becoming a part of the series of forced Indian relocations referred to as the Trail of Tears.[12]

As the Indians ceded land, the Georgia government devised various ways to distribute it. On May 11, 1803, the legislature established a land lottery, with lotteries in 1805, 1807, 1820, 1821, 1827, 1833, and two in 1832. The Callahans signed up for every one of them. Over one hundred thousand Anglos claimed three-fourths of Georgia's land. John drew a lucky number in the 1820 lottery for 250 acres in Early County, and after his death his widow and eight children qualified in 1827 and 1832, winning a 160-acre parcel in the Cherokee districts and a 202½-acre tract in Muscogee County. His father, James, drew lucky numbers in 1820 and 1821, and Jacob won 200-acre and 40-acre plots in the 1825 and 1832 lotteries. In all cases, the Callahans sold their allotted land. James Hughes was eligible for both the 1832 and the 1833 lotteries, but he did not win. However, he learned how land was accumulated in Georgia. He also surely shared his fellow Georgians' belief that Indian lands should be owned and occupied by Anglos. James Hughes Callahan did not forget this lesson, nor did other Georgians who ultimately moved to Texas.[13]

Conflict between Anglos and Indians in Georgia also influenced frontier settlers in other ways. In 1796, the federal government began compensating settlers who lost property during Indian raids. Edward and his sons reported no losses, but over one hundred of their neighbors did, mostly stolen horses. From the late 1790s to the late 1820s, newspapers published numerous articles about Creek depredations and a few articles about Cherokee raids. Despite not witnessing Indian raids, Edward's grandson James Hughes surely read newspaper reports and overheard discussions of Creek and Cherokee barbarity, as defined by Georgians. Consequently, as will be seen during his time in Texas, he learned to mistrust Indians and adopted the prevailing attitude that they were inferior to Anglos.[14]

Slavery also influenced James Hughes's perspective on the world. Slavery was woven into the fabric of life in Jackson County as Georgia's cotton production increased from 1,000 bales in 1790 to 326,000 by 1839. By 1830 the enslaved population (220,000) almost equaled the white population (297,000). Jackson County, where James Hughes spent his youth, had almost 2,000 slaves in 1820 and 2,700 in 1830. Even though his father never owned a slave, in 1820 fourteen of twenty-one neighbors did. The Methodist Conference of the South, with which the Callahans' church was affiliated, recognized slavery as morally acceptable, and the Reverend James Glenn of the Antioch Methodist Church in the Callahans' parish owned four slaves in 1820 and eight in 1830. James Hughes undoubtedly read articles in local newspapers announcing slave sales, defending slavery, criticizing northern abolitionists, and promoting nullification and states' rights. By the time he was grown, he accepted the view of most Georgians that blacks existed to serve whites. However, because his family survived without slaves, he understood that land ownership alone was itself a means to financial security and independence.[15]

James Hughes was able to read newspapers because he was literate. Georgia had a partially funded system of education comprising state, local, and church-administered schools; in 1793 Wilkes County had free public schools for white children. He attended school in Jackson County, which had several free schools, including one at the Antioch Methodist Church, three miles from his home. He and his classmates learned the fundamentals of reading, writing, spelling, geography, and arithmetic. Textbooks were rare; however, *Webster's Elementary Spelling Book, Murray's English Reader, Woodbridge's Universal Geography,* and the *Federal Calculator* were found in early Georgia schools. James's siblings John, Wesley, and Mary claimed in the 1870 census that they could read and write. Although James Hughes was long since dead by that time, he had earlier demonstrated his ability in financial tabulations and handwritten letters. His writing was distinctive and clear, and his sentences were grammatically correct.[16]

As mentioned earlier, the Callahans were churchgoing Methodists. Edward's arrival in Wilkes County coincided with a second Methodist conference held there; within two years, the Methodist Church reported 430 members in the county. Methodism was also popular in Jackson County, where circuit-riding ministers were assigned, and in 1812 the second Methodist Sunday School opened there. The residents were reported to be "good, Christian, God-fearing people." The Antioch Methodist Church was established in Jackson County in 1799, about three miles east of the Callahan homestead. Edward and his family were probably founding members, and subsequent generations of Callahans continued to worship there, including James Hughes, who remained a Methodist throughout his life. Like his father, James, he even named two of his sons, Wesley and Asbury, after the two prominent Methodist circuit riders.[17]

Being a white man in the antebellum United States came with civic obligations, one of which was serving in the militia. In Georgia all white men aged sixteen to fifty were required to join, with each man providing his own weapons and mustering four times per year for training. Each company elected its captain, and this same procedure was used to select commanders at the battalion, regiment, and division levels. Each justice of the peace precinct was a militia district, and the captain of each company supplied the names of his men to the county tax collector and helped collect taxes. During elections, county officials designated voting sites within each militia district. Road teams—organized to construct or repair roads—were chosen from men within each militia district. Militia training also served other purposes. In addition to military drills, the men socialized, gossiped, drank whiskey, and heard election speeches.[18]

The Callahans also lived in a world organized loosely into classes, though on the frontier the lines between them often shifted. As self-sufficient farmers they belonged to a middle class that included craftsmen, merchants, teachers, and physicians who composed the majority of Georgia's Anglo society. Above them in the antebellum hierarchy were planters, a small segment of the state's population, and below them were the poorest whites, often called "Crackers," who were one-fourth of the white population. Historian Kenneth Coleman concluded it was the small artisan class together with the yeomanry that formed the backbone of Georgia's economic and social development. Although humble by nature, these hard-working folks exuded self-confidence. James Callahan's family clearly fit this description.[19]

Outside of work, the James Callahan family played an active role in the community, attending church and social events. Augustus B. Longstreet, a contemporary and discerning chronicler of Georgians' behavior in the early 1800s, humorously described dances, horse trading, singing, gander pulling, debates, shooting contests, political gatherings, and hunts. Men hunted and fished, held shooting contests and barn raisings, and used the militia muster to drink, gamble, and gossip. Women gathered to quilt, weave, sew, prepare food, and talk. Occasionally the whole community came together for weddings, cornhusking, dances, and logrolling. Whiskey was often the drink of choice, but the Methodist Callahans believed in temperance. Later, James

Hughes's Texas friends noted that he also seldom uttered a profanity, which did not fit the norm at Georgia's social events. He did, however, enjoy dancing, a pleasure he had learned during his early days in Georgia.[20]

James Hughes Callahan was certainly shaped by his life in the backcountry of Jackson County, Georgia. He attended school and left home a committed Methodist who neither drank nor cursed, although he did smoke a pipe. On hunting excursions, in shooting contests, and at militia musters, he showed his skills with a rifle. Moreover, he learned the basics of military organization and logistics, as well as the basics of leadership. He understood the essentials of animal husbandry and how to plant and harvest crops. Like his brothers, he had a trade—carpentry and wagon-building—that would prove vitally important during his time in Texas; these skills would save his life. He understood that his role in society involved an obligation to participate in local government and pay taxes. He also accepted his superiority over Indians and slaves. Thus, he departed Georgia with an outlook typical for many Anglos who embraced the westward movement in the United States during what would later be known as the Jacksonian era. Through the experiences of his ancestors, James Hughes believed that land ownership was the best path to financial security and independence and he had all the makings of a successful land developer. He carried these qualities with him in October 1835 as he left on an uncertain journey to Texas.

CHAPTER 2

The Georgia Battalion, 1835–1836

"Texas needed SOLDIERS, *not* resolutions*"*

On June 16, 1836, the crew of the *Pennsylvania* slipped the mooring lines as Samuel Collings took the helm to pilot his schooner away from Velasco, Texas, headed east toward New Orleans. Under the spell of the vessel's motion, the passengers settled into their own worlds. Most were veterans of the Texas Revolution; several had survived by chance while others had dodged a firing squad's bullets. Discharged, these ex-soldiers were returning to their homes in the United States. But one man, Colonel Juan José (Johann Josef) Holzinger, a German native and paroled Mexican army officer captured by the Texians, stood out. He had fought at Refugio and Coleto, and he, more than anyone else, had intervened to save prisoners of the Mexican army. Several rescued men spoke with him on the *Pennsylvania.* Although Holzinger had also saved his life, James Hughes Callahan, a man of few words, contributed little to the conversation. He probably listened closely, though, because much of what had happened would shape his future.[1]

In the fall of 1835, emotions from Texas had spilled over into the United States, pulling countless Americans, including Callahan, into the Texas Revolution. By that time, some 25,000 Anglos inhabited what would ultimately become present-day Texas, laying the foundation for a violent conflict. The Constitution of 1824 in Mexico had delegated autonomy to the states during a decade of settlement and conflict in Texas, which was increasingly regarded with suspicion by the central government. When Antonio López de Santa Anna became president, he abolished the Constitution and centralized the government, angering many regional leaders, including Texians. On

October 2, 1835, conflict erupted at Gonzales, fifty miles east of San Antonio de Béxar, when Mexican cavalrymen attempted to retrieve a borrowed cannon. Days later, Texians captured the presidio at Goliad and a ragtag army marched for San Antonio. The Siege of Bexar ended with the capture of the town in December 1835 and the surrender of General Martin Perfecto de Cos, whom Santa Anna had sent to crush the rebellion.[2]

Newspapers in the United States applauded the Texian triumph, and many communities, particularly in the South, sent money, supplies, and weapons to Texas, as well as men itching to fight. In Georgia, prominent leaders organized and equipped the Georgia Battalion. Georgians were well informed about Texas thanks to papers like the *Athens Athenian*, *Southern Banner*, *Macon Telegraph*, *Columbus Enquirer*, *Augusta Chronicle*, and *Milledgeville Reflector*. Texas politics received special attention; the *Telegraph* in 1834 labeled Santa Anna as "traitorous and hypocritical." An alarming letter in the *Enquirer* on September 25, 1835, predicted that Texans would declare independence and that Santa Anna had promised to dispatch 10,000 troops to stop them; the anonymous writer, probably James W. Fannin Jr., asked his fellow Georgians for help. The twenty-one-year-old Callahan was captivated by reports of Texas events. In November 1835 he quit his work as a coach maker and joined the Georgia Battalion.[3]

The news of the clash at Gonzales reached Georgia in November. Posted around Macon, a broadside with the headline "Texas and Liberty" attracted a crowd on November 10, 1835. Perhaps they had heard of a similar meeting in Mobile, Alabama, where $1,500 was raised and Alabama volunteers had already left Mobile and Huntsville for Texas. Dignitaries at the Macon meeting, including Lt. Hugh McLeod, a recent graduate of West Point, called for immediate action. McLeod declared "the struggle in Texas needed SOLDIERS, not *resolutions*," and he pledged to resign from the U.S. Army and volunteer. Among that evening's twenty-nine volunteers were William A. Ward, elected as the commander; Uriah Irwin Bullock, a company captain; and James Smith and John O. Allen, future privates in Capt. James Cochran Winn's company. The meeting ended after $3,141 had been collected. The emotional intensity led the editor of the *Telegraph* to write, "The Texas Fever had treated us worse than the Cholera! Our office is completely swept! Journeymen and apprentices, men and boys, devils and angels, are all gone to Texas. If our readers get an empty sheet or no sheet at all, don't blame us." Two days after the meeting, Ward advertised in the *Telegraph* asking volunteers to meet on the 18th. At a November 17 meeting in Girard,

Alabama, across the Chattahoochee River from Columbus, Georgia, thirty-five men, mostly Georgians, enlisted and elected William A. O. Wadsworth as their commander. Ward meanwhile journeyed to Milledgeville, where he encouraged local men to join him in defending Texas. Many did, including James C. Winn, son of prominent Gwinnett County politician Elisha Winn. During his stay in the Georgia capital, Ward also borrowed enough army-issue Yager rifles from the state arsenal to arm his recruits.[4]

Shortly after November 18, Ward led about eighty Macon and Milledgeville volunteers, including Callahan, to Columbus and on to Montgomery, Alabama, where they joined with other Georgia Battalion recruits. During the trip the volunteers stopped in Knoxville, Georgia, where the townsfolk prepared a feast and, inspired by McLeod, fifteen-year-old Joanna Troutman made a flag of white silk adorned with a solitary large blue star. Stitched on one side was "Liberty or Death" and on the other "*Ubi libertas habitat, ibi nostra patria est*" (Where liberty dwells, there is our country). The banner was delivered to Ward's men in Montgomery, and McLeod thanked Troutman with a letter assuring her that her work would "wave over fields of victory in defiance of despotism." By that time, Ward's weary command, including Callahan, had marched eighty miles in just a few days over bad roads to join Wadsworth on the last day of November.[5]

Montgomery feted the Georgia volunteers in the city's Shakespeare Theatre, where an oration by H. J. Harwell proposed that the Texas situation paralleled what the United States had faced with England in 1776. A committee undertook to collect money and to "furnish . . . clothes, arms, and ammunition." Fifteen men from the Montgomery area led by Isaac Ticknor enrolled; two of these, John Oliver and George Eubanks, later joined Winn's company. McLeod began to train the inexperienced troops, but he remained in Montgomery when on December 1 Ward and his men clambered aboard the steamer *Ben Franklin* to travel down the Alabama River to Mobile. William Fairfax Gray recalled the trip usually took two days, for which the steamer's captain, H. S. Slade, charged $15. Ward's recruits traveled free of charge, and Slade joined in entertaining them. After they arrived in Mobile, a committee wrote a letter that publicly recognized the patriotism and generosity of Slade and the crew of *Ben Franklin*. Slade declared it was his pleasure to assist "the brave and patriotic band of emigrants to Texas from Georgia in the merited cause of freedom and the rights of man." Of the 120 men listed on the *Ben Franklin*'s manifest, ninety-one joined Ward's battalion; thirty-four, including Callahan, mustered into Winn's company.[6]

At Mobile, Ward's men attended a feast provided by local citizens, and Ward recruited seventeen more volunteers. On December 6, his men scrambled aboard Captain Sutton's *Convoy* for the two-day voyage to New Orleans. The New Orleans *Commercial Bulletin* listed ninety-nine deck passengers, presumably all in Ward's contingent, and reported eight additional men that later joined the Georgia Battalion. New Orleans had become a hub for money, matériel, and men destined for the Texas Revolution, so Ward's recruits were not the only ones looking for transportation west while local merchants bickered—one group sent aid to Texas while the other tried to protect their lucrative Mexico trade. As setbacks for Texians increased, New Orleans became a prime sanctuary for refugees, and throughout the conflict, land speculators swarmed the city looking for bargains to buy from exiled Texians. In sum, New Orleans must have been an eye-opening experience for many of Ward's recruits, including Callahan. While his men gawked, Ward bought supplies and made transportation arrangements. He had $8,500 to spend, which included $2,700 contributed by Macon benefactors, funds collected in Montgomery and Mobile, and his own $5,600. He may well have collected additional money in New Orleans from Texas financial backers. A likely member of that group would have been William Christy, and the group often met at Banks' Arcade, a three-story, red brick office and store complex, which served as the meeting site for supporters of the Texas Revolution. There Ward surely met with Christy and others who contributed money and information. After the provisions had been arranged, 135 men, including twenty-seven collected in New Orleans, tramped aboard the schooner *Pennsylvania*. Authorities cleared the ship for departure on December 12, 1835. On the day they departed, the *Commercial Bulletin* reported that General Cos had surrendered, and Mexican soldiers were deserting.[7]

Callahan sailed to Texas with the Georgia Battalion, but Captain Delarue, the *Pennsylvania*'s skipper, deliberately neglected to mention his passengers when filling out his manifest. According to the paperwork, he carried only "ballast." Military support of a foreign rebellion was a violation of federal neutrality laws, which a court confirmed in December 1835. Thus Slade, master of the *Ben Franklin*, listed Ward's volunteers as "emigrants to Texas from Georgia"; the *Commercial Bulletin* included them among the deck passengers on Sutton's *Convoy*; and Delarue did not report them at all. In the Gulf of Mexico, other vessels also had their prows pointed toward Velasco (see map frontispiece). Capt. J. H. Graham guided the schooner *Santiago* westward with fifteen recruits; the schooner *America* under Captain Miner had cleared New York for Texas with John Sowers Brooks (a recently resigned U.S. Marine) and other volunteers on board; and the *Camanche* also left New York with even more recruits. On December 20, all four ships arrived at Velasco carrying a total of 220 volunteers. Three docked safely, but the *America* foundered and nearly capsized, and Brooks lost most of his baggage. Velasco was not impressive; it contained a few log huts situated on a "low marshy perrary [prairie]." Ward's men debarked, marched upstream three miles, and camped. They learned that while San Antonio had fallen, General Jose Antonio Mexía's landing at Tampico had failed and most of the Americans involved had been executed. Rumors circulated that the Texans would attack Matamoros, and that Santa Anna was boasting he would invade Texas with a force of 10,000 men. Callahan and his colleagues thus had every reason to believe a fight lay ahead.[8]

Ward traveled to San Felipe, the seat of the Texas government, to report the Georgians had arrived. After being commissioned into the Texas volunteer army, he returned to Velasco, where, on December 23, he and his officers wrote to Colonel Fannin pledging their "honor and preferment" as the "Georgia battalion." On Christmas Day, Fannin greeted them as "brothers in arms" and welcomed them to Texas. The Georgians organized and elected Ward as major in command of the battalion; Wadsworth, Bullock, and Winn became captains of three companies. Callahan was elected the third, or orderly, sergeant in Winn's company of fifty-four men. His subsequent experiences with the Georgia Battalion significantly shaped his future in Texas.[9]

Callahan's commanders in the Texas Revolution had a great impact on him. Fannin, just thirty years of age, had briefly attended West Point, fought at Gonzales, and led a company in the Siege of Bexar before the Texas government chose him to lead the Matamoros Expedition. He was brave in combat, but his letters reveal a lack of self-confidence, which would lead to indecision and tragedy. Ward was, like Fannin, a native Georgian about thirty years of age; he had no military experience but owned land and slaves and practiced law. That being said, all evidence indicates that he was a brave leader whom the Georgia volunteers respected. Winn, also a Georgia native, was born in 1812 and served as an ensign in the Gwinnett County militia from 1827 through 1830. Considering that Callahan lived in Jackson County near the Winns, he and Winn may have known each other before the Texas Revolution.[10]

In January 1836, two former members of the U.S. military, Lieutenant Brooks and Joseph M. Chadwick, trained the 600 to 700 volunteers at Velasco. In a letter to his sister, Brooks expressed his frustration with their inexperience and complained about having to drill the officers too. But the Georgia Battalion, which also received night training, impressed him. Hard work made them hungry. Corp. Samuel T. Brown of Bullock's company, recalled that in one month the men consumed the two months' provisions purchased by Ward. As Pvt. Daniel Baugh Brooks told his father, the men also devoured wild hogs, cattle, deer, fish, and shellfish. The Georgians enjoyed their liquor too, as they bought forty gallons of whiskey in early January. Moreover, the ranks remained mostly free of illness as the surgeons confined only eight to the hospital. Private Brooks might have been speaking for all when he asserted, "My health is better than it has been of late. I weigh more now than I have at any former period of my life."[11]

The excitement faded quickly for some. As 1836 commenced, the Georgia Battalion had 153 men, but by the end of January twenty had deserted. Eleven volunteers left Winn's company during this period, giving it a desertion rate of 22 percent, the highest in the battalion. Most of these men joined other Texas units, including six of the eleven from Winn's unit. Meanwhile, Capt. Isaac Ticknor's company of forty-four men from Montgomery joined Ward's Georgians, arriving at Velasco on January 18 aboard the schooner *Flora.* By the end of January, as Fannin prepared to embark on the Matamoros Expedition, the Georgia Battalion had 119 volunteers fit for duty, including Winn's company, reduced to forty men since three invalids remained at Velasco (table 2.1).[12]

On January 23, 1836, Fannin's troops boarded the schooners *Columbus* and *Flora* for the voyage to Copano (map 2.1), where Fannin had ordered several men to procure oxen-pulled carts and wait. The vessels docked at Copano on January 30 or February 1, after a strong wind delayed their crossing of the bar. Joseph T. Williams, of Bullock's company, told the *Southern Recorder* that the eight-day trip was boisterous and disagreeable. Copano must have presented a desolate sight with its solitary warehouse and the hull of a wrecked ship in the harbor. Waiting on shore, Hermann Ehrenberg of the New Orleans Greys described Ward's Georgians as "herculean and muscular figures" dressed "in brown hunting shirts and trousers and . . . well armed with pistols and guns." More important for Callahan, when he disembarked, he met Edward Craddock Pettus, who would later play a major

Table 2.1. Muster roll, Capt. James C. Winn's company upon enrollment, Velasco, Tex., Dec. 23, 1835, and their fates thereafter

Name/rank/age	*Residence*	*Remarks*
Deserted or left company at Velasco, Jan. 5–22, 1836		
John O. Allen, Pvt.	Bibb Co., Ga.	Served in Texas Navy on *Invincible*
N. R. Allen, Pvt.		Sick at Velasco
Reason Green Banks, Pvt.	Baldwin Co., Ga.	Joined Texas Army, Mar. 3, 1836; fought at San Jacinto
William Duncan, Pvt.	Talbot or Marion Co., Ga.	Texas Army, June–Sept. 1836; returned to Ga., dead by 1838
John T. Garner, Pvt.		
James (Livingston) B. Grice, Pvt., 25	Ala.	Fought at San Jacinto
Smith L. Havens, Pvt.		Texas Army, Mar.–June 1836
Abraham Lewis, Pvt.		Texas Army, Mar.–Sept. 1836; fought at San Jacinto
David Tarvin, Pvt.		
Durant West, Pvt.		
John Williams, Pvt.		
Left sick at Velasco when company sailed for Copano, ca. Feb. 1, 1836		
Allen Burks, Pvt.		Fought at San Jacinto
Aaron Samuel Mangum, Pvt., 24	Fulton Co., Ga.	Joined Texas Army; died Aug. 9, 1884, Sherman, Tex.
William W. Yearly, Pvt.		Davenport said Yearly deserted but returned to Winn's Co.; Miller claimed Yearly died in Goliad Massacre
Transferred at Goliad to regular service (Westover's Co.), Feb. 29, 1836; survivors of ill-fated Tampico Expedition		
Robert English, Pvt.		Massacred at Goliad, Mar. 27, 1836
E. J. D. Greynolds (Grinolds), Pvt.		Massacred at Goliad, Mar. 27, 1836
Henry Lewis Schultz, Pvt.		Massacred at Goliad, Mar. 27, 1836
Absent when company marched from Goliad to Refugio, Mar. 12–17, 1836		
John Barton, Pvt., 19?	Cincinnati, Ohio	Born in Ireland (?); fought at San Jacinto (?); Texas Army (?)

Name/rank/age	*Residence*	*Remarks*
Wounded at Refugio Mission, Mar. 14, 1836; remained when company withdrew, evening of Mar. 14, 1836		
William Shelton, Pvt., 15	Miss.	Bayoneted by Mexican troops, morning of Mar. 15, 1836
Christopher Winters, Pvt., 25		Bayoneted by Mexican troops, morning of Mar. 15, 1836
Captured near Refugio, Mar. 15–16, 1836		
Daniel Baugh Brooks, 2nd Lt., 21	Bibb Co., Ga.	Shot by Mexican troops, ca. Mar. 23, 1836
Separated from company during retreat from Refugio, Mar. 21, 1836		
John (Jonathan) Bright, Pvt.	Pitt Co., N.C.	Fought at Bexar, 1835; joined Winn's Co.; escaped; joined Texas Army
Martin Moran, Pvt., 18–20	Bibb Co., Ga.	Escaped; discharged from Texas Army, May 18, 1836; reenlisted to 1841
Surrendered near Dimitt's Landing, Mar. 22, 1836; chosen by Colonel Holzinger to remain at Victoria to build or repair boats		
James Hughes Callahan, 3rd Sgt., 21	Jackson Co., Ga.	Escaped ca. May 25, 1836; S. T. Brown said he saw Callahan at Victoria, ca. May 1, 1836

Sources: Allen, John O., Allen, N. R., Barton, John, Bright, John, Grice, James B., Grinolds, E. J. D., Moran, Martin, Box 2R245, KC, CAH; *Macon Weekly Telegraph*, Nov. 12, 1835; *Georgian*, Dec. 3, 1836; "Comments . . . in biographies of Fannin's men," DHC, TSLA; Kemp, "Veteran Biographies," Herzstein Library, San Jacinto; Last and first names, Land Grant Search, TGLO; New Orleans Passenger List, 1820–1945, RG 36, M259, R14, NAB; Havens, Smith L., File 000485, TGLO; *Daily Democrat*, Aug. 18, 1836; Speer and Brown, *Encyclopedia of the New West,* 408–9; T. Miller, "Fannin's Men," 532; Gammel, *Laws of Texas*, 3:681, 4:1183; S. Crosby to the Texas legislature, petition, Nov. 19, 1857, DHP; *Texas State Gazette,* Nov. 23, 1850, June 18, 1853; Literary Effort: "Sabina Brown's Mournful Story," DHC, TSLA; Mona Macy, Winters family descendant, e-mail, 2010; *Austin City Gazette*, Feb. 17, 1841; Mrs. W. C. Jones Sr. to Harriett Smither, letter, Jan. 27, 1936, HDP, CAH; Robert Casey, Brooks family researcher, e-mail, 2010; Casey and Casey, *Brooks Family History*, 7-212–7-214, 7-418–7-420; Brown, *History of Texas,* 1:628; *Voice of Sumter*, Nov. 28, 1837; *South-Western American*, June 8, 1853; *Georgia Citizen*, Apr. 23, 1853; Jenkins, *Papers*, 3:305–6, 322–23; Odintz, "Bullock, Uriah Irwin"; Davenport, "Notes from an Unfinished Study"; Davenport, "Men of Goliad," 1–41.

role in his life. It took several days to unload materials and reload them on the oxcarts. While some of the men did this, the remainder marched fifteen miles west to Refugio, where the officers established headquarters in the old mission of Nuestra Señora del Refugio (figure 2.1). Ehrenberg vividly recalled seeing the unique flag borne by the Georgia Battalion. At Refugio, Fannin decided to reorganize into a regiment, and in an election

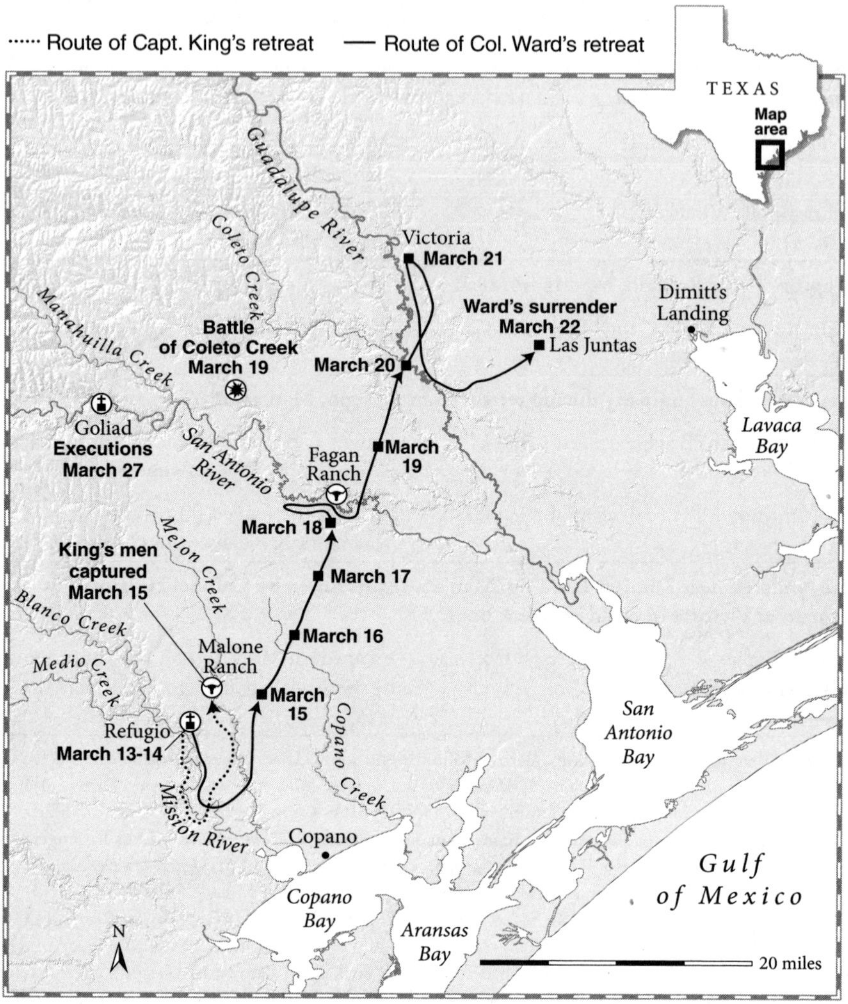

Map 2.1. Route of Colonel Ward and Captain King's retreat from Refugio, March 1836. Map by Carol Zuber-Mallison.

on February7, the men chose him as colonel and Ward as lieutenant colonel. Ticknor's company of forty-four men joined Ward's volunteers and the unit officially became the Georgia Battalion, while the remaining companies merged as the Lafayette Battalion. With Ward on the regimental staff, his men elected Dr. Warren Jordan Mitchell as his replacement. In Winn's company, Mitchell received twenty-one votes to Joseph M. Chadwick's twenty. At this point, the Georgia Battalion contained 163 men.[13]

Fig. 2.1. Refugio Mission, entrance, west side. Drawing by Juan E. Garcia commissioned by author. Author's collection.

In his January 4 letter, Fannin had declared he would conduct the Matamoros Expedition, and four days later he ordered his volunteers to rendezvous at San Patricio. But after arriving at Copano, he received several pieces of intelligence that drastically changed his opinion. The first arrived on February 6 from San Patricio, reporting that 1,000 Mexican soldiers led by General José C. Urrea would soon cross the Rio Grande at Matamoros. Fannin also learned that two schooners carrying more men, provisions, weapons, and munitions would not arrive—one had foundered on the sandbar at Velasco and a second had sunk in Matagorda Bay. During this time, Plácido Benavides, in Matamoros to rescue his captured brother-in-law, heard that the Mexican strategy was to lure Texian forces to Matamoros, where they could be defeated, and he reported this to Fannin. Fannin then abandoned plans to invade Matamoros and instead decided to proceed to and fortify the Goliad presidio and wait for Urrea (see map frontispiece).[14]

The Georgia Battalion joined the Lafayette Battalion for the march to Goliad, where they occupied the presidio, renamed Fort Defiance, on February 14. Brooks and Chadwick directed squads of soldiers as they strengthened walls, dug trenches, positioned cannons, and fortified the compound. Meanwhile, another 150 volunteers arrived, and Fannin faced challenges from two subordinates, James Grant and Francis White Johnson. Neither wanted to abandon Matamoros, so they kept independent commands, ostensibly to search for horses and act as scouts. Fannin vacillated. The first sign that he considered Goliad untenable came on February 18, when he took a trip to evaluate the possibility of withdrawing to Cox's Point or Dimitt's Landing but returned days later undecided what to do. On February 25, he received an appeal for help from William Barrett Travis, commanding at the Alamo, which was being enveloped by Santa Anna and 5,000 soldiers. Fannin marched the next day with 320 men, including the Georgia Battalion, but traveled only two miles before his wagons broke down, the oxen ran amok, and discipline vanished. After a night of freezing rain and sleet, and an officers' conference on the morning of the 27th, Fannin led them back to Fort Defiance. By this time, the Georgia Battalion was hungry, barefoot, ill-clothed, and doubting Fannin. Surgeon Joseph H. Barnard wrote of "discontent and murmurs and loss of confidence in their commander," which caused Fannin to ask to be relieved of command, blaming "circumstances . . . where I cannot retreat, but in disgrace." However, even in these dire straits, the volunteers commented on the fertile countryside and counted the acreage Texas would award them for their service. Callahan surely must have had similar thoughts.[15]

Despite the miserable conditions, some volunteers seemed to enjoy themselves, and most remained defiant. Private Brooks had the measles but claimed to have been cured. Capt. Burr H. Duval wrote, "You could at night hear the boys crowing, gobling, barking, bellowing, laughing and singing you would think them the happiest and best fed men in the world." The Georgians, fueled in part by seventy gallons of whiskey they received in mid-February, contributed to the raucous behavior. Occasionally a sense of realism emerged; Lieutenant Brooks admitted to his father that he anticipated defeat and to his sister, Brooks bluntly noted that he was in "a war of extermination." Concerning the enemy, Duval said his comrades never thought of retreat or surrender while lieutenants Thomas B. Rees and Benjamin Bradford anticipated an attack and noted the enemy did not accept surrender. Being a temperate man, Callahan probably did not engage in the drinking and raucous behavior, but he certainly understood the gravity of his circumstances, and he proved ready to fight. After Fannin marched back to Fort Defiance, his soldiers strengthened the defenses and mounted more cannons. He realized retreat was the prudent course of action, but he lacked the courage to order it and instead in his dispatches hinted at its necessity, hoping superiors would issue the order. Meanwhile, several in Winn's company requested reassignment. Three privates, Henry Lewis Schultz, Robert English, and E. J. D. Greynolds, joined Capt. Ira J. Westover's company in the Lafayette Battalion (table 2.1). These men had been members of Mexía's Tampico Expedition. Fannin also sent Pvt. John Barton of Winn's command to a Texas artillery unit, leaving Winn with thirty-six men.[16]

While Fannin dithered, the Texian cause suffered setbacks. Civilians fled the Goliad area as the two recalcitrant Texian leaders, Johnson and Grant, roamed farther south. On the night of February 26, 1836, Johnson's party of thirty men slept at San Patricio, thirty miles south of Fort Defiance (see map frontispiece). Meanwhile, Grant and twenty-six men set up camp at Agua Dulce, twenty-six miles farther south, and Plácido Benavides led his Tejano *rancheros* north to join him. None realized the danger they faced. General Urrea with 600 Mexican soldiers rode north from Matamoros, charged with destroying Texian detachments until he could rejoin Santa Anna, who surrounded the Alamo at San Antonio on February 27. A professional soldier, from a long line of presidio commanders, and the victor in previous battles in support of Santa Anna, Urrea overwhelmed Johnson's sleeping volunteers with a predawn attack on February 27 in a freezing rain. Urrea wrote that he killed sixteen and captured twenty-one Texians, but six, including Johnson, escaped to Refugio and sent an express rider to Fannin. In the meantime, Urrea attacked Grant on March 2, killing fourteen Texians and capturing six. The next day, an escapee wandered into Refugio, where Lewis Ayers bound his wound and took him to Goliad. By now the whole area was alarmed, Fannin's troops were on the alert, and Urrea watched for Fannin's response at Agua Dulce.[17]

As Urrea marched north from Matamoros, Fannin had little knowledge of his movements. Johnson and Grant had been more interested in corralling wild horses than gathering information. Furthermore, Fannin and many of his troops often treated Tejanos disdainfully, so they could not rely on them for reports. Urrea, on the other hand, took advantage of the willingness of the Tejanos to help. They scouted where the Texians camped, determined their strength, and reported to him. Thus, while Urrea was well informed about the Texian troops, Fannin, as well as Johnson and Grant, did not realize the proximity of Urrea's force until it was too late. This continued to plague Fannin as his situation deteriorated. On March 5, 1836, a courier arrived at Fort Defiance with word that Texas had declared independence. The men celebrated—cannons fired, soldiers paraded, bugles blared, and Troutman's banner flew from the flagstaff. On March 10, Fannin sent Capt. Amon Butler King and twenty-one soldiers with carts to Refugio to bring several families to Goliad. Two days later, a messenger arrived with news of the fate of the Alamo and its defenders. That same day, Fannin received an order from Sam Houston, general in chief of the Texas army, to withdraw to Victoria, but he decided to wait until King returned. Meanwhile, at Refugio, King found most of the families in the old mission but, incensed that Tejanos had looted Anglo homes, he decided to retaliate and after a fight arrested several. On March 12, King encountered a cavalry patrol from Urrea's force and immediately withdrew to the mission. The Mexican troopers attacked but met with accurate fire from King's men and retreated. King sent a courier to Fannin, who promptly ordered Ward with his Georgia Battalion to march to Refugio and rescue King and the families (see map frontispiece).[18]

The Georgia Battalion, accompanied by Ayers, left at three in the morning on March 13. Winn's company, including Callahan, trudged with the rest in an exhausting thirty-mile march. According to L. T. Pease of Bullock's company, they "marched most of the way in wet prairie, with the water often ankle deep." At one point, according to Lewis M. Washington of Bullock's company, Ward's volunteers pushed aside an enemy patrol sent to block the road. The battalion reached Refugio at two in the afternoon. Ward found King in the old mission and about one hundred of Urrea's cavalrymen across the river. He did not know that many more of Urrea's troops were only hours away. Once inside the mission, Ward evaluated his situation. His 203 troops had thirty-six cartridges per man and no artillery. Most of his men were barefoot, poorly clothed, and had few provisions. Water was also in short supply. Within the mission, in addition to the soldiers, there were eight families with children, four noncombatant males, and twenty Tejano prisoners. The mission itself did provide some reassurance that it could be defended. Nuestra Señora del Refugio (Our Lady of Refuge) was a massive stone complex completed in 1799. Closed in 1824, the structure had deteriorated, and settlers had used its materials for building houses and barns. Nevertheless, when the Georgia Battalion arrived, much remained intact (figure 2.1). The chapel with a single tower dominated the main building, which had some intact rooms. Men in the tower had a 360-degree view, while the three-foot-thick walls provided protection against cannon and rifle fire. Ward's men punched holes in the exterior walls, creating rifle ports. A cemetery, 150 feet long and 50 feet wide, lay on the western or front side; it was surrounded by a masonry wall, which had a 16-foot ungated opening with a stone arch. The mission lacked water, but the Mission River ran one hundred yards to the south.[19]

Ward on March 13, 1836, dispatched a night patrol composed of fifty men in King's and Ticknor's companies. They crossed the river and attacked the cavalry, killing several and forcing the rest to retreat. This success emboldened the Georgia Battalion but, with his troops exhausted and hungry, Ward decided to retire. At daybreak, his command scattered the remaining Mexican cavalry, capturing several horses. Callahan observed the nighttime raid from the mission and his squad probably participated in the dawn operation. In the meantime, King and Ward squabbled over who was the commander. Joseph W. Andrews of the Georgia Battalion recalled that King wanted to command the entire detachment. Samuel T. Brown, also of Ward's command, later wrote that most of the men vowed they would serve only under Ward. King angrily departed to attack a nearby ranch with his twenty-one men, eighteen from Peyton S. Wyatt's company, and Ayers. Ward then ordered a patrol to another ranch, where some of the men burned buildings and provisions while others scouted toward Goliad. Ward, in a quandary, decided to wait for King. Meanwhile, Urrea was marching toward Goliad when he learned about the Texians at Refugio. He detached 100 mounted men, 180 infantry, and a small cannon, and hurried to Refugio with them. Colonel Francisco Garay followed with the remainder. Urrea's arrival in Refugio increased his force there to nearly 410, including many Tejanos. Ward's patrol toward Goliad encountered Urrea's force and reported its presence. Anticipating a sustained fight, Ward ordered a squad to fill three barrels from the river, dispatched a rider to inform Fannin of the situation, and organized his defense. Urrea sent a detachment to engage the water party, and the ensuing skirmish left the Texians with two full barrels and a third leaking from a bullet hole. Meanwhile, according to Samuel G. Hardaway, Ward's men blocked the mission's entrances with benches and pews.[20]

According to Sabina Brown, a refugee in the mission, Urrea struck just before noon on March 14 with his infantry, which marched three lines abreast toward the mission's front. Ward had instructed his men to make every shot count, so when they fired a first fusillade, many Mexicans were killed or wounded. The Yucatan infantry battalion broke ranks and fled. Urrea ordered his cavalry to dismount and attack, but that failed. At this moment, King with his troops blundered into the rear of Urrea's force, and after a skirmish, took refuge in a thicket 600 yards east of the mission. Urrea claimed his troops killed eleven and captured seven. Nevertheless, his attacks had failed, and so Urrea withdrew, setting up a headquarters and hospital at Brown's home, a quarter mile north of the mission. While Urrea regrouped, Ward, his men, and the mission's other occupants reflected on their position. Pease claimed the Georgians believed their resistance would discourage any more attacks that day. Ward, however, realized this might not be the case, and his limited ammunition concerned him, so he dispatched another courier to Fannin, requesting aid and munitions. About two in the afternoon Mexican officers rallied their troops and began a second attack. The enemy columns marched toward the cemetery's entrance, where Ward and thirty-five volunteers waited. Firing through holes in the wall, the Georgians again stopped the assault. Washington crowed that the volleys were so deadly that the Mexicans retreated hastily, leaving many on the field. Brown claimed, "[T]his was the hardest fight of the day and the sulphur smoke rose high in the air and the rifles of the Georgians rattled like shot in a gourd, and they whooped for joy when they saw the Mexicans fall." A Mexican officer wrote to his wife that the Texians fought well, albeit from behind the cemetery wall. The Georgians later repulsed a third attack, although one Mexican officer reached the mission's door, inside the cemetery, before being shot.[21]

Urrea launched one more full-scale assault at nightfall, which was also rebuffed. Most participants' accounts say the fighting continued intermittently until about midnight. Henry Scott recalled that after sundown several of the Georgia Battalion sallied out to chase away Urrea's troops, who had camped nearby. Brown recollected that the Mexicans tried to set fire to the roof, and Urrea at one time engaged his four-pound cannon. A cannonball dislodged a piece of the mission's stone wall, striking Ward in the head. The cannon crew advanced to within thirty to fifty yards of the mission's door, but sharpshooting Georgians repeatedly killed cannoneers until they abandoned their gun. Urrea claimed that his men withdrew it, but by other accounts, the Texians hauled it into the mission as, according to Brown, their yells shook the rafters. Urrea correctly assumed that the Texians had little water, food, or ammunition so he decided to wait until daybreak before renewing any attacks, but he placed pickets to prevent escape. Meanwhile, Fannin sent two couriers in search of King and Ward, but Mexican cavalry captured and killed them. Anxious to retreat but not until he knew Ward's situation, at dusk Fannin sent a final messenger, colonist Edward Perry. Mexican cavalry caught him. Urrea read the note, which instructed Ward to march to Goliad, and decided to let Perry deliver it, hoping it would induce

Ward to evacuate the mission and allow the Mexicans to capture the Georgia Battalion.[22]

Reading Fannin's communication, and learning that Urrea had also read it, Ward took stock. His men were almost out of ammunition, so withstanding another sustained assault was unlikely. While the mission had strong walls, the Mexican cannon had practically battered down its doors. The defenders had suffered only light casualties and no deaths, but they had not eaten all day and had no food. They had finished the two-and-a-half barrels of water and were still thirsty. Ward also felt responsible for the women and children in the mission and had to decide how to handle his prisoners. One of King's patrol, Perry Davis, had straggled into the mission and described his unit's plight, so it was clear that King could not help. Ward believed his men had killed over a hundred Mexican soldiers, but he also realized that Urrea had reserves. Adding to his men's general misery, the weather had deteriorated; cold rain meant any withdrawal would be very unpleasant. Perry advised Ward not to take the road to Goliad as Mexican cavalry had that route covered. Instead, he recommended that he march east a few miles and then north toward Victoria. After some discussion, Ward told his men to prepare for a midnight exodus.[23]

The Georgia Battalion hurriedly prepared to march while tending to those left behind. One of the wounded, Abraham H. Osborn, resided in Refugio and had joined Ward or King on March 14. The battalion itself had two wounded soldiers, Christopher Winters and fifteen-year-old William Shelton, both privates in Winn's company. They needed water, so a patrol ventured to a nearby spring, dispersed Urrea's guards, and filled several gourds. Ward left two volunteers, Henry H. Wood of Bullock's company and William N. Simpson from Wyatt's company, to assist the wounded. At midnight, 159 men slipped through a window and marched five abreast between Urrea's sentinels, shielded by blustering winds and rain. Neither the pickets nor the women and children sleeping in the mission heard them leave. They simply marched from the mission under the strict discipline instilled by the training of Brooks and Chadwick. Under the circumstances, it was remarkable. Sergeant Callahan led his squad in Winn's company as the battalion escaped.[24]

The following morning Urrea realized his enemy was gone, so he instructed his troops to search the mission for survivors. Realizing every man faced death, Rebecca Ayers and another woman rolled the wounded Osborn, her brother, between two mattresses. Later, the bedding was taken to the Ayers residence with Osborn inside. Mexican soldiers discovered the two wounded Georgians, Winters and Shelton, and their caretakers, Woods and Simpson. The latter two along with Winters were killed immediately, but Brown intervened to save Shelton. Scott witnessed the macabre scene of the Mexicans yelling and bayoneting the wounded men. The other adolescent boy in the mission, E. N. Hill, remembered the wounded "were remorselessly butchered by the Mexican *officers* with their swords." Later, as she returned from the kitchen, Brown saw Shelton take his last breath as two soldiers wiped blood off their swords. With the mission secured, Urrea declared the building to be his headquarters and hospital.[25]

Garay had arrived at Refugio with the remaining 200 Mexican troops, so Urrea ordered him to attack King in the woods near the mission. King's volunteers repulsed Garay's assault, but their ammunition was nearly exhausted. As the Georgia Battalion slipped away, King and his men evaded Garay and started for Goliad, but they became lost. At daybreak on March 15, 1836, they crossed the Mission River at its junction with Melon Creek and marched to the Malone ranch north of Refugio (map 2.1). Their guns and powder were soaked while crossing the river, so when Mexican cavalry arrived at the ranch, they surrendered and returned to the mission as prisoners. At the insistence of his officers, Urrea ordered his soldiers to execute them. Colonel Juan Holzinger, a German-born officer in the Mexican army, noticed that two prisoners—Charles Jensen and Antonie Sayle—had Germanic names, so he arranged to spare them. Holzinger may have also saved Benjamin Digby Odlum and Francis Dieterich; both men lived in Refugio, were captured with King, and survived. Meanwhile, Rebecca Ayers barged into Urrea's headquarters with her children and convinced him to release her husband, Lewis. Mexican troops marched the remainder of King's company a mile down the San Antonio road. When the Texians were ordered to turn about, they were shot. Thirty-three men died.[26]

After escaping from the mission, the Georgia Battalion wandered aimlessly (map 2.1) and almost blundered into camps of Mexican sentinels. By daylight on March 15 they were headed southeast along the north bank of the Mission River. Arriving at the river's junction with Melon Creek, they observed hoofprints, leading Ward to conclude that a patrol had pursued them. This was the cavalry following King's men, who had crossed the same bridge six hours earlier. Ward ordered the bridge burned and led his men northwest along the east bank of Melon Creek before turning north toward Victoria. At dark, ten miles north of the mission, the battalion camped for the night with little water and no food. On March 16, Ward's troops marched north for several miles over a rolling prairie before halting for the night. Again, they did not eat all day, and they exhausted their water supply. Departing at daybreak on March 17, the Georgians trudged north, famished and thirsty. As dehydration became a major concern, Ward sent seven men to scout for water; they vanished. Ward and his remaining troops found water at their campsite but still had no food. The following day (March 18), the march continued to sap their energy. Finally, when camped near Nicholas Fagan's ranch (map 2.1) near the San Antonio River, they found cattle to slaughter. Somewhat refreshed, the men resumed their slog on March 19 but trekked up and down the river before finding a ford. Late in the afternoon, they heard explosions to the west; it was Fannin fighting Urrea at Coleto Creek. Ward and his men wanted to march in that direction but were dissuaded by their lack of ammunition. The distant gunfire ceased as night fell.[27]

That evening Ward's men slaughtered more beef and left the next morning (March 20) restored. They camped that night on the Guadalupe River, three miles southeast of Victoria (map 2.1). In the morning, Wadsworth with Samuel A. J. Mays, Joseph T. Wilson, and Joseph B. Tatum approached the home of a Tejano family and obtained food that Tatum carried to the battalion. As Wadsworth, Mays, and Williams walked toward Victoria, Mexican soldiers captured Wadsworth and Mays but shot and killed Williams. Meanwhile, cavalry spotted Ward's troops. In the ensuing fight, Ward's men used their last ammunition; historian Harbert Davenport concluded that at least seven Texians were killed, including Private Brooks from Winn's company. Dismayed, Ward and 142 men withdrew to swampy, timbered bottomland along the Guadalupe. In the hasty retreat, thirteen slipped away, including two, John Bright and Martin Moran, from Winn's company. Ward led his shrinking command on an all-night march down the north bank of the Guadalupe in an effort to reach Dimitt's Landing. At sunrise on March 22 he led his men into a large motte and sent out two squads—one to find cattle and the other to scout Dimitt's Landing. The team scouting for cattle found a Mexican patrol and told Ward that enemy troops had them surrounded. Meanwhile, Urrea's soldiers captured the two men dispatched to Dimitt's Landing, who then led Urrea to the thicket that concealed the remnant of the Georgia Battalion.[28]

By the time Urrea captured the Georgia Battalion, he had already secured the surrender of Fannin and his men. After Ward's men escaped from the mission at Refugio, Urrea had marched for Goliad with 200 infantry and cavalry. Meanwhile, Santa Anna ordered reinforcements to Goliad—Colonel Juan Morales with 500 troops and three cannons. Fannin, learning of King's fate and Ward's retreat, marched toward Victoria. Mexican and Texian forces met on an open plain near Coleto Creek. At mid-afternoon on March 19, 1836, a fierce encounter began that lasted until dark. The next morning, Urrea received reinforcements and decided to resume his attack, but after a few cannon shots Fannin surrendered, and he and his men were marched to Goliad. Learning from Fannin's correspondence that Ward was headed to Victoria, Urrea occupied that place on March 21. Urrea claimed locals surrendered six Anglo prisoners and his patrols killed or captured another twenty, but this contradicts what Ward's survivors wrote. Urrea did discover Texians fleeing down the north bank of the Guadalupe and pursued them with 200 infantry and a cannon. At two-thirty in the afternoon, he captured the patrol sent by Ward to scout Dimitt's Landing, then placed his troops around the woods concealing the Texians and sent a prisoner to tell Ward that unless they surrendered immediately, they would all die.[29]

Urrea's diary and his battle report provide the victor's account of Ward's surrender, while the recollections of Brown and Washington give the perspective of the captive Georgians. Urrea claimed the terms were unconditional, and that Ward decided in only five minutes to surrender himself with six other officers and ninety men. Brown recalled in November 1837 that Ward, Mitchell, and Ticknor negotiated with Urrea and reported that, as prisoners of war, they would be marched to Copano and shipped to New Orleans, to be exchanged. Washington wrote in April 1853 that Holzinger came under a white flag and offered the same terms given to Fannin, which were: surrender their arms and promise never again to fight against Mexico, and then they would be sent to New Orleans. Both Washington and Brown remembered that Ward argued against surrender, telling his troops he had no confidence in "*Mexican Honor*" and that he would "rather die than surrender." He believed his battalion had a good chance to whip the Mexicans; at worst, he thought a large number would escape. But his tired, hungry soldiers voted overwhelmingly to capitulate. Ward, Mitchell, and Ticknor signed the agreement, and 129 men grounded their rifles. The prisoners and their captors spent the night of March 22 at Las Juntas, while Urrea ordered a cavalry squad to nearby Linnville to get provisions. The next day, Urrea and his men returned to Victoria with their prisoners. Brown said the Texians marched under heavy guard and at Victoria moved the Mexican army's provisions and baggage across the Guadalupe River.[30]

At sunrise on March 24, Urrea paraded the prisoners, and Holzinger selected sixteen with mechanical or carpentry skills to stay in Victoria. Four who had sore feet and could not walk and one who served as an interpreter were also detained. The other 108 prisoners, including thirty in Winn's company, marched under guard to Goliad, arriving on March 25 or 26. Holzinger chose only one mechanic from Winn's unit—Callahan (table 2.1). The coach-making skills he learned and practiced in Georgia meant he would not share the fate suffered by his comrades at Goliad. In December 1835, at Santa Anna's request, Mexico's Congress had mandated the death penalty for prisoners captured during the Texas rebellion. At Goliad, Urrea became reluctant to execute the hundreds of men he had captured. Santa Anna then sent an order directly to Colonel José N. Portilla, the Goliad commandant, demanding the prisoners be executed. Regardless of the new law and Santa Anna's threats, the men who capitulated under Fannin and Ward understood they would be sent to New Orleans, and Holzinger escorted Fannin to Copano Bay to arrange their transport. There were no ships, but Fannin returned in a good mood, and the prisoners believed that passage to New Orleans would begin soon. On March 26, Portilla received Santa Anna's order. A day earlier, however, Urrea had instructed him to treat the Texians as prisoners of war and put them to work repairing the fortress. Portilla agonized at the conflicting instructions.[31]

Before sunrise on Palm Sunday, March 27, 1836, Mexican sentinels rousted almost 450 slumbering men. Dr. Jack Shackelford talked to men of the Georgia Battalion that morning and recalled, "On passing the gate of the Fort, I saw Ward's men in line, with their knapsacks on. I inquired of them where they were going; some of them stated that they were to march to Copano, and from thence to be sent home!" This was not true. In three groups, they were marched onto the prairie, ordered to turn around, and shot. All but one of the Georgia Battalion, including all of Winn's remaining men, fell near the Bexar Road ford of the San Antonio River. The survivor in Ward's command, Brown of Bullock's company, fled unscathed (table 2.2).

He was one of just twenty-eight prisoners who escaped unharmed. Fannin and Ward heard the gunfire and the cries of their doomed men before a squad came for them. According to an eyewitness, Ward refused to kneel even when told that might spare his life. A firing squad dispatched him.

Table 2.2. Surrendered near Dimitt's Landing, Mar. 22, 1836; marched to Goliad; massacred, Mar. 27, 1836

Rank/Name/Age	*Residence*	*Remarks*
Capt. James Cochran Winn, 24	Gwinnett Co., Ga.	Daniel Brooks's uncle
1st Lt. Wiley Hughes	Baldwin or Bibb Co., Ga.	Son of James Hughes, Battalion Commissary
1st Sgt. Anthony Bates	Gwinnett Co., Ga.	
2nd Sgt. John Stephen Thorn		
4th Sgt. Wesley Hughes	Baldwin or Bibb Co., Ga	Wiley Hughes's brother
1st Cpl. John M. Gimble		
2nd Cpl. Walter W. Davis		Sometimes spelled Daws
3rd Cpl. Abraham Stevens		
4th Cpl. John M. Powers	Tallapoosa Co., Ala.	
Pvt. John Aldridge, 35–40	Unknown co., Ala.	Cousin Isaac Aldridge was in Bullock's Co.
Pvt. Josiah (Josias) Bradley Beall, 38	Campbell, Coweta Co., Ga.	
Pvt. John McAllister Bryson, 22		
Pvt. Michael E. Carroll, 24	Henry Co., Ga.	
Pvt. Thomas H. Cosby, 21	Jasper Co., Ga.	
Pvt. John Ely		
Pvt. George Eubanks, 19	Montgomery Co., Ala.	
Pvt. Dominic Gallagher		
Pvt. Wilson Helms, 24	Henry Co., Ga.	
Pvt. Green Lee, 24	Bibb Co., Ga.	Some records list first name as Grier or Greer
Pvt. Alexander J. Loverly		Sometimes misspelled Lyerly
Pvt. Joseph S. Loving, 28	Bibb Co., Ga.	
Pvt. Watkins Nobles, 28	Coffee Co., Ga.	
Pvt. John M. Oliver	Montgomery Co., Ala.	
Pvt. Patrick Osborn	Wilkes Co., Ga.	
Pvt. William Parvin	Houston Co., Ga.	

Rank/Name/Age	*Residence*	*Remarks*
Pvt. Anderson Ray, 25	Upson Co., Ga.	Moved from Edgefield Co., S.C., to Ga., 1834
Pvt. Gideon S. Ross		
Pvt. Thomas Rumley, 21–25	Bibb Co., Ga.	
Pvt. James Smith	Bibb Co., Ga.	
Pvt. Harrison Young		

Sources: Robert Casey, Brooks family researcher, e-mail, 2010; Casey and Casey, *Brooks Family History*, 7-212–7-214, 7-418–7-420; *Georgia Telegraph*, Nov. 22, Dec. 24, 1835; Mrs. L. W. to H. Davenport, letter, Mar. 24, 1943, DHP, CAH; Last name and first name, Land Grant Search, TGLO; Aldridge, *Aldridge Records*, 118–20; Beth Klein, Aldridge family descendant, e-mail, 2010; Beall, Josias, B., Box 2R245, KC, CAH; U.S. Census, 1830, Campbell County, Ga., Edgefield County, S.C.; Cummins, *Georgia Bealls*, 23, 52–53, 66; Elizabeth Rebecca Beall History, Beall Family Papers, privately held; General Name File, Virtual Vault, GSA: *Augusta Chronicle*, June 16, 1827; Georgia Military Affairs, 1830–1835, 6:212, microfilm 269/14, GSA; Houston, *Thomas H. Crosby*, 2–3; Miller, "Fannin's Men," 526; Montague, *History and Genealogy of the Montague Family*, 76; Ely, *Records of the Descendants of Nathaniel Ely*, 71–72; *Columbus Enquirer*, Feb. 12, 1836; John Eubanks to Thomas S. Gordon, Esq., letter, July 23, 1839, DHP, CAH; Marie Lee-Walker and Craig Lee, descendants of John Anderson Lee, father of Green Lee, e-mails, 2010; *Weekly Telegraph*, Apr. 16, Nov. 12, 1835, Dec. 11, 1838; *Columbus Enquirer*, Feb. 2, 1833; Huxford, *Pioneers of Wiregrass Georgia*, 210–11; John Nobles, descendant of Lewis Sanders Nobles, father of Watkins Nobles, e-mail, 2010; *Douglas Enterprise*, Sept. 19, 2001; *Telegraph and Register*, Jan. 30, 1836; David Robinson, Patrick Osborn descendant, e-mail, 2010; *Macon Telegraph*, July 23, 1835; Central Georgia Genealogical Society, *First Hundred Years and Ten Years of Houston County*, 188; Davine V. Campbell, *Land Records of Houston County*, 126; James F. Smith, *Cherokee Land Lottery*, 248; Joyce A. Morris, Ray family descendant, e-mail, 2011.

Although Fannin asked not to be shot in the head, he was killed with a headshot. There was one paradoxical sequel to the massacre. As the prisoners lined up to leave the mission at Goliad, James Hughes stood with his sons, Wiley and Wesley, both of whom had served in Winn's company while he worked in the regimental commissary. Somehow, James had bribed a guard into sparing him but either did not or could not save his sons, so they perished. Perhaps weakened by the shock of what had transpired, several days later he contracted an acute illness and died.[32]

Meanwhile, in Victoria the sixteen prisoners retained by Holzinger busily repaired boats and bridges (table 2.3). Thomas J. Smith remembered that the Guadalupe River at Victoria was flooding, so twelve carpenters and four men wielding axes were to build a boat. Recaptured Goliad survivor Isaac D. Hamilton, who was returned to Victoria, also recalled being forced to help with boatbuilding. Thus, Callahan and the others constructed the means for Mexican troops and provisions to cross the river at Victoria. When Urrea and his division marched north toward the Colorado River on March 31,

Table 2.3. Men from Georgia Battalion detained at Victoria, Mar. 24, 1836

Company	*Name*	*Reason detained*	*Discharge date*
Wadsworth	James H. Neely	Mechanic	Unknown
	Joseph Callaghan	Mechanic	May 21, 1836
	Joseph H. Gamble	Mechanic	June 2, 1836
	Andrew Jackson Hitchcock	Mechanic	June 2, 1836
	Thomas Horry	Mechanic	May 30, 1836
	John C. P. Kennymore	Mechanic	May 17, 1836
	Edmond Durain	Unable to march	Unknown
Bullock	John (James) H. Barnwell	Mechanic	May 31, 1836
	Roderick Pierce Hammock	Mechanic	June 4, 1836
	Thomas J. Smith	Mechanic	June 15, 1836
	John T. Spillers	Mechanic	May 26, 1836
	Thomas G. Stewart	Mechanic	May 22, 1836
	William L. Wilkinson	Mechanic	May 17, 1836
	Benjamin Mordecai	Unable to march	June 15, 1836
	Lewis M. H. Washington	Unable to march	May 9, 1836
Ticknor	Edward Patterson	Mechanic	May 30, 1836
	John O'Daniel Jr.	Mechanic	May 26, 1836
	D. [S.] Greene	Unable to march	Unknown
	William Welsh	Interpreter	June 1, 1836
Wyatt	John James "Doc" Lumpkin	Mechanic	Unknown
Winn	James Hughes Callahan	Mechanic	June 9, 1836

Sources: Ornish, Ehrenberg, 316; Service Records: Alavez Telesoforo—Republic of Mexico, DHC, TSLA; E. Owens, *Story of Her Life*, 10; Coalson, "Alavez, Francita"; Last and first name, Discharge dates, Republic Claims, TSLA; *Dallas Morning News*, Sept. 13, 1931; W. N. Rowell and H. Davenport letters, 1936, DHC, TSLA; S. Moore, *Savage Frontier*, 2:154, 182, 277, 290, 306–7, 310, 341, 344, 3:12, 37, 131, 135, 166–67, 189–90, 211, 224, 226, 275, 314, 362; Spurlin, *Texas Volunteers*, 237, 242; *Texas Register*, Sept. 9, 1840; Gulick et al., eds., *Papers of Mirabeau Buonaparte Lamar*, 1:392.

most of the mechanics stayed at Victoria, although Holzinger took along a few unidentified men. Callahan remained in Victoria, where Colonel Telesforo Alavez took charge of the Mexican troops and prisoners. Alavez's wife joined him, as was typical in many armies of that era. Francita Alavez had been in Goliad on Palm Sunday and saved a few men that day. While Alavez was in command at Victoria, some of Ward's men were also slated for execution. With animated protests, Francita convinced him to cancel the killing. Nine-year-old Elizabeth McAnulty Owens, a Victoria resident, recalled seeing Francita guard the men with her voluminous skirt. Callahan was in Victoria at this time, but no records reveal whether he or any of the other mechanics were thus spared.[33]

Brown of the Georgia Battalion wandered until April 20, when he was captured again by Urrea's troops ten miles from San Jacinto and remained with them during the Mexican retreat after Santa Anna's defeat on April 21. Urrea arrived in Victoria between May 10 and 13, and Brown encountered four men from the Georgia Battalion who had been "detained there after the surrender, on account of their being mechanics: William Wilkerson [William L. Wilkinson], John Kinneman [John C. P. Kennymore], Barnwell [James (John) H. Barnwell], and Callahan [James Hughes Callahan]." According to an endorsement on his discharge papers written by Acting Secretary of War William H. Jack, Callahan escaped from his captors about May 25. He was not on the May 27 list of prisoners provided by the Mexicans to the Texians, so the circumstances surrounding his escape remain unknown. On June 9, he was discharged from the army at Velasco (table 2.3). All the other men retained at Victoria were discharged before June 9. Thus, the records indicate that Callahan was among the last prisoners from the Georgia Battalion to obtain his freedom. In any case, with his discharge approved, Callahan collected $106 and planned his journey home to Georgia.[34]

In retrospect, the Georgia Battalion became victims of their own inexperience, while their foes benefitted from professional leaders. Too, intelligence collected by Tejanos provided Urrea with accurate knowledge of enemy strength and location. In contrast, Ward often overestimated the Mexican numbers. Without adequate reconnaissance, the Georgians believed they faced an enemy force five to eight times their size, when in fact Urrea's force was just three times larger. Ward, like Fannin, failed to send scouts into the field to locate the enemy force and estimate its size. Thus, Ward, Fannin, and most of their men died in part because of inadequate intelligence, a key responsibility of a commander. From his experience at Refugio, Callahan had the chance to learn the value of effective reconnaissance, a skill he would need in the future.[35]

The Georgia Battalion's lack of military experience has been attributed to youth by many historians, who claimed that most of the volunteers were under twenty-one years of age. A closer look at Callahan and his comrades in Winn's company suggests otherwise. Ages could be found for twenty-one of the fifty-four enrolled at Velasco on December 23, 1835. Of the twenty-one, 81 percent were at least twenty-one years old, and 57 percent were twenty-four or older. John Aldridge was the oldest at 41. If Winn's company is typical, then most of the Georgia Battalion were not as young as previously claimed. What is true is that most of these volunteers had little military experience or training. This is supported by Lieutenant Brooks, who complained about having to drill officers and enlistees "in the elementary school of the soldier." For Winn's men, the evidence is again incomplete, but military records in Georgia suggest that only three—Winn, William Parvin, and James Bradley Beall—had prior training. It is entirely possible that any familiarity with military procedures evidenced in later life by Callahan, the sole survivor of Winn's company, reflected the training he got in the field with the Georgia Battalion.[36]

Estimating the exact number of enemies killed after a battle is fraught with uncertainty, and this is true of the fight at Refugio. Urrea's men killed about forty of Ward's troops, including thirty-three of King's men executed and four slain inside the mission on the morning after Ward escaped. The latter two figures match historian Harbert Davenport's estimate that the Texians lost thirty-seven men at Refugio. But Urrea said his troops put to death eight inside the mission, and he also claimed that another eleven of King's contingent were killed in the fighting. The number of Mexicans killed is also contested and estimates by the Texians are consistently too high. Bradford approximated enemy losses at 150 killed and 162 wounded; Richard Rutledge estimated 153 dead and 170 wounded. Scott, Hardaway, and John A. J. Hitchcock all said Urrea suffered about 200 casualties. Washington later claimed 500 Mexicans were killed and wounded and Pease roughly concurred with a count of 400. Sabina Brown stated that the pile of Mexican dead stood "as big as twenty cords of wood." In contrast, Urrea claimed he lost 11 killed and 37 wounded. A Mexican officer wrote to his wife that the Mexican killed and wounded were 40. On the other hand, General Vicente Filisola, who took charge of the Mexican army after Santa Anna was captured, reported that Urrea lost 16 dead and 53 wounded. In the end, the total Texian and Mexican casualties at Refugio may never be known.[37]

It is also difficult to assess the number of soldiers sent by Fannin from Goliad to Refugio. Ayers said Ward had 120 troops, while Samuel Brown recollected 125, Bradford 131, and Hitchcock 130. Sabina Brown remembered that 100 troops came with Ward. Bullock, who was sick at Velasco, heard that 120 had been sent. However, Davenport postulated a different number after meticulously recreating the muster rolls for Fannin's command. By his calculation, when the Georgia Battalion arrived at Refugio there were 45 in Bullock's company, 42 in Ticknor's, 37 in Wadsworth's, and 36 in Winn's. To these should be added Bradford and 21 soldiers from Wyatt's company whom Bradford claimed were at Refugio. Thus, Ward had 182 soldiers upon his arrival, and King's 21 brought the total to 203 at the mission. Davenport's estimates are about 30 percent greater than participants' recollections. While this discrepancy is difficult to explain, his figure seems more plausible. Davenport also says that Ward surrendered 129 men, of whom 21 were held in Victoria and 108 went to Goliad. Interestingly, Urrea reported to Santa Anna that 90 enlisted men and ten officers surrendered; he did not mention the 21 men in Victoria. Perhaps he misreported the number in an effort to evade orders to execute all prisoners. Only one Texian who surrendered with Ward, Samuel Brown, ever said how many gave up, insisting it was 85. Since both Brown, who was exhausted and possibly shell-shocked, and Urrea had reasons to be inaccurate, their estimates should be disregarded in favor of Davenport.[38]

An examination of the losses each company in the Georgia Battalion suffered—combat, detention, escape, and execution—reveals surprising disproportionality. Winn and Wadsworth had the highest mortality at 92 percent and 86 percent, while almost one-third in the Wadsworth and Bullock companies managed to live. Why these two sets of companies had such different survival rates is a mystery. Only three of the thirty-six men (8 percent) of Winn's company survived, highlighting the fortunate outcome for Callahan, who was not executed because his vocation, coach-making, saved his life.[39]

What motivated the men of the Georgia Battalion to risk, and most to lose, their lives in Texas? Patriotism represented one enticement; Ward stated this was one of his motives. Some had financial difficulties in Georgia and Texas offered a new start. James Hughes, for example, faced financial woes, as did his son Wesley. Basil Lamar of Bullock's company swore that he "took [Henry] Pierce Hammock [of Bullock's company], who was in jail for debt, and enrolled him to go to Texas . . . [and paid] Wiley [Wesley] Hughes [of Winn's company] out of debt to enable him to go to Texas." Others, like Private Brooks, volunteered because their wives had abandoned them, and others were merely searching for adventure. Undoubtedly free land lured many to join. This may have been particularly relevant to Georgians as land there had become increasingly difficult to acquire after the state lottery ended. Texas compensated its soldiers with its major resource, land, and volunteers in the battalion discussed how much they would get. Of Winn's company, all fifty-four (or their heirs) got grants with the exception of three deserters—N. R. Allen, John T. Garner, and David Tarvin—and Henry Lewis Schultz, who never applied. Callahan received two grants, each for 640 acres.[40]

Local newspapers kept the volunteers' families abreast of the volatile situation in Texas, albeit with some inaccuracies. On January 14, 1836, Fannin's letter appeared in the *Messenger,* noting he had mustered into service two hundred volunteers from Georgia under Ward. The Georgia press continued to provide updates as Santa Anna mobilized his troops. Accounts of his obliteration of the Alamo defenders, and Urrea's capture of both Fannin and the Georgia Battalion, appalled Georgians. On April 21, the *Southern Banner* declared that "Col. Fannin ordered the Georgia Battalion, consisting of 150 men under Colonel Ward to attack Mexicans at Refugio, numbering 600 men, which force they routed, killing 250 Mexicans, without loss of one man." One week later the *Macon Telegraph* provided a sadder, but more accurate, account: "Maj. Ward and the Georgia battalion . . . were at length overpowered by numbers and all put to the sword but five who escaped." The paper identified two who escaped: Rutledge and David I. Holt. The *Federal Union* on May 12 published affidavits from Z. S. Brooks, Wilson Simpson, and Dillard Cooper, of Shackelford's Red Rovers, who declared that near Dimitt's Landing the Georgia Battalion were captured and many perished in the massacre at Goliad. One day later, the *Columbus Enquirer* reported the capture and execution of King's men, In the last week of May, the *Macon Telegraph* published Urrea's report on the Refugio battle, Ward's surrender, and the executions of his men. The paper again included a list of escapees: "Joseph Andrews (our informant), David I. Holt, Lewis Washington, [Robert ?] Dickinson, Monroe Bullock, Samuel Hardaway, and Benjamin Mordecai, all Georgians." By month end, Georgians thus knew that most of the battalion had perished, though the publication in the June 2 *Macon Messenger* of documents signed by Santa Anna acknowledging the independence of Texas meant that the cause for which they fought and died had not failed.[41]

It was June 1836 before an inkling of Callahan's fate appeared in print. Dashing hope of his survival, the June 9 *Macon Telegraph* proclaimed that "Among the Volunteers from Macon who were killed are . . . James Calahan." Two weeks later, however, the truth emerged when the same newspaper published a firsthand account from Joseph W. Andrews of Ward's command. Andrews provided a list of prisoners who had survived, including Callahan. Meanwhile, with his June 9 discharge in hand and $106 in his pocket, Callahan waited at Velasco for a ship to New Orleans. On June 16, he clambered aboard the *Pennsylvania*, joining other Anglo veterans and Holzinger, recently released from custody. Captured near Matagorda Island, Holzinger had been conveyed to Velasco, where he was interrogated about the role he and Urrea played in the Goliad massacre. William Jack then informed Holzinger that due to his generosity with captive Texians, Texas President David G. Burnet freed him and provided transportation to New Orleans.[42]

Considering the others aboard the *Pennsylvania* (table 2.4), conversations were no doubt interesting. Callahan encountered four men—Hammock, Hitchcock, John O'Daniel, and Edwin Patterson—detained with him at Victoria by Holzinger. There were also two others from Winn's company: James (Livingston) B. Grice, who had deserted in January at Velasco but later fought at San Jacinto, and Martin Moran, who had escaped during Ward's retreat from Refugio. One passenger, Ehrenberg, had fled during the Goliad massacre but was subsequently recaptured by Holzinger. Three other fortunate Goliad survivors also were aboard: Alvin E. White and doctors Shackelford and Joseph E. Field. The latter two had fought at Coleto Creek and, after Fannin's surrender, were assigned by Urrea to tend Mexican soldiers. On the day of the massacre, Garay sent them to a tent away from the other Texians, where they joined White. Another passenger, John H. Tyler, had been ordered by Fannin to join the artillery branch of the Texas army and thus missed Goliad. Field, Shackelford, and Ehrenberg wrote accounts of their service in the Texas Revolution, but none commented on this voyage. Conversations about Refugio and Goliad must have occurred, reinforcing the lessons Callahan had learned. Given his actions in later years, he realized that mobile armed forces dominated foot soldiers and superior firearms were essential. He had experienced the disastrous effects of Fannin's indecisive leadership; in the future, men would often comment on Callahan's resolve, describing him as absolutely fearless. Callahan's strong aversion toward Mexicans was rooted in the violence at Refugio, his time as a prisoner, and the loss of so many friends at Goliad. What he had endured also desensitized him; in future years, he would appear unperturbed by death. On a more positive note, Callahan's time in Texas helped him to imagine his life on a larger scale, and the vast empty lands of Texas beckoned.[43]

Table 2.4. Passenger list, schooner *Pennsylvania*, departed Velasco, Tex., June 16, 1836, arrived New Orleans, June 22, 1836

Name	*Age*	*State or country of origin*	*Military unit and remarks*	*Profession*
Boodis, William	21	Georgia		
Callihan (Callahan), James H.	22	Alabama	Georgia Battalion (Ga. Bttn.), Winn's Co.; detained at Victoria	Coachmaker
O'Daniel, John	25	Philadelphia	Ga. Bttn., Ticknor's Co.; detained at Victoria	Coachmaker
Errenbury (Ehrenberg), Hermann	19	Prussia	With Fannin at Goliad; Mobile Grays; escaped massacre	Clerk
Field, Dr. Joseph E.	30	Maine	Fought at Bexar, 1835; with Fannin at Goliad; detained; provided medical services	Doctor
Grice, Livingston B.	25	Alabama	Ga. Bttn, Winn's Co.; fought at San Jacinto	Blacksmith
Hammock, Henry P. (Roderick Pierce)	30	Georgia	Ga. Bttn., Bullock's Co.; detained at Victoria	Carpenter
Hitchcock, John	19	Georgia	Ga. Bttn., Wadsworth's Co.; detained at Victoria	
Holsinger (Holzinger), Col. Johan	40	Germany	Fought under Gen. Urrea at Refugio and Coleto; surrendered to Texas Army	Mexican Army
Kiege, Edward M.	24	Texas		Texas Navy
Mole, Jacob	24	(illegible)		Clerk
Moran, Martin	20	England	Ga. Bttn., Winn's Co.; escaped during Ward's retreat	Clerk
Paterson (Patterson), Edwin (Edward)	26	Alabama	Ga. Bttn., Ticknor's Co.; detained at Victoria	Carpenter
Robinson, John	31	Scotland		Farmer
Shackelford, Jack	45	Virginia	With Fannin at Goliad, Shackelford's Co.; detained; provided medical services	Doctor

Name	*Age*	*State or country of origin*	*Military unit and remarks*	*Profession*
Tyler, John H.	40	Kentucky	Reassigned to Texas artillery, Feb. 29, 1836	Farmer
White, Elvin (Alvin) E.	30	Vermont	With Fannin at Goliad; Colonel Garay saved him; General Urrea took him on the march north where he escaped	Carpenter

Sources: Arrivals, June 22, 1836, New Orleans Passenger Lists, 1820–1945, RG36, M259, R14, NAB; *New Orleans Bee*, June 23, 1836; *Dallas Morning News*, Sept. 13, 1931; W. N. Rowell and H. Davenport letters, 1936, DHC, TSLA; "Comments . . . in biographies of Fannin's men," DHC, TSLA; Literary Effort: "Sabina Brown's Mournful Story," DHC, TSLA; Davenport, "Notes from an Unfinished Study"; Davenport, "Men of Goliad," 1–41; H. David Maxey, comp., "Index to Military Rolls of the Republic of Texas, 1835–1845," *TSHA Online*, http://www.tshaonline.org/supsites/military/rep_cont.htm, accessed Dec. 17, 2011; Brister, "Holzinger, Juan Jose," *HBTO*; Juan Holzinger, ACSH, DAM, SEDENA; Roell, "Shackelford, Jack," *HBTO*. See Ornish, *Ehrenberg*, for Ehrenberg's biography.

On June 22, 1836, the *Pennsylvania* passengers debarked at New Orleans. Only four—Field, Moran, Hitchcock, and Callahan—ever returned to Texas. But that was in the future. Callahan spent a few days in New Orleans and then boarded the steamboat *Leonidas*, arriving at Mobile on June 30. Where he traveled from Mobile is not certain. The *Pennsylvania*'s manifest said he was bound for Alabama. Yet, the June 23, 1836, issue of the *Macon Telegraph* claimed that he hailed from Columbus, Georgia. Eventually, according to James Wilson Nichols, he returned to his family's farm in Jackson County, Georgia.[44]

The citizens of Georgia honored the sacrifice of the Georgia Battalion. In March 1837, Gwinnett County dedicated a monument to Winn and Sgt. Anthony Bates. Almost twenty years later, Georgia attempted to fund another memorial. The state arsenal had provided rifles to the battalion as it mobilized, and in 1856 the Georgia governor informed his Texan counterpart, Elisha M. Pease, that William F. Fannin, a relative of James Fannin, was authorized to receive payment for the guns from the state of Texas. Samuel G. Hardaway, of Bullock's company, had instigated this request. The Texas legislature approved a payment of $3,000, and Fannin told Pease that the money should be used to construct a monument in Texas to honor the battalion. Fannin died shortly thereafter, and that memorial was never built. In 1883, the Texas legislature authorized $1,000 for a monument to the battle at Refugio. A pink marble obelisk was erected in the city's central plaza at the same time that the city of Goliad and the state erected a cenotaph to honor Fannin. In 1913, the state purchased the old Fort Defiance complex, and in 1929 it bought the site of the Fannin massacre. The Texas Centennial resulted in a citizen-led effort to build a monument to Fannin's men on the site where they were buried; Davenport gave the address at the dedication. Finally, in 1976 the citizens of Shackelford County erected a granite monument to the battalion that was dedicated by Lady Bird Johnson. This is the only Texas memorial to the Georgia Battalion except for a statue of Joanna Troutman, who sewed the flag they brought to Texas. In 1913, Governor Oscar B. Colquitt arranged for her remains to be moved from Georgia to the Texas State Cemetery, where a bronze likeness of Troutman marks her grave. Nearby lies Callahan, who actually returned to Texas during his lifetime to secure his spot in history.[45]

CHAPTER 3

The Families of Johnson and Sarah Day, 1794–1836

"Brother Day denied the charge"

"December 15, [1830] [I]t was of Gods own will and free grace that I was once more delivered of my sins though like a heddious Mountain of sin and unbelief I was made to rejoice and give God the praise and glory. [M]y companion professed to be forgiven of his sins."[1]

Sarah Medissa Day married James Hughes Callahan at Seguin, Texas, in March 1843. How they met and the story of their married life are central to this narrative. In many respects they had similar upbringings, and both eventually migrated to Texas, he alone and she with her family, in search of land and prosperity. Having met James's family, we can better understand Sarah by following her kin—the Hembrees and Days—as they journeyed from Virginia to North Carolina and finally to South Carolina. The attitudes of her parents, Johnson and Sarah Hembree Day, like those of the Callahans, were formed in the early years of the United States. Tensions between religious groups, poor harvests, disputes between relatives, and the lure of free land led Sarah's parents to believe that Texas could offer a better life, so they moved there in 1836.

David Hembree (Sarah's great-grandfather) was born in Virginia about 1728 and settled in Lunenburg County. In the mid-1700s, he joined the tide of migration moving over the border into Granville County, North Carolina, where he became a prosperous farmer. In 1754 he volunteered to fight the French but was dismayed when his company became an undisciplined rabble. In the 1760s, English authorities suppressed North Carolina's

Regulator tax revolt, and creditors foreclosed on debtors. David lost three lawsuits for unpaid debts, so he sold his land and moved to South Carolina. By 1767 he and his family lived on 500 acres in the Tyger River valley of Craven County. This region endured significant changes due to the Regulator revolt, evangelical Christianity, and the American Revolution. In 1765, New Light Baptists formed the Tyger River Baptist Church, which David, his family, and brothers joined. When South Carolina embraced American independence, coastal patriots sent agents to convince backcountry settlers to join them. They found support in most areas but encountered some resistance, particularly from New Light Baptists. When the Tyger River Baptist Church split and internecine warfare erupted, David and his brothers sat out the war. Then, to avoid the religious animosity and seek better economic prospects, David sold his property and in 1792 bought land on Twenty-Six Mile Creek, a tributary of the Savannah River, in the Pendleton District. Over the years, he bought several more parcels there and by 1809 owned nearly 900 acres. At eighty-one years of age, he began selling his property; he sold 500 acres for $600 to his son James. When David died later that year, his estate inventory suggested he had become a fairly wealthy and literate man. His religiosity, willingness to relocate, and hunger for land were to one degree or another inherited by three generations of descendants, although a settled farm life would not be their destiny.[2]

David and his wife, Elizabeth, had four children; James H., their first, was born on March 27, 1759. James, who was about eight years old when his family moved to Craven County, spent his childhood on the South Carolina frontier, and like his father was influenced by the New Light Baptists. During the Revolution, he married Asenath, the sixth child of Job Felton and his first wife. The Feltons lived in Chowan and Rowan Counties, North Carolina, before moving to South Carolina during the Revolution, settling on the Tyger River near the Hembrees, and attending the same church. Asenath and James had at least nine children. Sarah, the future mother of Sarah Medissa, was born on August 6, 1795, in the Pendleton District. James claimed that until 1800 "he was wild and reckless." He ignored the church and like most of his neighbors gambled and drank. Having settled in the Pendleton District by 1790, he served on the first petit jury, but few other records mention him and he apparently had no property. As he approached forty years of age, he could not have anticipated his evangelical transformation, which greatly affected Sarah.[3]

As the nineteenth century began, only 8 percent of white adults in the South Carolina backcountry attended church. In a decade, that number had tripled as the Second Great Awakening spread. James succumbed to this evangelical fervor. His conversion was transformative—in July 1801 the Mountain Creek Baptist Church, where he delivered his first sermon in 1800, ordained him as a Baptist preacher. When the Salem Baptist Church split from the Mountain Creek Baptist Church, James served as its minister from 1813 until his death in 1849. He preached at other churches, with most of his ministries in Anderson County at the Salem, Hopewell, Mountain Creek, and Lebanon Baptist Churches. He led church inquiries that excommunicated members for sins that included defamation, intoxication, intemperance, lying, fornication, adultery, horse racing, and disobeying church rules. His family did not escape judgment; granddaughter Asenath Hembree was excommunicated for an extramarital pregnancy and grandson John Hembree for fornication.[4]

James did not just chase backsliders. On November 5, 1803, delegates from nine Baptist churches in the Greenville and Pendleton Districts met at the Salem Baptist Church and formed the Saluda Baptist Association. James was a founding member, and over the years he wrote the association's circulars, chaired annual meetings, served on committees, and preached keynote sermons. In 1818 he became a founding member of the nondenominational Pendleton Bible Society, which distributed hundreds of bibles. In 1832, the Saluda Baptist Association baptized 1,275 converts, a 130 percent increase in members. However, missionary zeal led to a conflict. Younger ministers at the 1835 Association meeting advocated foreign missions, Sunday schools, an educated ministry, and temperance. However, older ministers, including seventy-six-year-old James, angrily resisted. The next year, younger ministers led the association in joining the South Carolina Baptist Convention and adopting its tenets. James then led his church and others to form the antimissionary Fork Shoals Association. Although he never publicly changed his antimissionary views, before James died, he told a friend that he "manifested deep and heartfelt grief that he ever assumed such an attitude."[5]

In addition to his religious activities, James practiced Thomsonian medicine. In 1791 Samuel Thomson became convinced an herbal mixture had saved his wife's life. While the medical community persuaded most state legislatures, including South Carolina's, to outlaw Thomsonian methods, many backcountry practitioners sought immunity. Among seventy-five petitions asking the South Carolina Assembly to allow Thomsonian practitioners to receive payment was one signed by James and twenty-five of his neighbors, but the Assembly rejected all requests. James also augmented his income by farming. In 1809 his father sold him 500 acres along Twenty-Six Mile Creek. James extended his holdings by 140 acres between 1820 and 1827, and his ownership of one slave in 1820 and three in 1840 suggests that he tried cotton production. He eventually sold his land, including tracts to two sons and two sons-in-law in 1816, and his remaining twenty-four acres in 1843. He preached his last sermon at Salem Baptist Church on March 17, 1849, signed his will two months later, and died at the age of ninety on August 16, 1849. Asenath died on September 8, 1852; both were buried in the Old Salem Cemetery next to the church in which James had long served as pastor.[6]

James H. Hembree's will provides a telling insight into his personality and relationships. He wrote, "Four of my children has been advanced above the rest—John and James, Winney Heaton & Polley Bowen. I have gave land to these four." He left $100 each to his oldest son, Amariah, and his daughters Didama and Mahala. He gave $5 to his oldest daughter, Hepzibah, but left $20 to her daughter, who might have been his favorite grandchild. Lastly, James wrote, "For my beloved daughter Sally [Sarah] Day—she lives far off in Texas, I therefore bequeath her one dollar." Moreover, he directed that the remainder of his estate be equally divided amongst three sons and four daughters. He intentionally chose not to give any to Hepzibah and Sarah. His will shows that he had favorites among his children. Baptist historian T. H. Garrett characterized him as "a plain, rugged, solid flat stone, symbolic of the rustic manners, the firmness of purpose and unbending will." He tolerated no person who disagreed with him, and he was willing to turn his back on those who did, including Sarah, future mother-in-law of James Hughes Callahan.[7]

Sarah Hembree later wrote in her prayer journal: "Sally [Hembree] Day was bornd August 6th 1795 of religious Parrents. When I was an infant my father was called to the ministry. . . . I was awakened to see my self a sinner at seven years of old but I went on sinning and praying. At 19 years old I was married date 1814." Johnson Day was the man she married, and he took her to Texas. She would never have met him if Johnson's grandfather Edward had not moved to South Carolina. Edward was born on October 13, 1728, in St. John's Parish, Prince George's County, Maryland, and about 1750 he married, a union resulting in five boys, including Ballard (christened

May 21, 1761). In 1765, as tobacco production spread and tension escalated between common men and the landed gentry, Edward moved his family to Loudoun County, in northern Virginia. By 1775 Loudoun was one of the most populous Virginia counties, with growing Baptist and Methodist churches. Locals openly criticized the English government and, once the Revolution began, exhibited a pronounced intolerance for Tories. Almost 2,000 Loudoun County men volunteered to fight, but none of the men in the Edward Day family joined them. By 1786, Ballard Day and two brothers left Loudoun County, and Edward and his other children departed two years later. In 1790 Edward and some of his family were living in Fairfield County, South Carolina, with Ballard, a single man, settled nearby. By 1800 Edward was in the Pendleton District, and 1804 records show he was given approval to form the Big Creek Baptist Church. He died in 1810. His estate, valued at $686, was typical for a Pendleton District yeoman farmer.[8]

Ballard Day carried forward his father's legacy. He was six years old when his family moved to Loudoun County. Little is known about his adult years in Virginia except he worked as an overseer on George Summers's plantation. Again, no records place him or his brothers in the army during the Revolution. In 1786 he left for Fairfield County, where he married seventeen-year-old Sylvia, a daughter of neighbors Abraham and Dorcas Mayfield. In 1775 Abraham had settled in Camden District (later Fairfield County), where he married, bought a 425-acre plot, and had seven children. Abraham was a typical yeoman farmer, periodically buying and selling land. By 1795, he moved to a 200-acre farm on Rocky Creek in the Pendleton District, where he joined the Big Creek Baptist Church, founded by Edward Day; Abraham even preached there on December 11, 1824. He died in 1826. In many ways his daughter Sylvia was similar to her husband, Ballard; both were children of itinerant Baptist yeoman farmers.[9]

Ballard and Sylvia Day, who eventually had eight children, bought 100 acres in Fairfield County in 1794. Following his father and in-laws, Ballard moved his family in 1800 to the Pendleton District, where he purchased 100 acres on Rocky Creek. By 1810, he owned 564 acres six miles east of Anderson village. Like most upcountry farmers, he raised pigs and his wife had a loom, but he was among the 30 percent who bred sheep, and he occasionally owned slaves, so he likely raised some cotton. Ballard was also a Baptist, so he and Sylvia joined the Big Creek Baptist Church. This was the church his father founded and where Sylvia's father was a deacon, and in

1801 Ballard was its representative to the regional Bethel Baptist Association meeting. During the years that he worshipped there, he was often asked to resolve disagreements, and he was not among those expelled or chastised.[10]

In early 1815, Ballard began to get his estate in order. He gave land and money to most of his children. However, he did not do this for his second oldest son, Johnson; instead, he sold him 100 acres for $200. Ballard's estate was worth about $1,500, and in his will he wrote that when Sylvia died, the farm and assets were to be distributed among their children, excluding Johnson. Ballard died in early April 1815 and was buried near his farm in what would become Dorchester Cemetery. Sylvia eventually joined her son Hezekiah in Tishomingo, Mississippi, where she died about 1835. Through hard work and perseverance, Ballard had become a prosperous farmer with considerable property. But the fact that Johnson was the only son to whom he sold, rather than gave, land suggests that the old Baptist had strong feelings about his second son's character.[11]

It would seem as though Johnson Day and Sarah Hembree would follow the example of their parents. However, both lost their evangelical fervor as adults, and a drinking habit haunted Johnson. That being said, the young couple must have met at the Big Creek Baptist Church, and they married in 1814, when she was nineteen years old and he was twenty. Their life together was interrupted by Johnson enlisting in the South Carolina militia toward the end of the War of 1812, which almost caused him to miss the birth of his first child, James Milford Day, on April 11, 1815. After his return, he and Sarah had three more children: Sylvia (born January 13, 1816), Mary M. (December 6, 1818), and Mahala J. (December 10, 1820). Church was not part of their lives, and Sarah's prayer journal contained references to Johnson's predilection for whiskey.[12]

Johnson and Sarah stayed on the Rocky Creek farm he bought from his father until January 1822, when they sold their place and purchased a 200-acre farm near Anderson, earning a $110 profit. Nevertheless, in March 1822 they moved to Tuscaloosa County, Alabama, a move they never explained. When they left South Carolina, conditions there were not favorable for yeomen farmers since the Panic of 1819 cut cotton prices and the value of paper currency, making it hard to pay debts, while soil depletion decreased crop yields. In March 1820, Congress authorized the sale of federal lands in Alabama, and by 1821 tracts in the Tuscaloosa District were just six dollars per acre. Having moved with their parents to find better economic opportunities, Johnson and Sarah left South Carolina for Alabama.[13]

Neither the journey nor the destination proved to be pleasant. The most popular route led to Athens, Georgia, and then into central Tennessee and south to Tuscaloosa. The trip must have been especially arduous for Sarah, for, in addition to managing four children, she was pregnant. The area around Tuscaloosa had for centuries been a homeland for the Creek Indians, who had only recently left after years of conflict. Just three years after Alabama became a state in 1819, Tuscaloosa was a thriving community with a county courthouse, Masonic lodge, stores, hotel, and churches. But William Ely also wrote in 1821 that it was "despicable rough dirty & [with] uncomfortable rotting log cabins" and that the locals "dissipate their time & money, & would their morals if they had any. . . ." It is uncertain what Sarah and Johnson did once they arrived. No records indicate that they joined a Baptist church, but Tuscaloosa's saloons may have welcomed him. Sarah delivered her fifth child, Sarah Medissa Day, on December 18, 1822. One month later the family moved again, to Hall County, Georgia, where they probably stayed with Sarah's brother Amariah, a farmer. After a few months, the Days returned to South Carolina and bought a 200-acre farm on Beaverdam Creek in Anderson County. However, on January 29, 1825, Johnson sold this and purchased 119 acres on nearby Beaver Creek, six miles east of Sarah's father's farm.[14]

Unfortunately for Johnson, he returned to farming in Anderson County as the price of cotton plummeted and the price of corn varied by 50 percent. Droughts and occasional floods and caterpillar infestations also ruined many crops. On August 20, 1831, the *Charleston Courier* declared: "For the last seven years there has not been two full crops of cotton and corn made." Certainly, the Days did not starve, but prospects seemed bleak. During these hard times, Sarah delivered another daughter, Hepzibah Clemons, on February 6, 1825. Somehow the children were fed and clothed—Sarah and her daughters almost certainly spent many hours spinning and weaving. They were also educated, either at home or in private rural schools, since later records indicated they could read, write, and add and subtract.[15]

In 1825, when Sarah and Johnson settled on Beaver Creek, the nearest Baptist churches were at Neal's Creek, two miles east, and Mount Tabor, four miles south. Salem Baptist, the church where Sarah's father, James H. Hembree, was pastor, lay six miles to the west. The main minister for Neal's Creek and Mount Tabor was Sanford Vandiver, a progressive preacher who challenged James on the issue of foreign missions. In 1828, Sarah rededicated herself to the church, and that June she wrote in her prayer journal,

"It pleased God to give my spirit rest from My troubles of sin for a while." Perhaps her hardscrabble life had become overwhelming, or maybe pleas from her father and Vandiver proved compelling. She implied that Johnson's drinking contributed to her return to the church. However, this commitment was short-lived, as she admitted that "being sadly opposed by A companion and the troubles Of this world with shame of Confess I turned again into the beggerly elliments of this world." Sarah was caught between her commitment to a wayward husband and desire to satisfy spiritual needs.[16]

With bleak economic prospects and smoldering conflicts over religion, Sarah and Johnson moved by 1830 to Lancaster County, South Carolina. There they settled near Johnson's mother, Sylvia, and his brother Alfred. Sarah delivered their sixth daughter, Elizabeth Caroline, on October 9, 1830. There are no clues as to how Johnson supported his family. His crippled mother had three sons living with her and owned two slaves; Johnson may have worked for her. He may had been lured by the small gold rush developing in Lancaster County. Regardless, whatever he pursued did not make him wealthy. However, in this new location, in proximity to his family, Johnson returned to the church. Sarah joyously wrote, "[In] the year 1830 which Was the 35 year of my life December 15 it was of Gods own will and free grace That I was once more delivered Of my sins [and] my Companion Professed to be forgiven of his sins About this time Christmas day wee was Baptised." The change affected at least some of their children. Sarah's next entry exclaimed that on "the 25 Of January Sibby was Baptised." Sibby, or Sylvia, was their fourteen-year-old daughter. When Sarah delivered her last child, a daughter, in November 1832, she and Johnson named her Meekness Amanda.[17]

In the 1830s, thousands of South Carolinians migrated to other states, while immigration into the Palmetto State almost ceased. Depleted soil, poor harvests, and low income led 200,000 to leave by 1860. In 1835 the *Camden Journal* noted that "the old and the young are preparing to emigrate, and the inquiry is not whether you are going, but when do you go." Encouraging this exodus were articles extolling the virtues of Texas and western Tennessee. Johnson and Sarah left South Carolina again on January 1, 1833, for Hardeman County, Tennessee. They sold their Beaver Creek land for $150. Sarah wrote, "we got to Tennesse Bolliver first of February." By all indications, they traveled alone. Sarah did not describe travel conditions during the month-long journey, but other travelers left accounts. Late in 1827, Henrietta Fitzhugh suffered through the "bitterly cold" nights in southern Tennessee and described a road near Bolivar "as beautiful if it was not quite so stumpy." According to Fitzhugh, Bolivar was a "very pretty flourishing looking place [with] some very pretty buildings," but she added that the "good folks seem to think much more of amusements and making money than educating their children & bringing them up with religious & moral habits." Bolivar lay in Hardeman County, which was named after Thomas J. Hardeman, a War of 1812 veteran. The Hardemans later relocated to Gonzales, Texas, and there crossed paths with Sarah Day, her children, and grandchildren. Sarah never explained why her family moved to Bolivar, but Johnson's uncle, Hanson Day and a son had settled there in 1828. Sarah and Johnson lived near Hanson outside the village of Toone, on the banks of Mill Creek, a tributary of the Hatchie River, which was navigable to the Mississippi River.[18]

On the third Sunday in 1833, Sarah, Johnson, and Sylvia joined the Mill Creek Baptist Church, presenting letters of good standing from their church in South Carolina. Johnson bought six acres of Mill Creek bottomland, though this small plot could hardly have provided sufficient support for his family. He had several ploughs, so he may have leased land, worked on other farms, or labored at the landing on the Hatchie. He did earn some respect. In 1835, he signed the will of Jacob Pirtle, a local political leader, and in September 1834 members of the Mill Creek Baptist Church sent "Brother William Sills, and Brother Johnson Day" to the Big Hatchie Baptist Association. However, sometimes Johnson ran afoul of fellow Baptists. In March 1834, church minutes noted, "Brother Day came forward with an acknowledgement to the Church for disorder of intoxication. The Church agree[d] to forgive the Brother." Johnson resorted to whiskey again during his trip to the Association meeting. His church's November 1834 minutes stated, "There is reports in circulation; saying Brother Johnson Day . . . has been gilty of drinking to much." At the December meeting, church members confronted Johnson about the intoxication accusation, but according to the minutes, "Brother Day denide the charge against him; and he continued in fellowship." After this, he briefly stopped drinking whiskey or drank only in moderation.[19]

Johnson must have found it almost impossible to eke out a living on the land he owned. Moreover, the constant surveillance of the Mill Creek Baptist Church members rankled him. In May 1836, the church clerk recorded, "Old Sister Day [meaning Sarah] . . . spoke for letters of dismission; and it was granted." The October 1836 church minutes revealed Johnson's troubles:

"The Saturday before the Lord's day in October, 1836; the Church met. . . . Brother, and Sister Day, [had] applied for letters of dismission. The Church granted a letter to Sister Day; but as there was report of Brother Day drinking two much, The Church objected giving him a letter." One year later, the Mill Creek Baptist Church members once more deliberated on the matter: "As Brother Johnson Day, last October, applied for a letter of dismission; but as there was a report against him for drinking to much; The Church did not grant him a letter unless he came forward and made satisfaction, but he did not, and moved of [off] in this situation . . . he is excluded from fellowship." Sometime during the summer of 1836, Johnson Day once more moved his family, this time to Texas.[20]

From the time Sarah and Johnson settled in Hardeman County, it would have been hard not to hear about Texas. In December 1830, William A. Mathews, an agent of DeWitt's Colony, arrived in Bolivar, and organized eighteen families who left and settled near Gonzales, Texas. In 1835, Hardeman County resident Mark R. Roberts wrote to *empresario* Sterling C. Robertson in Texas, inquiring about cotton production there. More importantly, after his wife died in 1835 Thomas J. Hardeman, with his brothers, Blackstone and Bailey, and twenty-five other families, relocated near Gonzales, where they participated in the Texas war for independence. Texas was also a hot topic in local newspapers, as well as those in New Orleans, Memphis, and Nashville. Accounts of escalating tensions between Mexicans and Texians were on everyone's lips, while the news of Sam Houston's victory at San Jacinto gave Texas an even more seductive aura. On June 29, 1836, the *Nashville Banner and Nashville Whig* reported, "no more emigrants are now wanted in Texas 'but those intending to settle down as cultivators of the soil.'" Other accounts stressed that Texas was safe for residents. Johnson, having fallen out of favor with his church, was certainly contemplating another move, and Texas looked good. The date of his departure from Hardeman County is unknown, but June 1836 seems likely; Hanson Day moved at that time to Lawrence County, Tennessee. Since Sarah asked for a letter of dismission from the Mill Creek Baptist Church in May, they had a month to prepare for yet another journey.[21]

The trip to Texas realigned the Day family. The oldest daughter of Sarah and Johnson, Sylvia, disappeared. The last record of her was when she joined the Mill Creek Baptist Church in 1833. Sarah noted in her journal when each daughter married and to whom, but not Sylvia. The Days, with their son and remaining six daughters, arrived in Memphis after a few days of travel; the town, according to Virginian James D. Davidson, was a "miserable looking place." They did not linger but crossed the Mississippi River on a steam ferryboat to Arkansas and drove west. On this route a fortuitous event occurred: the Days met the Nicholses. George Washington Nichols lived with his wife, Mary Ann, and their four sons and five daughters at Grandee Lake, a day's ride from the west bank of the Mississippi. James Wilson Nichols, their fifth child, wrote a memoir, *Now You Hear My Horn*, describing his family's adventures as they migrated from Tennessee to Texas, as well as his life as a Texan. He described the families' first meeting:

> In the summer of 1836 Father sold out in Arkansas to moove to Texas and his destination was San Antonio, but about a week before we was ready to start one evening som moovers drove up and baught som corn and fodder from Father and drove out and camped. After supper Father went out to the camp to chat and find out whare they was mooveing to and I went with him and we found out that their names was Day and that they was mooveing to Texas. This was the Johnson Day family, Milfords father, and Father and the old man Day mad a covenant that night to git togeather, travil togeather, and settle togeather.[22]

The Nicholses later played prominent roles in the lives of the Days. George Nichols was born about 1795 in Charleston, South Carolina. His son James claimed that George fought in the 1814 Battle of Horseshoe Bend and in 1815 at New Orleans. Before then, George's family moved to Franklin County, Tennessee, where in 1812 he married fourteen-year-old Mary Ann Walker. While there, she gave birth to six children: Solomon Grundy (born June 24, 1813), Thomas R. (January 8, 1815), John Walker (ca. 1816), Martha Hannah (ca. 1818), James Wilson (December 27, 1820), and Nancy (ca. 1821). Around 1823, the Nicholses moved to Madison County, where two more daughters joined the family: Elizabeth (ca. 1824) and Meriah (Mary) E. (ca. 1829). By 1830, the Nicholses relocated to the Grandee Lake farm in Crittenden County, Arkansas, where Mary Ann delivered their last child, Charlotte (ca. 1831). The Nicholses held a measure of prestige in their community, and one son, John Walker, was elected justice of the peace in 1835. Nevertheless, George, like Johnson, sold his property, and they left for Texas together in the fall of 1836.[23]

The oxen-drawn, two-wagon train with four adults and sixteen adolescents followed the Memphis–Little Rock Military Road, as did most Texas immigrants who traveled by land. Stumps dotted the roadbed, rain washed out sections, and swampy bogs appeared. Judging from the tenor of James Wilson Nichols's narrative, the Days and Nicholses worked well together. At Little Rock, ferries carried them across the Arkansas River, whence they traveled southwest along the post road into Louisiana and on to Natchitoches, where they arrived about December 10, 1836. The convergence of the land and river routes to Texas, Natchitoches was a gateway for colonists recruited by Stephen F. Austin and other *empresarios*. During the Texas Revolution, many volunteers passed through, including David Crockett of Tennessee and the New Orleans Greys. Not everyone appreciated Natchitoches; Mirabeau B. Lamar claimed in July 1835 that it was a "town of filth, fever & feuds."[24]

It may have taken the wagons three or four days to travel forty miles from Natchitoches to the Sabine River, which marked the Texas border. As James Wilson Nichols noted, the Days and Nicholses arrived on the Sabine on December 16 and crossed on the Gaines Ferry. Johnson and Sarah Day stepped onto Texas soil with seven children—James (21), Mary (18), Mahala (16), Sarah (14), Hepzibah (11), Elizabeth (6), and Meekness (4). Their wandering days were almost over. None would ever leave Texas, nor could they have predicted the trials mingled with joy to come. At just fourteen years of age, Sarah Medissa Day had lived in Alabama, Georgia, South Carolina, and Tennessee. She had experienced hardship and religious conflict, as well as conversion. She must have absorbed the essential meanings of her experiences, which shaped her own resolution and determination. Soon she would have ample opportunities to demonstrate the depth of her fortitude.[25]

CHAPTER 4

The Day Families from Gonzales to Seguin, 1837–1839

"As a citizen and representative"

After the Gaines Ferry docked on the west bank of the Sabine River, yoked oxen plodded down the gangplank, yanking the covered wagons into Texas. Nearby stood James Gaines's store, saloon, and inn, where the Day and Nichols families paid their tolls and purchased more supplies. Johnson Day paid about three dollars for his family, wagon, several yokes of oxen, and other livestock to cross the river, a modest price to enter a new land. After three months on the road, the Days and Nicholses had reached Texas and, according to James Wilson Nichols, they made the trip without any major arguments. They were among the first of thousands who would make a similar journey. But their quest was not over; their ultimate destination was San Antonio, a few hundred miles farther southwest.[1]

From Gaines's Ferry the families trekked through East Texas to San Augustine (see map frontispiece). There lay the eastern terminus of the Camino Real or Old San Antonio Road, begun by the Spanish. In 1834 Amos A. Parker described the area as undulating red clay covered in oak and hickory trees with an occasional log cabin and small fields. During his 1834 travels, Benjamin Lundy wrote that in contrast to Louisiana's sandy deserts the region had fields of corn and cotton while houses were shaded by groves of china trees. The Days and Nichols must have been impressed. At thirteen miles per day, their caravan took two days to reach San Augustine. The town had been a point of entry for volunteer troops in the Texas Revolution and one of exodus for families during the "Runaway Scrape." Parker called it a small village with "two large taverns, three stores, a courthouse, and ten or a dozen dwellings," and he noted it had a school attended by students from the region. Both families decided to spend the winter there. James W. Nichols recalled that they "rented land from [Francis] Richards," who lived six miles east of town. Day's grandson, William Martin Hankins, recalled that Johnson delayed his departure until the next summer due to the unsettled conditions in Texas.[2]

One of the coldest winters of recent years swept across East Texas in January 1837. It was so severe that all but two of the Nichols's oxen died from exposure, and the Days lost some as well. James W. Nichols and his brother, John Walker, bought three or four yokes of oxen from John Thorn on the Angelina River. Needing forage for their livestock and food for their families, Johnson Day and George Washington Nichols planted corn in March 1837; Hankins later said that Johnson raised this crop on rented land. Two of their sons, John W. Nichols and James Milford Day, hauled freight to earn money, while James W. and Solomon Grundy Nichols delivered hay. Everything helped; James W. Nichols wrote that he caught two catfish: "The large one weighed 107 pounds, the small one 49 pounds." The entire party—eleven girls, five boys, and two married couples—were always preparing for the next leg of their journey. On the road, both families would have cornbread, bacon, and coffee, with milk from cows tied to Johnson Day's wagon. With the corn harvested, the group left for San Antonio, southwestward on the Camino Real. They traveled three or four days before arriving at the next town, Nacogdoches. During the Texas Revolution, Nacogdoches had been another staging point for volunteers and a refugee center. Here both families saw for the first time some distinctive Spanish architecture.[3]

From the Sabine to south of San Antonio, the Texas countryside is cut by a series of major rivers running northwest to southeast into the Gulf of Mexico. Leaving Nacogdoches, the Day-Nichols caravan reached the Angelina River and then the Neches. Continuing for several miles, they came to a fork in the roadway. They decided to avoid the direct, and more dangerous, western route into San Antonio. Instead, they traveled on the inner road toward Gonzales (see map frontispiece). Along the way they entered a grassy corridor, which stretches from the Trinity River across the Brazos to the Colorado. Lundy described one section of this prairie as "three miles wide, very large and beautiful, and equal to any I have seen within" Texas. The Trinity River was the largest waterway the Day-Nichols group had encountered since the Sabine, but Robbins's Ferry made the crossing easy. After several days, they arrived at the junction of the Navasota and Brazos Rivers, where another ferry carried goods and people across. Here was Washington-on-the-Brazos, where the Convention of 1836 had declared Texas independent. The families continued south to the Colorado River through one of the more desirable parts of Texas. Some prairies around the Colorado sprawled across thousands of acres of tall grass that beckoned cattle raisers, and farmers coveted the fertile soil. Eventually, the caravan arrived at La Grange, on the east side of the Colorado. Crossing over, the Days may not have realized that, except for short visits to Austin, none would ever again set foot on the east bank. They had arrived in their new homeland—the Guadalupe River Basin.[4]

From the Colorado, the caravan took the road to Goliad, but at the thirty-mile marker the path forked, and they rolled southwest to Gonzales. They initially enjoyed fair but unseasonably cold weather. Near the midpoint, a short spell of chilling rain was followed by cool, sunny days until the rain resumed for a week. The two families struggled to haul their wagons from the mud. In the spring of 1837, Harvey A. Adams described his experience on the way to Gonzales: "My wagon was sinking every moment deeper and deeper into the mire; until the bed of the wagon was almost settled in the water." Gonzales had been the headquarters of DeWitt's Colony and where the Texas Revolution began with a clash over a small cannon in 1835. The small town had paid a heavy price for independence when thirty-two Gonzales men joined the Alamo defenders and died there. The town was burned to the ground four days later as Sam Houston withdrew toward San Jacinto. When the Days and Nichols arrived, Gonzales was nearly uninhabited; the 1837 county tax roll listed twenty-nine men. No one in the Day and Nichols families ever said why they halted in Gonzales; James W. Nichols merely noted, "We mad[e] the trip to Gonzales and stopped thare."[5]

George W. Nichols and Johnson Day did visit San Antonio, sixty miles west, before choosing where to settle. James W. Nichols wrote, "Father had heard so much about old San Antonio in his early life he wanted to see the place." James W. and his brother Solomon G. went along, and James M. Day joined his father. They found a deserted town where seeing the barrel of David Crockett's rifle and attending a fandango were the only excitement they encountered. According to James W. Nichols, "Father and Day decided not to move to San Antonio and returned to Gonzales."[6]

The two families established new lives in Gonzales. By the spring of 1838, about one hundred families lived along the Guadalupe and San Marcos

Rivers, and Gonzales County was organized. In the February 1838 elections, Thomas R. Nichols lost his bid for constable, but Johnson Day was elected a justice of the peace. The commissioners court first met in October, as did the district court, but some officials started earlier; the county clerk issued his first marriage license on April 15, and Day was sworn in for the Gonzales town precinct on March 3. The diverse responsibilities of a justice of the peace made him a familiar figure. His purchase of 244 sheets of paper and ink in June indicates how busy he was, and he married two couples in that month. The town grew rapidly and again became a thriving place, according to an anonymous letter in the *Telegraph and Texas Register*. With the Texas General Land Office organizing, real estate agencies appeared. By April 1838, Byrd Lockhart and Thomas J. Pilgrim opened a Gonzales real estate agency. That same month, Edward Burleson organized a militia brigade to protect most of the counties south of the Colorado River. Gonzales County and Gonzales thus had many of the features of a thriving frontier settlement.[7]

For frontier families in the Republic of Texas, the first priorities were food, clothing, and shelter. With Gonzales razed to the ground, the Days had a dire need for shelter, but Johnson had an array of carpentry tools. Within months, he also had five cows and calves, and for planting, he owned several plows. There were stores, so Sarah purchased flour, coffee, sugar, pork, and beef, but provisions were expensive. Women spun cloth, blankets or quilts were used to make coats, and breeches and shirts for men were made from tanned deer hides. Beef hides were shaped for moccasins, shoes, or boots. In Gonzales, which had no churches until 1840, Johnson probably felt he had found a place where he could live free of others' expectations. He added alcohol to his list of priorities. From January through April 22, 1838, he bought four and a half gallons of whiskey, at $2.50 to $3.00 per gallon, from a store operated by William Wirt Alsbury and Henry Clinton Slade, and he drank another twenty-eight glasses of "spirits" on their premises. In a ten-week period from May through mid-July 1838, he bought eighty-five shots of whiskey and ten shots of brandy at Joseph D. Clements's store, and he also purchased two bottles of whiskey and one of wine.[8]

By the time the Day and Nichols families reached Gonzales, they had developed firm friendships. Some of these friendships, as James W. Nichols noted, led to marriages by bond, with couples living together. By the spring of 1838, the Republic's marriage laws were enacted and on May 2, 1838, Gonzales County Chief Justice Bartlett D. McClure married twenty-three-year-old James M. Day and twenty-year-old Martha Hannah Nichols. The couple had pledged their first six-month marriage bond in 1837 and renewed it six months later before marrying. They did not own property when they wed, but they bought a wagon and two yokes of oxen in July. James hauled freight for a fee and rented or squatted on land in Gonzales. On the same day, McClure married nineteen-year-old Mary Day and twenty-two-year-old John W. Nichols. Mary and John had also lived together under a marriage bond for one year. John supported his wife by tenant farming and hauling jobs. On that Wednesday, McClure also performed a third wedding—allegedly the first three-ring ceremony since the Revolution. Some months earlier, after the Day and Nichols families settled in Gonzales, George W. Nichols had sent James W. Nichols with a wagonload of grain to a gristmill near La Grange. There he met Billy Mitchell, Barney Wilson, Barrett Randle, Green Cunningham, John Rhodes King, and Henry Basil King. These men had walked from Stewart County, Tennessee, to La Grange. After meeting Nichols, they all decided to accompany him to Gonzales, where Henry met Mahala J. Day. It was they who joined in that three-ring service.[9]

Mahala's new husband, Henry, was a Stewart County native, born December 12, 1818. He lost his father, William, in 1825. His mother remarried (John James Anderson McNary Boyd), but Henry and his older brother John, perhaps hard-pressed by the financial panic in 1837, sold their portions of their father's estate and left for Texas. Like the other two grooms, King did not own land, paying only a poll tax in 1838 and 1839. In 1841 his younger brother, William George King, with his mother and stepfather, also moved to Gonzales County. Two of the King brothers would become prominent local officials, and Henry would serve as a ranger with his brother-in-law, James Hughes Callahan.[10]

Mahala's parents actually attended four weddings that spring. Two weeks earlier, on April 15, fifteen-year-old Sarah Medissa Day had married William W. Alsbury, with McClure officiating. They were the last couple in Gonzales County who had lived as husband and wife under the Spanish bond system. They were also the first to apply for a license to marry in Gonzales County under the new Texas law, and their wedding was the first in the county since independence. It is not certain when Alsbury had arrived in Gonzales, but it was late in 1837 since he and Slade opened their tavern and store then. His origins are also vague. The Alsbury family had been in Texas since the 1820s. Thomas Alsbury Jr. of Virginia operated a tavern in Hopkinsville, Kentucky, before he became one of the "Old Three Hundred" recruited by Stephen F. Austin. Two years before he died in 1824, he and three sons received land grants ranging in size from one-and-a-half to two leagues (one league is 4,428 acres). In 1828, according to his land application, William W. Alsbury arrived in Texas at the age of twenty-two. By 1830 he was in Matamoros, where on October 9, 1832, the U.S. consul noted that Alsbury had been a resident since August 1830, was a Mexican citizen, and held a Mexican government commission. According to parish records, he married Ramona Garza, and in 1830 they had one daughter, Maria Andrea. Three of his brothers fought in the Texas Revolution, but William's location during that time is unknown. However, on December 17, 1836, he sent Austin a package of seeds and plants from the Mexican borderlands, which suggests he still lived in Matamoros or South Texas. By late 1837, he had a business in Gonzales, where he courted Sarah. On February 28, 1838, Alsbury received a single man's grant of one-third of a league and on May 5, now married, he was granted an additional two-thirds of a league.[11]

By the summer of 1838, Johnson and Sarah Hembree Day had every reason to be optimistic. They owed money to businesses and individuals, but Johnson was well-respected as a justice of the peace. The land office would soon certify his headright of 1,280 acres, and their son and three daughters had married. Three girls remained single, but in a county teeming with bachelors it should not be long before they left home, too. Then on a foggy July 29, his forty-sixth birthday, Johnson died suddenly after a brief illness. The Day family has conflicting stories about his death. Day's great-great-grandson, Otho B. "Papa" Phillips, said he died of an insect bite. However, three other sources indicate the cause was acute dysentery. Grandson Hankins wrote that Johnson's death resulted from "a very unsanitary condition" that prevailed in that part of Texas. Johnson's daughter, Sarah Medissa, said in an 1840 deposition that "she was taken sick by the persistent diseases of the country" in the summer of 1838 and almost died herself. John W. S. Dancy, who visited Gonzales in August 1838, wrote that there had been much sickness in Gonzales and four had died. Johnson, like other early Gonzales settlers, was probably interred in Cemetery Square. When a rectory was constructed there in 1890, these remains were reburied in a common grave in the City Cemetery.[12]

Johnson Day died intestate, so his estate was adjudicated in the Gonzales County probate court. On August 27, 1838, James M. Day petitioned to be his father's administrator. When no one objected, Justice McClure appointed him, with Anson G. Neal and Eli Mitchell endorsing his $5,000 security bond. Johnson's estate provides a good insight into life in Gonzales County at that time. Debt was common for newcomers on the Texas frontier, and without banks neighbors and merchants lent money. Six weeks after Johnson arrived, he borrowed cash and bought goods on credit. He signed promissory notes totaling $384.45 to ten men, including his son James and future son-in-law Henry B. King. Notes became a form of currency to settle debts on the cash-starved frontier; for example, George W. Nichols and Johnson jointly borrowed $100 from Jacob Roberts, who signed a portion of the note to H. G. Henderson, who later transferred it to George W. Nichols. Johnson also had charge accounts at two stores, including one co-owned by his son-in-law, Alsbury. At the time of his death, Johnson's debts totaled $469.44. But he had money to spend periodically. He used his large wagon and three yokes of oxen to earn money freighting, and he had an excess of farming equipment to cultivate crops for neighbors. The family surely sold butter, cream, and milk; after all, they had five cows. Also, Johnson's son James had enough cash to loan his father money.[13]

Selling assets was the common way to settle an estate's debts, and appraisers determined Johnson's estate to be worth about $675, not including the value of the 1,280-acre land grant due him. An auction on October 6, 1838, yielded $645.87. Of sixty-nine articles sold, Sarah H. Day, her son, and two sons-in-law bought forty-five. She acquired all the household goods, a sidesaddle, and one cow and calf. James M. Day purchased the three yokes of oxen, a wagon, a rifle, three plows, saddlebags, carpentry tools, and a cow with its calf. Sarah acquired enough to support herself, and James obtained the necessities for expanding his freight business and growing crops, as well as the means to repair and protect his home. By the time Johnson's probate closed on November 28, 1838, Sarah received $151.08, and $37.94 went to each of the married children.[14]

Texas law required probate judges to appoint guardians for deceased males' children under the age of twenty-one, even if the mother was still living. Johnson left three unmarried, underage daughters: Hepzibah Clemons, Elizabeth Caroline, and Meekness Amanda. So, on November 28, 1839, Sarah pledged a bond of $10,000 and asked to be named her daughters' guardian, a request the judge honored. An unmarried woman on the Texas frontier during the 1830s faced many challenges, so caring for three minors placed a great burden on Sarah. As events unfolded, she would meet this challenge. One source of hope was Johnson's land grant. Since he had arrived after March 1836 and was a married man, he was eligible for a 1,280-acre grant. On November 17, the Gonzales County Board of Land Commissioners awarded its first grants; Johnson was forty-second on the list of second-class awards. When his estate closed, his heirs divided the acreage; Sarah received half, with the remainder equally divided among the seven children. This agreement was only the beginning of the ultimate location and distribution of the land—a saga that would involve Sarah's grandchildren.[15]

Like Gonzales, other Texas communities were reestablishing themselves after the war, and new ones were being created. On August 12, 1838, three weeks after Johnson Day died, Mathew Caldwell, Arthur Swift, and James Campbell joined Joseph S. Martin and agreed to sell a tract of land thirty miles west of Gonzales. The property occupied a slight elevation that placed any houses above the Guadalupe River floodplain. Two spring-fed streams, Mill Creek and Elm Springs, lay on the eastern edge, while another, Walnut Springs, "a rushing torrent fed by a large spring," formed its western boundary. In 1832, when Green DeWitt organized his colony, two settlers, Humphries Branch and his father-in-law, John Sowell, built their cabins near the site. When the Texas Revolution erupted, they abandoned the area. Branch was so disgusted that he and his family sailed for England, but not before he sold (for 300 pesos) the lower half of his league to Martin. Martin and his associates had three advantages for creating a new town: the assets of the area were well known, the land had been surveyed, and in nearby Gonzales, established pioneers were making it difficult for newcomers. John R. King recalled that "the old citizens were prejudiced against new immigrants they even refused to sell lots in Gonzales." Thus, when Martin announced his plan to plat a town on Walnut Springs, many settlers attended the planning event on August 12, including Sarah, her son James M. Day, and two sons-in-law, Henry B. King and John W. Nichols.[16]

Thirty-three men signed up as shareholders on August 12, 1838, and James M. Day was fourteenth on the list. Each pledged to: pay a deposit of $50.31 and the balance within twelve months; move to their lots by November 1; live there for one year; and build a house at least fourteen feet wide and sixteen feet long within six months. The shareholders congregated under the oak trees at nearby Elm Springs on September 22. They named the town Walnut Springs and agreed the lots would be divided into four categories: inner town blocks; one-acre garden lots surrounding the inner town blocks; five-acre timber lots along the Guadalupe River banks; and twelve-acre farm lots occupying an area to the north (map. 4.1).

By now, Swift and Campbell had surveyed the town lots, so the men drew for parcels. At a shareholders' meeting on November 1, French Smith was elected president. One agenda item had important implications for

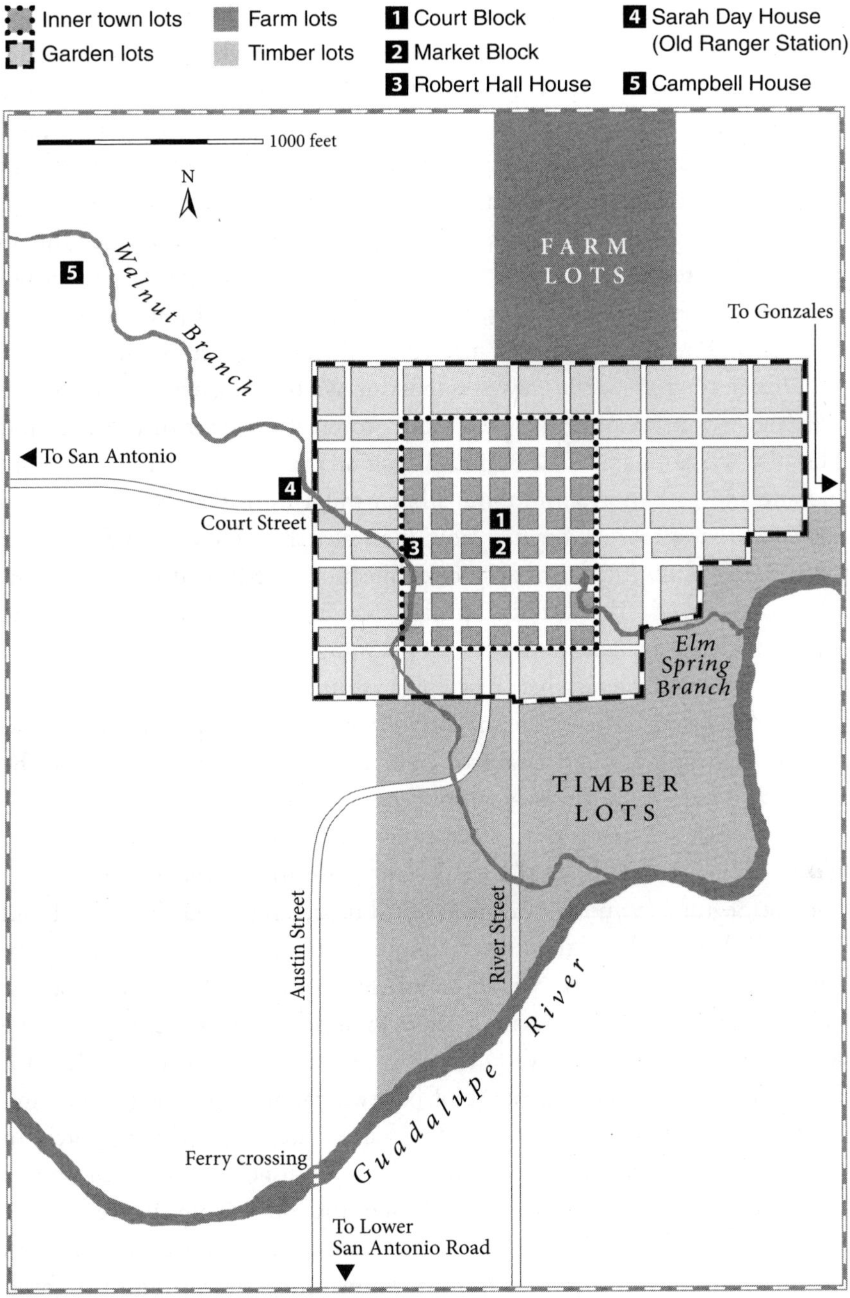

Map 4.1. Seguin township plats, 1839. Map by Carol Zuber-Mallison.

Sarah—the shareholders approved her "as a Citizen and Representative in lieu of Miles G. Dikes." She was the only woman afforded this status, and thereafter she attended the meetings and voted on issues. On August 12, 1839, she paid Dikes $50 and received deeds to five town lots and a one-acre garden plot. The other garden lots were distributed by lottery on November 15, 1838, and the drawing for the farm and timber lots followed on December 3. When all was settled, Sarah, her son, and two sons-in-law collectively possessed thirty-four town, sixteen garden, nine farm, and six timber lots. For all this, Sarah paid $93.50, James M. Day $105, Henry B. King $80, and John W. Nichols $126.50. All four considered this new village their permanent home.[17]

In December 1838, the new residents of Walnut Springs petitioned the Gonzales County Commissioners Court to create their own precinct and their plea was approved. The bounds began on the west at the Bexar County line and ran east to a point about fifteen miles from Gonzales. They also requested that a road be opened from Gonzales through Walnut Springs to the Bexar County line with a direct connection to San Antonio; the commissioners agreed. The Walnut Springs shareholders met for the last time on August 3, 1839, addressing street planning and inheritance of shares. One item on the agenda had particular significance. Dissatisfied with the settlement's original name, the shareholders voted to change it to either Tuscumbia or Seguin. By a margin of eighteen to seven, Seguin became the name, chosen to honor Juan Nepomuceno Seguín, Tejano hero of the Texas Revolution. The name proved appropriate as Seguin would be strategically important in the defense of the southwestern frontier of the Republic.[18]

Once Seguin's town lots had been distributed, landowners began to build houses. Robert Hall was the first to complete his log cabin, just downstream from where Sarah's house would stand. Sarah occupied her home about November 1, 1838, having chosen a prime location on the western edge of the one-acre garden lots along Walnut Springs Branch. She used walnut logs for the walls, ceiling joists, and frame of her two-room dogtrot log cabin, and planks and boards for the doors, window frames, flooring, and front porch. In 1846, her family renovated the structure, adding a stone chimney with a plank mantle and brick hearth on the south wall of the south room (figure 4.1).

The dogtrot was enclosed, and the outer and inner walls were coated with a layer of stucco. By then, the home was one of the largest and best-built houses in Seguin. On November 19, 1848, Capt. Seth Eastman sketched a landscape entitled "Seguin, Texas—looking north." Sarah's cabin appears on the horizon on the left side of the drawing (figure 4.2). The house served as

Fig. 4.1. Sarah Hembree Day's house—the Old Ranger Station. Author's collection.

Fig. 4.2. Seth Eastman, *Seguin, Texas, Looking North, November 1848*. From *Sketchbook, 1848–1849*. Graphite on paper. Collection of the McNay Art Museum, Gift of the Pearl Brewing Company (1961.5.80).

a mustering site and field hospital for local rangers, hence its being remembered as the "Old Ranger Station," as well as a popular venue for all-night dances. More important to Sarah were the lands for livestock and crops, and family living nearby—daughter Mahala and son-in-law Henry B. King lived immediately east across Walnut Spring Branch, while daughter Mary and her husband, John W. Nichols, settled 100 yards to the south. Sarah's house proved durable; it was lived in until 1955 and razed in 1965.[19]

Widows faced immense obstacles in the Republic of Texas, but few scholarly studies have been done on them, with the exception of a work on Colorado County by Angela Boswell. After studying the lives of frontier women, Ann Patton Malone wrote: "Female responses to frontier Texas varied in accordance with the position of each female in her life cycle. Pioneering . . . experiences were generally . . . liberating for the young, unmarried, newly married, and childless woman. But the same frontier presented terrifying challenges to women of childbearing ages and to mothers of small children." So, it is not hard to understand why many widows accepted the first marriage proposal they received. Sarah's life in Seguin provides a useful case study on a successful widow in antebellum Texas.[20]

Sarah never remarried and she appeared on the Gonzales County tax rolls from 1840 until 1846. Over this same period, the names of other widows changed, suggesting that each remarried, with the exception of one other: Sarah Seely DeWitt, widow of Green DeWitt, founder of the colony that bore his name. The two Sarahs represented economic extremes in the area; Sarah Hembree Day had little property, while Sarah DeWitt owned large tracts and several slaves. This illustrates one facet of widowhood in Texas—to some extent wealth determined the options a widow had. Sarah Day left no indication of why she never remarried. There were eligible men. Even George W. Nichols became available. According to James W. Nichols, there were only two widows in Seguin in 1839—Sarah Day and Rachel Sowell. If George approached Sarah, she rebuffed him, as he married Rachel. Sarah had endured a marriage that was disrupted by alcohol, had learned to be self-reliant, and retained the household tools from her husband's probate. Moreover, unlike many widows, she had a large support group in Seguin—three unmarried daughters, one married son, and two daughters with husbands. Sarah's wealth was in family, not money or property, and this provided her with an alternative to remarriage.[21]

Sarah and her extended family did well. There were catfish, perch, and bass in Walnut Creek and garden plots at her house. Sarah sold butter, so she had milk cows. Men hunted deer and turkey to distribute among Seguin's residents, and honey was collected and stored in deer skin bags. On one occasion, Sarah's daughter Mary baked twenty-six loaves of bread, indicating flour was available. And, of course, at this time in Texas corn and bacon were common and beef was also consumed. If the meals James Nicholson ate in nearby Bastrop in 1839 is an indication, Sarah's diet was varied. Nicholson consumed coffee, milk, buttermilk, butter, cream, beef, venison, chicken, fish, corn bread, flour pancakes, beans, peas, corn, pudding, soup, and grape pies. It is less obvious how Sarah acquired clothing, though she sewed clothes and even repaired shirts and trousers for neighbors. Women commonly spun thread, for which small plots of cotton were cultivated, and they wove fabric.[22]

Widows on the Texas frontier needed money, since taxes had to be paid, schools charged tuition, legal transactions required fees, and food had to be bought. Sarah earned cash by selling butter and washing and sewing clothes. The open prairie in front of her house provided grazing for her milk cows, and her three daughters milked cows and churned butter. Her washing jobs ranged from six to eight pieces, for which she charged an average of four bits (fifty cents) per garment. Margaret S. Henson has noted that to support their families, poor women often became laundresses. Sarah's house was conducive to this type of work because a series of steps carved into the earthen bank of Walnut Springs Branch provided access to a convenient supply of water, which was hauled in buckets to large wash pots and heated for the laundry.[23]

Socializing in isolated Seguin was more than a diversion; it was a necessity. Dancing was a major pastime, and the Old Ranger Station became a popular dance hall owing to its large interior and wide front porch. Gathering to worship was another opportunity to socialize. Beginning in 1839, Sarah hosted the first church services in Seguin at her home. She discussed her return to religion in her prayer journal begun in the spring of 1842, and it is from there that we know that in 1844 she turned her back on her Baptist fundamentalism and became a Methodist.[24]

If Sarah had seemed unwilling to challenge her husband during her marriage, she stood up for herself as a widow. When her neighbor John H. Russell accused her of committing an unsavory act, she filed suit, causing him to quit his accusations. Having become a shareholder for Seguin, Sarah made her way through the male-dominated community effectively. In this regard she fit Malone's description of a frontierswoman: "Stoic, fatalistic, taciturn, the women who participated most fully in the frontier experience were hardened as well as strengthened by it." But Sarah had an immediate cause for concern: incursions by Indians and Mexicans. When she looked west from her front porch, she could see to the horizon, where the blue sky hugged the prairie grass. It was thirty miles to San Antonio, with only an occasional log cabin to interrupt the landscape. Another local, Andrew J. Sowell, said the prairie stretched as far the eye could see, interrupted only by small mottes of live oaks. But the open expanse that Sarah looked out upon also held danger. As president of the Republic, Houston pursued a policy of peaceful coexistence with Indians. In the 1840s Lipan Apaches and Tonkawas roamed mostly peacefully in the Guadalupe River Basin after Texas officials signed peace treaties with them. Comanches and Cherokees were another matter. Along the western border, the former continued to raid. In the northeast, Anglos complained about Cherokee raids, resulting in a Houston-negotiated treaty with Chief Bowles, but the Senate led by Mirabeau B. Lamar rejected it. When Lamar became president in 1839, the stage was set for conflict.[25]

Trouble began in 1838 when, frustrated by Anglo dominance and encouraged by Mexican authorities, Vincente Córdova, a former Nacogdoches *alcalde*, sought to ally Tejanos and Cherokees in East Texas. On August 4 violence erupted when Córdova's men stole several horses and killed one local Texian. President Houston quickly journeyed to Nacogdoches and warned the Cherokees and Córdova. Nevertheless, matters festered and documents were found implicating the Mexican government in a plot with the Cherokees. Houston ordered militia into the field, and the pent-up frustrations felt by both Anglos and Indians led to bloodshed. By the end of 1838, Texians had conducted campaigns against the Kickapoos and Cherokees, resulting in the exodus of most Indians, but Córdova and his men escaped. As the spring of 1839 arrived, they began to maneuver south along a course that would pass between Gonzales and Seguin.[26]

While the turmoil had roiled North and East Texas during the summer and fall of 1838, Comanche raids came close to Seguin. On July 21 the *Telegraph and Texas Register* reported Comanches had committed depredations near San Antonio and Gonzales. A month later, Henry W. Karnes skirmished with Comanches thirty miles west of San Antonio; in October, Gonzales merchant Joseph D. Clements reported an Indian raid between the Colorado River and Gonzales; and in November, the newspaper declared that Comanches had killed ten men within three miles of San Antonio. These reports made people in Gonzales County uneasy, but what happened next terrified them. Ten miles southeast of Gonzales, Matilda Lockhart and four Putman children, ranging in age from two to seventeen, were seized by several Comanches. The raiders and their captives skirted around Gonzales, bypassed Seguin, and rode northwest. When the children did not come home, their families and neighbors began a search, found the young Putman boy's hat, and located the kidnappers' trail. Although Gonzales men searched for days, they did not recover any captives. The tragedy prompted Sarah and her neighbors to temporarily abandon Seguin for Gonzales. This incident accentuated Seguin's vulnerability and was a harbinger of the future.[27]

During the kidnapping crisis, the men of Seguin did not organize into a ranging company, but the episode taught them a lesson. On January 6, 1839, President Lamar endorsed a bill for a ranger company to be stationed at Gonzales. He chose Seguin founder Mathew Caldwell to be its captain instead of allowing the volunteers to select their leader. On March 16, Caldwell mustered his Gonzales Rangers into service and camped at Post Gonzales, about halfway between Seguin and Gonzales where Mill Creek joined the Guadalupe River. The new rangers patrolled along the road from Gonzales to Seguin and San Antonio. Thirty of the fifty-nine lived in or near Seguin, including Sarah's son James M. Day and sons-in-law Henry B. King and John W. Nichols (table 4.1). George W. Nichols and his three other sons, George H., James W., and Solomon G., also enlisted, as did John R. King, Henry's brother. In all, just eight local families provided twenty-four of the company's volunteers.[28]

Meanwhile, in early 1839 Córdova received a note from the Mexican commander at Matamoros requesting a conference. So, he collected forty Tejanos, several Biloxi Indians, a few freed slaves, and rode from the upper Trinity River toward Mexico. On March 25, when scouts informed Burleson that Córdova's contingent had crossed the Colorado near Bastrop and headed for Seguin, he mustered seventy-nine men. On March 29, Burleson's scouts found Córdova and his men camped on Mill Creek, six miles north of Post Gonzales. Córdova had stopped because he planned to burn Seguin to the ground; in preparation, he had sent men to reconnoiter the town. The raiders surely crept close to Sarah's house, considering its exposed position on the west bank of Walnut Spring Branch. Back at Mill Creek, Burleson sent his mounted men pell-mell toward the live oak motte sheltering Córdova's troops. In the ensuing melee, the Texians killed several, but a

Table 4.1. Seguin men in Caldwell's Gonzales Ranger Company, March 16–June 16, 1839

Capt. Mathew Caldwell	*Frederick W. Happle*	*David Reynolds*
1st Lt. James Campbell	Everett H. Harris	*Abram Roberts*
2nd Lt. Canah C. Colley	*Slaughter Henderson*	*Alexander Roberts*
1st Sgt. George D. Miller	David Henson	*James B. Roberts*
2nd Sgt. John R. King	*John S. Hodges*	*Jeremiah Roberts*
3rd Sgt. William N. Henry	Maury Irvin	*D. W. Russell*
4th Sgt. John Archer	Ebenezer R. Jones	*John H. Russell*
Privates	*William H. Killen*	*Ezekiel Smith*
M. L. Baber	*Henry B. King*	*French Smith*
Seth Baldridge	Henry McCulloch	*William Smith*
Nathan Burkett	*T. N. Minter*	*Andrew Jackson Sowell*
Curtis Caldwell	*George H. Nichols*	*Asa J. Lee Sowell*
William Clinton	*George W. Nichols Sr.*	*John N. Sowell Jr.*
James M. Day	*James W. Nichols*	John S. Stump
Miles G. Dikes	*John W. Nichols*	*James A. Swift*
S. Emmett	*Solomon G. Nichols*	*T. W. Symonds*
James Forrester	*William S. Osborn*	*Nathan Wadkins*
Daniel Grady	*James Pinchback*	*Isaac Wallace*
John G. Gray	*Daniel Noyes Poore*	John D. Wolfin
Thomas Grubbs	William Putman	

Sources: Gonzales Rangers, Mar. 16, 1839–June 16, 1839, Andrew Neill Papers, CAH; S. Moore, *Savage Frontier*, vol. 2, 1838–1839, 193.
Note: Italicized names are those who lived in the Seguin area or were town founders.

wounded Córdova retreated with a remnant of his force. Burleson spent the night in Seguin to protect its residents, who were considerably excited. Sarah and her six daughters were among the agitated townsfolk.[29]

Caldwell's camp was a few miles south of where the Burleson and Córdova fight erupted. At that time, Caldwell had ridden to Gonzales while sending half of his rangers to Seguin with Lt. James Campbell, leaving the rest at the post under Lt. Canah C. Colley. On the morning of March 29, Campbell sent out two patrols. The first was James W. Nichols, John Box Roberts, John N. Sowell Jr. and Andrew J. Sowell, who were instructed to scout north of Geronimo

Creek. Campbell ordered James M. Day, Thomas R. Nichols, John W. Nichols, Daniel Noyes Poore, and David Reynolds to patrol west, up the Guadalupe River. James W. Nichols and his three comrades reached Geronimo Creek, where they killed and skinned a couple of deer. In the afternoon, they heard weapons firing in the distance and saw buzzards swarming. Andrew Sowell headed for the fight, and after passing through a grassfire he joined Burleson's troops. The other three raced toward Seguin and found the town in a state of commotion as the residents had been told of the danger by two of Burleson's volunteers. By daylight the next day, Caldwell and the rest of his rangers arrived in Seguin, which was thus guarded by almost one hundred men. The women of Seguin spent much of the night preparing food for the famished men.[30]

Sarah was concerned about her son, but when a wounded David Reynolds walked into town with news of his patrol's skirmish with Córdova, her anxiety intensified. The Day patrol had found no sign of Indians, and on their way to Seguin they had decided to spend the night on the Guadalupe River and shoot turkeys in the morning. Sensing no danger, they placed no watch. Meanwhile, Córdova and his men crept around Seguin and headed for the river bottom, where at sunrise they blundered into the sleeping rangers. Day, roused by the sound of a snorting horse, saw an Indian trying to steal his mount and fired his rifle, precipitating a fight. He was wounded when a musket ball struck the back of his hip bone, exiting above his kidney. Firing their rifles as they retreated, the rangers dragged Day to the river and into the water, where they hid under an overhanging bank. As inexperienced fighters, the rangers were confused, but they held off their assailants and saved their friend's life. Córdova's men eventually quit the fight, riding away on stolen horses. A wounded Reynolds walked six miles to Seguin to report what had happened. Caldwell sent a cart to retrieve the wounded Day, who was in considerable pain. Back in Seguin, Day endured an extensive convalescence; the first wounded ranger Sarah nursed back to health in her home was her son. For the remainder of James's life, small fragments of bone occasionally emerged at the site of his injury, a painful reminder of his first fight. He was somewhat crippled, but he served again as a ranger and in the Mexican War. Partly because of being wounded in this action, Texas later awarded him land and a pension.[31]

Not surprisingly, the fighting against Córdova heightened anxiety in Seguin. Burleson's troops were exhausted and worried about their families; they gave up the chase and rode home. The next day, March 31, Caldwell's Rangers took up the pursuit. After capturing five horses from Day's men,

Córdova had led his men up the Guadalupe River, into the canyons and valleys of the Balcones Escarpment and onto the Edwards Plateau. Near the headwaters of the Frio River, they turned south and crossed the Nueces River into the chaparral. There they found a gauntlet of mesquite trees, cactus, rattlesnakes, and little grass or water. Unfamiliar with the environment, they struggled and even lost men to snakebites. The *Telegraph and Texas Register* received a report that Mexican traders near the Rio Grande had seen Córdova, who was not "anxious to return to Texas."[32]

By April 8, Caldwell's weary men returned to San Antonio. Texians read about their chase in the May 1 *Telegraph and Texas Register* in a letter from Andrew Neill, who said the rangers were unable to overtake Córdova but had provided protection for Gonzales County. San Antonio citizens celebrated their return and, according to Henry Eustace McCulloch, served a grand dinner. This episode left one legacy—Seguin had become a prime source of a cadre of rangers, who would often muster to meet threats by Indians, Mexicans, and rustlers. The May 21 *Telegraph and Texas Register* illustrated Seguin's importance: "The company at Gonzales was *protected* by a corps of rangers stationed at Seguin immediately on the frontier." Rangers began to use Seguin as their headquarters, and Sarah's house became their station. Ideally located on the west side of Seguin, the house faced in the direction of most threats, making deployments easy. The home's ample size and congenial atmosphere also made it a popular mustering place.[33]

One item of unfinished business remained. Burleson had captured about twenty men during the fight with Córdova. Among the prisoners were three black men, one of whom was little more than a teenager, and wounded. The Texians believed they were escaped slaves so Burleson ordered them sold. The teenaged prisoner was resigned to his fate, but the two older ones adamantly announced their intention to escape again. Burleson held a court-martial and the jury, composed entirely of Seguin residents, ordered the teenager sold and condemned the two older men. Andrew J. Sowell claimed the teenager sold for $800. The following morning Caldwell marched the two men to an oak motte west of Seguin and ordered them to dig their graves before rifle shots dispatched them. The execution took place half a mile from the Old Ranger Station, so it is almost certain Sarah and her daughters knew about this ugly scene. The other prisoners, all Tejanos, were tried in Bexar County district court and released.[34]

Córdova was not the only raider to raise an alarm in Seguin in early 1839. In mid-May another scare erupted a few miles west of Sarah's home. Manuel

Flores, a colleague of Córdova, had left Mexico for East Texas with plans to foster another Indian uprising. Flores and his men ambushed a survey party on Cibolo Creek, fifteen miles west of Seguin. The killing of the four surveyors caused local residents to panic. A ranger company from Austin cornered Flores, killing him and twenty-nine others. Until Seguin residents heard about the fate of Flores, they, including Sarah and her family, remained in a state of anxiety and vigilance. When the excitement subsided, Caldwell's Rangers were discharged on May 15, 1839.[35]

The area's growing population brought an array of new issues to be addressed. On July 1, the Gonzales County commissioners ordered new roads built from Gonzales to Austin, Gonzales to San Antonio, and Gonzales to Texana on the Navidad River. Texana was a port of entry, so Gonzales and Seguin had a link to shipping from the United States. Legal matters also became more numerous and complex. The Gonzales County district court heard forty-two civil cases in 1838–39, of which twelve were appeals of the probate judge's rulings on estates. Almost all of the appealed cases concerned men who had died in the Texas Revolution. In the summer of 1839, Sarah filed a slander suit against John H. Russell in a justice of the peace court. Sarah said Russell, Seguin's constable, had maliciously detained her and accused her of lying, which stigmatized her reputation. Sarah's dispute with Russell stemmed from his accusations against John R. King, the brother of her son-in-law Henry B. King, and against members of the George W. Nichols family. By the time of the district court's fall session, Sarah and Russell had settled their differences, splitting court costs, and the judge dismissed the case. This was the only time Sarah entered a district courtroom as either a plaintiff or a defendant.[36]

Crime in Gonzales County also increased in 1838–39 and local officials combatted it with varying degrees of consistency and success. The first men indicted for assault and battery in Gonzales County were Ezekiel Smith and his sons, French and Paris, all from Seguin. Other Seguin residents indicted for assault and battery include George W. Nichols, his daughter Nancy, his son John W., and John's wife, Mary (Sarah's daughter). The Nichols family were accused of assaulting John H. Russell's wife and their three children. John W. was found not guilty and the other three cases were dismissed. John H. Bibb, also from Seguin, was indicted for allegedly stealing four five-dollar bills. Constable Russell filed the complaint, but the jury found Bibb not guilty. Russell also charged John R. King with falsely claiming one of the bills. The judge agreed with King and ordered Russell to pay court costs. Russell's failed accusations against Sarah and John R. King ruined him financially, so he left Seguin. On October 9, 1839, his land bounty was auctioned on the courthouse steps to satisfy a debt, and in 1840, Russell sold his last Seguin lot to John W. Nichols, Sarah's son-in-law. Indictments for gambling, dueling, assisting at a duel, selling without a license, horse stealing, and killing an ox were also issued by the district court in the fall of 1839. In most cases the defendant was found not guilty or the case was dismissed. Seguin was a raucous town, and with about one hundred people it had two-thirds of the assault and battery cases in Gonzales County, and most of those indicted for all crimes were Seguin residents. Of course, this included Sarah and her family.[37]

By the end of 1839, much had changed for Sarah and her family. They had forged new lives in Seguin and the Guadalupe River Basin. They owned town lots and held bounty grants entitling them to hundreds of acres. They had built permanent homes, Sarah's being one of the most impressive and welcoming in Seguin. As a family, they had coped with the untimely death of Johnson Day, and Sarah had adapted to life as a widow. They had fought to protect their lives and property. Their chosen frontier attracted all kinds of newcomers, and Seguin assimilated a hodgepodge of strong personalities, just the kind that would vex a district judge. Some of these were Sarah and her family. However, a very different crisis loomed in Sarah's future—a sick, abandoned daughter.

CHAPTER 5

The Ranger Years, 1840–1841

"Avenging sword"

In June 1841, twelve Comanches stole cattle from ranches south and west of San Antonio and drove them west toward Uvalde Canyon. Capt. John Coffee "Jack" Hays led his company of Anglos and Tejanos in pursuit. At the entrance to the Frio River Canyon, Hays's men found the Comanches, killing ten and capturing two. Exhausted, Hays returned to San Antonio instead of riding up the canyon to the main Comanche camp. On July 10, Capt. James Hughes Callahan's Gonzales Minutemen had recently completed their third scouting patrol when Hays's courier raced into Seguin. Despite short notice, Callahan assembled sixteen men, all Seguin residents and all but two veterans of campaigns against Indians or Mexicans. In San Antonio's main plaza they joined Hays, twenty-five rangers from San Antonio, and fifteen Tonkawas. Hays then led this force west toward the Comanche camp. Such events were not uncommon for settlers in the Republic of Texas. Callahan and the members of Sarah Hembree Day's large family, including her daughter Sarah Medissa, often experienced frontier violence, and their hometown of Seguin played a pivotal role in military clashes from 1840 to 1845.[1]

Texians pushed their frontier west in many places after independence, but in the area around Austin, Seguin, and San Antonio the western boundary remained almost stationary, and all three towns were still exposed to Indian raids (see map frontispiece). The frontier from Austin to San Antonio spanned a unique area where the Blackland Prairie meets the Balcones Escarpment. The latter's deep ridges and narrow valleys extend thirty miles west, then flatten into the Edwards Plateau. Southwest of a line from San

Antonio to Corpus Christi loomed the Trans-Nueces chaparral, a region of stunted grass and shrubs with little rainfall and few fresh water pools. Extreme weather was common in both regions: brutal summers, harsh winters, and flash floods in the spring. Indians, especially the Comanches, used the Edwards Plateau as a staging area for raiding Anglo settlements, while Mexico used the Trans-Nueces chaparral to invade both the San Antonio and Guadalupe River valleys.[2]

Seguin—where the Days and Callahans lived in the Guadalupe River Basin with their families—lay on this volatile frontier (see map frontispiece). The Comanches were the common foe of many groups on the Texas frontier. With a population of about 20,000 by 1840, they were the Texians' most powerful Indian enemy. As president of the Republic of Texas, Sam Houston sought peaceful relations with them. Tonkawas and Lipans, who coexisted with the Texians in the Colorado and Guadalupe River valleys, bided their time until they could get revenge against the Comanches, who were also their archenemy. After expelling the Cherokees from East Texas, President Mirabeau B. Lamar focused on the Comanches. He authorized campaigns against them led by George T. Howard, John C. Neill, Henry W. Karnes, and Edward Burleson. These alarmed the Comanches, who decided to pursue another treaty. This set the stage for the Council House Fight.[3]

On January 10, 1840, three Comanches rode into San Antonio and told Karnes they wanted peace, offering a Mexican captive as an indication of good faith. Karnes declined to negotiate, demanding instead the return of all white captives before discussions could begin. The leaders agreed, promising to return in one month. Texas officials sent troops to San Antonio and appointed Adjutant General Hugh McLeod and Seguin resident William G. Cooke to conduct the negotiations. On March 19, sixty-five Comanche men, women, and children rode into the main plaza with one prisoner, Matilda Lockhart, the girl captured east of Gonzales in December 1838. Lockhart, scarred and disfigured, said that she had been beaten with a burning stick and reported other captives at the Comanche camp. McLeod, Cooke, and Col. William S. Fisher led twelve Comanche leaders into the Council House, a stone structure that had once served as the Spanish governor's home. The Texans then demanded to know where the other captives were. One Comanche responded that Lockhart was their only one; other groups held other prisoners. Fisher ordered soldiers inside the Council House and told the Comanches they were prisoners until the other captives were released. Pandemonium erupted as the twelve bolted for the door; shooting began, and in less than a minute all twelve Comanche leaders lay dead. Outside, Comanches and Texians scattered, and hand-to-hand combat ensued. When the fight subsided, sixty-three of the original sixty-five Comanches were either dead or prisoners. The Texians lost seven killed and eight wounded. One prisoner, an old woman, was sent to negotiate an exchange of the apprehended Comanches for Anglo captives. In the end, seven, including some Mexicans, were returned, and the Comanches who had not been exchanged managed to escape.[4]

Reported widely by local newspapers, this event caused consternation throughout south Texas. From Seguin, James Wilson Nichols and John Sowell, his stepbrother, had joined in the fighting. Two other Seguin residents were also in the Council House fight: Cooke and Mathew Caldwell, who engaged in a rock-throwing contest with one Comanche. Afterwards, the four Seguin residents spread their own tales about the fierce combat. These accounts and those of the released captives increased the fear that Anglos felt about Comanches. Comanche raids almost ceased for several months, but then in July, Gonzales County Judge James Campbell of Seguin was ambushed while riding to San Antonio.[5]

The Council House Fight inflamed the Comanches. On August 4, 1840, almost 1,000 Comanche men and women rode out of the Balcones Escarpment north of Austin. They crossed the Colorado River, heading southeast along the watershed divide between the Colorado and San Marcos Rivers toward Victoria. Incredibly, the Comanches traveled sixty-five miles before any Texian discovered their presence. On August 5, ten miles east of Gonzales, the Indians chased and wounded Joel Ponton and killed Tucker Foley. Later that night Ponton walked to his farm, near present-day Hallettsville, and raised an alarm. On August 6, Comanches attacked Victoria, catching its citizens by surprise. The Texians mounted a vigorous defense, repulsing the raiders, who then assaulted Mexican horse traders and captured 500 horses. In the morning, Comanches attacked and were repelled again, but they killed several Texians and captured a slave girl with her child and Nancy Darst Crosby with her baby daughter, Mary. Riding to Linnville, the Indians stole horses until they had 1,500. They camped that night on Placedo Creek; at daylight baby Mary began to cry, prompting a Comanche to throw her on the ground and spear her. At sunrise on August 8, residents of Linnville saw a large horse herd and assumed it was Mexican drovers. Then several hundred Comanches charged, killing some citizens and capturing others, including Juliet Constance Watts. Most of the townspeople retreated to ships anchored in the harbor. There they watched helplessly as Comanches looted and torched the town, then withdrew at twilight, camping a few miles north.[6]

On August 6, thirty-six mounted Texians from the Lavaca River area, led by Adam Zumwalt, found Foley's body and buried him. In the meantime, alerted by an Austin post rider, Benjamin McCulloch assembled twenty-four men and rode northeast, joining Zumwalt. The next day they encountered sixty-five men from Victoria, commanded by John J. Tumlinson Jr., who led the entire force to Victoria, arriving on August 9. The Indians had left, so Tumlinson sent a courier to Texana for reinforcements while the men camped for the evening. After daybreak, the Texians found the now gaudily dressed Comanches, who escaped after a half-hour skirmish. The rangers killed a few raiders but lost one of their own—Benjamin Mordecai, who had served in the Georgia Battalion with Callahan. Meanwhile, word spread about the Victoria and Linnville raids. Caldwell organized rangers at Gonzales, and Tumlinson's volunteers joined him. Men from Seguin mustered, including James Milford Day, his brother-in-law John W. Nichols, and seventeen-year-old Eli Skaggs Hankins, who later married another of Sarah Hembree Day's daughters. About twenty-five men left Seguin to confront the Comanches. By now, rangers from Austin led by Felix Huston had assembled, and Burleson at Bastrop had organized another troop, including a dozen Tonkawas. Henry McCulloch sent a message that the Comanches were riding west for the Balcones Escarpment on a path parallel to Plum Creek. Caldwell gathered all the Texians about three miles east of Plum Creek, near present-day Lockhart (see map frontispiece), where, on the evening of August 11, Huston and Caldwell met. Outranked by Huston, Caldwell reluctantly relinquished command, although most of the men wanted him to lead an attack.[7]

At sunrise, Henry McCulloch sent word the Indians were close, and yet another courier reported that Burleson's men and Tonkawas were minutes behind. While the Texians waited for Burleson, Comanches passed about a mile away. James W. Nichols described their appearance: "Thare was six or eight chiefs all dressed in guada aray, one having a cap mad[e] from the face or mop of a buffalo . . . with ten yards of red ribon tied to each horn, another with a two story bee gum silk hat [and] ten yards of each color, red, green, and blue ribon . . . , another had a green silk umbrilla streached over him, another that was kilt had on red top boots, blue cloth pants, and coat with the coat hind part before and buttoned up behind." Others also later wrote vivid accounts of this colorful cavalcade. When Burleson arrived, the Texians numbered about 185, so Huston ordered an attack in a hollow square formation. When the Indians refused to engage, it became obvious that Huston's plan would not succeed; instead, the Comanches continued west with their stolen horses and plundered goods. Finally, Burleson's and Caldwell's men spontaneously broke into a galloping frontal assault. A melee erupted, with each ranger and every Comanche seeking to inflict a deadly wound. Henry McCulloch wrote a few days later about his experience: "I had the pleasure . . . of hearing the whiz of the arrow as well as that of the leaden messenger of death and had the satisfaction of avenging the wrongs of my country. . . ." The Texians lost one killed and nine wounded; three of the nine were Seguin residents. Nichols suffered a hand wound, but his brothers and James Milford Day escaped injury. The Comanches escaped but estimates of their losses ranged from 52 to 138, while historian Donaly Brice says they may have lost more.[8]

When the dust settled, Texians rounded up stray horses, mules, and cattle, and collected other booty. The following morning, they divided the spoils by drawing lots. They also set aside goods the rightful owners could claim later, although some men arriving after the fight were not successful at reclaiming their property. Nichols's saddletree had been split by bullets, and when he saw his brother John with several, he chose a better one "of the Childresses make." Nichols used that saddletree for the rest of his life. He also wrote that he rode home on a new horse, while John Jenkins took a mule, and Robert Hall collected a pack mule and some dry goods. James Milford Day did not mention what he got, but undoubtedly, he did not leave empty-handed.[9]

Atrocities committed by Comanches and Texians during the Linnville Raid encouraged both sides to see the other as brutal. Nancy Crosby, whose baby daughter was skewered, was herself lanced to death at Plum Creek, but Juliet Watts survived an arrow's excruciating removal. Comanche women also died at Plum Creek. Nichols killed one but refused to shoot another, and he and others were horrified when Ezekiel Smith seized a wounded Comanche woman and cut her throat, a gruesome act that shocked even Smith's own son. The Comanches suffered a devastating blow and retreated 150 miles to the western edge of the Edwards Plateau. Lamar ordered Col. John H. Moore to pursue them, and on October 24 his men surprised the Indians in their camp, killing several, capturing many, and burning the village. After three defeats, the Comanches never again mounted a significant attack in Texas, though they did conduct small raids. At the same time, Texians had learned to fear the Comanches. Sarah Hembree Day and her neighbors anxiously awaited news of their menfolk in the Plum Creek fight; Robert Hall's wife received his blood-soaked shoes and thought he was dead until he walked in the front door days later. The memory of such dread lasted decades.[10]

Many Texians who fought at Plum Creek were new to Indian warfare, but they saw the futility of using standard tactics, like Huston's failed hollow-square attack. They experienced firsthand how a ferocious, rapid attack by mounted men firing weapons on the run could rout a superior, well-armed force. Hall remembered the men charged with a fierce yell, a characteristic of future ranger charges. These lessons applied elsewhere would earn worldwide fame for the Texas Rangers. The Texians also learned the value of repeating pistols and rifles, which suited this style of warfare. A year earlier, the Texas Navy had purchased 1,500 revolvers and repeating rifles from the Colt Firearms Company. Many of these were now in general use, and some were used at the Council House Fight and Plum Creek. Alsey S. Miller in Caldwell's company fired a seven-shot Paterson Colt rifle. In the Moore raid, one captain carried a ten-shot Colt carbine that performed very well, according to the *Telegraph and Texas Register.* While these first repeating pistols and rifles were clumsy to use, their effectiveness impressed the Texians, and within a year or two, several Seguin rangers would be carrying one, or two, Colt revolvers.[11]

Weapons and tactics were important, but effective leaders were essential. Caldwell, Burleson, and Huston were examples of the old guard who had defeated Mexico and placed the Republic on the world map. Nonetheless, new leaders would be needed for defending the Texas frontier. Of the men who fought at Plum Creek, three future leaders emerged—Hays and the McCulloch brothers, Ben and Henry. All had lives that centered on Seguin. Moreover, the twenty-five Seguin residents who fought at Plum Creek would often appear on future ranger muster rolls. James Hughes Callahan joined them on October 1, 1840, when as a lieutenant he rode out of San Antonio's main plaza as one of 180 Texians with Maj. George T. Howard. The week before, Callahan and thirty-three others from Gonzales and Seguin had volunteered to join Caldwell's Gonzales Rangers. The men elected Callahan as lieutenant, even though he was new to the area and had no previous ranger experience. Apparently, they recognized his leadership abilities.[12]

Callahan had returned to his parents' home in Jackson County, Georgia, after his service with the Georgia Battalion, but he had returned to Texas by the early spring of 1837. According to James W. Nichols, Callahan's parents strongly objected to his return to Texas, so he remained with them until the next spring, when a love affair collapsed. By then the Panic of 1837 caused the prices of Georgia cotton and other crops to fall, and credit from banks dried up. It was difficult for skilled workers, too, as wages fell as much as 50 percent. Moreover, Georgia had no more free land to distribute. Callahan concluded that his land bounty in Texas, awarded for his wartime services, offered the best opportunity. He told Nichols that he landed at Galveston on April 7, 1837. He was not alone. The March 28, 1837, *Telegraph and Texas Register* reported that several vessels had brought many new emigrant families to Texas. On May 1, the *Charleston Courier* claimed that a thousand emigrants arrived in Texas each week despite the threat of Mexican armed ships. According to the *Courier*, two schooners were captured on April 4, three days before Callahan landed at Galveston. While the Republic had designated Galveston as an official port of entry, Texas advocate Jacob De Cordova said that Galveston in 1837 consisted of a few frame houses, and naturalist John James Audubon described it as a "rough village . . . the whole population seemed both indolent and reckless." Callahan found little of interest and did not tarry long.[13]

From Galveston, Callahan travelled to Houston, which had become the capital of the Republic in January 1837. The town had been laid out by John K. and August C. Allen in 1836, and by the time Callahan arrived, had become a riotous and raunchy community. President Houston lived in a log cabin with a dirt floor, while others dwelt in clapboard houses. Congress met in the town's largest building. The first anniversary of San Jacinto was celebrated in April 1837, and the festivities amplified the city's raucous atmosphere during Callahan's visit. Land records offer the best clue as to what he did next. In August 1838, he had his military bounty warrant for 640 acres surveyed on land located fourteen miles east of Gonzales at the crossroads of the Old La Bahía Road to Goliad that connected San Antonio and Gonzales with Houston. This property lay in the path of the raiding Comanches in August 1840, near where Foley would be killed. In June 1839, Callahan bought a town lot in Velasco. Two months before the Comanche raid, he purchased 492 acres of the William Killen Survey located eight miles east of the Plum Creek battle site. Callahan does not appear on any muster roll of a unit that fought at Plum Creek; but, like many other men, he arrived after the battle and soon learned that Caldwell was mustering a ranger company.

Having no family ties or apparent business obligations, the Georgia expatriate and former revolutionary decided to enlist and was made a lieutenant by his fellow volunteers.[14]

Callahan's experience as a sergeant in the Georgia Battalion had prepared him for a lieutenant's duties. In 1840, rangers were loose bands of unruly, brawny men with varying degrees of battle experience. When not on duty, they gambled, wrestled, and sometimes fought among themselves. Enlistees had to provide their own weapons, ammunition, and horses, and they elected their officers. But by 1846 they earned a reputation as skilled horsemen and tough fighters, known as "Los Diablos Tejanos." Resilience and adaptability were indispensable for rangers who endured harsh conditions on the Texas frontier. They lived on parched corn, coffee, and game meat, and slept in the open. A durable, lightweight saddle held a lariat and carried a few clothes in saddlebags, and the typical ranger also had a rifle or shotgun, pistols, and a knife. Most men were adept at land navigation, possessing valuable surveying skills used in exploring unknown territory. They related to one another informally, and units operated seemingly without a fixed command structure; a captain earned his men's respect, and sometimes their votes, during every patrol. The best captains showed sound judgment under duress and faced danger fearlessly. Callahan's fearlessness, reserved demeanor, and quiet confidence made him a first-rate ranger, and he was regularly elected as a captain. President Lamar's aggressive policies accelerated the rangers' development during the early 1840s, providing Callahan and his comrades with many opportunities to improve their fighting tactics against both Indian raiders and Mexican troops.[15]

Howard's campaign, in which Callahan first served as a ranger lieutenant, was described by the *Telegraph and Texas Register* as an "avenging sword" against the Indians. Howard rode against the Comanches, proceeding west from San Antonio and then north to the headwaters of the Colorado River. This was intended to be a pincer movement, trapping the Indians between Howard moving from the south and Colonel Moore's forces riding west from Austin. Howard selected two infantry companies of the Texas army and called for volunteers to join them. Two companies from Bexar County formed, one composed of Anglos led by John R. Cunningham and the other of Tejanos commanded by Salvador Flores. Caldwell brought thirty-four men from Gonzales County, at least nine of whom came from the Seguin area (table 5.1). The result was an interesting mix. Cunningham's men included Chief Justice John Hemphill of the Texas Supreme Court and

Table 5.1. Caldwell's Gonzales Rangers, Sept. 25–Nov. 16, 1840

Officers	
Capt. Mathew Caldwell	*William H. Killen*
1st Lt. James Hughes Callahan	William R. Lockhart
2nd Lt. Christopher B. Acklin	Green McCoy
1st Sgt. W. W. Warren	*Benjamin McCulloch*
2nd Sgt. William Mitchell	John D. Perenfold
3rd Sgt. George D. Miller	*Wilson Randle*
	Jeremiah Roberts
Privates	
Tillman Berry	J. R. Smith
Green Cunningham	Darwin M. Stapp
Mark W. Dikes	Philip Stiffey
Bryant Donley	Alonzo B. Sweitzer
Patrick Donnelly	Creed Taylor
Daniel Grady	Josiah Taylor
William N. Henry	Rufus Taylor
Nathaniel G. Hudson	Nathan Trotter
J. W. Hunt	William Tumlinson
William J. Kellett	*Calvin S. Turner*
	Francis Williams

Sources: S. Moore, *Savage Frontier,* 3:140; Caldwell, Mathew, Gonzales Rangers 1840, Oversize 401-717, Folder 8, RTMR, TAGD, TSLA; last and first names, Republic Claims, TSLA.
Note: Italicized names are those who lived in or owned property in or near Seguin, Texas.

two congressmen from Bexar County. William Wirt Alsbury enlisted as a Spanish interpreter.[16]

On the first day of October 1840 Howard led his command out of San Antonio, crossed the Medina, Sabinal, and Frio rivers, and rode onto the Edwards Plateau near the headwaters of the Nueces River. Descending the plateau toward the south, the men wandered across Pissane Creek and crossed Las Nuras Creek, a tributary of the Rio Grande, and by October 12

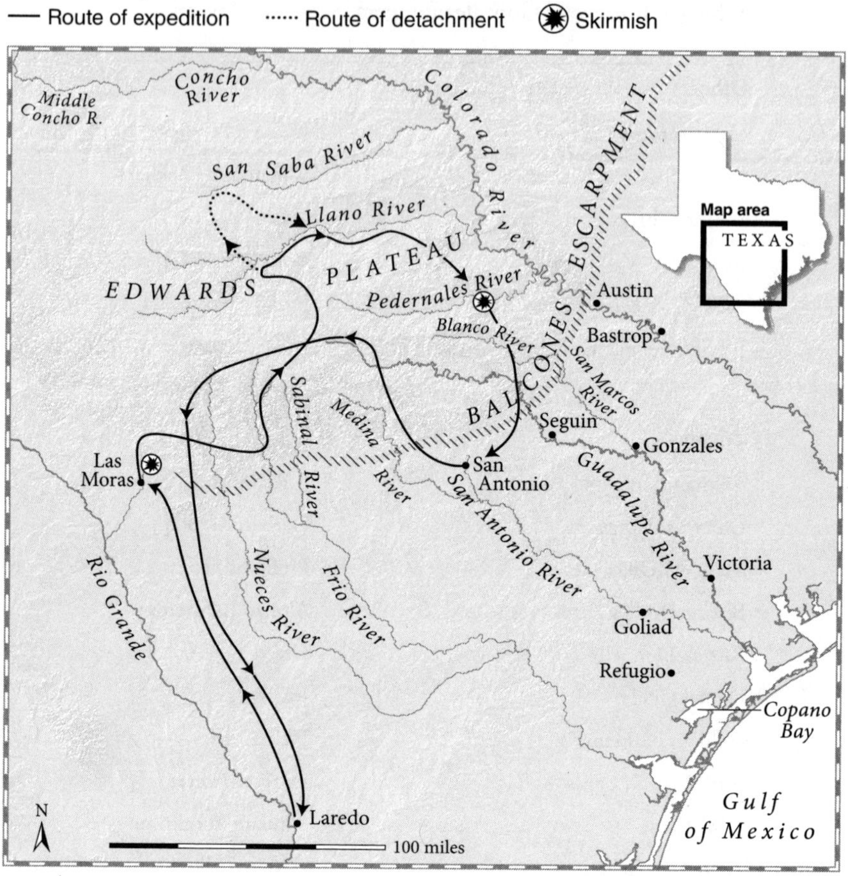

Map 5.1. Route of Major Howard's expedition, fall 1840. Map by Carol Zuber-Mallison.

they reached the banks of Turkey Creek, several miles west of present-day Uvalde (map 5.1). Discovering a recent Indian trail, the rangers dumped much of their baggage, left a guard detail, and rode west in pursuit until they lost the trail. At daybreak on October 13, the Texians located hoofprints, and Howard dispatched Caldwell and a Tejano, who returned reporting that the Indians had discovered them. Fearing the Indians would escape, the Texians hurried to the Comanche village at Las Moras Springs, where they found most had fled, but a few were still packing their horses. The Texians charged pell-mell through the camp and chased Indians several miles across the chaparral. The *Galveston Gazette* reported the Howard's men encountered sixty Comanches, who left buffalo robes and 100 horses. The Texians killed four Comanche men and a woman while losing only one of their own, though a few were wounded. Howard called off the pursuit after concluding his men's horses were exhausted. By late afternoon, the Texians regrouped in the vacant Comanche village, where they gathered horses and mules, guns, and buffalo robes, and destroyed tents and provisions. The *Houston Morning Star* said that sixty mules were needed to carry the buffalo robes. The next day, Howard marched east with 125 mules and horses. Some of his men piled several buffalo robes on a mule and topped these with a brass kettle whose loud clanging frightened the mules, causing them to run amok and stampede the horses. The fleeing horses and mules took with them many of the buffalo robes.[17]

When the Texians arrived at the Frio River, Howard turned north, following the river to its headwaters and onto the Edwards Plateau toward Moore's force. Some of Caldwell's Rangers, including Ben McCulloch, left Howard's command, riding to San Antonio with what remained of the captured horses, mules, and buffalo robes. Once on the Edwards Plateau, Howard's troops rode north to the headwaters of the Guadalupe River, then turned west to the source of the Llano River (map 5.1). Howard sent Cunningham's company on a scouting mission north to the San Saba River while he led the rest of his force down the Llano and over the watershed divide to the Pedernales River. On November 5, a patrol discovered twenty Comanches and chased them until they outran their pursuers. By then, Howard had been in the field for thirty-five days, and his men were tired and hungry. Violating orders not to fire weapons, nine of Caldwell's Rangers shot a deer and roasted it on a campfire. That night Comanches attacked the deer-roasting party and took three horses, though the Texians claimed to have killed one of the Indians.[18]

On November 6, 1840, Cunningham returned from his scouting mission and reported that he had seen no recent Indian signs. Howard concluded the Comanches had fled west and, with provisions running low, he returned to San Antonio, where he discharged the local volunteers on November 11. Callahan stayed in San Antonio while Caldwell and eleven rangers rode to Seguin and Gonzales. They had been in the saddle nearly fifty-three days. Howard assured the people of San Antonio that the Indians had crossed into Mexico. However, when Comanches killed some San Antonio Tejanos in December, Howard organized another pursuit, leading to a surprise pell-mell attack at Las Moras Springs. As at Plum Creek and in Howard's earlier attack at Las Moras, a frontal assault with repeating weapons won the day. A few weeks later, Moore's Rangers used the same tactic on a Comanche village along the Colorado River. In 1840, Texians had learned to attack; subsequent actions by Callahan indicate he absorbed these lessons.[19]

Callahan learned more than tactics during his first expedition as a ranger. After Howard's and Moore's campaigns, the Comanches retreated beyond the Edwards Plateau. Raids on settlers continued into the late 1870s, mainly by small bands, but they were limited mostly to the area from the Colorado north to the Red River and along the roads from Austin and San Antonio to El Paso. Callahan also saw how Texian notions of democracy and merit applied to the selection of officers. The Gonzales Rangers included men with prior ranger experience—Ben McCulloch, for example, a former captain—who were willing to serve as privates, while they elected the novice Callahan as their lieutenant. In his future ranger stints, Callahan served as a captain but also took his turn as an enlisted man. Finally, Callahan considered settling in San Antonio, but as he later told James W. Nichols, "he took an aversion on first sight as it then was almost entirely inhabited by Mexicans." While many Texians were prejudiced against Tejanos, Callahan's animosity was deeply embedded in his experiences with the Georgia Battalion.[20]

Callahan left San Antonio riding alone to Seguin, but along the way his horse became lame. He walked the last few miles to George W. Nichols's house. While he spent his first few weeks in Seguin with the Nichols family he purchased five town lots for $40 on January 5, 1841. He built a cabin and attended frequent shivarees (rowdy dances) that Sarah Hembree Day hosted at her house. He did not realize it then, but he had found a new home.[21]

Seguin was still exposed to raids by horse thieves and Indians, while the civil war in Mexico between federalists and centralists sometimes spilled over into Texas, mostly in the Trans-Nueces chaparral. Concerns about the Republic's debt load led its Congress to defund the army and, as a substitute, supplement the militia with rangers. While the ranger companies mustered under the authority of the adjutant general, each frontier county organized a company of twenty to fifty-six volunteers to protect their neighbors. As before, the volunteers elected their officers and provided their own mounts, provisions, and weapons, but they were exempted from county and state taxes. Each captain could determine his mission, and during 1841 companies from every frontier county conducted dozens of campaigns in response to Indian threats. Meanwhile, the three ranger companies controlled by the adjutant general, led by Hays and Antonio Pérez in San Antonio and John T.

Price in Victoria, patrolled the Trans-Nueces chaparral, and Lamar ordered three expeditions by Texas militia.[22]

None of these events occurred in or around Seguin. Nevertheless, thirty-two Seguin residents, including Sarah Hembree Day and Callahan, petitioned the Texas Congress for a company. Their request was honored, and the Gonzales Rangers, later organized at Seguin, were headquartered at Sarah's house and led by Callahan. Meanwhile, in the spring of 1841, Indians raided Seguin, and according to James W. Nichols, stole several horses, including Callahan's favorite. Infuriated, Callahan mustered twenty-six men for a twenty-day scout. After obtaining supplies in San Antonio, they rode northwest toward the Llano River and struck an Indian trail. Scouts Simon Wesley Cockrell, Andrew Jackson Sowell, and Nichols followed it to the junction of the Concho and Colorado rivers. They were on the path taken by the Howard Expedition into Comanche territory, which Cockrell knew well since he had been a Comanche prisoner as a boy. They continued along the middle fork of the Colorado to the site of present-day Colorado City and then headed west to Big Spring, where they expected to find a Comanche camp. At this point, Callahan and his men were about 275 miles northwest of Seguin (map 5.2a).[23]

Callahan found a recent Indian encampment at Big Spring and a trail leading into the dry plains. The next waterhole, according Cockrell, was "80 miles distant" at Lost Creek. The horses endured two-and-a-half days without water on the trail before the Texians found a dry spring on the third day. Cockrell told his comrades that the closest water was a seep spring another two-and-a-half day's ride away. Having exhausted their water supply, some wanted to end the chase so Callahan asked for a vote—twelve wanted to press on, eight said no, and six abstained. The next morning the thirsty men reconsidered, and this time only six wanted to continue. They then argued about the shortest distance back to the last water they had encountered. Following the majority's advice, the rangers wandered for another day before taking the correct trail to Big Spring. By then, John R. King's "tong was so swollen that he could hardly [close] his mouth." By the time Callahan and his weary men returned to Seguin, they had been away for forty-six days and apparently accomplished nothing.[24]

A tired Callahan had been home for only a few days in late April 1841 when Benjamin McCulloch called for men to chase Indians who had stolen horses at Gonzales. McCulloch did wait two days so the volunteers could furnish themselves with provisions and shoe their horses (table 5.2).

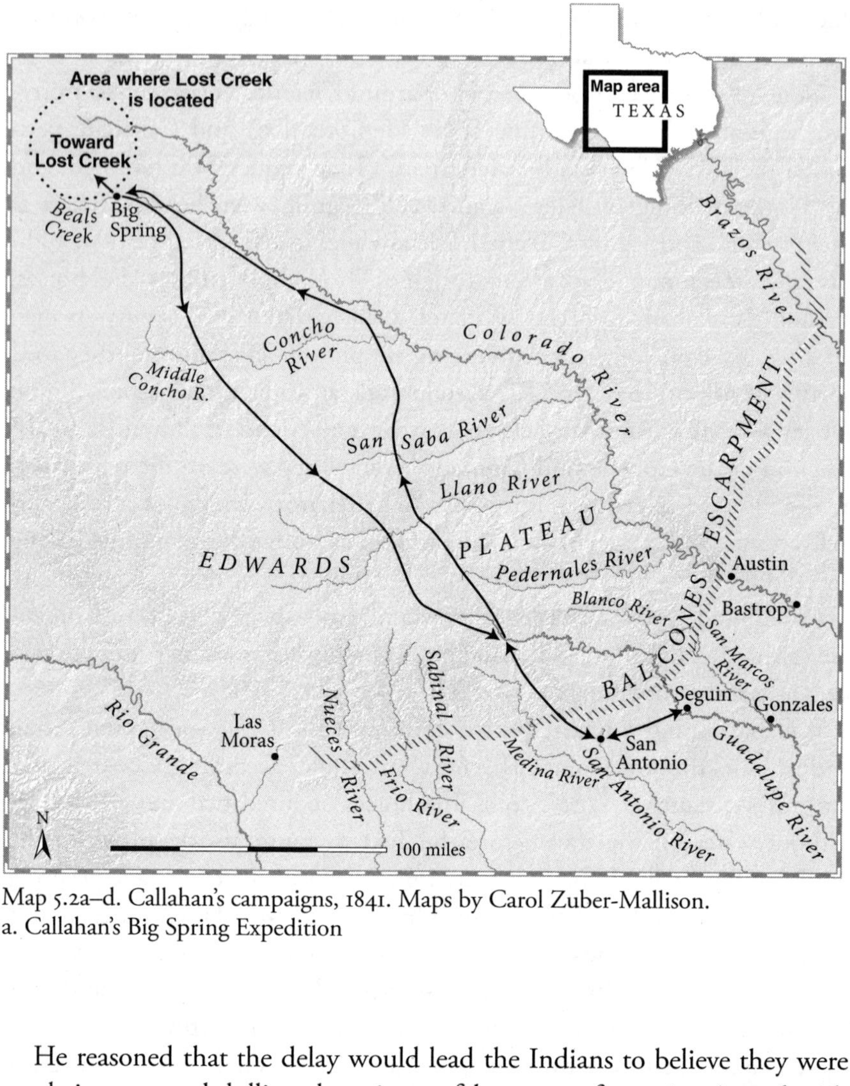

Map 5.2a–d. Callahan's campaigns, 1841. Maps by Carol Zuber-Mallison.
a. Callahan's Big Spring Expedition

He reasoned that the delay would lead the Indians to believe they were not being pursued, lulling them into a false sense of security. Armed with about 100 rounds of ammunition each, eighteen men followed a trail up the San Marcos River, then turned up York Creek and over the watershed divide to the Guadalupe, which they crossed near present-day New Braunfels. They continued westward, keeping the Guadalupe in sight, then after about forty-five miles (near present-day Boerne), McCulloch turned northwest for another thirty miles to Johnson's Fork of the Guadalupe (near present-day Kerrville) (map 5.2b). The rangers then meandered up Johnson's Fork onto the Edwards Plateau. Pushing through the scrub brush, they found

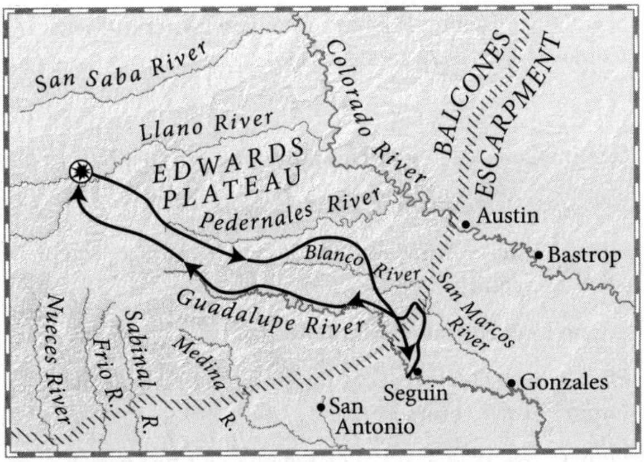

b. Benjamin McCulloch's Llano River Expedition, April

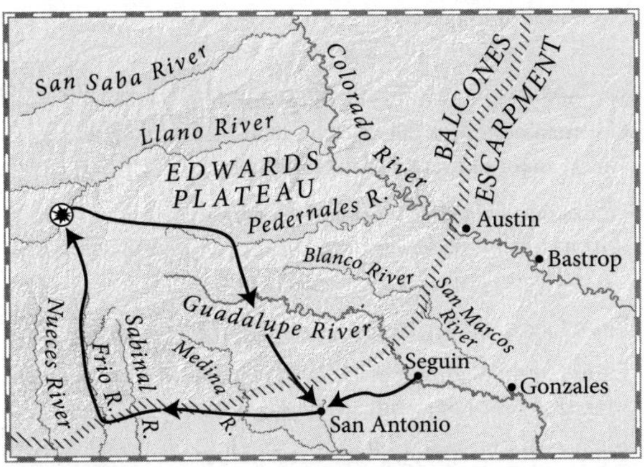

c. Jack Hays's Llano River Expedition

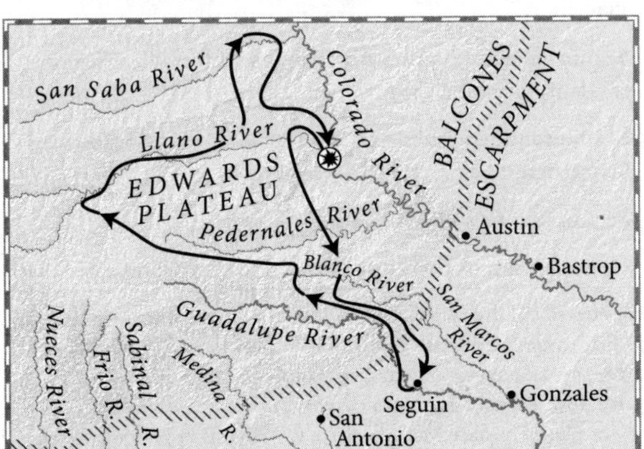

Carol Zuber-Mallison

d. McCulloch and Callahan's Gonzales Minutemen campaign, fall

Table 5.2. Benjamin McCulloch's Rangers, April 1841

Name	*Residence and fighting experience*
Capt. Benjamin McCulloch	Seguin; San Jacinto; Robbins, 1836; Peach Creek, 1839; Córdova, 1839; Plum Creek, 1840
Privates	
James Hughes Callahan	Seguin; Goliad survivor; Howard Campaign, 1840
Canah C. Colley	Gonzales; Córdova, 1839; Texas Army, 1836–37
Archibald Gibson	Gonzales; Texas Army, 1836–37; Plum Creek, 1840; son of DeWitt colonist
William Anderson Hall	Seguin founder; Texas Army, 1836–37
Eli T. (Skaggs) Hankins	Plum Creek, 1840; ward of Hinds family; Hinds nephew; future Callahan brother-in-law
(Eli) Clemmons Hinds	Plum Creek, 1840; ward of grandfather; his first patrol; Hankins's uncle
William P. Kincannon (Kinkennon)	Gonzales; San Jacinto
Green McCoy	Son of De Witt colonist; Hankins and Hinds cousin; Coleman's Rangers, fall 1836; Elm Creek, Jan. 1837; Plum Creek, 1940; Howard Campaign, 1840
Henry Eustace McCulloch	Gonzales; Benjamin's brother; Chance survey team skirmish, fall 1838; Peach Creek, 1839; Córdova 1839; Plum Creek, 1840
Alsey Silvanus Miller	Plum Creek, 1840
William Morrison	Plum Creek, 1840; son of De Witt colonist; Kimble Ranger, Mar. 1836 (did not to ride to the Alamo)
Thomas R. Nichols	Seguin; Córdova, 1839; Plum Creek, 1840
Wilson Randle	Seguin founder; Plum Creek, 1840; Howard Campaign, 1840
James B. Roberts	Seguin resident; brother Abraham was a founding Seguin resident; Córdova, 1839
Jeremiah Roberts	Seguin founder; Texas Army, 1837; Córdova, 1839; Howard Campaign, 1840
Arthur Swift	Seguin founder; his first patrol
William (P.) Tumlinson	Gonzales; son of DeWitt colonist; Howard Campaign, 1840

Sources: Kemp, Veterans Biographies, Herzstein Library, San Jacinto Museum; last and first names, Land Grant Search, TGLO; last and first names, Republic Claims, TSLA; Brown, *Indian Wars*, 84–85; S. Moore, *Savage Frontier*, 1:90–91, 168, 184, 216; 2:9–10, 179, 185, 193; 3:106–107, 140; *Muster Rolls of the Texas Revolution*, 25, 56, 130, 133, 152, 165, 188, 209; *Twentieth Century History of Southwest Texas*, 2:401–2; Transcript of Autobiography of Henry Eustace McCulloch, p. 1, BHMFP, 1798–1961, CAH.
Note: Residence is based on Deeds, bks. A–B, Gonzales County, CC; First Minute Book of Seguin, p. 3, TSLA; or another reliable publication. Unless noted otherwise, each ranger was listed on TR, 1840–42, TAC, Gonzales County.

another Johnson's Fork, this time of the Llano, and proceeded north until they camped to let their tired horses rest.[25]

Before daylight the McCulloch brothers and Canah C. Colley discovered the Indians' horses in a small ravine where Johnson's Fork met the Llano. McCulloch halted the rangers, reconnoitered the encampment, and arranged his men within sixty yards of the sleeping Indians. At daybreak, one brave wandered to the camp's edge, spotted the Texians, and shouted an alarm. Henry McCulloch recalled, "As if by magic every Indian sprang from his pallet and Ben's party fired on and charged them, killing them dead on the ground, but as the Indians were encamped or were sleeping in the edge of the brush, they fled into it where it was too dark to see them and made their escape." Disappointed at the skirmish's brevity, the rangers nevertheless took the Indians' horses and other property. Historian Josiah W. Wilbarger claimed that they killed four and all others escaped, while another historian, John Henry Brown, wrote that five were slain and eight of the remaining twenty-two escaped unharmed.[26]

Brown also named the members of the company, although Henry McCulloch in his memoir added Colley, to the muster roll (table 5.2). Eight resided in Seguin, five in the Plum Creek valley, and four in Gonzales. This distribution indicates that in one year the region's frontier had moved west, farther from Gonzales, and that more men were living in the Seguin area. All were less than thirty years old, which was consistent with other ranger companies at this time, and two, Eli S. Hankins and Eli Clemmons Hinds, were just eighteen and seventeen years old. For two rangers, Hinds and Arthur Swift, the skirmish was their first combat, but the others had prior experience. One, William S. Morrison, had promised to join Capt. George C. Kimble on his way to the Alamo in March 1836 but quit at the last moment. Benjamin McCulloch thus had a seasoned band of rangers. Their method of trailing their foes without detection, followed by an attack at daylight, had evolved from lessons learned at Plum Creek and other recent encounters. Again, some used repeating carbines and pistols; Alsey S. Miller owned a seven-shot Colt rifle. The attack at Johnson's Fork demonstrated the rangers were more than a match for their foes.[27]

For clever men such as the McCullochs and Callahan, these expeditions had an additional benefit. They had the opportunity to identify tracts of land they could later claim for themselves or others. Henry McCulloch recalled that, after the fight with the Indians, Callahan and Wilson Randle explored up the Llano. Finding land that suited them, they planned to return in the fall and survey tracts. In fact, during October 1841 Benjamin McCulloch returned with a team and plotted land for Callahan, Sarah Hembree Day, and other Gonzales County residents. Callahan later acquired the land (Sion D. Green Survey) where the spring 1841 skirmish was fought, while Randle claimed 640 acres on the opposite bank of the river.[28]

Back in Seguin, Callahan organized the Gonzales Rangers authorized by Congress. By May 7 he had twenty men on a two-week patrol, and by the end of the year another thirty-three had signed up for at least one stint (table 5.3). During that eight months, Callahan conducted ten two-week patrols and eighteen spy missions, providing Gonzales County, including Seguin, with an umbrella of protection. During that time no reports of any Indian incursions appeared in area newspapers or in accounts written by county residents. Callahan submitted dozens of muster and payroll accounts to the adjutant general, and these indicate his men spent more time in the field than most ranger companies during 1841. The documents also reveal something about Callahan's character: he could rapidly raise a company, paid attention to details, and followed regulations—all commendable traits that would serve him well in the future.[29]

A demographic profile of the men enrolled in the Gonzales Rangers offers insight into social undercurrents in the Republic of Texas, at least in Gonzales County. While the ages of all fifty-three men cannot be documented, many are known. Seven of the volunteers were over thirty years of age—George W. Nichols (45), Ezekiel Smith (60), Miles G. Dikes (34), Hugh G. Henderson (31), Joseph S. Martin (31), Jeremiah Roberts (32), and John A. M. Boyd (40). Having been a DeWitt colonist, Joseph D. Clements was also surely older than thirty. Several others were in their twenties, including Callahan, James Milford Day, the Nichols brothers, Ben McCulloch, the King brothers, the Sowell brothers, John Baker, James Foster, Arthur Swift, and Robert Hall. Many had come to Texas to fight for independence, and several had remained and joined the Texas army. Considering when several of them arrived in Texas, it is reasonable to assume that about 80 percent of the rangers were thirty or younger. Four may have been younger than twenty-one, since from 1840 to 1842 they did not pay taxes, as the law required for those twenty-one and older. One was Samuel Jennings Denyer, who was sixteen years old. Callahan clearly commanded a group of young men with a few older ones. Most of his rangers, although young, had military experience. Five had fought in the Texas Revolution, ten had served in the Texas army, and twenty-six had been in at least one skirmish against Indians or Mexicans.

Table 5.3. James H. Callahan's Gonzales County Rangers, 1841

Name	*Residence, Experience, Remarks*	*Dates of Patrols and Spy Missions*
Capt. James H. Callahan	Seguin; Goliad survivor; Howard, 1840	***Patrols***—May 7–21, June 7–21, July 7–9, *July 11–26, July 28–Aug. 6*, Aug. 8–10, Aug. 12–17, Oct. 24–Nov. 7, Nov. 9–23, Nov. 25–Dec. 2
1st Lt. William P. Kinkannon (Kinkennon)	Gonzales; San Jacinto	***Patrols***—May 7–21, June 7–21, July 7–9, *July 11–26, July 28–Aug. 6*, Aug. 8–10, Aug. 12–17, Dec. 4–18 ***Spy***—Sept. 21–23
2nd Lt. James Milford Day	Seguin founder; Córdova, 1839; Plum Creek, 1840; future Callahan brother-in-law	***Patrols***—May 7–21, June 7–21, *July 11–26, July 28–Aug. 6*, Aug. 8–10, Aug. 12–17, May 24–25 ***Spy***—Nov. 6–10, Nov. 17–21, Nov. 25–29
1st Sgt. John R. King	Seguin founder; Córdova, 1839; Plum Creek, 1840; Karnes, 1839; brothers, Henry B. and William G. King	***Patrols***—July 7–9, Aug. 12–17, Dec. 5–20 ***Spy***—Aug. 8–11, May 28–June 2, Aug. 20–27, Oct. 5–9, Nov. 6–10, Nov. 23–24
2nd Sgt. Allen A. Crane (Crain)	Seguin; future brother-in-law of Isaac A. Faris	***Patrols***—May 7–21, June 7–21, *July 11–26, July 28–Aug. 6*, Oct. 24–Nov. 7, Nov. 9–23, Nov.25–Dec. 2, Dec. 5–20 ***Spy***—Aug. 20–27, Sept. 7–20
3rd Sgt. Isaac A. (F.) Faris (Ferris, Farris)	Seguin; Texas Army, 1838	***Patrols***—May 7–21, June 7–21
4th Sgt. Asa Jarmon Lee Sowell	Seguin; Córdova, 1839; Plum Creek, 1840; George W. Nichols's stepson; A. J. Sowell's brother	***Patrols***—May 7–21, June 7–21, Dec. 4–18 ***Spy***—July 11–14, Aug. 8–11
1st Cpl. James W. Nichols	Seguin founder; father, George W.; brothers, John W. and Thomas R.; Córdova, 1839; Plum Creek, 1840	***Patrols***—July 7–9, July 28–Aug. 6, Aug. 12–17 ***Spy***—July 11–14, Nov. 17–21, Nov. 25–29
John Baker	Seguin; son of DeWitt colonist; Plum Creek, 1839; sister married Thomas R. Nichols; sister married J. D. Clements	***Patrols***—May 7–21, June 7–21 ***Spy***—July 7–9

(*continued*)

Table 5.3. (*continued*)

Name	*Residence, Experience, Remarks*	*Dates of Patrols and Spy Missions*
William Baker	Gonzales	***Patrols***—July 28–Aug. 6, Aug. 12–17, Oct. 24–Nov. 7, Nov. 9–23, Nov. 25–Dec. 2
Tillman Berry	Son of Francis Berry, DeWitt colonist; Plum Creek, 1840; Howard 1840	***Patrols***—May 7–21, June 7–21
Ira Bisbee (Bisby)	Plum Creek, 1840; Texas Army, 1836–38	***Patrols***—Aug. 12–17, Oct. 24–Nov. 7, Nov. 9–23, Nov. 25–Dec. 2, Dec. 5–20 ***Spy***—July 7–9, Aug. 18–20, Aug. 28–Sept. 5, Sept. 7–20, Sept. 25–30, Oct. 5–9
J. (John) A. M. Boyd	Seguin; early Gonzales settler; stepfather of Henry B. and John R. King	**Patrol**—Dec. 4–18
José María Cárdenas	Seguin	***Patrol***—Aug. 8–10
Joseph D. Clements	Gonzales; DeWitt colonist; escaped Goliad; married John Baker's sister	***Patrol***—Aug. 12–17 ***Spy***—May 24–25
William Clinton	Seguin founder; Córdova, 1839; d. 1849	***Patrols***—May 7–21, June 7–21, *July 11–26, July 28–Aug. 6,* Dec. 4–18 ***Spy***—Aug. 8–11, Nov. 25–29
Simon W. Cockrell (Cockrill)	Gonzales; early Gonzales settler; Texas Army, 1836	***Patrols***—May 7–21, June 7–21
Canah C. Colley	Gonzales; early Gonzales settler; Córdova, 1839; Texas Army, 1836–37	***Patrol***—Dec. 4–18
Samuel J. Denyer	Not on tax rolls; 16-year-old Maryland native; arrival date in Texas unknown	***Patrol***—June 7–21, 1841
Mark M. Dikes	Gonzales; DeWitt colonist; Howard, 1840; brother, Miles G. Dikes	***Spy***—July 7–9, Oct. 20–28, Oct. 30–Nov. 4
Miles G. Dikes	Gonzales; Seguin founder; DeWitt colonist; Córdova, 1839	***Patrol***—Aug. 12–17 ***Spy***—July 7–9, Aug. 8–11, Aug. 20–27, Oct. 20–28, Oct. 30–Nov. 4, Nov. 12–16
James Foster	Seguin	***Spy***—Sept. 25–30

Name	Residence, Experience, Remarks	Dates of Patrols and Spy Missions
Robert Hall	Seguin founder; veteran Texas Revolution; Texas Army, 1836–37; Plum Creek, 1840	***Patrols***—July 7–9, Aug. 8–10
William A. Hall	Seguin founder; Texas Army, 1836–37	***Patrols***—May 7–21, June 7–21, Oct. 24–Nov. 7, Nov. 9–23, Nov. 25–Dec. 2, Dec. 4–18 ***Spy***—Oct. 11–19
Frederick W. Happell (Happle)	Seguin; Córdova, 1839; arrived in Texas, 1837	***Patrols***—*July 11–26, July 28–Aug. 6*, Oct. 24–Nov. 7, Nov. 9–23, Nov. 25–Dec. 2, Dec. 4–18 ***Spy***—Aug. 28–Sept. 5, 1841
Hugh G. Henderson	Seguin founder; San Jacinto; Córdova, 1839	***Patrols***—*July 11–26, July 28–Aug. 6*, Dec. 4–18 ***Spy***—Aug. 28–Sept. 5, Sept. 25–30
David Henson	Seguin; Peach Creek, 1839; Córdova, 1839; arrived in Texas, 1837	***Patrols***—May 7–21, June 7–21, *July 11–26, July 28–Aug. 6* ***Spy***—Sept. 7–20, Sept. 25–30, Oct. 5–9
Henry B. King	Seguin founder; Córdova, 1839; brothers, John R. and William G. King; future Callahan brother-in-law	***Patrols***—July 7–9, July 28–Aug. 6, Aug. 8–10, Aug. 12–17, Dec. 4–18 ***Spy***—Aug. 18–20, Oct. 5–9, Nov. 6–10, Nov. 25–29
William G. King	Seguin; brothers, John R. and Henry B. King	***Patrols***—*July 11–26, July 28–Aug. 6*, Aug. 8–10 ***Spy***—May 28–June 2, Aug. 20–27, Oct. 11–19
Joseph S. Martain (Martin)	Seguin founder; early Gonzales settler	***Patrols***—Oct. 24–Nov. 7, Nov. 9–23, Nov. 25–Dec. 2 ***Spy***—Aug. 18–20, Aug. 20–27, Sept. 7–20, Sept. 25–30, Oct. 5–9, Oct. 11–19
Benjamin McCulloch	Seguin; San Jacinto; Robbins fight, 1836; Peach Creek, 1839; Córdova, 1839; Plum Creek, 1840	***Patrols***—*July 11–26, July 28–Aug. 6*, Oct. 24–Nov. 7, Nov. 9–23, Nov. 25–Dec. 2, Dec. 4–18
Andrew Neill	Seguin founder; Texas Army, 1836–37; Karnes, 1839	***Patrols***—Aug. 8–10, Oct. 24–Nov. 7, Nov. 9–23, Nov. 25–Dec. 2

(*continued*)

Table 5.3. (*continued*)

Name	*Residence, Experience, Remarks*	*Dates of Patrols and Spy Missions*
George W. Nichols	Seguin founder; Córdova, 1839; Plum Creek, 1840; sons, James W., John W., and Thomas R.; married Sowell brothers' mother	***Patrols***—May 7–21, June 7–21, *July 11–26, July 28–Aug. 6,* Aug. 8–10, Dec. 5–20 ***Spy***—Nov. 6–10, Nov. 17–21
John W. Nichols	Seguin founder; Córdova, 1839; Plum Creek, 1840; future Callahan brother-in-law	***Patrols***—July 7–9, *July 11–26, Aug. 8–10,* Aug. 12–17, Dec. 4–18 ***Spy***—Nov. 6–10, Nov. 17–21
Thomas R. Nichols	Seguin; Córdova, 1839; Plum Creek, 1840; married John Baker's sister	***Patrols***—May 7–21, June 7–21, *July 11–26, July 28–Aug. 6,* Aug. 8–10
L. (Lewis) L. Peck	Seguin; Plum Creek, 1840; not on tax rolls; 1840 Postmaster, Lowell, Gonzales County	***Patrols***—Oct. 24–Nov. 7, Nov. 9–23, Nov. 25–Dec. 2, Dec. 4–18
George W. Price	Seguin; 1846 tax roll, Guadalupe County; Texas Revolution veteran	***Patrols***—Aug. 12–17, Oct. 24–Nov. 7, Nov. 9–23, Nov. 25–Dec. 2 ***Spy***—Sept. 21–23
James B. Roberts	Seguin; his brother Abraham resided in Seguin and was a founder; Córdova, 1839; arrived in Texas, 1839	***Patrols***—July 7–9, *July 11–26, July 28–Aug.* 6, Aug. 8–10, Oct. 24–Nov. 7, Nov. 9–23, Nov. 25–Dec. 2 ***Spy***—May 28–June 2, July 28–Aug. 6, Aug. 8–11, Aug. 18–20, Oct. 11–19
Jeremiah Roberts	Seguin founder; Texas Army, 1837; Córdova, 1839; Karnes, 1839, Howard, 1840	***Patrols***—May 7–21, June 7–21, Aug. 8–10, Dec. 4–18 ***Spy***—July 28–Aug. 6, Nov. 12–16, Nov. 25–29
Arthur Smith	No information	***Patrols***—*July 11–26, July 28–Aug. 6*
Byrd Smith	Gonzales; arrived in Texas, 1840	***Spy***—Oct. 20–28, Oct. 30–Nov. 4, Nov. 17–21
Charles A. Smith	Seguin (1840 gave land for Methodist church); arrived in Texas by Nov. 1839	***Patrols***—July 7–9, Aug. 8–10 ***Spy***—Sept. 21–23, Nov. 23–24, Nov. 30–Dec. 4
Ezekiel Smith	Seguin; arrived in Texas, 1837; Córdova, 1839; Plum Creek, 1840; father of Paris Smith; 60 years old	***Patrols***—May 7–21, June 7–21, July 28–Aug. 6, Aug. 8–10 ***Spy***—May 24–25, Nov. 23–24, Nov. 30–Dec. 4

Name	*Residence, Experience, Remarks*	*Dates of Patrols and Spy Missions*
Paris Smith	Seguin; brother French a Seguin founder	***Patrols***—May 7–21, June 7–21, July 7–9, Aug. 12–17 ***Spy***—May 24–25, Sept. 21–23, Nov. 12–16, Nov. 23–24, Nov. 30–Dec. 4
Andrew Jackson Sowell	Seguin founder; brother of Asa J. Lee and John N. Sowell Jr.; father was DeWitt colonist; Córdova, 1839; Plum Creek, 1840; Texas Revolution; Texas Army, 1836	***Patrols***—May 7–21, June 7–21, July 7–9, Aug. 8–10, Aug. 12–17 ***Spy***—July 8–17, Sept. 7–20, Nov. 17–21
John N. Sowell (Jr.)	Seguin; brother of Asa J. Lee and Andrew J. Sowell Jr.; father was DeWitt colonist; Córdova, 1839; Plum Creek, 1840	***Patrols***—July 7–9, Aug. 8–10, Dec. 4–18 ***Spy***—July 28–Aug. 6, Aug. 8–11
William C. Stiffey	Texas Army, 1836	***Spy***—May 24–25, May 28–June 2
Arthur Swift	Seguin founder; arrived in Texas, 1836–37	**Patrols**—Aug. 8–10, Dec. 4–18 **Spy**—Aug. 18–20, Aug. 28–Sept. 5, Oct. 20–28
Calvin S. Turner	Seguin; not on tax rolls; Howard, 1840; sister married Andrew Jackson Sowell	***Patrols***—*July 11–26, July 28–Aug. 6*, Oct. 24–Nov. 7, Nov. 9–23, Nov. 25–Dec. 2, Dec. 4–18
Samuel Turner (Towner)	Seguin; not on tax rolls; arrived in Texas, 1840	***Patrols***—May 7–21, June 7–21, Oct. 24–Nov. 7, Nov. 9–23, Nov. 25–Dec. 2, Dec. 4–18
John B. Veach	Seguin	***Patrols***—July 28–Aug. 6, Aug. 12–17 ***Spy***—May 28–June 2, Sept. 21–23, Nov. 17–21, Nov. 30–Dec. 4

Sources: Kemp, Veterans Biographies, Herzstein Library; last and first names, Land Grant Search, TGLO; *Muster Rolls of the Texas Revolution*, 9, 50, 56, 72, 84, 86, 88, 98, 130, 133, 175, 187–88, 195, 207, 209, 229, 256; S. Moore, *Savage Frontier*, 1:168, 184, 2:179, 193, 198, 230, 3:106–7, 140; last and first names, Republic Claims, TSLA; Rather, "De Witt's Colony," 163–72; *Texian Advocate*, Mar. 2, 1849; Sowell, *Rangers*, 107, 414; Fretz, *Brief History of John and Christian Fretz*, 327–28; *San Luis Advocate*, Sept. 28, 1840; U.S. Census, 1850, Gonzales County; Sowell, *History of Fort Bend County*, vi. Residency is based on Deeds, bk. A, 173, 205, 286, 306; bk. B, 15–19, 30, 312, 427, 465; bk. C, 2–3, 10–11, 46, 503, 506, 519–21, 582–84, 591–92; bk. D, 7, 10–11, 197–99, 280–81, Gonzales County, CC; First Minute Book of Seguin, p. 3, Call Number 2-231/971, TSLA; or another reliable publication or document. Unless noted otherwise, each ranger was listed on TR, 1840–42, TAC, Gonzales County.
Note: Italicized dates indicate Callahan Rangers in Hays's Llano River campaign.

A few had served in the U.S. Army or in militias; George W. Nichols fought at Horseshoe Bend and New Orleans. Only fifteen men had no documented combat experience. The majority knew how to fight, and some had repeating pistols or rifles. They were a formidable fighting force.[30]

Where the Gonzales Rangers lived highlights the westward shift of the frontier as the region's population grew. Thirty-eight lived in and around Seguin; seven near Gonzales, thirty miles east; and two near Plum Creek. While a few years earlier it might have been difficult to find almost forty men living in the Seguin area, the increased population made it possible for Callahan to recruit that number of volunteers. Since Callahan lived in Seguin, it was logical that the muster was there, and nowhere was better than Sarah Hembree Day's house. Seguin and Gonzales were vulnerable to Indian raids coming from the region between the San Marcos and Guadalupe Rivers, about fifteen miles west and northwest of Seguin, so Callahan concentrated patrols in that vicinity. The Gonzales Rangers began patrolling on May 7, 1841, and continued until late December, each patrol lasting two weeks. On several occasions, especially between August 18 and December 4, Callahan sent out spy patrols consisting of four to five men; these rode the frontier for three to eight days, and according to payroll and muster rolls they received extra pay. On three occasions, Callahan dispatched a small spy contingent to range ahead of the main body of rangers. Using both scout and regular company patrols, he effectively protected Seguin and Gonzales from Indian raids.[31]

Callahan led all eleven ranger patrols conducted during this period, except for the last (December 4–18), which was commanded by Lt. William P. Kinkannon. Not surprisingly, Seguin men participated in about two-thirds of the patrols; James Milford Day, the King and Sowell brothers, and the Nichols and Smith families joined the most frequently, though Allen A. Crane, William Clinton, Calvin S. Turner, and the Dikes brothers also volunteered many times. In contrast, men from Seguin and Gonzales seem to have alternated on spy patrols. It is also interesting to note that most of Callahan's men enlisted more than once. Only five men served just one stint and of these, two resided outside of Seguin—C. C. Colley from the Plum Creek area and Joseph D. Clements of Gonzales—while two—Jose Maria Cardenas and George W. Price—lived in the Seguin area. After the rangers returned from the June 7–21 patrol, sixteen-year-old Denyer joined the ill-fated Santa Fe Expedition and became a prisoner for a year. On two occasions Callahan and his troop joined other companies in operations that reached beyond their usual patrols. They rode with Hays in July and with Benjamin McCulloch in November.[32]

During the last week of June 1841, Indians stole cattle near San Antonio, prompting Hays to lead a pursuit by sixteen Anglos and Captain Salvador Flores's twenty Tejanos. The Gonzales Rangers joined them to fight the Comanches, and Callahan thus met the man who is considered to be the epitome of a Texas Ranger in the pre–Civil War era. Hays was a short, thin man, only twenty-four years of age in 1841, but his stature and self-effacing manner masked a fearless and effective leader. Hays was a perfect mentor for Callahan, who was five years his senior and may have first met Hays in Seguin. Hays fell in love with Susan Calvert, after meeting her at one of the dances at Sarah Hembree Day's house, and it was likely there that Callahan first saw Hays.[33]

Hays and his rangers traveled west from San Antonio along the southern edge of the Balcones Escarpment for eighty-five miles to the mouth of Uvalde Canyon, where the Frio River exits from the Edwards Plateau (map 5.2c). Hays reported that he fought ten Indians there, killed eight, captured two, and confiscated horses and property. In the skirmish one ranger was slightly wounded. Deciding not to venture to the main Indian camp, Hays returned to San Antonio by July 1 to rearm and recruit more volunteers before returning to the pursuit. Hays could not recruit enough rangers in San Antonio, so he contacted Callahan, who had the nearest frontier company, and also asked Flacco to bring his Lipan warriors. Callahan brought sixteen men to San Antonio. Many of the Gonzales Rangers with him were veteran rangers, the most prominent of whom was Benjamin McCulloch (table 5.3). Fourteen of Callahan's sixteen had fought in a ranger company within the last two years. Henry McCulloch in writing about this venture noted that his brother, Ben, and others joined Callahan hoping to fight Indians, but added that Ben also wanted to locate and survey lands.[34]

Hays left San Antonio for the second time in July 1841 with twenty-five men from that city, about fifteen from the Seguin area, and a similar number of Lipans and Tonkawas. The ride west was dry and hot. Hays's troops arrived at the site of the previous fight on the Frio River, hoping to find the Comanche encampment, but the Comanches had fled after killing a few prisoners. So they followed their trail thirty miles north to where the West and East prongs of the Frio meet (present-day Leakey). Hays's report reflected the challenges posed by the terrain: "We pursued at a great disadvantage, the Indians having designedly picked the worst road possible, and burned the whole Country. Our Horses and Men were much starved and worn down by the time we had reached the head waters of the Llano." On the Edwards Plateau the scrub brush thinned, making it easier for the scouts to find fresh Indian trails, which converged at a Comanche encampment at the headwaters of the South Fork of the Llano River (map 5.2c). Here the rangers slept until the following morning, when Comanches discovered them and fled, sounding an alarm. Hays's troops pursued the warriors until they were attacked by fifty, who were covering the retreat of the main body. A running fight, lasting two hours, covered six miles over the jagged terrain. Benjamin McCulloch killed several Comanches with his long-range rifle and at some point, Callahan's men dismounted and attempted to dislodge some Indians who were on a craggy ledge high above them. A ranger was wounded in the melee but the Texians believed they killed and wounded ten Indians. Hays concluded he had encountered almost two hundred Indians herding six hundred horses and that there was another large camp near the headwaters of the Guadalupe. Considering the exhaustion of the rangers and their horses and the burden of several wounded men, Hays decided not to go further and he led his men back to San Antonio, arriving on August 4. Two days later, after twenty-seven days in the saddle, the Gonzales Rangers returned to Seguin, where Callahan discharged his exhausted volunteers.[35]

Back in Seguin, Callahan's Rangers settled into their regular routine, punctuated by periodic spy missions or an occasional two- to five-day patrol. This continued until October 24, 1841, when fifteen men served continuously until December 2. Forty days in the saddle indicate their intent was a long-range expedition beyond the San Marcos and Guadalupe Rivers. Apart from the length, the other unusual aspect was that Benjamin McCulloch again joined Callahan's company. Very little is known about this campaign; historians give it sparse attention, but family traditions and government documents reveal an interesting aspect of the relationship between Callahan and McCulloch. The Austin *Daily Bulletin* placed the expedition geographically on the San Saba River, and ten years later, Callahan told Caldwell County neighbor William N. Trainer that he rode through the Blanco River valley in November 1841 on a scouting trip with Benjamin McCulloch. He vividly remembered that the "grass was as tall as the spurs on a man riding a horse." They rode northwest thirteen miles and then traversed the Devil's Backbone, a ridge that separated the canyons of the Blanco and Guadalupe Rivers (map 5.2d). They crossed in succession the Little Blanco, Blanco, Pedernales, Llano, and San Saba Rivers. Survey records of the Llano River from the mouth of Johnson's Fork and the North Fork of the Llano (all in present-day Kimble County) confirm McCulloch's objective. He arrived in that area by October 20, 1841, four days before Callahan mustered his rangers in Seguin (table 5.3). Antonio Coy, a frequent member of Hays's companies, served as one of McCulloch's chainmen until October 28, when he was replaced by George Price, a Gonzales Ranger. Coy's replacement with Price indicates that McCulloch and Callahan cooperated in surveying the area. In fact, from October 20 to November 1 McCulloch and his team completed about thirty surveys.[36]

Taken together, the *Daily Bulletin* article, Trainer family oral tradition, and government records indicate that Ben McCulloch and Callahan planned separate trips that allowed them to join each other. On October 24 Callahan led his men, with Price but without McCulloch, along the Devil's Backbone beyond the headwaters of the Pedernales and Blanco Rivers. He met McCulloch four days later near the junction of the North and South Forks of the Llano (map 5.2d) and learned that he had plotted the Sion D. Green Survey, a grant that Callahan had purchased in 1838, and a survey in Callahan's name. The Green property had been the site of the Hays fight with the Comanches in the spring of 1841. Callahan had shown both pieces of property to McCulloch at that time, and he intended for McCulloch to return and plot the surveys. By the fall of 1841 Callahan bought other land grants, which he also had McCulloch survey at the same time. He met with him to see if McCulloch surveyed the tracts in the locations he had chosen. McCulloch's surveys coinciding with Callahan's patrols during the fall of 1841 are an example of how ranger activities promoted multiple Texian goals—land speculation, defense of the frontier, and opening up new lands for settlement by pushing the Indians west.

With his survey tasks completed, McCulloch joined Callahan's Rangers, and they scoured the area and chased a band of Waco Indians, killing two (map 5.2d). One of the smaller Indian groups in Texas, the Wacos had been depleted by disease and campaigns by the Cherokees, Spanish, Mexicans, and Texians. By 1840 the survivors were confined to the upper Trinity and Brazos Rivers, whence they occasionally made hunting forays to the Colorado River near the junction of the San Saba and Llano Rivers. This minor skirmish against a tribe that was not a critical menace to settlers is an example of how aggressive the Texians had become.[37]

Callahan established his reputation in the 1840 and 1841 Indian campaigns, and his participation in future expeditions would soon solidify his repute as a capable commander. The popular image of the brave and courteous, yet also individualistic and well-armed, Texas Ranger is of course a stereotype that obscures the diversity of those who served on the frontier before the Civil War. Callahan's Rangers varied from the eccentric to the hardened, further testing his skills as a leader. An examination of Gonzales County records offers fleeting insights. Of the fifty-three men who served under him, eleven were indicted from 1839 through 1843 for crimes that included dueling, assault and battery, rioting, gambling, selling without a license, altering a brand, larceny, and killing an ox. In all but three cases, the indictments were dismissed, or the defendant was found not guilty. During the same years, almost half of Callahan's men appeared in court for civil disputes, including debts, deed disagreements, divorce, jury duty refusals, and probates. On the other hand, seventeen served on juries, some on multiple occasions, and five were appointed to serve as road overseers. The Gonzales Rangers were probably no different than their peers in other frontier counties, but what is notable is that Callahan made them into an effective military command, a testament to his leadership.[38]

Lamar's policy of using volunteer companies was partially successful. In northern Texas the Indians were pushed farther west, and in the southwest the frequency of Indian attacks declined. In March 1841, a Bexareño told the *Telegraph and Texas Register* that "the country is assuming the appearance of peace and prosperity." By the end of 1841, not all Texians supported the volunteers, and there were complaints about the program's cost along with accusations of fraud, misuse of funds, and inadequate oversight. In July 1841, Gonzales resident William D. Miller wrote, "The system is too much disjointed to be effectual." The editor of the *Telegraph and Texas Register* concluded that the ranger system encouraged land speculators to locate land at public expense and fostered cattle thefts, and he further complained that costs were double the $65,000 appropriation. The volunteers were clearly under fire from many of the same people they defended.[39]

While Callahan's Gonzales Rangers were an effective force, since the Comanches were not able to dominate the Guadalupe River Basin, he and his men did use patrols as opportunities to search for land. Callahan and Ben McCulloch did exactly what the editor condemned as land speculation. The Gonzales Rangers also contributed to the cost overruns. Surviving payroll records indicate Callahan invoiced the Republic for at least $10,325 in 1841. But this was far less than the $700,000 the Republic spent on its army in 1840, and the volunteers demoralized the Indians and moved the frontier west, both of which were goals of the Lamar administration. Texian casualties from Indian raids also decreased from thirty-three killed and fifty wounded in 1839, the last year of Houston's first administration, to five killed and seven wounded in 1841. Although rangers in 1841 cannot claim sole credit for this, they contributed, and Callahan's Gonzales Rangers are entitled to their share of recognition.[40]

A vitriolic presidential election dominated Texas politics during the latter half of 1841. Houston campaigned again for the presidency, focusing his platform on the debt accumulated by the Lamar administration. On election day, Houston soundly whipped David G. Burnet, the man Lamar hoped would succeed him. While President Houston could not reverse many changes made by the Lamar administration, he was determined to return to his frontier policy of treaties and trade relations with Indians. Thus, the era of state-funded, county-organized rangers came to an end. Soon, though, troubles with Indians and Mexicans would force Houston to authorize ranger companies, and leaders such as Callahan would be needed again in the spring of 1842.[41]

CHAPTER 6

The Ranger Years, 1842–1843

"Capt Calleghan cooley . . . called on the men not to be excited"

Hearing that Mexican General Adrián Woll had captured San Antonio, armed men from the Colorado and Guadalupe River valleys poured into Seguin, and by September 12, 1842, Col. Mathew Caldwell had nearly two hundred volunteers. The rangers molded bullets and filled powder horns, while women prepared meager provisions, mainly corn and beef, for them. The news about San Antonio was confusing but two disturbing facts stood out—Woll had captured several prominent Texians and raised the Mexican flag. With 1,300 troops, he posed the greatest threat to Texas since the 1836 revolution. Once again, residents of Seguin organized to fight, with women such as Sarah Hembree Day and her daughters providing logistical support for the men marching forth under the leadership of officers such as Caldwell and James Hughes Callahan.[1]

Mirabeau B. Lamar's success in subduing Indians had diverted the attention of most Texians from the Rio Grande border. In the Trans-Nueces chaparral, brigands stole livestock and threatened settlers. Adding to the chaos, some on both sides of the river plotted to create a third country—the Republic of the Rio Grande. By 1839, centralist General Mariano Arista dominated northern Mexico, forcing the federalists, who sought support from the Texas government, into the Trans-Nueces chaparral. Mexican politician Antonio Canales, with a mixed force of Mexicans, Americans, Tejanos, Texians, and Indians, invaded Mexico twice and was defeated, causing him to switch sides. Mexico interpreted Texas's support of Canales as interference in its internal affairs, an impression reinforced in 1840 when Lamar sent the Texas Navy to support the Yucatan rebels. Likewise, Canales's duplicity caused Texians to be suspicious of Tejanos, wondering if their loyalties lay with Texas or Mexico.[2]

While Texas's hold on the Trans-Nueces chaparral was tenuous, it was entirely absent in the upper Rio Grande valley of present-day New Mexico, where Texians also claimed territory. Believing Mexicans around Santa Fe would welcome Texians, Lamar authorized an expedition to assert Texas's claim over the territory. During June 1841, Col. Hugh McLeod led a caravan north and west from Austin. Caldwell commanded a company while Samuel J. Denyer, who had recently served under Callahan, enlisted, as did Gonzales County resident Anson G. Neal, who had endorsed James Milford Day's bond as executor of his father's estate in 1838. William Wirt Alsbury, the spouse of Sarah Medissa Day Alsbury, was the expedition's Spanish translator. Content with leading the Gonzales Rangers, Callahan remained in Seguin. By August, the Santa Fe Expedition was lost, famished, thirsty, and beleaguered by Comanches. Its Mexican guide had deserted and McLeod had no map, so on September 17 the last Texian surrendered to Mexican troops. The prisoners endured an arduous trek and by the end of 1841 were held captive in Mexico City or Perote Prison. It was not until December 8 that Texians learned the expedition had failed when excerpts from the Mexican newspaper *El Siglo XIX* were reprinted in New Orleans and Texas.[3]

Sam Houston, who succeeded Lamar as president, was determined not to provoke either Mexico or the Indians. Nevertheless, after returning to power, Antonio Lopez de Santa Anna made reconquest of Texas a top priority. He ordered General Arista to set his sights on San Antonio and on November 24, 1841, he issued a draft plan. Using the two-pronged strategy Santa Anna had employed in 1836, Arista planned to send Brigadier General Ráfael Vásquez across the Rio Grande at Laredo with nine hundred men to take San Antonio, while Lieutenant Colonel Ramón Valera would cross at Mier and attack Refugio and Goliad. By the time Arista finalized his plans, the troops available to Vásquez had dwindled to 425, but he believed San Antonio's Tejanos would welcome the Mexican army and Texians there could be cowed. On January 9, 1842, Arista issued a threating proclamation, hoping to convince many Tejanos and Texians to rejoin Mexico, and then he launched his invasion.[4]

On January 21, Valera crossed the Rio Grande with two hundred cavalrymen en route to Corpus Christi, and four days later Vásquez's reduced force moved into Texas. Arista's proclamation shook the Tejano community and many departed San Antonio, seeking safety in the countryside.

But Texians dismissed the idea that Mexico had either the courage or the capacity to invade, as the *Telegraph and Texas Register* insisted. Meanwhile, Houston heard from Gonzales resident Washington D. Miller that Mexico had stopped trade on the border, but a more alarming report came from San Antonio mayor Juan N. Seguín, who received a message from Vásquez that indicated his city could be occupied in March. On January 30, Seguín dispatched a warning to Houston, resigned as mayor, and retired to his ranch near Seguin. San Antonio resident Mary Maverick recalled that friendly Mexicans warned her to leave as well.[5]

Seguin residents worried more about Indian raids and paid little attention to any threat from Mexico until Vasquez was in Texas. At the full moon on the last weekend in February, Sarah Hembree Day held a dance at her home. John R. King, who stood guard, fired on a band of Indians attempting to steal horses. The same Indians killed John Lee Witter in Gonzales County on February 25, 1842. Meanwhile, Anglos in San Antonio concluded that the invasion threat was real, so they formed a safety committee and sent two men to Laredo to reconnoiter. The spies were stopped at the Nueces River by Vásquez's lead company and ordered back to San Antonio. A second Texian scouting party left San Antonio on February 26 but was detained by a Mexican patrol. When the committee appealed for aid to nearby towns, a few men from Seguin led by Andrew Neill rode to San Antonio, where residents had elected Jack Hays as their leader and established martial law. Having no news from the last two spies, Hays sent a trusted Tejano to investigate, but he was also captured. By then, San Antonians were panicking, and three-fourths of the city's population left by February 27. Mary Maverick, along with several other women, numerous children, and a few older men, fled to Seguin, arriving on March 3. Meanwhile, Neill implored Seguin residents to stay at home, but Hays added a postscript pleading for men to hurry to San Antonio. Maverick found families loading their possessions into wagons and abandoning farms in what became known as the "Runaway Scrape of '42." As they hurried east, about forty men from the Guadalupe and Colorado river valleys assembled at Seguin for a fight.[6]

Hays had no idea of the composition of the Mexican force bearing down on San Antonio, so on March 2, he dispatched Ben McCulloch and Alsey S. Miller, who found Vásquez crossing the Hondo River, forty-five miles southwest of San Antonio. They counted the invaders, rode south to the Nueces River and ascertained that no reinforcements were following, then hurried north and turned east toward San Antonio. By that time, Vásquez had sent a mounted patrol under Captain Calixto Bravo to cut communications between San Antonio, Austin, and the lower Guadalupe River. Bravo did not meet any Texians, but he passed not far from Sarah Hembree Day's house. Early on the morning of March 4, Texians left Seguin for San Antonio. They halted at Cibolo Creek, elected Callahan as their captain (table 6.1), and then pressed on, arriving that evening with a second group of twenty-five volunteers from DeWitt County, led by Capt. Daniel Boone Friar.[7]

Vásquez on March 3 camped on the Medina River, thirty miles southwest of San Antonio, and sent scouts to reconnoiter the city. They watched as several Texian units arrived, including Callahan's and Friar's men. The next day, a seven-man Texian patrol was fired upon by the lead contingent of Vásquez's force, but they evaded the Mexicans and located the enemy's camp on Leon Creek, eight miles from the city. Gonzales County resident Creed Taylor, a member of this patrol, estimated the Texians faced between 750 and 1,000 foes. In fact, Vásquez by then had almost 700 men, including 200 Tejanos and a few Indians. The Texian patrol returned to San Antonio early in the morning on March 5, at the same time as McCulloch and Miller. Hays, realizing he faced a formidable force, organized a defense with 107 Texians and two cannons. Among their captains were two from Seguin, Callahan and French Smith. Later that day a nine-man patrol encountered a man bearing a white flag and a letter, which demanded that the Texians surrender. After learning that reinforcements would not arrive despite the pleas of the safety committee, Hays convened his officers, who voted five to four to withdraw from San Antonio. The officers from Gonzales and Seguin, including Callahan, voted to retreat. Hays sent an armistice commission to Vásquez while his men dismantled the cannons. The remaining merchants of San Antonio blew up their stores after distributing cigars and liquor as volunteers scoured the town for anything of value. James P. Kinkannon and John Bibb, both from Gonzales County, almost set off an explosion when Bibb touched his lighted cigar to a powder trail leaking from a keg. Taylor recalled that merchant John Twohig used gunpowder kegs to prepare a trap in his store; they later exploded, killing several Mexicans. As the Texians withdrew, enemy cavalry harried them until Seguin volunteers counterattacked. That night, March 5, the Texians camped on Cibolo Creek, twelve miles west of Seguin. Hays dispatched an urgent plea to Austin for aid, while Samuel Highsmith sent a note to Seguin that San Antonio had fallen, and they should seek safety in Gonzales.[8]

Table 6.1. Volunteers, James Hughes Callahan's Ranger Company, Vásquez invasion, March 1842

Name	*Residence*	*Military Experience and Remarks*
Capt. James H. Callahan	Seguin	Howard 1840, Llano 1841, Big Spring 1841, Gonzales Minutemen 1841
A. A. Crain	Seguin	Gonzales Minutemen 1841
H. D. (Taylor) Conn	unknown	Rusk Expedition 1838, Kickapoo Expedition 1838
Thomas Hill	unknown	Rusk Expedition 1839
David Henson	Seguin	Peach Creek 1839, Córdova 1839, Gonzales Minutemen 1841
Eli Skaggs Hankins	Plum Creek	Plum Creek 1840, Llano 1841
William G. King	Seguin	Gonzales Minutemen 1841
William R. Leonard	Gonzales	Settled in Texas, 1842
Edward Mallock	Plum Creek	Settled in Texas, 1842
Benjamin B. Peak	Seguin	Settled in Texas, 1842
James Ramsey	Gonzales	Settled in Texas, 1842
Jeremiah Roberts	Seguin	Tex. Army 1837, Córdova 1839, Howard 1840, Llano 1841, Gonzales Minutemen 1841
P. (Pitkin) Taylor	Gonzales	Creed Taylor's brother
John B. Veach	Seguin	Gonzales Minutemen 1841
J. Vandevner (Vandeneer)	unknown	unknown
Joseph L. Baker	Gonzales	Died 1850, DeWitt County
C. C. Colley	Gonzales	Tex. Army 1836–1837, Córdova 1839, Howard 1840, McCulloch 1841, Gonzales Minutemen 1841
C. C. DeWitt	Gonzales	Plum Creek 1840
Miles G. Dikes	Gonzales	Córdova 1839, Gonzales Minutemen 1841
Robert Hall	Seguin	Tex. Revolution 1835–1836, Tex. Army 1836–1837, Plum Creek 1840, Gonzales Minutemen 1841
David Hodges	Gonzales	unknown
John Seaborn Hodges	Gonzales	Córdova 1839
Charles F. Harwood	unknown	unknown
Lt. John R. King	Seguin	Córdova 1839, Plum Creek 1840, Gonzales Minutemen 1841, Big Spring 1841

Name	*Residence*	*Military Experience and Remarks*
Andrew Neill	Seguin	Córdova 1839, Karnes 1839, Plum Creek 1840, Gonzales Minutemen 1841
French Smith	Seguin	Tex. Army 1836–1837, Karnes 1839, Gonzales Minutemen 1841
Andrew J. Sowell	Seguin	Córdova 1839, Plum Creek 1840, Big Spring 1841
Asa J. Sowell	Seguin	Tex. Rev. 1835–1836, Tex. Army 1836, Córdova 1839, Plum Creek 1840
John N. Sowell	Seguin	Gonzales Minutemen 1841
Arthur Swift	Seguin	Córdova 1839, Plum Creek 1840, Gonzales Minutemen 1841
Calvin S. Turner	Seguin	Córdova 1839, Plum Creek 1840, Gonzales Minutemen 1841
Isaac H. Turner	Seguin	Llano 1841, Gonzales Minutemen 1841
William R. Turner	Seguin	Howard 1840, Gonzales Minutemen 1841
William S. Turner	Seguin	unknown
John Henry Brown	Victoria	Plum Creek 1840
Two unknown men	—	unknown
Creed Taylor	Gonzales	Tex. Revolution 1835–1836, Howard 1840, Plum Creek 1840

Sources: TR, 1841–43, TAC, Gonzales County, TSLA; S. Moore, *Savage Frontier*, 2:29, 71, 131, 179, 184–85, 193, 230; 3:106–8, 138–39, 222, 337; *Muster Rolls of the Texas Revolution*, 84, 88, 130, 222; Vásquez Campaign (commander James H. Callahan) [Mar. 1–Apr. 1,] 1842, Oversize 401-714, Folder 6, RTMR, TAGD, TSLA; Baker, *Texas Scrap-Book*, 627; last and first names, Land Grant Search, TGLO; last and first names, Republic Claims, TSLA; Mortality Schedule, U.S. Census, 1850, DeWitt County; J. Brown, *History of Texas*, 212; Creed Taylor Narrative, Vásquez Invasion, Box 1, Folder 52, JTDSP, DRT; *Texas Democrat*, June 24, 1845; U.S. Census, 1850, Lavaca County; *TSG*, Aug. 7, 1852.

Note: Howard 1840–Howard Campaign, fall 1840; Llano 1841–Hays's fight, Llano River, spring 1841; Big Spring 1841–Callahan Expedition, spring 1841; Gonzales Minutemen 1841–Callahan's Gonzales Minutemen 1841; Rusk Expedition 1838–Rusk campaign against the Cherokees, summer 1838; Kickapoo Expedition 1838–Rusk campaign against Kickapoo Indians, fall 1938; Rusk Expedition 1839–Rusk Trinity River campaign, winter 1839; Peach Creek 1839–Ben McCulloch's fight on Peach Creek, Gonzales County, spring 1839; Córdova 1839–fight against Córdova near Seguin, spring 1839; Plum Creek 1840–fight against Comanches, August 1840; Tex. army–individual served in Republic of Texas army in year(s) noted; Karnes 1839–Karnes's Comanche Expedition, June 1839.

Sarah Hembree Day, her daughters, and the few other citizens who remained in Seguin were shaken by the news. Rumors circulated that 14,000 soldiers were tramping toward San Antonio and Sarah knew her house was first in line if Vásquez came to Seguin. Her matter-of-fact entry in her prayer journal for that day—"March, Seguin, the Beginning of the War. [O]n the fifth, Retreat from St Antona"—may reflect a studied attempt to avoid panic. Maverick was more candid. She was at the Capote Ranch six miles east of Seguin and recalled: "I took a shaking ague and could not speak for the chatter of my teeth. . . . We were in fact seized with a genuine 'panic.'" By evening a resigned inertia set in, and after dinner they all sat on a log waiting for the Mexicans to arrive. According to Sarah, on March 8 the remaining families left Seguin. Their departure was observed by Captain Antonio Pérez, a scout sent by Vásquez. Sarah's unhurried exodus may be explained by crucial information received by Hays on March 6. He learned that Vásquez had no reinforcements, and many Texians were on the way to help. This altered his outlook. Hays sent foraging parties to obtain beef and corn, and dispatched rangers to stampede Vásquez's horse herd. On March 7, he moved across the Guadalupe to the east bank, camping at Seguin. Miles Bennett recalled the Texians spent the night molding bullets, making corn dodgers, and drying beef. As Hays regrouped, Vasquez's men sacked San Antonio, packing their plunder on carts and 132 mules. The following morning, March 8, they began an orderly but hasty retreat. The rear guard under Bravo skirmished with Indians near the Medina River, and on March 12 several of Hays's Rangers briefly saw Bravo's troops. On March 13, Vásquez led his men across the Rio Grande, and the next day he drafted a report to Arista in which he admitted that his horses and men were worn out.[9]

Meanwhile, Sarah, her daughters, and other Seguin residents made their way to Gonzales. The thirty-mile journey took three days and was a chaotic, pell-mell dash in wagons and carts, or on horseback and foot. Some refugees, Maverick noted, were troubled by the desolate, deserted homes they saw as her caravan traveled to Gonzales. In Gonzales, Sarah and her family found a place to stay, which must have been difficult as the town was crowded and folks were in a state of panic and easily spooked. One night an elderly man rushed into the village in an excited state claiming a large band of Indians was riding toward Gonzales. As the news spread, more of the area's inhabitants raced to Gonzales, where the available men prepared to defend the agitated citizens. The old man proved to be delusional, but the people's panic was very real.[10]

While San Antonio's residents were preparing for a hurried escape, Valera led his two hundred Mexican cavalrymen north from the Rio Grande at Mier. Rains and swollen rivers slowed their progress and drained the stamina of the troops and horses. Nevertheless, on March 3, forty of Valera's men occupied Goliad, while the area's Anglos fled to Victoria. The next day, Valera took Refugio, then his soldiers killed a band of Lipans and captured their horses, which they butchered and ate. When Valera did not hear from Vásquez, he began retreating to the Rio Grande. In the meantime, a Mexican patrol roamed to San Patricio, where they defeated Texan volunteers in a skirmish and then withdrew, meeting Valera on the Nueces River on March 7. The Lipans, angry at the assault on their band, dogged the retreating Mexicans, attacking them on March 10, inflicting many casualties and dispersing their horses. Chastened, Valera led his exhausted men across the Rio Grande into Mexico.[11]

The incursions by Vásquez and Valera reignited calls for war with Mexico, and Houston was pressed to authorize an invasion. Meanwhile, six hundred Texians arrived at San Antonio by mid-March and another five hundred camped near Goliad. Callahan, who had not joined in pursuing Vásquez to the Rio Grande, remained in San Antonio as men poured into the town. Texas Vice President Edward Burleson left Austin after calling for a muster at San Antonio, and by March 15, he was with the volunteers at Mission Concepción, where they confirmed his leadership by vote. In the meantime, Houston appointed Alexander Somervell as commander and sent him to San Antonio. Sensing the volunteers resented him, Somervell returned to Austin, leaving Burleson in charge. On March 17, more officers were elected, and Callahan became a lieutenant in Capt. Louis P. Cooke's company. At Austin, an infuriated Houston ordered Somervell back to San Antonio. A two-day standoff ensued between Somervell and Burleson while Callahan and the troops waited in a persistent rain. On April 1, Burleson capitulated and dismissed the units under his command, giving each man the option to join Somervell. Callahan, like most, decided to return home and was discharged on April 2. Since almost all of the volunteers departed, Somervell disbanded the rest. There was no imminent threat of invasion, and men preferred to return to spring planting rather than serve under a commander whose motivation and leadership was uncertain. Taylor later wrote that most of the Texians were disgusted and discouraged, and the *Telegraph and Texas Register* blamed the debacle on Houston.[12]

By mid-summer, the impulse to invade Mexico waned and Texians resumed their daily routines. James W. Nichols recalled: "After we ware rid of the Mexican army . . . everything seemed to lull down in perfect forgetfulness." While many San Antonio residents had not returned home by the time the district court met in September, most in the Seguin area were home by the end of spring. "May the 21 Came back to Seguine," Sarah recorded in her prayer journal. She must have been infuriated at the desolation she found. Texian volunteers had looted homes and slaughtered livestock. Nichols wondered who was worse, Mexicans or these Texians. On the other side, Santa Anna was not pleased with the Vásquez raid. However, Arista decided that Texas could muster, on quick notice, only a hundred or so men to confront an invasion, and Tejanos, when given the option, would support Mexico, so a second raid should be launched.[13]

An analysis of the other Seguin-area defenders who were at San Antonio when Vásquez arrived reveals that Arista was not wrong. Only 16 of the 53 Gonzales Rangers who had served in 1841 joined the 107 men who initially defended San Antonio during the 1842 raid (see tables 5.3, 6.1). Conspicuously missing were the Nichols men (except for James W. Nichols), Henry B. King, and James M. Day. They may have been helping families and neighbors before joining the defense force; San Antonians Sam Maverick and Anderson Hutchinson escorted their families to Gonzales and returned home. The absent Gonzales Rangers may have been among the seven hundred men in San Antonio by mid-March. However, it is odd that many Gonzales Rangers who lived in Seguin did not join Callahan when he rode to San Antonio earlier. Of 38 volunteers with him then, 19 lived in Seguin, 10 in Gonzales, 2 in the Plum Creek valley, and 1 in Victoria, while the residences of 6 are unknown (table 6.1). Although four had no combat experience, most of them had fought Indians or Mexicans, including Eli Skaggs Hankins, who later became Callahan's brother-in-law. In sum, the force Vasquez confronted was clearly insufficient to defend San Antonio, but if Hays had had more veterans like those with Callahan, he might not have retreated.[14]

Callahan's role during the Vásquez raid indicated his status, and growing pragmatism, as a leader. It was the third time he had been elected by peers to lead them. After Vásquez retreated, the influx of hundreds of volunteers, along with political leaders such as Burleson, changed the dynamics, and in the election on March 17, politics played a dominant role. Cooke, a member of the Texas Congress, became a captain. Nevertheless, Callahan was elected the first lieutenant in Cooke's company. That was another good choice. Callahan was proving to be a careful leader, one who would not waste men in lost causes. When Hays polled his officers during the armistice on March 5, Callahan voted to withdraw. Later, when the volunteer force dissolved in chaos at San Antonio, Callahan went home with his men. In both cases, he showed one measure of a good leader—he chose to fight when he could win and to retreat when he could not.[15]

According to Sarah Hembree Day, Seguin's citizens quickly returned to their ordinary routine. Spring was the planting season, but an already difficult year was made more challenging by unpredictable weather. Heavy rains in April destroyed the young crops. By the end of summer, second crops had been planted, and a visitor told the *Telegraph and Texas Register* that local farms were flourishing. Seguin residents also watched for Indians. In June, the paper claimed that near Seguin Jose Antonio Navarro's son was wounded. The paper reported another attack in August near San Marcos Springs, thirty miles northwest of Seguin, but three Tejanos captured in early September admitted that a gang of fifty men had committed the depredations in a manner that implicated Indians. To protect the area, Houston authorized Hays to enroll 150 rangers, but he could only find 50. This time Callahan and most of his men in Seguin did not join Hays. George W. Hockley, the Secretary of War and Marine, defended the volunteers' failure to respond, noting they had families to tend. In fact, Seguin residents did not perceive a significant threat. Taylor recalled that the locals were lulled into a sense of security and did not believe another invasion would soon occur.[16]

Santa Anna blamed Arista for the failure of the Vásquez raid, and he also doubted the general's loyalty. Arista, claiming ill health, resigned on May 28, 1842, and was replaced by General Isidro Reyes. On June 5, Santa Anna told Reyes that General Adrián Woll was to organize another invasion with the objective of occupying San Antonio and conducting a reconnaissance down the Guadalupe River to the coast. By August, Reyes was in Coahuila, where Woll had 1,539 troops, and on August 25 they began crossing the Rio Grande. Reyes and Woll selected an unorthodox route to San Antonio. The Mexicans forded at an obscure pass and marched north to the Balcones Escarpment, then turned east to San Antonio. By mid-August hints of an attack had begun appearing in Texas newspapers, and at the end of the month one of Hays's men reported unfamiliar Mexicans in San Antonio. Local citizens became frantic on September 9, when reports surfaced that 1,500 Mexican troops were approaching. The next morning the district court was suspended and the judge and lawyers, along with about 100 Tejanos and 75 Anglos under Hays, organized a defense. At first, they mistakenly believed brigands were approaching, so Hays led a five-man patrol to determine the threat's nature. As a precaution, a courier was sent to the Guadalupe River valley requesting that 50 to 100 volunteers ride to San Antonio. For the second time that year, Callahan, Sarah Hembree Day's extended family, and other Seguin residents found themselves at war.[17]

Woll's army on September 10 arrived at Leon Creek near San Antonio, where he had his men rest, intending to surround the city that night and capture it the next morning. He assumed that he remained undetected and could mount a surprise attack, but when four Tejanos appeared it became clear that the Mexicans' presence was known. By midnight they blocked most of the city's exits and at 4:30 A.M., under a heavy fog, they marched toward the plaza with their band blaring. Texians and Tejanos rallied to their posts and blindly fired toward the music, killing several soldiers and wounding many. Infuriated, Woll sent a colonel forward with a white flag, and he returned with four commissioners. Woll insisted the Texians capitulate but agreed to a half-hour truce. Realizing how many Mexicans they faced, the Texians surrendered. Sixty-two men stacked their arms and congregated in the plaza, but eight evaded the Mexicans, making their way to Seguin. Among those captured were a district judge, a former vice president, a district attorney, two Texas Congressmen, and several lawyers and businessmen. Shortly after their surrender, sixteen wrote a letter to Texas authorities saying they had been treated humanely and requesting that Mexican prisoners be equally respected. On September 15, Woll released ten prisoners and sent the remaining fifty-two to Mexico. Two captives were particularly important to Callahan and the Day family: lawyer Andrew Neill, who was representing Sarah Medissa Day Alsbury in a lawsuit, and William Early Jones, an attorney and Texas Congressman who had lived near Callahan in Jackson County, Georgia.[18]

Hays had left San Antonio before the surrender and withdrew east along the Guadalupe River, calling for volunteers to rendezvous with him at Seguin and asking other residents to stay in their homes. San Antonio mayor John W. Smith, who had also escaped, sent a plea for help to Gonzales and Mathew Caldwell, recently returned from a Mexican prison. Caldwell also asked men to assemble at Seguin and dispatched messengers east and north, requesting reinforcements. Participant James Ramsay later wrote that the first volunteers arrived on September 12 and slept in John R. King's gallery. At Seguin, when the men selected their officers, Caldwell was elected commander, and companies formed under Hays, Friar from Cuero, Ewen Cameron from

Victoria, and James Bird of Gonzales. Callahan became the first lieutenant in Bird's company of rangers from Gonzales and Seguin (table 6.2). The chaos of Woll's raid disrupted the normal practice of keeping muster rolls, which has made it difficult to explain why Callahan was a lieutenant rather than a captain. Bird did not create a roll, or it was lost. Historian Stephen L. Moore compiled a roll for his company, but this does not corroborate the eyewitness accounts that sixty came from Gonzales and Seguin. Comparing Moore's tabulations with other records reveals that thirty lived near Gonzales and nineteen around Seguin. Thus, with more men from Gonzales, it becomes clear why Bird was elected the company's captain and Callahan of Seguin became its lieutenant. In fact, both were proven leaders. Moreover, most of their men had served in Texas campaigns, with only nine admitting to being novices. Fourteen had been in Callahan's Gonzales Rangers, and fifteen rode with him during the Vásquez invasion; most of these lived near Seguin. Bird's company was a strong unit, which explains why it did well in Caldwell's fight with Woll at Salado Creek.[19]

Bird's company was also tightly knit through kinship and business relationships. Charles Braches jointly operated a mercantile store in Gonzales with Caleb Brown. Based on claims filed, every man in the Turner family volunteered to fight; however, according to family stories, the father, William S., did not fight but loaned his rifle to one of his sons. The three King brothers—Henry B., John R., and William G.—fought side by side. James W. and John W. Nichols were at Salado Creek while their brother Thomas was posted at the San Marcos River, organizing and sending provisions. Their father, George W., was unable to take part as he was recuperating in Seguin from a fistfight, but Ezekiel Smith and his son French participated. Six Texians who fought at Salado Creek would later become brothers-in-law—Callahan, Solomon Brill, James M. Day, Eli S. Hankins, Henry B. King, and John W. Nichols. The Sowells and Turners intermarried. These connections further strengthened Bird's company.[20]

In preparing to fight, the Texians had only a few hours to gather supplies and ammunition. It was again a community effort, and fortuitously someone with the skills required to manage the logistics was present—the former commander of the Texas army commissary, Valentine Bennet, who had just returned to Gonzales. Santa Anna had freed all the Santa Fe prisoners except José Antonio Navarro in June 1842. One was Bennet, who had traveled to Gonzales with Caldwell, a fellow Santa Fe prisoner. Bennet set up his commissary at Sarah Hembree Days' home in Seguin and began collecting corn,

Table 6.2. Reconstructed muster roll, James Bird's Company, Woll invasion, Sept. 1842

Name	*Residence*	*Military experience and remarks*
Capt. James Bird	Gonzales	Tex. Revolution 1836, Cherokee 1839, Howard 1840, Burleson 1840, Plum Creek 1840
Lt. James Hughes Callahan	Seguin	Tex. Revolution 1836, Howard 1840, Llano 1841, Big Spring 1841, Gonzales Minutemen 1841, Vásquez 1842
Miles S. Bennet	Gonzales	Cage 1838, Flores 1839, Karnes 1839, Plum Creek 1840
C. (Charles) Braches	Gonzales	Plum Creek 1840
Solomon W. Brill	Seguin	Tex. Revolution 1836, Tex. Army 1836–1837
Dr. C. (Caleb) S. Brown	Gonzales	Plum Creek 1840
Rev. Daniel Carl	Gonzales	Tex. Army 1839–1840
James M. Clark	Gonzales	unknown
C. (Canah) C. Colley	Gonzales	Tex. Army 1836–1837, Córdova 1839, Howard 1840, McCulloch 1841, Gonzales Minutemen 1841, Vásquez 1842
John A. Cummings	Gonzales	Santa Fe 1841
J. (John) H. Darst	Gonzales	unknown
Rollo M. Davis	Gonzales	unknown
James Milford Day	Seguin	Córdova 1839, Plum Creek 1840, Gonzales Minutemen 1841, Vásquez 1842
Clinton C. DeWitt	Gonzales	Plum Creek 1840
Miles G. Dikes	Gonzales	Córdova 1839, Plum Creek 1840, Gonzales Minutenmen 1841, Vásquez 1842
Andrew H. Erskine	Seguin	unknown
James T. Foster	Gonzales	Gonzales Minutemen 1841
Archibald Gibson	Seguin	Tex. Army, 1836–1837, Plum Creek, 1840, McCulloch 1841
Daniel Grady	Seguin	Córdova 1839, Howard 1840
John A. Green	Gonzales	unknown
E. S. (Eli Skaggs) Hankins	Gonzales	Plum Creek 1840, McCulloch 1841
David Hodges	Gonzales	unknown
John S. (Seaborn) Hodges	Seguin	Córdova 1839, Vásquez 1842
Archibald Jones	Gonzales	Tex. Army 1836–1837
Isham G. Jones	Gonzales	New immigrant, 1842
Henry B. (Basil) King	Seguin	Córdova 1839, Plum Creek 1840, Gonzales Minutemen 1841, Vásquez 1842

Name	*Residence*	*Military experience and remarks*
John R. King	Seguin	Córdova 1839, Plum Creek 1840, Gonzales Minutemen 1841, Big Spring 1841, Vásquez 1842
William G. King	Seguin	Gonzales Minutemen 1841
Byrd Lockhart (Jr.)	Gonzales	Burleson Mounted Rifles 1836
William Lockhart	Gonzales	Rusk Expedition 1838, Howard 1840
Morris May	Gonzales	Rusk Expedition 1838
James Nash	Gonzales	New immigrant, 1839
James W. (Wilson) Nichols	Seguin	Córdova 1839, Plum Creek 1840, Gonzales Minutemen 1841, Big Spring 1841, Vásquez 1842
John W. (Walker) Nichols	Seguin	Córdova 1839, Plum Creek 1840, Gonzales Minutemen 1841, Vásquez 1842
J. R. North	Gonzales	unknown
William Polk	Gonzales	unknown
B. (Benjamin F.) Powers Jr.	Gonzales	unknown
Wilson Randle	Seguin	Howard 1840, McCulloch 1841
A. Sehsan (unknown)	unknown	unknown
Solomon Simmons	Gonzales	Tex. Revolution
Byrd Smith	Gonzales	Gonzales Minutemen 1841
French Smith	Seguin	Córdova 1839, Plum Creek 1840
Peter D. Smith	Gonzales	New immigrant
Arthur Swift	Seguin	McCulloch 1841, Gonzales Minutemen 1841, Vásquez 1842
William Tumlinson	Gonzales	Howard 1840, McCulloch 1841
C. (Calvin) S. Turner	Seguin	Howard 1840, Gonzales Minutemen 1841, Vásquez 2842
I. (Isaac) H. Turner	Seguin	Vásquez 1842
William R. Turner	Seguin	Vásquez 1842
William S. Turner	Seguin	Vásquez 1842
Jesse Zumwalt	Gonzales	unknown

Sources: Last and first names, Republic Claims, TSLA; TR, 1841, 1842, 1843, TAC, Gonzales County, TSLA; U.S. Census 1850, Gonzales, Guadalupe, and Caldwell counties; S. Moore, *Savage Frontier,* 1:84, 76, 160; 2:35, 85, 203, 278, 308, 344; 3:106, 138; *Muster Rolls of the Texas Revolution*, 69, 213, 254; last and first names, Land Grant Search, TGLO; Loomis, *Texan-Santa Fe Pioneers*, 214.

Note: Bolded names are brothers-in-law. See *Note* table 6.1 for description of fights; others are: Cage 1838, fight on the Leon River, October 1838; Flores, 1939, fight against Manuel Flores on the San Gabriel River, May 1839; Santa Fe '41–Expedition to Santa Fe, N.M., 1841; Burleson's Mounted Riflemen, July–Dec. 1836.

beef, lead, and powder. According to Ramsay, the Texian volunteers camped nearby at James M. Day's house. Sarah Hembree Day and four daughters parched corn and dried beef, while Mary Nichols, another of Sarah's daughters, baked twenty-six loaves of bread. A heavy rain on September 12 hindered but did not stop their preparations. Meanwhile, William "Bigfoot" Wallace and another ranger arrived from Austin with a keg of gunpowder and bars of lead that Bennet parceled out. As before, not all of the volunteers behaved well. Fayette County resident Harvey Alexander Adams passed through Seguin and observed that "the people of this town appear to be very kind; they have been very much imposed upon by Some of the volunteers who show their patriotism by infringing upon the rights of Citizens."[21]

Caldwell left Bennet in Seguin, detailing James M. Day, Jim Alley, "old man Dunken," and three Nichols brothers—Solomon G., Thomas R., and John W.—to stay behind and forward provisions to the volunteers. Caldwell led his mounted command on a muddy slog to Cibolo Creek, where they bivouacked until September 17 as more recruits arrived and patrols scouted Woll's positions. The atmosphere was somewhat festive, according to James W. Nichols, as the men played cards, sang songs, wrestled, and ran foot races. Miles S. Bennet, Valentine's son, remembered that the command was mostly "young, light-hearted and buoyant" volunteers, with several more mature men. Twenty-eight-year-old Callahan was among the latter. About midnight on September 13, Caldwell sent ten men to find Hays, camped on Salado Creek; they rode all night in unremitting rain. Hays spent September 14 and 15 trying to determine Woll's strength and intentions. Meanwhile, Woll ordered Juan Seguín, Antonio Pérez, and about 150 mounted horsemen, mostly Tejanos, to reconnoiter the road to Gonzales. Seguín reached Cibolo Creek south of Caldwell's camp and sent patrols along the stream; other than three men swimming in the creek, two of whom they killed, Seguín's men found no Texians, but, leery of riding deeper into enemy territory, they refused to ford the stream. On September 14, Seguín told Woll that his horses were worn out, so he sent most of his men to San Antonio but continued to patrol until September 17, when he returned, reporting there were no Texians at Goliad or Corpus Christi. Inexplicably, he did not find the Texians organizing at Seguin and on Cibolo and Salado creeks.[22]

Meanwhile, Caldwell received a report that Pérez with 250 men was riding to Gonzales, so he notified the people living along the Guadalupe River. More than twenty volunteers rode for Cibolo Creek, where they arrived on September 17. That evening, Caldwell ordered his men, now numbering

203, to the east bank of Salado Creek. Ramsay wrote that the full moon shone bright as the men arrived about midnight on Salado Creek, six miles east of San Antonio, and camped in a ravine running east to west, parallel to the bank. They staked their horses, posted pickets, and prepared food without fires. Once settled, Callahan, as officer of the guard, ordered three men to ride back toward the Cibolo to make sure no Mexican patrol had discovered the new camp. Benjamin B. Peck, a Seguin gristmill owner, rode a scrappy mule and an unnamed man had a mustang, while a "Mr. White" from Cuero straddled a large American horse. White was inexperienced in fighting and easily spooked. About a mile from camp, the trio spotted a lone rider. When this stranger yelled, White raced back to the encampment and rushed through, shouting "Mexicans Indians" and stampeding the horses. Chaos ensued until "Capt. Callaghan [Callahan] cooley taking his pipe out of his mouth called on the men not to be excited—secure there horses . . . —Fear & excitement had rather stopped," wrote Ramsay. This is a good example of Callahan's ability to remain calm in a chaotic situation and his effectiveness as a commander. Moreover, sending a patrol to scout the trail illustrates another aspect of his growing military acumen. After the excitement, the men drifted into sleep, expecting to fight in the morning.[23]

With all his troops gathered in an ideal defensive situation on the east-west section of Salado Creek, Caldwell intended to force Woll to attack. James W. Nichols remembered that the forty-foot-wide, deep creek blocked an attack from the rear or south, while a steep bluff on the west was also an effective barrier. On Caldwell's left, the creek made a sharp turn to the north, protecting that flank from attacks. On the east side of the creek, in front of the Texians, was a slow-rising plateau with scattered mottes of live oak, pecan, elm, and mesquite. Two ravines snaked up the watershed divide so that the right wing of their position was anchored on one and the left wing on the other. This forced Woll to cross Salado Creek and attack from the east over an open prairie on the upper slope of an incline, a position that encouraged the Mexican soldiers to fire their weapons high.[24]

At sunrise on September 18, French Smith arrived at the Texian camp, accompanied by twenty men from the Guadalupe River valley and several head of beef. Two volunteers with Smith were James M. Day and John W. Nichols, who had stayed behind at the commissary. The famished Texians slaughtered the cattle and broiled the meat as Hays left camp with thirty-seven men mounted on the fittest horses, hoping to entice Woll to attack. Hays and his men, shouting and waving their hats, rode within a half mile of the Alamo and were chased by Mexican cavalry and mounted Tejanos led by Pérez. Meanwhile, most of Woll's infantry marched in pursuit. In this helter-skelter chase, Hays and his riders safely, but barely, crossed Salado Creek and halted behind the Texians' line as the mounted Mexicans stayed out of range. Two hours later, Woll and his infantry appeared with two cannons. Meanwhile, Caldwell sent another appeal for help as his men fell into line, many of them still eating. Caldwell had almost 220, while Woll's forces consisted of 300 cavalry, 400 infantry, 100 Tejanos, and 65 Cherokees. Caldwell positioned his troops with Cameron on the far right, Bird at center right, and Callahan in the lead with fifteen men. To Bird's left were Zumwalt and then Friar, while squads of Hays's company had been scattered throughout the line or placed in reserve. To begin the battle, Hays with several others charged twice, leaving several Mexicans dead and wounded while two Texians suffered minor injuries. When Woll countercharged, many Mexican troopers were unhorsed, and several more lay dead or wounded on the ground.[25]

By two in the afternoon, the skirmishing had lasted three hours. Woll repositioned his units and commenced an artillery barrage that, according to Nichols, only succeeded in breaking tree limbs overhead, causing no harm but annoying the horses. With each round, the gunners lowered their aim until the projectiles cut the grass on the embankment without any damage. Unable to rout the Texians, Woll ordered a combined charge by his cavalry and infantry. When ordered forward, Texians crawled out in small groups, but most stayed behind the embankment shooting in pairs; as one fired, the other man reloaded. The Mexicans suffered heavy losses as they marched downhill, their shots going over the heads of the concealed Texians. After another three hours of desultory fighting, with night approaching, Woll tried another frontal assault. The Mexican infantry advanced firing as the cannons boomed. Zenas N. Morrell described them as advancing with music playing and lances, guns, and swords gleaming. Callahan must have been reminded of Refugio in 1836. Meanwhile, on Caldwell's right wing, Vicente Córdova, who had eluded Burleson in East Texas in 1839, rallied forty Cherokees and struck at the junction of the Bird and Cameron companies. It was the greatest threat the Texians faced that day. Miles Bennet reported, "Captain Callahan made a detail of fifteen men, of whom I was one, to guard against surprise in that corner." Córdova and the Cherokees crawled close to the Texians and an intense firefight exploded. Nichols recalled that the yelling Cherokees fought like demons, launching a phalanx of arrows, while Callahan's men shot them as quickly as they appeared. Regrouping, they tried to gain the rear of the Texians, which resulted in bloody hand-to-hand fighting. By the time the Mexicans and Cherokees retreated, Córdova and ten to thirty-five of his men lay dead.[26]

Woll prepared to assault the Texian line again, but he was told that enemy reinforcements were approaching. It was Capt. Nicholas Dawson with fifty-two men. Woll halted his attack and ordered his cavalry and two cannons to confront the approaching riders. Mexican troopers surrounded Dawson, and cannon fire devastated his unlucky Texas volunteers, killing thirty-six and forcing fifteen to surrender. One of two men to escape was Alsey S. Miller, who made a spectacular getaway to Seguin. His news of the Dawson massacre led residents to fear the worst for Caldwell and his men. Andrew J. Sowell recorded his father's recollection that the women in Seguin expected the Mexican cavalry to attack at any moment. They were relieved when Caldwell sent a report later that evening that the Mexican army had retreated. Caldwell remained unaware of Dawson though Robert Hall, one of the Texians from Seguin at Salado Creek, recalled they heard cannon and musket fire to the east. Under a bright moon, a few men, including Hall and Morrell, who feared his son might have been in the fight, ventured forth to investigate. Morrell described seeing thirty-five mangled bodies, many of them friends. Considering Callahan's experiences at Refugio and Victoria and the massacre of his comrades at Goliad, it is easy to imagine how he felt as he helped bury the slaughtered Texians.[27]

As Woll withdrew to San Antonio, two other companies of volunteers joined Caldwell. Meanwhile, on September 19, many Tejanos in San Antonio, fearing reprisals, began fleeing to Mexico. That same day, as they trudged south in a driving rain, Mexican soldiers sought shelter in San Antonio and Texians hunkered down on Salado Creek. At sunrise on September 20, Woll marched toward the Rio Grande with the fifteen Dawson prisoners. The Texians, now numbering nearly 325 and growing by the hour, camped that night on the Medina River within eight miles of Woll's soldiers. The next morning, September 21, Caldwell's men debated whether to attack and another one hundred Texians arrived under the command of Col. John Moore. Woll's army, reduced to 500 soldiers, marched south as Hays and his scouts caught up with the Mexican rear guard, with Caldwell's troops following close behind. The next day a sharp skirmish raged at a Hondo River crossing before Caldwell decided, due to the late hour, to halt his attack, resulting in a rapid retreat by the Mexicans. The next morning, acrimony between Caldwell's men and Moore's newcomers led Caldwell to stop his pursuit and return to San Antonio, whence most, including those from Gonzales and Seguin, chose to march home. Noah Smithwick, one of the reinforcements, said he learned that tired, hungry, married men were less eager to fight than single men. Callahan's vote to return was another indication of his careful calculation of when to fight and when to retreat. He may have been tired of fighting, as James W. Nichols later wrote, but he also had a personal reason—he was hoping to build a family.[28]

The Mexican and Texian forces trudged away from each other on September 23. Woll's troops marched for six days before arriving at the Rio Grande. In a proclamation, Woll declared that they had killed, captured, or wounded more than 600 Texans. The Mexican consul in New Orleans repeated Woll's unrealistic estimate, but Woll became more conservative in later reports. To Reyes, he wrote that he had captured 67 Texians and killed 133, and the number of wounded must have been immense. On October 11, 1842, after hearing from a San Antonio resident, Woll amended the number of Texians killed at Salado Creek to 170 and those wounded on the Hondo River to 17, while he added a warning that Houston planned to raise 3,000 men to invade Mexico. Woll claimed that he lost 30 men killed and 81 wounded in three clashes with the Texians, and that none of his men were captured. Caldwell concluded that his losses were 6 killed and 11 to 13 wounded, but his figures did not include Dawson's volunteers or 52 civilians captured at San Antonio. Clearly, Woll's reports of the casualties he had inflicted were inconsistent, and Texian estimates do not clarify the situation. However, it is reasonable to conclude the Mexican losses were about 20 percent of Woll's force. Including Dawson's men and the San Antonio prisoners, the Texians lost about 120, almost 35 percent. By any measure, losses on both sides were high.[29]

One reason for substantial Mexican casualties may be the use of multishot weapons by Callahan and the Texians. In San Antonio, Woll confiscated two seven-shot rifles and one five-shot rifle. These belonged to the fifteen or so Hays men who had remained on September 11, so the data suggests that 20 percent of the rangers had such weapons. From Dawson's men, the Mexicans collected five seven-shot rifles and one five-shot, indicating that 11 percent of them had a repeating firearm. Mexican reports also claimed that 100 pistols were confiscated, but they did not indicate if any were repeaters. It is not known how many of the 220 men with Caldwell at Salado Creek used a multishot weapon, but some certainly did. Creed Taylor had spent seventy-five dollars on a Colt five-shooter but lost it in the race from the Alamo. Assuming 13 percent of the Texians, an average of those in Hays and Dawson's commands, carried a multishot rifle or pistol, then the twenty-eight volunteers who had these weapons were carrying firepower equal to at least 140 men with single-shot weapons, a considerable increase in firepower.[30]

On September 20, 1842, when Caldwell left Salado Creek to pursue the Mexicans, he assigned Lt. Henry E. McCulloch to care for thirteen wounded men. With no transportation, McCulloch faced a quandary until Solomon Brill drove up in a captured cart with blankets. At that time Brill, a graduate of a New York medical school, was courting Hepzibah Clemons Day, a daughter of Sarah Hembree Day, and he transported the wounded Texians to the Old Ranger House in Seguin. One man, Sam "Scotch" Callaghan, requested to be left alone and was placed in an empty house where, though tended, he soon died. Six men stayed with Mary and John W. Nichols; of these, Taylor, Jesse Zumwalt, John Law, and Solomon Simmons quickly healed and left for their homes, but Simon Cockrell and Rollo Davis required more extensive recuperation. Thomas Ingles Smith and five others were hospitalized at the Old Ranger Station, where Sarah and her daughters cared for them. Two of the four wounded at the Hondo River, Archibald Gibson and Cicero Rufus Perry, also convalesced in Seguin. By the time Caldwell returned to San Antonio, Seguin citizens had provisioned about 400 men, and provided medical care for at least fifteen wounded.[31]

After Caldwell quit his pursuit of Woll and led his men to San Antonio in late September 1842, most returned home, but some joined a new campaign to invade Mexico. Callahan and his future brothers-in-law, with one exception, did not join this expedition, nor did any member of the King or Nichols families, but others from Seguin did, not anticipating the eventual tragic outcome. Houston again sent Somervell to San Antonio to organize an army and march to the Rio Grande. Somervell marched south in mid-November with 1,200 troops. They were plagued by supply shortages and floundered through a bog, sapping their strength and resolve. After about 450 turned back toward San Antonio, Somervell reached the Rio Grande but did not cross. Small groups of disgusted soldiers left for home, further undermining morale, and on December 11 another 190 abandoned the expedition. Eight days later Somervell called off the project and led 200 to Gonzales. The remaining 307 Texians were determined to invade Mexico and organized under William S. Fisher. After crossing the Rio Grande on December 19,

Fisher's men fought a Mexican army at the village of Mier. With significant losses, the Texians surrendered and were marched toward Mexico City as prisoners. Five weeks later, they attempted an escape, but only four succeeded and the remaining 176 were recaptured. Santa Anna ordered every tenth man to be shot. The selection process was excruciating: those who drew a white bean lived, but a black bean meant death by firing squad. The surviving Mier prisoners, including Ezekial Smith of Seguin and Isaac Zumwalt of Gonzales, marched to Perote Prison, where they joined the Texians Woll had seized in San Antonio and at the Dawson massacre. Several died before Mexico succumbed to pressure from the United States and England to free them. On March 24, 1844, the last thirty-five Texians captured during the fighting around San Antonio were released. The remaining 107 men taken at Mier, including Smith and Zumwalt, were freed in September.[32]

The Mexican forays into Texas, and the involvement of various Tejanos, strained the relationship between Texians and Tejanos. Tejanos dominated the city council of San Antonio until 1842, but the resignation of Juan Seguín prompted many to leave the city. Antonio Pérez, the seasoned, respected ranger captain of San Antonio, relocated to Mexico, as did Seguín. However, some Tejanos continued to live near the town of Seguin; José Cárdenas and Manuel Flores, for example, appeared on the Guadalupe County tax rolls into the mid-1850s. Moreover, José Antonio Navarro operated a ranch on Geronimo Creek, six miles north of Seguin, and his brother Luciano lived nearby. Navarro, an officeholder during the Spanish, Mexican, and Republic eras, and a signer of the Texas Declaration of Independence, was convinced by Lamar to join the Santa Fe Expedition in 1841. This resulted in his capture, from which he returned to his ranch in 1845. Prior to his imprisonment, Navarro's place was known for its efficiency, and Navarro was respected as an honest and capable rancher. After his capture, his son operated the ranch, and the tight control that the elder Navarro exercised over the place disappeared and men with questionable character began to come and go, leading to conflict.[33]

Andrew J. Sowell recalled that in the summer of 1843 Seguin area settlers were harassed by Mexican horse thieves. In Nichols's account, the motley crew living at the Navarro ranch had dissipated into criminals, including "Cristova Arouba," whose wife was the head cook. Nichols claimed that Arouba, who kept a quiver of arrows, had stolen horses in San Antonio, leaving an arrow-killed carcass behind. Nelson Lee, another chronicler of this episode, identified the thief as "Christolphle Rublo," whose father was an overseer of Navarro's ranches. According to Lee, Rublo had not inherited his father's ethics and was cunning and treacherous. The misspelling of Spanish surnames by Nichols and Lee obscures the identity of the leader of the horse thieves. In fact, Navarro had an overseer, Ramón Rubio, who started managing Navarro's Atascosa ranch in 1832 and in 1840 moved to the Geronimo Creek ranch. The man discussed by Lee and Nichols was Cristobal Rubio, Ramón's son. By 1843, his activities concerned Anglos near Seguin, and their fears were soon confirmed. "One light moon they swooped down on us and stole six or eight horses and amongst the rest Captain Callahans fine saddle horse," wrote Nichols. In Lee's version, Callahan had padlocked a chain around his horse and secured the other end inside his house. The morning after the raid, by Nichols's recollection, Callahan was calm, but Lee recalled that he was astonished and profane. It did not take him long to conclude where the horses were hidden, and he was proven right when Nichols and James M. Day followed hoofprints to Navarro's ranch. Callahan gathered men from Seguin, listed by Nichols as himself, Day, John W. Nichols, Jim Roberts, Hardin Turner, Calvin Turner, Joe Williams, John Sowell, Asa Sowell, Andrew Sowell, and Nelson Lee.[34]

Callahan's group rode toward Navarro's place. According to Nichols, they asked no questions at the ranch and even rode around it up a creek onto York Creek ridge. By then they were about eight miles north of Seguin, where according to Sowell, Day led them to the rustlers' hideout. Continuing on, Nichols wrote, they found a new trail and, with Callahan in the lead, followed it until they came upon "a deep ravine in a small prairie containing good grass." York Creek ran through this prairie, and over the years it had created the gully. Lee recalled that Day, with his fingers to his lips, halted and pointed through a small opening to a dozen Mexicans and two dozen horses. Nichols remembered that Callahan and his men cautiously ambled along the trail until encountering hobbled horses in the gulley and a smoking campfire. Lee described it as "a robber's retreat, no more admirable selection could have been made," with trails providing ingress and egress on two sides. Callahan and his men tied their horses and crawled through the tall grass to the edge of the prairie. Without being detected, they had penetrated the lair of Rubio and his men. Lee noticed that some of the bandits were mending saddles, moccasins, and shirts, while others slept on the grass. Nichols recollected a different but equally tranquil scene where the robbers sat around a fire eating. By now it was near sundown and Callahan told each man to choose a target. Nichols recalled Callahan said: "'Take good aim, boys, Fire!'" Lee later wrote that each shouldered his rifle and fired, causing the Mexicans to jump like an electric shock hit them, including Rubio, who sat behind a pile of blankets and buffalo skins. By now Callahan's men were firing revolvers. Five of the bandits were killed but three, including Rubio, ran toward the horses. The posse watched the thieves mount the unsaddled horses, including Callahan's, and escape through the opposite entrance of the prairie. Callahan and his men ran to their horses and commenced a chase toward the Guadalupe River. Sowell remembered that Callahan on a faster horse left the others behind. Lee recalled that Rubio was riding Callahan's stolen horse, which may account for his determination to catch the thief.[35]

By the time Callahan and Rubio reached the east bank of the Guadalupe River, their horses were exhausted. Rubio abandoned his mount, jumped into the river, and waded toward a small island. Callahan also dismounted and jumped into the river, intending to capture or shoot Rubio. On the island, according to Sowell, a dramatic scene played out. Rubio's carbine misfired and so did Callahan's rifle, since both guns had gotten wet in crossing the stream. Staring at each other, both combatants worked quickly to reload their weapons, completing the task at the same time. Rubio's gun failed again, and while Callahan's made a loud pop it did not discharge. Callahan commenced to reload again while Rubio swam to the opposite bank. When his weapon failed a third time, Callahan in disgust gave up the chase and rode to Seguin leading his prized horse. Day and the others had returned to the robbers' campsite. In their haste, the rustlers had left saddles and other articles, along with a dozen horses, which the Texians took with them. Nichols wrote, "That broak up the band." Hays later shot and killed Rubio in San Antonio.[36]

The Rubio episode illustrates the challenge historians encounter. The story has been told in different ways by three men all claiming personal knowledge of what happened. According to Sowell, the Rubio event occurred in 1843, and Lee agreed. Nichols, however, contended that Callahan's Gonzales Rangers were still active, so the year was 1841. The historians who have written about this incident do not clarify the issue. But newspaper articles in the *Telegraph and Texas Register* and *Clarksville Standard* verify that the episode occurred in May 1843. The more challenging question for historians is the accuracy of the surviving accounts. Many of the stories told by Sowell and Nichols are supported by government documents, contemporary newspaper reports, or written accounts by peers. Some of Lee's recollections have been challenged by historians. His description of his captivity among the

Comanches has been deemed implausible by Melburn D. Thurman and Gary Clayton Anderson. But Lee may not be dismissed entirely. Gonzales County records, including tax rolls and a ranger muster, and statements by Nichols leave no doubt that Lee lived in Seguin from 1841 through 1843, and Nichols said Lee joined the assault on Rubio. Lee's recollections of the Rubio event, except for his faulty dating, are supported by other sources.[37]

The conflict between Rubio and settlers at Seguin, although a local event, is another example of the deteriorating relationship between Anglos and Tejanos. Each had developed deep suspicions about the other, and it is instructive to note that individuals such as Rubio were called Mexicans, as if they belonged in Mexico. Anglos remembered the plight of Texians imprisoned after the Santa Fe Expedition and raids by Vásquez and Woll, while the Mier Expedition fiasco further inflamed Texians' emotions. On the other hand, since Texas independence, Tejanos had increasingly experienced losses of their liberty and possessions, especially land. Juan Seguín and Antonio Pérez were not the only Tejanos who fled to Mexico. That Lee and Nichols concluded Pérez organized the horse-theft gangs in the area illustrates how suspicions had deepened. The growing influx of immigrants from the United States began to tilt the demographic profile of South Texas toward the Anglos, further reducing the Tejano sphere of influence.[38]

The years 1840 through 1842 were particularly difficult for the people of the Guadalupe River valley. "Seldom . . . does a people pass through a more gloomy period than we experienced in the fall of 1842," Zenas N. Morrell recalled, "Widows among us wept . . . mothers mourned. . . . Our crops on the Guadalupe were all consumed." Although Mexican incursions and Indian raids ended, people did not easily forget their fears. As elsewhere in Texas, animosity between Anglos and Tejanos endured. Seguin's location on the cultural frontier between Anglos and Tejanos could have made it an arena for even greater conflict, but except for the Rubio episode, it appears to have avoided, until the 1857 Cart War, the ethnic clashes that flared elsewhere. In 1841, 25 of 107 signers of a petition to create a new county in the area were Tejanos, and three years later a member of Prince Carl of Solms-Braunfels's party said he heard Spanish as often as English in Seguin. Until the late 1850s, José Antonio Navarro had two leagues, Manuel Flores one league, and Luciano Navarro and José María Cárdenas 620 and 340 acres, and no one contested this. They hired Tejanos who lived on their land, and Spanish surnames appeared on tax rolls. Tejanos were indicted for gambling, but less often than Anglos. Nevertheless, Anglos and Tejanos in the area did not form social bonds, other than commercial relationships, and only one Tejano joined a local ranger company: Cárdenas served in Callahan's Gonzales Rangers. Callahan's experience did leave him with prejudices toward Mexicans, and he said as much to James W. Nichols. But, like many of his neighbors, he respected success and would accept anyone's help in vital matters such as business or frontier defense.[39]

Callahan became a leader during this difficult period for the Guadalupe river basin. He demonstrated fearlessness on several occasions: at Las Moras, twice on the upper Llano River, on the San Saba River, at Salado Creek, and during his face-to-face confrontation with Rubio. His leadership was confirmed when, at every opportunity, local men selected him to be their captain or lieutenant. "He seemed to have been born to command," Nichols wrote about Callahan. His ability to calm the nervous men on the first night at Salado Creek, and later his leadership of his fifteen-man platoon in stopping the assault of Córdova and his Indians, demonstrated, as Nichols also noted, that he was cool and brave in a fight. Henry E. McCulloch, who served with and under Callahan on many occasions, later wrote, "As a fellow soldier and intimate friend of his, I wish to say that in my opinion a braver, better soldier never fought under any flag and a more honest or true man never broke bread." But, by 1843 Callahan was tired. In two years, he had spent almost 370 days in the saddle away from home, so when Hays asked him to join yet another ranger company, he declined. Callahan's ranger days were over, and he was ready to embark on a new endeavor.[40]

CHAPTER 7

Sarah Hembree Day's Extended Family, 1837–1849

"Good wife"

In September 1837, when Seguin's original settlers drew for town lots, attorney Andrew John Neill received Lot 6 in Block 31 and established his office there. From his front door Neill could see the court and market squares to the south and southwest. Looking down Court Street to the west, he could see Sarah Hembree Day's house, the Old Ranger Station. As a lawyer he was privy to all manner of information, from personal tribulations to financial transactions, and as the town grew, so did his caseload in the district courts of Gonzales and San Antonio. On September 28, 1841, a diminutive young lady came into Neill's office, sat down, and asked for his help in obtaining a divorce. Neill began transcribing her deposition: "The Petition of Sarah Medissah Alsbury formerly Sarah Medissah Day of said county would most respectfully represent to the Honorable Court. . . ." The story of the Day family in Seguin offers a good insight into the dynamics of a community as it matured from a frontier settlement into a flourishing town with bustling commerce and a well-established legal system. For Seguin, this transformation occurred within a decade. Sarah Hembree Day's son and six daughters were part of this evolution as they married, had children, and divorced. Their marital situations offer a fascinating narrative that can be compared with trends in other Texas counties and across the United States.[1]

After Spain conquered Mexico, the Spanish imported their customs, culture, religion, and legal system, and these remained after Mexico gained its independence. It was under Spanish law that land was distributed by Mexico to settlers, women were permitted to own property, and the concept of community property was implemented, which allowed a husband and wife to share ownership. More importantly, sons and daughters inherited equally. While husbands retained the right to control the property and divorce was virtually impossible, annulments and separations were more easily obtained than under English common law. This differed from the colonies in English North America, whence came the United States, birthplace of most of the settlers who came to Texas during the Mexican era. While single women could manage their own property under English law, once married the wife surrendered this right to her husband, who could make decisions without consulting her. Furthermore, daughters could not inherit property. During the colonial period, divorce was difficult. Little changed after independence; women gained some rights for property and legal proceedings, but in general they remained subservient to their husbands. Divorce laws liberalized gradually and the grounds for divorce expanded to include impotence, habitual intoxication, cruelty, adultery, and bigamy, among other reasons. Divorce laws did vary from state to state and by region, with district courts handling the cases in the North while legislatures controlled the matter in the South.[2]

Anglos who settled in Texas in the 1820s and early 1830s had an affinity for English common law as modified by the local governments of the United States, and so as the Republic crafted its own legal system, officials were faced with a conundrum—Spanish or English law? Being pragmatic, they adopted Spanish law for property matters and English for other matters. This hybrid created a unique legal environment, particularly in the areas of divorce and property law. Like the U.S. Constitution, the Texas Constitution of 1836 did not directly address divorce. Legislation in 1837 allowed cases to be filed in district courts, but many litigants still sought a decree from the legislature. On January 1, 1841, Texas gave district courts full authority to settle divorces. The law defined three criteria for divorce: cruel treatment, abandonment, or adultery. There was gender bias: to qualify for divorce a husband had to leave his wife and live with another woman, but the wife only had to be unfaithful once. To prevent fraud, the legislation required both the wife and husband to be residents of Texas and there had to be witnesses, except when the grounds were adultery.[3]

Divorces during the Republic of Texas have been sparsely examined by historians, but Francelle Pruitt and Angela Boswell have studied divorce

Table 7.1. Divorce cases in four Texas counties, 1837–1849

County	*Spouse filing (no. of cases)*	*Grounds for divorce*
Colorado 1837–1845	Husband (9) Wife (13)	Adultery–2, Abandonment–3, Cruelty–4 Adultery–1, Abandonment–3, Cruelty–9
Gonzales 1837–1845	Husband (2) Wife (6)	Adultery and abandonment–2 Abandonment–3, cruelty–1, abandonment and cruelty–2
Harrison 1841–1849	Husband (5) Wife (14)	Combined—3 adultery, 11 abandonment, 10 cruelty
Washington 1841–1849	Husband (2) Wife (1)	Adultery–1, Cruelty–1 Abandonment–1

cases in several specific counties—Colorado, Harrison, and Washington. In another study, Robin Sager explored cruelty as the basis for divorce in 358 cases filed in thirty-four counties from 1840 to 1860. These inquiries indicate that divorce was a fact of life in the Republic of Texas, where, just as in the antebellum United States, it became more common as the grounds broadened. A comparison of the eight divorces filed in Gonzales County from 1837 to 1845 with those during roughly the same period for the counties studied by Boswell and Pruitt reveals some interesting trends (table 7.1). With the exception of Washington County, which had only three cases, wives were more often the plaintiff, and cruelty was most frequently the reason given. For husbands who filed, abandonment was the most common reason. Sager observed that in these communities, prospective jurors and judges were familiar with the individuals and circumstances. Moreover, since the defendant was seldom present to contest the divorce, it is not surprising that the plaintiff, most often the wife, prevailed.[4]

The eight divorces in Gonzales County during the Republic period illuminate pertinent aspects of marriage in that era: finding a spouse, roles of husbands and wives, owning property, surviving on the frontier, and premarital pregnancy. Six of the eight cases were filed by women, including Sarah Medissa Day Alsbury, who was only the second woman to obtain a divorce in Gonzales County. All of them can be considered pioneers for women's rights in Texas. Five of the women who filed—Alsbury, Sarah Nash Tumlinson Bruner, Margaret Mary "Polly" Salmans Power Gray, Emmeline McGloane Hill, and Mary Harris Ashby Smothers—declared their husbands had abandoned them, and four added charges of cruelty. The fifth, Gray, filed because her husband had married and was cohabitating with another woman. She may have done this because she had been indicted for adultery and bigamy in Gonzales County. There seems to have been an arrangement between the district judge and her attorney for the charges to be dropped against her and her new husband if she got a divorce; the indictments were dismissed on the same day that her divorce was finalized. The Republic did a poor job of keeping records, and ascertaining marital status beyond a verbal declaration was sometimes difficult. In any case, after a certain length of time, a wife may have presumed an absent husband had died and she could remarry without risking the crime of bigamy. The sixth woman who filed, Prudence Hardin Nash Kimble Holdridge, did so on grounds of abuse, though her claims of "ill treatment, vulgar and abusive language and repeated threats of violence" were similar to other testimonies. It is interesting that the men who filed for divorce, James Bird and Mark W. Dikes, did so on grounds of abandonment and adultery by their wives.[5]

The melding of Spanish and English law gave women some protection when it came to portioning property after divorce. In five of the Gonzales County cases filed by wives, property was clearly mentioned; only Alsbury did not make any property demands. Alanson Holdridge lost his right to sell Prudence's land and had to reimburse her for cattle he had sold. Hill, Bruner, Gray, and Smothers, or their children, received their share of the community property. Moreover, the property a wife brought into the marriage was relevant to a future husband. Dikes's apparent motive for pursuing a legal conclusion to his first marriage was his impending union with Dianna Perry, who inherited a considerable amount of land from her father. It was in his best interest to ensure that his next marriage, with its increase in wealth, was safe from any future accusation of bigamy. The empathy of district judges and juries toward the female plaintiffs in these six cases was noteworthy. Juries awarded a divorce to each woman except Hill, who died in 1843 before her case came to trial, and Smothers, whose petition was dropped due to John Bates Smothers's death in 1846. This was usual in most of the Texas counties studied by Boswell and Pruitt, and an analysis by Christopher Morris of a Mississippi county in the same period indicates that such was not unusual elsewhere in the antebellum South. Even when the district court in Gonzales County indicted Gray for bigamy and adultery, the district judge and attorney dismissed the case after she obtained a divorce from her second husband. Gray's first husband and oldest son had been killed by Indians, and at the time of her divorce proceedings two other sons were captives of the Comanches, making her a very sympathetic figure. Holdridge was also a well-known and respected woman whose second husband died in the defense of the Alamo. The jury would also have been aware of her third husband's cruelty by virtue of her connections in the community.[6]

Alva Fitzpatrick advised his nephew in 1849 that it was hard to make it in Texas without a good wife. Frontier circumstances led many people, especially women, to seek spouses for the support they provided, but this concern may have been lessened in Texas by laws that allowed women to own property. While Holdridge stated when she remarried that she was looking for a companion to protect her and her children, Hill was not in a rush and she waited five years before solemnizing another commitment. Smothers entered into a marriage of necessity during the Runaway Scrape in 1836; when the chaos subsided, her relationship became toxic. The aftermath of the divorces in Gonzales County is instructive. Hill died before her case was decided and Bird died during the Mexican War without remarrying. Dikes married Perry within seven months of his divorce, and Alsbury married James Hughes Callahan immediately after her divorce was finalized. Holdridge remarried a fourth time to Claiborne West, a successful farmer who signed the Texas Declaration of Independence. Bruner married Jeremiah Roberts, one of Seguin's founders, and had seven children with him before his death in 1866. When Gray's relationship with John Fitzpatrick ended, she resumed using her first husband's name, Power, and in 1877 died at her son's home. Smothers died unmarried at her own home in 1893.[7]

Of course, despite similarities, each marriage and divorce is also unique. While Sarah Medissa Day's divorce from William Wirt Alsbury shared some aspects with others discussed here, closer examination reveals fascinating dimensions of their marriage and personalities. On September 28, 1841, in the presence of her attorney Andrew J. Neill, Sarah listed the grounds on which she wished to obtain a divorce. She swore that a short time after they married, she had a prolonged illness but William neglected her, and when she could not care for herself, he made no effort to provide her basic necessities. After three months of marriage, she asserted, William had abandoned her. She added that she would have died had her mother not sheltered her, and in the intervening three years he had provided no aid. Moreover, Sarah avowed that in the few months of being together she was faithful and had lived since "wholly in a retired manner." Next, she told the court she did not know where to find William, whom she had told before he left that she would file for divorce as soon as the law permitted. While the accusations were harsh, Neill constructed her petition so that it met the requirements set forth in the January 6, 1841, law. Sarah could have asked for financial support but did not, and she said she would pay her costs for the lawsuit. Even though William had used their marriage to obtain two-thirds of a league of land (2,800 acres) Sarah made no claims on it. In sum, her petition was designed to avoid obstacles that would delay the divorce. In Gonzales on Saturday, October 9, 1841, Sarah's petition was considered by Judge Anderson Hutchinson, who decreed that even though William had vanished, he was ordered to appear at the next term. This order was published in the *Austin City Gazette* as was customary. No issues of the paper from October 1841 into 1842 have survived; however, subsequent court proceedings indicate that Sarah's petition was published. Thus, it seemed that by the next court term in March 1842 she would be divorced.[8]

Although Sarah claimed not to know where William was, various records document his whereabouts. At the time of their marriage on April 15, 1838, he co-owned a mercantile store in Gonzales. Sarah asserted that three months after they married, she contracted a serious illness and William abandoned her. Her father, Johnson Day, died on July 29, 1838, during this epidemic, so William left as early as the end of July. While his partnership submitted a bill to the executor of Day's probate in the fall of 1838, it is not clear if the business still operated or who presented the bill. By December 1 William had a new mercantile partner, Charles Larabee, in Austin. He next appears as the translator in the 1840 campaign led by Maj. George T. Howard, when James Hughes Callahan, Sarah's second husband, served as a lieutenant in Mathew Caldwell's company. In late December 1840 Alsbury spent time in Seguin when he bought two cows, a calf, and a heifer. By March 15, 1841, he returned to San Antonio, where two of his brothers lived. Three months later he went to Austin and joined the ill-fated Santa Fe Expedition. He was one of ninety men surrendered on September 17, and a few days later he and his fellow prisoners set off on a harrowing 1,500-mile journey to Mexico City. William and three others escaped but were captured by Puebla Indians and returned. On December 27, eighty-seven captives arrived in Mexico City and were quartered at Santiago Prison. Smallpox and typhoid ravaged them, food was inadequate, and prisoners worked in chain gangs to repair roads and sometimes were beaten. On June 16, 1842, Santa Anna succumbed to international pressure and freed them. Marched to Vera Cruz, William and the others boarded the *Rosa Alvina*, which sailed on August 12. They landed at Galveston on August 21 and it is unknown where William went after disembarking, though he had another brother living there.[9]

At the time Sarah filed for divorce in October 1841, William had been a prisoner of Mexico for three weeks, and when he arrived in Mexico City in December, Sarah's divorce notice had appeared in the *Austin City Gazette*. William could not have read this, but his brothers in San Antonio and Galveston could have. Whether Sarah knew of William's plight or not, she and her attorney did not anticipate complications with her divorce; both expected she would prevail in the March 1842 district court term in Gonzales County. But, due to the Rafael Vásquez raid, the court was canceled, and cases were rescheduled for the fall. Then Sarah's expectations were thwarted when Adrian Woll raided Texas in September, capturing the district court judge and Sarah's attorney. With the fall term canceled, there seemed little hope of a successful outcome anytime soon. Sarah had one other option—legislative relief. On December 14, 1842, she sent a petition to the Congress of the Republic of Texas, swearing that in "March 1838" she married William, who left and since afforded her no protection. She requested the "passage of a law, divorcing the said William Allsbury and herself a vinculo matrimonii." Sarah summarized her earlier deposition, though she misstated the month of her marriage (April) and subtracted two years from her true age (fifteen) at the time she married. Neill's law partner, Michael Erskine, probably composed the writ, and Sarah sent it to her senator, James Webb of Travis County. She could not have submitted the plea to William E. Jones, the representative from Gonzales County, since he had also been captured by Woll. On January 14, 1843, the Texas House approved about twenty divorces, including Sarah's, but the Senate tabled the bill before Congress adjourned on January 16.[10]

By now Sarah was frantic and pregnant. Her fate lay with the judge of the March 1843 district court term in Gonzales County. On Monday, March 13, visiting judge William Jefferson Jones pounded the court into session and took up the case of *Sarah M. Day v. William W. Alsbury*. Although the defendant did not appear, a jury heard arguments and awarded Sarah a divorce so she could marry Callahan. Ironically, the same court indicted Mary Gray for adultery and bigamy. William could have known that Sarah had filed for divorce. By late September 1842 he had joined John C. "Jack" Hays's company after the Battle of Salado. Hays participated in the pursuit of Woll, and on December 5 his men captured two Mexicans near Laredo. Alsbury was detailed to guard one but during the night he fell asleep and, despite being severely wounded, the prisoner escaped. William was arrested, although the disposition of his case and where he went afterwards are unknown. After he failed to attend the 1843 divorce hearing, he never made any effort to fight the case or file a counter complaint. Evidence suggests he next lived in Galveston. During November 1846 he was a private in Company D, First Texas Foot Riflemen, composed of men from Galveston, including his brother Hanson Alsbury, who was the regimental quartermaster. That month, William and five members of Company D skirmished with Mexicans near the Rio Grande at Camargo. The final piece of evidence placing him in Galveston is his probate record showing he died in the fall of 1850. His estate amounted to thirty-eight dollars.[11]

Sarah, having finally divorced William, must have hoped to do better with her next spouse. On March 25, 1843, the Gonzales County clerk issued a marriage license to "James H. Calahan" and "Sarah Madissa Day," and the following day, Justice of the Peace H. G. Henderson married them in Seguin. The journey they began in early 1843 would last for a decade and a half, but it also marked a parting of the ways for the Callahan and Alsbury families, and this had significance later. It is not certain how Sarah met James, but there are three possibilities—a dance, a ranger muster, or a church meeting, all events held at the Old Ranger Station where Sarah had lived with her mother, Sarah Hembree Day, since 1838. According to James Wilson Nichols, Callahan loved to dance, but he also served in several companies that mustered at the Old Ranger Station. Or, perhaps they met at one of the church meetings Sarah Hembree Day hosted in her home after converting to Methodism, Callahan's denomination. Whatever the occasion of their first encounter, descendants say that Sarah Medissa Day and James Hughes Callahan fell in love soon after they met, and by September 1841 they were a couple.[12]

Ideas about marriage and the family were evolving in Texas and the United States during the antebellum era. The Victorian notion that marriage should be based on romantic love that led to conjugal love was widespread, and gender roles within marriages solidified. Husbands were to provide for and protect wives and children, while wives cared for the family by cooking, making clothes, and delivering children. Finding a mate depended principally upon where one resided—neighbors married neighbors—and peer or family pressure encouraged many to marry at a young age. The geographic and legal situation of Texans, especially those on the frontier, also shaped marriage, with property and survival being two prime motivations. When Sarah filed her divorce petition in September 1841, she met the law's requirement for a woman to have been abandoned for at least three years, and her relationship with James pushed her to act. September was the only month in 1841 that he did not take the Gonzales Rangers on a patrol, suggesting that he and Sarah had decided to marry, or at least he supported her in getting a divorce. They may have been in love, as family members insist, but they certainly made good partners. Sarah at eighteen years old was considered to be in her prime for producing children and being a helpmate. James had demonstrated he could protect and provide for a wife. He had property; by 1841 he owned 1,032 acres in Gonzales County and several lots in Seguin and Velasco. The Vásquez and Woll raids delayed Sarah's divorce, which may have caused anxiety because she was pregnant when she married James, but in the 1830s up to one-third of brides in the United States were pregnant when they married. Texians, particularly on the Republic's frontier, were further removed from social and religious constraints of more settled regions. In the case of James and Sarah, family and community both knew of her first failed marriage and how events had delayed her divorce. By the fall of 1842 they were living together, and neighbors accepted them as a married couple. At any rate, twelve days after her divorce was final on March 13, 1843, they married.[13]

The Callahans began their married life in a house built on a five-acre timber lot whose west side backed onto Walnut Creek. James had bought this property in the spring of 1841, six months after arriving in Seguin. Little is known about their years in Seguin except that he raised cattle, bought and sold land, and performed common civic duties. He and Sarah joined the local Methodist Church and continued to attend various social events, including shivarees. Also, in that house Sarah gave birth to three boys—Wesley Hughes (August 1843), James Sanford (July 5, 1844), and Josiah Asbury (1847). By all indications, the Callahans were a happy family.[14]

By marrying Sarah, James joined the large Day family led by matriarch Sarah Hembree Day. At the time, she still had three single daughters at home—Hepzibah Clemons, Meekness Amanda, and Elizabeth Caroline—but three children had married years earlier. James Milford Day had wed Martha Hannah Nichols in 1838, and by 1846 they had three boys. Also, in 1838, Mary M. Day married John Walker Nichols, and by 1847 their family included two daughters and one son. In later years they had two more boys and a girl. Another daughter, Mahala J. Day, wed Henry Basil King in 1838, and by 1848 they had three sons and three daughters. These three marriages illustrate family connections in Seguin. In 1841, Henry King's mother, stepfather, two younger brothers, and two sisters moved to Seguin. Two of the marriages connected Sarah Hembree Day's family to the George Washington Nichols family, which included another three sons and four daughters, who themselves had intermarried with other families in town. Thus, James and Sarah had many family members living near them, and their stories are essential for understanding subsequent events in the Guadalupe River Basin.[15]

Very little is known about the personalities of Sarah Hembree Day's daughters except what comes through family histories. Sarah Medissa, for example, is recalled as having a streak of independence and speaking candidly. Elizabeth's granddaughter, Mildred Hankins Norris, wrote that Elizabeth was a self-sufficient, independent frontier woman. According to Brill family tradition, Hepzibah's exceptional beauty caused men to ride out of their way just to see her. All three women were excellent seamstresses since, like most mothers of her time, Sarah Hembree Day taught her daughters to sew and knit. Elizabeth's granddaughter recalled that she once made a highly prized, beautiful dress and also that she gave her black knitted gloves. Sarah Medissa made clothes for her children and sewed various household items. All of the Day daughters were religious. By the standards of their time, each had all the makings of a good wife.[16]

Sarah Medissa was not the only daughter of Sarah Hembree Day to have a premarital pregnancy. On May 25, 1845, twenty-year-old Hepzibah married forty-four-year-old Solomon William Brill. Brill had arrived in Seguin in 1838 and settled in with Hepzibah by 1843, as their first child, Louisa, was born on June 2, 1844. Brill was born in Dutchess County, New York, on April 23, 1801; according to Brill family history, he earned a medical degree in New York, and in 1832 went to New Orleans during a cholera epidemic. In addition to employing his medical expertise, Brill made caskets. He stayed in New Orleans until the spring of 1836, when he joined Colonel Charles Harrison's regiment of Kentucky volunteers, who had sailed down the Mississippi River bound for the Texas Revolution. Harrison's men traveled aboard the side-wheeler *George Washington* up the Red River to Natchitoches, where they disembarked and marched to San Augustine, Texas. Pvt. Robert Hall, the enlistment officer for the regiment, later wrote, "I enlisted Solomon Brill, who made a good soldier and became a famous Texan."[17]

Harrison next led his men on a long trek to Camp Johnston, where on June 16, 1836, Brill joined the Texas army. Conditions were harsh, according to Hall, as the men ate mostly beef and many died from dysentery. By midfall, most decided Mexico would not invade, so they asked for discharges.

Brill was discharged on October 25, and the following day he joined Colonel Juan Seguín's cavalry in San Antonio. The enlistment officer described Brill as "5 feet and 8 inches, complexion dark, eyes Blue, and hair dark." He was a private but was promoted to quartermaster sergeant responsible for securing provisions, horses, and munitions. Seguín's cavalry fought one skirmish with Mexicans and another with Tonkawas, and lost most of their horses after a second Tonkawa raid. Brill struggled to procure supplies as Seguín reported that his troopers were mostly barefoot and naked and that he had a shortage of horses. Brill also participated in one of the more somber rituals ever to occur in San Antonio. The bodies of the Alamo defenders killed on March 6, 1836, had been burned and left scattered. Seguín was ordered to collect the ashes, conduct a solemn ceremony, and bury them. In February 1837, remains were gathered from three locations, placed in a black casket, and interred as San Fernando Cathedral's bell tolled and Seguin's troops fired three volleys. Brill told his family that he built the walnut casket, but he did not reveal the location of the burial site until he was on his deathbed, when he said the Alamo defenders were buried twenty steps from the southeast corner of the mission. From April 1837 until the spring of 1838, Seguín's companies had few assignments, so on April 14, 1838, they were discharged.[18]

After his release, Brill went to Houston, where on April 18 he received a second-class donation land grant for his military service. He sold the certificate for $500, rode to Seguin, and on July 19 purchased a town lot. Brill worked as a cabinet maker, joining a future brother-in-law in this endeavor, but he also used his medical skills after he fought at Salado Creek, when he carted the wounded to Seguin to oversee their care. That being said, cattle raising was of greater interest to him than either medicine or carpentry. Between 1842 and 1850, his herd increased from 18 to 150, the largest owned by any of Sarah Hembree Day's sons-in-law. Along with their four children, Solomon and Hepzibah became a vital part of the Day family.[19]

Elizabeth wed Eli Skaggs Hankins, who came to Seguin to join ranger companies in 1841, 1842, and 1843. It is not known when or how they met, but they were married on December 31, 1846, when Sarah Hembree Day wrote in her prayer journal: "Lord bless the both I say." Eli, born January 1, 1823, in Knox County, Kentucky, was the first child of Melinda and John Hankins, who later moved to Wayne County, where her parents, Levi and Susannah Hinds, and several siblings lived. When Melinda and John died in 1833, Eli Skaggs and his sister, Ruth Ann, became wards of Levi and Susannah. Members of the Hinds family began settling in DeWitt's Colony in

1833, and the Hinds's three sons, James B., Gerron, and Thomas Shelton, fought in the Texas Revolution. In 1836, Levi and Susannah, along with their younger children, Clarissa and Eli Clemmons, and grandchildren, Eli Skaggs and Ruth Ann, came to Texas. They traveled along the Cumberland River and down the Mississippi River to New Orleans, and from there sailed by schooner across the Gulf of Mexico, docking near Brazoria.[20]

After May 1838, when the Texas General Land Office began to distribute land to war veterans, Levi's three sons received their shares, ranging from 640 acres to a league, and located their claims in Gonzales County. Levi had settled with his minor children and grandchildren in Brazoria County on the edge of Bailey's Prairie, but he died and in the guardianship proceedings Eli and Ruth Ann became the wards of James B. Hinds, their uncle. His farm was situated at the junction of Plum Creek and its tributary, Clear Fork branch, eight miles north of Gonzales and adjacent to his brother Gerron's farm. Eli was living with his uncle when he participated in the fighting at Plum Creek. Eli's children recalled that one of his greatest desires as a young man was to own a horse, saddle, blanket, and rifle, and he became an expert marksman and fearless rider. After Plum Creek, Eli next joined Ben McCulloch for his raid against the Comanches on the Llano River in April 1841. Having fought alongside his future brother-in-law Callahan in 1841, Eli again served under him during the Vásquez and Woll invasions in 1842. He was one of the first on the scene after the Dawson Massacre. In 1843, Eli joined Hays twice—June 1–July 15 and October 1–November 10. During his first stint, he participated in the killing of Cristobal Rubio. Later, during his second term, Eli escorted recently released Mexican soldiers, captured during the Woll invasion, from San Antonio to the Rio Grande. Then in early November, Hays led his rangers in a skirmish with the Mexican bandit Leandro Garza and his gang. By the end of 1843, at just twenty years of age, Eli was a tough, experienced frontier veteran.[21]

When Eli was eighteen, Probate Judge Edmund Bellinger ordered James B. Hinds to provide a complete inventory of Eli's assets. Hinds swore on September 28, 1841, that Eli was due $250 as a share of his grandfather Levi's estate. When Eli turned twenty-one, he and his uncle agreed on a settlement, with Eli receiving 300 acres of land and Hinds released from his guardianship. Eli's tract was in the southeast corner of the James B. Hinds survey, with its west boundary on the east bank of Plum Creek. By a stroke of fate, Eli avoided by two weeks a long delay in obtaining title to his land since his uncle died on December 12, 1845, and his probate continued for ten years. Thus, when Eli married on the last day of 1846, he could provide for his new wife and their future children. He had not only his Plum Creek land but also a 320-acre plot in Gonzales County that he received in March 1846 for his military service. He and Elizabeth certainly needed the support; their first child, a daughter, arrived in June 1848 and by 1853 a son and another daughter had joined the family.[22]

Augustus David "Gus" Pharr Jr. and Meekness Amanda "Meeky" Day courted for a year before they married on June 3, 1849, in Seguin, with District Judge William E. Jones officiating. Gus was twenty-six years of age and Meeky nineteen. In her prayer journal, Sarah Hembree Day wrote, "Meekey was married on the 3rd of July [June]. O may the Lord bless her abundantly in this world and save her in his kingdom. Above is my prayer, Amen." Her new son-in-law, born on June 22, 1823, in Warren County, Mississippi, was the only child of Elizabeth Bailey and Augustus David Pharr Sr. Elizabeth was a strong-willed, beautiful girl who defied her father to marry Pharr, a farmer, on December 8, 1821. Just three years later, twenty-three-year-old David died, leaving seventeen-year-old Elizabeth with an infant son. She moved to Austin's Colony to live with her father, James Briton Bailey, who had relocated there in 1818 near the Brazos River, on land later known as Bailey's Prairie. Elizabeth's brother-in-law, Samuel Pharr, lived nearby. The 1826 census indicates she was independent and self-sufficient, listing her as "Elizabeth PHARR, widow, farmer, and stockraiser, bet[ween] 16–25 yrs," with "(1) males bet[ween] 1–7 yrs."[23]

Gus Pharr spent his formative years around his grandfather. Bailey was a tough, gruff, colorful character who loved whiskey and liked to brawl. He fought in the War of 1812 before leaving Tennessee, under threat of prosecution, to head for Texas, where he settled before Stephen F. Austin founded his colony. Bailey resisted efforts by Austin to expel him, so Austin included him among his original three hundred colonists. Bailey was elected first lieutenant in the militia and Mexican authorities later promoted him to captain, and in June 1832 he led an attack on the Mexican fort at Velasco, one of the first times Texians had notions of an independent country. Six months later, on December 6, Bailey died and left an eccentric request to be buried erect, facing west, with his rifle in his arms, and a jug of whiskey at his feet. Another influential man in Pharr's life was his stepfather, David H. Milburn, a devout Christian whom his mother married on October 24, 1826. Milburn was one of Austin's original settlers and became a plantation owner and successful merchant in Marion (née Bell's Landing). There, Gus Pharr, with the four Milburn children, spent much of his childhood in comfortable circumstances. Bell's Landing and the nearby communities of Bailey's Prairie, Brazoria, and Velasco became prosperous, dynamic Anglo enclaves during the colonial era. Professionals and tradesmen came with other immigrants on ships that also brought in goods and carried away bales of cotton to New Orleans. Gus Pharr attended school, watching as his community evolved into a hotbed of the independence movement. He was too young to fight, but militia mustered at the Milburn plantation in July 1835 and an influx of volunteers later came through, including the Georgia Battalion. Euphoria turned to panic when the Alamo fell and Sam Houston retreated. During the Runaway Scrape, Elizabeth and David fled with the five children. David's sole contribution to the Texas Revolution was to lend one horse to Houston's army.[24]

How the Milburns avoided the conflict and when they returned to their plantation is not known, but one year later David bought two lots in Columbia and the family split their time between the farm and the town. By 1837 David and Ammon Underwood became successful partners in a mercantile enterprise. Because she had arrived in Texas by 1826, Elizabeth was eligible to receive one league and one labor (177 acres) of land, and in May 1838 she was awarded her donation bounty. David died on August 10, 1840, but he stipulated in his will that fifteen-year-old Gus should have a good education and thus Gus was provided with a tutor in 1841 and had access to a newly opened academy in Brazoria. He volunteered during the Vásquez and Woll raids and had a miserable experience. He served against Lieutenant Colonel Ramón Valera in March 1842, when Texian troops subsisted solely on beef, resisted the imposition of non-elected officers, and even deserted. Gus later joined his neighbors in slogging through rain, floods, and mud, arriving in San Antonio after Woll retreated but in time to witness Texas leaders squabble over who was in command. In spite of this sorry spectacle, Gus joined the disappointing Somervell Expedition. Faced with choosing to march into Mexico or go home, he chose the latter. He was discharged on January 20, 1843, and paid $80.25 for three months and seventeen days of military service. With one exception in 1855, Gus never enlisted in a ranger company, nor did he fight in the Mexican War or Civil War. He returned to Brazoria County and became a farmer and rancher.[25]

Little is known about Gus Pharr's adult years in Brazoria County. However, religion played a central role. His stepfather was a pious man, and he and Pharr's mother, Elizabeth, attended Presbyterian services in Columbia every Sunday. One year after David died, Elizabeth married Claiborne Rector, a local farmer who was the son of Joseph Morgan Rector, a Methodist minister influential in establishing the denomination in Texas, including a church in Columbia. Elizabeth converted to Methodism, and Gus met Amelia B. Rector, Claiborne's sister, at their church. The young couple married on June 4, 1846, but Amelia died a few months later. Tragedy struck again when Elizabeth died in May 1847. She had no debts, but she left no will concerning her major asset, a certificate for a league of land. Benjamin F. Milburn, her oldest child with David, took charge of settling the estate. On May 24, 1847, he, Gus, and Claiborne Rector filed a notarized agreement at the Brazoria County clerk's office. Rector surrendered all claims on Elizabeth's estate by the two children he had with her. For $600, Gus sold half of the land due to him but retained one-fourth of the one-league certificate. The death of both his wife and mother left Gus with money, land, and no ties to Brazoria County. He sold his cattle and by mid-1848 settled at Seguin, where he married Meeky. She delivered the first of their nine children, Ellen Elizabeth, on November 9, 1850.[26]

Sarah Medissa was not the only one among her siblings to remarry. On September 2, 1846, one week after giving birth to her third child, Martha Nichols Day died. As a widower, James Milford Day faced caring for a week-old baby boy, John Merrian, and two young sons, six-year-old William J. and two-year-old James Milford Jr. It was an overwhelming task for a frontiersman, but luckily his mother, Sarah Hembree, took charge of his three sons. Seeking a diversion from grief, James M. Day joined Capt. Henry E. McCulloch's frontier protection company. The annexation of Texas by the United States had led to war with Mexico in May 1846. With so many Texans joining the army and flocking to Mexico, the people on the frontier were left unprotected, so the new state government ordered the creation of frontier companies. McCulloch mustered his volunteers into service on October 22, 1846, at San Marcos, twenty-three miles northwest of Seguin. Of ninety men who enrolled, at least eighteen lived around Seguin. They received thirty dollars per month and had to furnish their horses, arms, and clothes. James M. Day arrived riding a forty-dollar horse and sitting on a ten-dollar saddle. On November 13, Sarah Hembree Day wrote about her anxieties and hopes when her son left. She worried that he might not return and prayed that he would "turn from the evil of his ways," probably a reference to his gambling. McCulloch's men patrolled south to New Braunfels, north to Austin, west up the Guadalupe River, and north as far as Fredericksburg, which, like New Braunfels, had been recently settled by German immigrants. Nichols later wrote that they never fought Indians or Mexicans, though he said they must have done some good since no raids occurred. While the patrols were boring affairs, the paymaster reimbursed the men for their time and, since he was only a few miles from his home in Seguin, James was able to court Margaret Susan Hudson.[27]

Gen. Zachary Taylor's army west of Monterrey, Mexico, had a dangerously long supply line from its warehouse at Camargo, and its wagon trains came under regular attack by Mexican bandits, guerrillas, and army patrols. On March 15, 1847, the *Democratic Telegraph and Texas Register* reported the dire straits at Camargo when one hundred laden wagons, escorted by two cavalry companies, were captured. This news caused considerable excitement, and the state ordered three companies to Camargo, including McCulloch's. James M. Day and his comrades arrived in Mexico at the end of March 1847. Nichols recalled that they rode from San Antonio to King's Ranch, and then crossed the Rio Grande and camped at Mier. Here the Texans received conflicting messages, so Nichols was placed in charge of a courier detail sent to General Taylor's headquarters and Day accompanied him. Mexican guerrillas hovered around the Texans but did not attack. Arriving in Monterrey, the men visited the battleground and attended a fandango. By May 1847, Mexican threats dissipated, so the Texans were ordered home. McCulloch's company went to Hamilton's Valley, at the junction of the Llano and Colorado Rivers. Day, who had become a sergeant, took a leave of absence and in Seguin on June 27, 1847, married Margaret. Sarah Hembree Day wrote, "I do give up the little boys to their step-mother. May The Lord guard, guide, and direct both parents and children." James was discharged on October 17, 1847, and, like other Seguin men with families, he chose not to reenlist.[28]

Born in 1828, Margaret was the daughter of widow Frances Hudson, who moved to Guadalupe County because her sister and brother-in-law, Jane and Bonaparte Nicholson, had settled there. According to her descendants, Frances Hudson and her husband had four children before he died. Margaret settled with James M. Day in his house on the west bank of Walnut Springs Creek and took charge of the three young boys from his first marriage. She and James had four children of their own—Henry Milton (1848), Meeky Ann (1850), Caroline Jane (1851), and Sarah (Sally) (1852).[29]

It is often difficult to assess motivations for a marriage, but it is easy to believe that fifteen-year-old Sarah Medissa, living with a widowed mother, married William Alsbury for need more than love. Certainly, for Prudence

Hardin Nash Kimble Holdridge, the necessity of having a helpmate was more important than a loving relationship. For James M. Day, his children's needs were a strong factor in his decision to marry Margaret, although later events would show that their mutual affection was important. In an era where men and women had to work together, especially on the frontier, it is understandable that when one partner did not carry their weight, divorce was not uncommon. The Texas Congress passed laws supporting this reality and also protecting the property rights of both men and women. Eight divorce cases in Gonzales County from 1838 through 1845 illustrate how the laws allowed partners to escape bad relationships and left some with the resources to make better choices concerning a new spouse. Not everyone was lucky. Necessity sometimes kept couples together; those with limited financial resources simply endured each other in exchange for protection and stability. James W. Nichols recalled a woman he met on the road from Seguin to Indianola; she said she was leaving her husband. A few days later he found her walking back to Seguin; she had decided it was best for her to return home. At the same time, extramarital pregnancies sometimes provided another impetus for marriage. Wide age differentials did not impede marriages on the frontier, where emigration or military service often had a significant effect on the number of available males.[30]

Sarah Hembree Day did not have to make the hard choices others made. She was a loyal and productive helpmate until her husband died, and as a widow her resilience and the support of her large family helped her survive on the unforgiving Texas frontier. She faced many hardships, but unlike some Texas widows of her generation, she found no reason to marry again. She may not have been desirable, not necessarily because of her age, but because she had little money and her land lay in a remote region still infested by roaming Comanches. Her six daughters absorbed their mother's adaptability and willpower. Interestingly, most of the deeds for Brill family lands were in Hepzibah's name, which suggests Day women could dominate a household. With one exception, after 1847 none of their husbands joined a ranger company or participated in combat expeditions. That includes James Hughes Callahan, whose marriage to Sarah Medissa Day was another successful union within the extended Sarah Hembree Day family. The stories of her daughters and their husbands illustrate many aspects of the changing culture and society of the Guadalupe River Basin, and how these continued to evolve as Texas developed on the southwestern frontier of the antebellum United States.

CHAPTER 8

From Seguin to Prairie Lea, 1843–1853

"Field of civilization"

Sarah Medissa and James Hughes Callahan began their married life in a dynamic era of Texas history. The most significant event was the 1845 annexation of Texas by the United States and the subsequent war with Mexico. Texas became a major staging area for the U.S. Army, which became a permanent presence with San Antonio as its main base. To protect Texans from Indians and Mexican bandits, forts were constructed along the Rio Grande and the western frontier north to the Red River. San Antonio also became a staging point for migration and commerce. Many soldiers who came to fight stayed, and immigrants swarmed into Texas. The state population grew from 142,000 in 1847 to 213,000 in 1850, and by 1860 it was 604,000. The first organized migration of Germans came just before annexation, settling from the coast up the Guadalupe River Basin (see map frontispiece). The Seguin area became a popular destination for them, and after a few years, German and French were spoken in San Antonio along with English and Spanish.[1]

Social, economic, and political trends evident in the United States manifested themselves in the Guadalupe River Basin as well. Temperance became an organized movement, and religion took a strong hold. Believing in the value of education, Texas leaders founded schools. As the frontier pushed west, cattle raising and cotton production became important economic endeavors; with cotton came slave labor. Yeoman farmers persisted in large numbers, but they were joined by merchants, professionals, and even plantation owners. Since the arrival of the Anglos, Lipans and Tonkawas had peacefully coexisted with them in the Guadalupe River Basin, but the influx of immigrants increased the demand for their removal. These changes directly affected Sarah and James, as well as other members of the extended Day family, as they coped with a multifaceted society, acquiring wealth and enjoying more options than Texians had in the past. The word "Texian" disappeared from the daily lexicon, and Texas residents become forever known as Texans.

Political boundaries within Texas changed as well. Gonzales County from 1837 through 1845 conformed to the borders of the DeWitt Colony. The first state legislature in March 1846 created thirty-one new counties, including Guadalupe County, organized from parts of Gonzales and Bexar Counties with Seguin as its seat (map 8.1). On December 16, 1847, men living along Plum Creek asked the legislature to create a new county, to be called Plum Creek County, and in March 1848 it became one of eleven new counties, but instead of Plum Creek it was named Caldwell, in honor of Mathew Caldwell. The new county, carved from Gonzales and Bastrop Counties, with Lockhart as its seat, bordered Guadalupe County, with the San Marcos River between them.[2]

Texas conducted a census in 1847 to establish the number of representatives the state should have in Congress, and the 1850 census added another snapshot of the demographics of Guadalupe, Caldwell, and Gonzales Counties. The 38 percent population increase for all three from 1847 to 1850 was greater than the 34 percent growth rate for the state, which reflects the region's popularity. Foreigners, mostly Germans, accounted for about one-third of the tri-county increase, with the majority settling in Guadalupe County. By 1850, slaves were 33 percent of the population of Gonzales County, but just 20 percent each in Guadalupe and Caldwell. This difference contributed to Gonzales County having more improved acres, growing five times more cotton, and producing more horses, cattle, hogs, potatoes, and corn than the two other counties combined. The profiles for 1850 demonstrate that Gonzales County was more of a plantation-style economy. Guadalupe County was the top producer among the three of wheat, oats, sheep, and wool, and it was the only one that grew tobacco, thanks to more German farmers. Moreover, nonagricultural enterprises operated mostly in Guadalupe. In their analysis of agriculture in antebellum Texas, historians Randolph B. Campbell and Richard G. Lowe wrote that Gonzales, Guadalupe, and Caldwell Counties were like the pre–Civil War South. While this may have been true by 1860, census data indicates this had not happened in Guadalupe and Caldwell Counties by 1850.[3]

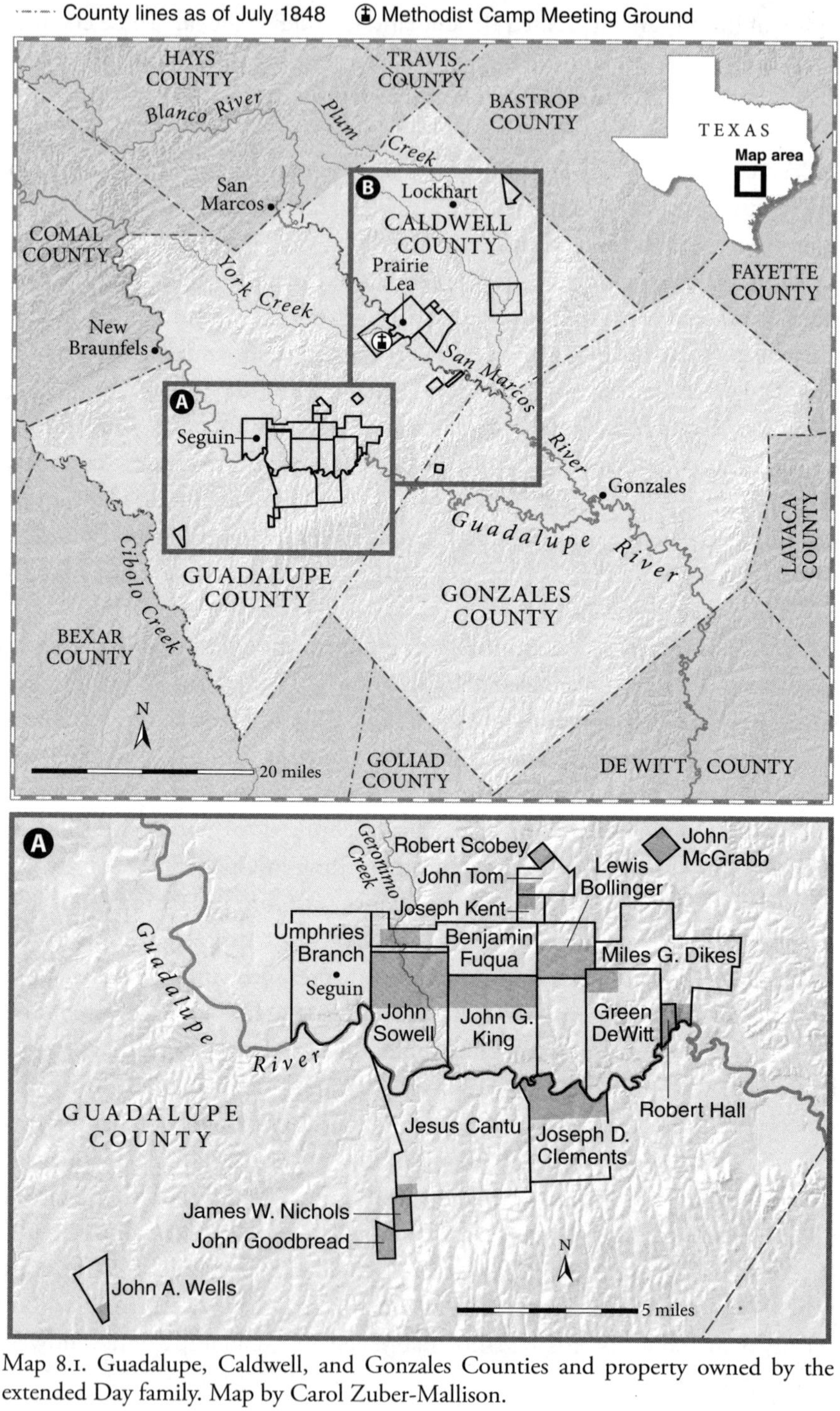

Map 8.1. Guadalupe, Caldwell, and Gonzales Counties and property owned by the extended Day family. Map by Carol Zuber-Mallison.

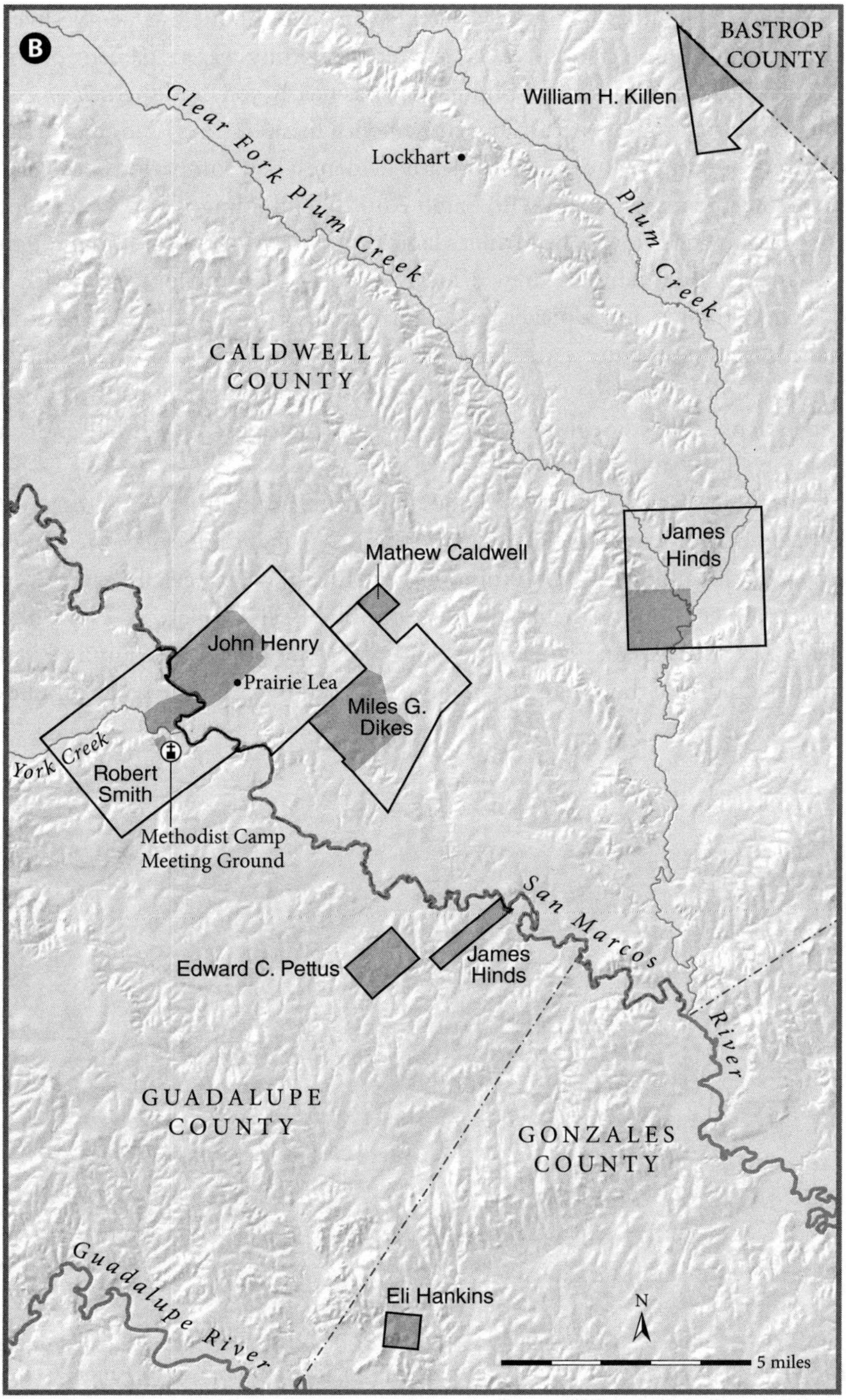

B
BASTROP COUNTY
William H. Killen
Clear Fork Plum Creek
Lockhart
Plum Creek
CALDWELL COUNTY
James Hinds
Mathew Caldwell
John Henry
Prairie Lea
Miles G. Dikes
York Creek
Robert Smith
Methodist Camp Meeting Ground
San Marcos River
Edward C. Pettus
James Hinds
GUADALUPE COUNTY
GONZALES COUNTY
Guadalupe River
Eli Hankins
N
5 miles

When Guadalupe County was created in 1846, about 250 people lived in Seguin, so Sarah Hembree Day's extended family was 12 percent of the population. By 1854, Seguin's population was nearly 500, and the *Ledger and Texan* reported that it was an active town with brisk business and many new concrete buildings. The change is clearly evident when comparing Seth Eastman's 1848 pencil drawings with Sarah Ann Lille Hardinge's 1852 watercolor and graphite drawings. The former's landscape shows log cabins lining rough dirt streets; Eastman also drew a local house—a dogtrot log cabin with a detached kitchen and a picket fence, surrounded by mottes of live oak and walnut trees (see figure 4.3). Hardinge shows painted clapboard and stucco houses, buildings, and a new courthouse. Carriages and fashionably dressed pedestrians traveled Seguin's wide, graded streets (figure 8.1). It had indeed become a busy and prosperous place.[4]

Sarah Hembree Day, her son James Milford Day, and the Nicholses never left Seguin, but the Brills, Pharrs, Kings, and Callahans relocated three miles east to farms along San Geronimo Creek. Livestock, especially cattle, was their main economic pursuit. By the 1850s, the Brills, Callahans, Days, and Nicholses accumulated large herds, and while the other three families had smaller holdings, they were not inconsequential; together the seven families

Fig. 8.1. *Seguin on the Guadalupe River, Texas*, ca. 1852, by Sarah Ann Lillie Hardinge (1824–1913). Watercolor over graphite drawing on paper. Courtesy of Amon Carter Museum, Fort Worth, Texas.

owned almost seven hundred head of cattle. Their herds' annual increase indicates they had numerous head to sell each year. As an indication of their value, in 1850 S. G. Cunningham paid $25,000 for livestock from farms along the Guadalupe River. Thus, livestock, especially cattle, represented real wealth, not just a decent income. Each of the seven families also possessed at least one wagon, with oxen or draft horses, which could be employed to transport other farmers' goods for a fee. Transporting local products to the Gulf Coast could be profitable; John W. Nichols once hauled 106 bushels of pecans to the coast for shipment to New Orleans. During April 1843, 20,000 bushels of pecans were exported from the Guadalupe and San Antonio river basins, earning $40,000. Cowhides were another commodity hauled to the coast for export.[5]

The September 18, 1852, *Texian Advocate* highlighted the importance of cattle along Texas's coastal plains, especially up the Guadalupe River valley, where a blend of Tejano and Anglo cattle raising practices emerged between 1830 and 1860. Callahan and his brothers-in-law were among the men who participated in this hybridization, with six of the seven recording their brands and earmarks with county officials (figure 8.2).

The brothers-in-law learned how to rope and throw cows from skilled, experienced Tejanos in the Seguin area, then spent three or four months each year taking care of their herds, cooperating in cow hunts and checking on each other's cattle. Some of them also worked for others; Solomon W. Brill managed attorney Andrew J. Neill's livestock. In the beginning, they sold cattle to neighbors and hauled hides to the coast for shipment to the New Orleans market, but by the mid-1850s long cattle drives to distant markets were commonplace. What the brothers-in-law told the census taker and tax collector reflects their lives as cattlemen.

Their horses were used as mounts and wagon teams rather than as commodities. They raised just enough hogs for their consumption, and none had sheep, though they purchased wool locally. All the families except the Pharrs milked cows and produced butter; James M. Day's family churned 780 pounds, so they had extra to sell. The Kings and Hankinses together collected 450 pounds of honey—adequate to supply all seven families. They planted sweet potatoes for their larder, with a few bushels left over to sell. Four brothers-in-law harvested enough corn to meet their family's needs, but Callahan harvested 1,000 bushels. No one harvested any cotton, reinforcing the notion that they were cattlemen who planted food crops mostly for family needs.[6]

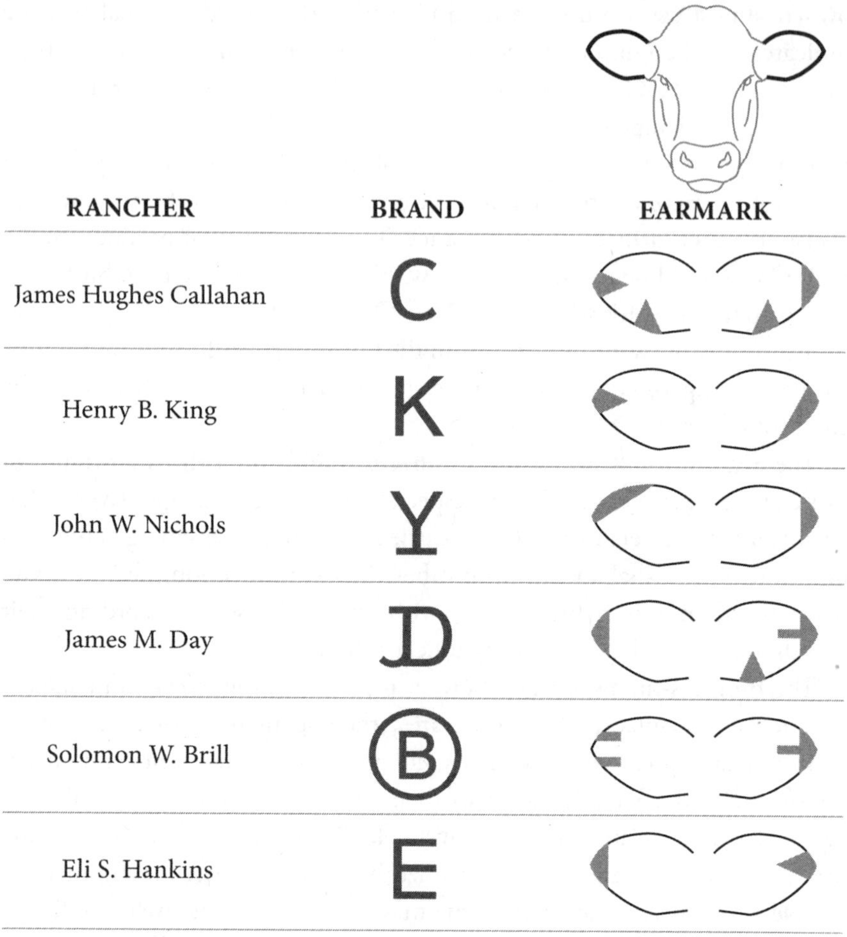

Fig. 8.2. Marks and brands for Callahan and his in-laws. Illustration by Carol Zuber-Mallison. Author's collection.

The Callahans did not stay long on San Geronimo Creek. In 1848, Sarah and James with their three sons moved to Caldwell County and helped found Prairie Lea (map 8.1). Their first daughter, Armiseda Catherine, was born at this time. Prairie Lea, the oldest township in Caldwell County, was situated just fifteen miles from Gonzales, Seguin, San Marcos, and Lockhart, with Austin, the state's capital, forty-five miles to the northwest and San Antonio the same distance to the southwest. In 1834, Joseph S. Martin paid John Henry 125 Mexican pesos for 1,200 acres, and he later purchased an adjoining 1,081 acres. In 1842, Martin sold Callahan 300 acres and also contracted Callahan to build a house for him. In 1845 Callahan acquired 350 adjacent acres. In 1851, Callahan bought more land, paying $300 for three hundred acres in the Robert Smith Survey, across the San Marcos River in Guadalupe County. These transactions were the genesis of Prairie Lea. By 1852, people passing through said the fertile valley of the San Marcos River around Prairie Lea was dotted with farms and ranches, while the town had a school, two stores, a post office, a hotel, and a Masonic lodge. Callahan opened the first store, became the first postmaster, and built a road from Lockhart to Prairie Lea and on to Seguin. He, David F. Brown, and Thomas M. Hardeman established Prairie Lea Academy, near the public well and Callahan's store and house, on eight acres they secured from Martin in 1851 and 1854. Dissatisfied with circumstances in San Augustine County, the Shiloh Baptist Church moved to Prairie Lea in 1853 and settled in "The Meeting House," next to Callahan's house. Callahan and seven other men bought eight more acres in the Smith Survey and developed the Methodist Camp Ground to serve the area's Methodist congregations. Prairie Lea's status as a village was formalized in 1852 when Martin asked Arthur Swift to plat the town. Callahan's store increased the taxed value of its merchandise from $300 to $2,200 by 1853, indicating it was modestly successful. With a growing population all around him, Callahan had positioned himself well for continued prosperity.[7]

People with cash wanted store-bought goods, as illustrated by the advertisements in the October issues of newspapers in 1853, and this included members of the Callahan and Day families. Based on an 1856 inventory of household belongings, Sarah Medissa Callahan bought manufactured cloth by the yard and ready-to-wear clothing, including shirts for her husband. When Seguin merchant Louis Hipp died in 1852, his estate was auctioned and Sarah Hembree Day's extended family bought several dozen pairs of shoes, many shirts and pairs of pants, over fifty yards of cloth, two hats, three coats, several dresses, a couple of capes, four bonnets, two shawls, sheeting, lace fringe, and garters. Sarah and her relatives also purchased dishes, saucers, cups, knives, forks, spoons, pitchers, glasses, mirrors, chairs, buckets, tubs, barrels, pounds of almonds, dozens of cans of sardines, and carpentry tools. It is evident that the extended Day family enjoyed the evolving array of household comforts.[8]

While the Callahans and Days and their relatives did not live a life of ease, they did not want for much either. Bacon, beef, cornbread, and coffee were the basic staples of the Texan diet. Ferdinand von Roemer, a visiting

German scientist, complained that "supper consist[ed] of coffee, warm cornbread, and fried bacon." Texans did vary their diet. Historian C. Allen Jones noted that they also ate chicken, fish, wild game, sweet and Irish potatoes, pumpkins, cabbage, turnips, melons, peas, pecans, grapes, and peaches. Sweeteners included honey, molasses, and unrefined sugar. Vegetable seeds were widely available, and women did most of the gardening, growing beets, carrots, lettuce, and beans, according to the *Democratic Telegraph and Texas Register*. In late summer, roasting ears were consumed, and in the fall shelled corn was ground and baked for cornbread and hoecakes. Milk cows lactated throughout the year, so butter and cheese were available. A cold-water spring served as a refrigerator and beef could be slaughtered anytime. According to the 1850 agriculture census, Sarah Hembree Day's family had plenty of beef, hogs, corn, butter, sweet potatoes, and honey, while the women certainly had gardens.[9]

There was always work to be done. Hogs roamed freely; after the first frost, they were rounded up and butchered. Salted hams, sausage, and bacon hung in smokehouses for curing. The area was fortunate since a salt marsh lay in the eastern part of Gonzales County. During butchering, fat was trimmed, tossed into large iron kettles, and heated over a wood fire. The rendered products were lard and cracklings. A portion of the lard was stored in crocks and used for cooking, with the remainder set aside. Throughout the year, kitchen and fireplace ashes were collected in the ash hopper. Water was slowly dripped through the hopper to produce a lye water that was mixed with the lard. This mixture was heated until solids formed to be skimmed off and placed into molds, resulting in lye soap. Lye water was also mixed with dry corn to produce hominy. Gardens and fields had to be fenced to protect crops from livestock, so men chopped down trees, split rails, and built fences. Eastman's drawings of Seguin suggest the zigzag-rail fence was popular. In the late winter, topsoil was turned over; a man with a team of oxen could plow one to two acres per day, so Callahan planted twenty acres for his 1850 harvest of one thousand bushels of corn. Sweet potato slips were planted and at harvest the rows were plowed, raising the yams to the surface to be gathered by hand; one acre produced about one hundred bushels. Considering the corn and potato yields, Callahan and his brothers-in-law spent an aggregate of about one hundred days in 1850 to cultivate thirty acres.[10]

While men tended the fields, women also had great responsibilities. Washing and ironing clothes was laborious, with Mondays designated as washing day. Fortunately, Sarah Hembree Day had Walnut Springs Creek steps from her back door and daughters to help. They filled three or four large iron pots with water and maintained a fire beneath each until the water boiled. They shaved lye soap into the first pot and soaked the laundry, whites first, in the steaming water, scrubbing each piece on the washboard. They successively rinsed the clothes in the remaining pots and, after wringing the excess water, pinned each garment on the clothesline. Once the items were dry, the women ironed each piece—including sheets, towels, and bedspreads—with heavy irons heated on the wood stove. Sarah worked long hours on laundry and ironing days since she washed clothes for her family and for several men who paid her; she even repaired clothes for men in the town.[11]

Good food, plenty of exercise, and clean clothes did not protect Texans from disease. Yellow fever and malaria appeared almost every year in the summer along the coast and in 1844 killed four hundred people in Galveston. Gonzales, Seguin, and Prairie Lea generally escaped these two maladies but not cholera, smallpox, dysentery, and croup. Smallpox vaccinations were available but not enough people in Seguin were vaccinated. Sarah Hembree Day recorded a smallpox outbreak in February and April 1849, and again in June 1852, when the dead included the town's two tailors. Smallpox was known to be highly contagious. When Samuel K. Nelson died during the outbreak of 1849, the administrator of his estate had to reduce the price of his clothes to just pennies before anyone would purchase them. Texas public health measures were rudimentary in the 1850s, usually relying upon quarantines when epidemics broke out.[12]

Health remained a constant concern of antebellum Texans in the Guadalupe River Basin, as three personal diaries from that time indicate. Sarah Hembree Day wrote 108 entries in her prayer journal between 1843 and 1853, and on twenty-seven occasions she complained of acute or chronic sickness. Her comments about physical well-being indicate not only how important her health was to her but also how frequently she, and likely her neighbors and family, were ill. Elise Tipps Wuppermann, another Seguin resident, kept a diary with monthly or daily entries from 1850 through 1865. Her family experienced sickness about twelve times each year, most often fever, dysentery, colds, headaches, chills, and toothaches. During these years, two of her children died. Occasionally, her husband, Otto, submitted to bleedings, while Elise undertook sweating and water treatments, and each swallowed a variety of pills sent by friends or dispensed by local pharmacists. Hermann Seele, a native of Hildesheim, Germany, arrived in December 1843 and by

1844 lived in New Braunfels. Seele wrote in his diary almost every day in 1844 and 1845, documenting his health in detail. Two weeks after his arrival he exhibited symptoms of malaria and took quinine. During 1845, he was sick on twelve occasions, four of which lasted one week, and he noted that other New Braunfels residents had similar illnesses. Seele's bouts and Sarah's and Elise's ailments reinforce the notion that health was precarious in Texas at the time.[13]

Sick patients had little help because qualified physicians were in short supply. According to historian Pat Ireland Nixon, a person had three paths to becoming a doctor—attend a certified medical school, study under a licensed physician, or claim the title without training. Thus, many doctors were incompetent, and the practice of medicine was often based on faulty understanding of disease origins and the efficacy of treatments. In the 1850s, two doctors, Caleb S. Brown and John E. Park, practiced in Seguin, while Prairie Lea had James Fentress and David F. Brown, but it is uncertain what training each man had. The primitive state of pharmaceuticals did not help matters. Quinine was used to alleviate malaria symptoms, and it was thought that mercury-based calomel cured cholera. Laudanum, an opiate derivative, was used for a variety of diseases and it was beneficial for gastrointestinal illness. Texans relied upon patent medicines and remedies, most of which contained sarsaparilla and were advertised in newspapers to cure just about any malady. By 1852, Seguin residents could purchase such potions at the town's new drugstore.[14]

Before the Texas Revolution, Protestant missionaries began to establish churches. Progress was slow, and the number of regular churchgoers by 1845 was merely 15 percent of the population, but by the mid-1850s many Anglos and slaves exhibited religious fervor. In the San Marcos and Guadalupe river valleys, the Callahans, along with others in their extended family, participated in this shift. Methodist congregations were in the majority, although Baptists had a visible presence. The success of the Methodist church in Texas was in large part due to its circuit preachers. In December 1838, the Mississippi Conference assigned several preachers, including Joseph Perkins Sneed, to Texas, and at the December 1840 Texas Conference, Samuel Millett, a Seguin resident, begged for a church to be established at Seguin. So, in early 1841 Sneed rode into Seguin and organized a church, although it was another eight years before funds were raised to construct a sanctuary. From 1841 through 1855, thirteen circuit preachers tended this church; prominent among them was John Wesley DeVilbiss. He was not an exciting preacher, but his prayers were electrifying, and it was said that when he began to pray, sinners either pleaded for mercy or fled in fear. Membership records are incomplete, but "Captain James H. Callahan" joined in 1844, when DeVilbiss was the minister, as did John R. King. Sarah Hembree Day had begun holding nondenominational Sunday school classes at her home in 1839, and she longed to join a congregation. The passion of DeVilbiss at an 1844 revival, combined with the attendees' enthusiasm, prompted Sarah and all but one of her children to be baptized into his church.[15]

For Sarah Hembree Day, religion was personal and fundamental, and as a Christian she believed she had to be committed to living her faith. Illustrative of her devotion was her study, for the year before her conversion to Methodism, of the *Book of Martyrs*, a sixteenth-century, multivolume treatise about the persecution of Protestants by Catholics. Her entries in her prayer journal had a pattern. The first sentences commented on her health or expressed gratitude to God. Next, she lamented her spiritual weakness, pleaded for a return to righteousness, and often beseeched God to protect her children. Comments on the weather, family visits, and church or camp meetings often followed. Her entry for June 22, 1845, reveals her religious perspective on illness: "This is the second day since the Lord has been pleased to afflict me severely with pain and sickness, but I do rejoice in my affliction knowing that he chastened whom he loveth. . . ." In her October 13, 1848, entry she had just returned from a camp meeting physically and spiritually energized, and while a comment on grasshoppers may seem incongruous, it reflected her worldly concerns. By 1851, Sarah was conflicted as she witnessed the beginnings of the Baptist and Presbyterian churches in Seguin. Moreover, she was worried since her son James M. Day's 1839 wound had debilitated him so much that he had applied to the Texas legislature for financial support. She wrote on March 16, "This day we have heard three sermons preached and saw a Presbyterian Church organized. . . . O thou God of Israel be pleased to have mercy on my son for he is sorely afflicted. . . ." Sarah turned fifty-eight years old on August 6, 1853, and was preoccupied with death and her delicate health: "Another Birthday has rolled around and I am still alive but not in good health. . . . For I am so afraid . . . that when my Heavenly Father shall call for me that I shall die with a frown on my countenance. O God forbid."[16]

Sarah often wrote about her family in her prayer journal. Even though six of her children joined the Methodist Church in November 1844, she worried about her family's spiritual health. She thought her prayers were answered at a June 1848 revival when Meeky, Hepzibah, and Mary and John W. Nichols confessed their sins, and the next year all four were baptized again. By the end of 1849, the Seguin Methodist Church had 232 white and eight black members, and Sarah's family comprised a significant portion of the congregation. Nevertheless, tension had arisen between Sarah and some church members. In April 1845, they had voted her out of the church. Sarah wrote in her journal: "It appears that there is got up A prejudices in the Methodist Church against me and they Do turn me out of their fellowship." Neither she nor anyone in her family ever said what caused her dismissal. Theological differences are a real possibility considering she was the daughter of a fundamentalist Baptist preacher. It is also conceivable that someone frowned upon the frequent dances she hosted. Whatever the conflict, it was resolved, and she rejoined the Methodist Church.[17]

Sarah's break with Methodism later became permanent. In September 1850, she attended a regional association meeting of Baptists at Gonzales, where a church had been established in 1841. On New Year's Day in 1852, her journal revealed her longing for a Baptist church and also her suspicion of missionaries, a view her father had espoused. After a few months of prayer, on May 16, 1852, she wrote: "I have joined the Baptist Church and I hope the Lord will bless the church and Pastor and me." The Methodists in Seguin agreed to share their sanctuary with the Baptists, but in August cooperation between the denominations collapsed and she complained that the Methodists tried to prevent Baptists from holding services. The congregations overcame their differences, but for a while Sarah's extended family was divided by faith, with the Callahans and Kings continuing to attend the Methodist Church. The Baptist Church did not have a resident pastor for two years, but sporadically a preacher attended the congregation. One such circuit preacher was James Huckins, financial secretary of Baylor University, making his annual revenue-generating tour of Texas. By late 1853, the Seguin congregation was large enough to have a full-time pastor.[18]

The Callahans remained active Methodists after moving to Prairie Lea. James served as the primary trustee after he and others in August 1848 paid fifty dollars for eight acres on the west bank of the San Marcos River to provide a campground for the Methodist Church. This site, which played a vital role in recruiting new members, was across the river from Prairie Lea and the Callahans' house. The first camp meeting was held that September, and the following year the *Texas State Gazette* advertised the second, pointing out that preparations were being made to accommodate a large crowd.

It soon became a successful annual event, and in 1851 a newspaper reported that more than fifty people had professed religion. By 1853, Methodists in Prairie Lea had established their church, congregating at the meeting house near the Callahans' store. Sarah Medissa and James Hughes Callahan were among its founding members.[19]

Religious fervor in antebellum Texas resulted from the Second Great Awakening, which also spawned various reform movements, most notably temperance. Baptists, Presbyterians, and Methodists led in organizing temperance societies, with women in prominent roles. Texians were known for heavy drinking, but over time the Republic's Congress authorized cities to license sellers of alcoholic beverages and forbade gambling in establishments selling alcohol. After the Mexican War, the tidal wave of immigrants included many teetotalers. Sons of Temperance societies appeared, and one of the first was organized in Brazoria, where Augustus Pharr lived. In 1849, the first statewide convention of the Sons of Temperance met, fifty villages petitioned for a charter, and weekly meetings were held in Houston, Galveston, and Austin. That same year, Seguin became the first town in west Texas to install a Sons of Temperance society, and in 1850 Lockhart residents in Caldwell County formed theirs. After the 1853 Sons of Temperance state convention in Austin, legislators passed a local option law, giving counties and cities authority to regulate the sale of alcohol. Lockhart and Seguin then forbade the sale of liquor in quantities of less than one gallon, closing saloons. Guadalupe County indicted its first person for selling liquor in 1854, as did Caldwell in 1857. Temperance had arrived in the Guadalupe River Basin.[20]

The Sons of Temperance movement remained quite popular in Seguin and surrounding communities. Several local men led at the state level, and area women often played key roles in proceedings. Memberships were not recorded but, considering the destructive drinking of Sarah Hembree Day's husband and her religious devotion, she must have joined the female branch of Seguin's Sons of Temperance. Teetotaler James Hughes Callahan likely was a member of the Guadalupe or Caldwell County chapters, along with some of his brothers-in-law; James M. Day and Henry B. King owned shares in Seguin's Sons of Temperance building. Callahan's friends and business associates were active at the local and state level, including John D. Pitts, A. M. Lindsey, Edward Burleson Jr., and Clement R. Johns of San Marcos; Horace Eggleston and Clinton C. DeWitt of Gonzales; and Thomas H. Duggan, John Ireland, Andrew J. Neill, and Henry E. McCulloch of Seguin. Within a decade there was a shift from a wide consumption of alcohol to its restricted availability. For lifelong teetotalers like the Callahans, it must have been a welcome triumph.[21]

Reformers also focused on education. Anglo settlers who arrived in antebellum Texas generally had a working knowledge of reading, writing, and arithmetic. Sarah Hembree Day and her extended family were not unusual in being literate, and the evolution of schooling in the Guadalupe and San Marcos River valleys reflects their interest in educating their children. The Republic in 1839 reserved three leagues of land in each county for schools, but this initiative failed to generate revenue due to cheap land prices and lack of surveys. Meanwhile, itinerant teachers opened small schools, while larger schools incorporated to offer courses from primary through college classes. Guadalupe College in Gonzales was established in 1841, but schools of this type were expensive. The 1845 Constitution laid out a bold plan to fund public schools, and teachers held their first statewide meeting at Austin in March 1846, but little was done until 1854, when Governor Elisha M. Pease used federal money from the Compromise of 1850 to endow education. Even this proved inadequate, and private schools continued to flourish. While Texans struggled to provide for public education, Sarah's youngest daughters and grandchildren began their schooling. In 1846 and 1847 Sarah sent Caroline and Meeky to Celia Rector's and Miss C. E. Madden's one-room school in Seguin. Madden and Rector never reported their tuition costs or courses taught, although Sarah indicated one class included science. Courses and tuition at other academies do indicate what was generally taught and the cost. Austin's Masonic Institute offered a curriculum in reading, writing, and arithmetic for ten dollars per session, and classes in science and language for twenty dollars per session. Celia Rector was the sister of Claiborne Rector, who married Augustus Pharr's mother, and Pharr's first wife was Celia's younger sister. Madden was an experienced teacher who had organized female academies in San Augustine and Galveston. As students under Madden and Rector, Caroline and Meeky received a solid education.[22]

Educational opportunities in the region improved in 1848 when several men, including William E. Jones and Michael Erskine, established Guadalupe College. The next year another group, including Jones and Andrew J. Neill, asked the legislature for the authority to develop Guadalupe High School. Both groups merged their efforts and for $5,000 built a two-story stone schoolhouse, which opened in 1850 for the first class of 110 male and female students. The school taught spelling, reading, writing, math, science, geography, history, and English. The basic fee for primary school was eight dollars, orphans did not pay, and children who required boarding were fed and housed with local families for eight to ten dollars per month. Eighteen-year-old William Tom Jr., who gave the commencement address for the spring term, captured the mood: "It may be said by the next generation, that education, on a firm, fundamental basis in Western Texas, had its inception in this building. Here the American, Castillian, and the German, the rich, poor, and the orphan can acquire that power." Guadalupe High School quickly gained a reputation for academic excellence. An August 1852 issue of the *San Antonio Ledger* proclaimed that it was among the top-rated in the state. By 1855 the class size had increased to 165 pupils, but teaching children turned out to be easier than financing the school. It went bankrupt, and on January 1855 the sheriff sold its assets for $3,800 to another group of investors, who operated the school for two more years until giving it to the Methodist Church. In the meantime, with funds from the Compromise of 1850, the legislature allowed counties to create public school districts. In March 1854, the Guadalupe County commissioners established eleven districts, and in 1856 the state amended the process, providing independent school districts with the authority to tax and receive a per capita subsidy.[23]

Three years after the Callahans moved to Prairie Lea, four community leaders decided their children needed a school. On June 7, 1851, Martin sold four acres for one dollar to newly organized trustees Callahan, David Brown, and Thomas M. Hardeman. One year later a writer for the *Galveston Weekly News* rode through the region and congratulated its citizens for their willingness to support education and hire excellent teachers. The Prairie Lea Male and Female Academy had opened near the Callahans' home. Sarah Hembree Day had sent her two youngest daughters to a one-room school, but her grandchildren enrolled in public schools that received state and local support. The editor of the *San Antonio Ledger* lamented that Bexar County, the most populous in the state and one of the wealthiest, did not have a fine school like Seguin's. Sarah Medissa and James Hughes Callahan took a leadership role in establishing Prairie Lea Academy to benefit not only their children but generations of future scholars.[24]

Thanks to significant in-migration of new settlers, and their slaves, during the antebellum period, the Guadalupe River Basin underwent a dramatic ethnic transformation in which Anglos, Tejanos, Germans, free and enslaved Africans, and various Indian cultures intermingled and at times collided. Historian Timothy Matovino likens such a mixture to a "stew pot," in which each culture enriched the others, but integrative assimilation was almost absent. And sometimes conflict erupted. As the 1840s and 1850s progressed, the relationship between Anglos and the local Indians deteriorated. Anglos brought with them the notion that Indians should be removed as the Cherokees and other tribes had been in the 1820s and 1830s. It was a process Callahan, his extended family, and many of his contemporaries had witnessed, and their parents, relatives, and local and national politicians had espoused. After annexation Texans, particularly new arrivals, blamed Lipans for killing and stealing livestock so, despite years of relative harmony and cooperation with Anglos against the Comanches, the Lipans and Tonkawas were both forced to cede their tribal lands. By 1850, the Tonkawas moved north to the upper Brazos River valley, while the Lipans relocated west of San Antonio to the Leona, Frio, Nueces, and Llano rivers, and they eventually moved west of the Rio Grande into Mexico.[25]

Relations between Tejanos and Anglos were more nuanced. Many Tejanos had fought alongside Texians for independence, but despite finding a common foe in Indians, they seldom formed an alliance. Interaction between Anglos and Tejanos was affected primarily by land, racial bias, and suspicions of disloyalty. By the mid-1850s, Anglos had wrested control of much Tejano-owned land along the Texas coast and in the Rio Grande Valley. The Guadalupe River Basin, where huge swaths of land were first owned by a few Tejano families, experienced similar shifts. The Veramendi Survey occupied western Guadalupe County and eastern Comal County; needing land for his German immigrants, Prince Carl of Solms-Braunfels bought the property. Many Anglos wondered if Tejano loyalty lay with Mexico or the Republic. The exodus of San Antonio Tejanos to Mexico during the raids of 1842 and the alliance of prominent Tejanos Juan Seguín and Antonio Peréz with the Mexican government increased suspicions.[26]

For Tejanos in the Guadalupe River Basin, cultural relations were complex. Intermarriage did not occur, but until the 1850s Tejanos and Anglos in Guadalupe County generally coexisted peaceably. In 1846, men in Solms-Braunfels's caravan said that they heard Spanish in Seguin as often as English. Ten percent of the voters in an 1849 constitutional referendum were Tejanos, and Guadalupe County in 1850 had five prominent Tejano landowners. Through 1853, Tejanos were less likely to break the law than Anglos and Germans, and courts did not seem to be biased against them. Moreover, in 1851 Tejanos were equally represented with Anglos and Germans in the high school. Despite his misgivings, James Hughes Callahan valued the expertise of Tejano cattlemen. However, the Tejano population of Guadalupe County dropped from fifty-four in 1850 to eighteen by 1860. How animosity developed between Tejanos and Anglos in Guadalupe and Caldwell Counties is uncertain, but the Cart War of 1857 was a turning point in the Guadalupe River Basin. Until then, Tejanos and Anglos mingled together for shopping in town, livestock wrangling, attending school, and even playing cards. However, after the mid-1850s apparent enmity toward Tejanos resulted in most abandoning Guadalupe County.[27]

During the 1840s in Germany an oppressive political climate and economic depression caused many Germans to flee to America. Texas became a prime destination in 1844 with the founding of the Adelsverein led by Solms-Braunfels. The Adelsverein was "a significant effort to establish a new Germany on Texas soil by means of an organized mass emigration." Within three years, over 10,000 Germans sponsored by the Adelsverein arrived in Texas, with almost an equal number migrating independently. Most went to the future Comal County, which became the center of German settlement while others claimed a substantial swath of land up the Guadalupe River Basin. By 1850, one quarter of the white population in Guadalupe County were German immigrants. There were very few Germans in Caldwell County, though of the four German families there, three lived near Prairie Lea. Thus, Sarah Hembree Day's extended family was adjusting to the growing presence of German settlers. Most of them became farmers, though many continued their professions. In Seguin, Peter Kessler and Frederick Winstrot started a tailor business, and Louis Ransaw opened a shoemaker shop. By 1852, Louis Hipp, a Swiss German, owned the largest dry goods store and served as a justice of the peace. Otto Wuppermann of Dortmund came to Texas in 1848 and initially farmed, but he later opened a mercantile store in Seguin and in 1854 settled on the Little Blanco River, where he raised horses and founded a new settlement called Middletown. While living in Seguin, Elise and Otto Wuppermann became friends with the Brill, Pharr, and Day families and also with Luciano and José Antonio Navarro. Julius Bose was a San Geronimo neighbor of the Days, Brills, and Pharrs. Although he had multiple degrees from Leipzig University, Bose became a farmer in Guadalupe County and later sheriff of Comal County. He served with Augustus Pharr on road patrols. Hipp, Wuppermann, and Bose were atypical in that they associated with Anglos. Most Germans confined themselves to their own community as language was a significant barrier to integration, as were their liberal views, particularly regarding slavery. Moreover, as German language newspapers revealed, Germans often expressed haughtiness toward Anglo neighbors.[28]

Slavery was present in Texas under Spanish and Mexican rule, but it expanded quickly with the arrival of Anglo settlers. At the time of the Texas Revolution, slaves were almost 15 percent of the population, and the institution of slavery was strengthened by the Republic's constitution. The proliferation of Texas slavery laws illustrates its importance, and the growth of the slave population emphasizes the institution's centrality. Texas's slave population grew from about 5,000 in 1836 to 182,000 in 1860, while the free white population increased from 30,000 to 412,000. In Gonzales County, the number of slaves had increased from 31 in 1839 to 323 by 1850, and by 1860 there were more than 1,000 slaves in Gonzales, Guadalupe, and Caldwell Counties. When the Civil War began, at least a third of the local inhabitants lived in bondage.[29]

Considering that most settlers along the San Marcos and Guadalupe rivers migrated from southern states where cotton production dominated, it is not surprising that slaves became such a substantial segment of the population. However, James Hughes Callahan and his brothers-in-law, because they raised cattle, seldom had slaves. Eli S. Hankins, according to his son, disapproved of slavery, and two others, James M. Day and Henry B. King, never owned or leased any slaves. John W. Nichols owned one slave for three years, and in 1857 Solomon W. Brill and a partner rented Big Maria and her four children for one year. In 1854 Augustus Pharr paid Alfred Bailes $500 to lease thirteen-year-old Louisa for one year. Callahan had the most extensive holdings in the family, yet these involved few bondsmen. In 1847, he paid $600 to N. S. and Harriett Rector for forty-year-old George, whom he kept for one year. In June 1853, Callahan gave $1,100 to Ann and T. P. Johnson for twenty-seven-year-old Mary and her two-year-old daughter Amy; he owned both for a year and one for an additional year. In January 1855, Callahan signed a one-year lease with George P. Smith for Humphrey and Ester and her daughter. One year later, he signed a one-year lease for Amanda and her child. Based on the gender and age of the slaves bought or leased by Day, Nichols, Brill, and Callahan, they sought house servants more than field hands. Moreover, the short-term leases indicate that they had no intention of accumulating slaves. Thus, Sarah Hembree Day's extended family was similar to 75 percent of their neighbors who engaged in what historian Randolph B. Campbell has called "intermittent slave ownership." Nevertheless, with the exception of Hankins, Callahan and his brothers-in-law were typical in their acceptance of slavery.[30]

The personal interaction of the Callahans and their relatives with the various groups in the Guadalupe River Basin generally reflected the views they brought with them from the South, shaped further by their individual experiences with Indians, Tejanos, Germans, and slaves. The same can be said for their politics, which can be ascertained in the few instances that the votes of men from Guadalupe and Caldwell Counties were recorded. In the 1846 election for the United States representative for the Second District of Texas, Callahan voted for William Early Jones, while his brothers-in-law Brill, Day, and King voted for Timothy Pillsbury. Jones had argued against annexation, while Pillsbury was an ardent supporter, and their positions became a key election issue. From the votes cast, it is evident that Sarah Hembree Day's extended family did not agree on annexation. In March 1849, the legislature proposed amending the state constitution to require the election of several state officers, including district judges, previously appointed by the governor. King, Brill, and Nichols voted for the amendment, but Hankins and Callahan did not. Callahan and Hankins thus signaled they believed in a centralized state government, a view not commonly supported by Texans.[31]

James Hughes Callahan and his brothers-in-law seldom sought elected office, having little time outside their ranching and farming commitments, but it was sometimes unavoidable given the population size. In 1841 the voters in the Seguin precinct of Gonzales County elected Henry B. King as their constable for two years; he did not seek reelection. In the first election after the formation of Guadalupe County in 1846, King was elected as one of two justices of the peace and voters put James M. Day on the commissioners court. Both served one term. The commissioners court was responsible for constructing and maintaining the local road system and for organizing patrols to scour the roads for escaping slaves. Additionally, the commissioners set the tax rate, approved the budget, and authorized the construction of buildings. Commissioners also had other responsibilities; for example, when Guadalupe County was created in 1846, Day and the other court members met on August 7, 1846, and swore in the elected county officials, selected thirty-six jurors for the district court, and appointed a county treasurer. Later, Day and his colleagues built a courthouse, certified the initial tax roll, issued a second-class headright for 1,280 acres to the heirs of Johnson Day, funded the county's expenditures, and completed a road to New Braunfels. In 1852, the voters in precinct 3 of Caldwell County elected Callahan to their commissioners court; he served one year before he resigned. During his term, he supported building the county's first jail—a sturdy "16 feet square" structure with three-feet-thick walls constructed of three layers of one-foot square logs secured by iron rods.[32]

To build and repair roads, county commissioners met quarterly, assigning men from the various precincts to three-month stints. From 1843 through 1853, Callahan and his brothers-in-law built or repaired roads that linked Seguin to Gonzales, Lockhart, Bastrop, San Marcos, and Prairie Lea (table 8.1). Road assignments came with useful opportunities. Callahan proposed and then constructed the Bastrop road to pass Henry B. King's house,

Table 8.1. County Commissioners Court road assignments for James Hughes Callahan and his six brothers-in-law

Name	*County*	*Road patrol*	*Road trail blazer*	*Road supervisor*	*Road overseer*	*Road hand*
James H. Callahan	Guadalupe,	—	Aug. 1846	—	—	—
	Caldwell	May 1849, May 1850, Aug. 1851	Aug. 1848, Aug. 1851	Sept. 1848	Sept. 1848, Feb. 1849, Feb. 1851	Feb. 1850, Feb. 1852
Solomon W. Brill	Guadalupe	Feb. 1849, Aug. 1849	Feb. 1853	—	Feb. 1848, Feb. 1851	—
John W. Nichols	Guadalupe	Oct. 1847, Apr. 1848, Aug. 1848, Nov. 1849, Aug. 1851, May 1852	Aug. 1846	—	—	—
James M. Day	Gonzales,	—	—	—	Jan. 1844	—
	Guadalupe	—	—	—	—	—
Henry B. King	Guadalupe	Feb. 1849, Aug. 1849	Aug. 1851, Mar. 1853	Nov. 1851, May 1854	Jan. 1848, Feb. 1850	—
Augustus Pharr	Guadalupe	Feb. 1849, Aug. 1851	Feb. 1853	Feb. 1853	—	—
Eli S. Hankins	Caldwell	—	Aug. 1848, Feb. 1849	Feb. 1849, June 1850	June 1850	Sept. 1848, Feb. 1850, Feb. 1851, Feb. 1852, Feb. 1853

Sources: CCM, bk. 1, p. 24, Gonzales County, CC; CCM, bk. A, 1–7, 18–19, 24, 27, 34, 46–47, 50, 53, 62, 89, 91, 96, 105, 125, 127–31, 148, 166, Guadalupe County, CC; CCM, Vol. A, 1–2, 6, 8, 15, 17, 21, 32, 34, 39, 43, 54–55, 64–65, 74, 88, 90–92, 95, Caldwell County, CC.

thence to the Callahan crossing on San Geronimo Creek and along the Callahan trail to York Creek and Martin's Ford on the San Marcos River, ending near Prairie Lea. Brill was the overseer of this road in February 1849 and 1851, while King served in 1850. When a group of farmers suggested changes in 1853, Brill and Pharr were two of five men ordered to assess the request. They determined the alteration was impractical, reporting a more direct route ran from Seguin to Pharr's farm, then joined the road to Callahan's Ford on the San Marcos River; Pharr directed that project. In August 1851, five men, including King, suggested a road be constructed to Blackstone Hardeman's farm on the San Marcos River. Two years later, the commissioners told King and four other men to examine the Hardeman road, and they recommended a route from Seguin across Mill Creek at King's place and thence to the San Marcos River; King supervised its construction. In Caldwell County after 1848 Hankins was charged with locating bridges and supervising their construction; he chose locations near his farm and Callahan's. Other residents certainly built roads to suit themselves as did Callahan and his kin, but the latter did their work well. Today the Bastrop road is Prairie Lea Road (County Road 232), and a bridge spans Callahan's Ford. Hardeman's road is the Old Seguin-Luling Road (County Road 204). State Highway 90 follows a roadway that James W. Nichols first blazed in 1846. Hankins's and Callahan's contributions include State Highway 80 (Luling to Prairie Lea to San Marcos), State Highway 183 (Lockhart to Luling to Gonzales), and the State Highway 183 bridge over the West Fork of Plum Creek.[33]

Another responsibility for county commissioners was to enforce Texas's livestock laws. Horses and cattle grazed freely, but the law protected owners by requiring strays to be identified, appraised, and held until someone could claim the property. A public notice of detained animals had to be issued, and an individual could be remunerated for pasturing the animal. In February 1850, the Guadalupe County Commissioners Court ordered payment to ten men holding strays—James M. Day received $18.75, the most awarded to anyone, and Henry B. King was paid $4, a more common compensation. Obviously, the brothers-in-law wanted their livestock protected, and when the occasion arose they also acted as good stewards of the estray law.[34]

A fair judicial system relied on ensuring a jury of peers was available for all courts. Justices of the peace and county courts drafted men for jury duty, and for a district court session names were drawn based on the tax roll. The summoned men attended the first day of the district court and sixteen were assigned to the grand jury; the remainder served on petit juries. Between 1843 and 1853 in Guadalupe and Gonzales Counties, Callahan's brothers-in-law were members of a grand or petit jury in almost every district court. However, Callahan was never summoned, nor was Hankins. James M. Day's petit jury duty in May 1844 is especially noteworthy. The jury found Edward D. Davis guilty of murder and sentenced him to death by hanging, the first capital conviction in Gonzales County. Considering the extensive kinship and business connections in antebellum Seguin, it was almost impossible to avoid having a juror consider a case involving a relative or friend. On one occasion, Day's father-in-law, George W. Nichols, and brother-in-law Augustus Pharr were members of the grand jury that indicted him for playing cards, and when George W. Nichols's divorce case was heard, Day, as a juror, decided in favor of his father-in-law. In another trial, Day's brother-in-law, John W. Nichols, was a member of the jury that said Day was not guilty of gambling. Clearly, kinship could influence an outcome.[35]

Indictments from Gonzales, Guadalupe, and Caldwell Counties indicate the types of criminal activity there. Gambling indictments occurred most frequently; Day was indicted on three occasions. However, defendants were convicted in less than one-quarter of the 114 gaming indictments, and then most were fined five to twenty dollars. Assault and battery was the second most common cause for indictment, though the rate in this tri-county region was lower than the state average of 60 percent calculated by historian William R. Hogan. This is difficult to explain, as the obvious interpretation—that men in these counties were less violent—seems simplistic. The men in Guadalupe County stole far more cattle than did residents of Gonzales or Caldwell Counties, but Solomon W. Brill accounted for six of the twenty-two cattle theft indictments in Guadalupe. Only one horse was among the twenty-eight instances of stolen livestock. Other indictments included cutting trees without permission, an affray, swindling, selling without a license, trespassing, rioting, disturbing a religious meeting, public indecency, and harboring, trading with, or abusing a slave. The six recorded instances of bigamy and adultery undoubtedly understate the frequency with which both occurred. Louise, the consort of German-born John Goldberg, is an example of the few women indicted for bigamy or adultery.[36]

Indictments rarely led to convictions from 1843 to 1853. Charges were quashed or dismissed in about half of all cases, and of the remaining, only a quarter resulted in a guilty verdict. Once indicted, the odds of being convicted by a jury were about 10 percent. Penalties varied considerably. In Guadalupe County, men stealing trees were fined between $10 and $100, while assault and battery warranted fines ranging from one cent up to $101. Convicted of playing blackjack, Samuel Tease was fined $1,000 on two occasions, but John W. Hall, guilty of assault with intent to kill, had to pay only five dollars. The arbitrary dispensing of punishment seems significant enough to imply that kinship and business relationships between defendants, jurors, and judges were influential, and to some extent jurors may have deliberately nullified the law. However, if settling differences in court instead of through physical confrontation is a measure of civilization, the residents of Guadalupe, Gonzales, and Caldwell Counties were very civilized. District courts heard twice as many civil cases as criminal. Half of the former concerned overdue loans. Without banks, neighbors borrowed money from each other and often sold on credit, and when debts were outstanding, the issue could be contested in court. One third of the civil cases involved land disputes—deeds, titles, and partitions. The remainder included probate disputes, bond forfeitures, divorces, errant jurors, naturalization oaths, and a smattering of other suits.[37]

From 1843 through 1853, King, Pharr, and Hankins never appeared as a plaintiff or defendant in a civil or criminal case. While Callahan was never indicted in a criminal case, he made three court appearances in civil suits. After a hung jury, Henry McKinney asked that his case against Callahan be dismissed at his expense. Callahan's complex lawsuit against James and Robert Patterson ended with a decision by the Texas Supreme Court that a wife's property brought into a marriage was afterward controlled by her husband. Callahan, King, Pharr, and Hankins never failed to repay a debt. Moreover, when Day, Nichols, and Brill were sued for a debt or contract dispute, the cases were dismissed, except for one loss each by Day and Brill. Only Brill sought relief for damages by a third party; he won. In general, Callahan and his kin were diligent in paying debts, forthright in business and personal relations, and not litigious.[38]

Of the brothers-in-law, only Brill spent time in court after being indicted. Examining his trek through the judicial system provides insight into antebellum Texas's evolving, and at times unpredictable, legal structure. Beginning in the spring of 1852 Brill faced multiple accusations of stealing hogs or cattle, and over a twelve-month period he was indicted six times. Twice the charges were dismissed; in three other cases a petit jury found him not guilty. However, on May 8, 1854, the same day that he was declared not guilty of stealing a beef, the same jury found him guilty of stealing Andrew Neill's oxen. It began on April 21, 1852, when Neill told a Guadalupe County grand jury that Brill stole one of his cattle. Grand jurors Augustus Pharr, Brill's brother-in-law, and John C. Sheffield, both later witnesses for Brill, surely told the grand jury what they knew. Nevertheless, Brill was indicted, arrested, and released on bond. In four subsequent court terms, Brill's attorney employed a variety of delay tactics, but the district judge overruled each objection. On May 8, 1854, the court heard testimony in the case of *Texas v. Solomon Brill.* The story was complicated. In October 1851, Dr. J. M. Anderson's overseer, driving an oxen-pulled cart, stopped at Neill's house. Neill told the jury that he recognized one ox as his, but Anderson testified he paid Pharr fifty dollars for it. In turn, Pharr said Brill bought the steer from Neill. In Brill's defense, Sheffield claimed that Brill had charge of Neill's cattle and a second witness, A. M. Ferguson, heard Neill boasting that Brill had authority to sell any of his cattle. Swearing he never had such an arrangement with Brill, Neill admitted that they talked about it but added that while he sold Brill several head, he never sold the one in question. The jury convicted Brill and sentenced him to a year in the penitentiary. Two days later, Brill's attorney asked for a new trial. In the meantime, Brill refined his defense, and his extended family rallied to help. He admitted being "thrown off guard" by Neill's testimony, which led him to forget that Pharr, King, John W. Nichols, and neighbor H. C. Fountain could vouch for him. Brill's purchase of the ox from Neill, Fountain wrote, was well known in the neighborhood. The three brothers-in-law swore that for several years Brill had authority over Neill's cattle. Despite this new evidence, Judge Thomas J. Devine denied the motion for a new trial but released Brill on bond, prompting Brill's attorney to appeal to the Texas Supreme Court.[39]

The Supreme Court justices concluded that, because of a new law that went into effect seven days before Brill was found guilty, he should be imprisoned while on bond. The justices had not considered any evidence. This news set off a panic in Brill's family, but all was not lost. William Early Jones, retired Guadalupe County district judge and former associate justice of the Texas Supreme Court, filed a brief at the request of Callahan. Without documentation, it is not clear if Jones conferred with his friend, Governor Pease, but they probably discussed the case. Meanwhile, 205 Guadalupe County citizens—including the sheriff who arrested Brill, three of Brill's brothers-in-law, and witnesses Sheffield and Ferguson—sent a petition for clemency to Pease, who received a similar plea from nine of the twelve jurors. Both appeals highlighted the new evidence that Judge Devine and the Supreme Court refused to consider. After reviewing the matter, Pease wrote that he doubted that Brill should have been convicted. On March 20, 1855, he issued Brill a pardon, the first ever for a resident in Guadalupe County. Brill's case illustrates the influence of family and personal connections on judicial outcomes at that time, as well as the effectiveness of having a persistent and imaginative defense attorney.[40]

Historians typically divide Texas's pre–Civil War past into the Republic and antebellum periods, identifying annexation by the United States as a watershed moment. This is undoubtedly true at the state and national level, but transitions at the local level can have their own cycles. For Sarah Medissa and James Hughes Callahan, their families, and their neighbors in the San Marcos and Guadalupe River valleys, the years from 1843 into 1853 form a distinct period. During this time their frontier transformed from an unpredictable, hazardous area where settlers fought the elements, defended themselves against Indians, and battled invading Mexican armies into a more stable, safer place populated by increasingly prosperous residents. In 1853 the *Galveston Journal* highlighted this transition. Now with 500 people, Seguin had one of the best schools in the area, three hotels, several churches, nine dry goods merchants, two groceries, one drugstore, two restaurants, three blacksmith shops, and two shoemakers. Even nearby Prairie Lea had a well-respected school, two churches, two doctors, and Callahan's store, as well as a post office, blacksmith shop, gristmill, and cotton gin. If the services of a larger town were required, the county's road system allowed access to the wider world.[41]

Scholars have studied similar transitions in other Southern towns. Christopher Morris discusses the evolution of Warren County, Mississippi, in the 1830s. There a rapid population increase led to a shift from a sparsely settled Anglo region cemented by mutually supportive, interrelated families to a society joined together by expanding commerce and family wealth held jointly by the strengthening rule of law. It may be argued that the Seguin region passed through a similar transitional point between 1843 and 1853, with 1850 the pivotal year. But while William Tom Jr.'s vision of a "field of civilization" may have been realized, it was not wholly embraced by all. Having observed and experienced the process of creating and building new communities, by 1853 Callahan was ready to try again. Likely feeling hemmed in by strangers and seeking the financial rewards of land speculation, he decided to move west again. The Callahans sold their home on the San Marcos River and traveled west over the Devil's Backbone to the Blanco River, where they planned to develop their own "field of civilization."[42]

CHAPTER 9

Brazoria County, 1837, to Rio Blanco, 1853

"All are land-hunting"

In February 1838, commissioner Thomas Blackwell unbolted the door of the Brazoria County land office. As the men swarming outside rushed in, Patrick C. Jack elbowed his way to the front. When interviewed about his eligibility, Jack swore he was single and had arrived in Texas before May 1835. Witnesses William B. Aldridge and Anson Jones declared they knew Jack and that his statement was truthful, so the county land commissioners awarded him "369 acres augmentation," an addition to the land previously given to him by Mexico. Similar scenes were repeated many times as Texas officials gave away millions of acres to attract settlers and reward others for service.[1]

County land commissioners faced a formidable task. For two years, veterans of the Texas Revolution and new settlers had been clamoring for certificates so they could acquire land. The delay had begun in the Congress of the Republic of Texas, where debates about land allocation seemed unending. As the opening day for land offices approached, confusion mounted and pandemonium followed. One commissioner later wrote, "Now Sir please imagine to yourself a Board crowded with near 200 applicants on the first day of the opening of the land office and on subsequent days from 50 to 100 more." James Hughes Callahan waited his turn at Brazoria; he was number 175, and in the following months 698 more applicants lined up to claim certificates. Speculators hovered, looking to buy land from anyone willing to sell. District Judge Benjamin C. Franklin of Brazoria County cornered

Callahan and paid an unknown amount for his 1,476-acre first-class bounty certificate. Callahan's career as a Texas land speculator had begun.[2]

Land ownership has been inextricably linked with the development of the United States. The Day, Hembree, and Callahan families, in moving from Virginia and Maryland to Georgia and the Carolinas, became part of a massive relocation of early Americans seeking property. This migration continued into Texas, where unique laws created new opportunities for acquisition, development, and speculation. Studies of land ownership in Texas often focus on the holdings of the archetypical land baron, but most Texans struggled on small farms and ranches. The story of land acquisitions and sales by Sarah Medissa and James Hughes Callahan and their extended family is more typical of most Texans, especially those who arrived during the Republic period. A detailed examination of properties held by them also illustrates the complexity of acquiring and selling Texas land during this era.

The history of Texas land ownership is as unique as its political history. Spain sent colonists, priests, and soldiers to establish populated areas around San Antonio, Nacogdoches, and Goliad, as well as along the Rio Grande borderland. Many received land grants, but relatively few actually settled on them. After independence, Mexican authorities concluded that more settlers would provide a barrier to the threat of Americans and Indians, and so they continued with the late Spanish-era *empresario* effort. The deals brokered by Moses Austin and then his son Stephen F. Austin provided settlers with a large swath of almost free land; immigrants would receive one league and one labor for less than the cost of 640 acres of public land in the United States. Other empresarios quickly joined the effort that brought almost 30,000 Anglos to Texas by 1835. Among these pioneers was the James C. Neill family, in Austin's Colony, and the Francis Berry family, in Green DeWitt's settlement. Both would cross paths with the Callahan family.[3]

Early Texas settlers obtained titles to the bottomlands of major rivers and their primary tributaries, as these areas were the most desirable. During the Texas Revolution, the Republic government was cash poor but promised land to those who joined the struggle. It was a great incentive, so men like Callahan came, as did others. After the Texans won independence, it was not long before surviving veterans, or relatives of those who had fallen, and postwar immigrants demanded their land. The formidable task of distribution fell to the Texas General Land Office. For pre-1836 settlers, the Republic accepted all titles issued by Spanish and Mexican officials. Texas soldiers received bounty and donation grants, and to encourage immigration the Republic offered headright grants to new settlers. Bounty grants, ranging from 320 to 1,280 acres, were awarded to any man who had served prior to October 1, 1837, while donation grants, usually 640 acres, were issued to veterans of various battles. First-class headrights (4,605.5 acres to families, or 1,476.1 to single men) went to those arriving before Texas's Declaration of Independence on March 2, 1836. Second-class headrights (1,280 or 640 acres) were awarded to those settling between March 2, 1836, and October 1, 1837; and third-class (640 acres) and fourth-class (320 acres) headrights were given to arrivals between October 1, 1837, and January 1, 1842.[4]

Grants were distributed by issuing a certificate for a specific amount of land to the eligible person at authorized local offices, which were overseen by the Texas General Land Office. The certificate holder could sell for cash, as Callahan did, or he could locate the acreage and embark on the process of claiming the property. Land became a reliable source of income, and even wealth, in antebellum Texas. Almost half of the veteran bounty and donation warrants were sold by the original recipients. To obtain land, a certificate holder selected an unclaimed parcel and arranged for a survey by an authorized surveyor. A field surveyor produced field notes and a plat, which went to a supervising surveyor, who forwarded the material to the General Land Office, where it was drawn on the master map. Once the certificate had been exchanged and land was awarded, the county clerk provided a deed and handled all future transactions. The flexibility of the system and demand for land created enticing opportunities for speculators and developers, honest and unscrupulous alike. Americans have a deserved reputation as speculators, Texans no less so, but the rules in Texas were different. Under Mexico, immigrants had to live on their property and land speculation was prohibited. There was one exception: Mexicans and Tejanos could acquire up to eleven leagues that they could sell. Some took advantage of conflict between the state of Coahuila y Tejas and Mexico's central government and obtained nearly 500 leagues with the intention to sell, prompting Texians, once independence was won, to void these transactions. With large-scale speculation thus discouraged, Texas developers had to buy grants or small parcels. While the wealthy had an advantage, men of lesser means, like Callahan and his in-laws, still had opportunities to acquire land and participate in the development of the state. The population explosion of the 1840s and

1850s created a ready market for them as people seeking land flooded into Texas.[5]

General Land Office regulations prohibited the acquisition of large parcels, which meant that most deals were for less than a thousand acres. Some individuals did acquire impressive amounts of land, but most Texans dabbled on a smaller scale, Callahan and his family among them. Less than a year after Texans won independence, *Niles Weekly Register* reprinted a letter that said, "I learn from the intelligent southern men that a tremendous rush is already making from the south and south west into Texas, where lands can be had for little or nothing. . . . So Texas lands will, for some time, present an abundant field for speculation." But speculation was risky and could ruin a man. An anonymous Texan's letter to the *New Orleans Daily Delta* captured the mood: "All are land hunting . . . but are as much at a loss in their selection as children in a toy-shop." Like the Republic, many Texians were land rich and cash poor. They used land to pay debts, to create wealth by buying and selling, or to access cash. How they handled land depended on their goals, circumstances, philosophy, appetite for taking risks, and backgrounds. The experience of Callahan and his in-laws reflects all of these.[6]

Due to her status as an unmarried widow, Sarah Hembree Day's land dealings were few and focused upon obtaining a home and garden plots (table 9.1). However, one exception was the second-class headright due to her husband, Johnson Day, which she and her children inherited upon his death in 1838. James Milford Day, his father's executor, swore to the Gonzales County land commissioners that his father was married and arrived in Texas

Table 9.1. Land transactions in Texas by Sarah Hembree Day

Date	*County*	*Size*	*Remarks*
Aug. 1839	Gonzales	Seguin–5 TL, 1 GL	Paid $90.50; from Apr. 1845–Sept. 1855 sold 6 lots, $124
Nov. 1845	Guadalupe	Seguin–1 TL	Paid $20 to James M. Day; sold, Aug. 1854, $200
Nov. 1845	Guadalupe	Seguin–1 TL	Paid $14 to Asa Sowell; no sale record
Aug. 1849	Kimble	1,280 acres	Texas General Land Office, awarded to Johnson Day heirs; sold in the 1880s
June 1857	Comal	Pittsburg–1 FL	Paid $50, no sale record (Blanco County courthouse burned, 1876)

Sources: Johnson Day, Land Grant Search, TGLO; Deeds, bk. A1, 20-21; bk. B, 276, Guadalupe County, CC; Deeds, bk. E, 646, Blanco County, CC; Deeds, bk. B, 276, Gonzales County CC.
Note: TL: town lot; GL: garden lot; FL: farm lot

in February 1837, so he was eligible for 1,280 acres, which the commissioners awarded to his heirs. Sarah paid her future son-in-law, Callahan, ten dollars in silver and ten dollars in gold to have the land located and surveyed. Callahan had seen the property he wanted for her during his time with Benjamin McCulloch in April 1841. The following October, McCulloch and his two chainmen were on the Llano River near the junction of the north and south forks (present-day Kimble County) when Callahan led rangers to the area and pointed out the parcel to be surveyed for the Day heirs. He did the same for one tract due him, four plots for the heirs of George Kimble, a third of a league for Sion Green, and 320 acres due Henry P. Redfield (map 9.1).[7]

This indicates where land was available in 1841. During the first years of the Republic, the choice plots of land were in the bottomlands of major rivers and their tributaries close to the coast. For example, in March 1838, the *Matagorda Bulletin* reported that new plantations were appearing on the Colorado River. By the time Sarah claimed her grant, only riverfront property further west remained. She kept her Kimble County land and bequeathed it to her children, who sold it in the 1880s. However, her most useful acquisitions were six lots she purchased in 1838 as Seguin was established. As her health declined, she started to sell these, which included her homestead, earning a profit of about $210, but by 1857 she bought a farm lot in the emerging village of Pittsburg, on the Rio Blanco. This opportunity arose because in March 1855 the U.S. Congress authorized land bounties for soldiers who served in the War of 1812. Johnson Day had volunteered, so she applied and received 160 acres in Watonwan, Wisconsin. Selling it gave her an unexpected windfall. As a widow, Sarah, like many Texas women, had little access to credit and was not wealthy enough to invest in property ventures. Despite that, land ownership brought her financial security as she aged, and she took advantage of bounties for her deceased husband. Her land provided a place to live and a means to support herself and her dependents, as well as some cash, so that she never became a liability for her family.[8]

The sale of donation and bounty grants provided many Texans with the opportunity to become self-sufficient. The Brill family was a good example. Solomon W. Brill was entitled to four parcels of land awarded by the Republic—three for military service during the Revolution and one because of the date he arrived. In all four cases he applied at the earliest opportunity and, like many awardees, sold his certificates (table 9.2). His awards totaled 4,676 acres, but he had no intention of residing on any of it. Instead, his sales earned him $950, about twenty cents per acre. Four individuals bought his

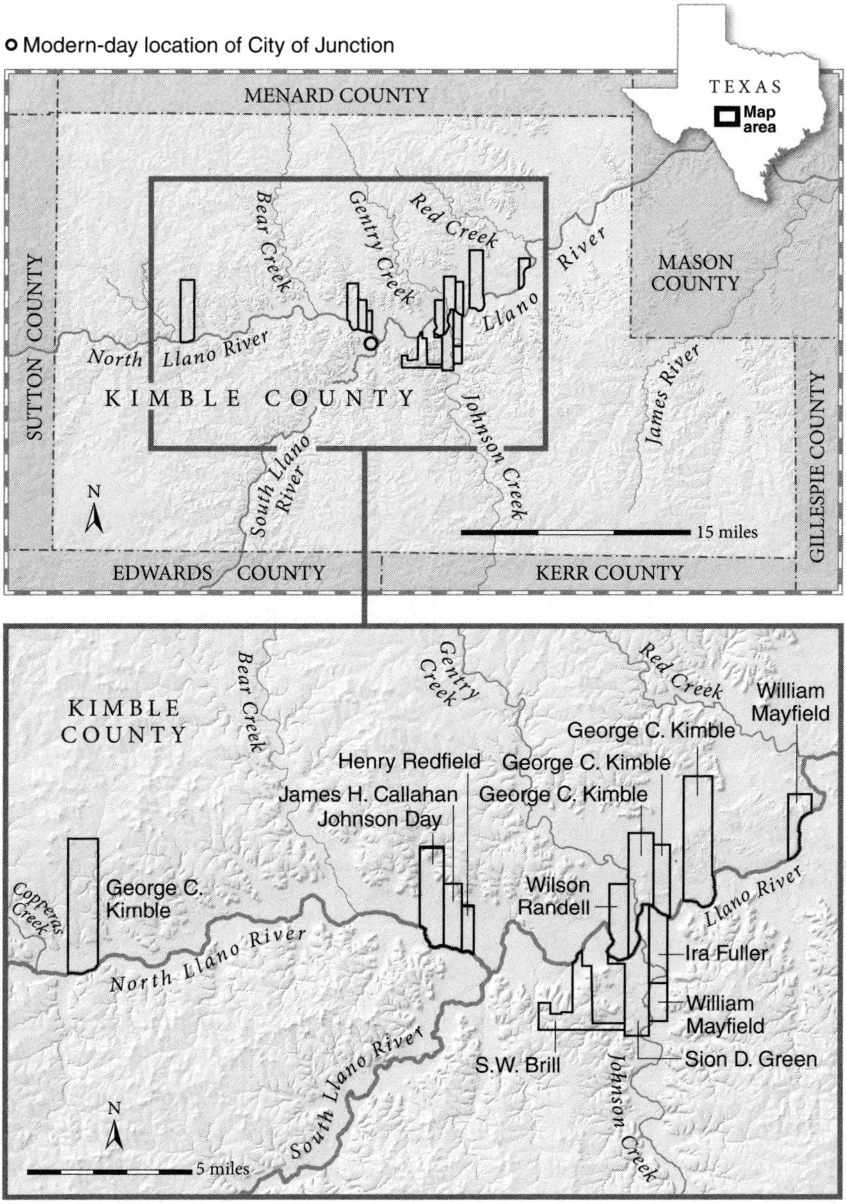

Map 9.1. Callahan and his in-laws' land, Kimble County. Map by Carol Zuber-Mallison.

Table 9.2. Land transactions in Texas by Hepzibah C. and Solomon W. Brill

Date	*County*	*Acres*	*Remarks*
Apr. 1838	Chambers	1,280	Texas General Land Office (TGLO), Republic of Texas Army, Oct. 1836–1838; sold certificate, $500
Nov. 1844	Bandera	1,476	TGLO, in Texas before Mar. 2, 1836; sold certificate, $100
Aug. 1845	Lampasas	640	TGLO, Republic of Texas Army, June–Oct. 1836; sold certificate, $100
July 1881	Kimble	1,280	TGLO, 1880 Tex. Legislature awarded land to indigent veterans of Tex. Revolution; sold certificate, $250
July 1838	Guadalupe	unknown	Seguin–1 town lot (TL); Paid $15; sold, Sept. 1853, $20
unknown	Guadalupe	52	Paid unknown amount, Fuqua Survey; sold 52 acres, June 1846, $250
Oct. 1852	Guadalupe	50	Paid, $200, Fuqua Survey; Hepzibah bought this land; sold 15 acres, Feb. 1876, $150; sold 1.3 acres, railroad company, Mar. 1899, $150
May 1855–1857	Guadalupe	52	Paid $900, San Geronimo Creek; Hepzibah bought this land; sold 19 acres, railroad company, May 1875, $400
Mar. 1887	Kimble	182 6/7	Hepzibah's share of Johnson Day estate; sold 182 6/7 acres, $15

Sources: Solomon Brill, A. Crawford, Ira Bisbee, J. Sydnor, Sarah Cloud, Land Grant Search, TGLO; Deeds, bk. D2, 20, Bexar County, CC; TR, 1857, 1861, 1864, 1867, 1870, 1873, 1877, 1881, TAC, Guadalupe County, TSLA; Deeds, bk. C, 222; bk. D, 540; bk. E, 45; bk. F, 258; bk. N, 17, 524; bk. O, 19; bk. 15, 61, Guadalupe County, CC; Deeds, bk. A, 472, Kimble County, CC.

certificates. The first was Alexander C. Crawford, who despite having four bounty certificates himself, was a small-time speculator, buying certificates from four men. Brill sold his second bounty to Ira Bisbee, a one-time buyer who settled on Plum Creek and served as a ranger under Callahan. Brill sold a third certificate to John S. Sydnor, a low-volume speculator who, in addition to two bounties he was awarded, bought one Texas land scrip and fourteen land certificates. Sarah H. Cloud, an early Kimble County settler, bought Brill's fourth certificate (map 9.1). She wanted land on which to live and was not interested in speculation. Brill's experiences indicated that many speculators bought relatively little land, and women sometimes participated.[9]

When he arrived in Seguin in 1838, Brill bought a town lot, where he and Sarah Hembree Day's daughter Hepzibah lived early in their marriage. In 1852 they sold it and moved to a larger tract on San Geronimo Creek. The Brills had previously owned land on this stream, but for an unknown reason they sold it in 1846. Interestingly, the 1852 purchase of fifty acres was made by Hepzibah and not Solomon, and she was also the sole buyer in an 1855 transaction that gave them another fifty-two acres adjacent to their homesite (see map 8.1, table 9.2). This purchase was prudent; the farm lay parallel to the road that ran to Gonzales, and later the railroad bought a right-of-way through the property. It is not certain why she is listed as the purchaser in these transactions, but one possibility is that Brill's felony conviction complicated owning land in his name. Taking a broader view, her ownership demonstrates the opportunities that Texas law provided to women when it came to owning real estate that were not available in most other states in that era. It also may indicate that she inherited some of her mother's resilience and was the dominant partner in the marriage. Hepzibah and Solomon lived a simple life. He forwent his physician's training, and they owned horses, cattle, and hogs that roamed the countryside. They showed no ambition to speculate in real estate, or for that matter, to seek other opportunities that involved owning and working more land. They used the sale of his certificates to supplement their income and develop their homestead on San Geronimo Creek. By the end of the 1850s they had set the course for the remainder of their lives—they were simple yeomen, or plain folks.[10]

The Hankins' land acquisitions illustrate the different methods of distribution used in Texas and also highlight a fiercely debated decision made by the Texas Congress. Eli inherited property, received a third-class headright, and bought land. As a ward of his grandfather Levi Hinds, in November 1845 Eli received a portion of Levi's estate, 300 acres on Plum Creek. He and Elizabeth lived modestly there, downsizing to 128 acres in 1848 and selling another fifty acres one year later before moving to Prairie Lea in 1853 (see map 8.1, table 9.3). Unlike his brother-in-law Brill, Hankins did not get land for military service, despite the fact that he fought at Plum Creek in 1840, served in ranger companies in 1841, 1842, and 1843, and volunteered during the 1842 Mexican raids. Texas politicians made a distinction between men who fought in the Revolution and those who later repelled Mexican invasions or battled Indians. The latter did not get land but did receive cash, often years after their service. Hankins did obtain some land as a Republic-era immigrant. While he arrived in the summer of 1836, he did not reach

Table 9.3. Land transactions in Texas by Elizabeth Caroline and Eli Skaggs Hankins

Date	*County*	*Acres*	*Remarks*
Jan. 1846	Gonzales	320	Texas General Land Office; sued to recover headright; sold 320 acres, Nov. 1886, $160
Nov. 1845	Gonzales	300	Paid $300, Hinds Survey; sold 122 acres, Mar. 1848, $150; sold 50 acres, July 1849, $75. No record for the sale of the remaining 128 acres was discovered.
Apr. 1853	Caldwell	100	Paid $1,000, J. H. Callahan, Henry Survey; deeded 1 acre for Prairie Lea Cemetery; sold 69 acres, Aug. 1856, $552; estate sold 31 acres, Jan. 1913, and 29¼ acres, Gilliland Survey, $4,000 (see entry below)
Aug. 1856	Caldwell	27	Paid $432, Gilliland Survey; 1874, half interest in Tennison's mill; purchased, $1,200, Jan. 1878, Tennison's other half interest, $1,200; bought ¼ acre, Oct. 1881, $30; bought 2 acres, Oct. 1882, $20; estate sold 29¼ acres, Jan. 1913, $4,000 (see entry above)
Oct. 1867	Caldwell	90	Paid $180, Reavill Survey; sold 90 acres, Jan. 1874, $700
June 1871	Caldwell		Town lot (TL), paid $10, Eli Hankins et al., trustees for Shiloh Baptist Church, Prairie Lea
Jan. 1881	Caldwell	60–70	Paid $1,000, Gilliland Survey; Elizabeth sold 60 acres, Dec. 1888, $1,000
Feb. 1885	Gonzales	6¼	Gristmill; undivided interest with Bellinger and Miller; sold ⅓ undivided interest, Mar. 1886, $700; sold ⅔ undivided interest, Dec. 1886, $800
May 1882	Kimble	182⁶⁄₇	Elizabeth Caroline's share of Johnson Day estate; sold, May 1882, $167

Sources: Deeds, bk. E, 174; bk. G, 219; bk. I, 169; bk. K2, 414–15, Gonzales County, CC; Deeds, bk. A, 93; bk. B, 387; bk. C, 352; bk. F, 701; bk. G, 32, 105, Caldwell County, CC; Deeds, bk. A, 379, Kimble County, CC; E. (Eli) Hankins, Land Grant Search, TGLO; TR, 1846–48, TAC, Gonzales County; TR, 1848–88, TAC, Caldwell County, TSLA; Caldwell County, Nonpopulation Census Schedules, Texas, 1850–80, MT1134, R10, R21, NAB.

maturity until 1841, and as a single adult the Gonzales County land commission gave him a third-class bounty of 320 acres. In one respect, he was fortunate that a parcel of this size still remained in Gonzales County, but it was not desirable land, being on the watershed divide north of the Guadalupe and San Marcos rivers. Eli must have identified the land earlier since he staked out his survey nine days after receiving a certificate on January 29, 1846. He lost interest in the property, never paid an annual tax, and forty years later had to sue for its recovery, which he then sold for fifty cents per acre, a price indicating the value of land lacking a ready source of water.[11]

In 1853, Eli and Elizabeth purchased 100 acres in the John Henry Survey from Sarah Medissa and James Hughes Callahan (see map 8.1, table 9.3). At this time, they also set aside one acre for the Prairie Lea community cemetery. Even though they lived in a small town, up to the Civil War they continued to have livestock holdings ranging between 40 and 190 head of cattle and 50 and 75 hogs, indicating that they used the open range to support their livestock. They appear to have been averse to, or too poor for, the risks inherent in land speculation and instead followed a pastoral way of life much like the Brills. However, the Hankins had a long-term ambition that would take them away from ranching. In August 1856, they bought twenty-seven acres on an adjoining survey where a sluice of the San Marcos River flowed, and after the Civil War they owned a gristmill and began a milling business that remained in the family into the twentieth century.[12]

In many respects the life of Augustus Pharr, who married Sarah Hembree Day's daughter Meekness, mirrored that of his brother-in-law Hankins. Although he arrived during the Mexican era, Pharr like Hankins was too young to fight in the Texas Revolution, so he qualified only for a third-class headright of 320 acres (table 9.4). While both men benefited by inheriting Texas land, Pharr's inheritance was considerably greater and in a prime location. Nevertheless, once married, he did not succumb to speculation schemes but rather remained close to Sarah's extended family, following the yeoman example of the Brill and Hankins families. Despite owning a significant amount of land, Pharr did not sell or even use most of this land. Before marrying, he claimed his grant and had it surveyed in Gillespie County; he and Meekness never lived on this tract, though they paid the annual taxes and kept it for three decades (table 9.4). In the settlement of his mother's estate in Brazoria during 1846 and 1847, Pharr received two parcels of land—thirteen acres in Brazoria County that he sold for $100—and half of his mother's league in Milam County, of which he quickly sold an undivided half for $600. Six years later, he sold the remaining 1,151 acres for one dollar per acre to Guadalupe County resident Thomas H. Duggan, a small-time speculator. Though there is no record that he and Meekness had a town lot in Seguin, they seemingly lived there because he was in business with Brill. After two years of town life, they bought 342 acres on San Geronimo Creek, three miles east of Seguin (see map 8.1), where the Brills joined them in

Table 9.4. Land transactions in Texas by Meekness Amanda and Augustus Pharr

Date	*County*	*Acres*	*Remarks*
Sept. 1847	Gillespie	320	Texas General Land Office (TGLO), arrived in Texas by Jan. 1842; sold 320 acres, May 1874, $320
Feb. 1846	Milam, Lee	2,302	TGLO, Pharr share, mother's estate, Milbourn Survey; sold 1,151 acres, May 1847, $600; sold 1,151 acres, Dec. 1853, $1,151
May 1847	Brazoria	13	Undivided interest, Phar's mother's estate, Brazoria County; sold, Jan. 1858, $100
May 1851	Guadalupe	342	Paid $800, John Sowell Survey; sold 171 acres, May 1853, $513; sold 85½ acres, Jan. 1855, $500; sold 85½ acres, Jan. 1857, $2,500
Jan. 1856	Comal	500	The Pharrs did not make a Jan. 1856 payment of a $1,100 note when a purchaser of the Sowell Survey defaulted; Callahan's estate cancelled this sale
Nov. 1871	Blanco	Blanco–1 TL	Paid $15 to James M. Day; sold, July 1872, $80
N/A[a]	Blanco	Blanco–1 TL	Sold Apr. 1873, $60
N/A[a]	Blanco	Blanco–4 TL	Pharr's estate, Meeky sold, Apr. 1876, $220
ca. 1859[a]	Blanco	Blanco–5 TL	Paid $25; sold by heirs of Pharr, July 1894, $300
Apr. 1879	Kimble	182 6/7	Meeky's share of Johnson Day estate; sold, Apr. 1879, amount unknown

Sources: Elizabeth Milbourn, Augustus Pharr, Land Grant Search, TGLO; Deeds, bk. M, 163, Gillespie County, CC; Deeds, bk. D, 408; bk. H, 367, Brazoria County, CC; Deeds, bk. E, 407, Guadalupe County, CC; Deeds, bk. C, 636; bk. D, 308, 754; bk. E, 407, 812; bk. G, 185, Guadalupe County, CC; Deeds, bk. 1, 569, 572; bk. 2, 20, 313; bk. 14, 173, Blanco County, CC; Deeds, bk. A, 466, Kimble County, CC; TR, 1848–58, TAC, Guadalupe County, TSLA; PL, bk. H, 1–8, 220–21, Comal County, CC; Deeds, bk. A, 466, Kimble County, CC.

Note: TL: town lot.

[a] The records were incinerated when the Blanco County courthouse burned in 1876.

ranching. Unlike the Brills, within two years the Pharrs began selling their homestead piecemeal; the final parcel sold in 1857, netting $2,500. Before completing the sale, the Pharrs looked to the Texas frontier and on January 1, 1856, purchased 500 acres from the Callahans' speculative venture and settled on the Rio Blanco in Comal County.[13]

Speculation occurred where town and garden lots were in demand, as well as on larger rural tracts. These were two distinct markets, but Mahala and Henry B. King did well in both. The first bewildering transaction occurred during an 1838 fall meeting of the Gonzales County land commissioners. Having arrived before October 1, 1837, Henry was due a first-class bounty, but he declared he was a single man despite having been married to Mahala for six months. He actually qualified for 1,280 acres instead of the 640 he received (table 9.5). He did not pursue his right to the additional land, perhaps because what he got was correct for his marital status prior to the law's stated deadline. In September 1838, he and Mahala were among the original settlers of Seguin, buying ten town, three garden, three farming, and two timber lots (table 9.5). They settled about one hundred yards east of her mother's house. Within a year the Kings began to buy and sell lots in Seguin, and by 1853 they had sold their original lots. However, they also bought an additional six town lots, one timber lot, and three and a half garden lots that they eventually sold, almost doubling their $210 investment. In 1846, they purchased their first larger tract—fifty-two acres on the east bank of San Geronimo Creek, close to the future homesteads of the Brills and Pharrs (see map 8.1). Through a series of transactions, they increased their land holdings, eventually buying the Bollinger Survey along Mill Creek, south of Prairie Lea (see map 8.1, table 9.5). Their accumulation of land coincided with expansion of their cattle herd. Ultimately, their initial investment of $425 earned about $2,510. In total, according to the tax rolls from 1845 to 1854, their wealth grew from $100 to almost $4,000. While the Kings were minor players in Texas land speculation, the growth in their income must have been welcome.[14]

Like Henry King, John W. Nichols filed for his headright as a single man, although he was eligible for a married man's allowance. Moreover, he did not take possession of the land, so he had to refile in 1845 (table 9.6). Even then he did not have a tract surveyed but, like many others, sold the certificate, in his case sixteen months later to Michael H. Erskine for thirty dollars. Later, he and Mary dabbled in the risky practice of purchasing certificates during the Court of Claims period of the late 1850s. At that time, all eligible recipients and their heirs were offered a final opportunity to claim land due them; however, speculating on the certificates was unpredictable and riddled with fraud. For $250, G. W. Jackson, a resident of Kerr County, sold Nichols his right to a 960-acre headright due his father, Thomas Jackson, who had died at the Alamo (table 9.6). Nichols had the property surveyed, but the General Land Office voided the claim since it had been platted elsewhere. Of 430 filings with the Court of Claims, 259 were withdrawn, and Mary and John were among the many people taken advantage of by unscrupulous men. Having lost $250, they ended their venture into Court of Claims certificates.[15]

Table 9.5. Land transactions in Texas by Henry Basil King and his wives

Date	*County*	*Acres*	*Remarks*
Nov. 1838	Gonzales	640	TGLO, 3rd-class headright; King never claimed the certificate
Aug. 1839	Gonzales		Seguin, paid $86, 10 TL, 3 GL, 2 TML, 3 FL; Oct. 1839–June 1853, sold 16½ lots, $420
1841–44	Gonzales		Seguin, paid $14, 4 TL; sold, Oct. 1845, $100
Oct. 1845	Gonzales		Seguin, paid $25, 2 GL; sold, June 1853, Feb. 1858, $55
Aug. 1846	Guadalupe		Seguin, paid $30, 2 TL, 1 TML; sold, Aug. 1846–Aug. 1853, $62
Dec. 1846	Guadalupe	52	Paid $52, Fuqua Survey; sold, Sept. 1850, $600
Aug. 1850	Guadalupe	504⅔	Paid $150, John R. King, Bollinger Survey; sold, Sept. 1850–Jan. 1857, $2,100
May 1852	Guadalupe		Seguin, paid $24, 1 GL; no sale record
Feb. 1854	Guadalupe	375	Paid $275, Kent Survey; sold, Sept. 1855, $833
March 1855	Guadalupe	70	Paid $261, Kent Survey; sold, Aug. 1856, $127
Dec. 1855	Guadalupe		Seguin, paid $42, 5/237 interest, Sons of Temperance Building; never sold his share
Feb. 1856	Guadalupe		Seguin, paid $50 half interest, 1 GL; no sale record
Aug. 1856	Guadalupe	196½	Paid $1,000, A. J. Sowell Survey; May 1858 placed 80 acres in trust for $1,700 loan due Jan. 1860; sold to John Nichols, 129 acres, Dec. 1867, $400
Jan. 1858	Caldwell		Prairie Lea, paid $24, 1 TL; no sale record
Oct. 1858	Caldwell		Prairie Lea, paid $120, 4 TL; divorce settlement, lots awarded to Eliza King
Oct. 1860	Caldwell		Prairie Lea, paid $45, ½ TL; sold, Jan. 1860, $10
May 1882	Kimble	182⁶⁄₇	Mahala's share of Johnson Day estate; H. C. King sold 37 acres, $120, and W. H. Kishbaugh sold 36 acres, $20, May 1882; John R. King sold 10.4 acres, July 1888, $40; no record of when the other King heirs sold the remaining 99 acres

Sources: H. (Henry) King, Land Grant Search, TGLO; Deeds, bk. A, 279; bk. B, 30, 278, 398; bk. D, 291, 381; bk. E, 65; bk. F, 171, Gonzales County, CC; Deeds, bk. A, 12, 26, 30, 57, 73, 76; bk. B, 55, 59, 70, 303, 556; bk. C, 297, 303, 556; bk. D, 83, 312, 631, 780; bk. E, 112, 256, 598; bk. F, 47, 310, 314, 524, 746, 765; bk. G, 186, 475, 489, Guadalupe County, CC; TR, 1845–54, TAC, Guadalupe County, TSLA; Deeds, bk. G, 213, 260; bk. H, 111, 328, 756, Caldwell County, CC; Deeds, bk. A, 474; bk. 4, 116, Kimble County, CC.

Note: TL: town lot; GL: garden lot; FL: farm lot; TML: timber lot

Table 9.6. Land transactions in Texas for Mary and John W. Nichols

Date	*County*	*Acres*	*Remarks*
May 1845	Gonzales	640	Texas General Land Office, in Texas by 1838; sold certificate, Sept. 1847, $30
Aug. 1838	Gonzales		Seguin, paid $126, 10 TL, 2 GL, 3 FL, 2 TML; sold, Aug. 1849–Nov. 1867, $306
Oct. 1840	Gonzales		Seguin, paid $20, 1 GL; sold, Apr. 1850, $12
May 1842	Gonzales		Seguin, paid $50, 1 GL; no sale record found
July 1842	Gonzales		Seguin, paid $40, 1 TL, 3 GL, 2 FL, 4 TML; sold, Aug. 1845–Jan. 1847, $262
Feb. 1843	Gonzales	50	Paid $1, sheriff's sale, Sowell Survey; 50 acres in homestead, Aug. 1881
June 1844	Gonzales	200	Paid $600, Sowell Survey; sold 100 acres, Oct. 1849, $400; 100 acres in homestead, Aug. 1881
Mar. 1848	Guadalupe	177	Paid $177, Dikes Survey; sold, Feb. 1862, $150
Sept. 1848	Guadalupe	177	Paid $34, Robert Hall Survey; sold, June 1855–Nov. 1855, $260
Dec. 1850	Guadalupe	1,476	Paid $100, ⅓ interest, Clements Survey; sold, June 1855, $2,000
June 1852	Guadalupe		Seguin, paid $20, 1 TL; sheriff's sale to settle lawsuit Nichols lost in JP court, Nov. 1867, $18
May 1853	Guadalupe	177	Paid $177, Scobey Survey; sold, Jan. 1856, $600
Mar. 1854	Guadalupe	2	Paid $150, saw- and gristmill on Geronimo Creek; sold, Aug. 1854, $420
unknown	Guadalupe	60	Paid unknown amount, Tom Survey; sold, Aug. 1859, $150
Sept. 1855	Guadalupe	320	Paid $320, Miller Survey; sold, Sept. 1855, June 1857, $640
Feb. 1856	Guadalupe	25	Paid $240, Sowell Survey; 25 acres in homestead, Aug. 1881
Mar. 1857	Guadalupe	960	Paid $250, Thomas Jackson bounty certificate; invalid certificate
July 1857	Guadalupe	320	Paid $250, John Goodbread bounty certificate; sold certificate, May 1858, Feb.1880, $400
Dec. 1857	Guadalupe	130	Paid $400, Henry B. King, Sowell Survey; John traded to his wife for ½ interest, Johnson Day Survey, Kimble County, Oct. 1865; sheriff's sale to settle lawsuit lost in district court, $25
Apr. 1858	Guadalupe		Seguin, partition of Campbell estate, 9 TL, 1 GL, 2 FL; sold, Mar. 1859, Oct. 1875, $210
Mar. 1868	Guadalupe	320	Mary paid $300, James W. Nichols, Nichols Survey; sold, Jan. 1869–Oct. 1871, $700
Nov. 1881	Kimble	182 6/7	Mary's share of Johnson Day estate, Kimble County; sold, Nov. 1881, $90

Sources: John W. Nichols, Thomas Jackson, Land Grant Search, TGLO: Deeds, bk. N, 598, Gonzales County, CC; Deeds, bk. A, 202, 266, 278, 298; bk. B, 286, 298, 312; bk. C, 604; bk. D, 125, 202, 404, 407; bk. E, 259; bk. F, 31, Gonzales County, CC; Deeds, bk. A, 107, 139; bk. B, 15, 62–63, 348, 655, 716, 774; bk. C, 136, 568–71; bk. D, 381, 397, 822; bk. E, 56, 562, 566, 571; bk. F, 226, 306, 388–89, 438, 441, 499; bk. G, 159, 348, 387, 551; bk. H, 117, 119, 138–39, 257; bk. I, 258; bk. J, 345-46, 397–99, 441, 471; bk. N, 219; bk. S, 183, Guadalupe County, CC; TR, 1845–54, TAC, Guadalupe County, TSLA; Mortgage bk. A, 189; bk. B, 59, 254, Guadalupe County, CC; DCM, bk. E, 69, 92, 288, Guadalupe County DC; Deeds, bk. A, 477, Kimble County CC.
Note: TL: town lot, GL: garden lot; FL: farm lot; TML: timber lot

As some of the initial Seguin settlers, Mary and John paid $126 for ten town, three garden, three farm, and two timber lots, and over the next twenty years obtained another twelve town, six garden, three farm, and three timber lots (table 9.6). The bulk of the latter became the focus of a dispute with James Campbell, who was killed in 1840. They contended that Campbell sold them these lots, but the administrator of Campbell's estate disagreed, and after eighteen years in the district court, the matter was settled in favor of the Nicholses. Mary and John also invested $130 in other town lots but by 1859 had sold most of their Seguin property, earning about $750. Like the Kings, Mary and John were small-time speculators, supplementing their income, but they were also the first among Sarah Hembree Day's family to acquire a homesite on San Geronimo Creek east of Seguin. In February 1843, for just one dollar at a sheriff's sale, they bought fifty acres in the Sowell Survey (see map 8.1, table 9.6). The following year they purchased more acreage and eventually owned a 255-acre homestead. Like their in-laws, they used their land to raise livestock. Moreover, their decision to settle on San Geronimo Creek and encourage their relatives to follow contributed to family cohesion. Mary and John continued to invest in real estate with moderate success. Beginning in 1848 they purchased parcels near Mill Creek totaling 911 acres for $1,100 and sold most of it for $1,650. John also joined two other locals in buying 4,400 acres in the Joseph D. Clements Survey (see map 8.1). The trio paid $300 for the tract, which they sold for $2,000 five years later; John netted $566. With their land sales, less the loss for the fraudulent Jackson bounty, Mary and John had total real estate profits of about $2,000.[16]

Like his two brothers-in-law, Nichols and King, James Milford Day applied for a single-man's headright despite being eligible for that of a married man. Michael Erskine paid thirty dollars for the 640-acre writ and sold it for $100 to a recently retired local district judge and attorney, William E. Jones, who settled on the platted parcel on the edge of the Texas frontier along Curry Creek. Separately in 1851, Guadalupe County representative Thomas H. Duggan filed a petition on behalf of Day, who had been wounded in the 1839 Vicente Córdova raid. The petition for 4,428 acres was approved and Day sold it to Morgan C. Hamilton for $480, who also acquired fifty-two certificates totaling 25,000 acres. Hamilton made a profit of thirty dollars by selling the certificate to Middleton T. Johnson, who also purchased forty such certificates (table 9.7). The tract was finally surveyed on the Rio Grande, thirty-nine miles southeast of El Paso. Clearly, for Day cash in hand was of more use than remote acreage. Fortunately, opportunists were willing to give cash for a certificate, and Erskine and Hamilton were typical speculators. Day's dealing in certificates represented a change in economic focus for him. Before the death of his first wife, Hannah, in September 1846, he invested only in lots within Seguin. As an original settler he received ten town, three garden, three farm, and two timber lots, which over time he sold, and he also bought and sold other town property, earning a profit of nearly $400 (table 9.7). After marrying Margaret Susan Hudson, Day in 1850 moved to a 70-acre tract on San Geronimo Creek, near the Nicholses and Brills (see map 8.1). Five years later, wanting space to develop their cattle herd and after having earned $3,400 from land sales in Guadalupe County, Susan and James Milford Day moved fifty miles from Seguin to a 210-acre ranch adjacent to the Callahans on the Rio Blanco.[17]

When James Hughes Callahan returned to Texas in April 1837, land was a powerful lure. He claimed his first warrant for 640 acres in Houston on December 29, 1837 (table 9.8). The site that he chose for his grant showed that he had become familiar with the area between Houston and Gonzales. His plot was a half mile south of the intersection of two thoroughfares—the Old Bahia Road to Goliad and the Gonzales road linking Houston to San Antonio. It was surveyed in August 1838 and patented three years later. There is no evidence that he lived there; however, if he did, it was in the path of the invading Comanches during the Linnville Raid of August 1840. In 1845 Callahan sold 320 acres to Alsey Miller for $300, and two years later he sold the other half for an unknown sum to A. W. G. Davis (table 9.9). Thus, Callahan was among the majority of veterans who had their property surveyed. By patenting his bounty and retaining it for some years, he earned several hundred dollars profit.[18]

Callahan was also eligible for a single man's first-class headright of 1,476 acres because he had arrived before the Texas Declaration of Independence. In the spring of 1838, he claimed this warrant from the Brazoria County land commission and sold it to Benjamin C. Franklin for an unknown price (table 9.8). Franklin did not have the property surveyed until 1849, when he discovered that he had lost Callahan's certificate. To minimize fraud, state law required him to advertise the misplaced writ in a newspaper. When no one objected, he obtained a duplicate certificate and in 1850 located a parcel along the Colorado River near Columbus. However, the surveyor made an error and platted the acreage on an existing deed, so the General Land Office voided Franklin's survey and returned the warrant. In 1851, New Orleans merchant and small-scale land speculator Erastus H. Harris paid

Table 9.7. Land transactions in Texas by James M. Day and his wives

Date	*County*	*Acres*	*Remarks*
Dec. 1851	El Paso	4,428	Tex. Legislature, relief for James M. Day; sold certificate, $400
Nov. 1838	Kendall	640	Texas General Land Office; arrived in Texas before Feb. 1838; sold, June 1845, $30
Aug. 1838	Gonzales		Seguin, paid $105, 10 TL, 3 GL, 3 FL, 2 TML; sold Nov. 1839–June 1875, $458
Sept. 1840	Gonzales		Seguin, paid $25, 1 FL; sold, July 1847, $33
Jan. 1841	Gonzales		Seguin, paid $25, 1 TML; sold, Oct. 1855, $250
July 1843	Gonzales		Seguin, paid $60, 1 TL; sold, Apr. 1846, $60
July 1845	Gonzales		Seguin, paid $50, 1 GL; sold Sept. 1850, $400
Aug. 1845	Gonzales		Seguin, paid $100, 1 GL, 1 FL; sold, Sept. 1850, $400
Nov. 1847	Guadalupe		Seguin, paid $20, 1 TL; sold, Aug. 1851, $20
Oct. 1850	Guadalupe	640	Paid $400, J. G. King Survey; sold, Sept. 1852, $700
Sept. 1852	Guadalupe	70	Paid $630, San Geronimo Creek; sold, Dec. 1855, $2,000
Dec. 1855	Guadalupe		Seguin, paid $16, 2/237 interest, Sons of Temperance Building; sold, Oct. 1861, $5
Nov. 1865	Guadalupe	320	Paid $650, Estell [Estill] pre-emption grant; sold Dec. 1866, $700
1855	Comal	201	201 acres, north bank of Rio Blanco; sale likely occurred in late 1855
June 1857	Comal		Pittsburg, paid $26, 1 TL; no record found for when Day sold this lot
Aug. 1857	Kimble	640	Paid $300, John Page Survey; sold February 1860, $640
Apr. 1858	Kendall	320	Paid $100, John M. Lonis for certificate; sold half interest, $100, Sept. 1858; uncertain when or if Day sold remaining half interest
unknown	Blanco		Blanco, paid unknown amount, 1 TL; sold to brother-in-law Pharr, Nov. 1871, $15
Apr. 1879	Kimble	182 6/7	J. M Day's share of Johnson Day estate, sold to son W. J. Day, Apr. 1879, $250
Sept. 1879	Blanco	4	Paid $5; sold, Nov. 1882, $100

Sources: James M. Day, Morgan Hamilton, M. T. Johnson, Land Grant Search, TGLO; Gammel, *Laws*, 3:1047; Deeds, bk. B, 297, 400; bk. C, 299, 581; bk. D, 53, 156, 406–7; bk. F, 92, Gonzales County, CC; TR, 1845, TAC, Gonzales County, TSLA; Marriages, bk. A, 5, Guadalupe County, CC; Deeds, bk. GT, 300, 434; bk. A1, 20, 28; bk. B1, 9,173; bk. B, 73, 228; bk. C, 322, 327; bk. D, 66, 245, 453–54, 458, 563; bk. F, 422, 429; bk. I, 202; bk. N, 129, Guadalupe County, CC; Deeds, bk. E, 645, Comal County, CC; TR, 1846–54, TAC, Guadalupe County, TSLA; PM, bk. C, 212–14, Comal County, CC; PL, bk. H, 223–27, Comal County, CC; Deeds, bk. 3, p. 382, bk. A, 467, Kimble County, CC; Deeds, bk. 1, p. 569; bk. 6, p. 412, Blanco County, CC.
Note: TL: town lot; GL: garden lot; FL: farm lot; TML: timber lot

Table 9.8. James Hughes Callahan records at Texas General Land Office (TGLO)

Date	*Grant type*	*Acres*	*County*	*Remarks*
Aug. 1838	Milan 1st class	1,476	Erath	Arrived in Texas before Mar. 2, 1836; sold (unknown amount) bounty to B. C. Franklin
Dec. 1837	Gonzales bounty	640	Gonzales	For participation in Texas Revolution; surveyed, 1839
May 1839	Bexar donation	640	Kimble	For participation in Texas Revolution
Nov. 1838	Bexar 2nd class	640	Kimble	To Ira Fuller; in Texas before Sept. 1836; Fuller gave Callahan 213 acres for arranging a survey; surveyed, 1841
June 1838	Bexar 1st class	3,498	Kimble	George Kimble's heirs; in Texas, 1831. For this and the next two Kimble entries, Callahan paid $125 to Prudence Kimble, George's wife, and she gave Callahan 1,749 acres to have land surveyed
Dec. 1838	Bexar bounty	640	Kimble	George Kimble's heirs, for his death at Alamo; Callahan received 320 acres
Dec. 1838	Bexar bounty	1,960	Kimble	George Kimble's heirs, for his service in Texas Army and death at Alamo; Callahan received 980 acres
May 1839	Bexar 1st class	1,476	Kimble	To Sion Green, Georgia Battalion; Callahan arranged survey for 492 acres
Feb. 1846	Bexar bounty	320	Kimble	To Henry Redfield, service in Texas Army, Feb.–Mar. 1836; certificate purchased by Callahan on unknown date for unknown amount
July 1858	Court of Claims	—	—	Application by heirs of Callahan for donation and bounty awards; invalid

Sources: Gammel, *Laws*, 1:925–26, 951–54, 982–83, 1094, 1134, 1324, 1367–68; T. Miller, *Bounty and Donation*, 24–27, 38, 40, 42–43, 887; James Callahan, Land Grant Search, TGLO; Deeds, bk. C, 343–44; bk. F, 170–71, Gonzales County, CC; Deeds, bk. A, 29–30, Lavaca County, CC; T. Miller, *Public Lands*, 30–31; *TTR*, June 3, 1846, Aug. 23, 1849.

Note: George Kimble's heirs received one league (4,428 acres) and one labor (177 acres) for a total of 4,605 acres. Kimble had previously received one-fourth of a league (1,107 acres) so the land board concluded the heirs were due an additional 3,498 acres. Misspelled Kimbill in the TGLO documents.

Table 9.9. Land bought and sold by James Hughes Callahan in Brazoria, Gonzales, Guadalupe, Lavaca, and Caldwell Counties

Date	*County*	*Acres/TL*	*Remarks*
June 1839	Brazoria	1 TL	Paid $7 at sheriff's sale, Velasco; no sale record found
July 1839	Gonzales	492	Paid $256 for undivided ⅓ of 1,476 acres on Plum Creek; Dec. 1845 sold 246 acres for $130; Jan. 1847 sold the remaining 246 acres for $500
Jan. 1841–Mar. 1848	Gonzales / Guadalupe	8 TLs	Paid $115 for 8 TLs in Seguin; from July 1841 through Oct. 1851 sold these 8 TLs for $125
Aug. 1841	Gonzales / Lavaca	640	Surveyed Bounty Claim (see Table 9.8); Oct. 1845 sold 320 acres for $300; Jan. 1847 sold the remaining 320 acres for an unknown amount
Oct. 1842; Mar. 1845	Gonzales / Caldwell	650	John Henry Survey; for 300 acres Callahan build a $250 house and paid an extra $200; later paid $525 for an additional 350 acres; Apr. 1853 sold 100 acres for $1000; Dec. 1853 sold 250 acres for $410; Jan. 1854 sold 300 acres for $4000
Aug. 1846	Guadalupe	320	J. R. King Survey; paid $700; Jan. 1847 sold for $400
Sept. 1846	Guadalupe	175	Benjamin Fuqua Survey on Geronimo Creek; paid $800 (cash $364 plus a $436 note at 10 percent); no sale record found
Dec. 1846	Guadalupe	1 TL	Callahan et al., trustees for the Seguin Methodist Church, paid $10
Mar. 1847	Guadalupe	300	Robert Hall Survey; paid $200; Apr. 1847 sold 100 acres for $100; no sale record found for the remaining 200 acres
Aug. 1848	Guadalupe	8	Callahan et al., trustees, Methodist Church campground, south bank of San Marcos River, paid $50
Jan. 1849	Guadalupe	160	R. Smith Survey, York Creek, paid unknow amount, deal voided when, J. Peterson, husband of the seller, refused to provide a deed
Jan. 1851	Caldwell	68¼	Miles Dike Survey, San Marcos River, paid $100; Aug. 1851 sold for $75
June 1851	Guadalupe	300	R. Smith Survey, York Creek, paid $300; Sept. 1852 sold for $600
June 1851	Caldwell	4	John Henry Survey, Callahan et al., school trustees for academy, paid $1
Feb. 1852	Caldwell	177	M. Caldwell Labor Survey on Seals Creek, paid $265; Sept. 1852 sold 100 acres for $27 and a $110 note, buyer defaulted; May 1853 sold 177 acres for $265
Feb. 1852	Caldwell	400	M. G. Dikes Survey, paid $300; Apr. 1854 sold 100 acres for $210 and a $200 note due in Jan. 1856; no sale record found for the remaining 300 acres

Sources: Deeds, bk. C, 330; bk. D, 403–4, Brazoria County, CC; Deeds, bk. A, 240–42, 280–81; bk. B, 394–95; bk. C, 8, 343, 349–50, 463–64; bk. D, 197–98; bk. E, 201–2; bk. F, 170, 407–8, Gonzales County, CC; Deeds, bk. A, 10–12, 23–24, 34–35, 57–60; bk. B. 16–17, 67–68, 81–82, 147–48, 682–84; bk. C, 50–51, 225–26, 639–40; bk. D, 72–73, 602, Guadalupe County, CC; Deeds, bk. A, 29, Lavaca County, CC; Deeds, bk. A, 615–16, 675; bk. B, 89, 224–25, 684–85; bk. C, 42, 70–71, 302, 352, 648; bk. D, 315, 323–24, 338, Caldwell County, CC; TR, 1848, 1852, TAC, Caldwell County, TSLA.

Note: TL: town lot

Franklin $147, adding the Callahan grant to his seven other certificates. A few months later, Harris's writs were sold to land developer Richard B. Kimball for $1,120, an average of $140 each. Kimball was a business partner of Jacob R. De Cordova, a vocal promoter of Texas land. Kimball purchased many certificates and in 1850 surveyed 27,000 acres along the Brazos River, ninety miles northwest of Waco. English naval officer Sir Edward Belcher brought a group of English tradesmen and their families to settle on Kimball's property as the Colony of Kent. Excited about his seemingly successful enterprise, Kimball started another development project, adding Callahan's warrant to others for a total of about 60,000 acres. He arranged for the surveys to be platted seventeen miles northwest of the Colony of Kent on the headwaters of the Paluxy River. This tract was called Kimball Block, and Kimball sold land there for one to two dollars per acre. Meanwhile, stranded without tools and living in huts, many Colony of Kent immigrants died, and the remainder fled. Kimball's failed Colony of Kent doomed his second project. It was years before a settler bought any of the Callahan survey in the Kimball Block.[19]

Callahan meanwhile focused on his own land development project on the upper Llano River. On May 13, 1838, he swore to the Brazoria County land commission that Sion D. Green had fought with the Georgia Battalion and was eligible for a 1,476-acre donation (table 9.8). Green gave him 492 acres in exchange for Callahan arranging a survey. Callahan had Green's land surveyed on the Llano where he and McCulloch's Rangers had skirmished with Comanches months earlier (map 9.1). In 1846, Callahan convinced his brother William to buy his share of Green's survey, but William never completed the deal. On May 1, 1839, Callahan claimed a 640-acre donation grant, which he also located on the Llano. Ira Fuller of Fort Bend County agreed to give him one-third of his 640-acre second-class headright when Callahan arranged for the parcel to be surveyed; Callahan again located this tract on the Llano. Prudence Hardin Nash Kimble Holdridge provided even more property. Her second husband, George Kimble, died at the Alamo, and his heirs were entitled to 6,098 acres. Callahan paid $125 to Prudence, who agreed to give him one-half of each of her four parcels of land if he had them surveyed. When he bought a certificate for 320 acres from Texas veteran Henry P. Redfield, Callahan had a total of 4,814 acres located on the upper Llano (map 9.1, tables 9.8, 9.10).[20]

As noted earlier, Callahan was very familiar with the upper Llano, having participated in the April 1841 fight there (see map 5.2). After the skirmish he

Table 9.10. Land sold by James Hughes Callahan in Kimble County

Date	*Acres*	*$ value*	*Remarks*
May 1846	492	300	Callahan pledged to sell Green Survey to William Callahan, his brother; sale never completed
June 1847	640	320	Callahan Survey to Bruce Campbell, 6-month note
Nov. 1847	—	—	2-year extension Campbell note; defaulted
Feb. 1852	640	640	To Wm. Moore, Callahan Survey
May 1851	213	50	To H. G. Henderson, Fuller Survey
Aug. 1851	450	400	To William R. Conner, first-choice rights for 450 acres from any Kimble Survey
unknown	300	unknown	To John R. Frances (Francis), second-choice rights for 300 acres from any Kimble Survey
May 1852	2,279	500	To Henry E. McCulloch, the remaining acres from the four Kimble Surveys

Sources: Deeds, bk. O2, 347–48; bk. P1, 338–39, Bexar County, CC; Deeds, bk. 3, pp. 200–201, 267–68; bk. 18, pp. 519–21, Kimble County, CC; Deeds, bk. B, 194, 247, Guadalupe County, CC; Deeds, bk. B, 405; bk. F, 186, Gillespie County, CC.

had walked the area and identified locations that suited him. During the fall of 1841, he arranged for McCulloch to survey the land and, to ensure the best would be his, led his rangers there and pointed out the tracts. The land lay at the junction of the north and south forks of the Llano, where rocky but fertile bottomland was bounded by abundant water (map 9.1, table 9.10). Settling titles proved more troublesome. Fuller did not file his documents until 1850, while Holdridge created even more complications. She and Callahan held an undivided interest in each plot, requiring both to agree before any land could be transferred. Meanwhile, she was divorcing her third husband, so nothing could be done until that was final. She then remarried, creating more delays since she had to obtain her new husband's consent for any settlements. By 1849 Callahan was so exasperated he filed suit in the Gonzales County district court, which claimed that it had no jurisdiction. Nevertheless, his legal action prompted Holdridge and her children to settle the issue, and in 1850 they agreed on a division.[21]

The dealings with Holdridge caused Callahan to reconsider his vision, or maybe he saw another opportunity. In any case, by 1847 he began to sell his holdings on the upper Llano (map 9.1). In June he sold his 640-acre donation grant to Bruce Campbell, who signed a promissory note for $320, but Campbell defaulted even after an extension. However, this benefitted

Callahan as two years later he sold the property for $640 (table 9.10). After Fuller filed his documents, Callahan sold his one-third interest to Guadalupe County Judge H. G. Henderson for $50. After Callahan and Holdridge's heirs signed a final agreement, he sold 750 of his 3,049 acres, earning several hundred dollars, and in 1852 he received $500 from Henry E. McCulloch for the remainder. This episode illustrates the difficulties of buying certificates and having a tract surveyed and patented. What Callahan's plans were for this land are unknown, but considering the number of acres, he must have had something in mind. If he only acquired the tracts as an investment, he made a profit of nearly $1,600. Alternately, his vision may have included a town surrounded by farms and ranches. If so, he underestimated the threat of Indian raids; it was not until well after the Civil War that settlers populated the upper Llano.[22]

Callahan also acquired substantial property elsewhere in Texas. Before settling in Seguin, he bought a town lot in Velasco and land on Plum Creek (see map 8.1, table 9.9). His decision to relocate to Seguin was confirmed when he bought five town lots there and later purchased a one-acre garden and a five-acre timber lot. The latter was ideally situated since it backed up to Walnut Creek; he built a house there, which became his first home with Sarah Medissa. Over the following decade, they acquired three more town lots, bringing their total to eight at a cost of $115; they eventually made a meager profit of ten dollars on these properties. During this time, Callahan was also one of the trustees who purchased a lot where the Methodist church was built. Starting a trend for their family, the Callahans next moved to Geronimo Creek, where they bought 795 acres at the spot still known as Callahan Crossing (see map 8.1, table 9.9), but another opportunity arose. The founder of Seguin, Joseph S. Martin, had bought land on the San Marcos River and contracted Callahan to build a house for him there. In addition, Martin offered Callahan 300 acres for $450. Martin's vision of a new village must have been appealing; Callahan bought another 350 acres and in 1848 moved to what would become Prairie Lea, building his own home a half mile east of the river on what is today Callihan Road along Callahan Creek (see map 8.1). Callahan expanded his holdings when he obtained 300 acres on York Creek across the San Marcos River in Guadalupe County. By 1851, the Callahans were settled in Prairie Lea, with 950 acres and a mercantile store. Callahan joined eight other men to buy land for a Methodist campground (see map 8.1) and was instrumental in arranging support for the new Prairie Lea Academy. The Callahans did well in Prairie Lea; their wealth increased from $1,825 at marriage to $9,235 in 1852, placing them within the top 10 percent of Caldwell County residents. Thus, by 1853 the economic future for Sarah and James looked promising.[23]

The Callahans' success reflected that of both the state and their family. In 1847, two years after annexation, the state's population was 147,000, increasing to 212,000 by 1850 and 604,000 in 1860. The army and migrants to California injected much cash into the economy and created a greater demand for goods, services, and land. The total wealth of Sarah Hembree Day's extended family grew from $985 in 1843 to $18,749 in 1854, an eighteen-fold increase. This affluence depended largely on cattle, as their herds grew from none in 1843 to 534 head in 1854. During the same time, their land holdings grew from 2,570 to 7,365 acres, while they bought and sold almost 10,000 acres and nearly seventy-five town lots. One component of this growth was a new breed of developers, prominent among whom was Jacob R. De Cordova. He had organized supplies for the Texas Revolution in New Orleans, then after independence settled in Galveston and Houston, whence he was elected to the legislature. Over the years, De Cordova bought Texas certificates, accumulating claims to nearly one million acres, and he and his brother established a flourishing business. His most innovative investment was near Seguin. In 1831 Antonio María Esnaurrizar received an eleven-league (48,620 acres) tract; it occupied parts of Guadalupe, Hays, and Comal Counties. De Cordova, with three San Antonio businessmen, subdivided this to be sold in parcels ranging from 85 to 640 acres. He became the manager and built a large house there. To promote the project, he made numerous trips around Texas and the United States and advertised in his brother's Austin newspaper, the *South-Western American*. As sales progressed, the tract size decreased to as few as seven acres. De Cordova's approach caught the attention of many, including Callahan and William E. Jones.[24]

In 1845, expecting more immigrants, Texas leaders offered additional public lands though preemption grants to any resident. Homesteaders could live on an unsurveyed 320-acre plot, make improvements, and after three years obtain a deed for $160. In 1854 the offer became 160 acres at no cost. These terms were more attractive than those offered for public land by the United States. The problem in Texas was that, by 1845, settlers had been claiming public lands for more than two decades. Most property east of a line from Dallas to San Antonio to Corpus Christi had been distributed, and even beyond that much of the choice bottomland had been claimed. Thus, while the terms were generous, the quality of public land was not ideal. However, one section not far from San Antonio was desirable and available—the Rio Blanco valley.[25]

Callahan first visited the Rio Blanco valley in 1840 and 1841. The area lies between the Pedernales and Colorado Rivers to the north and the Guadalupe to the south. The Rio Blanco originates at three powerful springs in northeast Kendall County and flows southeast for forty-five miles as Martin's Fork until it meets the Little Blanco River, which begins in eastern Kendall County. The two branches join to form the Rio Blanco (known today as the Blanco River), which flows into the San Marcos River east of San Marcos. Spanish explorers first reached the white limestone banks in 1721 and gave the river its name, and by 1835 a few league-sized surveys had been platted as part of Benjamin Milam's colony. Callahan first crossed the valley with the 1840 expedition led by Maj. George T. Howard and was there again in the 1841 spring and fall campaigns under McCulloch. During his spring 1841 trek, the prairie grasses were green and near their maximum height and flowers appeared resplendent in yellow, red, pink, and blue. While he admired the lush valleys, rolling hills, and fertile bottomlands, most memorable to Callahan was the tall prairie grass, which he later told William Trainer touched "the spurs on a man riding a horse." The area made a deep impression on him, and by 1853 he had a plan to develop land there.[26]

Callahan was influenced by a pattern of other emerging settlements dotting the region. After New Braunfels was founded in 1845, German immigrants moved up the Guadalupe River valley for fifty miles, creating several villages, including the communalist Bettina community and the prospering town of Fredericksburg at the headwaters of the Pedernales River. While a few stopped in the Rio Blanco valley, it remained largely unoccupied. By 1849 Guadalupe County leaders realized the economic value of Fredericksburg and they decided to link Seguin and Fredericksburg by a road that integrated into a larger network connecting Lavaca on the coast with El Paso. The Rio Blanco and the Little Blanco River lay in the direct path of this proposed road, making the vacant land more desirable. About thirty miles upstream from New Braunfels, Curry Creek joins the Guadalupe (map 9.2). In 1847, Bastrop County resident Samuel B. Patton built the first house along Curry Creek and soon other families moved there, including retired Guadalupe County district judge William E. Jones and sheep rancher and *New Orleans Picayune* co-owner, George W. Kendall. By 1853, Curry Creek was the focus of a community of one hundred residents stretching six miles

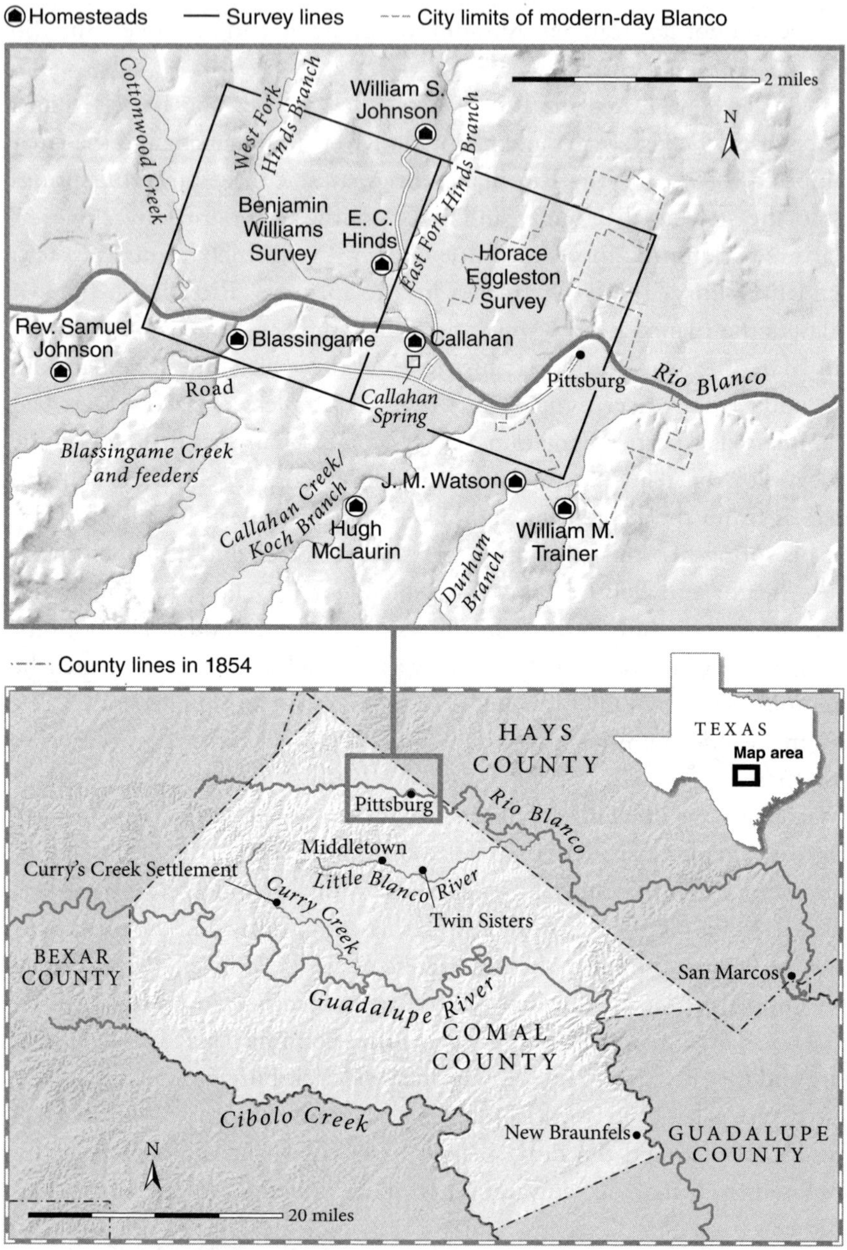

Map 9.2. Location of the Eggleston and Williams Surveys, Rio Blanco, Little Blanco River, Curry Creek, and the villages of Pittsburg, Curry's Creek settlement, Middletown, and Twin Sisters, 1855. Map by Carol Zuber-Mallison.

along its banks. Sawmills and gristmills buzzed, while fields of cotton and grain were attended by two dozen slaves.[27]

Prior to settling on Curry Creek, Jones had been a deputy surveyor for Comal County and surveyed several plots before buying bounty warrants, one being the 640-acre certificate awarded to James Milford Day. Jones later surveyed several other parcels along Curry Creek and in the valleys of the Rio Blanco and Little Blanco River. Thus, he was very familiar with local property owners and vacant land. Because both men were born and raised in Jackson County, Georgia, where they lived only a mile apart, Callahan and Jones may have known each other there, but in Gonzales County they developed a friendship and a mutual interest in land development. The best property had been claimed on Curry Creek, but they had two other good choices—the Rio Blanco and Little Blanco. Except for a few one-league plots, most land on the Little Blanco was being surveyed into preemption grants of 320 acres. However, on the most desirable portion of the Rio Blanco were five adjacent one-league surveys that were centrally located, being just thirty to forty miles from Austin, San Antonio, San Marcos, New Braunfels, and Fredericksburg. Before long, Callahan focused on two one-league parcels, the Benjamin Williams and Horace Eggleston Surveys (map 9.2). Neither had been subdivided and both had fertile river bottom grassland, a spring-fed creek, and lots of pecan and oak trees. Callahan understood the ownership of each to be uncomplicated, which proved to be true for the Williams land but not for the Eggleston tract. Callahan's plan required capital, so he liquidated his property holdings to accumulate cash. The timing of this suggests that he began planning this venture in 1852, when he made the first of many land sales, including property on the Llano River (table 9.9). All told, over two years he collected nearly $6,800 to invest in his new project on the Blanco.[28]

The original settlers on this portion of the Rio Blanco were members of the Milam Colony, but the fifty-two colonists had been insufficient to satisfy Milam's contract with the Mexican government. However, despite the contract's cancellation, in 1835 Mexican authorities gave the colonists their promised land, so the property was surveyed and logged in the records of Austin's Colony. The Williams and Eggleston surveys had remained vacant since then. Upon arriving in Texas, Horace Eggleston had settled in Gonzales, where he opened a store but left during the Texas Revolution. He and his wife, the former Sarah Ann Ponton, returned to Gonzales by the mid-1840s, settling on land that she had inherited. At the time of the 1835 survey,

Benjamin Williams was living in Austin's Colony. When hostilities erupted in the fall of 1835, he volunteered for the Texas army and was discharged on January 20, 1836, when he joined his family in the Runaway Scrape. He never returned to Texas and in 1837, using a Texas agent, he advertised the sale of half of his league on the Rio Blanco, having previously sold the other half.[29]

Purchasing the Williams Survey was straightforward, though the deed passed through the hands of several speculators before reaching Callahan (map 9.2). Half was sold to Fort Bend merchant Robert E. Handy, who sold it to his business partner, William Lusk. Acting as an agent for New York speculator William S. Pierson Jr., Swante Swenson bought it for $276 in 1849. Though the date is uncertain, Texas jurist and legislator Robert M. Williamson acquired part of this half of the Williams Survey and in 1850 sold it for $1,000 to Texas Supreme Court Justice John Hemphill. Thus, by 1852, Pierson and Hemphill owned undivided interests in one-half of the Williams Survey. In the meantime, in May 1837, Williams sold the other half of his league to William Houston, younger brother of Sam Houston, president of the Republic. Three years later Jabez Dean bought Houston's half for $2,000. By the time Callahan was considering land on the Blanco, Dean also owned half of the Eggleston Survey. In 1853, Callahan paid Hemphill $500 for his part of the Williams Survey, and he gave Pierson a down payment of $554 and two notes totaling $2,150 for his share. Callahan then enlisted Dean as a partner in his development plan. Dean agreed to take the western half of the Williams Survey, leaving Callahan the eastern half, which included the Rio Blanco and a spring-fed creek. At the same time, Dean gave Callahan 300 acres in the southwest corner of the Eggleston Survey (map 9.2).[30]

Callahan and Dean were therefore partners by 1853, but how they first met is not clear. In the fall of 1846, Dean told land commissioners in Washington County that he arrived in Texas before 1842. He may have settled in Texas during 1841, since he appears on the 1840 census in Davidson County, Tennessee, and then in July 1841 appears on a ship's manifest for a trip from Texas to New Orleans. However, he could have visited Texas earlier since before 1837 he loaned money to the Texas government and in March 1838 he sold land in Washington County. Dean obviously had an interest in Texas, and in 1841 he was appointed as the agent for the Nashville Texas Emigrant Society. He and his family settled on a 500-acre farm in Washington County, where, as the Society's representative, he became engaged in land speculation. Although he sold his 1,280-acre warrant, during the early 1840s he bought six leagues (26,568 acres) in Fayette, Matagorda, Fort Bend, Lavaca, and Houston Counties for $27,000.

He must have financed these purchases with the Society's money since in the 1850 census he claimed he was a mechanic with an estate valued at $2,000.[31]

When the Rio Blanco deed transactions were completed in the spring of 1853, Callahan resigned his seat on the Caldwell County commissioners court and moved his family there. He made several trips, driving livestock, hauling building materials, and employing local hands to help build his house. People first learned about the Callahans' plan to establish a town when the July 9, 1853, *South-Western American* reported it was destined to be "one of the most thriving settlements in the upper country." H. R. Crawford noted in the *Texas State Gazette* that the road from Seguin to Fredericksburg went through the "Callahan settlement on the Blanco." Though a mere boy, Andrew J. Sowell recalled his family's 1853 trip to the Rio Blanco over the rugged Devil's Backbone road. Callahan's final move must have required several wagons, considering his well-established household in Prairie Lea. At any rate, the seven Callahans—James, Sarah, and their children Wesley Hughes, James Sanford, Josiah Asbury, Armiseda Catherine, and William—were the first family to settle on the upper Rio Blanco.[32]

The Rio Blanco valley was "wild and beautiful looking," according to Sowell. The clear river teemed with fish, the region was full of deer, bear and turkey, and there were also wild bees. Given the local food sources, the only supplies needed, according to Sowell, were "flour, meal, coffee, tobacco," but acquiring those items involved a two-day round trip to San Marcos. Sarah and James chose for their homesite a wide, level space in the most fertile area, bounded on the east by a spring-fed stream, later called Callahan Creek. The spring, the most productive along the Blanco, spewed volumes of cold water from six underground fountains, forming a pond sixty yards long and twenty-five yards wide. The water flowed north from the pond for two hundred yards along a narrow channel before it joined the Rio Blanco. Under a canopy of pecan trees, ten yards west of this brook, the Callahans built a four-room clapboard house.[33]

Even while settling his family, Callahan remained busy with his development project. Sowell recalled that almost immediately there was an exodus from Guadalupe County to the Rio Blanco area. The Sowells and Turners settled six miles north of Callahan on Cypress Creek, another Rio Blanco tributary. Callahan promoted the valley as ideal for horse ranching, causing the William N. Trainer family of Caldwell County to move to Flat Creek, four miles east of the Williams Survey. The Lindemann family came from New Braunfels, and Hugh McLaurin from Caldwell County occupied a

320-acre preemption grant. By 1854, the Rio Blanco valley was attracting an increasing number of immigrants, including other families settling on preemption grants.[34]

Eli Clemmons Hinds, Callahan's Caldwell County neighbor and cousin of his brother-in-law Eli S. Hankins, bought 556 acres in the Williams Survey, paying Callahan $700 for his first sale (map 9.2). The Hinds family constructed a log cabin on the banks of a brook they named Hinds Creek. According to their family biographer, they were on the Rio Blanco by the end of 1852. Hinds, known as Clem, and his wife, Catherine, were the type of settlers that Callahan wanted on the Rio Blanco. Both came from families that had arrived in DeWitt's Colony, survived the Republic, and thrived in the years after annexation. Clem inherited part of his father's headright and received a bounty of 640 acres, both on Plum Creek. He fought with McCulloch's Rangers in April 1841, where he met Callahan for the first time. During the Adrian Woll invasion, Clem was a scout under Jack Hays. On November 7, 1844, he married Catherine, the daughter of John McCoy Jr., who also lived on Plum Creek. The Callahans and Hinds became friends in Prairie Lea, and when the opportunity arose to move to the Blanco, Clem and Catherine followed Sarah and James.[35]

On February 1, 1854, Callahan made his second land sale. For $525 Mary and Woodson Blassingame purchased a 177-acre plot in the south section of the Williams Survey (map 9.2). This parcel fronted on the Blanco and was bisected by a spring-fed stream that was known as Blassingame Creek. Woodson and Mary, who lived in Arkansas at the time, authorized their son Thomas Blassingame and son-in-law W. K. Holmes to negotiate and sign the deal; they made a $160 down payment and signed a two-year note. In 1853 one of the two Blassingame sons, who lived in Hays County, was a survey chainman for William E. Jones and Andrew M. Lindsey and must have recognized the potential of Callahan's venture. Thus, according to the family oral tradition, Mary and Woodson were encouraged to join their children in Texas. Callahan's cash flow had been boosted by the sale of his land in Caldwell and Guadalupe Counties, and he had paid his note to Pierson. For the Williams Survey parcels he had collected $860 in cash, and he had the promise of another $365 within two years. Yet this was not enough to realize his grand vision in creating a community. He needed more capital, so he entered into a partnership with five men, and when Michael Erskine presented him with a chance to increase his income substantially with a single cattle drive, he eagerly accepted.[36]

CHAPTER 10

Erskine Cattle Drive to California, 1854

"The cattle stompeded last night"

A pregnant Sarah Medissa Callahan stoked the fireplace on the cool morning of April 20, 1854, as she and her mother began preparing breakfast for their large family. It was James's last morning before driving Michael H. Erskine's cattle to California. Breakfast over, he strapped on his two six-shooters and, taking his rifle and shotgun, walked out on the porch to his saddled horse. Riding to Seguin's market square, James met his brothers-in-law John W. Nichols and Augustus Pharr and stepped into his lawyer's office to have his will witnessed and signed. He then rode to *El Capote* Ranch, where he joined thc other drivers. He would be paid $1,500 for leading the cattle drive, about one dollar per mile on a trek he anticipated lasting six months.[1]

By the late 1700s, cattle raising in Texas was well established in the lower Guadalupe and San Antonio River valleys, with the livestock often driven south into Mexico. The first cattle drive to the east took place during the American Revolution, when the Spanish supported the war against Britain. After Texas won its independence from Mexico, drives to New Orleans from the lower Guadalupe became common, and ambitious Texans began considering taking herds west to the burgeoning California markets. In 1854, nearly twenty-five herds totaling almost 15,000 head were driven 1,600 miles from Texas to Los Angeles. Erskine, a wealthy Guadalupe River Basin rancher, organized a herd of almost 1,100 longhorns and hired Callahan as his trail boss. Needing money for his land development project, Callahan embraced the opportunity. Erskine's diary of the expedition recorded Callahan's expertise in handling men and cattle, navigating the harsh terrain, and coping with Indians, factors that contributed greatly to making Erskine's one of the most successful Texas cattle drives in 1854.[2]

Callahan traveled through the territory acquired by the United States after the Mexican-American War. The army surveyed several roads from Kansas to California, and Capt. Philip St. George Cooke blazed his route southwest from Doña Ana on the Rio Grande in New Mexico to the San Pedro River valley in Mexico, then north to Tucson, and on to the Gila River and Yuma and then across the desert to San Diego and Los Angeles. Cooke's road deviated into Mexican territory, but army engineers reported it was the best route for a southern railroad to California. Ambassador James Gadsden, a railroad investor, convinced Mexico to sell the territory for $10 million. Thus, in late 1853 the border shifted south, accommodating the railroad and most of Cooke's trail. The *Democratic Telegraph and Texas Register* advised anyone making a drive to California to use Cooke's route from El Paso, and Callahan did. To reach El Paso, Callahan rode along trails established by both the army and an expedition that had been funded by Bexar and Travis County officials. In 1849 John S. Ford and Robert S. Neighbors left Fredericksburg, traveled northwest along the Colorado River, turned west and crossed the Pecos River, skirted the Davis Mountains, and continued to El Paso. At the same time army engineers led by Lieutenants William F. Smith and William H. C. Whiting departed San Antonio, passed through Fredericksburg, and more or less followed the Ford–Neighbors road to El Paso. On their return, Smith and Whiting rode southeast down the Rio Grande, turned east through the Davis Mountains along Limpia Creek to Comanche Springs (present-day Fort Stockton), and trekked to the Pecos River. From there, they continued southeast to Las Moras Creek (future site of Fort Clark) and on to San Antonio. The Ford–Neighbors trail became known as the upper road to El Paso, the Smith–Whiting alternative was the lower road. Callahan herded Erskine's cattle along the latter.[3]

Texas ranchers believed, and rightly so, that California was a great market for their cattle. With the discovery of gold, its non-Indian population of 8,000 exploded to 130,000 by 1850, and then to 300,000 in 1855. Cattle ranches were the mainstay of California's economy, but once the gold rush began, their herds were quickly depleted. This lack of supply, along with the surge in wealth generated by gold miners, drove prices up. A single beef cow sold for $10 to $13 in 1850, but by February 1853 cattle prices in San Francisco had risen to $100 to $150 per head. Texans were not the only ranchers attracted by such potential profits. Buyers swarmed the Mississippi River valley, and in July 1853, the *Daily Missouri Republican* reported that 102,828 cattle were en route to California. It is disputed when the first cattle were driven from Texas to California, but Texans drove about 15,000 head to California in 1854, and Callahan had 1,054 of those.[4]

As an Anglo rancher in Texas, Callahan used equipment that represented a blend of traditions from England and Spain modified by environment and innovation. The Mexican saddle is a good example. The Moorish saddle brought by the conquistadores underwent a 200-year evolution, enabling a *vaquero* to remain seated while roping a 1,500-pound bull. Features of the vaquero saddle were incorporated in Richard Hope's wooden saddletree, which was popular among Anglos. Many others copied Hope's saddle, including Rice & Childress of San Antonio. James W. Nichols owned a Childress saddle, and certainly Callahan and most of his drovers sat on a Childress or Hope saddle. Waterproof saddlebags held clothes, food, and ammunition, while a rolled-up blanket was also tied behind the cantle. A long, plaited rawhide or twisted horsehair rope hung on the front skirt, and a canteen and rifle scabbard were strapped to the saddle. The vaquero curb bit made horses more responsive. Finally, in addition to rifles and shotguns, Erskine gave his men six-shooters, the 1851 Colt Navy being the most popular; Callahan had two on his belt. All Texans carried a large knife, usually called a "Bowie" regardless of design. Callahan's attire reflected a similar blend of traditions and innovations. Vaqueros favored wide-brimmed sombreros, but most Anglos wore straw or felt hats. Big roweled spurs were a vaquero hallmark that Anglos did adopt. By 1850, durable denim or corduroy pants tucked into leather boots were common. Cotton shirts were cool, but most men had a heavy flannel top or a wool *serape* for cold nights, and by 1850, waterproof India rubber ponchos, blankets, and coats could be bought. Bandannas protected the neck and face. Another recognizable feature of cowboy attire adopted from the vaqueros was leather leggings, or chaps, that protected legs from thorny brush like that encountered on the trail to California. Erskine's drovers thus wore colorful, functional outfits.[5]

Wrangling longhorn cattle required competent horsemen riding trained, durable horses and working as a team. Callahan and others were good riders and stockmen, but they learned much from their Tejano neighbors. Considering the amount of livestock owned by prominent nearby Tejanos such as José Cárdenas and the Navarro brothers, Anglos had ample opportunity to observe vaqueros. Anglos also learned about Texas livestock. The longhorn's progenitor, the *criollo*, came from Andalusia to Mexico, then moved north into Texas, where they proliferated. Meanwhile, the English brought breeds to North America that interbred with criollos in border areas, developing into hardy longhorns that thrived in the brush country. Longhorns could endure long drives, so the cattle collected by Erskine in 1854 were certainly longhorns. Texas mustangs were also Andalusian stock brought to Mexico. Strays roamed freely, and early visitors to Texas commented on the many wild horses roaming the prairies between the Gulf Coast and the Llano Estacado. Mustangs were agile, strong, and tireless, characteristics of value to cowboys and vaqueros alike. Erskine's men, including Callahan, rode mustangs.[6]

Erskine himself had adapted well to Texas ranching. Born a Virginian, family tradition contends that he was raised to be "a gentleman . . . kind, Christian, generous, and hospitable to a fault." He also had an entrepreneurial spirit. He married in 1817 and, after fifteen years farming and ranching in Virginia, relocated to Huntsville, Alabama, and later Bolivar, Mississippi, where he raised cotton and speculated in land. In 1840 he settled north of Victoria, Texas, but moved to Gonzales County after being attacked during the 1840 Comanche raid. Erskine became one of the most prosperous men in the area as a rancher, attorney, and land speculator. Although he did not claim land in 1841, he paid taxes on 29 cattle and 12 slaves. By 1842 he owned 26,568 acres, 60 cattle, and 17 slaves, and by 1853 the number of his cattle and slaves increased to 755 and 31, and he also owned 57 horses. The increase in real estate came when he bought the six-league El Capote Ranch, which occupied four miles of the western bank of the Guadalupe ten miles from Seguin. He left the ranch's management to his sons, John Paulee Erskine and Andrew Nelson Erskine. Meanwhile, when Guadalupe County formed in 1846, Erskine was elected its first chief justice and became a founder of Seguin High School. His law partnership with Andrew J. Neill prospered, as did El Capote Ranch, where Erskine had a two-story home built on a bluff overlooking the river valley. Key to Erskine's success was his financial backing. His sister Mary Jane married Hugh Caperton of Monroe County, Virginia (now West Virginia), whose estate was valued at $500,000 in 1847. His daughter Catherine Haynes married John Christopher Blucher Ehringhaus of Elizabeth City, North Carolina. Ehringhaus was a wealthy merchant and banker, and Erskine borrowed money from him and Allen Caperton, Erskine's nephew, to finance the operation of El Capote and his land speculations, acquiring almost 50,000 acres in a dozen or more Texas counties.[7]

The investment by others in driving cattle to California attracted the attention of the entrepreneurial Erskine. Among these, James Campbell, whose daughter described him as "a wide traveler, full of the spirit of adventure," stands out. He had settled in San Antonio by 1840, and ten years later opened a store in Eagle Pass. In 1853 he led a drive to California, earned a sizable profit, and on his return spoke freely about prospects for future sales there. Campbell almost single-handedly prompted the wave of Texas cattle drives that started for California in 1854. James Bell, a drover in John James's herd who also kept a diary, mentioned Californian Jonathan D. Holliday, a "great, big, elephant looking man" who had made two trips from the Midwest to California, taking several hundred emigrants and cattle. When he arrived in Texas in the spring of 1854, he drew attention while advertising California's virtues and his intention to buy cattle.[8]

Erskine was not alone in driving cattle to California in 1854; almost two dozen Texans drove cattle there that year (table 10.1). John James, a native of England, was a land developer before he and his brother-in-law, Nova Scotia native James Robert Sweet, started a mercantile business in San Antonio. Sweet also invested in mining and land, and by the early 1850s had a prosperous freighting business to El Paso. James, like Erskine, organized a herd, hired drovers, and led his caravan to California, while Sweet hired a trail boss to lead his drive. Joseph H. Beck lived in Victoria County before moving to San Antonio, where he raised cattle and speculated in land. Beck organized his herd as did Sweet, paying the costs but hiring a man to drive his cattle to California. The results of such ventures were mixed. Alabamian Charles Lynn Pyron stayed in Port Lavaca after his Mexican War service, then married and moved to a Bexar County ranch by the old San Jose Mission, where he sold real estate and rented pasturage. He drove 600 cattle to California, accompanied by a "right clever crowd" of forty men that included doctors, lawyers, carpenters, wheelwrights, blacksmiths, printers, and grave-diggers. The result disappointed him, so he sold his ranch and became a San Antonio hotelier. Howard Rhine, a prosperous Clarksville merchant, had a partly successful drive in 1853, then tried again in 1854 but arrived with only about half of his herd. He subsequently dissolved his mercantile business. Post and Hedges, early San Antonio merchants, did worse, arriving with 74 of their original 400 cattle. Others lost drovers. Henry Matson, who had a general store and saloon in Eagle Pass, heard of Campbell's 1853 success and sold his business to drive 400 cattle to California; his partner was killed when Indians attacked the herd.[9]

Driving cattle to California was not for the fainthearted, but Erskine had advantages over his competitors. He had access to money, and his abundant self-confidence was complemented by his hiring of Callahan. Callahan proved to be a prudent leader who made wise decisions and had the ability to meld together a diverse set of personalities and ethnicities into a reliable team. Erskine's drive is also notable because of its documentation. His diary provides great insights into such an undertaking from the perspective of a herd owner focused on maximizing profits. His notations provide an interesting contrast to the diary of James C. Bell, a novice drover for John James, who followed closely behind Erskine. Bell focused on the cowboys' skills, routines, diets, interactions, and experiences. Both diaries are given an added dimension by considering the written impressions left by independent travelers heading from Texas to California around the same time. The result is a vivid perspective on a well-organized, well-led cattle drive that arrived in California in much better shape than many others.[10]

Erskine prepared carefully for his venture. Campbell gave him a list of waypoints and watering holes along the trail, and a man named Varnal also suggested a route that had plenty of grass and water (map 10.1). With $18,000 borrowed from his Virginia nephew Oliver Beirne and $5,000 from his wealthy brother Alexander, Erskine bought a herd of 1,054 cattle from Tom O'Connor, a prosperous rancher in Refugio County. He also acquired seventy-five horses, a trio of oxen-pulled wagons to carry supplies, and a horse-drawn carriage for his own transportation. He hired about forty men as drovers, but only paid a dozen; the others worked for food and passage to the California gold fields. Callahan was promised $1,500 to act as the trail boss. A fellow entrepreneur, he left his pregnant wife and their five children in Seguin, where they were surrounded by family, to take advantage of an opportunity to finance his development project on the Rio Blanco.[11]

The drive commenced on Sunday, April 23, 1854, and the first weeks tried the patience of drovers and cattle alike. In his diary, Erskine scribbled, "First night stompeded on the Cibilo [Creek], lost some cattle. Stompeded next night, we lost but few." The crew learned from their mistakes, and the following day Erskine noted that the cattle were quiet. Driving around San Pedro Springs on the north side of San Antonio, Callahan parked the herd two and a half miles west of the city for five days, while Erskine purchased salt, provisions, ammunition, and other essentials, filling three wagons and the horse-drawn carriage that he called an ambulance. Even before the drive was fully underway, one of the cowboys, Levi Hinds, stole a horse and left. As Erskine and Callahan would discover, desertion was a common feature of drives. Callahan led Erskine's herd away from San Antonio on May 1, and after two uneventful days they had gone forty miles through Castroville and on to Quihi. Castroville, on the Medina River, was the last town with a hotel and restaurant for several hundred miles. Travelers noted its beautiful setting, and the butter, eggs, and milk that could be bought there and in Quihi. The drovers' good fortune was short-lived, however, as on May 3 a storm stampeded the herd. It took the crew a day to round up 800 head, then the cattle stampeded again and it was a full week before they moved on. They managed to find all but sixty steers, thirty-seven of which eventually wandered to San Antonio. Five men deserted after this ordeal. Erskine sent Callahan to San Antonio and Seguin for more men, horses and money while he moved the herd another thirty miles to the Sabinal River, where he camped at Thomas B. Hammer's ranch (map 10.1). During that week another hand, Hampton, deserted, taking a mule, a horse, and two guns. Callahan returned on May 20 with seven horses, six Tejanos, and one Anglo. The deserters were all Anglos, so for Callahan, pragmatism trumped prejudice when he recruited Tejanos, realizing they were more reliable and had greater expertise than Anglos. Bell, riding behind Erskine with James's herd, had little better luck with his start, and like Erskine's men he and his comrades welcomed the cold water of Hondo Creek.[12]

Following the trail he had ridden during the 1841 Indian campaigns, Callahan led Erskine's herd from the Sabinal to the Frio River, where they camped on May 21. For two consecutive nights, storms made the animals skittish, but Erskine and Callahan were gaining experience in handling a large herd by doubling the night watchmen. Other nearby herds were not as fortunate. Although there were Indians raiding in the vicinity, Erskine's herd had a quiet passage to Fort Clark. Again, some were not so lucky; Indians attacked Pyron's herd, killing two steers. Then on May 27 a thunderstorm stampeded Erskine's cattle, and it took until June 2 to round up 933 head. Callahan kept the herd at Maverick Creek during two storms and drizzling rain to allow the drovers time to retrieve the runaway cattle. They also may have needed a break after traveling the desolate trail from Fort Inge to Fort Clark (map 10.1). The resourceful troops at the latter post grew vegetables that, according to Bell, they shared with drovers, and another

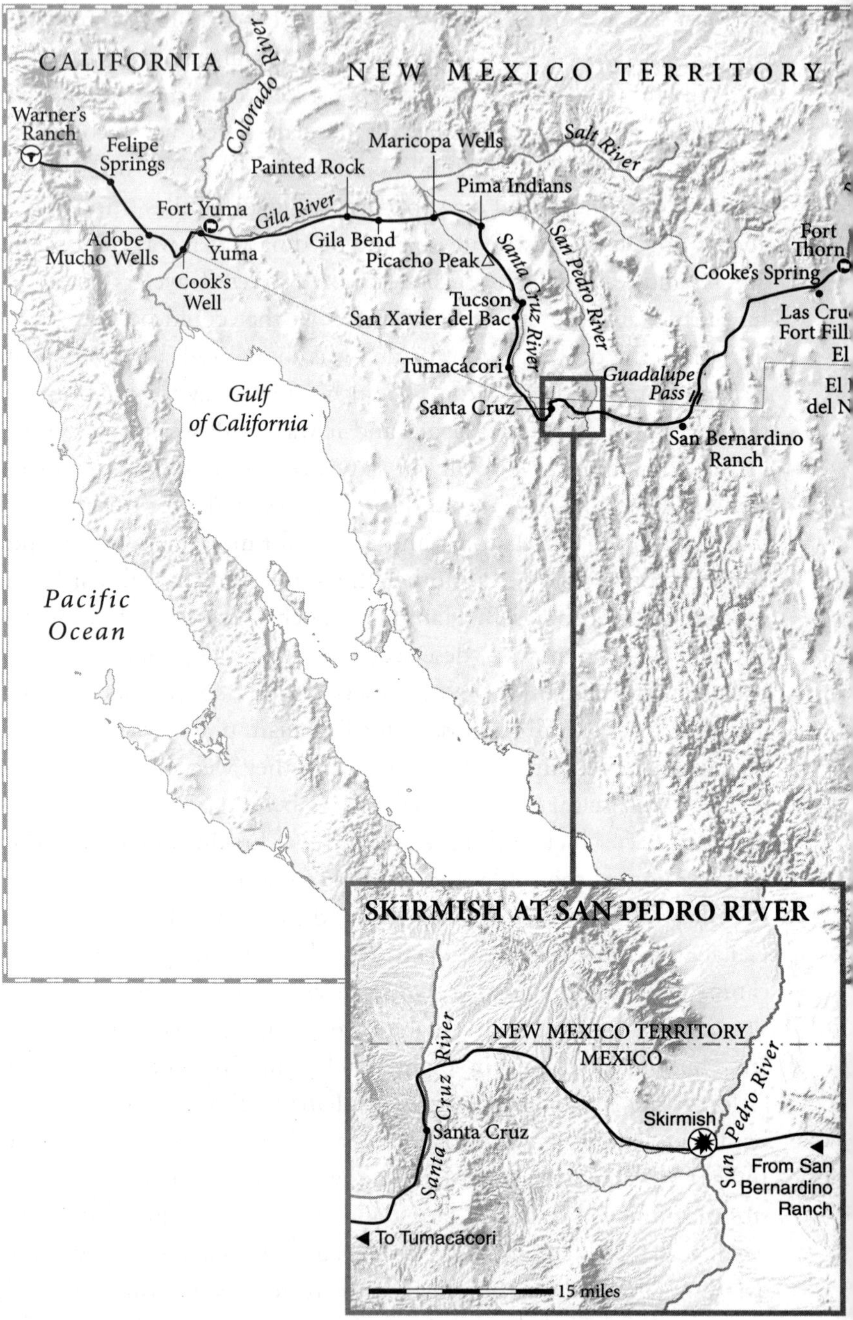

Map 10.1. Route of Erskine cattle drive, Seguin, Texas, to Warner's Ranch, California, 1854. Map by Carol Zuber-Mallison.

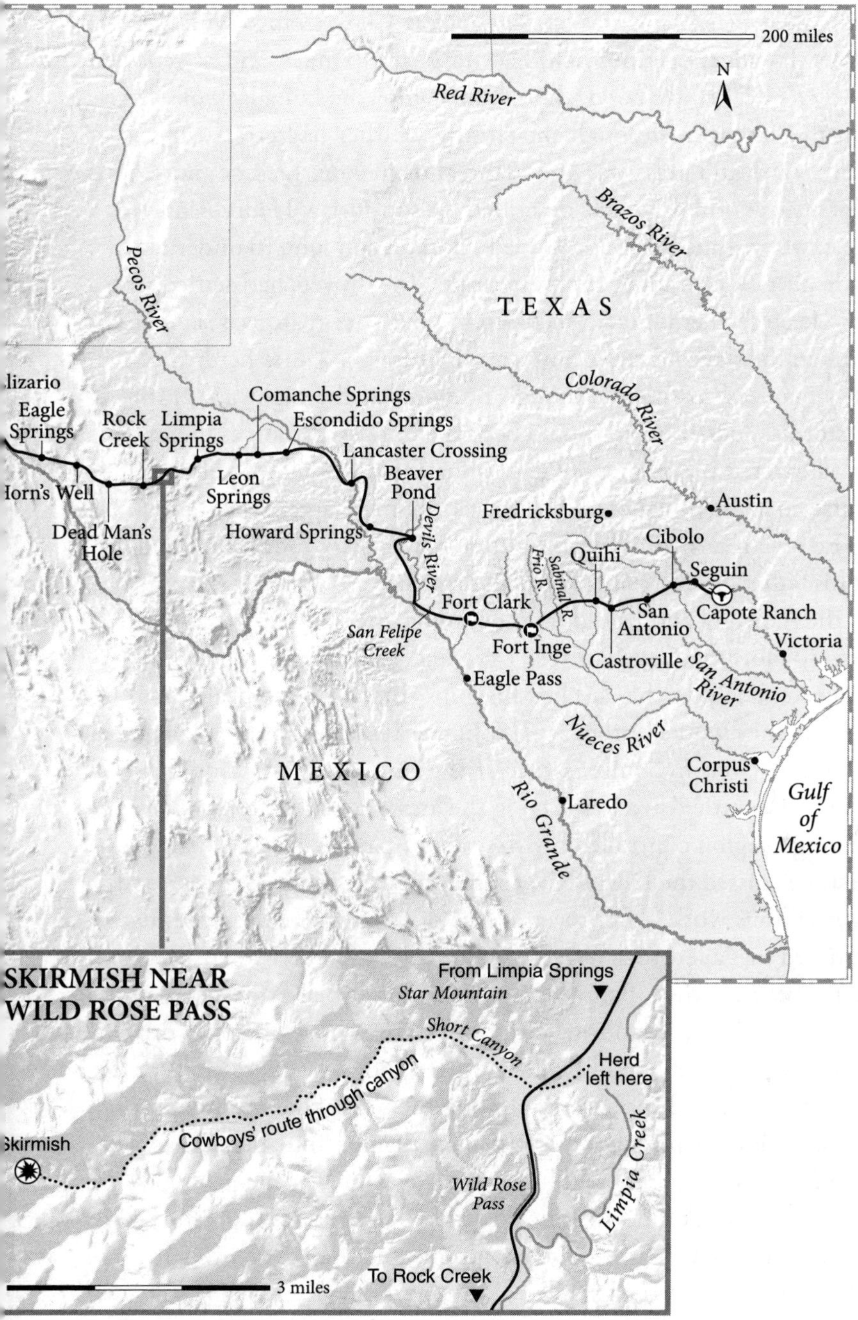
200 miles
N
Red River
Brazos River
Pecos River
TEXAS
Colorado River
lizario
Eagle Springs
Rock Creek
Limpia Springs
Comanche Springs
Escondido Springs
Lancaster Crossing
Leon Springs
Beaver Pond
Iorn's Well
Dead Man's Hole
Howard Springs
Devils River
Fredricksburg
Austin
Cibolo
Quihi
Frio R.
Sabinal R.
Seguin
Capote Ranch
Fort Clark
San Antonio
Fort Inge
Castroville
Victoria
San Felipe Creek
Eagle Pass
San Antonio River
Nueces River
MEXICO
Corpus Christi
Rio Grande
Laredo
Gulf of Mexico
SKIRMISH NEAR WILD ROSE PASS
From Limpia Springs
Star Mountain
Short Canyon
Herd left here
Cowboys' route through canyon
Skirmish
Limpia Creek
Wild Rose Pass
To Rock Creek
3 miles

traveler recalled that Las Moras Springs at Fort Clark teemed with fish. By the end of May 1854, Erskine's herd had traveled 190 miles, and he reported that the men's health was good, though he complained of a lack of exercise riding in the carriage. Although the stormy weather had created havoc, it did ensure water and grass was abundant, thus making Erskine more optimistic for a successful drive. He described his son-in-law Henry Maney as a first-rate cowboy, although he depended upon his son John to undertake the most difficult task of finding runaway cattle. The drovers had settled into a routine to keep the herd intact. According to Bell, the guard was six men for two hours in the day and three hours at night for the James herd. Callahan similarly organized his men, although he doubled the night guard during thunderstorms. Such routines would become more important as the Erskine cattle herd entered the immense Chihuahua Desert, where water and grass were sparse, and the threat of Indian attacks loomed larger.[13]

John Erskine returned to camp on June 2 with sixty-four recaptured cattle, and his father gleefully noted the herd totaled 933. The drive resumed by eight in the morning and halted in the evening after traveling ten to fifteen miles. Every morning Callahan rose early and rode ahead in search of the next campsite. Each day he checked his guns; Erskine periodically fired his to make sure they worked properly. On June 6 Callahan found a good spot on the Devils River, five miles south of the future site of Camp Hudson (map 10.1). The cattle drive was leaving the area known as the *Comancheria* and entering a region controlled by Mescalero Apaches. As Callahan led the herd west, he crossed the Devils River sometimes five to seven times per day, making it tedious work. After seven weeks of hard trailing, tempers flared; Erskine noted that a few men began to complain but settled down after John Erskine threatened to whip them. In the James camp, Bell expressed a strong dislike for the Mexicans and an old Comanche who worked as drovers, but while Erskine's men could be ill-tempered, no overt expressions of disdain were made toward the Tejanos among them. Erskine's team approach to meals contributed to cohesion. His men divided into messes, and the responsibility for cooking rotated through each group. Callahan stopped the herd about every week, and Erskine had a beef slaughtered, cut into strips, dried, and distributed. This was not foolproof, since due to wet weather, the beef dried at Maverick Creek spoiled within four days, but luckily someone shot a deer. The James crew, on the other hand, had a Tejano cook with a wagon who prepared the meals for everyone. Bell recalled that they ate well but were quick to complain if they had to eat bacon too frequently.[14]

After leaving the Devils River, most of June passed rather pleasantly. Erskine's drovers spent one day and two nights at a well-watered spot where they shod horses, washed clothes, and bathed. At an army camp near Live Oak Creek, the future site of Fort Lancaster, they purchased clothing and boots. Other than noting the availability of water and grass, Erskine seldom mentioned a location's appearance, but on June 21 he wrote that they parked the herd near "Comancha Creek [Springs] a pretty stream, for bathing and fishing"; this was the future site of Fort Stockton (map 10.1). Taking breaks was standard procedure; Bell recorded similar interludes for James's crew. Until El Paso, the cowboys enjoyed the luxury of mail, as a postman, Henry Skillman, rode up and down the trails, and it was not uncommon to meet commercial wagons. Erskine worried about Indian attacks, but his diary entries report no Indian signs until near the end of the month. There were no stampedes, and his herd at the end of June numbered 929, a decrease of only four during the month. The most exciting sight during June was the cowboys' first view of a prairie dog town. Bell was less sanguine about Indians. Several graves he saw along the Devils River alarmed him, and just one day after passing over the Pecos River the edgy James crew mounted their horses at two in the morning when Indians were reported nearby. Callahan did have to work hard to find water and grass, a task made more difficult by the herds ahead and the beginning of the hot, dry season. Although the wagons carried water for cooking and drinking, Callahan had to find water for the stock. Fortunately, he did so almost every day, but four times he camped overnight without water for the cattle, once for two consecutive nights. In this section of the trip, the James herd spent seven nights with no water, once three days in succession. Thus, Callahan's decision to drive his herd a greater distance one night proved correct, as did his habit of riding in front of the cattle with a Tejano partner, cutting an arc back and forth looking for grass, water, and Indians. Toward the end of the month they saw signs of Indians for the first time. On June 29 three oxen were stolen, and Erskine suspected Indians since a Tejano saw moccasin tracks.[15]

That night Erskine's crew camped overnight in the Davis Mountains at the north entrance to Wild Rose Pass, near the base of Star Mountain (map 10.1). Feeling vulnerable to a more damaging raid, Callahan decided to recapture the oxen. He took thirteen men up a rugged canyon, engaged some Mescaleros, and returned with eight horses, two mules, and two donkeys. Callahan kept one of the horses and Erskine bought nine animals for $300, which was divided among the men who participated in the encounter.

Callahan's account of the fight was published in Seguin's *Texan Mercury*, and an extract was republished in the *Standard*. Callahan noted they rode through country with steep canyons and high peaks, the roughest that he had seen, and after twelve miles they found fifty Mescaleros camped in a narrow gorge with one entrance and one exit. Scouts Woodson Jett and Pedro Suvio crawled within two hundred yards before being discovered, when a firefight erupted. The Indians retreated but a few almost cut off Callahan's men and nearly captured their horses. A frontal assault drove away the Indians and, now mounted, the drovers charged the camp, capturing the twelve livestock. Not content, Callahan decided to attack again and led his men to within thirty yards of the foe. Both groups fired their weapons incessantly until Callahan realized the Indians could not be dislodged. Firing as they withdrew, the cowboys left the canyon and returned to the herd. This report illustrates Callahan's leadership. His use of Suvio as a scout reveals his pragmatism; he put aside prejudice in choosing the best individual for a job. Callahan never lost sight of his tactical position. He understood an assault was the most effective way to defeat his foe, but he ensured that he had the full support of his men before ordering a charge. He also realized when retreat was the best option. The skirmish seems to have deterred retaliation by the Apaches; Erskine wrote in his diary the next day, "No disturbances last night."[16]

In July, Callahan led Erskine's cattle across 280 miles of one of the most desolate regions of the United States during the hottest and driest season (map 10.1). The first 150 miles had very little water; another cattleman, John Dunlap, lost 700 head to thirst there in 1854. With daytime temperatures over one hundred degrees and nighttime lows in the fifties, Callahan and Erskine chose to drive their cattle at night. The day after the first nighttime trek, Callahan found water twice and pushed the caravan sixteen miles farther. While other drovers, such as Bell with James's herd, also chose to travel at night and wrote about the beauty of the nighttime landscape, Erskine in his diary remained focused on business, recording the location of water and grass and continually fretting about Indians. He was right to worry; other stockmen, including Campbell, lost hundreds of cattle to Indians in this region, and at least two drovers were killed. The number of carcasses between Eagle Springs and the Rio Grande impressed the Erskine and James hands. When Skillman drove along this trail, he complained of an overpowering stench forcing his men to cover their faces with bandannas. Callahan saddled horses, tied the remainder to the wagons, and doubled the day and night guards. Likewise, James kept ten horses saddled, ready for an

Indian attack. This became a daily routine until the herds arrived at the Rio Grande.[17]

Erskine's herd crossed the worst stretch over four days, completing the final forty miles in twenty-four hours. His drovers drank the water stored in casks on the wagons but the cattle had no water, and the horses, mules, and oxen had only what the cowboys could haul by bucket from two shallow wells at Van Horn's Well and Eagle Springs, neither of which were adequate. A traveler in 1857 wrote that Van Horn's Well was a funnel hole a few feet deep and wide, while another remarked that water just "ozzed out of the ground" at Eagle Springs. At the Rio Grande, Erskine boasted, "We have accomplished what no other man has done—Traveled 100 miles in 3 days with a drove of cattle of 875 head & not lose one." He knew his success was due to the hard work of Callahan. Before reaching the river, they left Jett behind with fifteen hands and two oxen-pulled wagons to round up stragglers. Jett's crew made it to the Rio Grande a few days later with forty steers. In sum, Erskine reported, since June 27 his herd had decreased by just eleven cattle. Losing a mere three head to the well-armed Apaches was impressive, especially considering they saw Indian signs at every watering hole. The drovers saw the flicker of Indian campfires in the mountains at Van Horn's Well and Eagle Springs, so Callahan's doubling of the guard must have dissuaded most from raiding. James, riding a week behind, lost seventy-five cattle on the same trek, and he fired three of his Mexicans when he reached the Rio Grande.[18]

At his camp about six miles from the Rio Grande, Callahan organized the cattle into groups of 100 to 200 and drove each to the river separately to drink for the first time in three days. Henry Maney recalled that Callahan chose an ideal way to manage the cattle because if they smelled water, they became uncontrollable. It was much easier for the cowboys to handle small groups of thirsty cattle because the risk of stampede was high. Callahan let them recuperate as they moseyed upriver for several days toward El Paso (map 10.1). The James herd, close behind, stayed at its Rio Grande camp for five days while James himself searched for lost cattle and eventually found fifty. Erskine's herd reached El Paso on July 20, 1854, having enjoyed plenty of water and grass during the last week of traveling, which was made difficult only by the sandy road. While the wagons were repaired in El Paso, Callahan pastured the herd fifteen miles north at James W. Magoffin's ranch on the Rio Grande. The hands rotated shifts so each man had free time in town, and much to Erskine's annoyance several got drunk and Phillipe ran off on

Garcia's horse. He of course was not the only vexed owner; Bell was amused to see that the James men camped near the town in order to attend a fandango. Erskine stayed in town with Magoffin, as did anyone of distinction. He also made $400 by selling ten steers to the local army garrison, so it was a good visit. Callahan led the herd, once recuperated, into the Mesilla Valley on July 26. As they passed Fort Fillmore, Erskine spent thirty-five dollars for 700 pounds of flour and eighteen dollars for four harnesses. Two days later, they camped near Doña Ana, an area admired for its productive soil. Travelers the previous year were astounded by the harvest of corn, wheat, and beans, and claimed that fruits and vegetables grew profusely. The only excitement logged by Erskine during this phase occurred on the last day of July, when a snake bit a steer and Hinds's horse. Evidently, after deserting the herd near San Antonio, Hinds had returned.[19]

After traveling north up the Rio Grande for three days, Erskine's herd forded the river and stopped near Fort Thorn; they were 800 miles from San Antonio, at the halfway point (map 10.1). During a two-day layover to fix the mule-drawn wagon, Erskine stayed with the fort's commander and negotiated an exchange of fifteen steers for fourteen oxen. On their final night there, Erskine had four of his drovers—John Lackey, Pat McGuier, and two men known only as Malone and Leander—jailed for drinking and insubordination. He left Lackey, McGuier, and Malone at Fort Thorn, allowing only Leander to continue with the herd when it departed on August 5. Since Robert Caperneck also quit at that point, Erskine noted that there were thirty-four in the crew after he hired two hands from the fort. With only two opportunities to replenish provisions before arriving at Warner's Ranch in California, it was time for the men in charge to streamline their outfits for maximum efficiency. While Erskine reshuffled only part of his crew, the drovers of another herd disbanded completely. Behind Erskine, in El Paso, James discharged several men and hired replacements. If Bell's diary is any indication, racial tension continued to fester among the James crew. Near Fort Thorn, Mexicans working for James debated returning to San Antonio but decided to continue. Such friction did not seem to occur in Erskine's crew.[20]

Over the next five days, Erskine's herd covered almost eighty miles to the Mimbres River (map 10.1). Water was scarce, and the cattle drank only twice, though the men, horses, and oxen partially slaked their thirst at Mule's and Cooke's Springs. Just before entering Cooke's Pass in the Mimbres Mountains, they were approached by Apaches who claimed that Indians west of the Rio Grande were friendly; wary, they gave the Indians a steer. At about the same point a friendly Apache ate with James's crew, but Bell believed the visit was for reconnaissance. Continuing west, Erskine counted his cattle on August 16 and recorded that he had 882. Since 35 head had been sold, killed, or given away since the last count of 915 on July 11, he had picked up 2 strays. From the Mimbres, the trail passed over the Continental Divide, through Guadalupe Pass, and across the Mexican border. Much of this route lay within the Gadsden Purchase, which Boundary Commissioner John Russell Bartlett described: "As far as the eye can see stretches one unbroken waste, barren, wild, and worthless." But Erskine's men found plenty of water and grass, and they easily covered 155 miles in nine days. Although Erskine did not mention frequent showers, Bell said it rained often, including an afternoon deluge when he could not retrieve his gum coat and rode into camp soaking wet. Riding from Guadalupe Pass into Mexico and down 1,000 feet, Callahan led Erskine's herd eight miles through a dry creek bed, arriving at the deserted San Bernardino Ranch (map 10.1). Here the Texans camped on the prairie. The trail ran parallel to and ten to twenty miles south of the new international boundary, following the Spanish road connecting Chihuahua and Tucson. Erskine continued to enjoy better luck than some of his competitors. When the James herd stopped overnight at the San Bernardino Ranch, two steers were killed by lightning. According to Bell, conflict within the James crew regularly became violent. Two German drovers, one of whom Bell described as paranoid, often provoked trouble. James had to intervene when a gun was drawn, and on another occasion the suspicious German challenged Bell to a duel. Moreover, the undercurrent of racial prejudice was exacerbated when two Mexicans deserted, taking four of the best horses, three six-shooters, and two rifles.[21]

This stretch of the trail was beautiful in its harshness but made perilous by the Apaches. *New Orleans Picayune* correspondent John E. Durivage wrote that the road was littered with "broken wagons, and harness" and "for twelve miles it was very hard work for the animals," but the view was "romantic in the extreme." Asa B. Clarke declared it "one of the prettiest valleys" he had ever seen. Wild cattle, known to attack men, roamed the plains; while it was tempting to kill and eat them, their meat was inedible. Driven herds depended on rainwater ponds, which fortunately were kept replenished by rain. Callahan led the way as his crew descended into the San Pedro River valley. Here Cooke's Wagon Road went north, but in 1854, Texas cattle herds headed west up a fertile canyon and crossed the divide into the Santa Cruz River valley (map 10.1). Bell was impressed with the San Pedro Valley: "Upon the whole this is the most habitable place since we left San Antonio." Erskine agreed that the roads were fine and the grass plentiful. Erskine's luck changed that night when his herd stampeded and he lost 111 cattle; after a day spent regrouping, 47 head were still missing. An Indian shot at some of his hands, a warning of the ever-present danger. The best trailers unsuccessfully scoured the canyons, so on a rainy August 30, the herd continued to Santa Cruz while Callahan and seven drovers remained behind, searching for more. The next day, Erskine found a note tacked to a tree on the trail and read about Indian attacks on three herds ahead of him (table 10.1). Significant numbers of cattle had been lost, and one drover had been killed. Two days later Erskine's men, after double teaming over a treacherous mountain road, were met by several herd owners and hands, concerned that the slow progress of Erskine's caravan was an indication that he had also been attacked. They told Erskine that another herd had been raided nearby; not only was every head lost, but one of the cowboys had been murdered. A few days later, when James led his herd into the San Pedro River valley, he was startled to see a fresh grave with a note from Erskine telling him that this cowboy was killed and 100 cattle were stolen when Apaches attacked Beck's herd.[22]

Late on September 2, 1854, Callahan and his crew, driving forty-seven recovered steers, caught up with the main herd camped south of Santa Cruz village. Bell thought the Santa Cruz River valley was a "beautiful . . . desirable place for farming purposes," and others agreed with him. As the first inhabited place since Fort Thorn, Santa Cruz made a welcome haven. Bell and the others enjoyed the local produce—apples, peaches, and quinces—smoked the homegrown tobacco, and admired the village's woven blankets. Several herds were parked at Santa Cruz, and of course recent Indian attacks became the main topic of discussion. There was a general feeling of anger and the need for retribution. Maney recalled that Callahan called for volunteers to join him. By Monday, September 4, he had fifteen of Erskine's men, twenty-three from other cattle drives, and twenty-five Mexican soldiers from the local presidio, and he prepared to retaliate against the Apaches. The Mexican lieutenant and his troops had not subdued the Apaches in the area, but they had become familiar with the valleys and mountains. The San Pedro and Santa Cruz Rivers have an unusual proximity to each other (map 10.1). The San Pedro begins in Mexico and flows north to join the Gila River about 100 miles east of present-day Phoenix. West of a dividing ridge,

Table 10.1. Cattle herds driven from Texas to California, 1854

	Departure		*Herd Size*		
Herd Owner(s)	*Point*	*Date*	*Start*	*End*	*Remarks*
Erskine	Seguin	Apr. 22	1,054	814	Arrived Warner's Ranch, Oct. 29
Oliver, Montgomery	Austin		400	—	Mescaleros stole 200 at Eagle Springs; stopped near Tucson to mine gold
Pyron, Edwards	San Antonio	Mar. 27	600	—	40 men; May 5, Leon Springs, no losses; repulsed Indians, Eagle Springs; Creswell wounded, San Xavier Mission; Aug., Tucson
Wallace	—	—	—	—	May 25 at Devil's River
Matson, Whitney	San Antonio	Apr. 10	400	—	Value $10,000, 40 men; lost few cattle, Limpia Creek; Miller drowned, Ft. Fillmore; Apaches killed Whitney, San Pedro River
Post, Hedges	San Antonio		400	74	Lost 176 head, 2 men killed, Eagle Springs; arrived Warner's Ranch
James	San Antonio	June 1	700–1,000	—	30 men with 6-shooters and rifles; lost 100 head before Santa Cruz; 125 poisoned, Cooke's Wells
McRea, Rankin	Victoria	July 13	700	—	17 men with revolvers; lost 125 head, Devil's River; Dec., near San Diego
Grayson	Brazos River		500	—	Lost 12 head before El Paso
Franklin, Dean	Bastrop		—	—	Lost no cattle before El Paso; herd of 250 at Rio Mimbres
Dunlap	Bell County		1,500–1,900	—	On May 11 no losses; 700 head died of dehydration Dead Man's Hole to Eagle Springs; Apaches stole 20 horses, killed Houston, San Pedro River; had 450 head at Santa Cruz
Fairchild, McClure	San Antonio	May	—	—	Lost 100–200 head to dehydration before El Paso; Apaches stole 350, San Pedro River; arrived destitute in Los Angeles
Beck, Bryant	San Antonio		400	—	May 9 at Devil's River, no losses; lost 200 head to thirst before El Paso; Apaches stole 160 head, perhaps entire herd, San Pedro River

(*continued*)

Table 10.1. (*continued*)

	Departure		*Herd Size*		
Herd Owner(s)	*Point*	*Date*	*Start*	*End*	*Remarks*
Pendleton	Bastrop		—	—	Lost 100–140 head, San Pedro River
Holliday	San Antonio	July 11	1,000	800	At Cooke's Pass, 1,000 head, 50 men, 8 wagons, 75 horses/mules; Nov. near Yuma; late Nov. arrived San Diego
Unknown	—		—	—	Aug. 21, near Pima village, Apaches stole 600 head, killed 50 people
Rhine	Clarksville		1,140–1,300	640	Lost few head before El Paso; 40 head died, Cooke's Wells; arrived Warner's Ranch
McKinley	Port Lavaca		—	200	5 men killed at Tubac; arrived San Diego with 20 men, Dec. 5
Campbell	San Antonio		500	100	Indians stole all cattle, Eagle Springs; U.S. Army recaptured 250; arrived Los Angeles, Jan. 1855
Shackleford	Bastrop	May 1	—	—	
Unknown	Lockhart	Apr. 1	700	—	
Griffin	San Antonio	Early May	—	—	
Tully, Sweet, & Co.	San Antonio		—	—	Attacked at Limpia Creek, Mrs. Wall killed; late Aug., Tucson; arrived Warner's Ranch, early Oct.
Unknown	—		—	—	G. Sutton claimed Texans with 1,100 cattle started a settlement at Yuma.
Poer	Clarksville		700	—	
Unknown	San Antonio		1,000	—	30 immigrant wagons with families

Sources: Sacramento Daily Union, May 5, Sept. 4, 6, 18, Dec. 13, 18, 1854; Hoover and Kyle, *Historic Spots*, 224; *TSG*, March 28, May 27, July 29, Aug. 5, Nov. 4, Dec. 2, 1854; *Daily Placer Times and Transcript*, Aug. 26, 1854; Erskine, *Diary*, 43–45, 65, 76–79, 93–94; Bell, "Log," pt. 2, pp. 297, 305–7; pt. 3, pp. 47, 57, 59; *Texan Mercury*, Apr. 29, May 13, 20, 1854; *Daily Alta California*, June 16, Aug. 1, Sept. 3, 9, Oct. 7, Nov. 7, 1854; *San Antonio Ledger and Texan*; Mar. 30, May 4, 18, June 1, 8, July 20, 1854; *Western Texan*, Apr. 13, 20, May 18, July 20, Oct. 19, 1854; *Nacogdoches Chronicle*, Mar. 28, 1854; *Daily Placer Times and Transcript*, July 17, Sept. 27, Nov. 7, 24, Dec. 18, 1854; *California Farmer and Journal of Useful Sciences*, Nov. 30, 1854; *TST*, Feb. 17, 1855; *Alamo Star*, May 20, 1854; *Texas Planter*, Nov. 8, 1854; *Clarksville Standard*, Sept. 23, 1854; *Galveston Weekly News*, Nov. 7, 1854; *NOP*, Oct. 29, 1854; *Los Angles Star*, July 21, 1854: *Neu Braunfelser Zeitung*, May 5, 1854.

Note: Rhine drove a herd in 1853, lost most of his cattle, and ten of his drivers were killed. *Clarksville* (*Tex.*) *Standard*, May 28, June 28, Oct. 1, 1853; Marrin and Sheppard, *Paradise*, 14, 24–25, 54, 62, 187.

the Santa Cruz begins in the United States, meanders south for 50 miles to the town of Santa Cruz, then makes a horseshoe turn before continuing north to Tucson. Apaches raided both valleys, with the mountains providing cover. Maney recollected Callahan's posse left at sunset, rode up the Santa Cruz for three hours, then turned east over the watershed divide. By the early hours of morning, the men were close to the border, moving into the San Pedro basin along a small tributary. The Texans and Tejanos were armed with six-shooters, shotguns, and rifles, and the Mexican troops carried old carbines, swords, and lances.[23]

During the ride, two false alarms caused the men to rally and in one case fire their guns. Wild horses instigated the first alarm, and in the second instance Teck, a Tejano with Erskine's crew, triggered a commotion when he wandered away after drinking mescal given him by the Mexican soldiers. Callahan's men were clearly nervous and feeling vulnerable. On the valley's floor where a creek paralleled the river, Callahan sent two drovers and a Mexican soldier ahead to reconnoiter. One reported that about fifty Apaches were driving cattle down the San Pedro on a path that converged with the creek on which Callahan's posse was riding. Callahan slowed his pace, intending to fight where the streams met (map 10.1). After thirty minutes, a second scout reported that the Indians had camped at the junction. Maney recalled that Callahan ordered his men to tighten girths and check guns, then he "pulled off his hat, put spurs to his horse, and said 'Charge.'" The yelling attackers surprised the Apaches. The mounted warriors fled, leaving their dismounted companions to bear the brunt of the assault. After the initial contact, Callahan's men focused on killing dismounted Apaches, including one with a rifle who shot and killed a Mexican soldier. A few pursued mounted warriors. William Ramsey and the Mexican lieutenant caught an Apache who turned his mount and tried to lance both pursuers but missed. The lieutenant slashed the Indian's skull with his sword, almost scalping him as he fell dead from his horse. Maney and three soldiers chased two Apaches riding one horse; when one slid off, he was roped by a trooper and dragged while a second Mexican lanced him repeatedly. The fighting degenerated into hand-to-hand combat and long-range sniping as Indians escaped into tall grass along the river. When Callahan rode to the edge of the brush, dismounted, and asked for volunteers to follow him, several Texans and Mexican soldiers did so. Ramsey and John Lewis entered from the west and were charged by an Apache, who was wounded by Ramsey's shotgun blast. The injured Indian waded upstream, where he was killed by Lewis with three shots from his six-shooter. Callahan, a revolver in each hand and a Mexican private behind, was charged by another warrior as he crept along the bank of the river. Maney watched as Callahan's gun misfired twice; when Callahan ducked under a lance thrust and jumped into the water, Maney shot the Indian.[24]

The twenty-one Apaches killed that day were scalped by the Mexican soldiers, since cash was awarded for scalps. One Mexican soldier was slain and two drovers slightly wounded; in addition to the livestock captured, a fifteen-year-old Mexican boy who had been kidnapped four years earlier was rescued. Erskine claimed that sixty to sixty-five animals were brought back. Within twenty-four hours of the fight, Callahan and his men drove the livestock the forty-five miles to Santa Cruz and were welcomed by the firing of guns and the ringing of the church bells. The widow of the Mexican soldier was given sixteen steers for her loss, and Erskine said that his crew got thirteen cattle, one horse, and one mule, which he bought for $425. The remainder was divided among the other herds. In this skirmish, like the one near Wild Rose Pass, Callahan demonstrated his combat leadership and his successful use of a surprise attack. As he did with his drovers, Callahan led a disparate group to achieve a goal and exhibited a fearlessness many acquaintances later emphasized. The San Pedro River skirmish is one more example of Erskine's good judgment in hiring Callahan to lead his herd to California.[25]

After dividing the livestock and having two drovers quit, Callahan again led as Erskine's drive departed for Tucson, eighty miles north (map 10.1). Leaving on September 10, the caravan arrived at its destination eight days later, having crossed the Mexican border near present-day Nogales and ridden by the picturesque mission villages of Tumacácori, Tubac, and San Xavier del Bac. In a rare entry about things other than grass, water, and Indians, Erskine wrote that San Xavier del Bac was "a handsome Church of brick" in a "small village inhabited by Pimo Indians." Bell was unimpressed by the countryside or its inhabitants en route to Tucson, and continued to disparage Mexicans, but he did admire the towering saguaro cactus. While he and others continued to regard San Xavier del Bac as miserable, they were impressed by the church and the amazing variety of fruit trees that grew in the vicinity. At San Xavier del Bac, Callahan rode ahead to locate a camping place on the edge of Tucson; while Erskine agreed the water was good, he complained that the grass was poor. With the onset of the Gold Rush, Tucson had become a major transit point, so it was well developed despite its remoteness. The presence of a Mexican garrison that had not yet departed provided a welcome respite from the monotony of the drive. Erskine traded various items with the presidio's captain and bought 100 pounds of unsifted flour for six dollars. In the meantime, the priest's and captain's sons stole John Erskine's vest, which he retrieved, and that night Callahan joined the captain and priest for dinner. James's men attended a fandango, and Bell also ate with the Mexican commandant and a priest. He wrote:

> Our first dish was rice cooked with some ingredients to make it palatable, and *Chili Verde* (green pepper) in a separate dish, but to eat together, second was Beef, Squash, quinces, whole Peppers, Green Beans, cooked seperatley, but all, on the table in one dish; third, dried beans, and Peppers to eat with them, fourth, desert [*sic*], boiled flour Pudding with almonds in it, and Peach Marmalade for sauce. A large glass tumbler with a pitcher of water composed our drinking tableware. The thin well baked Torttilla, common to this country, accompanied the meal.

Callahan must have eaten a similar meal, which Bell claimed was one of the best he had ever had. While no one was impressed by Tucson or its inhabitants, the low prices and abundance of food were commented upon by virtually every chronicler.[26]

After spending a day in Tucson, where two more drovers quit, Erskine's herd left on September 19, 1854, following the dry Santa Cruz riverbed northwest toward the Gila River. A drenching downpour fell on September 21, and after a seven-mile hike they watered the cattle at the base of Picacho Peak (map 10.1). The next opportunity for water came two days later at a large pond that Erskine called Gila Lagoon. Callahan found a campsite eight miles beyond with adequate grass and access to the Gila River. Four days behind Erskine, the James crew found water near Picacho Peak, but they discovered Gila Lagoon was dry, so they had to push to the river before the cattle could drink. Erskine and James were lucky; the ninety miles from Tucson to the Pima villages was normally dry and treacherous, the trail littered with discarded debris, animal skeletons, and human graves. During his slog to the Gila River, Durivage nearly died of dehydration and heat exhaustion. In Clarke's group, several horses gave out and they had to shoot others too weak to continue, and he saw several men who were stragglers unable to keep up with their groups. For two days Erskine's men trailed twenty-five miles along the west bank of the Gila River, stopping in Pima villages to trade. Erskine gave the Pimas needles and threads, but complained that they still stole more plus shirts, knives, and hatchets. He mused, "They require to be watched close." Bell was more irritated by the Pimas, writing that their begging was annoying and they stole his hobble and canteen. He concluded, "On the whole I believe they are a great set of scoundrels." Their experiences contrasted inexplicably with those of other travelers, who were enamored with the Pima and Maricopa tribes and did not complain about thefts.[27]

Instead of continuing to follow the Gila, Callahan led the herd in the cool of the night across forty-five miles of formidable desert until they reached the river again. Erskine never hinted at any hardships on this leg of their journey; he merely wrote, "Fine road." It took James's herd thirty hours to cross the same desert. Camping on the night of September 30, Erskine was about 300 miles from Warner's Ranch, his destination. Between him and Fort Yuma lay ninety miles of harsh valleys and steep, rocky buttes. Although Bell complained about the miserable, rocky road, he admired the mountainous scenery, stating it was unsurpassed by any he had seen. Steep bluffs ran into the river, blocking livestock from water. Erskine described how Callahan guided his herd across the Gila at a low-water crossing and, finding water and good grass, they recrossed the river for the night's camp. James, on the other hand, crossed the Gila three or four times, to avoid climbing the buttes, and found less grass. The exertion took its toll. Bell wrote, "I am doged [*sic*] tired of this trip . . . one trip does for a lifetime." Another traveler, C. C. Cox, was more emphatic: "I am sure that no sane man will ever travel this route a second time." Two men with Erskine, Payne and Arnold, had the same opinion and simply quit. Erskine's hands finally exited the mountains on October 11 and found a small lake and plentiful grass to park their herd while Callahan and John Erskine rode to Fort Yuma to determine the best way across the Colorado River. The Erskine cattle now numbered 868.[28]

On October 13 Callahan and John rode back to Erskine's parked herd, having concluded the cattle, horses, and wagons had to be ferried across the Colorado, which was about eighteen feet deep and flowing swiftly. The ferry was expensive, and Erskine was skeptical of their report, so he paid to have one-fifth of his herd ferried. The following day only 100 cattle could be forced to swim the river, so Erskine had to accept the cost and ferried the remainder. By this time the cattle had gone without food for three days and were agitated, then on October 20 Erskine noted that some had eaten careless weed, which could be toxic. By the time they arrived at Cooke's Well, forty head had strayed, so a few cowboys fanned out to retrieve them. At Fort Yuma, the James herd caught up with the Erskine crew and thereafter remained a day behind. Twenty-four hours after Erskine had fed and watered his herd near Cooke's Well, James lost 125 head when his cattle gorged on careless weed. Bell watched in horror as the animals died. In addition, James lost his oxen, forcing him to abandon his wagons and carry essentials in the ambulance for the final miles to Warner's Ranch. Bell returned to Yuma to buy oxen and retrieve the wagons. He arrived at Warner's Ranch on November 12 after learning another drive had lost forty head to careless weed. Callahan's cattle-raising sense saved Erskine from a similar loss.[29]

By the third week of October 1854, Erskine was 110 miles from Warner's Ranch and had again crossed into Mexico (map 10.1). Progress was slow as deep sand bogged the wagons; even Erskine pushed and pulled for several miles. Finally, at midnight on October 21, his herd, minus several strays, arrived at Adobe Mucho Wells, where there was water. Over the next week, they covered ten to fifteen miles a day and crossed the border for the last time. Callahan located water every day. The *Sacramento Daily Union* said that recent rains left pools on the desert and grass was plentiful, although Erskine complained it was the "coarse kind not good for cattle." More cattle strayed, a few died, and even horses faltered as men searched for stragglers as far back as the Colorado River. Most of the men rejoined the group by the time the herd climbed the last sand dune heading for Felipe Springs, the first fresh water since the Colorado. Topping the ridge, Erskine and his drovers had their first view of the extensive valley below and their destination—Warner's Ranch. After a hazardous journey of 1,600 miles and six months since leaving Seguin, Erskine and his herd arrived on October 29.[30]

Erskine's caravan had indeed been fortunate during the drive from Yuma to Warner's Ranch, across what is known today as the Yuha Desert. Traveling in 1851, an unknown Texan described the area as "destitute of everything except desert shrubs, and reminds one . . . of the great Sahara desert." Durivage's trek was typical of the experience of most people. He saw scores of dead mules and an endless string of discarded clothes, wagons, guns, and trunks. Cox eloquently described crossing this inhospitable terrain: "On on we rolled, hour after hour passed by—not a tree, a sprig of grass or living creature to be seen . . . throughout the day the sun shone hot and scorching, glimmering on the sand, like heat from a furnace." To drovers and argonauts alike the sight of Warner's Ranch was a great relief. Connecticut native John T. Warner went to California in 1831, settling in Los Angeles and becoming a

Mexican citizen. In 1837 he married Anita Gale, a ward of former California governor Don Pío Pico. Pico's brother obtained a grant for *Aguas Caliente* in 1840 but abandoned the property when Indian raids proved troublesome. The vacancy allowed Warner to acquire the Pico grant in 1844, and the addition of another large parcel increased his acreage to 26,700. The property, which became known as Warner's Ranch, was a broad, fertile valley, surrounded by mountains and watered by hot and cold springs. It lay astride the road to Los Angeles and San Diego, so many passersby wrote about its great beauty and the variety of produce grown there. Erskine and Callahan camped near the old ranch house, where the cowboys used the hot and cold springs to wash away months of grime and sweat. After weeks of eating dried beef, they surely consumed the local produce with delight.[31]

Needing a place to fatten his herd over the winter, Erskine sent Callahan and others to find valleys with adequate water and grass. Upon returning from the San Luis Rey area, Callahan reported that Warner's Ranch pastureland was superior and the herd should remain there. Erskine agreed. Now at trail's end, the cowboys who intended to try their luck in the gold mines headed north to San Francisco, but Erskine kept a few hands to tend the livestock. He and the remaining hands repaired a corral and branded 814 head. Bragging about their efficiency, Erskine doubted "if so many cattle were ever branded before in so short a time." The roping skills of Callahan and the other men, especially the Tejanos, impressed their boss.[32]

Erskine left Seguin with 1,054 head of cattle and camped at Warner's Ranch with 814, a loss of 240. On various occasions during the trek he recorded the number of cattle he had. The largest drop occurred in May with the first stampedes, which showed his men's inexperience. The second significant loss happened during the drive from Fort Yuma to Warner's Ranch in October and November, which reflected the hazards of that stretch of the trail. Though smaller, the shortfall between Tucson and Fort Yuma in September and October revealed the impact of the desert and the buttes along the Gila River. The losses were not all due to runaways. Erskine slaughtered 25 to feed his men. He also sold or exchanged 76—40 in San Antonio (recovered from a May stampede), 4 at Quihi, 21 in El Paso, 2 at Fort Thorn, and 9 at the Colorado River. Four were given away, 4 died near the San Pedro and Santa Cruz rivers, and 7 were left behind, between Limpia Creek and the Rio Grande. The drive from Fort Yuma took its toll when 2 oxen drowned, 2 steers died, and 17 cattle were left because they could not keep up, though some of these may have been retrieved by men sent to find them. Erskine recorded that only four escaped, including one that swam the Rio Grande, though occasionally he scribbled: "lost [cattle] we can't account for." Only three oxen were stolen by Indians. While Erskine's numbers are incomplete, almost 140 of his missing 240 head could be accounted for; of these, 106 were butchered, sold, or given away. Thus, his unaccounted loss was under 10 percent, a remarkable achievement. On a few occasions the herd was augmented. In Limpia Canyon his men found three strays, another joined at Rio Mimbres, and two calves were acquired near Eagle Springs. The largest boost came after the skirmish at the San Pedro River, when Callahan brought back captured cattle, of which thirteen were bought by Erskine. Nearly eighty horses left El Capote Ranch with Erskine's herd, and Callahan brought several more with him. The only horse not completing the journey was left at Carrizo Creek, forty-four miles short of Warner's Ranch. The drive started with three wagons and nineteen yoke of oxen. Of these, other than the three stolen at Limpia Canyon, only one other yoke went missing, at the Colorado River crossing. Erskine never noted if any wagons were discarded. He rode in an ambulance, a buggy with a short wheelbase towed by a pair of horses or mules, which evidently survived the trek to Warner's Ranch.[33]

Erskine did very well in comparison with many of his competitors. At least twenty-five herds were driven from Texas toward California in 1854, totaling 14,000 to 15,000 cattle (table 10.1). News reports and records concerning the number that arrived are imperfect, although the failure rate was significant. Bell asserted that by October 29 over 4,000 cattle had crossed the Colorado at Fort Yuma. However, two months earlier a newspaper reported twice that number of Texas cattle bound for California, and by May 1855 the Soberanes family in Monterey County, California, claimed 10,000 cattle from the 1854 Texas drives had passed their ranch. Among the herd owners were some substantial losers. Fairchild and McClure lost all of their 500 cattle and arrived in Los Angeles destitute. Beck and Bryant fared marginally better, losing 360 out of 400, while Campbell started with 500 and lost 400. Dunlap began with 1,500 and had 450 at Santa Cruz with another 500 difficult miles to go. Post and Hedges, who left San Antonio with 400, arrived at Warner's Ranch with 74. After losing half of a herd, Oliver and Montgomery stopped to mine gold at Tucson, and a wagon train with 1,100 cattle remained at Fort Yuma and started a community. The most unfortunate was an anonymous caravan attacked by Apaches near the Pima villages; the entire crew of fifty was killed and their 600 head were stolen. Nevertheless, some drives had fewer losses. Of the 1,140 cattle he started with, Rhine drove 640 into Warner's Ranch. Pyron and Edwards, McRea and Rankin, and James seem to have led successful drives, too. As for Erskine, his success reinforces the *Texas State Gazette's* claim that an "experienced Captain [Callahan] was at the bottom of [Erskine's] good fortune."[34]

Given the number of herds, between 800 and 1,000 drovers took part in the 1854 Texas drives to California, though not all finished the journey. A look at Erskine's cowboys provides some insight into this cohort. Most of his fifty-two men can be identified (table 10.2). Four were related to Erskine: sons John Paulee and Michael Henry Erskine; son-in-law Henry Maney; and Thomas Ignatius Johnson, the brother-in-law of son Andrew. The ages of ten drovers are known; if this small sample is representative, then most were in their mid-twenties. Many had worked on cattle ranches, but none had experienced a long cattle drive. When six Anglos left after an early stampede, Callahan replaced them with six Tejanos, knowing their expertise would help raise the overall efficacy of the crew. Being familiar with Tejano ranchers in Guadalupe County, Callahan hired José Cárdenas, son of a longtime Guadalupe River ranchero, and the others were probably from that county too. Thereafter, when Callahan rode out on a mission, he took along a Tejano, and Erskine always made sure one went with drovers to look for strays. In both fights, Callahan relied on Tejanos, including at least one who was a lead scout. Clearly Tejanos were a key part of Erskine's success. The lure of gold in California was a primary motivation for many drovers. Erskine paid only twelve hands; the others worked for food and transportation. This may have contributed to instability; the first six who deserted found the strenuous work too high a price to pay for the uncertain promise of gold. John Lackey, who was fired at Fort Thorn, also chose to return to Texas. Most of Erskine's hands stayed in California and many went to the goldfields. His two sons, John and Michael, did, as did Bell, the diarist of the James herd. Few found gold, and some, such as Rufus Byler and Charles Proctor, went back to Texas within a year or two. At least one drover never got near a goldfield nor returned home: William Waters died of typhoid in December 1854 at Los Angeles. For many who stayed in California, their decision to join a cattle drive changed their lives since they avoided the Civil War. And some met other needs by enlisting with Erskine, like John Box Roberts, who had abandoned his wife.[35]

The drive did not end for Erskine and Callahan at Warner's Ranch. After branding the cattle and selecting the men who would tend the herd into

Table 10.2. Men of 1854 Erskine cattle drive to California

Name/Age	*Remarks* (Texas origin point, role, key experiences on drive)
Michael Erskine, 60	Guadalupe County; owner
James Hughes Callahan, 40	Comal County; trail guide; ex-Ranger
John Paulee Erskine, 35	Guadalupe County; Erskine's son; wintered herd, Warner's Ranch
Michael Henry Erskine, 20	Guadalupe County; Erskine's son; wintered herd
Henry Maney, 24	Guadalupe County; Erskine's son-in-law; San Pedro River skirmish
Thomas Ignatius Johnson, 23	Guadalupe County; Andrew Erskine's brother-in-law; Limpia Creek fight; San Pedro River skirmish; wintered herd; returned to Texas, 1855
Shelton	Caldwell County
Joe Shelly and son Matt	Wintered herd; with herd, 1855-56; worked in Erskine mine, 1858; returned to Texas, 1859
Levi Hinds, 27	Caldwell County; stole horse, left Apr. 31; later returned; snake bit his horse near Doña Ana
Karn (Kain?)	Deserted, May 11
Davis	Deserted, May 11; returned; left Warner's Ranch, Nov. 2
Polish man	Deserted, May 11
Polish man	Deserted, May 11
Bennet	Deserted, May 11
Hampton	Deserted and stole mule, horse, saddle, bridle, gun, six-shooter, May 15
Perfecto	Guadalupe County; joined the drive May 20; wintered herd; quit, July 1856
Teck	Guadalupe County; joined the drive May 20; San Pedro River skirmish
Pedro Suvio	Guadalupe County; joined the drive May 20; Limpia Creek fight
Garcia	Guadalupe County; joined the drive May 20; retrieved stolen horse at Fort Thorn
Monte	Guadalupe County; joined the drive May 20; left Warner's Ranch Nov. 9 with horse, saddle, bridle, gun
José Cárdenas, 26	Guadalupe County; joined the drive May 20; late arrival at Warner's Ranch with 7 stray steers
Woodson Jett	Bexar County; joined the drive May 20; Limpia Creek fight
John Box Roberts, 39	Bastrop County; San Pedro River skirmish; to Los Angeles, Calif., Nov. 10, 1854; Columbia, Calif., Oct. 1856
John Lewis, 28	Guadalupe County; San Pedro River skirmish

(*continued*)

Table 10.2. (*continued*)

Name/Age	*Remarks* (Texas origin point, role, key experiences on drive)
J. H. French	Left Warner's Ranch for Los Angeles, Calif., Nov. 10
Alfred J. Mann	Limpia Creek fight
John Lackey, 36	Limpia Creek fight; fired at Fort Thorn
Pat McGuier (McGevis)	Limpia Creek fight; fired at Fort Thorn
Rufus Byler, 20	Guadalupe County; Limpia Creek fight; San Pedro River skirmish; wintered herd; went to Texas, 1856
William Watson	Limpia Creek fight; left Warner's Ranch, Nov. 1
William Waters, 23	Limpia Creek fight; died of typhoid, Los Angeles, Calif., Dec. 1854
Fred Miller	Limpia Creek fight; left Warner's Ranch, Nov. 4
Charles Porter, 24	Caldwell County; Limpia Creek fight
Robert Caperneck	Limpia Creek fight; quit at Fort Thorn
Sheppard	Wounded at San Pedro skirmish
Daffin	Left Warner's Ranch, Nov. 8
Phillipe	Stole horse and deserted at El Paso
Malone	Fired at Fort Thorn
Leander	Jailed at Fort Thorn but continued with herd; wintered herd; with herd, 1856
Two unknown men	Joined at Fort Thorn
Markes	Limpia Creek fight; left the herd at Santa Cruz
Sluder	Left the herd at Santa Cruz
White	Left the herd at Santa Cruz
Payne	Left the herd at Yuma
Arnold	Left the herd at Yuma
Charlie Baker	Left the herd at Yuma
Brown	Left Warner's Ranch, Nov. 1
Boatright	Left Warner's Ranch, Nov. 2
Atwood	Left Warner's Ranch, Nov. 2
May	Caldwell County; left Warner's Ranch, Nov. 2
Frankenburg	Left Warner's Ranch, Nov. 4
Franklin	Left Warner's Ranch, Nov. 6
Matterson	Wintered herd

Sources: Erskine, *Diary,* 27, 43–46, 50–51, 56–68, 78–79, 89, 91–94, 97, 101, 127, 129, 133, 136, 138, 156; U.S. Census, 1850, Guadalupe County, Tex.; *Clarksville Standard,* Sept. 2, 1854; Sowell, *Texas Indian Fighters,* 683, 686; U.S. Census, 1860, Caldwell, Comal Counties, Tex.; *Ledger and Texan,* July 10, 1856; *Daily Union,* Dec. 6, 1854; U.S. Census, 1870, Mariposa County, Calif.; TR, 1876–70, TAC, Guadalupe County, TSLA. *TSG,* Dec. 2, 1854.
Note: Shelton was one of four brothers—Lemuel, Samuel, Stephen, John. May was one of four brothers—Leonard, Morris, Albert, or Milton. John M. Lewis lived near El Capote Ranch.

the spring of 1855, Erskine, Callahan, Maney, Roberts, and a man identified as "Mr. F." left for Los Angeles on November 10. The 113-mile trip took five days. Leaving Los Angeles, they traveled by stagecoach to San Pedro, a hacienda converted into a bustling port. On November 23 the Texans boarded the SS *America*, a three-masted sidewheeler departing for San Francisco. After four days at sea, the ship passed through the Golden Gate and docked. It was not Callahan's plan to go to San Francisco; he had wanted to sail from Los Angeles to Panama and then to Texas. Erskine's correspondence reveals he did not have the means to pay Callahan in Los Angeles, so they continued to San Francisco, where Callahan did visit his friend John C. "Jack" Hays, California's surveyor general. Erskine had no better access to funds there but promised to have his son Andrew pay Callahan. With no reason to extend his stay, Callahan was eager to go home, and on December 2 he and Maney left San Francisco on the SS *Sonora,* a two-masted sidewheeler bound for Panama. After a voyage of almost two weeks, Callahan and Maney began the second part of their journey, a trip across the Panama isthmus. Transiting the isthmus was chaotic, starting on the Pacific side with changes from larger to smaller lighters and a search for hotels and food in Panama City, a noisy, dirty place where gunfights were common. To reach the Caribbean side, Callahan and Maney rode donkeys over a high ridge into a tropical forest filled with screeching monkeys, exotic birds, lush orchids, and acres of coconuts and tropical fruit. About ten miles into the forty-mile journey, the caravan emerged onto a swampy plain at the railroad terminus. There a long train of passenger-filled carriages were enshrouded by the engine's cinders and billowing smoke. This was the first railroad both Texans had ever seen. After rattling thirty miles to the port at Aspinwall (now Colón), they boarded the three-masted sidewheeler SS *Falcon,* sailed on December 17, and spent six days plying the Caribbean before landing in Havana, Cuba.[36]

In the 1850s Havana was a hub with vessels from many ports. Following a three-day layover, Callahan and Maney by mid-afternoon on December 26 embarked on the steamer SS *Philadelphia*, which arrived in New Orleans four days later. If lucky, they caught the December 31 departure for Galveston and Indianola; otherwise, they waited for the twice-weekly packet sailing on Wednesday, January 3. Callahan was certainly in Seguin on January 13, 1855, when he signed legal documents. Gone for 250 days, he had reunited with his wife and children, and he was introduced to newborn daughter Mahala Caroline.[37]

Erskine stayed behind with his cattle, working hard to get the best price. After a long trek, cattle needed fattening, so his herd moved slowly northward until by the summer of 1855 they grazed on the grasslands near San Francisco. Erskine anticipated making a handsome profit, calculating that with his total cost at $34,500 he had to sell each head for no less than forty-four dollars. In a July 31, 1855, letter to his son Andrew, a fretful Erskine exclaimed, "James sold his cattle for $45 per head. I think it is a Great sacrifice. He got all cash." The man who bought the James herd offered a similar price to Erskine. Now Erskine revealed a mercurial personality as, despite being encouraged to do otherwise, he held on to his cattle herd, confident in his ability to get a better price. By doing so, he irritated his family and creditors and was eventually thought to have lost touch with reality. But he was not alone—in October 1854 the *Texas State Gazette* had reported that many Texas herd owners in California were refusing to sell and waiting for better prices in the coming year.[38]

Back at El Capote, Andrew Erskine expected his father to sell his cattle quickly and return home to settle the ranch's debts. This did not happen, and what ensued was a series of increasingly vitriolic letters. Sometimes the elder Erskine or one of his two sons who stayed in California sent drafts to Andrew, usually $1,000 at a time. In the meantime, Erskine invested in potatoes, a copper mine, and a crop of oats and wheat, which became infected with rust. During this time, Callahan visited Andrew, demanding money, until finally in February 1856 Erskine sent $3,000 with instructions that he be paid first. Trust between Andrew and his father ended in late 1856 when Erskine announced that he and sons John and Michael were investing in a gold mine. Later letters do not mention cattle, though Erskine's grandson recalled the cattle were sold in 1857. By January 1858, Erskine and his two sons were working a gold mine in the Kern River area and Andrew's epistles became caustic as he juggled the mortgages held against El Capote. Erskine's last letter from California, dated April 18, 1859, offered yet another dose of optimism: "No change has taken place since my last . . . I hope in my next [letter I] will be able to give you some favorable account of things here." Five months later Andrew received an unexpected letter from his brother Michael, who confessed: "There are many devils like ourselves that are delving into the earth with vain hope that something equal if not surpassing the Comstock [lode] will be their reward but I fear many will be doomed to disappointment." In 1859, Erskine returned to Seguin, believing he could salvage his reputation and beloved ranch. His failures had forced him to borrow money from his nephew to pay for his passage home. Not a man to dwell on mistakes, he began anew. Joe Shelly rejoined him at El Capote, and in the fall of 1860, Erskine organized another cattle herd. Shelly drove the livestock to New Orleans, while Erskine traveled ahead by ship and arranged a sale. A second drive months later was equally profitable, so he organized a third herd and again made a good profit. Choosing to ride horseback from New Orleans back to the Guadalupe River valley, Erskine died en route on May 12, 1862, in New Iberia, Louisiana.[39]

At the onset of the Civil War, the Erskine family's finances were in disarray and the mortgages totaled more than the value of El Capote. Andrew and Johnson, his brother-in-law who had worked as a drover on the 1854 cattle drive, joined other locals in Company D, Fourth Texas Infantry, which was assigned to the Texas Brigade in the Army of Northern Virginia. Six weeks after his father died, Pvt. Andrew Erskine was mortally wounded at Gaines' Mill. Two months later, Lieutenant Johnson was killed at the Battle of Second Manassas. John and Michael sat out most of the war in California. The former returned to Texas in 1864, taking on the task of saving El Capote. He established a successful Texas-to-Kansas cattle trading company, but in August 1872 he was murdered in Kansas City. Michael arrived back in Seguin in 1868 but never returned to El Capote. Instead, he became a banker and cattleman in San Antonio, married late in life, and died in 1923, having outlived all his brothers. In the 1870s the Erskine family lost El Capote and today the original house, restored and relocated, is on the campus of the National Ranching Heritage Center at Texas Tech University in Lubbock.[40]

Henry Maney, Erskine's son-in-law, having accompanied Callahan to Texas across Panama, resumed his legal practice, and was elected Guadalupe County judge. During the Civil War, he was hospitalized and captured at Albuquerque. Paroled, he returned to Seguin and was elected to the Texas legislature, became a Republican, and was a delegate to the 1868 Texas Constitutional Convention. Appointed by the governor as a district judge, Maney embarked on a provocative tenure, feuding with courtroom lawyers and defying the Texas Supreme Court. He was removed by the legislature in 1874, but Guadalupe County voters again elected him county judge. In 1879 he sought his district's seat for Congress and lost. He retired from public service, living in San Antonio until he died on July 13, 1920, at the age of ninety-one.[41]

While the decline of the Erskine family and its influence within the Guadalupe River Basin still lay in the future, Callahan pondered his next step.

Reunited with his growing family, and certainly expecting to get his $1,500 for leading Erskine's cattle herd to California, he was eager to return to his Rio Blanco farm, ranch, and land development venture. He had his own livestock and land to tend, as well as plans to sell more property to finance further expansion. He had again shown that he had the leadership skills and durability to make his schemes a reality, if the right opportunities arose. He was just forty-one years of age, and he looked forward to many more years of hard work and service in Texas.

CHAPTER 11

Pittsburg Land Company, 1853–1856

"Comfortable home at a fair price"

One of the tasks for the district clerk of Comal County was auctioning land when a parcel was offered in a public sale. Today the clerk would be calling for bidders on a one-half share of the Horace Eggleston league. Eggleston, as the original owner of the league, had it platted on Martin's Fork of the Rio Blanco in May 1835, but sold it two years later. After several transfers, speculators Jabez Dean of Washington County and Joseph Fowler Jr. of New Orleans owned equal undivided halves. Then Fowler died and thirty-eight heirs claimed a portion of his estate. They and Dean could not agree on an equitable division, so the district judge ordered Fowler's half to be sold from the Comal County courthouse steps on the first Tuesday in July 1855. On that hot morning, the district clerk began by describing the property and the terms of the sale. Bidding was brisk, but two partners offered $1.94 per acre, a total of $4,295.55. These buyers, James Hughes Callahan and his partner, William E. Jones (figure 11.1), signed a twelve-month note and took possession of half of the league. With additional partners John D. Pitts and Andrew M. Lindsey, who bought the other half, the Pittsburg Land Company was launched.[1]

Callahan had returned to the Guadalupe River Basin at the end of the first week of 1855 after the cattle drive to California. He found a growing family, his wife, Sarah Medissa, having given birth to daughter Mahala Caroline, bringing the total number of their children to six. He initially focused on reestablishing his farm and ranch on the Rio Blanco. The fields needed to be fenced, plowed, and planted, and the livestock rounded up, branded, and earmarked. At the same time, Sarah had a house to clean, meals to cook, and

Fig. 11.1. William Early Jones portrait. Courtesy Fred Riley Jones, San Antonio.

clothes to wash, iron, and mend. Facing an immense workload, they decided to lease two slaves, a field hand and a housekeeper. By 1855, the dynamics of slavery in Texas had changed as the demand rose and prices increased. Enterprising owners hired out their slaves, and some bought slaves with the intention of leasing them out. An adult female could be leased for about $125 per year, and a male for $200, far less than the cost of buying them. This provided families such as the Callahans a way to be engaged in slavery.[2]

George P. Smith of Missouri was one of the enterprising speculators who profited from slave leasing in Texas. In 1850, thirty-three-year-old Smith lived in Cooper County, Missouri, with real property valued at $2,500 and no slaves; nearby was sixty-four-year-old Collin Johnson, who owned twelve slaves. The two men embarked on a slave-renting business, and in 1854 Smith moved to Guadalupe County, Texas, where over the years he paid taxes on between twenty-two and forty-six slaves. Johnson owned several of these slaves. Smith used some of these bondsmen on his own ranch, but he also hired out several. Looking to lease a slave, Callahan consulted with business acquaintance George B. Hollamon, and they signed together for the lease of two slaves. Acting as Johnson's agent, Smith leased Humphrey and Ester, with her daughter, to the two men, who paid $150 for Ester and pledged to pay $220 more upon returning both slaves on December 25, 1855. It is certain Callahan intended to use them first.[3]

By February 1855, Callahan, his family, and the two slaves had made their way along Devil's Backbone, across the Little Blanco River, and into the Rio Blanco valley. Upon their arrival at the homestead, which had been vacant for nine months, the women and girls assumed responsibility for the house, while Callahan and the two older boys checked on the cattle and hogs. Humphrey chopped firewood and split rails. Jones, Callahan's partner, probably visited; he lived in Curry's Creek, ten miles southwest. Five years earlier Jones had been among the first from the Guadalupe River valley to settle on Curry Creek, a spring-fed, meandering tributary of the Guadalupe. By 1855 he had a farm, shingle mill, and general store in the growing settlement. Because of Callahan's absence, Jones had much to discuss, and of greatest importance were the increasing Indian raids. Unless the frontier was safe, it would be difficult for Callahan and Jones to attract buyers to the Rio Blanco. Moreover, the complex ownership of the Eggleston league was unresolved, and without undisputed control of all of its land, the Pittsburg Land Company would not survive.[4]

Callahan's sole motivation for leading the cattle drive to California had been money, but he had returned home without the $1,500 Michael H. Erskine owed him. The Pittsburg Land Company was important to Callahan, and he needed to complete the purchase of the Eggleston Survey. He had full possession of 2,224 acres of the Benjamin Williams Survey (see map 9.2), so he could market land there to buyers. To do that, he placed an advertisement in one of Austin's premier newspapers, the *Texas State Gazette*. He provided his contact details and the names of five men who vouched for his character: John D. Pitts, Andrew M. Lindsey, Francis W. Chandler, Thomas H. Duggan, and John Henry Brown. Pitts, Lindsey, and Chandler became partners with Callahan and Jones in the Pittsburg Land Company. The valley of the Rio Blanco did offer great potential for ranchers, and thus for the Pittsburg Land Company. With its tributary of the Little Blanco

River and nearby Curry Creek, it formed a distinct part of the watershed for the Guadalupe River (see map 9.2). The profusion of porous white limestone along its length functioned as a sink, collecting rainwater into multitudes of interconnected aquifers that emerged as numerous springs spewing forth immense quantities of water. These include the headwaters of the Rio Blanco, Callahan Springs on his homestead, Cold Springs around which Pittsburg was platted, Twin Sisters Springs on the Little Blanco, and the source of Curry Creek. The thin soil in the area was not ideal for farming, but it generally had enough rain for native prairie grasses to proliferate, with bluestem and grama varieties dominating. When Callahan commented that the "grass grew as tall as the spurs on a man riding a horse," he was referring to these. Mesquite trees were not often found in the area because Indians annually burned the grass. Given these features, it was small wonder that Callahan and other ranchers moved to the Rio Blanco valley.[5]

There were few previous settlers to compete with Callahan and his partners. About 1700, Comanches had forced the Lipan Apaches south from the Llano Estacado and into the region. As the nineteenth century began, decimated by European diseases and constant warfare, the Lipans left the Rio Blanco valley, moving into the lower Guadalupe River Basin. After their departure, the Comanches consolidated the Rio Blanco area into the *Comancheria*. Their dominance waned with their defeats in 1840 and after Texas was annexed by the United States. With the Indian threat diminished, by the early 1850s Anglos and Germans began to settle on the Rio Blanco, Little Blanco, and Curry Creek. The first leagues granted in 1835 included those for Eggleston and Williams, but they were not developed. The remoteness of the area discouraged settlers, but this changed as the settlement line moved west, bringing rangers such as Callahan, who rode through the Rio Blanco region a handful of times (see maps 5.1, 5.2b, 5.2d). After Jones settled on Curry Creek, he urged Callahan to relocate and join him in bringing more settlers to a frontier that remained relatively empty.[6]

Before leaving for California, Callahan had sold two parcels from the Williams Survey on the Rio Blanco. Eli Clemmons Hinds paid $700 for 556 acres, placing him on the river's north bank, almost opposite Callahan's house (see map 9.2). Two sons of Woodson Blassingame purchased 177 acres for their father, promising to pay $525, and staked a plot west of the Callahan homestead. Callahan planned to sell his remaining 1,500 acres in the Williams Survey, and he also intended to broker land in the area owned by others. Soon brothers-in-law Augustus Pharr and James M. Day would move to the Rio Blanco. With these transactions in progress, the growing Pittsburg Land Company, and his ranching, Callahan anticipated prosperity. His wealth did increase during his first years on the Rio Blanco when his taxable assets in Comal County grew from $2,000 in 1853 to $5,665 by 1855. He was certainly an up-and-coming rancher and realtor typical of those who migrated from the Texas coastal plains up the river valleys and onto the Edwards Plateau.[7]

Hinds moved into a house he built on his Rio Blanco property, and the Blassingame brothers, Thomas and Luther, constructed a two-room dogtrot log cabin for their parents, Mary and Woodson Blassingame, who with four wards settled there in early 1855. Several men left Caldwell County and settled in the Rio Blanco area within a few miles of the Callahans. Among them were William N. Trainer, William S. Johnson, and Hugh McLaurin. Texas Revolution veteran Jesse L. McCrocklin and his son-in-law A. J. Kercheville moved from Washington County to McCrocklin's league, five miles east of Callahan. The next year brought the Reverend Josiah Cox, the Reverend Samuel Johnson, John M. Watson, Robert Page, and German-born John Lindemann Sr. with his son-in-law, Richard B. Goar, and son, John Lindemann Jr. Other arrivals included brothers-in-law Joseph R. Burleson and James C. Stephenson, and the William H. Babb family. The dominance of one-league surveys along the river meant that most who came with 320- or 160-acre grants were pushed to the higher elevations and generally lacked a ready water source. However, Callahan and the Pittsburg Land Company had two of the area's riverfront leagues, which made their land attractive.[8]

Two valleys nearby also drew settlers because they had available water and plots smaller than a league. Six miles south was the Little Blanco (see map 9.2), which from 1853 through 1856 became a popular location for 320- and 160-acre preemptions. The claimants included Joel Cherry and his three sons, brothers W. C. and William McKinney, William K. Holmes (Blassingame's son-in-law), George Lang, brothers Isaac and Solomon Tanner, John C. McKibbin, Christian Speiser, W. A. Blackwell, George McKinney, E. Benjamin George, John Tinney, John B. Green, Joseph Williams, R. M. Hokit, Ferguson Kyle, Otto Wuppermann, and brothers James C. and Francis M. Martin. These families resided in the upper reach of the Little Blanco, where Wuppermann began a village, Middletown, as a competitor to Pittsburg, the village planned by the Pittsburg Land Company. The local landmark was Twin Sisters peaks, where another community, Twin Sisters, grew up three miles downstream of Middletown. Germans dominated Twin Sisters, including Carl and Hermann Jonas, Jacob Keller, Johann Kraus, Carl Bechstadt, August Boenig, Henry Buemmer, August Dietz, A. Eggleing, Marius Erfurt, Alex Reszezynski, Christian Schmidt, and Andrew Wagenfuhr Sr. and Jr. Obviously, communities along the Little Blanco flourished.[9]

Settlers came early to Curry Creek (see map 9.2), ten miles southwest of Callahan's house. After 1846, Germans flocked up the Guadalupe River from New Braunfels to establish several villages, and Sisterdale, five miles west of the Curry's Creek settlement, became the hub of the area's German communities. Interestingly, Curry's Creek was settled largely by Anglos. Samuel B. Patton and his three sons were the first to settle there. The Jones family came next, followed by the Reverend Daniel Rawls, J. D. Brown, brothers Jesse and John Lawhon, William Sansom and his son John W., W. H. Clopton, John S. Hodges, James M. Pruitt, Carl Klemme, Neil Robinson, Edward Kriegner, George W. Saunders, J. B. Powell, N. P. Rector, and Carl Kaiser. The community extended along Curry Creek, with families operating cattle ranches, cotton farms, dairies, and gristmills and lumber mills. The area's first Masonic lodge and school was organized there, and by the end of 1855 a post office opened and stagecoaches regularly stopped. The most well-known resident was George W. Kendall, a founder of the *New Orleans Picayune* and survivor of the Santa Fe Expedition, who had a large sheep ranch a few miles northeast of Curry's Creek, near present-day Kendalia.[10]

By early 1855 the Rio Blanco area was becoming settled. March was the time for planting a garden, for which Sarah was responsible in addition to household chores. Her two oldest boys, Wesley Hughes and James Sanford, joined their father in wrangling livestock. German immigrant Otto Wuppermann, writing to his father, expressed astonishment at how children in Texas performed chores considered only suitable for adults in Germany. The small community social scene included dances and church gatherings. The Reverend Rawls of Curry's Creek started Methodist meetings in 1854 and John M. Watson opened a school. Compared to Seguin and Prairie Lea, the area in 1855 was undeveloped, but the people seemed committed to improving their conditions. A young man riding through that year spent the night with a family of six who lived in a large one-room cabin. He found a boiling coffee pot and a roaring fireplace and was feted with a "supper of bread, bear meat, venison, honey, and coffee." Surprisingly, he also found comfortable sleeping arrangements: the floor was covered with deerskins and several mattresses.[11]

Slavery was a part of this growing Southern frontier community. There were almost four dozen slaves in Curry's Creek, while there were a handful on the Rio Blanco, where Blassingame brought a slave and Hinds owned three, and one slave on the Little Blanco. Male slaves usually tended fields, though some in Curry's Creek worked in the gristmills and lumber mills. While tax rolls do not show a slave's gender, likely several females, like Ester, were house servants. Of course, slaves on the frontier faced unique dangers, such as Indian raids, but slaveowners still brought field hands and housekeepers with them, while others leased them, as the Callahans did with Humphrey and Ester. As part of the spring tasks in 1855, Callahan sent Humphrey to split rails and turn the sod in preparation for planting. Humphrey must have found tilling difficult as Texas had suffered an extended drought; according to one farmer in the area, trying to till was akin to "plowing sandstone." To make matters worse, hard freezes from February into March delayed planting. By April 1, the weather warmed and rains sporadically appeared, so with crops in the ground, farmers and ranchers turned to other chores. With almost 300 head of cattle and hogs, many of which had not been branded while he was gone, Callahan faced more than a week of branding, earmarking, and castrating. Dividing the tasks, each day Callahan sent Humphrey to the fields, while he took Wesley and James with him to tend the livestock.[12]

April 13 was pleasant and by noon the temperature was near 79 degrees. After working cattle all morning, Callahan and his sons stopped at the spring near their house to wash before lunch. They found Humphrey sitting on a log, clad in a long winter coat. The Callahan boys later commented that his heavy coat seemed odd considering the day's warmth; both of them were "in shirt sleeves." Earlier that day they had noticed Humphrey had a six-shooter and a large butcher knife. The presence of both weapons surprised them, and they may have told their father about it. Seeing the knife and revolver for the first time at the spring, Callahan demanded that Humphrey give him the weapons. The slave angrily refused, declaring that "his master allowed him to carry arms & he intended to do so." Alarmed, Callahan sent Wesley to fetch a shotgun from the house; when he returned, gun in hand, Humphrey sprinted for a horse tied to a nearby fence. Callahan shouted for him to stop and surrender his pistol and knife. Ignored, Callahan threatened to shoot Humphrey, whereupon the slave retorted, "That is just what I want you to do," and pulled the revolver from his coat pocket. Callahan emptied the shotgun and started firing his six-shooter. Badly wounded, Humphrey ran to a thicket and disappeared. The gunshots attracted the attention of others. Thomas S. Johnson, Hugh McLaurin, and Jacob Kercheville arrived, searched for the fugitive, and found his body 500 yards off the trail leading from Callahan's spring. They saw two wounds, and also found his knife and six-shooter. Investigating further, in the smokehouse they found bags of shot and powder in a trunk. News spread quickly. Callahan described the incident in a letter to his friend, Thomas H. Duggan, who became the source for an article in the *Texan Mercury*. The newspaper claimed Duggan heard that Humphrey harassed the Callahan family for several nights in succession by attempting to break into their house. Each time Callahan scared Humphrey away, usually finding him near the woodpile beside the house. The paper claimed Callahan feared Humphrey would harm his family; however, this conflicted with the impression of the Callahan boys. They were surprised by the slave's actions, claiming that up until April 13 "Humphrey had got along very well" with the Callahan family, and neighbor Thomas S. Johnson later swore he "knew Callahan to be kind to slaves."[13]

Undoubtedly, a slave's existence on the 1855 Texas frontier was harsh and oppressive. Adding to their misery, Humphrey and Ester were isolated from their familiar community near Seguin. It is impossible to comprehend the state of mind of either Callahan or Humphrey, but what is surprising is when Duggan had visited Callahan in March, he had seen Humphrey with a pistol. But an armed slave on the Texas frontier was not unknown. For example, a slave found the body of Thomas Neal near Fredericksburg. Neal had been killed by Indians, and the slave fired his own rifle to warn the neighborhood of an impending attack. Interested in protecting his slave chattel, it is conceivable that George P. Smith, Humphrey's owner, loaned him the knife and pistol for protection. Given Callahan's reaction to Humphrey, it is reasonable to conclude Humphrey did not have Callahan's permission to be armed. When Callahan saw the six-shooter, he decided to disarm Humphrey, who was loath to surrender his weapons, and a fatal conflict ensued. Callahan was remorseful and told James W. Nichols that he regretted killing Humphrey, an act that caused him "grief until his dying day."[14]

The laws concerning violence toward slaves provided that an Anglo could be indicted for abuse, including murder, but circumstances precipitating the act, such as threatening behavior by the slave or escape attempts, were taken into consideration. Of utmost concern was protecting a slave owner's property, and even if criminal charges were not pursued, civil action often was. No inquest followed Humphrey's death. However, Collin Johnson sued, seeking compensation for his loss, and a judge ordered Callahan to pay him $1,200. The killing of Humphrey followed the usual pattern in Caldwell, Guadalupe, and Comal Counties in that no criminal inquiry ensued. Between 1854 and 1856, there were sixteen newspaper reports of Anglos or Tejanos killing or injuring slaves in that area, including the Callahan incident, but indictments were rare. One of these incidents occurred on the Rio Blanco in 1856 when a Mr. Hays shot what he believed was a prowling Indian who turned out to be an escaping slave. Of course, many altercations between Anglos and slaves were never reported, which may explain the lack of indictments. But such was not the case with Callahan, whose letter to Duggan about Humphrey led to his case being publicized.[15]

While coping with his ranch and farm, Callahan still needed to gain full possession of the Eggleston league (see map 9.2). The legal tangle concerning Jabez Dean and the heirs of Joseph Fowler Jr. was only partly resolved by auctioning the latter's share of the tract at the Comal County courthouse in July 1855. The challenge for the five partners of the Pittsburg Land Company was to secure clear title to all the Eggleston Survey, part of which Dean still owned. Each of them—Callahan, Jones, Chandler, Lindsey, and Pitts—had skills or connections necessary for the success of their venture, and all had the ambition of opening the Rio Blanco valley to settlement. But they came from very different backgrounds.

Chandler, an attorney from Massachusetts, had represented the Fowler heirs in the lawsuit that prompted the auction of their interest in the Eggleston Survey. Arriving in Texas in 1846, he established a legal practice with Andrew J. Hamilton in La Grange and served in Benjamin McCulloch's command in the Mexican War. As an attorney, it was said that "no one against whom he had a just claim for collection could hope to escape" payment. Relocating to Austin in 1852, he was active in the Independent Order of Odd Fellows and the Baptist church. After an unsuccessful run for district attorney, Chandler joined the Know-Nothing Party and then helped organize the Constitutional Union Party, which opposed secession. Like many of his peers, Chandler accumulated wealth in land, purchasing town lots and land grant certificates, and he also acquired parcels in Bexar and Guadalupe Counties as a result of his work with estates and claims. Representing the Fowler heirs made him valuable to the Pittsburg Land Company, and he became a partner just twenty-two days after Callahan and Jones won the auction.[16]

Lindsey was a second-generation Texan whose childhood was infused with aspirations to develop land. His father, a respected surveyor, platted Galveston

Island, plotted land in Bexar County, surveyed the Military Road to the Red River, and helped create the town of San Marcos. His children were raised to be shrewd dealers in real estate, and their long list of transactions reveals their success. Having never married, Lindsey was devoted to his sister and brother and committed to protecting the family's investments. Besides owning land, Lindsey also conducted surveys, especially on the Rio Blanco and Little Blanco, making him a valuable partner. Surviving records from the Pittsburg Land Company suggest that he was punctilious and uncompromising as a businessman, which made him difficult. He was an advocate of the Know-Nothings and may have influenced other partners to join this party.[17]

Pitts spent his youth in Georgia, moving in the early 1830s from Washington County to Stewart County, where he farmed 2,200 acres, became an influential community member, and founded the city of Florence. Professionally, he was a civil engineer and land developer, but a flood or subsequent lawsuits devastated his development project. So, he left Georgia for Texas, persuading eleven families to join him. In 1847, he was appointed the engrossing secretary of the House of Representatives for the second Texas legislature, and afterward the adjutant general. During this time, he moved to the community of Stringtown on the road from New Braunfels to San Marcos. He was instrumental in founding a school and Methodist church there, and worked with Callahan to establish the first Methodist campground near Prairie Lea. He also founded the Texas Bible Society and was an early advocate of temperance. With six others, Pitts organized the first Masonic lodge in Hays County. He owned an extensive library, and he was a founding trustee of two institutions of higher learning. In addition to his civic interests, Pitts bred prime racehorses and was the first to raise sheep in Hays County. Like his partners, he invested in land, buying property in Hays County and along the Rio Blanco.[18]

Jones and Callahan were the senior partners in the Pittsburg Land Company, and their long-term friendship indicates they had much in common. Russell Jones Sr., William's paternal grandfather, settled in Wilkes County, Georgia, in 1780 and later relocated to Jackson County. In 1806, Russell Jones Jr. married Sophia Harris, and they had seven children, their fifth being William Early. They lived on Cabin Creek, one mile from the Callahans. Russell Jr., a wealthy planter who owned nearly thirty slaves, was prominent in community affairs. William attended Franklin College (now University of Georgia) and became a practicing attorney at twenty-three, four years after marrying Caroline Randle. In 1835 he bought and edited several newspapers, and during this period he also served in the Georgia House of Representatives. His younger brother Augustus joined the Texas Revolution, fighting in 1835 at Goliad, Lipantitlán, and Bexar. After being discharged on January 1, 1836, Augustus was sent to the United States to solicit funds and men, but he returned in time to fight at San Jacinto. Back in Jackson County after the war, Augustus persuaded William, their parents, and four siblings to move to Texas in 1840.[19]

Within months of arriving in Texas, William's father and youngest son died. Sophia, his mother, found life on the frontier difficult. She objected to her daughter Leticia's marriage and to her sons dividing her husband's assets, notably the slaves they brought from Georgia. Even after establishing themselves in Gonzales County, Sophia and Leticia yearned to return to Georgia. Leticia discouraged relatives from moving to Texas, complaining if the family could sell what they owned, they would leave since there was "nothing but Mexicans, Indians, rascals & thieves here to associate with." But William was determined to stay. He settled south of the Guadalupe River between Seguin and Gonzales, using a one-third league donation grant that he had bought in 1838 for $1,300. Once settled, Jones entered the social and political scene and was elected to the Republic's House of Representatives for two terms. He also practiced law, and during this time he and Callahan became close friends.[20]

As a first-term congressman, Jones proved to be a tightfisted fiscal conservative, an advocate of probate law that protected Texans' assets, and an opponent of foreign wars and Texas's annexation by the United States. When not in Congress, Jones continued his legal practice, appearing primarily in the Fourth District Court, which encompassed counties along the Guadalupe and San Antonio Rivers. His life abruptly changed during the 1842 fall term at San Antonio. He, Judge Anderson Hutchinson, attorney Andrew J. Neill, and others were taken from the courtroom as prisoners of the Mexican army. A surrender agreement with General Adrian Woll was negotiated by a committee that included Jones. They then marched under guard into Mexico to Perote Prison, arriving in a freezing norther. By that time, Neill had escaped to Mexico City, gotten a British passport, ridden to Vera Cruz, and sailed to the United States. Jones's ordeal at Perote changed his views. The conditions were as wretched as they were rumored to be. He was forced to haul sandstone while chained to another prisoner to deter escape. Hutchinson was in charge of a group that carried out "manure" every day. Texan and American prisoners petitioned the U.S. government to intervene, and President John Tyler sent Waddy Thompson to obtain their release. On March 22, 1843, after a three-month confinement, Jones, Hutchinson, and Samuel Maverick were delivered to Thompson. They were the first San Antonio captives freed. The three rode to Vera Cruz and on April 9 boarded the USS *Vincennes*. When they arrived in New Orleans, Hutchinson left to join his wife in Mississippi. Jones and Maverick boarded the schooner *New York* for Galveston, and from there Maverick went to San Antonio and Jones rode to east Texas, where he delivered speeches highlighting the harsh treatment of Texian prisoners in Mexico. Jones's imprisonment had radicalized him, and he now wanted to invade that country. The *Clarksville Standard* endorsed him for the vice-presidency, but by the end of the summer he returned to his farm and prepared to attend the Eighth Congress of the Republic of Texas.[21]

Jones resumed an active role in his second term in the Congress of the Republic. As chair of the foreign relations committee, he requested access to documents exchanged between Texas and England, France, Mexico, and especially the United States about annexation, which Jones opposed. President Sam Houston's refusal frustrated the Congress and inflamed Jones's already negative opinion of him. Also galling to Jones was Houston's veto of a bill to compensate Thompson for obtaining the release of the prisoners held by Mexico. As chairman of the Judiciary Committee, Jones advocated a change in the probate law to protect estates by establishing prioritization of debts and voted against a bill making it easier for a nonresident woman to transfer her Texas property without the consent of her husband. During the session, Jones sat on various special committees; one recommended the restriction of liquor sales. When a fight developed over the location of the Texas capital, Jones led the faction that denounced Houston's attempts to move the seat of government from Austin. Jones's final action as a congressman was to resign. After his release from Perote Prison, Judge Hutchinson had submitted his resignation. On February 4, 1844, the House and Senate held a joint election to fill the Fourth Judicial District vacancy. Jones had resigned his seat before the vote and, as the sole candidate, won unanimously.[22]

In the Republic era, district judges also served as associate justices of the Texas Supreme Court. Jones attended the 1844 and 1845 Supreme Court sessions and wrote nine of the thirty opinions issued. Jones's opinions were cogent and sophisticated and caught the attention of the U.S. chargé d'affaires, who proclaimed that Jones was the "most eloquent man that I have ever heard speak in Texas." None established precedents, but at least one affected a future partner. Reflecting the dominant attitude toward Indians in Texas, the Supreme Court made a significant ruling in *Herbert v. Moore*. The court, having concluded Indians were not a nation but rather wards of the state, concurred that postliminy (property taken in a time of war is restored to its prior owner) did not apply. This ruling underscored a historical contention that would come into play in Callahan's later expedition into Mexico.[23]

Jones presided over the Fourth and Second District courts from 1844 to 1851, signing the minutes with his distinctive flourish. He heard hundreds of cases affecting the fortunes and lives of almost everyone in the Guadalupe River Basin. He was the first judge to hold court in Comal, Guadalupe, Caldwell, Hays, and Williamson Counties, setting standards and tutoring officials in a district court's proper functioning. A few of his counties were unlike other judicial districts in Texas; he coped with Tejano, German, and Anglo defendants, plaintiffs, and jurors, arranging translations to and from English, Spanish, and German. Reports of his courtroom manner have not survived, but if his attention to detail in editing the court's minutes are an indication, he was meticulous in his conduct and must have expected the same from all present in the courtroom. The range of criminal cases he handled in Gonzales, Guadalupe, and Caldwell Counties is undoubtedly representative of his usual caseload. Citizens and judges took any *habeas corpus* hearing seriously, and one decided by Jones reveals his vision of justice. In Guadalupe County, a Tejano accused of stealing cattle claimed he was jailed without a bail hearing, and after listening to all parties Jones ruled the man was illegally incarcerated and ordered him to be freed on bail. Jones apparently believed in an equitable application of the law for all citizens. Certainly, this gave him a good reputation, enhancing his value as a business partner.[24]

Jones's performance as a district judge also enhanced his ties to his community. Texas attorneys, even immigrant lawyers from the United States, were licensed to practice by a district judge after being interviewed by experienced lawyers. In Comal, Guadalupe, Gillespie, and Fayette Counties, Jones administered several hundred U.S. citizenship oaths, primarily to German immigrants. Jones cemented his reputation for being fair in civil cases; often in land litigation, plaintiffs and defendants waived a jury trial and asked him to rule in their cases, such was their confidence in him. In a Guadalupe County case, Solomon Brill objected to Jones's brother, the plaintiff, being an estate's administrator, and Jones removed him. His impartiality was tested again in the 1849 fall term when Callahan asked Jones to rule in his lawsuit against James Patterson et al. When Jones declared in favor of Patterson, Callahan appealed to the Texas Supreme Court and lost. This was not unusual for Jones—out of seventy-three of his decisions appealed to the Texas Supreme Court, less than one third were reversed. His focus on fairness extended to women as well: his rulings helped both Prudence Holdridge and Emily Barker to retain property in difficult divorce cases. His activism extended to education, and while serving as a judge he and several others sought state charters to establish schools in Seguin, one of them the acclaimed Guadalupe High School. However, his legalistic focus did lead him, when the school declared bankruptcy in 1855, to sue successfully for a reimbursement of his donation.[25]

Personal changes led Jones to leave the bench and start a new career on Curry Creek. On Christmas Day 1847, Caroline Randle Jones acknowledged receipt of a divorce petition filed in the Guadalupe County district court by her husband. Jones declared that he had been a "good husband," treating his wife with the "greatest kindness, affection, & indulgence," but his hope for her "love and society" for the remainder of his life faded when she became "addicted to intemperance & to habitual excessive intoxication by ardent spirits." Two days later, the couple filed a joint declaration agreeing on a division of property and the care of their only surviving child, sixteen-year-old Willis. The judge kept the real and personal property, including slaves, and became sole guardian of Willis. Caroline agreed to an annual annuity of $250, though Jones could make, and Caroline could request, a one-time payment of $2,500 instead. An amended petition moved the hearing to Comal County. On March 7, 1848, Jones as judge gaveled the district court into session there and immediately appointed David C. Vanderlip to preside. Both parties were present as Judge Vanderlip swore in twelve jurors. After both submitted depositions, the jury awarded Jones a divorce on terms identical to the agreement he and Caroline had signed. She left Texas to live with her sister, Emaline Chandler Randle Holt, in Alabama and later in Tennessee. On July 20, 1848, the judge married Keziah Rice Rector Baxter, a twenty-six-year-old widow, and they settled on Jones's homestead on the Guadalupe, a few miles west of Seguin. On April 2, 1849, Keziah delivered twin boys, the first of seven children she would have with Jones.[26]

In May 1851, Jones decided not to stand for reelection. In a letter to the *Texas State Gazette,* he cited his long-standing ill health as the main impediment to continuing his judicial career. He also expressed a desire to leave public life to tend his "private affairs." Jones was alluding to his land investment along Curry Creek, where he had constructed a shingle mill. He sold his 606 acres on the Guadalupe River for $6,000 and bought James M. Day's 640-acre land warrant, which he had surveyed on Curry Creek. In the summer of 1851, Jones moved his family to the nascent community and with additional property created what his son called "one of the finest ranch-farms." An 1853 visitor claimed the family lived in a "beautiful mountain residence" supplied with "cool . . . mountain spring water" near a "first rate saw mill running by water and a great abundance of cypress timber." Jones did continue to practice law, appearing in the district courts of Comal and Guadalupe Counties, but he also began surveying on the Rio Blanco and Little Blanco with the intent of establishing the Pittsburg Land Company in tandem with Callahan. It was not Jones's first venture in development. He had begun buying land on the west bank of the Guadalupe in 1844, and within four years he accumulated almost 950 acres; in 1850 he acquired another 1,070 acres nearby. The sale of his 606-acre homesite demonstrated his acumen: the buyer, John H. Morrison, agreed to be responsible for the annuity to Caroline. The balance of the debt was to be paid to Jones over three years on an interest-bearing note. During the next few years, Jones sold his other Guadalupe County land, grossing $10,600, which he invested in the Pittsburg Land Company and other ventures along Curry Creek.[27]

Jones was thus a great asset for his new partners in the Pittsburg Land Company. As an individual, he was popular and well-respected. He was known to be scholarly but also adept at engaging people; on one occasion when the debate in the Republic's Congress turned rancorous, he calmed tempers with a "beautiful little speech, in his usual appropriate and happy manner." In the courtroom, he dispatched cases "with commendable facility" and his charges to juries were made in a "concise . . . [and] lucid manner." His political and legal reputations were matched by his business savvy, strong economic resources, and devotion to his community. Sometimes this led him to be a man of contradictions: he opposed secession but served as a militia captain during the Civil War; he was a slave owner but freed a black-Indian woman; he confounded Democrats by running for lieutenant governor as a Know-Nothing and playing an active role as a Republican during Reconstruction. And while Jones sought a quiet country life, as matters turned out, he and Callahan would have more than enough adventures. In 1855, however, the former congressman and judge seemed a good partner for the ranger captain and cattleman, and together with the young lawyer from Austin and two experienced land developers they seemed poised for success.[28]

Jones and Callahan worked together to acquire, plat, and market the Eggleston Survey in 1855. Dean was initially included in the planning, since he was useful in dealing with the owners of the other half of the survey, and at some point, Callahan and Jones invited Lindsey and Pitts into the partnership. They may have become doubtful about Dean's long-term participation, but his death one year later solved that problem. With the partners in place, the next step in forming the Pittsburg Land Company was to purchase the land from the Fowler heirs. It is almost certain that Callahan, Jones, Lindsey, and Pitts suggested that Fowler's heirs hire Chandler, then advised him to file suit on their behalf against Dean. When the Comal County district judge ordered the land sold at an auction in July 1855, Jones and Callahan became the highest bidders for the half share of the Eggleston league. Later, Dean's half was sold for $3,321 to the partnership of Jones, Callahan, Lindsey, Pitts, and Dean. Thus, Dean kept a one-tenth share, but after he died this was sold to Chandler.[29]

Callahan, Jones, Lindsey, Pitts, and Chandler may not have had complete possession of the Eggleston Survey in July 1855, but they acted as if they did. On July 25, the five signed "an article of agreement" merging their interests into a single unit encompassing the entire league, with each man owning an equal share and dividing expenses evenly. Chandler ensured that the partners had clear title to the Fowler share since, at the auction, he instructed the district clerk to issue a deed to all five men, even though two had only signed a promissory note for the property and had not paid in cash. The new owners made their first sale to Eli C. Hinds, giving him almost 300 acres on the western edge of the league. Hinds already owned land in the Williams Survey and paid $600 for this adjacent part of the Eggleston Survey. Additionally, the partners sold 320 acres for $550 to Callahan; this was where he had built his home, the most desirable parcel along this portion of the Rio Blanco. Callahan and Dean had made this arrangement when they divided the Williams Survey. Lastly, the five men agreed to plat a town around "Cold Springs," creating a village to be known as Pittsburg.[30]

Before signing the agreement on July 25, 1855, the Pittsburg Land Company partners had provisionally agreed on the terms when all five were together on July 3 in New Braunfels. Eager to start their project, on July 16 Lindsey had ridden to the cold springs on the Rio Blanco, stayed at Callahan's house, and "commenced to lay off [the] town," which took seven days, according to his diary. Platting the lots was hard work, and Lindsey used four chainmen: Hugh McLaurin, Joe Burleson, James C. Stephenson (Burleson's brother-in-law), and George Boon. Callahan and William Trainer also helped for a day. Reflecting the influence of religion, even on the Texas frontier, the crew did not work on Sunday and instead attended the

Reverend Josiah Cox's sermon. Lindsey returned to work on August 14, taking two days to finish platting the town. On July 17, he laid out the acreage for Callahan and Hinds, as well as a parcel recently sold to James M. Day.[31]

The Pittsburg Land Company partners set aside 520 acres for their town, which was centrally located in the Eggleston Survey on the south bank of the Rio Blanco where it made a ninety-degree bend (figure 11.2). The public

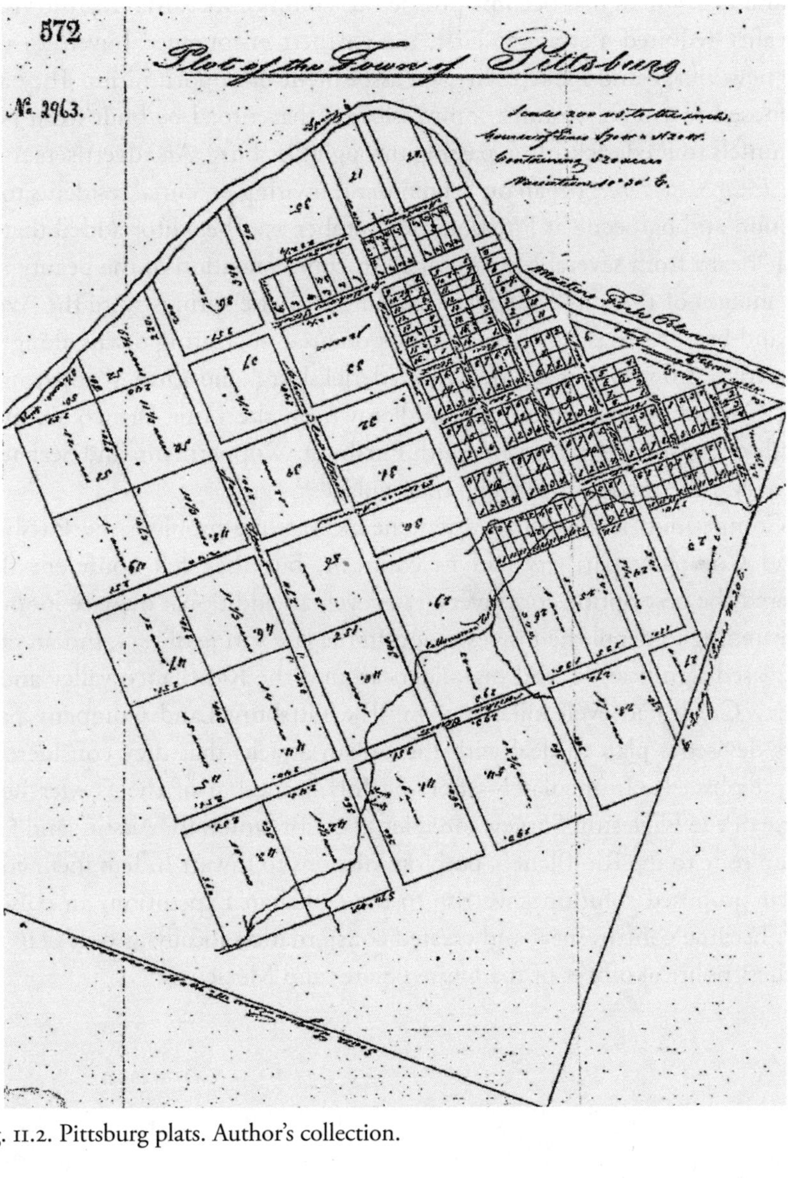

Fig. 11.2. Pittsburg plats. Author's collection.

square was situated on the northeast side, next to the cold springs. Lindsey plotted 209 half-acre town lots and thirty-seven farm lots, ranging from three to seventeen acres. Streets running north and south were named Jones, Chandler, Lindsey, Trainer, Democrat, American, Spring, and San Marcos; the east to west streets were Callahan, Blanco, San Antonio, First, Second, and Third. One farm lot was designated as the cemetery. Pittsburg was thus a typical Texas frontier town modeled in the manner of Seguin, Gonzales, and Prairie Lea, which had become prosperous communities. Making the vision a reality required a strategy. First, the partners encouraged buyers to visit the new village and make their own assessment of opportunities. They also proposed to Comal County commissioners that a road be built from New Braunfels to Fredericksburg, passing through Pittsburg. An advertisement in the *Texas State Times* began on September 1, inviting potential residents to an auction and barbecue at Pittsburg on October 25. The editor added that he had "heard from several sources much in commendation of the beauty and advantages of this city *in embryo*," adding that the springs were the "coldest and best in Texas." Others saw the potential in creating towns along the new route from New Braunfels to Fredericksburg, and Otto Wuppermann and Conrad Seabaugh started Middletown on the Little Blanco six miles south of Pittsburg. To compete with Pittsburg, Wuppermann and Seabaugh requested the road pass through their village.[32]

Competition from other entrepreneurs was one problem the Pittsburg Land Company partners had to confront, but they felt confident they offered the best option for buyers. However, an additional menace loomed, threatening to derail their investment. In the late spring of 1855, Indian raids increased significantly, and marauders around the Rio Blanco valley and at Curry Creek had even killed a man. The Pittsburg Land Company partners devised a plan to deal with the Indian attacks that they considered a major obstacle. Immediately after the July 3 auction of the Fowler heirs' share of the Eggleston Survey, Jones left New Braunfels for Austin, and Callahan rode to the Rio Blanco, both on missions to thwart Indian incursions. Their proposed solution gave rise to the Callahan Expedition, an episode that became controversial and created consternation locally as well as in the highest political offices of the United States and Mexico.

CHAPTER 12

The Callahan Expedition, 1855, Context

"¡Pero es tan solo un río!"

Success for the Pittsburg Land Company seemed assured after the partners obtained the deed for the Eggleston Survey, but they still faced two challenges. Collectively they had to repay loans of almost $8,000, but they were confident that could be done. Of greater concern were increasing Indian raids. However, these were resourceful and determined men, not easily dissuaded, and willing to use their many connections. They implemented a plan that became the 1855 Callahan Expedition, undertaken so the Pittsburg Land Company could protect its investment.

Complex local, national, and international trends merged in Texas in 1855 to create a volatile environment. By 1855 the Texas frontier extended from Gainesville on the Red River south to Fort Mason and Fort Clark, and then terminated at Fort Duncan on the Rio Grande (see map frontispiece). Westward expansion was accompanied by a debate between U.S. and Texas officials over the role of the army and local defense forces. On the national stage, the argument for the abolition of slavery increased in intensity, while in Texas, slave owners were alarmed about slaves escaping into Mexico. Moreover, Texans continued to be suspicious of Seminole and Maroon enclaves south of the Rio Grande in Coahuila. Meanwhile, persistent centralist (conservative) and federalist (liberal) disagreements in Mexico created an opportunity for the rise of a powerful *caudillo* in the north at the same time that filibustering efforts by some Texans increased tension on the border. This was enhanced by intensified Indian depredations, for which Lipan Apaches, recently displaced to Coahuila, were identified as the primary culprits. National and local leaders in the United States and Mexico, inexperienced in dealing with such problems, were unwilling to make concessions to secure a resolution. It was a political powder keg, and James Hughes Callahan lit the fuse with his expedition.

Over the decades, scholars have proposed contradictory explanations for the Callahan Expedition, and some even inserted fabrications into their analyses. Three primary perspectives on the expedition have emerged. First, some focus solely on the directive from Governor Elisha M. Pease to Callahan, which authorized him to pursue and punish raiding Indians. Second, some historians concluded that slave reclamation from Mexico was the campaign's primary motive. Third, others proposed that filibustering—the private, armed takeover of sovereign territory—was the goal. Each explanation deserves consideration, but for the Callahan Expedition to be fully understood, it must be examined within the historical context, coupled with a closer look at key personalities and locations.[1]

During the 1850s, conflicting ideologies regarding the expansion of slavery threatened to tear apart the United States. Passage of the Kansas-Nebraska Act in 1854, which negated the 1820 Missouri compromise, escalated sectional conflict, and chaos ensued when proslavery Missourians packed the Kansas polls, resulting in violent conflict that subsided but did not end when U.S. Dragoons were sent from Texas. (Dragoons were mounted infantry.) Republicans' primary strength derived from northerners who favored the abolition of slavery, while the Democrats survived by becoming the party of the South, embracing slavery. Abolitionists intensified their acts of civil disobedience, while organized groups began providing sanctuary to escaped slaves, and in this milieu the topic of Texas slaves escaping to Mexico became a focus. Slavery remained the prominent concern of most Texan politicians, and they sided with the Democrats and the rest of the South.[2]

Filibuster entered the American lexicon during the same era. Historian Robert E. May made two distinctions concerning the 1850s definition of filibuster: it included private military forces that invaded a country, and it excluded expeditions that had their government's explicit or implicit permission. The most prominent expeditions were led by Narciso López in Cuba and William Walker in Mexico, Nicaragua, and Honduras. Southerners, including Texans, supported these with the idea of expanding slavery, and foreign governments came to believe the United States gave tacit approval to adventurous, armed, ostensibly private expeditions in order to gain more territory. Between 1850 and 1853 along the Mexican border, José María de Jesús Carvajal led campaigns using Texan filibusters. Articles in Texan and Mexican publications reported other Rio Grande filibustering forays, including a few in 1855 that historians later conflated with the Callahan Expedition. Unsurprisingly, Mexico considered an armed Texan group near the border, filibuster or not, as a threat to its national security.[3]

To many residents of Texas and the United States in the 1850s, the Rio Grande was a distinct border that divided people of different customs and nationalities, but this perception ignored geography and history. The area on either side of the Rio Grande (Rio Bravo in Mexico) was a connected space that contained a river but was not divided by it. For centuries, crossing it had been unimpeded by any formality. Anthropologist José Dávila said it well: "¡Pero es tan solo un río!" (But it's just a river!) A broad chaparral stretched for about seventy-five miles on either side of the Rio Grande (map 12.1). In Texas, the Nueces River formed the northern boundary; in Mexico, the southern periphery followed the Rio Salado in the upper chaparral with an indistinct margin in the lower region. Between these two lay a ruthless, barren, and often desert-like territory where the weather was unremittingly harsh. While rainfall was usually scarce, during thunderstorms it could be torrential, creating raging streams without warning. Amid such harsh conditions, the most ruthless residents gathered. Maj. William Emory found this area well suited to hide outlaws and Indians. Lydia Spencer Lane, wife of an army lieutenant, recalled the region as "a dreary, desolate country, where nothing lived but Indians, snakes, and other venomous reptiles." Later, ethnohistorian James F. Brooks characterized the chaparral as "La Gran Ladronería" that had become "a *place* and a *process* organized around systemic thievery." Theft, murder, and worse were common, and traveling required precautions to avoid being ambushed. Officials struggled to maintain order, especially on the Mexican side. "Nomadic Indians kill cattle, steal horses, and bring death to the shepherds" was a common refrain. One Mexican official complained, "On the ranches, they were assaulting, robbing, or destroying everything they found." To make matters worse, some authorities joined in the criminal activity.[4]

All political lines in Texas faded when one issue was discussed: frontier security. On this subject, Texans shared a common goal. The violence in the chaparral often spilled into adjacent regions such as the Rio Blanco valley. Settlers on both sides of the Rio Grande by the 1850s concluded that marauding Indians were the principal threat, and the Treaty of Guadalupe

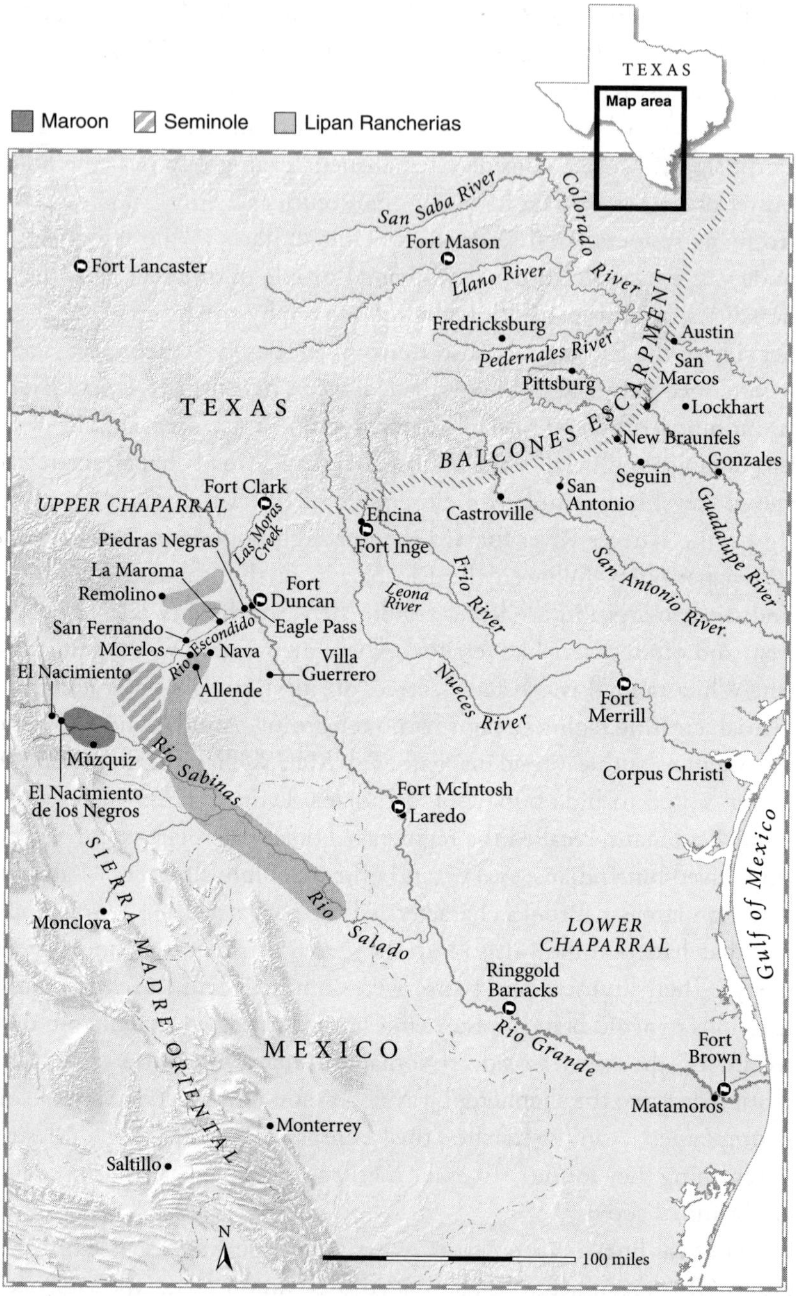

Map 12.1. Trans-Nueces and the Rio Salado chaparrals in Texas and Mexico and the Eagle Pass and Piedras Negras region, with locations of key towns and Seminole, Maroon, and Lipan rancherías, 1855. Map by Carol Zuber-Mallison.

Hidalgo in 1848 required both national governments to stop depredations originating in their territories. When Texas was a colony and republic, the primary defenders were rangers and militia, but after 1848 the U.S. Army became responsible for ensuring Texans' security. However, over time Texans' criticism grew increasingly strident as the Indians outmaneuvered the army. The problem was that federal and Texas officials had no common strategy. The army built forts on the frontier to protect the Texans. Initially, almost 1,000 mounted regular troops occupied these posts, but by 1849 they had been replaced with 300 dragoons supplemented by 1,000 infantry and 100 artillerymen. Federal officials also sought treaties that defined boundaries neither the Indians nor Anglos could cross. This plan was flawed due to renegade Indians still raiding and Anglos ignoring the boundaries. Indian reservations created in 1854 failed for the same reasons. Texans, on the other hand, wanted the Indians removed and expected the federal government to pay for rangers to do this. Every army general was loath to ask for rangers, believing they would cause more problems. Nevertheless, federal officials eventually asked Texas governors to muster ranger companies to work with the army, and sometimes a governor sent rangers into the field. From 1849 through 1853, almost two dozen ranger companies mustered. Army reports of Indian skirmishes during these years were revealing: eighteen in 1850, zero in 1851, one in 1852, and zero in 1853. These numbers convinced Texans that army infantry was ineffective except when supported by Texas Rangers. As the *Texas State Gazette* declared: "The idea of repelling mounted Indians, the most expert horsemen in the world, with a force of foot soldiers, is here looked upon as exceedingly foolish."[5]

The debate escalated in 1854. Pease had been governor for a year, and Gen. Persifor F. Smith had commanded the Department of Texas for four years. Both were very familiar with the situation and the mood of the people, but as the next two years would demonstrate, they did not agree on a solution and did not communicate effectively. Throughout 1854 almost every Texas newspaper printed reports of Indian raids. In March, the *San Antonio Ledger* criticized the army and doubted if confining Indians to reservations would stop the violence. A May editorial in Seguin's *Texan Mercury* captured the sentiments of southwest Texas: "The only force capable of achieving this difficult and dangerous task is the gallant and skillful Texas Ranger." Concerned citizens in eight counties sent petitions to Pease and Smith asking for mounted troops. Those in Webb County claimed several citizens had been killed by Indians, who stole horses and cattle in an area occupied by

500 army infantry. Individuals also sent warnings: William E. Jones warned Pease that settlements were in danger of being eliminated by Indian depredations. In a July 1854 letter replying to a petition from Bexar County, Pease urged Smith to send effective forces to the frontier. By mid-summer 1854, General Smith considered the menace of great concern and, with his troops spread thin, he asked Pease to organize six ranger companies. The governor scheduled a muster for November 1 and notified Smith and also the Secretary of War. Somehow Smith's and Pease's communications failed. In Austin, the army mustering officer refused to enroll the rangers, claiming that the muster order had been postponed. Pease was embarrassed and, in a November letter, scolded Smith while declaring that the six companies would be mustered into service anyhow. The general had depleted the governor's patience and goodwill. During the next crisis, Pease would act unilaterally.[6]

By early 1855, mustering officers had ushered into service companies led by John G. Walker, William R. Henry, and Charles E. Travis. These were posted at Fort Clark, where they defended against incursions in the upper chaparral. Meanwhile, the companies of Giles S. Boggess, William Fitzhugh, and Patrick H. Rogers rode the western frontier from their base at Fort Chadbourne. Subsequently, on March 10, General Smith reenlisted only the companies of Walker, Henry, and Travis. The reduced ranger force concentrated on the region southwest and west of San Antonio. Incomplete records exist for Travis, but the activities of Henry and Walker are well documented. Henry's actions have particularly influenced interpretations of the Callahan Expedition. Meanwhile, Indian raids continued. Citizens in the Rio Blanco area, along with those near San Antonio, grew increasingly agitated with what they saw as inadequate protection by ineffective federal troops and too few rangers. When Pease next responded, Callahan emerged as the leader for an enhanced ranger force, but he did so within the context of a brewing conflict resulting from Henry's activities.[7]

Henry, the grandson of American Revolutionary War patriot Patrick Henry, had settled in San Antonio after serving with the Second Florida Dragoons in the Mexican War. On December 11, 1850, he married a Tejana, Consolación Urrutia, whose father was a cartman. One year later, he bought the Navarro Stable in San Antonio, and in 1854 he was elected city marshal. The noted Texas Ranger John S. "Rip" Ford characterized him as brave but egotistical, adding that he was disrespectful of his superiors. An opportunistic adventurer, Henry's grandiose ideas included filibustering. In March 1855, while under army orders as a ranger captain, Henry offered his services to

General Ángel Trías, governor of Chihuahua. When rebuked, Henry insulted Trías by letter and solicited funds from Texans to organize a filibuster into Mexico. The project failed. Nevertheless, Henry took what few men he had and camped on the Leona River at the recently abandoned Fort Inge, whence he volunteered his services to Santiago Vidaurri, the new *caudillo* of Nuevo León. Vidaurri refused his offer. A few weeks later, Henry tried to organize volunteers to join Vidaurri, who again rejected him. On this occasion, the *National Intelligencer* castigated Henry, who defended himself in a letter to the *Texas State Times*. Not dissuaded, Henry crossed the Rio Grande with a force of forty men intending to "foment a revolution." Mexican authorities arrested them and escorted them back to the Rio Grande. Henry probably used this foray to try to catch runaway slaves, as it coincided with an attempt described by Frederick Law Olmsted. When his last venture collapsed at the end of August 1855, Henry and his men returned to San Antonio.[8]

Henry became a well-known and often not very well-liked figure. The *New York Times* reported that the spring 1855 fiasco provoked both Texas officials and General Smith. A lack of discipline by his rangers also led to inexcusable losses of property and livestock in D'Hanis, a village near Castroville. Authorities later discovered this scandal occurred while Henry was intoxicated. Additionally, American and Mexican army officers alike complained about Henry's incursions across the Rio Grande. Henry's criticism of General Smith, published in the *Texas State Times*, was a good example of the disrespect for superiors that Ford had noted, and officials on both sides of the border considered him a man to be avoided. In the first week of April, when Smith dismissed the three remaining ranger companies, Henry had arranged for his volunteers to send a censure resolution to Pease. Back in San Antonio in September 1855, Henry continued his crusade, writing a flattering letter to Pease asking for another command. Pease did not reply. Obviously, Henry was eager for yet another adventure on the Rio Grande, and the Callahan Expedition provided him a chance.[9]

The Callahan Expedition also offered a convenient stage for others to advance their ambitions. Santa Anna resumed power in Mexico in the early 1850s; in response, liberals Juan Álvarez and Ignacio Comonfort proclaimed the Plan de Ayutla, which called for removing Santa Anna, revising the Mexican constitution, and reestablishing representative government. By the spring of 1855, Santiago Vidaurri took advantage of the turmoil to establish a power base in north Mexico. Born in Nuevo León in 1809, Vidaurri had worked as a bureaucrat in local and state offices. His years in government service provided him with an extensive network of allies, while his political, business, and military insights made him a formidable leader. Vidaurri's charisma and fluency in English meant he was extraordinarily suited to meeting the needs of the border populace. He realized that collaboration with Texans was essential, so he promoted open trade. Although he opposed slavery, he would compromise if it increased his revenues and helped him acquire modern arms. Vidaurri overthrew the centralist governor in Nuevo León and seized Monterrey, the capital, while his allies occupied other towns and later combined Nuevo León with the states of Tamualipas and Coahuila with him as the head of government. However, southern factions blocked him from incorporating the state of San Luis Potosí. Their leaders feared that Vidaurri aspired to establish a new republic, and his contact with Texas slave owners and filibusters amplified their concerns. Luckily for him, the Callahan Expedition presented an opportunity to show his loyalty and deflect his opponents' protests.[10]

With the Callahan Expedition, Vidaurri had the aid of Colonel Edvard Emil Langberg. In 1835, the twenty-four-year-old Danish aristocrat had migrated to Mexico, where he joined Santa Anna's army. After graduating from the Colegio Militar as commander of the student corps in 1837, he returned in 1839 as a professor with the rank of captain. Rapid promotions to lieutenant colonel and colonel occurred in 1841 and 1846. During the Mexican War, Langberg fought in battles near Monterrey and Mexico City and was decorated for valor. More important, by the early 1850s he commanded troops in northern Chihuahua and Coahuila and consolidated a power base on the Rio Grande near Piedras Negras. He knew the region's geography and worked with the United States and Mexico Boundary Survey. Skilled at political reinvention, he had survived frequent changes of power. However, in 1854 his relationship with the recently returned Santa Anna soured. Suspecting his life was at risk, Langberg spent time in San Antonio and Austin in the spring of 1855 (map 12.2), becoming noted for his violin concerts. Here he met men who would later request his assistance in extraditing fugitive slaves. Attracted to the hotbed of exiled Mexican liberals in New Orleans, Langberg joined the intrigue. In June, sensing changes were afoot in Mexico, he decided to return to Coahuila but lingered in Texas for two months, where he again played concerts and visited with prominent friends in Austin and San Antonio. On this occasion, he made a specific proposal to extradite escaped slaves in exchange for fugitive Mexican peons. Langberg during the last week of July 1855 crossed the Rio Grande into Piedras Negras, where he accepted an appointment from Vidaurri as commandant of the

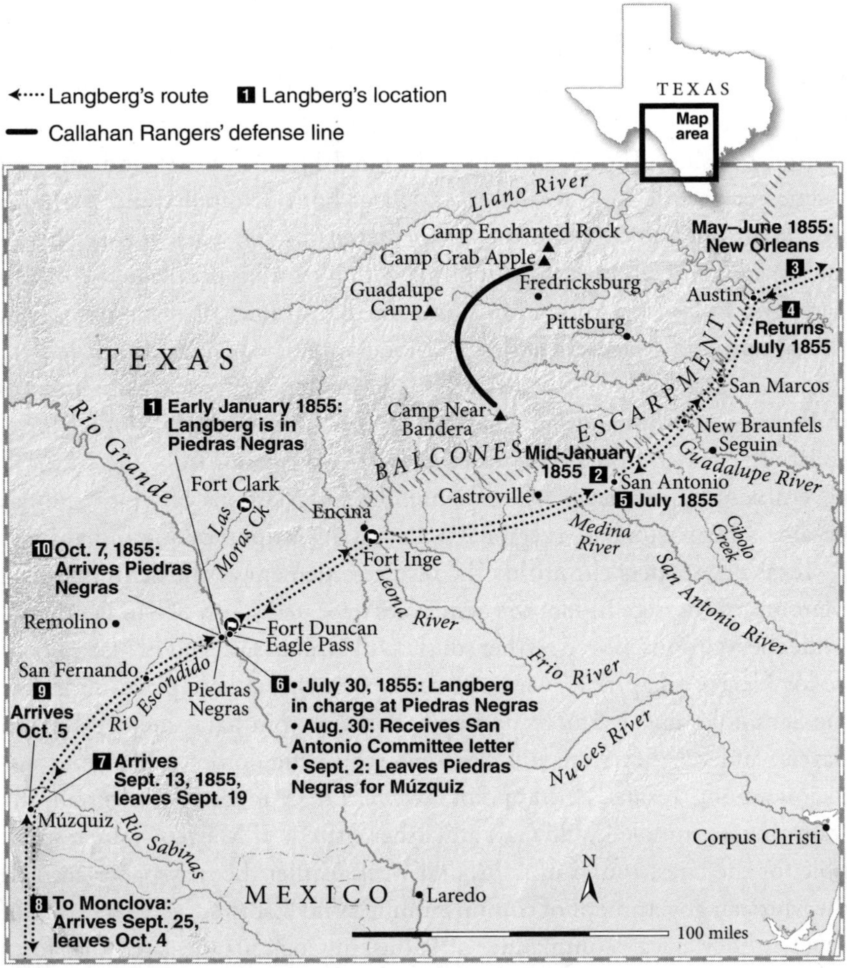

Map 12.2. Locations and routes of travel for Langberg (January–July 1855 and July 30–October 7, 1855). Map by Carol Zuber-Mallison.

garrison. Piedras Negras, like those in other towns on the Rio Grande, had been created to fulfill the requirements of the Treaty of Guadalupe Hidalgo. To combat Indians, Mexico posted regular soldiers and National Guard, while in nearby pueblos, citizens joined militias, which were at times armed by the state. Langberg commanded the garrison, auxiliary troops, and militias at Piedras Negras during the Callahan Expedition.[11]

Langberg's constituency included one unusual collection of people: communities of Seminoles and Maroons that had been established south of

Piedras Negras. Under Spanish rule, Florida was a haven for runaway slaves, and over time they founded Maroon communities. Meanwhile, Spanish Florida donated land to Creeks, who assimilated with other tribes, forming the Seminoles. Over time, the Seminoles and Maroons developed a symbiotic relationship. The United States acquired Florida in 1819 and initiated a series of wars leading to the expulsion of both Seminoles and Maroons to Indian Territory. A charismatic Seminole leader, Coacoochee, better known as Wild Cat, became dissatisfied with life for his people in the Indian Territory, so he led a migration south. In the summer of 1850, Seminoles, Kickapoos, and Maroons settled at Monclova Viejo, several miles west of Piedras Negras. Wild Cat was granted land in exchange for assisting militias in fighting Apaches and Comanches, and the Maroon leader, John Horse, collaborated with him and received the rank of captain from the Mexican government. Thus, the alliance of Seminoles and Maroons with local militias became a cornerstone in a regional policy to thwart plundering Indians.[12]

Texas newspapers chronicled the 1850 resettlement of the Seminoles and Maroons in Mexico. In 1853 the Seminoles relocated south of San Fernando, while the Maroons moved farther south to El Nacimiento and El Nacimiento de los Negros (map 12.1). Mexican authorities chose these places to isolate the Seminoles and Maroons and protect them from harassment by Anglo slavers, and yet they were still close enough to the border to generate suspicion among Texans. An 1854 *San Antonio Ledger* reporter was certain the "notorious Seminole [Wild Cat] and other citizens of Mexico" were responsible for the latest round of raids, and weeks earlier the newspaper accused the Mexican government of commissioning Wild Cat to steal Texas cattle. In August the Mexican commander of Parras, in Coahuila, declared that forty Lipans and Seminoles with ten Mexicans constituted a horse-thieving gang residing near the frontier. By August 1855, the *Texas State Times* considered the Seminoles to be such a serious menace that Texans were justified in pursuing them. Riled by these accusations, Wild Cat threatened to hang U.S. soldiers stationed at Fort Duncan. On the other hand, he was not considered a typical Indian. The *Texas State Gazette* received a report claiming that Wild Cat and fifty of his men were baptized, and Eagle Pass resident Jane Cazneau asserted that he dressed neatly and displayed a dignified attitude. All the same, Texans mistrusted Wild Cat and his band, especially after Col. Joseph Plympton reported that Wild Cat and Mexican General Gerónimo Cardona had an agreement in which the Seminoles stole horses from Texas and Cardona kept half of each herd.[13]

Seminoles and Maroons were not the only Indian settlers near Piedras Negras. Unlike the U.S. policy of concentrating Indians on reservations, Mexico employed a decentralized approach. Efforts began in the 1820s and expanded substantially from 1853 through 1855, with Coahuila in the vanguard. Extended Lipan family groups were settled in locations ranging from the northwest at Remolino southeast along the Salado and Sabinas rivers to sites near Laredo (map 12.1). These small settlements, termed *rancherías*, usually contained three to five families, or about twenty-five to fifty inhabitants. If raids occurred, officials could identify the offending ranchería, and militia, with Seminole and Maroon support, could punish the raiders. However, government officials benefited by purchasing the plunder, mostly horses, when Lipan raiding parties returned from Texas. Don Armando, who maintains the tribe's oral history, claimed that by the early 1850s the Mexican army and Lipans had a symbiotic relationship, with the Lipans trading stolen livestock for material goods. Thus, Lipans found a market for stolen goods among government officials, Mexican citizens, and even the Seminoles and Maroons. This of course enraged Texans, who were the focus of many raids.[14]

Mexico truthfully could no more control their rancherías than the United States could handle its reservations. In 1849, Captain Francisco de Castañeda wrote about peaceful Comanche, Lipan, and Mescalero villages, but the next year Mescaleros and Lipans attacked Seminoles near Villa del Guerrero. The following year, as relations soured again, officials cautioned Seminoles and Maroons to avoid contact with Lipans, and later that year the Seminoles accused Lipans of stealing their cattle and threatened to retaliate by kidnapping Lipan wives and children. In June 1851, the Seminoles had their chance for revenge when a joint force, including Kickapoos and Maroons, fought Lipans and Comanches. By late 1851, after Fort Duncan officers returned fifty Mexicans captured by Lipans and Comanches, tranquility slowly reemerged. In September of the next year, Lipan chief Coyote appealed for peace, and Mexican officers dispatched a commission to arrange a truce. However, several Lipans crossed the Rio Grande into Texas and stayed there. Throughout 1852 and into 1853, Mexican officials made several visits to Lipan villages, hoping to sign a peace treaty, but just as often the Lipans crossed the Rio Grande into Texas. Animosity flared again in August 1853 when a band of Lipans killed a young boy near Abasolo. Militia, with Seminoles, hounded them until the Lipans crossed into Texas, where they sold the horses stolen in the raid. After August 1853, there were few reports of clashes between Lipans and other Indians or Mexican citizens, but tension persisted within this apparently peaceful coexistence.[15]

Texans had good reason not to celebrate the apparent peace south of the border. By 1853, many northern Coahuilans had become weary of fighting Indians and were receptive to peaceful overtures, which the Lipans periodically made. The Mexican government signed a treaty with the Lipans, causing those in Texas to migrate south of the Rio Grande, settling near San Fernando and on the Rio San Antonio and Rio Salado. From their new rancherías, the Lipans raided into Texas, returning with livestock that they sold or traded to locals. They even stole horses from the U.S. Army, causing Fort Duncan's commander to ask permission to cross into Mexico, a request refused by Mexican officials. Violence perpetrated by Indians remained infrequent in Mexico throughout most of 1854 and into 1855, according to reports that local leaders submitted to the state government. This quiet phase corresponds to the upswing in depredation reported in Texas. In essence, the perpetrators set their sights on Texas and generally left Mexican villages and rancherías in peace. The Callahan Expedition would abruptly end this symbiotic serenity.[16]

Texans considered the Lipans to be devious, treacherous, and cunning, but they also observed a clever resourcefulness that allowed Lipans to exploit their enemy's weaknesses. Diplomatically astute, Lipan leaders negotiated alliances against their enemies, and although small in number they created an inordinate amount of havoc. With all Lipans concentrated in Mexico by early 1855, they were ready for the next raiding season and Texans along the frontier knew what to expect. General Smith informed the adjutant general to be ready, but what they did not realize was that the ever-vigilant Lipans had observed the precipitous removal of the Second Dragoons from Forts Duncan and Clark in May 1855. The Lipans knew that with this powerful mobile force out of the way, effective federal resistance to raids had all but disappeared.[17]

It is relevant to note that the hundred or so Lipans who crossed into Mexico in 1854 were the last organized kinship group of their culture. When Apaches centuries earlier had migrated to the southwest, one faction amalgamated with Indians from Mexico. These, the Lipans, settled in family groups in what would become south central Texas, including the Guadalupe River Basin. Caught between expanding empires of Comanches and Spanish, the Lipans slowly dwindled as they were driven farther south. They did ally with the Spanish and later the Anglos against the Comanches, but their alliance with the Republic of Texas ended when Anglos killed two Lipans, one of them Chief Flacco's son. Disillusioned, Flacco led his band to Coahuila. In May 1854, Chiquita's band was accused of murdering an Anglo family, but in fact Tonkawas were guilty. Disgusted, Chiquita led his band into Mexico after being invited by the governor of Coahuila. Once in Mexico, Chiquita's followers joined Lipan rancherías close to San Fernando, near Remolino twenty miles west, and in the chaparral from Allende down the Río Salado (map 12.1). Another small Lipan group arrived later that year after spurning an invitation to settle on one of the two reservations along the upper Brazos River in Texas. The new arrivals joined other Lipans in collaborating with Mexicans, selling them horses and other goods stolen in Texas.[18]

While Indians who stole livestock were an obvious threat to Texans, the presence of the Seminoles and Maroons were of particular interest to slaves and slave owners in Texas. Slaves regarded them as a haven and owners as a threat. As early as 1850, and increasingly so by the decade's midpoint, Texas slave owners devised numerous approaches to retrieve runaways that included bargaining with Wild Cat, bounty rewards, dispatching slavers, filibustering, lobbying Congress, and cajoling the army. Even with pressure by prominent Texas politicians, the army refused to cooperate, and Congress balked at enacting legislation beyond the 1850 Reclamation of Fugitives from Labor Act. However, the federal government did try to negotiate an extradition treaty, which Mexico declined. Some slave owners sought another alternative by promoting the formation of a country between Texas and Mexico, but filibustering failed to create the Republic of Sierra Madre. These invasions only hardened Mexico's resolve to support fugitive slaves and the Seminole and Maroon settlements. After all, Wild Cat, John Horse, and their militias had contributed to repelling various incursions.[19]

Texans persisted in chasing runaway slaves in Mexico despite their failure to find any significant numbers of them. Raids into Mexico seldom returned with escaped slaves, while those that did generally found only one or two. According to Coahuila records, attempts to recover escaped slaves there occurred mostly at Villa de Guerrero in 1851. Local official Manuel Flores in March told the Saltillo government that an American had died attempting to take a black man to Texas, and later he reported several Americans had tried to transport blacks across the border. In October, Guerrero's alcalde reported that Tom Crawford had captured two black men and was requesting passports to return them to Texas. No slavers were reported entering Coahuila in 1852 and 1853; however, in October 1854 the governor issued a warning that 500 *filibusteros* intent on capturing blacks were expected. Significantly, the Coahuila archives mentioned no American slavers in 1855, but in Guerrero, officials arrested two Mexicans who had seized two escaped slaves and tried to carry them into Texas. At least according to Mexican documents, slavers had little success in repatriating fugitives.[20]

The persistence of Texans in chasing escaped slaves over the Rio Grande has influenced many interpretations of the Callahan Expedition. Much of this scholarship has been based on a pronouncement made by John S. "Rip" Ford in 1855 that 4,000 slaves had fled to Mexico. Ford had served in the Republic of Texas Congress and as an army officer and ranger captain before being elected to the Texas legislature. He edited several newspapers, including the Austin-based *Texas State Times* from 1852 to 1857, so he was well-known and respected. His approximation of 4,000 fugitive slaves over a ten-year period suggests that 400 escaped each year. However, German abolitionist Ferdinand Kapp estimated only 150 slaves ran away in Texas during 1853. In contrast, the 1860 census analyst Joseph Kennedy calculated that an average 20 escaped each year. What accounts for the differences in these estimates? Articles and reward advertisements from Texas newspapers in 1854 and 1855 document that 177 slaves escaped, about 90 each year, and about 40 percent were captured or killed, thus casting grave doubt on Ford's estimate. Moreover, a few were recaptured on the northwest frontier, indicating that nonslave states or territories, not Mexico, were their destination. In another dataset, as of March 2018 the ongoing Texas Runaway Slave Project reported that about 2,600 slaves had escaped from 1836 through the end of the Civil War—almost 100 per year. In sum, the records show the number of slaves escaping to Mexico was small. That said, the issue was not inconsequential. For slave owners, even one escaped slave was one too many.[21]

Mexican reports again corroborate the impression that few slaves escaped across the Rio Grande. This may be due to paucity of documentation, as even the Archivo General del Estado de Coahuila holds few records. One exception is documentation for David Thomas, a slave who fled from Texas in 1849, with his daughter and grandchildren, and settled in Allende. Moreover, references to *los negros* after 1850 generally refer to Maroons, not fugitive bondsmen. Still, a few escaped slaves were reported to authorities; for example, in 1853 the mayor of Nadadores near Monclova saw three runaway slaves in his village. In 1855, only two reports of escaped slaves appeared in correspondence by Coahuila authorities. Occasionally Mexicans tried to take fugitive bondsmen back to Texas, as noted earlier in Guerrero, but the lack of documentation concerning escaped slaves in Coahuila seems remarkable if hundreds or thousands escaped from Texas between 1846 and 1855. Nevertheless, believing Ford's exaggerated estimate, Texas slave owners wanted a formal mechanism through which they could retrieve their property. Given the length of the Rio Grande border, the success of any reclamation effort was problematic, but the increase of such efforts during the summer of 1855 led some historians to conflate slave hunting and the Callahan Expedition.[22]

With the 1855 seizure of Nuevo León by Vidaurri and Langberg in command at Piedras Negras, Texas slave owners sensed a new opportunity. While in Texas, Langberg had endorsed exchanging escaped slaves for fugitive Mexican peons. His proposal had three points: he would accept military help from Texas if requested by the Mexican government; Texas would provide 2,000 armed men ready to enter Mexico; and he would be paid $80,000. In late August 1855, Langberg was contacted by some Texas friends, members of the "San Antonio Committee" for slave recovery. In 1854 and 1855, recovery was a recurrent theme at community meetings, especially in counties where Indian raids were less common. Most endorsed an extradition treaty, but other options included increases in rewards for the return of fugitive slaves and a bounty for the capture or indictment of individuals who assisted escapees. A few resolutions resulted in local vigilance committees, and two such committees proceeded with actions that culminated in a dialogue with Mexican officials. In addition to the San Antonio Committee, "The Directing Committee" of slave owners meeting in Bastrop set in motion another plan.[23]

In June 1855, the Directing Committee at Bastrop commissioned Bennett Riddells to contact Vidaurri. Riddells carried a written proposal prepared by San Antonio resident Hanson Alsbury that included elements of Langberg's scheme. Alsbury's participation in both the San Antonio and Bastrop committees reflects the broad collaboration across counties by leaders in the slave recovery movement. Initially, Vidaurri sent Riddells back to Texas, advising him to obtain a formal proposal from the Texas government. When Riddells returned to Mexico in early October 1855, he informed Vidaurri that Pease had no legal power to negotiate an extradition agreement. Nevertheless, Riddells said that the governor had suggested an alternative that would accomplish the same results, and that the Directing Committee guaranteed the legislature would ratify it. Texas slave owners wanted to reclaim their escaped slaves, and Vidaurri was pragmatic enough to accept an arrangement if it also achieved his goals. Riddells is a mysterious figure. From 1850 to 1852 he was the U.S. consul in Chihuahua, where he operated a hotel for several years after marrying a local woman. Pleading poverty, he resigned as consul and moved to Mazatlan in 1853. How Riddells became involved with the Directing Committee or what became of him is unknown. Nevertheless, his activities in 1855 caused a few historians to link him to the Callahan Expedition.[24]

The involvement of Riddells and Alsbury reveals the prominence of San Antonio as a base for slavers. By 1855, San Antonio had become a cosmopolitan community of 7,000, but it was divided. Germans lived on the eastern edge while Anglos, as many northerners as southerners, occupied the northern section. Tejanos and immigrant Mexicans resided in La Villita on the southern periphery. The population was almost equally split between the three groups, although slaves were few in number. The army headquarters were in San Antonio, and military spending contributed greatly to prosperity and growth. Within range of Indian attacks, local citizens urged state and federal officials to increase the military, including ranger companies, and many of the latter, mustered in 1854 and 1855, rode from San Antonio into the chaparral. It was not hard to recruit—there were countless unemployed adventurers, including many former soldiers. When not employed in productive jobs, these vagabonds often engaged in illegal activities, and recruits for chastising Indians or hunting slaves could easily be found in all parts of the city.[25]

Southwest of San Antonio, in the upper chaparral, the twin towns of Eagle Pass, Texas, and Piedras Negras, Coahuila, on opposite sides of the Rio Grande, provided a good base for an intriguer like Langberg. A major trade and smuggling route from Saltillo had existed for decades at a nearby crossing, Paso del Águila. In 1849 Capt. Sidney Burbank selected a site nearby for Fort Duncan; as the post grew, tents and straw structures were replaced by permanent structures. With the rush to the California gold fields, the Eagle Pass area became a staging station and a stop on the San Diego–San Antonio mail route. Nevertheless, in 1855 it was a "wretched place to live," according to Lydia Spencer Lane. Piedras Negras was even less appealing. Olmsted labeled it a "wretched-looking Mexican town" composed of caves, mud-walled houses with thatched roofs, and a commercial center of adobe, one-story structures with two-wheel carts scattered helter-skelter. In August 1850, Colonel Juan Manuel Maldonado established a garrison, La Colonia Militar de Guerrero en Piedras Negras, across the Rio Grande from Fort Duncan.

With two armies and thriving commerce, legal and otherwise, citizens began to enjoy an energetic and sometimes violent existence. Drinking, gambling, and prostitution flourished. The atmosphere attracted characters who willingly dealt in contraband or at the very least looked the other way.[26]

Callahan would lead his expedition through Piedras Negras toward San Fernando de Rosas (present-day Zaragoza). A smooth road, thirty feet wide, followed the course of the Rio Escondido and connected Piedras Negras to San Fernando; about halfway between them was the village of La Maroma (map 12.1). Slightly west and parallel to the Rio Escondido was the Río San Antonio, both supplying abundant water to irrigate crops that grew bountifully around the pueblos. In San Fernando, straight, wide streets and avenues formed square blocks for business and residential buildings, and an aqueduct supplied water for drinking and irrigation. Colorful adobe houses topped by cement roofs stood in town, while thatched roof *jacales* sat farther out. Olmsted remarked that Kickapoos, Lipans, and Seminoles mingled in the community like "they were masters of the town," illustrating the symbiotic relationship between the Indians, locals, and authorities. San Fernando and nearby pueblos had a militia, into which Indians were sometimes conscripted.[27]

The events that would bring Callahan into this area may have begun with the schemes of Henry, Riddells, Alsbury, Langberg, and Vidaurri, but they were defined by the decisions of three other men: Governor Pease, General Smith, and Captain Burbank. Texans elected Pease to two terms as governor in the 1850s, after he fought in the Texas Revolution, helped write the Republic's constitution, and served in a variety of public offices before and after annexation. Thus, Pease was an experienced politician. Smith, a brevet major general, commanded the Department of Texas during Pease's two terms. During the Mexican War, Smith commanded a brigade with distinction at Monterrey, Vera Cruz, Contreras, and Churubusco. He became the first commander of California's Pacific Division before coming to Texas. A cautious, methodical administrator and an indefatigable leader with good organizational skills, Smith failed to grasp the dynamics of the Texas border. By 1855 he was also a sick, obese man who could hardly walk, afflictions that affected his ability to be an effective commander. Burbank, the child of a career army officer, had graduated from West Point and fought in the Seminole Wars, but he had not served in Mexico. He founded Fort Duncan, and he returned to that command in 1855. Having spent five years in charge of posts on the Rio Grande, Burbank had ample exposure to the border's political and military intrigues. In many respects, he was like Smith. Cautious and pedantic, he appeared to hesitate in a crisis, waiting to see which way the political winds blew before taking a stand.[28]

In the early fall of 1855, the Callahan Expedition ignited a powder keg that was primed to explode. A long list of conflicts and schemes reached a crescendo, and the border towns of Piedras Negras and Eagle Pass found themselves at the center of a storm. Political instability in Mexico and the threat of filibusters put Mexican officials along the Rio Grande on high alert, and the allure of Mexico as a haven for runaway slaves inflated suspicions in Texas concerning the border at a time when the national debate on slavery was reaching epic proportions. Added to this, the inability of the army to stop Indian raids came under scrutiny against a backdrop of persistent attacks from rancherías in Mexico. Texans demanded the mobilization of rangers. A respected leader, Callahan, was selected by Governor Pease, who provided explicit instructions about his objective. In theory, the Callahan Expedition seemed a straightforward assignment; the rangers had retaliated against Indian raids many times before. No one, least of all Callahan, anticipated what transpired during his mission. It proved a brutal awakening for him.

CHAPTER 13

The Callahan Expedition, 1855, Preparation

"Follow them up and chastize them wherever they may be found"

If a single event set the Callahan Expedition in motion, it was the brutal killing of an Anglo by Indians near the Rio Blanco. Early on May 26, 1855, a Saturday, two unarmed men rode through a swarm of grasshoppers into an open field searching for cattle on William E. Jones's Curry Creek ranch. Suddenly, five Indians crawled over the creek bank and charged them. In a helter-skelter pursuit, Sebron, a young slave, escaped, but the overseer, Jesse Lawhon, did not. Using every ruse, including sliding down a thirty-foot cliff, Lawhon was unable to shake his pursuers. His naked body was found stretched over a bush; he had been bludgeoned and shot through with arrows and bullets. The brutality of his murder lit the fuse of a charged powder keg.[1]

Throughout 1854 the Blanco River valley had experienced uncommonly dry weather, and prospects for rain in 1855 remained bleak as James Hughes Callahan and his Pittsburg Land Company partners settled on a development strategy. In July 1855, partner Andrew M. Lindsey began platting town and farms lots for the new village of Pittsburg, and the five men agreed on a marketing plan that included an auction and barbecue in October. Prompted by Lawhon's death, they also adopted another objective: quelling Indian raids in the valley. A few days after the May attack, Jones had sent a letter to Governor Elisha M. Pease insisting the government should prevent further atrocities. He also wrote an evocative account of the incident, which was published in area newspapers. When Indian raids continued, Jones rode from New Braunfels to Austin on July 3 to urge Pease to create a company of Texas Rangers under the command of Callahan. Francis W. Chandler, who lived in Austin, probably accompanied Jones to the Governor's office. The other partners encouraged young men in the Guadalupe River Basin to enlist, and Callahan contacted Ed Burleson Jr., whom he wanted as his second in command. On July 5, 1855, the Callahan Expedition began when Pease invited Callahan to form a ranger company.[2]

By the summer of 1855, even skeptical Gen. Persifor F. Smith recognized the Lipans posed a threat to Texans from their rancherías inside Mexico. In November 1854, Texas Indian agent George T. Howard had reported that the Mexican government had invited the Lipans in Texas to settle in Coahuila near San Fernando and Remolino, while to the southeast more Lipan rancherías stretched almost to Laredo (see map 12.1). Beginning in March 1855, Texas newspapers were again reporting Indian raids along the frontier. A March 3 letter to the *Texas State Gazette* reported that two men had been killed near Fredericksburg. That same day, another reader wrote that Indians had killed cattle and horses on the San Saba River. Eagle Pass rancher Benjamin Thomas told the *San Antonio Texan* about his complaints to Mexican officials concerning horse thefts by Lipans, adding that he might have to abandon his ranch. Later in March, the *Texas State Gazette* reported that on the Pedernales River five horses were stolen, as well as four near the San Saba crossing, and Indians had ridden within 25 miles of San Antonio. A month later, the editor sarcastically noted that the army "cannot do more than keep their weapons and quarters clean." Other editorials followed, complaining about the army's ineptitude and the need for a constantly employed force of local men.[3]

According to the local newspapers, hostilities continued through July, with Lawhon one of many casualties. Lipans mortally wounded a Mexican ranch hand and stole horses at a Cibolo Creek ranch northeast of San Antonio. One week later, subscribers read of seven horses being stolen from Leon Springs, nineteen miles from San Antonio, and yet another on Cibolo Creek. Reports came from as far away as El Paso, where the U.S. Boundary Commission had twenty-three mules stolen. Meanwhile, raiders made their third excursion for the year in the San Saba River valley, stealing several horses. Raids spread south as Indians took a cowboy's mount near the Medina River, west of San Antonio. Editors once more blamed the army: "there is evidently a want of distribution of military force in the Indian country." A Fredericksburg woman fretted that her husband could not earn a livelihood hauling provisions since Indians stole his horses. The editors of the *San Antonio Ledger* and *Texas State Gazette* not only wrote about the raids' devastating effect on frontier families but also claimed the violence convinced many potential immigrants to go elsewhere. Medina River residents announced that unless the frontier was protected, they would have to abandon their homes. Meanwhile, George W. Kendall, the *New Orleans Picayune* co-owner, now a sheep rancher near Curry's Creek, chastised authorities for a lack of mounted forces on the frontier, which, if present, he insisted would restore confidence to existing inhabitants and induce others to settle.[4]

Jones's lengthy narrative on Lawhon's murder placed him in the vanguard of advocates for rangers to stop Indian raids. First published in the *Texas State Times*, it presented a haunting, grisly description of Lawhon's killing. Just weeks later, the *Texan Mercury* recounted the attack to a wider readership. In a note to Smith, Pease pointed out that Lawhon's murder took place in an area devoid of troops, and that it was one of several events in which the perpetrators escaped. He warned that citizens planned to confront the next attackers, creating the potential for a general war. In another letter, on June 20, Pease asked Smith to send mounted troops into the region for protection. Smith did not. In addition to writing to the *Texas State Times*, Jones and others wrote to the governor. Pease responded that he was pressing for a reply from Smith and assured Jones that he was not an "indifferent spectator of your sufferings." In the meantime, Pease suggested residents should organize for their own defense, as he expected raids to continue. This exchange signaled to the Pittsburg Land Company partners that the governor was receptive to forming a ranger company. Pease's attitude, and that of Texans in general, was not without justification. During 1855, both Texas and Kansas were volatile hotspots, and there was a Sioux uprising in the Upper Plains. Smith stripped the southern frontier of troops since he had to send units north.[5]

In 1855 there was a clear shift in the location of Indian raids in Texas. In 1854, there were more than fifty attacks, 60 percent of which took place south of the Colorado River, and most of those in the chaparral along the Nueces River. Only occasionally were residents targeted in the Blanco and Guadalupe River valleys. Of significance to Texans, army fights with Indians were infrequent, even when ranger companies joined them in the field. Editorials criticized the lack of effective government protection, and residents sent several petitions to the governor asking for greater safety. During the first six months of 1855, Indian raids almost disappeared in north and west

Texas, while south of the Colorado, unlike in 1854, most attacks occurred in the southern and eastern parts of the Edwards Plateau, and only rarely in the chaparral. Forty raids took place from the San Saba through Fredericksburg and into the Blanco, Guadalupe, and Medina River valleys, concentrating just west of San Antonio. Army and ranger fights with Indians then decreased. This geographic shift in raiding and decline in fighting correlates to the posting of army and ranger companies in western and northern Texas in 1855, leaving the Hill Country undefended. Ironically, this movement of defenders came when there were fewer cattle drives and wagon trains for raiding parties to target in the west; and, in the north, the settlement of Indians on the Brazos River reservations reduced raids. While citizens all over Texas still complained, and newspaper editorials, particularly in Austin and San Antonio, remained frequent and strident, it was Jones's neighbors who had the most reason to excoriate the army and clamor for ranger companies.[6]

While the location of Indian raids shifted in the time from 1854 to 1855, the gruesome intensity of the attacks did not change. It is impossible to determine the exact number of deaths, the amount of destruction, or the number of livestock stolen. However, an approximation from newspapers alone suggests that almost 1,000 head of livestock were lost, and fifty to one hundred Texans and Tejanos were killed during this period. In March 1854, Hamilton P. Bee claimed Indian raids near Laredo had resulted in the "death of nine men, several wounded, and the stealing of hundreds of horses and cattle." In May 1854, residents near San Patricio reported the killings of six American and thirty Mexican mustangers. These examples were outliers, since most raids left one or two individuals dead. Significant for Jones, in March 1854, people were killed on the Blanco in Callahan's neighborhood. Three events south of the Colorado in 1855 in particular galvanized people and newspaper editors: the slaying of the Forrester family along the Medina River, the murder of Lawhon, and a grisly attack in June 1855 that left two men dead near Encina on the Nueces. For the Pittsburg partners, the raids became personal when a band of Indians in late June 1855 hit Sisterdale, Curry's Creek settlement, and the Callahan homestead.[7]

While the raids in Texas south and west of San Antonio intensified from 1854 to 1855, Texans were aware that attacks south of the border were declining, which led to conclusions that would shape the Callahan Expedition. By 1854 the border area in Texas and Coahuila contained numerous Indians, including Lipans, Seminoles, Kickapoos, Mescaleros, and Comanches. Just as in Texas, Mexican officials believed Lipans, Mescaleros, and Comanches were the chief raiders. An 1873 Mexican government study, conducted to prove that both states suffered equally from Indian raids, in fact indicated that the number of attacks in Coahuila each year was about half that in the contiguous area of Texas, though losses were still considerable (276 people killed, 92 wounded, and 52 captured along with 2,289 horses stolen and 2,474 cattle rustled). Furthermore, records found in the Músquiz Collection and Luis Alberto Guajardo Papers at Yale University and the Archivo General del Estado Coahuila indicate that the number of raids and related fights with frontier defenders substantially decreased in this area from 1854 to 1855. U.S. Army officers reported in 1854 that Mexican military officers, including Coahuila's governor, General Gerónimo Cardona, colluded with Indians, especially Lipans and Wild Cat's Seminoles, to steal Texas horses and split the rewards. For Texans, this confirmed that the Indians had shifted from raiding in Mexico, where authorities either ignored or colluded with them, to South Texas, which had been left vulnerable by the deploying of army troops and Texas Rangers elsewhere.[8]

On July 5, 1855, Jones arrived in Austin intent on convincing Pease to order a ranger company into the field; he brought with him a petition from settlers in the Rio Blanco and Curry Creek areas. The petition tallied the recent raids, and Jones attached it to his July 5 letter to Pease. In a June 30 letter to the *Texas State Times*, Jones had blamed Smith for the calamities on the frontier, accusing the general of living a life of luxury in Corpus Christi. Jones's second letter also conveyed the anger of a community under siege. He described cattle butchering and mule thefts from Julius Dresel and Christoph Rhodius near Sisterdale, reported that Callahan's cattle were shot, and that the Hinds and Blassingame families had been harassed. Near Curry's Creek settlement, Indians chased the Reverend Daniel Rawls and later visited Jones's place. He told Pease in no uncertain terms that the locals could no longer sustain these assaults. Jones had relocated his family to San Antonio, indicating his fear. His bluntness jolted Pease into authorizing a ranger company to protect frontier settlements. The governor did not wait for federal approval, and only later did he inform Smith.[9]

Jones's two letters to the *Texas State Times* and the governor were not the only ones that stirred Pease into action. Jones in an earlier missive claimed that the public had not been fully informed about Indian raids, noting that since the murder of the Forrester family, seldom had a week passed without a raid between the Nueces and Colorado. Moreover, Jones complained that officials treated the reports with contempt, although almost $100,000 worth of horses and cattle had been stolen or destroyed. He worried that settlers would abandon their homesteads, and he demanded protection. In closing, Jones promised to continue to "impress upon the public mind the extent and character of the depredations." Pease sent a copy of this letter to Smith. Kendall, Jones's neighbor, wrote in the *New Orleans Picayune* about the army's ineffectiveness and Smith's obstinate attitude and reluctance to call out mounted volunteers. This article was also published in newspapers across Texas. Earlier, Ed Burleson Jr. told the *Texas State Times* that settlements on the Blanco and Guadalupe Rivers would disband unless protection was furnished. Then in late June, foreshadowing the Callahan Expedition, Burleson told the same newspaper that residents had outfitted themselves to chase the next Indians who attacked, and he planned to accompany them. The letters of Jones, Kendall, and Burleson together facilitated the Pittsburg Land Company partners' plan to stop the Indian raids.[10]

Jones did his best to keep his cause in the pages of the *Texas State Times*. He reported that locals followed Lawhon's killers to the Devil's River. On their return, the men encountered a band of Tonkawas, whose leader alleged that Comanches had killed Lawhon and intended to continue raiding the frontier from the Colorado to the Rio Grande. According to the Tonkawas, 200 or 300 Comanches operating together planned to establish their base camp in Mexico. Jones continued to criticize Smith for incompetence, but he also shamed Smith for treating petitions with disdain. After visiting Pease, Jones rode to San Marcos, whence on July 7 he wrote again to the governor, saying that he had received additional alarming reports that Indians had stolen thirty horses from Hermann Fisher, who lived ten miles from Callahan. Jones added that a man who lived between Jones and Callahan found a campsite near the Twin Sisters Mountains. He also noted that Felix Kyle, who lived on the Little Blanco, had lost nine horses. Defining his role, Jones told the governor, "I will endeavor to keep you advised of everything of importance connected with this subject." His tenacity made him effective in reporting Indian depredations and pressing for action, which led to the Callahan Expedition.[11]

Goaded by Jones and convinced that the raids were authentic, would continue, and the army would do nothing, Pease instructed Callahan to organize a ranger company to protect the settlements along the Guadalupe and Rio Blanco. The company would serve for three months, had to provide its own weapons and food, but could depend upon the legislature to reimburse expenses. Pease expected the rangers not to attack peaceable Indians nor molest citizens and their property. Callahan was to patrol the frontier, and if he encountered Indian raiders, he was "authorized to follow them up and chastize them wherever they may be found." Pease's action met with general approval in Texas. The *San Antonio Ledger* lauded the governor's promptness in defending the frontier and noted that "Captain Callahan [was] a gentleman who has seen much service against the Indians." Soon, other Americans, even as far as New York, read the news of Pease's directive to Callahan. To Callahan, these instructions were reminiscent of orders he had received more than a decade earlier. They focused on Indian raids, with no mention of filibustering or slave hunting.[12]

On July 25, Pease modified his instructions to Callahan, telling him of a Bexar County Committee's petition for a volunteer unit to be posted in Medina and Bexar Counties and relaying a promise from Smith to send troops into the region. The governor therefore told Callahan to station a portion of his men to provide protection west and south of Medina and Bexar Counties and to keep the remainder along the upper Guadalupe. What Pease did not know was that by the time his modified instructions went out, Callahan and his rangers were already in the field. In both of his directives, on July 5 and 25, Pease seemed to doubt that Callahan could recruit enough rangers. However, by July 20 Callahan had mustered into service seventy-four privates, one farrier, two buglers, four corporals, four sergeants, and two lieutenants. With a total of eighty-eight, including himself as captain, Callahan successfully raised not only his first Texas Ranger company since 1842, but also his largest ever. For rangers like Callahan, who had led patrols for the Republic of Texas, fighting Indians was familiar, but they could scarcely imagine the greater potential ramifications of their actions in the new political climate.[13]

After instructing Callahan twice in raising a ranger company to fight Indians, Pease reiterated their purpose in a response to the Bexar County Committee. Their July 12 petition, signed by 123 citizens, had warned that without protection their frontier would be abandoned. They recalled eight raids in 1854 and an additional fourteen since March 1855. Pease responded to the Bexar petition on July 25, the same day he directed Callahan to post some of his company on the Medina River. He informed the citizens of Callahan's command and his directive to Smith to provide protection for Medina and Bexar Counties; he also reassured them that authorizing more rangers remained an option if Indian raids continued. The petitioners shared the concern of the Pittsburg Land Company partners regarding the attacks; the Indians were the instigators and they had to be stopped. Both would closely watch the progress of the Callahan Expedition.[14]

As volunteers began to congregate at Pittsburg, John D. Pitts inspected and mustered the company—another example of the active role that Pittsburg Land Company partners took in the Callahan Expedition. The recruits elected Callahan as captain, Edward Burleson Jr. as first lieutenant, and William O. Kyle as second lieutenant (table 13.1). Burleson came with a sound Texas pedigree. His father, Ed Burleson Sr., commanded the Texian army in the Siege of Bexar and later served as a vice president for the Republic. The younger Burleson joined Jack Hays's Texas Mounted Rifles during the Mexican War, and his ranger service since then had involved more than one scrape with Indians. He married into the prominent Claiborne Kyle family, so Second Lieutenant Kyle was his brother-in-law. In April 1855, Burleson and Kyle together wrote to the *Texas State Times* describing the Indian raids in the Fredericksburg and Rio Blanco areas and proposing a ranger company be stationed nearby to protect residents. Three months later, they mustered as lieutenants in the Callahan Expedition.[15]

With mustering and officer elections completed on July 20, Callahan prepared to lead his men on their mission. Modern historians have concluded that his company was composed largely of experienced rangers; however, this is not correct. The eighty-eight recruits can be stratified by age: older than 35—six (7 percent); 27 through 35—thirteen (15 percent); 23 through 26—twenty-three (26 percent); and 16 through 22—forty-six (52 percent). Thus, sixty-nine (78 percent) were 26 or younger. An examination of muster rolls for ranger companies in previous years reveals only six of the sixty-nine (9 percent) had served as rangers; thus most of Callahan's Rangers were young novices. In the older two groups (nineteen men), about one-third had prior ranger service, with the participation of some extending back to the Republic. In sum, of the eighty-eight rangers enrolled, only about twelve (nearly 14 percent) had prior ranger experience. Of the twelve, only Callahan, Burleson, and James M. Patton could be described as experienced rangers, and just four had served in the Mexican War. Callahan's command was actually typical for the period. Since annexation, the rangers had become primarily young new arrivals with little concept of the hardship and danger that ranger duty entailed. The *Texan Mercury* editor lamented: "There are scores of individuals in the State who are called Rangers, but they are not of the original, genuine stamp. Three-fourths of them are 'green horns;' the others mostly 'riff-raff, tag-rag and bob-tail.'"[16]

Pease was understandably surprised that Callahan was able to muster his company by July 25, so soon after his authorization. An evaluation of enrollment periods for companies in previous years reveals a recruitment period of weeks, and even months, before a muster. An explanation of how Callahan was able to recruit so quickly may be found in an analysis of where his men resided. Three-fourths lived in Guadalupe, Caldwell, or Comal Counties; most were either friends of Callahan or knew him by reputation. Enlistments by county were Caldwell—23, Comal—23, Guadalupe—21, Hays—12, Travis—7, Bexar—1, and Bastrop—1. In Comal, 19 came from the Rio Blanco or Curry's Creek settlements, while in Caldwell County 14 lived in Prairie Lea; 37 were neighbors of Callahan. It helped that Callahan had a reputation as a ranger, and that he had extensive business and kinship networks. Also, accounts of Indian mayhem created a groundswell for intervention, and Jones's letters deserve credit, aided by Jones's own reputation as a former district judge. Moreover, Burleson, Lindsey, and Pitts resided in Hays County. All of these counties had plenty of new young arrivals. Texas's population increased almost 200 percent from 1850 to 1860, and most newcomers were males. In Caldwell and Guadalupe Counties, about 40 percent of the men owned no land but had a horse; newcomers often worked as hired hands and were not tied to family or real estate. Given these factors, two weeks to recruit seems right. As Private John Campbell recalled, Callahan was "quick to begin the execution of [his] orders, and hastily equipped his force."[17]

Texas historian John Gesick has inferred that the counties where the Callahan Expedition recruited linked the company to groups advocating the capture of escaped slaves in Mexico. However, none of the men's names are found in lists of known attendees at meetings held to discuss recapturing fugitives. Nevertheless, evidence of slave ownership by a ranger or a close family member could reflect how important slavery was to them. Surveying the 1850 and 1860 censuses and tax rolls for 1854, 1855, and 1856, only sixteen names (18 percent) emerged, suggesting a minority of Callahan's Rangers had a direct link to slave ownership. Moreover, the eight Burleson and Tom men represented three slave-owning families, so if only families are considered, direct ownership falls to 12.5 percent. Just two of the men resided in Bastrop and Bexar Counties, where runaway slaves had become a major topic in meetings that led to overtures to both Santiago Vidaurri and

Emilio Langberg. Thus, it is certain the efforts by the slave owners there did not translate to men joining Callahan, and so no evidence supports Gesick's supposition.[18]

With his men mustered, Callahan quickly prepared them. Although the volunteers had to provide their own weapons, horses, food, and forage, Callahan needed extensive preparation for a ninety-day mission, and what he did in a few days illustrates his leadership, planning, and logistical competence. Of utmost importance was inspecting the recruits' firearms. Like most Texans during this period, they were well armed. Based on the values of the arms listed in his muster rolls, most of Callahan's men had three firearms (table 13.1). Transplanted Yankee Stanton Denison, a San Antonio resident, was amazed that every Texan openly wore at least one six-shooter, and most had two belted around their waists. As the 1855 photograph of Private D. A. T. Walton (figure 13.1) demonstrates, Texans had six-shooters and "Bowie" knives, and the *Texas State Times* confirmed that rangers carried "mostly rifles and six shooters." Some of Callahan's recruits had Walker Colts, though most had lighter 1851 Colt Navy models. Muzzle-loading rifles remained common, and many who served with Callahan also had shotguns. Callahan's experience led him to focus on firepower, and in addition to the munitions brought by each man, he bought 5,000 Walker and 3,000 Eley waterproof percussion caps, 170 pounds of lead, 50 two-pound bags of shot, and 50 two-kilogram bags of rifle powder. The Callahan Expedition thus had the ability to fire as much as 800 rounds in a minute.[19]

While the volunteers brought some food with them, Burleson obtained "2,263 Rations of Subsistence," enough for almost four weeks, from Thomas Durham, a San Marcos merchant; one of his sons had joined Callahan's company. Immediately before his departure, Callahan dispatched Burleson with another list of supplies, including 5,270 rations, to Austin merchant Swante Swenson. Pease had authorized a three-month muster, and Callahan's purchase from Swenson ensured he had sufficient supplies. These actions, including acquiring the munitions mentioned earlier, indicate that Callahan intended to remain in the field for the full term. Flour, cornmeal, bacon, coffee, sugar, and dried beef comprised the common subsistence rations. A couple of tents, requisitioned from Swenson, along with other camp supplies completed the baggage. Thirteen mules and ten packhorses carried this load. Before departure, the farrier examined the hooves of 113 animals, replacing worn horseshoes, and the men test-fired their weapons. Callahan looked out for the volunteers' health by contracting with twenty-three-year-old Comal

Table 13.1. Muster roll, Capt. James H. Callahan's Ranger Company

Name	Rank	Age	Residence	Value: Horse	Value: Arms	Remarks
James H. Callahan	Capt.	40	Rio Blanco	$150	$100	Lost 1 six-shooter
Edward Burleson Jr.	1st Lt.	29	San Marcos	150	100	Acting QM
William Kyle	2nd Lt.	25	San Marcos	150	75	
Constantine M. Conly (Connally)	Sgt.	24	Prairie Lea	85	75	
William H. Word (Ward)	2nd Sgt.	28	Prairie Lea	120	50	Lost horse, saddle, bridle
Joel B. Sanders	3rd Sgt.	24	Prairie Lea	125	75	Horse captured at river
Riley Lewis	4th Sgt.	24	Seguin	100	60	
Charles Taylor	1st Corp.	18	San Marcos	85	75	
Benjamin Elam	2nd Corp.	25	Prairie Lea	75	50	
Thomas B. Boon	3rd Corp.	19	Prairie Lea	120	75	
William F. McMurrain	4th Corp.	23	Prairie Lea	120	75	
John McCoy	1st Bugler	16	Rio Blanco	100	50	
Isaac Tanner	2nd Bugler	18	Rio Blanco	75	75	
Jacob Roberts	Farrier	30	Seguin	100	75	
Samuel L. Alridge	Pvt.	40	Prairie Lea	100	25	
John A. Baughn	Pvt.	24	San Marcos	85	75	Lost gun
Zachariah P. Bugg	Pvt.	24	San Marcos	150	75	Lost gun, pistol
Aaron Burleson	Pvt.	22	Austin	125	75	
David C. Burleson	Pvt.	19	San Marcos	100	75	
B. Eustace Benton	Pvt.	18	Seguin	100	75	Wounded at Escondido, lost horse
Henry W. Bridges	Pvt.	19	Seguin	120	75	
Jacob F. Byler	Pvt.	25	Seguin	100	75	
Edward Burleson	Pvt.	20	San Marcos	75	75	
Luther Blassingame	Pvt.	20	Seguin	85	20	Horse captured at river
Paul Brotson (Brotze)	Pvt.	20	Comal	85	20	

(*continued*)

Table 13.1. (*continued*)

				Value		
Name	*Rank*	*Age*	*Residence*	*Horse*	*Arms*	*Remarks*
Robert Copender	Pvt.	20	Seguin	65	75	
William A. Carry	Pvt.	20	Prairie Lea	100	75	Horse captured at river
John (F.) Campbell	Pvt.	21	Curry's Creek	75	75	
William C. Campbell	Pvt.	22	Curry's Creek	100	70	
William H. Clopton	Pvt.	21	Curry's Creek	75	65	Killed at Escondido, lost horse
Thomas A. Carey	Pvt.	21	Curry's Creek	75	60	Horse captured at river
Henry (S.) Davis	Pvt.	21	San Marcos	85	75	Horse captured at river
Samuel Durham	Pvt.	27	San Marcos	150	75	
James (A.) Darby	Pvt.	23	Seguin	85	75	
Isham L. Davis	Pvt.	24	Lockhart	100	75	Horse captured at river
William A. Dewooddie	Pvt.	22	Onion Creek	100	75	
Jack Ellis	Pvt.	25	San Marcos	100	75	Commissary Sgt.
Lemuel Fentress	Pvt.	30	Rio Blanco	100	75	
Joseph G. Hines	Pvt.	20	Lockhart	120	50	Horse captured at river
John Hoffler (Haufler)	Pvt.	22	Comal	85	50	
Bedford Hamet	Pvt.	23	Austin	100	50	
John F. Hamilton	Pvt.	24	Austin	75	30	
Tilford D. Hines	Pvt.	27	Seguin	100	20	
Elijah Harris	Pvt.	29	Prairie Lea	75	25	
Rufus Hynyard (Hinyard)	Pvt.	30	Cibolo	100	20	
William J. Johnson	Pvt.	23	Lockhart	100	20	
Thomas Johnson	Pvt.	21	Rio Blanco	85	35	Horse captured at river

Name	Rank	Age	Residence	Value Horse	 Arms	Remarks
Albert Jones	Pvt.	19	Austin	65	30	
Polk R. Kyle	Pvt.	19	San Marcos	100	—	Wounded at Escondido
John H. Lesseman (Lessmann)	Pvt.	19	Comal	65	25	
John A. McCrocklin	Pvt.	20	Rio Blanco	100	30	Horse killed at Escondido
Jonathan J. Miers	Pvt.	18	Prairie Lea	85	15	Horse captured at river
Francis M. Martin	Pvt.	20	Rio Blanco	85	35	Horse lost at river
Thomas N. McKenzie	Pvt.	22	Prairie Lea	135	15	
Charles T. McGehee	Pvt.	18	Bastrop	150	40	
Adolphus Norman	Pvt.	20	Curry's Creek	75	35	
Benjamin O'Banion	Pvt.	26	York's Creek	125	10	
Robert Page	Pvt.	20	Rio Blanco	100	35	Horse captured at river
Thomas Pullum	Pvt.	40	Plum Creek	120	20	
William A. Pitts	Pvt.	24	Seguin	125	18	Lost 1 six-shooter
James M. Patton	Pvt.	44	Curry's Creek	120	35	Lost pack mule at Escondido
William Pearson	Pvt.	22	Curry's Creek	150	35	
Benjamin F. Patton	Pvt.	21	Curry's Creek	85	35	Wounded at Escondido
James Pogue	Pvt.	19	Austin	125	75	
Robert Ruse	Pvt.	27	Austin	75	70	
Daniel B. Shuler	Pvt.	23	Lockhart	75	60	
William Snell	Pvt.	23	Austin	100	75	
George W. Shuler	Pvt.	21	Lockhart	75	60	
Samuel G. Smith	Pvt.	40	Prairie Lea	85	75	Horse killed at Escondido
Johnson Snibble	Pvt.	30	Comal	100	60	

(*continued*)

Table 13.1. (*continued*)

Name	Rank	Age	Residence	Value: Horse	Value: Arms	Remarks
Augustus Smith (Schmidt)	Pvt.	27	Bexar	125	75	Killed at Escondido, lost equipment
Lafayette Stokes	Pvt.	30	Guadalupe	125	40	Lost horse, equipment
Oscar Starke	Pvt.	22	Guadalupe	135	75	
John W. Sansom	Pvt.	21	Curry's Creek	100	75	
Velarius B. Sanders	Pvt.	21	Cibolo	100	75	Lost rifle at Escondido
George W. Tom	Pvt.	19	Seguin	100	65	
Solomon Tanner	Pvt.	20	Rio Blanco	75	75	Horse captured at river
William Tom (Jr.)	Pvt.	22	Seguin	115	75	Lost gun
(Hughes) Simpson Tom	Pvt.	18	Seguin	150	50	
David Walton	Pvt.	25	Seguin	150	65	
Hezekiah Williams	Pvt.	18	Seguin	90	75	Horse captured at river
Emanuel Wydick	Pvt.	24	Prairie Lea	85	85	Horse captured at river
Robert W. Ware	Pvt.	24	Prairie Lea	85	50	Horse captured at river
Peter W. Williams	Pvt.	24	Lockhart	125	75	Horse captured at river
John R. Wilcox	Pvt.	18	Lockhart	75	35	
Edward Wayland	Pvt.	30	Curry's Creek	85	75	
James L. Weems	Pvt.	22	Seguin	100	65	
Ewel M. Wright	Pvt.	18	Prairie Lea	100	75	Wounded at Escondido

Sources: MR, Callahan, July 20, 1855, Oversize 401-723, Folder 6, TRMR, TAGD, TSLA; List of *Power of Attorney,* 1855-59 (bulk 1855-56) Box 401-1185 Folder 1, TRR, TAGD, TSLA.
Note: Order of entries reflects that of the original muster roll. Names in parentheses correct the spelling or clarify the person's identity. Pvt. Edward Burleson is the brother of Aaron Burleson and the cousin of 1st Lt. Edward Burleson Jr. and Pvt. David C. Burleson.

Fig. 13.1. D. A. T. Walton with pistol and knife, ca. 1855, D.A.T. Walton Collection. Courtesy of Bryan Wildenthal Memorial Library, Sul Ross State University, Alpine, Texas

County resident James G. Barbee, a physician, to be the company's surgeon. All of these preparations took just a few days, so Callahan led his men into the field before Pease sent the July 25 letter modifying his orders. In another example of the centrality of the expedition to the success of the Pittsburg Land Company, the partners signed their development agreement on the day the Callahan Rangers departed.[20]

The pattern of Indian raids in 1854 implicated three potential perpetrators. In West Texas, Mescaleros were responsible for attacks on mail carriers, wagon trains, and cattle drives. Along the settlement line, Comanches, riding from the Llano Estacado, and Lipans, coming from the western Balcones Escarpment or Mexico, were considered the culprits. In 1855 the dynamic changed. Mescaleros still controlled West Texas, but many Comanches settled on their Brazos River reservation, where, according to Indian agent Robert S. Neighbors, they "greased their rifles and hung them up," though a renegade band moved farther north into the Texas Panhandle. However, the Lipans were in northern Coahuila (see map 12.1) and seemed to be focusing their raids on South Texas. Today it is impossible to be certain which tribe made the 1855 raids from the San Saba River to west of San Antonio. The locations indicate any roaming band of Comanches or Lipans could have been responsible, and Texans had little difficulty in blaming both groups. Nevertheless, most Texans came to believe that the Lipans were the primary perpetrators.[21]

While Callahan's men organized and deployed, Indian attacks continued, with seventeen farms and ranches and a stagecoach raided during July 1855. On Sunday, July 1, Indians chased Reverend Rawls on his way from Curry Creek to preach at Pittsburg. However, during the next few weeks most of the raids, including one by seventy-two warriors, occurred west and south of San Antonio. On July 16, men from Goliad and Karnes Counties chased horse rustlers toward the Rio Grande and swore the thieves were Lipans living in Mexico who crossed the Rio Grande fifty miles south of Eagle Pass. Texans became more anxious upon hearing 300 Lipans had stolen 1,500 horses. From mid-July, the raids mostly occurred west of Castroville along the road to Eagle Pass, beginning when a young boy, Charles Eichhorn, outran several Indians. On July 15 near the Medina River, New York traveler Dr. J. D. B. Stillman said Indians had stolen all the horses in the neighborhood. A week later, Indians raided three ranches south of San Antonio and drove off almost 100 horses, and the next week they hit four places near Encina, where they destroyed corn and watermelon fields. About the same time, three miles west of D'Hanis during a rainstorm, thirteen Indians attacked a stage bound for Eagle Pass, but when a passenger shot one of them, they dispersed. The Lipans were again considered to be the culprits, since Eagle Pass was where they often crossed the border.[22]

At Enchanted Rock, Callahan couriered his first report to Pease on August 10, remarking that he had received Pease's July 25 order. Callahan first deployed his rangers in an arc from north of Fredericksburg south along the upper Guadalupe, with Kyle commanding the northern sector and Burleson leading the southern group. Pease's July 25 modifications caused Callahan to shift one-fourth of his company south to "Camp Near Bandera," on the Medina (map 13.1). A second group of twenty-two men remained near the

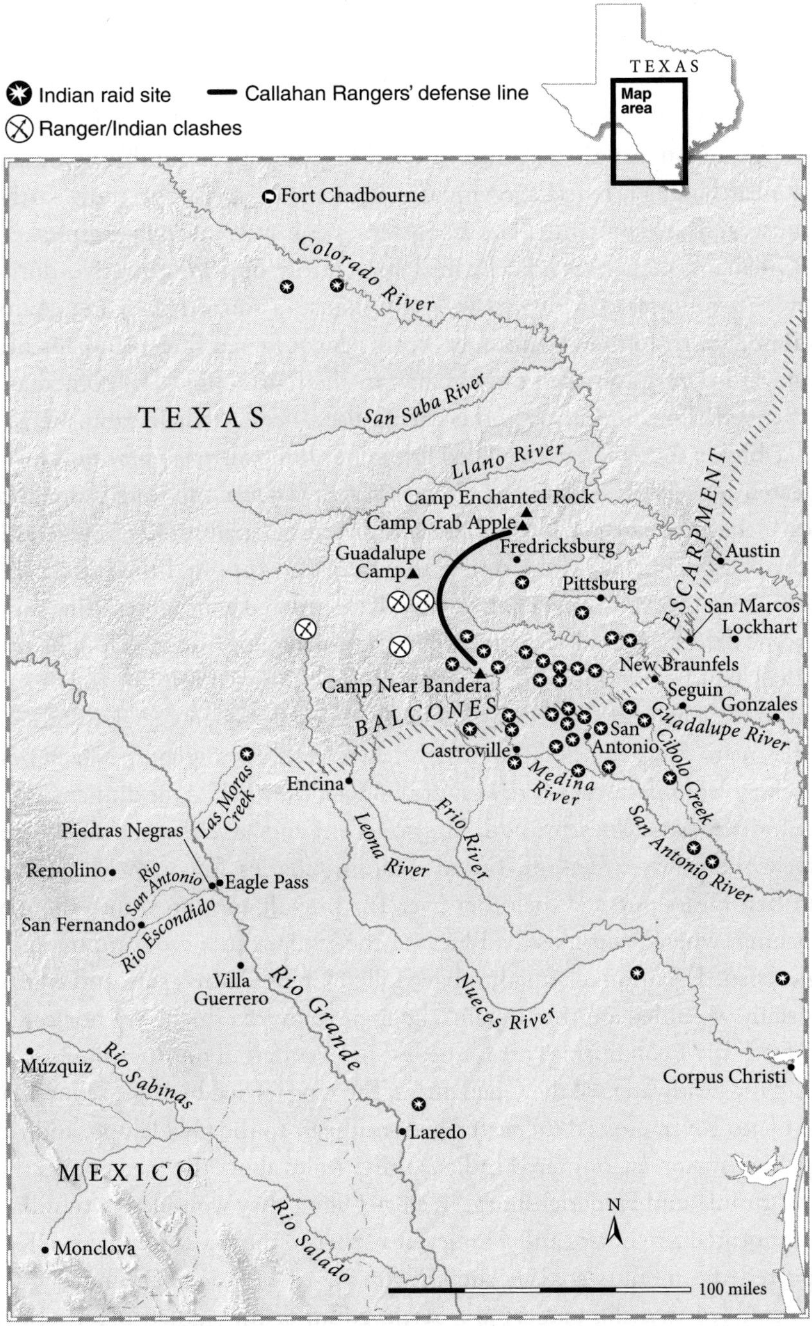

Map 13.1. Locations of the Callahan Rangers' defense line, campsites, skirmishes, and Indian raids, August 1855. Map by Carol Zuber-Mallison.

Guadalupe headwaters while a third, posted at Enchanted Rock, guarded the north. Meanwhile, Callahan led twenty-two toward the Llano, an area with which he was familiar. It was thus Governor Pease who initiated the first repositioning of Callahan's Rangers to the south in the direction of Eagle Pass. About August 20, Callahan ordered Burleson to establish a command post near Bandera. Foreshadowing Callahan's evolving plan to move farther southwest, Burleson rented two houses for a commissary and a hospital.[23]

Callahan's men had not enrolled for patrols or administrative duties; they had volunteered to fight. In early August, a squad led by Pvt. Aaron Burleson, with John W. Sansom as scout, encountered fifteen Indians near Boneyard Springs on the north branch of the Guadalupe. The combatants exchanged shots and arrows, but the Indians fled. At their campsite in a cedar brake, the Texans discovered a butcher knife, arrows, fifty pounds of uneaten horseflesh, and several stolen horses. When none were claimed by locals, the men auctioned the herd and, needing spare mounts, several of them bought horses. Interestingly, the men who captured the horses split the auction proceeds. Several days later, Kyle ordered another scouting party into the field. Riding along a branch of the Guadalupe, the men fought with a small band of warriors. Again, there were no casualties, but the Texans captured a small horse herd, which locals claimed. When Callahan ordered Burleson to Bandera, Sergeant Riley Lewis led the vanguard. Near Hicks Creek, seven miles west northwest of Bandera, they halted for dinner. When ten Indians passed nearby, Pvt. Simpson Tom and several comrades chased five, while privates Sansom, David Walton, Charles Taylor, F. M. Martin, and Ben Hines pursued the other five. The pursuit continued into the next morning, when Walton's squad located the Indians in a cedar motte and a fight ensued. Sansom claimed to have killed Chief Castro's son, and Martin mortally wounded another Lipan. The men recovered thirty-five horses stolen from the Leon Springs area. The last fight occurred on August 28, again along the headwaters of the Guadalupe. The rangers, led by Kyle, scouted up the Llano River, crossed the watershed southeast to the Guadalupe, and riding downstream encountered Indians thirty miles above the road connecting San Antonio and Fredericksburg. In a brief fight, they wounded two Indians and captured five horses and a mule. In a letter to the *Texas State Times*, Kyle reported the mounts sold at auction for $31 to $85 each. Ominously, the paper added that the rangers also retrieved an arrow-riddled bloody shirt, blue cotton pants, and a hat, all of which looked like they belonged to a small boy.[24]

The younger, less experienced volunteers were obviously eager to fight Indians, and some were clearly interested in financial rewards. They became disgruntled when they had to return their booty to the rightful owners, and in the last instance, Kyle sold the animals before announcing their capture, preventing locals from reclaiming their horses even though the animals were branded and easily identified. The camping, raiding, and retreating toward the Rio Grande suggested the raiders were Lipans, while citizens did identify some captured horses, validating Texan suspicions that Indians had stolen the horses. Finding Indian arrows and other tools at the camps and skirmish sites only confirmed this conclusion. The bloody shirt indicated the raids were violent and potentially deadly. Because the rangers during August patrolled west of the defense line, and their skirmishes occurred in the middle and southern part of the region they were trying to protect, the area near San Antonio remained exposed to raids, much to the concern of local residents.

Lipan raids commonly began when thirty or so men, led by two or three experienced leaders, departed the rancherías. After a few nights of travel, the group would establish a base camp, using dense oak, cedar, and mesquite thickets for concealment. The band then dispersed into small groups of three to six, traveling on foot or double mounted bareback on horses. Raids frequently took place under a full moon, with August and early fall being the favored times. The smaller bands periodically returned to the base camp with their booty, and when the horse herd reached a sufficient size, the group returned home, traveling at night. After much practice, Lipan raiders were stealthy and, having developed an uncanny sense of where danger might be found, easily evaded pursuers.[25]

This pattern meant the number of raids exploded during August 1855, with accounts of thirty-nine appearing in newspapers and letters to the governor (map 13.1). The raiding parties avoided the defensive line established by Callahan and, because only two raids came north of the Guadalupe, must have approached from the south or southwest. The initial eight raids occurred during the first days of August and were scattered at Fort Clark, Laredo, San Patricio, and near Bandera Pass. More than 200 horses and mules were stolen, though several were recaptured. While a single Texan was killed by the Lipans at Laredo, according to Col. William W. Loring, the fight near Fort Clark left eight raiders dead. At Bandera Pass the Indians, besides stealing horses and mules, again destroyed watermelon fields. The raids happened while the full moon transitioned into a quarter moon; in mid-August, when the sky was dark, no Indian incursions were reported. The rampaging resumed in earnest in the last week of August as the full moon reappeared. Raiders hit east of San Antonio at Cibolo Creek and the San Antonio River, and later near Fort Merrill they struck a group of cowboys herding livestock. A few days later, fifty miles west of Corpus Christi, Lipans stole a Tejano's horses and fled into Mexico at the Dos Hermanos crossing, halfway between Laredo and Eagle Pass. West of San Antonio, ranches lost horses at Culebra and Hondo creeks and at Leon Springs. In an incident behind Callahan's perimeter, Indians chased a fifteen-year-old boy near Fredericksburg.[26]

At the height of the full moon, there was a flurry of incursions, hundreds of livestock were lost, and gruesome murders occurred (map 13.1). Invaders hit southwest of the Medina River, along the Atascosa River, again near Fort Merrill, at a residence on the Hondo River, and at another ranch on the Medina where a Tejano was killed. Striking within the city limits of San Antonio, Indians stole two horses and killed one near San Pedro Springs, while another band passed along Culebra Creek. Fourteen miles from Fort Chadbourne, raiders killed two Anglos. Meanwhile, an attack at Bandera Pass was repulsed, with five Indians reported to be mortally wounded. Southeast of San Antonio, a rancher lost several horses, and Levi English chased several Lipans, claiming to have killed five. East and north of San Antonio, the ranches along Cibolo Creek turned out to be a favorite target, with dozens of horses taken. The brutality of the raids on August 30 and 31 reverberated throughout the region. Indians struck W. R. Elam's farm, captured a young black woman, and disemboweled her. Continuing southeastward, the Indians lassoed Reverend John McGhee's young son and lanced him repeatedly while dragging him. Not finished, on the last day of August, a small band of Indians attempted to enter Smithson's Valley, several miles west of New Braunfels. The raiders then raced to James S. Hodge's home on Curry Creek, where, as the family watched, two Indians took four horses. The raiders continued up the Guadalupe and escaped.[27]

To Austin and San Antonio area residents, the incursions appeared bolder, more violent, and wider in geographic scope. As a result, citizens became terrified and now believed Smith's July promise of more federal troops was insincere. Capturing local sentiment, the *Texas State Times* editor proposed that if Mexico allowed the Lipans to raid from their territory then Texans had the right to pursue them to their camps. Back in action on September 1, the Bexar County Committee forwarded to Pease a new petition that listed recent atrocities and asked how depredations could transpire near the most populous Texas county, especially after numerous appeals. They also complained that the federal government did not believe victims, misrepresented their motives, and removed the only effective force, the dragoons. The petitioners insisted that another company of mounted volunteers was necessary to make sure the Indians in Mexico "feel in their own homes the evils which they inflict."[28]

An alarmed Pease rushed from Austin and by September 5 stood on the doorstep of Smith's headquarters in San Antonio, which he found vacant. Smith had relocated to Corpus Christi, hoping it might restore his deteriorating health. Pease's outrage at the violence was intensified by Smith's absence, which he expressed in a lengthy letter. Maj. James Belger let Pease review his dispatch to Smith concerning the murder of McGhee's son, so Pease took the opportunity to write that the brutal details of the killing had been confirmed by reliable sources. He added that Smith's reluctance to acknowledge the reality of the Indian raids had become an irritant to him, the victims, and Texans in general. Pease's mordacious note informed Smith the raids had almost disappeared where Callahan's company camped, and with that in mind, Pease recommended that mounted volunteers, in groups of thirty or forty, be stationed southeast of San Antonio in an arc northwest toward the headwaters of the Llano River. The governor admitted he would prefer to be relieved of the necessity of unilaterally mustering additional rangers and said he would delay doing so until he heard from the general. Both men were unable to grasp that the situation had spiraled beyond their control due to their inability to work together.[29]

While the South Texas frontier was under attack from Indians, Coahuila officials were distracted by political instability. Santiago Vidaurri's power struggle climaxed with an attack on the conservatives in Saltillo, Coahuila's capital, and he took control when his liberal army forced a surrender on July 24, 1855. National defense became his first priority when the authorities in Guerrero, a village on the Rio Grande, reported Texan filibusters had killed a young man and a dog. Four days later, the same city officials mustered 170 men to repel the filibusters. By the end of the month, three circumstances emerged that would have grave consequences for Callahan's Expedition: Vidaurri controlled northern Mexico, defending his new regime became his paramount concern, and he had been told that Texan filibusters were raiding along his border. With his July 1855 victory, Vidaurri gained more territory, but maintaining control was fraught with difficulties. His exhausted troops pursued their conservative enemies to San Luis Potosí while the Coahuila government was in shambles and vulnerable to threats from political rivals. Santa Anna, barely clinging to power in Mexico City, launched another propaganda campaign, accusing Vidaurri of plotting to renounce Mexico in favor of a new country—the Republic of Sierra Madre. Liberals in southern Mexico had divided opinions about Vidaurri: some trusted him, but others did not. With no money in the treasury, Vidaurri initiated import taxes to be applied in his state to Texas—Mexico's major trading partner. Thus, by the end of August, Vidaurri's major concerns had multiplied.[30]

By July 27, Colonel Emilio Langberg, a Vidaurri supporter, was appointed commander of north Coahuila (see map 12.2), and many municipal and military leaders pledged their allegiance to Vidaurri. Lieutenant Colonels Manuel Leal and Manuel Menchaca guaranteed the ability of their militias to defend their homeland, while local elections put men loyal to Vidaurri in official positions in the villages, including customs officials to collect his import taxes. Reorganization of the state's armed forces and auxiliary troops ensued, and by mid-August, Langberg assured Vidaurri that almost 1,500 troops could be raised in north Coahuila. In San Antonio, the *Bejareño* claimed the colonel commanded no fewer than 400 troops in Piedras Negras alone. Langberg spent most of his time at Piedras Negras implementing changes decreed by Vidaurri, and he socialized across the Rio Grande with U.S. Army officers and locals. The bulk of Coahuila's state and municipal correspondence in August focused on administrative matters, import duties, and national defense. Indians raids were seldom mentioned, which indicates they were not of great importance.[31]

Only twice in July and August did Mexican officials note Indian activity. On August 12, the central government sent a notice to several villages that the Seminoles continued to cross the Rio Grande, generating hostility on the other side. A week later, in the interior near Abasolo, Indians attacked shepherds. At the same time, on August 11, Texan filibusters drew attention at Villa de Rio Grande, and again seven days later at Guerrero. In response, the justice of the peace at Piedras Negras notified other villages to maintain vigilance and not allow Americans near the Maroon communities for fear of abduction. More concern for cross-border invasions from Texas developed in the third week of August. On August 22, Langberg directed Guerrero to send troops to block the fords of the Rio Grande, and three days later, he ordered Juan Valdez to march near Guerrero and stop any border crossings. Meanwhile, reports surfaced that Mexican deserters were intending to cross into Texas, and smuggling intensified after the implementation of import taxes, all of which increased the concerns of Mexican officials.[32]

Unaware of the escalating tensions below the Rio Grande, Callahan began to contemplate chasing the Lipans and chastising them, even if he crossed into Mexico. Border residents, army officers, and Indian agents were reporting that Indians, especially Lipans, were crossing into Texas to steal horses. A U.S. consul observed that in August 1855, Lipans in Mexico had taunted Texans at the Rio Grande. Some Texans accused Mexican officials of inciting Lipan incursions and sharing in the profit from the bounty, which was widely publicized in the region where Callahan and his rangers lived. James Wilson Nichols, brother of John W. Nichols, wrote that Antonio Peréz, the Tejano who had become a Mexican official, headed this enterprise. Thus, many Texans agreed with Callahan that Lipans in Mexico were a problem. Indian agent George T. Howard's 1854 spying mission near San Fernando was also widely reported. According to the *New Orleans Picayune,* Howard claimed Mexican authorities protected the Lipans who raided in Texas. Believing that he needed independent proof of Mexican and Lipan complicity, Callahan dispatched Augustus Schmidt, a private in his company, on a spying mission. Schmidt, a Swiss-German by birth, spoke Spanish fluently and, according to John W. Sansom, was acquainted with the region where the Lipans's rancherías were situated. Several Lipans boasted of their rustling ventures to Schmidt, and he returned with two horses he had purchased, both of which an Anglo claimed. For Callahan, Schmidt's findings proved the Lipans were his primary target.[33]

As he had done before, Callahan concluded that the best way to stop the raiding was to attack the Lipans where they lived. He wrote Burleson a revealing communication on August 31 that included the line: "I am bound to go to the Rio Grande." He cautioned Burleson to keep his intentions confidential, believing he should notify the governor before announcing his plans. The next day, September 1, Callahan wrote to Pease and summarized his dilemma (map 13.2). He explained that small parties, who scattered so as not to be trailed, had caused most of the depredations, and since he had been given the freedom to "chastize [*sic*] them wherever they be found," he intended "to follow them to their homes." The mission, Callahan continued, would commence on September 15. Sixty-five in his company would be joined by forty other volunteers, and the remainder of his men would continue protecting the area. He informed the governor that his rangers were

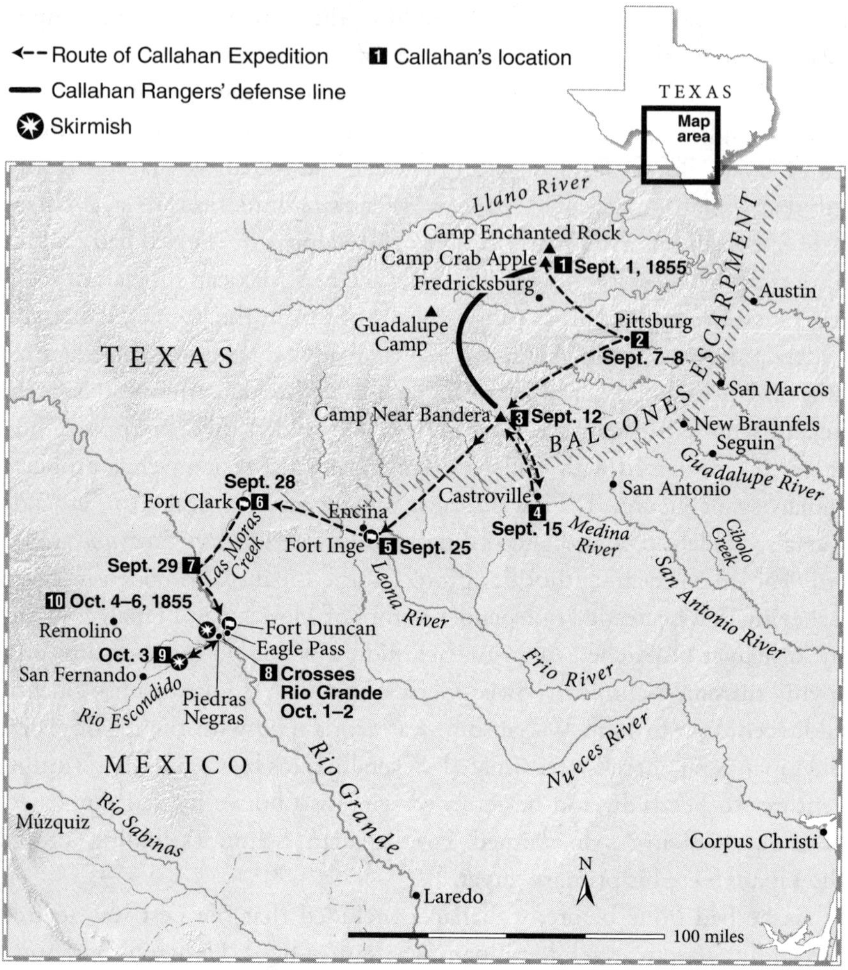

Map 13.2 Locations and routes of travel for Callahan (September 1–October 6, 1855). Map by Carol Zuber-Mallison.

healthy and ready for a fight, and he believed all would "accomplish some good." On September 8, 1855, Burleson, at Camp Near Bandera, penned two letters, one to Pease, the other to the *Texas State Times*. He wrote about leaving on September 15 to take the fight to the Indians. Pease thus had an additional warning of Callahan's intentions of crossing into Mexico and attacking the Lipans. Callahan's mention of other volunteers indicates that he invited them to join him. Some probably told others, including Pease, about what was afoot. Certainly, the expedition was no secret.[34]

As Callahan made ready for his campaign, tragedy struck. William Milford Callahan, born in Caldwell County on February 18, 1852, died suddenly on September 6, 1855. His father rushed home (map 13.2). William, the fifth child of James Hughes and Sarah Medissa Callahan, became the first person to be buried in the new Blanco Cemetery in Pittsburg. James Sanford Callahan, their second child, remembered the burial as heartbreaking. Sarah, her siblings, and her mother, Sarah Hembree Day, attended with their spouses and families, and others traveled from nearby Guadalupe and Caldwell Counties. When Jones, in a September 22 letter to Pease, wrote that he had seen Callahan about two weeks ago, he was referring to the younger Callahan's funeral. The death of his three-year-old son surely made Callahan miserable. But while at home, he asked his brothers-in-law and neighbors to issue a call for volunteers throughout the Guadalupe River Basin and at San Antonio.[35]

Callahan's business partners—Jones, Lindsey, and Pitts—attended his son's funeral. In spite of the personal loss and the alarming Indian raids, the Pittsburg Land Company had to tend to its future, so the partners discussed their project. With about six weeks before Callahan's muster would expire, the company announced in the *Texas State Times* its October 25 public auction of town and farm lots, which was to be accompanied by a barbecue. The partners expected a successful conclusion to the Callahan Expedition by that time. Middletown developers Conrad Seabaugh and Otto Wuppermann, who must have talked with the Pittsburg Land Company partners, also believed the Indian raids would diminish, and following the lead of the Pittsburg investors, they likewise advertised lots for sale and a public dinner on October 20. These events gave Callahan a timetable for resolving the Indian problem, and unquestionably he left the Rio Blanco resolved to cross the Rio Grande. Texans still clamored for action and appeared to have an effective plan when Callahan and his rangers departed to fight in Mexico. Focused on frontier defense, in response to both the concerns of the state and his fellow investors, Callahan put aside his grief for his son and rode south, unaware of the fiasco that would ensue when he encountered Mexican officials determined to protect their border and maintain Vidaurri's fragile government.[36]

CHAPTER 14

The Callahan Expedition, 1855, Plan

"We intend to hunt up the Lipans in particular"

San Antonio's main plaza had always been its social and commercial center. While street vendors, mainly Tejanas selling food, still congregated there in the mid-1850s, the city was transitioning into a cosmopolitan city where Spanish, English, German, and French could be heard. Situated on the plaza's west side was a new three-story hotel, the Plaza House. In August 1855, the owner, Hanson Alsbury, met with other prominent men, all members of the San Antonio Committee for slave reclamation, and prepared a letter to Colonel Emilio Langberg, commander of the Mexican troops in Piedras Negras, Coahuila. The letter contained a proposal for the return of fugitive slaves from Mexico to Texas. A series of loosely connected events and personalities have caused some historians to include this letter in the history of the Callahan Expedition, but recently discovered documents challenge their assertions. A new interpretation of the relationship between the San Antonio Committee and the expedition is overdue.[1]

In August and September 1855, most South Texans were concerned with Indian raids. September began with Thomas F. McKinney chasing the Indians who raided a ranch on the Rio Blanco, stealing horses and killing cattle and a settler (map 14.1). During the same week, as the full moon waned, eighteen miles north of San Antonio raiders took twenty-five of Elisha A. Biggs's horses and killed a man near Samuel Caruthers's farm on the Medina River. Southwest of San Antonio, on the Rio Frio, fifteen Lipans attacked Juan Rodriguez, who killed two of them. On September 2, near the junction of the Medina and Atascosa rivers, Indians attacked two Tejanos, but they captured one raider and tied him to a tree. In a skirmish on the Atascosa,

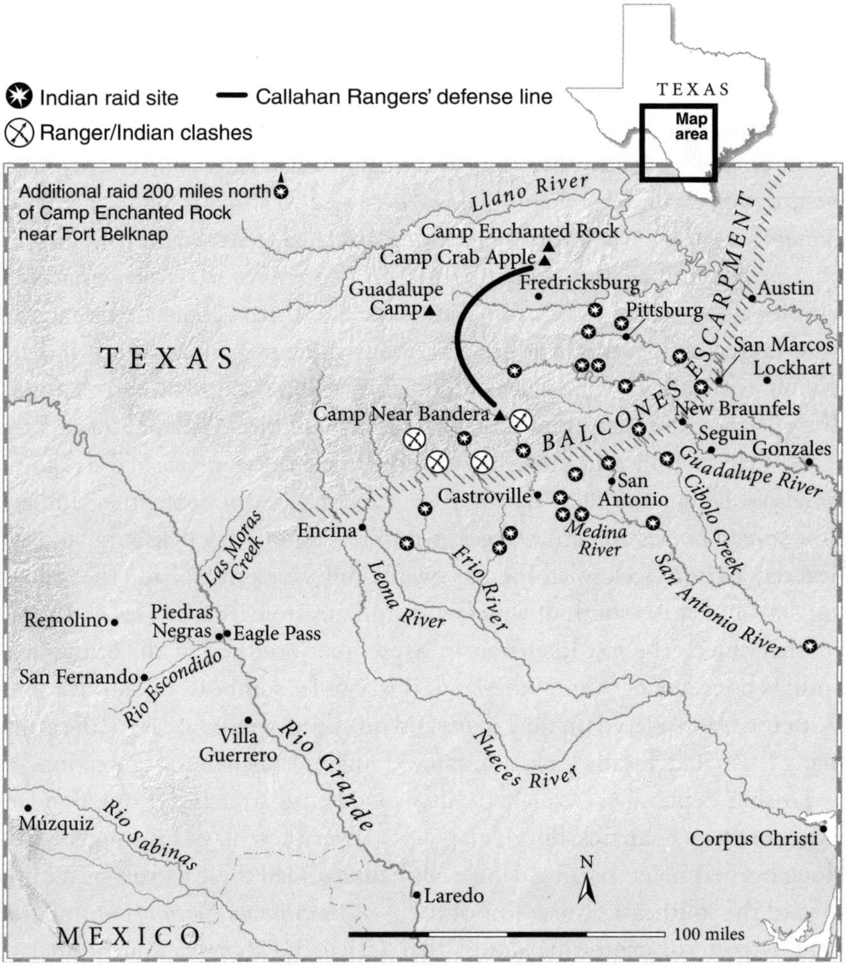

Map 14.1. Positions of Callahan Rangers' defense line, campsites, skirmishes, and Indian raids, September 1855 (last raid September 29, 1855). Map by Carol Zuber-Mallison.

Texans recovered twenty-eight horses and killed two warriors, but days later, twenty miles south of San Antonio, Indians stole twenty to thirty horses. West of Castroville, at Vandenburg, Indians ran off several horses, while four miles northeast of New Braunfels, near Hortontown, they shot a Texan's horse but he killed one of his assailants. Raiders chased a German-Texan near Sisterdale and attempted to steal Julius Dresel's livestock, frightening settlers in the upper Guadalupe River valley. The widespread nature of the raids suggested that several Indian bands were involved.[2]

Over the next two weeks, while Indian raids decreased, the area of attack grew more scattered (map 14.1). The attacks continued when John Leakey on the Sabinal River lost two horses, and a colt and cow were killed on the Guadalupe, near Curry's Creek. Fifteen miles southeast of Pittsburg at Hermann Fischer's store another horse was slain and half eaten, and twenty miles west of New Braunfels Johann Halm was chased by Indians but escaped. On September 17, again at Curry's Creek, Indians tried to steal James S. Hodges's horses, but gunfire drove them away. On September 10, Indians harassed families along Salado Creek, and nine days later three Cibolo Creek ranches were raided and sixty horses stolen. About the same time, twenty Indians ran off with horses from farms along the Medina south of San Antonio. The ghastliest deed occurred near Bandera, when thirty Indians attacked the R. N. Davis family and mortally wounded their thirteen-year-old daughter, Amanda. Four more raids occurred in the last week of September. Indians stole several horses on Grape Creek, ten miles east of Fredericksburg, and the next day Barton Beck spied Indians twenty miles west of Goliad. The following day, nine miles south of Castroville, Indians stole three horses and killed another three. The last incursion in September occurred at the Sutherland Springs homesite of John Sutherland, thirty miles southeast of San Antonio. With the blame placed on the Lipans and no effective response from the army, many frustrated Texans looked to James Hughes Callahan for protection.[3]

During September, Callahan's line of defense stretched from Bandera Pass north to Fredericksburg (map 14.1). Every few days his rangers rode along his perimeter; sensing danger, Indians avoided these patrols by raiding toward the southeast. The editor of the *Neu Braunfelser Zeitung* commented on this pattern, expressing doubt that Callahan's Rangers contributed to the region's security. Lt. Edward Burleson Jr.'s zone of responsibility was the south tip of the line at Camp Near Bandera, sometimes called Camp Ridley. With only eighty-eight men in the entire company, Burleson complained to the *Texas State Times*, "The space is too extensive for our number." However, the rangers did occasionally find Indians. On September 5 and 6, several of Burleson's men chased warriors who had stolen John Ridley's mules, recovering several. Two days later, Burleson wrote that Sgt. Riley Lewis and Corp. Charles Taylor had fought Indians, killing one and wounding another. Then on September 7, a two-man patrol arriving from Callahan's camp at Fredericksburg was fired upon near Burleson's headquarters.[4]

A fight on September 8, twelve miles south of Camp Near Bandera, was described by Burleson in a letter to the *Texas State Times*. He claimed that his rangers had shot Wild Cat's interpreter and sent him to San Antonio, and that evening Burleson made another remarkable assertion that his men had shot at John Horse, the Maroon leader, and wounded one of Wild Cat's men. Burleson actually wrote two letters on September 8; the first, which mentioned Wild Cat and John Horse, was sent to John S. "Rip" Ford, editor of the *Texas State Times*, and the second to Gov. Elisha M. Pease. The latter exists in two versions, but neither mention Wild Cat or John Horse. Moreover, Burleson explicitly wrote in the Ford letter that on the fifteenth they would leave on "a big scout in which I am sure we will get Mr. John [Horse]." To Pease, he promised to find the Indians' trail and "follow them up." These two letters confused some analysts looking at the Callahan Expedition later, but their differences do not obscure some obvious facts. Notably, all clashes between Callahan's Rangers and Indians in early September occurred near the southern tip of his line. After September 8, neither he nor Burleson reported fights. This indicates that the raiders rode east after crossing the Rio Grande, slipping south of Callahan's perimeter, then attacked inside the Texans' protective screen close to San Antonio. Importantly, Piedras Negras Comandante Manuel Menchaca confirmed that Lipans crossed the Rio Grande into Texas during September. Callahan therefore prepared for a mission directed at the Eagle Pass area when southwest Texas residents resumed their appeals for protection.[5]

Pease on September 6 replied to yet another Bexar County petition. Noting that he was actually in San Antonio, he defended mobilizing Callahan's Rangers, summarized his appeals to Gen. Persifor F. Smith for mounted troops, and promised to protect lives and property. It did not stop the appeals. On September 13, twenty-one Comal County citizens sent a blunt note demanding additional volunteer forces and informing Pease that they had created a committee to begin mobilization. The *Neu Braunfelser Zeitung*'s extensive summary of Indian incursions caused the German-Texans in the Guadalupe River Basin to join their neighbors in threatening to take matters into their own hands. Another petition, from Goliad, arrived on the governor's desk the same day as Comal County's. The seventy-one signees demanded authorization for a ranger company and threatened that the area's citizens were ready to call out volunteers to serve until the governor sent aid. A September 21 appeal from Bandera, with thirty-seven signatures, included a frightening account of the killing of the Davis girl and added that with thirty Indians in the area, people had stopped working to defend their homes. In the final September petition, citizens of Medina and Uvalde

Counties described the last twelve months of frequent raids, horse stealing, and the killing of cattle and hogs. Like the others, they proposed the same solution—more ranger companies.[6]

On September 22, William E. Jones reported to Pease on the late summer raids and the Callahan command's successes. Jones declared nearly one hundred Indians had raided between the Colorado and Nueces rivers. He blamed the Lipans, Comanches, and Wild Cat's Seminoles. Furthermore, Callahan had asked that Jones tell the governor that three or four extra companies were needed on the frontier. This message echoed Burleson's September 8 recommendation to Pease. Jones dispatched another missive on September 24, reporting Indians had driven off sixty horses from the Cibolo Creek area. No doubt Jones agreed with Callahan about how to stop the raiding, and since he wrote his September letters in Austin he may well have visited with Pease and told him that Callahan would take the fight to the Lipans in Mexico. Pease also surely read Burleson's letter in the *Texas State Times* about the plan to ride south. However, before Pease responded, Callahan's Rangers had assembled at Bandera, whence they rode southwest toward Eagle Pass. The Lipans, observing their movement, retired across the Rio Grande.[7]

After burying his son, Callahan had rejoined his troops in the field. On September 12 from Camp Near Bandera (see map 13.2) he issued two orders to Burleson, setting in motion a series of actions that resulted in a Rio Grande crossing by the Callahan Expedition. In his first order, Callahan directed Burleson to store 326 and 560 bushels of corn bought in Bandera and Fredericksburg. Each horse and mule consumed about one bushel of corn per week, and in August, Callahan had arranged for sufficient forage for his eighty-eight rangers' mounts and pack animals until the end of his muster. However, these extra bushels could feed an additional sixty-five horses and mules for one month. In his second order, Callahan instructed Burleson to obtain 1,560 rations of bacon and flour from San Antonio. July's and August's requisitions from Durham and Swenson would feed Callahan's Rangers until October 19, the mustering-out date. The additional rations would supply sixty more men for a month. The excess forage and rations indicate Callahan expected reinforcements totaling about sixty men and seventy mounts. He clearly intended to augment his forces for a larger campaign before his muster ended.[8]

As noted, Callahan and Burleson provided Pease with ample notice of their intent to cross the Rio Grande into Mexico while preparing to do so. Callahan's August 31 letter to Burleson plainly stated the Rio Grande was the objective, and the next day Callahan notified Pease that he planned to "follow them to their homes." One week later, Burleson told Pease that the rangers planned to "follow them up." Burleson also wrote the *Texas State Times* that a campaign would commence on September 15; Pease could not have avoided reading this letter. Then while in San Antonio, Burleson sent a dispatch on September 15 to Pease reporting that Callahan had started his expedition and that they intended to "hunt up the Lipans in particular." Pease, by now, had received four warnings of Callahan's goal to pursue the Lipans to Mexico. With reinforcements arriving, he had the means to accomplish this objective. Callahan also hired Russell Varnell, a resident of Encina on the Leona River, as a scout. Deliberately pursuing Varnell's knowledge of the Rio Grande borderlands is another indication of Callahan's intention. By mid-September Callahan had set in motion a plan he had contemplated for a month. Now, as more armed men rode to join him, Burleson collected and stored additional rations, and a competent scout provided expertise about the border at Eagle Pass and Piedras Negras.[9]

Nathaniel Benton's company of twenty-six men joined Callahan's Rangers after being mustered into service on September 15 at Castroville by Callahan (see map 13.2). From his base at Camp Near Bandera, Callahan passed through Castroville en route to or from San Antonio. Benton was a Callahan acquaintance in Guadalupe County, and his first wife's brothers were Benjamin and Henry E. McCulloch, long-time Callahan friends. Benton farmed near the site where the Reverend John McGhee's son was slain; at the time of that attack, Benton had organized a posse to pursue the Indians. When he returned from the chase, he and his men, augmented by additional volunteers, departed to join Callahan. Benton's son Eustace was already serving with Callahan, and one of the new recruits was John Wesley Harris, whose sister later married the elder Benton. Benton's recruits were similar to Callahan's men (table 14.1). Each had at least two and often three weapons, and they brought five pack horses and mules to carry the company's supplies and ammunition. Almost half lived in Guadalupe County, with the remainder from surrounding counties. Three (12 percent) were thirty-five years or older, while six (23 percent) were between twenty-seven and thirty-four, and the majority, seventeen (65 percent), were between sixteen and twenty-six. One, sixteen-year-old Charles Patton, was under the legal age for ranger duty, but he had an uncle and cousin in Callahan's ranks. Only Benton had fought in the Texas Revolution, while just three others (8 percent) had prior ranger or Mexican War experience. Henry B. King, a Callahan brother-in-law, had

Table 14.1. Muster roll, Capt. Nat Benton's Ranger Company

Name	*Rank*	*Age*	*Residence*	*Value*		*Remarks*
				Horse	*Arms*	
Nat Benton	Capt.	36	Seguin	150	75	
H. B. King	1st Lt.	32	Seguin	100	75	
Chas. (Charles A.) Reed	2nd Lt.	28	Gonzales	100	75	
F. M. Marshall	1st Sgt.	25	Seguin	100	75	Lost 1 shotgun
N. N. Cox	2nd Sgt.	19	Seguin	85	75	Lost horse, equipment
E. B. Millet	3rd Sgt.	18	Seguin	75	75	Lost 1 six-shooter
A. Wilson	4th Sgt.	20	San Marcos	65	30	
S. T. Burney	Pvt.	18	Seguin	50	75	
R. M. Bonner	Pvt.	23	Prairie Lea	100	75	Lost horse, equipment
J. S. Crump	Pvt.	28	San Marcos	100	120	Lost horse
Noah Cherry	Pvt.	20	Fredericksburg	85	75	Lost 1 six-shooter
V. B. Dixon	Pvt.	22	Gonzales	140	75	
N. N. Daughtery	Pvt.	28	Lockhart	125	75	
Thos. A. Evans	Pvt.	22	Fredericksburg	100	75	Lost horse, equipment, 1 six-shooter
Gustavus Fox	Pvt.	37	Clinton	100	50	Lost horse, equipment, pistol
Chas. Hurnaw (Hermann)	Pvt.	38	Fredericksburg	120	75	
J. W. Harris	Pvt.	21	Seguin	85	75	
H. K. Holland	Pvt.	24	San Marcos	100	75	Lost horse, equipment, KIA
S. J. P. McDowell	Pvt.	28	Lockhart	100	75	
R. B. Porter	Pvt.	24	Lockhart	125	75	
H. A. Perryman	Pvt.	21	Seguin	150	75	
Jas. Rodgers	Pvt.	18	Seguin	125	55	
M. F. Whiteaker	Pvt.	24	Lockhart	150	75	
W. T. (W. P.) Wall	Pvt.	33	Seguin	100	75	
S. Morrison	Pvt.	25	Seguin	90	75	
Charles Patton	Pvt.	16	Curry's Creek	50	40	

Sources: MR, Nathaniel Benton, Sept. 15, 1855, Oversize 401-723, Folder 1, TRMR, TADG, TSLA; *Power of Attorney Records*, 1855–59, Box 401-1185, Folder 1, TRR, TAGD, TSLA.
Note: Order of entries reflects that of the original muster roll.

served in ranger companies during the Republic of Texas. Charles D. Reed fought as a Texas volunteer in the Mexican War, and Gustavus Fox had seen previous frontier duty. Finally, like Callahan's Rangers, most of Benton's company had little or no direct involvement in slave ownership. Just six (23 percent) were members of slave-owning families, and only two (8 percent) of the six themselves owned slaves.[10]

Callahan commanded 114 men by the time Burleson returned to Camp Near Bandera on September 18 (see map 13.2). Sixty-five members of Callahan's company traveled with him, and twenty-three remained at Camp Near Bandera. Burleson posted a small squad under Sergeant Constantine M. Connally at Camp Enchanted Rock (map 14.1). With regular patrols between the encampments, Burleson hoped he could protect the settlements. It is not clear how Callahan determined the division of men, but the reluctance of some of them to invade Mexico may have been a factor. An eagerness to muster out appeared in a September 25 letter to Burleson from Connally and Pvt. Jack Ellis. Burleson even seemed inclined to cancel the mission; on the same day he sent a communication to Pease inquiring about the planned dismissal date in mid-October. Four days later, the governor replied that he would let Burleson know by October 15. Apprehension was rising in Callahan's ranks, and Burleson worried about his brother, David C. Burleson, one of two underage recruits in the company. So, he arranged for David to be a courier to Austin and miss the fighting in Mexico. The other young ranger, Charles McGehee, had pleaded with Burleson to be enrolled until he relented. McGehee remained with Callahan's and Benton's Rangers as they mounted their horses at Camp Near Bandera on September 18 and rode southwest in a soaking rainstorm (see map 13.2).[11]

While Callahan contemplated crossing the Rio Grande, plans laid by two groups in Texas and the evolving Mexican political scene defined circumstances that ultimately complicated his mission. The San Antonio Committee that met to discuss the recovery of runaway slaves, along with a similar group in Bastrop, focused on Langberg, who had visited San Antonio and Austin in the spring and summer of 1855 during his self-exile (see map 12.2). This also meant they relied on Santiago Vidaurri, who depended on Langberg's allegiance while securing his own power base in northern Mexico. Langberg in Texas had tendered a proposal to return escaped slaves and accept a 2,000-man Texan force, if the Mexican government requested it, but conditioned his acceptance upon being paid $80,000. The Texans hesitated, but then the Bastrop Directing Committee accepted a plan devised by San Antonio resident Hanson Alsbury. Alsbury and that committee proclaimed that Texans were sympathetic to the goals of insurgents in Mexico. Moreover, they declared that their committee had the authority and means to reclaim escaped slaves in Mexico. They offered to solicit funds and outfit 1,000 volunteers who would aid in founding an "Independent Republic in Mexico." These terms were analogous to Langberg's proposal. The committee entrusted their endeavor to Bennett Riddells, the former consul from Chihuahua, as their agent, instructing him to emphasize their support for Vidaurri and that their aid was not a filibuster. Carrying a copy of their broadside, Riddells departed for Monterrey in early July 1855, at about the same time that Langberg left San Antonio for Mexico (see map 12.2).[12]

Riddells arrived in Monterrey in mid-July, but Vidaurri held off substantive talks with him until after his military triumph at Saltillo, which Riddells observed as one of Vidaurri's entourage. Now in control of a victorious army, Vidaurri rejected the offer of 1,000 Texans, declared he could not negotiate treaties with private individuals, and proposed an alternative option to be considered by Texas's elected officials. The details of his plan are vague, but it included the return of runaway slaves. Riddells was back in San Antonio by August 18, when he declared: "Vidaurri is willing to deliver to their owners all fugitive slaves escaping to Mexico, and is anxious to make a treaty thereof." Riddells discussed his trip with the Bastrop Directing Committee, which endorsed Vidaurri's proposal and appointed Riddells and John S. Ford, the *Texas State Times* editor, to finalize an agreement in Monterrey. At this point, events become increasingly unclear. In an October 12 letter to Vidaurri, Riddells claimed he had met with Pease, and though the governor admitted he had no authority to negotiate with Vidaurri, he proposed a plan that accomplished the same goal—recovering fugitive slaves. Furthermore, Riddells alleged that, at a Bastrop meeting of representatives from many counties, he had been authorized to say that the Texas legislature would ratify the agreement and pass the appropriate legislation at the next session. This Bastrop meeting on September 10 must have been chaired by Alsbury. Thus, when Riddells left again for Monterrey, his allies believed their optimism for an arrangement with Vidaurri was well founded. Again, this meant the full cooperation of Langberg, who had pledged his loyalty to Vidaurri and in turn was appointed to command the garrison at Piedras Negras.[13]

Meanwhile, the San Antonio Committee met at the Plaza House in late August, shortly after Riddells returned from Mexico. Its relationship to the Directing Committee in Bastrop has been difficult to determine, but new documents clarify some of its actions. The San Antonio Committee sent an intriguing letter to Langberg on August 25 that offered a bounty for every slave returned from Mexico. James N. Fisk carried this letter to Langberg by August 30 (see map 12.2). The San Antonio Committee expected a positive reply from Langberg, based on his discussions in Texas and what Riddells reported after his meeting with Vidaurri. Indeed, the *El Bejareño* published a letter from a correspondent in Coahuila indicating Vidaurri did not oppose mutual extradition of criminals of all categories, including peons and slaves. Langberg's reply to San Antonio was optimistic, asserting the locals considered fugitive slaves more burdensome than useful, and they in turn expected Texas authorities to return runaway peons. He emphasized that a final decision would be made by Vidaurri, whom he believed would agree with him. Lastly, he suggested a joint commission should handle the logistics and costs of exchange. On August 31, Langberg forwarded the letter from the San Antonio Committee to Vidaurri, stating the proposal had merit. Vidaurri's reply was ambivalent, endorsing exchanges but again insisting governments should set the terms. In the same letter Vidaurri warned Langberg to be ready to repel an invasion. By that time, Callahan was eighty-five miles from San Antonio and riding for the border (see map 13.2), far from where Langberg's response to the San Antonio Committee would have been received.[14]

With little supporting evidence, some historians of the Callahan Expedition have written that the San Antonio Committee convinced Callahan to amend his objective and focus on capturing runaway slaves. Only one committee member had any association with Callahan, and the only document confirming the committee's involvement is the August 25 letter to Langberg. The original letter in English is not in any archive, and only the Spanish translation exists; it was published in two Mexican newspapers, the *Boletín Oficial* and *El Siglo Diez y Nueve* (appendix 1). Nevertheless, the letter's signees are the committee's members, and it is relevant to explore who they were and how they might be linked to Callahan. Except for two, the ten names as translated bear little resemblance to typical Anglo surnames, but all can be identified. Five names correspond to members in a similar 1854 committee: Onesimus Evans, J. S. McClelland, Asa Mitchell, J. M. Hill, and Russell Howard. In 1855 they were joined by Jean Baptiste Lacoste, William B. Knox, George Martin, and Xavier Blanchard Debray. None of these nine had direct links to Callahan. The tenth member, whose name was translated as Janbpusk in the August 25 letter, proved to be the most difficult to identify, and in fact he did have an inimical relationship with Callahan.[15]

Of the group, five were prominent business and political leaders. Evans was a successful merchant and former alderman and legislator whose wealth and health were declining; he died on October 6, 1855. McClelland had a cotton plantation and owned twenty-eight slaves in 1860, the most of any committee member. He had been a county commissioner and alderman. Lacoste had arrived in New Orleans from France in 1848 and then moved to San Antonio, where he was an alderman and owned a billiard parlor, a real estate enterprise, and a wine store. He had no slaves in 1855, but he and his wife would each have a house slave in 1860. Knox was sheriff of Bexar County in 1855, having defeated William R. Henry for the office. By 1857 he would be an alderman and working with Henry to raise funds for William Walker's filibuster in Nicaragua. His transport business prospered, and by 1860, like Lacoste, he and his wife would have house slaves. The anomaly among the business and political leaders was Martin, a livestock broker and alderman who apparently never owned slaves. While he supported the successful lawsuit of Harriet Arnold, a slave who sued for her freedom in Bexar County in 1846, he also joined with McClelland and Fisk in 1854 to offer a reward of $1,000 for anyone who apprehended someone was later convicted of helping slaves escape.[16]

The other members of the San Antonio Committee were businessmen. Mitchell was one of the Old Three Hundred of Stephen F. Austin's Colony, and he played several roles during the Texas Revolution. As a prosperous merchant, he became involved in virtually every aspect of San Antonio politics, though he never held an office. He was also active in the Methodist church, and he owned twelve slaves by 1860. Hill was the proprietor of a tavern on Cibolo Creek where the road from San Antonio to Austin crossed. He probably lived in Bastrop County, which is where he is listed in the 1860 census, but he attended both meetings concerning runaway slaves in San Antonio and paid taxes on three slaves in Bexar County in 1855. Howard was the younger brother of George T. Howard, under whom Callahan had served as a lieutenant in 1840. Russell served several times as the San Antonio city attorney, coinciding with the alderman terms of Martin and Lacoste. He never paid taxes on slaves, but in 1853 he advertised the sale of two slaves. Debray, who, like Lacoste, was a native of France, received military training at Saint-Cyr and arrived in San Antonio in 1852 after four years in New York. He was the copublisher of *El Bejareño* in February 1855. He never owned slaves, making him an unusual member of the San Antonio Committee, but he was Langberg's host and frequent companion in San Antonio, and Langberg directed his letters about the Callahan Expedition to Debray.[17]

The nine members of the 1855 San Antonio Committee so far identified had no direct relationship with Callahan, although he may have had chance personal or business encounters with some, and most of them surely knew him by reputation. However, the final member did have a prior relationship with Callahan, albeit an antagonistic one. Undoubtedly, Mexican officials translated and transcribed the name "Janbpusk" from the florid autograph of Hanson Alsbury from San Antonio, and the fact that Js are pronounced like Hs in Spanish supports this. That Alsbury sent Riddells to Mexico with a letter he signed as chair of the Bastrop Directing Committee and also signed the 1855 San Antonio broadside for the reclamation of slaves, places him in the middle of efforts to recover runaways, and thus indicates that he was a member of the San Antonio Committee. Furthermore, Alsbury participated in the 1854 San Antonio Committee for slave reclamation and he also joined nearly every social and political meeting in San Antonio during the mid-1850s. Alsbury's hotel, the Plaza House, served as a prime location for most of these meetings. Alsbury, Howard, McClelland, and Mitchell were all members of Alamo Lodge No. 44 of the Grand Lodge of Texas. Alsbury was therefore a leading figure in San Antonio and certainly the tenth member of the committee, making his ties to Callahan worth a closer look.[18]

Alsbury's father, Thomas, and his sons were members of Austin's Old Three Hundred, and Hanson established a legal practice and settled on a land grant located in modern Brazoria County. However, for his wife's health Hanson later moved to Biloxi, Mississippi, where he practiced law, speculated in land, and was elected to the legislature. In 1841, he and his wife and two children returned to Texas, settling in Galveston, where he opened a law practice focused on land speculation. During the Mexican War, Alsbury served as quartermaster in Col. Albert S. Johnston's regiment. After his oldest son died in October 1849, the family moved to a farm on Salado Creek five miles east of San Antonio. By 1854, Alsbury's wealth had grown to $9,400, including ten slaves, and he had fourteen slaves and $16,100 in 1855. He also engaged in local politics and civic matters. In addition to his legal work and plantation, his business enterprises included the hotel, a land agency, and a sawmill. Locals recognized him "for his constant segar and majestic promenade in front of the [Plaza House] and pleasant countenance." Alsbury's connection to Callahan was through William Wirt Alsbury, Hanson's older brother, who had been Sarah Medissa Day Callahan's first husband. As discussed in chapter 7, William had married Sarah in 1838, but she applied for a divorce in 1841 on the grounds that he abandoned her soon after their wedding. During this period Sarah's relationship with Callahan blossomed, and they were accepted as a couple well before her divorce from Alsbury and marriage to Callahan. From 1841 forward, Callahans and Alsburys avoided all public and private contact. Hanson Alsbury's presence on the 1855 San Antonio Committee strongly implies that Callahan would have had no association with it, just as he had avoided contact with his wife's first husband and his family in the past.[19]

Of the 1855 San Antonio Committee, Evans, McClelland, Mitchell, and Alsbury had the greatest investment in slaves. Although no evidence suggests that any lost a slave as a runaway, they had the most interest in protecting their human property. They cooperated with the Bastrop Committee and facilitated Riddells's participation, Alsbury was particularly influential in this regard. Knox and Martin, well known in Eagle Pass, could provide contacts and organize logistics if necessary. Howard provided legal advice and probably wrote the August 25 letter. Lacoste and Debray were the conduit between the committee and Langberg at Piedras Negras. The letter created problems for Callahan, and it has provided historians with an opportunity to redefine the objective of the Callahan Expedition. As Riddells traveled south through the lower chaparral to Monterrey on his assignment from the committee, the Callahan Rangers patrolled the Texas Hill Country, each unaware of the volatile political situation south of the Rio Grande.

During September 1855, Vidaurri focused on consolidating his hold in northern Mexico. With trade interrupted to the east and south, import duties on Texas commerce became the major source of funds for his treasury. Thus, he searched for ways to increase trade with Texas. At the same time, seeking to expand his power, he sent his army to capture San Luis Potosí, but a three-way stalemate ensued between Vidaurri's army, the conservative army, and the southern liberal army. To the east, in Tamaulipas, Vidaurri tried to cajole General Juan José de la Garza into joining him, but he vacillated. At the same time, a military impasse existed with General Adrian Woll at Matamoros. Meanwhile, Saltillo conservatives, realizing Vidaurri's vulnerabilities, began to grumble. Lastly, Vidaurri communicated tirelessly with southern liberals, particularly Juan Álvarez and Ignacio Comonfort, in an effort to boost support for his power base in northern Mexico. In sum,

Vidaurri needed no additional dilemmas at that time, especially not any intruders from Texas.[20]

Meanwhile in Piedras Negras, Langberg ended August 1855 by dining with U.S. Army officers and neighboring Texans. On August 30 he replied to the San Antonio Committee and couriered a copy of their letter to Vidaurri in Monterrey. Langberg also told Vidaurri about a second, more extraordinary letter that arrived the same day. From whom and how it appeared is unknown, and moreover, the original has not been found in any archive. Considering its contents and Callahan's stated objective, it is tempting to connect the two. To Vidaurri, Langberg wrote, "Today I send you two interesting communications, one about the Lipan Indians and another is a representation made by the San Antonio commission on black fugitives who are found in the states you control." Continuing, the colonel added a remarkable statement: "I should tell you that there is a general lively feeling in Texas and they have tried to form an expedition by introducing it through Las Moras." Langberg thus told Vidaurri three key points: Lipans were crossing the Rio Grande into Texas, the San Antonio Committee had offered a proposal to exchange escaped slaves for peons, and there were rumors that Texans planned to cross into Mexico where Las Moras Creek joined the Rio Grande. This was just days after Augustus Schmidt completed his scouting mission at San Fernando (now Zaragoza), thirty-five miles southwest of Piedras Negras, and it was his findings that convinced Callahan to invade Mexico. Thus, it is astonishing that one month before Callahan arrived at Las Moras on the Rio Grande, Langberg heard that an expedition planned to cross the border there. Locating the actual letter Langberg received about Las Moras and identifying its source would challenge historical perspectives concerning events on the Rio Grande in September and October 1855. Apparently, this second letter led Vidaurri to warn Langberg to watch for an invasion.[21]

In the meantime, Langberg provided vital support for Vidaurri as he dealt with threats from Woll in Matamoros and unrest in Saltillo. In a communiqué that arrived about September 1, Vidaurri told Langberg to prepare his troops to march to Monterrey. The colonel ordered San Fernando and other villages to send their companies to Piedras Negras, but he reminded Vidaurri about the need for frontier defense. On the same day, Langberg ordered Miguel Patiño to locate two hundred horses for the auxiliary troops in order to patrol the frontier and also march south. The next day, the colonel reported that he had 1,200 men, including Seminoles, mustering at Monclova. Days later Langberg left Piedras Negras for Monclova (see map 12.2). Still concerned about a Texas threat, on September 4 he issued an order to the commander at Villa Guerrero, twenty miles downstream from Piedras Negras, which resulted in Antonio Cosa and Tomás Pérez crossing the Rio Grande in search of filibusters. They reported no evidence of armed Texans near the border. Reassured, Langberg focused on his muster to support Vidaurri. In one case, Eagle Pass rancher Benjamin Thomas hired two Mexican deserters; needing them for his campaign, Langberg insisted upon their return and Thomas's arrest, but nothing happened. With his mobilization nearly completed, the colonel marched south, establishing his headquarters on September 13 in Múzquiz. There he ordered militias from villages near the Texas border dispatched to Monclova. When rain delayed this transfer, he sent an explanatory letter to Vidaurri that also reported there had been no hostile Texan movement on the Rio Grande. However, constant rain continued to disrupt his logistics.[22]

While Langberg prepared to support Vidaurri and watched the border, he also had to cope with Indians, especially Lipans. On September 1 he warned Monterrey authorities, a warning he repeated in a note to Vidaurri, that Lipans were threatening the peace, and he advised a campaign against the troublemakers. In August, a conflict occurred near Abasolo, about ninety miles south of the Rio Grande, when Lipans attacked a group of shepherds. Later, six Lipans crossed the Rio Grande, and Piedras Negras Comandante Manuel Menchaca instructed villages along the river to take precautions and stop them from crossing into Texas again. To defuse the situation, Langberg on September 19 ordered district officials to designate specific sites for Lipans to occupy. He was beginning to take measures to control raiding parties from Coahuila, but it was too little, too late as Callahan and Benton were now leading rangers toward the Rio Grande. When Langberg relocated to Múzquiz, he left Piedras Negras under the command of Menchaca with only a few men to oversee the customs house, indicating that his primary concern was supporting Vidaurri rather than policing Indians or guarding against a Texan incursion. Slogging through rain and mud, he led his troops away from the Rio Grande, expecting a fight to secure Vidaurri's power (see map 12.2).[23]

While garrisons in northern Coahuila hummed with activity, nothing was reported in Texas newspapers. Meanwhile, Callahan had his own internal struggles in late September 1855. Disgruntlement with orders and scouting tedium had become commonplace for him, but adding another company of men led by William R. Henry, with his scandalous past, provided a greater test of his leadership. Callahan led his rangers out of Camp Near Bandera on September 18, arriving at Fort Inge on the Leona River several days later (see map 13.2). According to a diary kept by Pvt. S. J. P. McDowell of Benton's company, the seventy-mile trip was a laborious wet and muddy trudge in incessant rain. Recently abandoned, Fort Inge was eighty-five miles west of San Antonio and sixty miles northeast of Eagle Pass. Henry and thirty-five armed men encamped there greeted the Callahan and Benton Rangers. Henry was renowned for his slaver and filibuster endeavors as newspaper reports in 1855, especially in July and August, chronicled his schemes. The *National Intelligencer* excoriated Henry for his fiascos, to which he indignantly replied. Still looking for a chance, on September 2 he had written a sycophantic three-page letter to Pease, requesting authorization to recruit and lead a ranger company. The governor never responded.[24]

Henry's participation in the Callahan Expedition has led several historians to conclude that the objective was slave recovery more than retaliating against raiding Indians. However, this assumption can be dismissed based upon where Callahan, Henry, and other key players were in September. Henry wrote his September 2 letter to Pease from San Antonio, a hotel ledger shows he also was there during the week of September 12–18, and by September 25 he was camped at Fort Inge. On September 12 from Camp Near Bandera Callahan sent Burleson to San Antonio to obtain more provisions. Burleson stayed at the same hotel as Henry September 12–18, returning to Camp Near Bandera by September 18. Callahan was at Camp Enchanted Rock on September 1, at his home on the Rio Blanco from September 7 to 9, at Camp Near Bandera on the twelfth, mustering Benton's men at Castroville on the fifteenth, at Camp Near Bandera on the eighteenth, and at Fort Inge on September 25. Riddells was in Austin on August 25, at Bastrop with the Directing Committee on September 10, and left for Mexico about the last day of September. Henry and Burleson were therefore staying at the same hotel, the Grayson House, as Callahan enrolled Benton's men. Henry undoubtedly talked about the Callahan Expedition with Burleson. During this time, Callahan also saw Riddells in San Antonio in mid-September, and William E. Jones's family was temporarily living in San Antonio at this time. Thus, Henry may have talked with Callahan, Jones, or even Riddells. In any case, Callahan had made his decisions concerning his expedition in early September before he met Henry or Riddells.[25]

Regardless of how he learned about the Callahan Expedition, Henry saw an opportunity and, without authority, independently organized his own ranger company. Nine months later, he submitted a muster roll claiming he enrolled thirty-six volunteers in San Antonio on September 10. However, it is more likely that he actually enrolled them nine days later after moving to Fort Inge. Based on where some of them lived—for example, William G. Sansom, James Campbell, Samuel Patton, and Willis Jones resided in the Twin Sisters and Curry's Creek area, and others came from Goliad—it seems more likely they would have joined at Fort Inge. Henry may have used the earlier date simply to claim a month's pay for his men. Unfortunately, no records exist today that list the participants in Henry's unauthorized July and August slaving and filibustering exploits, but there was some overlap in membership; Robert Augustine, one of Henry's constant companions, is an example. At Fort Inge, Callahan mustered Henry's company on September 25, increasing his total to 128. They were a two-day ride from Eagle Pass and Piedras Negras.[26]

Henry's recruits were experienced and more mature than the other two companies (table 14.2). Of the thirty-six he mustered, seven (19 percent) were thirty-five years of age or older, of whom three had served in the Texas Revolution or as rangers for the Republic of Texas, or both. Men between 27 and 34 years of age numbered 15 (42 percent), while 14 (39 percent) were 18 to 26, with five (14 percent) younger than 23. In the 27- to 34-year-old age group, five had been rangers for the Republic, and five fought in the Mexican War. Furthermore, nine of thirty-six (25 percent) had enrolled in Henry's companies in 1854 or 1855, or in other companies mustered into service from 1850 to 1854. Not counting duplications, a total of sixteen of Henry's men (44 percent) had military or ranger experience. Unlike Callahan and Benton, Henry did not record each man's residence. However, an examination of censuses and tax rolls for Bexar and nearby counties located sixteen. Many did not live in Bexar County; as noted earlier, several came from the Curry's Creek area. Interestingly, nine had a direct connection to slavery, signifying that slave ownership was more common for Henry's men than those in the other two companies.[27]

When the three companies organized into a battalion on September 26, the first order of business was electing officers. The election of Callahan as battalion commander with Henry as his second-in-command signaled that Benton's company would merge with Henry's. Arguments erupted concerning captainships and command, and there may have also been a dispute

Table 14.2. Muster roll, Capt. William R. Henry's Ranger Company

Name	Rank	Age	Residence	Value		Remarks
				Horse	Arms	
William R. Henry	Capt.	35	Bexar Co.	75	35	1 horse captured at Rio Grande
Huston (Houston) Tom	1st Lt.	30	Seguin	150	65	1 gun lost at Piedras Negras
Barney Riggs	2nd Lt.	28	Bexar Co.	80	60	
John M. Hort (Ford)	1st Sgt.	24	San Antonio	75	35	
Thomas McKinney	2nd Sgt.	28	San Antonio	80	55	1 horse captured at Rio Grande, 1 gun lost
Thomas Bingham	3rd Sgt.	25	San Antonio	75	40	1 horse captured at Rio Grande, 1 gun lost
James Campbell	4th Sgt.	18	Curry's Creek	80	55	
Robert Augustine	Pvt.	22	Bexar Co.	75	55	1 horse captured at Rio Grande
Jeremiah Campbell	Pvt.	18	San Antonio	70	65	1 horse captured at Rio Grande
Samuel Culbertson	Pvt.	28	San Antonio	80	55	
Benjamin F. Dye	Pvt.	24	San Antonio	55	50	1 horse captured at Rio Grande
Samuel L. Dorcy	Pvt.	20	San Antonio	80	60	
George Frazier	Pvt.	23	San Antonio	140	65	
Emory Gibbons	Pvt.	28	Encina	90	60	
Jessy Graham	Pvt.	30	San Antonio	100	60	
August Garner	Pvt.	28	San Antonio	80	65	1 horse lost at Escondido
John Gregory	Pvt.	30	San Antonio	90	60	Wounded; horse lost at Escondido (Piedras Negras?)
Russell Huston (Houston)	Pvt.	25	Bexar Co.	125	50	
Fabian L. Hicks	Pvt.	26	Bexar Co.	150	60	1 six-shooter lost at Escondido; horse captured at Rio Grande

(*continued*)

Table 14.2. (*continued*)

Name	*Rank*	*Age*	*Residence*	*Value* Horse	*Value* Arms	*Remarks*
Willis H. Jones	Pvt.	24	Curry's Creek	125	60	Lost horse, arms, equipment; killed at Escondido
Richard James	Pvt.	28	Cibolo Creek	90	60	1 gun lost at Escondido
John McCormick (McCormack)	Pvt.	27	Bexar Co.	100	60	
Colon (Colin) D. McRhea (McRea)	Pvt.	22	San Antonio	75	60	1 gun lost at Rio Grande
Jacob Obrian (O'Brian)	Pvt.	40	San Antonio	135	60	1 horse captured at Rio Grande
Francis Powers	Pvt.	45	San Antonio	100	55	
Samuel Patton	Pvt.	45	Curry's Creek	80	65	
James Peacock	Pvt.	45	Encina	75	65	1 horse, 1 gun, 1 spyglass lost at Rio Grande
William (G.) Sansom	Pvt.	45	Curry's Creek	100	60	
George G. Sutherland	Pvt.	26	Sutherland Springs	150	60	
Levin J. Sutherland	Pvt.	23	Sutherland Springs	150	60	
Robert H. Spence	Pvt.	28	San Antonio	100	65	1 pistol lost at Piedras Negras
Lewis (Louis) Sarison (Sarason, Sarisin)	Pvt.	27	Comal Co.	100	60	1 horse lost at Piedras Negras
James (W.) Summerville	Pvt.	30	San Antonio	100	55	
James Thompson	Pvt.	27	San Antonio	100	60	
John Russell	Pvt.	24	San Antonio	125	60	
Marion F. Gholson	Pvt.	28	San Antonio	180	60	

Sources: MR, Henry, Sept. 15, 1855, Oversize 401-724, Folder 18, Nov. 2, 1854, Dec. 14, 1854, Oversize 401-794, Folder 9, TRMR, TAGD, TSLA.
Note: Order of entries reflects that of the original muster roll.

about the expedition's mission. Henry was a divisive figure, and many knew his reputation. The next morning, Callahan gave the men an option. He declared those not wishing "to serve under Henry were permitted to organize." Benton's men then elected Benton as their captain, with King as first lieutenant and Reed as second lieutenant. According to McDowell, Callahan next spoke at length on his purpose, declaring "his intention to obey his orders to the letter." If crossing the Rio Grande became necessary, the objective was "to chastise the Indians" and not to molest persons or property in Mexico. He advised those who could not follow these orders to leave. No one resigned. Callahan thus aligned his orders with Pease's instructions, and neither contained any intention to recapture slaves.[28]

Pvt. John W. Sansom, a Curry's Creek resident in Callahan's company, described the renewed preparations for the expedition. Henry's experience had taught him the importance of unity, and he drilled the rangers for three days. The recruits had live-fire training sessions, and Pvt. Charles Patton of Benton's command was accidently wounded in the thigh. Competitions became physical, and in a wrestling match an opponent broke Pvt. James Darby's leg. Dr. James G. Barbee, the physician for Callahan's company, confined Patton and Darby to the hospital; since neither would be going with the expedition, they lent their weapons to others. Meanwhile, after having left the command at the Nueces River several days earlier, scout Russell Varnell returned on September 27 after finding Indian signs beyond the Rio Grande. Pvt. David Walton of Callahan's company recalled the battalion rode directly to Fort Clark and then turned south, riding down Las Moras Creek to its junction with the Rio Grande. It was this junction to which Langberg had referred four weeks earlier in his note to Vidaurri. On September 27, according to Walton, the rangers followed hoof tracks to a ford on the Rio Grande, thirty miles upriver from Eagle Pass, at the junction with Las Moras Creek. However, a *San Antonio Texan* correspondent reported it was September 29 when the Texans stopped where Las Moras joined the Rio Grande. Across the border, according to this writer, the trail led nine miles to an Indian camp and a herd of stolen horses. This obviously referred to Varnell's report and pointed in the direction of El Remolino, a Lipan settlement (see map 12.1). Importantly, the expedition's initial destination of El Remolino reinforces the goal of the Callahan Expedition as retaliation against Indians who had stolen horses in Texas. Furthermore, Callahan's strategic and tactical approach appears to have been sound as Col. Ranald S.

Mackenzie used a similar plan when he led a successful incursion in 1873 and punished the Lipans and Kickapoos at El Remolino.[29]

Callahan faced a flooding, raging Rio Grande at the mouth of Las Moras Creek. Heavy summer rains had created major hazards for the Texans since their July muster. While the August and September thunderstorms brought a welcome end to two years of drought, they made roads muddy and river crossings dangerous. Flooding interfered with the area's stage schedules, and even Langberg, then at Múzquiz, complained that the rains impeded his movements (see map 12.2). Without boats and unable to construct rafts, Callahan's battalion failed to ford the river at Las Moras. An October 9 news report by a *New Orleans Picayune* correspondent at Eagle Pass confirmed that the Texans at Las Moras, after unsuccessfully attempting to cross, rode downstream in search of an easier and safer place to traverse the Rio Grande. Leaving late on September 29, the Texans arrived near Eagle Pass the next day. For the first time in weeks, a warm, sunny day welcomed them and a near full moon lit the night. They camped four miles upstream from Eagle Pass and Fort Duncan. Here the rangers rested while the three captains visited Eagle Pass. Jesse Sumpter, merchant and saloon proprietor, recalled their arrival in his memoir. Interestingly, at this time he was the deputy sheriff for Eagle Pass, appointed by Bexar County Sheriff William B. Knox, a member of the San Antonio Committee. When three middle-aged Anglo men arrived early in the evening of September 30, Sumpter assumed they were slave hunting. According to Sumpter's recollection four decades later, the men were bragging, and he understood they intended to "go into Mexico and take them [slaves] out by force." Given the reputations of the men involved, Sumpter must have based his assumptions on Henry's boisterous behavior rather than Callahan's. Callahan was a modest and quiet man, and it seems out of character for him to have behaved as Sumpter described.[30]

According to Sumpter's memoir, "Alambejar" (a mangling of Langberg's name) was a Mexican colonel who had moved to San Antonio due to north Mexico's ongoing internecine warfare. There he met Callahan just prior to the expedition's departure from Camp Near Bandera on September 18. Once "Alambejar" settled his difficulties with Mexican officials, Sumpter wrote, he arranged for Callahan to cross the Rio Grande. However, "Alambejar" stipulated the rangers must neither "cross directly into Piedras Negras" nor "go through any of the Mexican towns." According to Sumpter, this explained why the Texans camped north of Eagle Pass, which kept them away from Piedras Negras on their way to San Fernando and gave "Alambejar" time to arrive there ahead of them. Sumpter was incorrect as far as Langberg's whereabouts, based on Mexican archives and newspapers, and likewise for Callahan's location (see maps 12.2, 13.2). After an early evening of gossip and intelligence gathering, the three captains rode out of Eagle Pass intent on implementing their plan. Luck was on their side as recent events in Mexico had led to the removal of 1,500 troops that could have stopped them, but at the same time other defensive forces had been alerted that Texans might be coming.[31]

In the meantime, Langberg had arrived in Múzquiz on September 13 with most of the troops from Piedras Negras (see map 12.2). Following Vidaurri's instructions, he issued orders to surrounding villages to muster their militias and rendezvous at Monclova. On September 18, rain delayed the departure of the militia, whose march was further impeded by a lack of supplies in Monclova. Most of the villages had difficulty providing support; for example, as late as October 1, Múzquiz officials had scraped together only ten pesos to help their men get to Monterrey. While mustering troops to help Vidaurri was the priority, Langberg remained concerned about raids, so he ordered the Indians to stay near their homes. Nevertheless, in a September 19 letter to Vidaurri, Langberg announced his imminent departure for Monclova.[32]

During this period, Lieutenant Colonel Manuel Leal, also at Múzquiz, dispatched two curious letters to Vidaurri. In the first, he condemned Langberg's delay and remarked that his militia would stay at Múzquiz to wait on Captain Miguel Patiño's men, who were still at Morelos near the frontier and unable to march due to rain. In the second letter, Leal reported malicious gossip directed toward Langberg, but assured Vidaurri the rumors had no credibility. Still anxious for reinforcements, a few days later Vidaurri pressed Langberg to march south. Finally, some of his units, including most of the regular troops from Piedras Negras, marched for Monclova. But Leal, with 500 men from Allende, Gigedo, Piedras Negras, and San Fernando, did not go with Langberg. His presence at Múzquiz, a two-day march from Piedras Negras, would have grave consequences for the Callahan Expedition. Langberg arrived at Monclova on September 25 (see map 12.2) and found the villages in the area also had difficulties sending men, and some were deserting. Three days later, he received a report from Menchaca, his commander at Piedras Negras, about Texans planning to punish the Lipans, which prompted him to issue instructions to Menchaca to defend the frontier. Meanwhile, waiting for reinforcements, Langberg remained at Monclova. Thus, as the Callahan Expedition marched from Fort Inge to Las Moras Creek and on to Eagle Pass, Langberg was in Monclova, Leal camped at Múzquiz, and Patiño remained at Morelos. All had been warned that Texans might be approaching, though they had no idea of the location of Callahan's Rangers.[33]

At Piedras Negras, Menchaca busied himself in the nearly deserted *presidio*, declining requests to forward more men to Músquiz. He was drawn into local law enforcement when two recalcitrant men were arrested, and their arms and mounts were confiscated. At one point, he complained about Lipans crossing the Rio Grande, causing the disruption of local commerce, and on September 23 he sent his communication to Langberg that Texans were reported to be at Arroyo Seco chasing Lipans but were not a threat to Mexico. Langberg was not as certain. He had earlier told Vidaurri that Texans were planning to cross the Rio Grande thirty miles north of Eagle Pass to confront Lipans residing there, and he had complained about the border troubles that Lipans were creating. His reply to Menchaca included instructions to call the Lipan leaders together and tell them not to cross the river. For their protection, their families were to move southwest into the Santa Rosa mountains, but some men were to remain and assist the militia. Menchaca was to emphasize that Mexico would protect them. Langberg also ordered Menchaca to send spies to follow the Texans; if they crossed the river, Menchaca was to notify him and retreat, harassing the invaders until Langberg arrived to punish them. Though it is uncertain, it is probable that Menchaca received Langberg's instructions on October 1.[34]

At some point during September 28, Menchaca was again informed of a potential threat. On this occasion, he wrote to Vidaurri that a Texan volunteer force had gathered at Arroyo Seco with the objective of attacking Lipans, who had recently crossed the Rio Grande into Texas. Menchaca repeated that, according to his sources and reports in Texas newspapers, the Texans had no orders to cross the Rio Grande. Nevertheless, he planned to maintain vigilance and was prepared to castigate any Texan who entered Mexico. At the time of his writing, Callahan's men were forty miles north, halfway between Fort Inge and Fort Clark (see map 13.2). Two days later, on September 30, as the Callahan Expedition rode from Las Moras Creek to Eagle Pass, Menchaca raised the first alarm that Texans were exploring the Rio Grande above Piedras Negras. That evening he ordered auxiliary troops from Villas de Rosas, Allende, Nava, Gigedo, and Guerrero to mobilize at Morelos and prepare to confront the Texans, if necessary. The villages responded, sending their militias toward Morelos. By now Callahan was committed to crossing the Rio Grande on the next day, October 1, 1855. He would find more than he ever expected when he did so.[35]

CHAPTER 15

The Callahan Expedition, 1855, Skirmishes

"We whipped them, four to one"

By early October 1855 it was no secret that James Hughes Callahan planned to cross into Mexico. On September 29, John S. Ford, the *Texas State Times* editor, confirmed rumors that Callahan's expedition against the Lipans was underway. Even Gen. Persifor F. Smith left Corpus Christi for his San Antonio headquarters. Once there, he claimed to be in "good health and fine spirits," but locals, less interested in his well-being than in the Indian depredations, assailed him with reports of recent raids. Defensively, Smith declared he had done all he could to protect the frontier, but his orders had been countermanded. Realizing the enormity of the situation, Governor Elisha M. Pease hurried to San Antonio, hoping Smith would agree to mobilize more Texan volunteers or army troops. The city was simmering with expectation when scout Russell Varnell rode into town and described the dire events unfolding near Piedras Negras and Eagle Pass.[1]

Returning to his camp north of Eagle Pass late on September 30, Callahan had ordered a march to Paso del Águila, the ford where his men planned to cross the Rio Grande (see map 13.2). The details of the crossing vary by source, but all agree that by October 2, save for a few men, the Callahan Expedition was in Mexico. Jesse Sumpter, the Eagle Pass deputy sheriff, was most specific. He claimed that, arriving at Paso del Águila, a detachment of Texans had hiked upriver to Eagle Pass and commandeered the ferry skiffs, taking them downstream. The crossing began on September 30 at Paso del

Águila and required three days as 111 rangers shuttled to Mexico, while several "backed out," staying in Eagle Pass. Pvt. John F. Campbell of Callahan's company recalled collecting several boats on the trip downriver, then crossing in the frail craft with horses swimming beside them. Pvt. John W. Sansom, also with Callahan, recollected that the crossing lasted only one day, October 1, but he criticized Callahan's lack of secrecy, which attracted the attention of United States and Mexican authorities. But both he and a writer for the *New Orleans Picayune* reported that an army lieutenant drowned while helping with the passage. This was Lt. William M. Davant. Lt. Richard W. Johnson wrote that Davant died on October 1 while looking for a passable ford over the flooded river. In a letter to Davant's family, Capt. John G. Walker said he was at Paso del Águila when Davant's boots filled with water, dragging him into the current. Obviously, knowing about the crossing led the army to help, not hinder, the Texans. Pvt. S. J. P. McDowell of Nathaniel Benton's company wrote that on October 1 Callahan ordered William R. Henry to secure the skiffs from the ferry owners, both Americans, who willingly lent their boats. Once on the far side, Henry, anticipating an attack, asked for reinforcements, and another twenty men joined him. This detachment guarded the west bank through the night, but fortunately no one attacked since the Texans were preoccupied with arguing among themselves.[2]

Sansom and Henry worried needlessly about Mexican resistance. The *Picayune* writer reported that the crossing at Paso del Águila made little headway until a Mexican, who was in command, let the Texans shuttle directly from Eagle Pass to Piedras Negras. Callahan confirmed this when he wrote to Pease that on October 2 some of his rangers crossed at Eagle Pass and the others three miles below. A correspondent for the *San Antonio Texan*, Sansom, and McDowell also said a few rangers crossed at Paso del Águila and the rest at Eagle Pass. Eagle Pass resident and ferryman Edward T. Moore, describing the ferries' seizure in a deposition years later, swore that at midday on October 1, ten mounted men charged through Eagle Pass and seized his ferry, allowing the remainder of the 101 men to cross at Eagle Pass, not below, in full view of local citizens and Fort Duncan soldiers. Rangers then rode through Piedras Negras without molesting any property and camped overnight three miles outside the village. John Newton, a Seminole who lived in Piedras Negras, told the same commission that the crossing was at Piedras Negras and the rangers' camp lay twenty miles beyond the town. Regardless of differing details about the river's crossing, by sunrise on the morning of October 3, 1855, a rear guard of about fifteen men remained on the Texas bank of the Rio Grande and 111 rangers were in Mexico without having clashed with military forces on either side of the border (see map 13.2).[3]

While Mexican authorities did not challenge Callahan's crossing, their accounts of what happened differ from Texan versions. According to Col. Emilio Langberg, who was not present when the Texans crossed, Piedras Negras residents owned and guarded the ferryboats, but each night they chained them on the American side of the Rio Grande. On the afternoon of October 1, Henry and twenty Texans seized the boats and became the first to cross, establishing a beachhead on the west bank. Passage of the other rangers took place that night and part of the next day, a process that Langberg estimated took eighteen hours. Langberg accused the U.S. Army of intentionally ignoring the invasion. By 1873, when the commission met, Mexican accounts changed, with twelve Texans seizing two Mexican ferries on Texas soil near Fort Duncan, then moving the skiffs downstream for all of the rangers to cross. Interestingly, an attempt by three filibusterers to take the same skiffs on September 14, 1855, resulted in a one-hour firefight with Mexican militia. The next day, Lieutenant Colonel Manuel Menchaca had complained to the commander at Fort Duncan, Capt. Sidney Burbank, who declared the raiders were civilians whom the army did not have the authority to arrest. The three attackers were never identified. Some believe they may have been Callahan's Rangers, but they were 135 miles away at Camp Near Bandera, Benton's men were about 120 miles northeast at Castroville (see map 13.2), and Henry was recruiting in San Antonio. Still, the contrast between that angry reaction and the quiet reception of Callahan just a few weeks later is intriguing.[4]

The Mexicans at Piedras Negras may have decided not to challenge Callahan's crossing because by early October 1855 most of the local troops had departed with Langberg to support Santiago Vidaurri. Sansom thought a small contingent of soldiers could have easily defeated the rangers on the first night when they were separated by the Rio Grande. Sumpter asserted that a half dozen armed Mexicans could have blocked the crossing. Nevertheless, with the October 3 sunrise, Callahan prepared to lead his men southwest toward San Fernando, bent on punishing the Lipans who had tormented his Texan friends and neighbors.[5]

The crossing of the Rio Grande understandably posed a quandary for the alcalde of Piedras Negras. Sumpter reported that many residents fled to Eagle Pass or the countryside. During the first night the rangers camped in Mexico, the alcalde and a delegation of citizens approached them. Callahan explained his mission against the Lipans, an indiscretion Sansom later condemned. According to correspondents for the *Picayune* and *San Antonio Texan*, the rangers were cordially received by most Piedras Negras residents. All Texan accounts agreed that the alcalde accepted the expedition's mission to punish bandits and Indians as long as the rangers spared Mexican property and lives. The alcalde even offered additional men and arms, which the Texans declined, according to McDowell and Callahan. Not only did the locals offer the rangers assistance, in an October 4 letter to Pease, Callahan wrote that the Texans had Langberg's assurance that as long as they did not molest Mexicans or their property, they would be allowed to castigate the Indians. This pledge was confirmed by a traveler arriving from Piedras Negras, who told the *Texas State Times* that Viduarri had ordered Mexican authorities to help Americans crossing the border to fight Indians. The traveler added that Callahan had forded the Rio Grande where Menchaca was waiting to cooperate with him. Thus, Texans had every reason to believe Mexico would support Callahan's effort to punish the Lipans.[6]

Callahan in a later letter to Pease described the communication from Langberg that led him and many others to be optimistic about the mission. While crossing the river below Eagle Pass, an American gave Callahan a letter written in Spanish and sent by express from Langberg. The missive informed the army at Fort Duncan that Callahan had permission to pursue Indians inside Mexico. Callahan then marched the remainder of his men to Eagle Pass and crossed over in full view of army officers. Whether army officers read and sent the missive to Callahan or never saw it remains unresolved, though it helps explain why Callahan openly forded the Rio Grande. Callahan kept this letter in his hatband. Langberg later denied giving any approval and declared instead that when Menchaca heard that Texans had captured the ferries, he immediately left for San Fernando. Once again Mexican and Texan accounts differ. Nevertheless, Callahan, reassured by the apparent support of local authorities, led his men deeper into Mexico toward San Fernando. He may have considered the situation akin to the San Pedro River skirmish in 1854, when the Mexican militia cooperated with him.[7]

The lack of Mexican resistance was temporary. After sending instructions on September 30, 1855, for the local pueblos' remaining militias to consolidate at San Fernando, Menchaca was the sole Mexican military representative at Piedras Negras. With Texans across the Rio Grande, on October 1 he sent another order to the militia, emphasizing several points. He reiterated Langberg's September 28 instruction that in the event of an invasion, local forces must assemble at Morelos under Captain Miguel Patiño and that additional volunteers should be enlisted; this included Lipans, whom Menchaca had told to stay nearby. Everyone was to stay at Morelos, prepared to move quickly if the Texans crossed the Rio Grande. Patiño had the authority to issue marching orders as conditions demanded, and if he was incapacitated, Captain Manuel Flores was to take command. Numerous Lipan rancherías were in the area (see map 12.1), while Wild Cat and his Seminoles living near Múzquiz were available to augment the troops commanded by Lieutenant Colonel Manuel Leal, then at Múzquiz. Meanwhile, the Maroons were farther away in El Nacimiento and El Nacimiento de los Negros, sixty miles from Piedras Negras on the far side of difficult-to-navigate mountain ridges and valleys, away from any invading force.[8]

Menchaca remained in Piedras Negras until late on October 1, so he knew Henry had confiscated the ferryboats and established a defensive perimeter on the Mexican side of the river. In accordance with his orders from Langberg, Menchaca told the alcalde to approach Callahan in a friendly manner while he prepared to confront the Texans deeper inside Mexico. Intending to fight, Menchaca also instructed the alcalde to move residents into his military post. Langberg later boasted about this deception when Callahan complained about the alcalde's treachery. Meanwhile, Patiño organized the militia and volunteers, including Lipans, at Morelos, and on October 2 he sent a request for reinforcements to Múzquiz authorities, which stunned them and Leal, who believed there was no danger near the border. Menchaca joined Patiño at Morelos on October 2, and that evening they consolidated their forces and waited for the Texans to advance.[9]

At twilight on October 2, Callahan and his men were camped on the outskirts of Piedras Negras near the road leading to San Fernando, with Menchaca and his troops bivouacked near Morelos (see map 13.2). Neither side sent scouts to determine the presence and size of the other force. Callahan saw no need; he had permission to enter Mexico in his hat. Meanwhile, Langberg in Monclova (see map 12.2), unaware of the events near Piedras Negras, continued to accumulate troops for his march to Monterrey, and Múzquiz authorities sent men to join him. October 3 began with a warning for Callahan: a Piedras Negras justice of the peace told him about Menchaca and his troops, but he ignored this vital information. Callahan later reported to Pease that on October 3 he led his rangers toward San Fernando en route to the Indian camp. From all accounts, this goal was plainly understood by the troops; even Henry later acknowledged that retaliation against Indians was the sole objective. Targeting the Indian encampment meant that from San Fernando the column would ride northwest to El Remolino, the original destination had the Texans crossed the Rio Grande at the mouth of Las Moras Creek.[10]

After riding fifteen miles from Piedras Negras, the Callahan Expedition stopped at noon by the Rio Escondido and rested for two hours. Reenergized, the rangers remounted and traveled several miles at a brisk trot when, suddenly, a Mexican appeared and warned them of an ambush ahead. Again, disregarding a warning, Callahan continued without deploying a lead scout. His men rode a short distance before noticing a cloud of dust hovering over a "lone mott of timber," about 500 yards ahead to the right. The column hesitated at a point near Hacienda de la Maroma on the east side of the Rio Escondido adjacent to Marcelina Creek (map 15.1, map 15.2; see map 13.2). As a seasoned ranger captain, Callahan should have dispatched scouts, just as he did at the San Pedro River in 1854, but for reasons unknown, on this occasion he did not. Moreover, Henry and Benton were experienced rangers, and neither of them challenged Callahan. One explanation for his lack of vigilance and dismissal of two warnings is that Callahan truly believed he possessed written permission to enter Mexico. Therefore, he expected no Mexican resistance.[11]

According to Pvt. David Walton of Callahan's company, Lipans had been watching the Texans advance into Mexico just as they had observed the rangers' patrols throughout August and September. Lipan leaders understood they were the target of the invading force. A prominent Lipan ranchería was located at Morelos near Captain Patiño's hacienda, and there were others near San Fernando and along the Río San Antonio. Living in the vicinity of the gathering troops, the Lipans had little difficulty uniting with militia by the morning of October 3. Doña Estela, a Lipan in Zaragoza (formerly San Fernando), recalled her great-grandfather's reminiscence of the October that *"rinchis"* [rangers] came to Mexico to kill the Lipans. He was one of several who joined the militia. Don Miguel, a Lipan from the Rio Escondido area, recalled his grandfather's story that scouts spotted the rangers crossing the Rio Grande and chose to unite with the Mexican troops. Zaragoza resident Doña Socorro's father said that his ancestors had a similar experience. Lipan descendant Percy Bigmouth told anthropologist Morris Opler that Lipans "fought on the side of the Mexicans" against the Texans. All this confirms that after Langberg's September 28 letter to Menchaca instructed him to

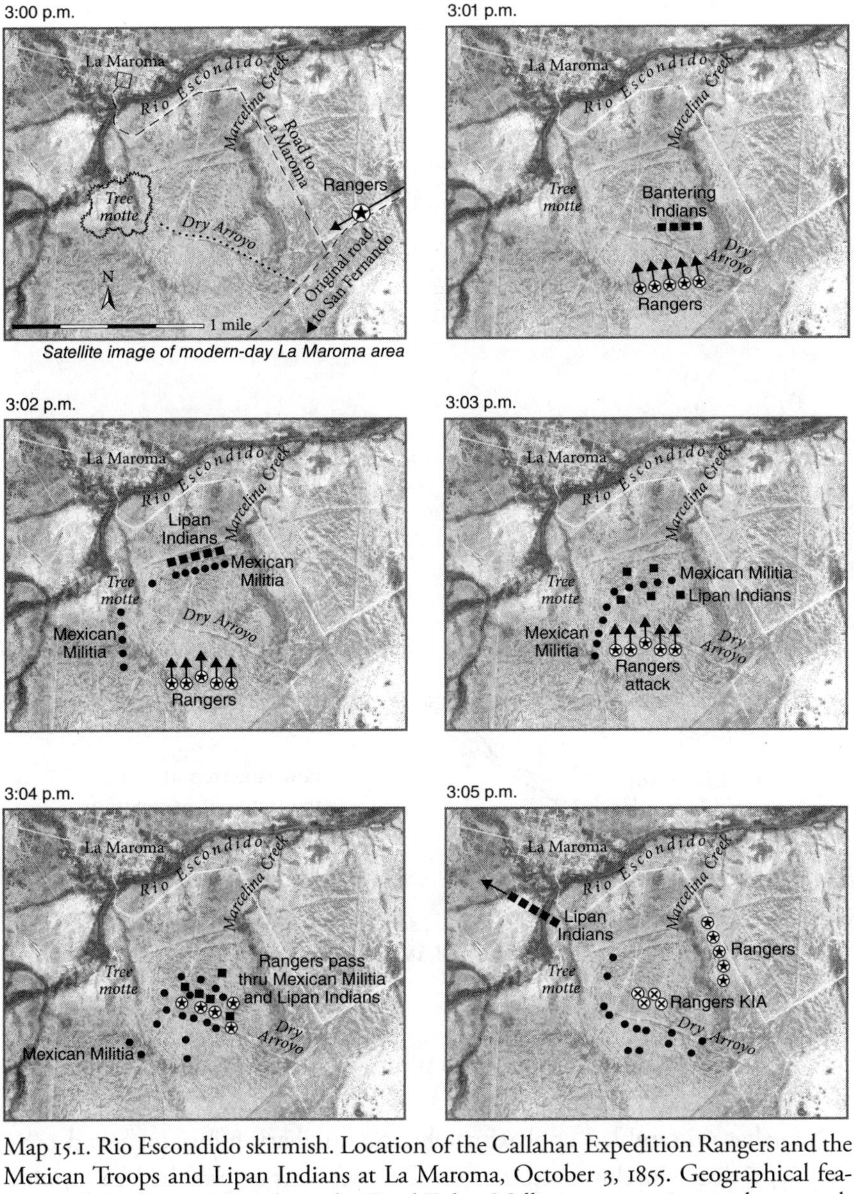

Map 15.1. Rio Escondido skirmish. Location of the Callahan Expedition Rangers and the Mexican Troops and Lipan Indians at La Maroma, October 3, 1855. Geographical features and combat positions drawn by Carol Zuber-Mallison are superimposed on a satellite photograph (2003). Satellite photograph courtesy of Maxar Technologies © 2020.

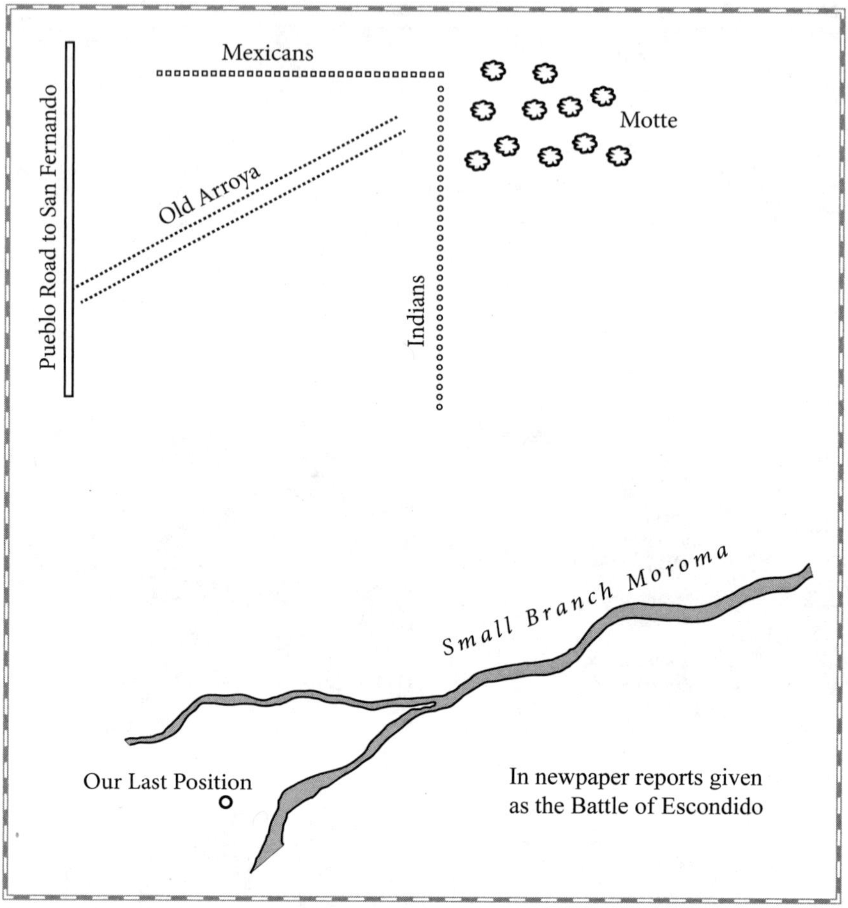

Map 15.2. McDowell's drawing of the Rio Escondido skirmish. Adapted from S. J. P. McDowell, *Galveston Daily News*, January 8, 1893. Illustration by Carol Zuber-Mallison.

order the Lipans to join any confrontation with Texans, the Lipans did join Menchaca.[12]

Menchaca assembled approximately 200 auxiliary militiamen and others. Departing Morelos at sunrise on October 3, they marched to a point near La Maroma on the Rio Escondido, arriving about noon. Menchaca's troops were insufficiently armed, and only a few possessed six-shooters. In this regard, they presented no match for the better armed rangers. However, because local men had mustered to fight Indians several times during the past few years, historian Luis García argues that their military skill, especially in guerrilla warfare, was significant. Thus, it is fair to infer that when confronted by the novice rangers accompanying Callahan, the Mexicans' fighting experience compensated for their deficiency in weapons. Menchaca moved his men to La Maroma because he had heard from the Piedras Negras justice of the peace that the Texans planned to spend the night of October 3 at San Fernando. He intended to intercept them before they reached the town. By early afternoon the Mexican forces congregated under a motte of trees along the east side of the Rio Escondido (map 15.1, map 15.2; see map 13.2). By chance, Menchaca had chosen an ideal position for an ambush—Campbell of Callahan's company remembered the Mexicans were hidden by an embankment where the river joined an irrigation ditch. The few horsemen with Menchaca unsaddled their mounts while awaiting the return of his scouts, who failed to locate Callahan. Then Callahan unexpectedly appeared. In a later report, Langberg claimed that Menchaca wanted to talk with the Texans about their intentions and who had given them permission to follow through on them. In another letter, he contradicted himself, making no mention of attempts to confer. Instead, he claimed that the rangers formed a line facing Menchaca's troops and dismounted, then suddenly remounted and charged the Mexican left wing.[13]

After their noon break, Callahan, Henry, and Benton had ridden in the lead while their rangers followed in a column. The men were relaxed and, according to McDowell, telling jokes. When the dust hovering over the large clump of trees came into view, they presumed the cause was grazing cattle and continued to ride forward until the motte was midway along their column (map. 15.1; map 15.2). Suddenly at 3 P.M., three or four horsemen approached the middle of the Texas line. The Texans initially believed they were herdsmen. As the horsemen came within two hundred yards, the rangers were startled to realize they were Lipans in war paint. The Indians yelled, hoping to lure the Texans into an uncoordinated charge, and one even rode close to Callahan's column, attempting to discharge arrows. Against orders, Zachariah P. Bugg and Daniel B. "Brent" Shuler fired their guns, breaking the leg of a Lipan's horse. According to Campbell, before they shot, arrows swirled through the ranks and over their heads. Not having seen the Lipans, Callahan rode down the line to reprimand the shooters and threaten to arrest the next man who fired without permission. When he saw the horsemen, he assumed they were Mexicans who intended no harm and so, wishing to speak to them, he rode forward. Meanwhile, rangers formed into a battle line along the road. Astonished at the Indians' appearance, Callahan halted, and Benton and Henry joined him as their men dismounted and tightened their saddle cinches (map. 15.1). The three were hastily discussing their situation when about two hundred Lipans emerged from the motte, forming a line to the right. Suddenly, two hundred to three hundred Mexicans, armed with lances, *escopetas*, and other weapons, sallied forth in a line on the left. The expertly deployed Mexican militia and Indians faced the rangers in an inverted V formation (map 15.1; map 15.2). To the Texans, it appeared as if they were being surrounded, and Campbell claimed they thought the Mexicans were trying to duplicate the Alamo.[14]

Discrepancies exist concerning the number of enemy who confronted the rangers. Texan accounts put the figure at anywhere from 350 to 1,000 Mexicans and Indians; the *Picayune* and *San Antonio Texan* reporters placed the number at around 600. Ludovic Colquhoun, a civilian accompanying the expedition, thought there were between 600 and 700, Callahan reported a similar estimate to Pease, and Campbell recalled a seven-to-one advantage for the Mexicans. By any measure, a much larger force with an advantage in position faced the rangers. The captains assessed their situation as they galloped to their battle line. There Callahan shouted: "We have been duped and all of us will be put to death if we do not win this fight. . . . There is no chance to escape. . . . Charge and fight." Having been in similar situations, Callahan understood his peril but displayed strong leadership by remaining calm. Prudently, he also, according to Sansom, sent three men to Texas to report the Texans were engaged in a forlorn struggle. However, Callahan wrote that he only sent Varnell to report the situation and appeal for reinforcements, which suggests that the other two who left, Marion F. Gholson of Henry's company and Valerious B. Sanders of Callahan's company, simply decided to flee. Several hours later, the two raced past Reading Black's house at Encina, and Varnell did reach San Antonio. Meanwhile, Callahan had decided upon an immediate charge, although Walton claimed that the men voted to attack, and Campbell remembered that Henry suggested the tactic. In any case, charging allowed the Texans to take advantage of their superior weaponry, especially the six-shooter. Ordered to hold their fire until they met the enemy, the entire command, screaming fiercely, charged into the right line of the enemy's V (map 15.1).[15]

The Texans named the fight the "Skirmish at Rio Escondido"; the Mexicans remembered it as the "Battle at La Maroma." Differences abound in the accounts of the combat, but all agree the fight was initiated by Callahan and reports from both sides described the intensity, violence, and confusion of the close fighting. In Menchaca's account, the Texans struck his troops with great velocity. The Mexicans resisted, though with difficulty, and eventually drove the Texans three hundred paces to a muddy arroyo, Marcelina Creek (map 15.1). Menchaca claimed his men killed eight to ten enemy during the melee, which at times devolved into hand-to-hand struggles. He also lauded the bravery of Captain Patiño, who killed one Texan with his own hands during the initial cavalry charge. Later, a three-man Mexican team fought its way to the creek's edge where the rangers had taken cover. The fighting continued until sunset, when Menchaca ordered what he described as an orderly withdrawal to San Fernando, which he justified by saying he had to replenish his ammunition. Based on what he was told, Langberg produced two accounts, both of which generally agreed with Menchaca. However, he criticized the decision to retreat, claiming Menchaca should have pursued the Texans after the engagement. Perhaps because Langberg was not present, his accounts are contradictory. In one, he wrote that the dismounted Texans had an advantageous position over the Mexican forces, and in the other he claimed the rangers had been repulsed, suffering the loss of ten men, thirty horses, and several pistols. These losses, he said, caused them to retreat in disorder to Marcelina Creek. There a Mexican detachment attacked the Texans lying in the creek bed and engaged in hand-to-hand combat in which four rangers were killed and four wounded (map 15.1).[16]

The Lipans' oral history of the fighting is largely consistent with the Mexican written accounts. Don Miguel, whose great-grandfather fought at La Maroma, tells of the ambush of the Texans and how the Lipans tried to surround the rangers after they took cover behind a creek bank, but the Lipans ran out of ammunition and the Texans escaped. Eight Lipan ranchería families are remembered to have allied with the Mexicans, and some stories include the point that the Mexican commander promised to reward them with material goods but later reneged. The fighting was remembered as being short but devastating and, according to doña Socorro, the Texans' superior weaponry killed many Indians.[17]

Texan accounts of the fight differ significantly from those of the Mexicans and Lipans. In an October 4 letter to Pease, Callahan said the Mexicans chose a superior position after having been warned of the Texans' arrival. However, once the shooting commenced, the Mexican forces fled in disarray. After their charge, the Texans occupied the enemy's last position, an outcome confirmed by the *Picayune* reporter. Acknowledging the enemy attack from the rear that left four rangers dead, Callahan said his men rallied behind a creek bank and fought for three hours until sundown, when the enemy rapidly retreated toward San Fernando (map 15.1). He recognized one Mexican trooper killed at the creek's edge as a man who had assisted the rangers in their Rio Grande crossing. A seriously wounded Mexican later reappeared at his home in Piedras Negras. Evidently these were members of the three-man team that Menchaca mentioned. Other rangers supported Callahan's account. McDowell remembered, "With six shooters and clubbed rifles we charged their ranks [and] killed about thirty of the enemy." He added that the charge demoralized the Lipans and created confusion in the Mexicans' ranks, while the rangers occupied the position selected by Callahan and tethered their horses. McDowell also recalled that the enemy recovered from their initial disarray and established a skirmish line near the road where the rangers began their attack (map 15.1). After setting a grass fire, with both sides firing at long range, the Mexicans retreated at sunset toward San Fernando.[18]

Texans regarded the engagement as a victory. According to Sansom, "the fight was short, sharp and decisive." The Mexican left wing broke, leading to hand-to-hand fighting as Indians mixed with Mexicans and both floundered in a muddy ditch (map 15.1). Sansom claimed the Texans' charge drove their enemy onto the prairie, where there was little cover, and then the Mexicans bolted upriver and out of range, where they remained until nightfall. A detachment, probably Menchaca's team, attempted to surprise the Texans by advancing up the creek bed, but after a sharp firefight they fled. After three hours, the Mexicans and Indians fell back and left the rangers in possession of the field. Lt. William O. Kyle agreed that "by and by we cleaned them." Campbell wrote that when the rangers struck, the advanced guard of the Mexicans was cut down, so the Texans charged the right wing and then circled and routed the left wing. He added that the Mexicans and Indians fled in confusion as the rangers occupied a horseshoe fortification. About four in the afternoon, the enemy rallied and attacked, after which firing continued without effect until nightfall. Walton recalled that the men "hurled themselves onto the enemy" and completely routed the Mexicans and Indians, capturing two cannons. Hicks said he had loaded his double-barreled shotgun with buckshot and during the charge he fired at a Mexican soldier, who ducked as the load went over his head, then turning left he felled an Indian with a full blast.[19]

In their frenzied charge, the rangers encountered a dry arroyo. Some of them were wounded or killed when their horses hesitated or failed to jump the ravine, eliminating the advantage of mobility. Most of these casualties occurred on the extreme left end of their line, where they were exposed to an enfilading fire from the Mexican right wing (map 15.2; map 15.1). Sumpter recalled being told that rangers were thrown from their horses but continued to fight until slain. Pvt. Eustace Benton lay gravely injured on the arroyo's edge, so Captain Benton, himself wounded but protected behind the creek bank, asked for men to carry his son to safety. Pvts. Fabian L. Hicks, Simpson Tom, and Wesley Harris responded. Hicks remembered seizing young Benton with bullets kicking up dust, but the trio carried Eustace to his father. The younger Benton had a bullet wound above one eye and a skull injury oozing brain tissue. Dr. James G. Barbee clipped the brain matter and applied a dressing. Sansom had a different memory, which had young Benton's injury occurring near sundown at an outpost 150 yards in front of the main body of Texans. In this version, he, William A. Pitts, Aaron Burleson, and Benjamin F. Patton rescued Benton. Pitts left yet another account, which described Benton's injury occurring as the rangers retreated. Captain Benton dismounted, intending to stay with his son, but riding by, Pitts scooped up the wounded private and carried him to Piedras Negras. Campbell had a fourth story, listing a different set of men who rescued the younger Benton and also noting that in his delirium Benton screamed and kicked while being taken to safety. The differing tales indicate how chaotic and violent the fighting was, as well as how the passage of time can affect memory.[20]

With night approaching and expecting Mexican reinforcements, Callahan ordered a withdrawal to Piedras Negras. He also sent Henry with a few rangers to shadow the retreating Mexicans; after several hours they reported the enemy had camped at San Fernando. Henceforth, Texan scouts provided frequent and accurate intelligence concerning the enemy. Leaving their dead on the field, the rangers rode twenty miles to Piedras Negras with the seriously wounded tied to their saddles. Later, Callahan updated Pease, reporting his men had killed or wounded sixty-five to seventy Mexican soldiers and Indians. Colquhoun, the *Picayune* and *San Antonio Texan* correspondents, Lieutenant Kyle, and Private Sansom estimated the enemy dead at forty to one hundred. During the early hours of October 4, 1855, Callahan's battalion arrived on the outskirts of Piedras Negras, where the weary rangers camped until sunrise (see map 13.2).[21]

Texan estimates of Mexicans and Indian losses varied, but they knew exactly who had been killed and wounded within their own ranks. Four Texans were killed at Rio Escondido—William H. Clopton and Augustus

Schmidt of Callahan's company, Hal K. Holland of Benton's company, and Willis Jones of Henry's company. Seven were wounded: Benton, Patton, Polk R. Kyle, and Ewel M. Wright of Callahan's company; Captain Benton and Lt. Henry B. King of Benton's company; and John Gregory of Henry's company. The Callahan and Benton companies sustained a casualty rate of about 10 percent, with Henry's loss being approximately 7 percent. Close ties among the rangers enhanced the losses. Jones lived on Curry Creek with his father, William E. Jones, Callahan's business partner. Clopton owned land next to the Jones homestead. Schmidt had explored San Fernando as Callahan's spy, but little more is known about him. The *Picayune* claimed he was a German living in San Antonio, but the *San Antonio Zeitung* asserted he was a Swiss émigré. Among the wounded, King was Callahan's brother-in-law, while Benton lived with his father and Kyle was the younger brother of Lieutenant Kyle. Patton resided at Curry's Creek with his father, Samuel B. Patton, a private in Henry's company, while his half-brother, James M. Patton, was in Callahan's company. Eighteen-year-old Wright lived in Prairie Lea. It is not known where thirty-year-old Gregory resided.[22]

Unlike Callahan, Menchaca's concerns about his military career may well have led him to under report his losses to superiors. His report listed four Mexican soldiers killed and three wounded. He never identified his casualties, noting only that two of the dead men came from Allende and one from Morelos. Initially, Menchaca said his troops counted five rangers lying dead near the arroyo and thirteen wounded men accompanying the retiring Texans, although in a later report, he claimed that up to thirty-eight rangers had been killed or wounded. He based this estimate on people in Piedras Negras, who allegedly counted the men returning to Texas across the Rio Grande. Menchaca, and later Langberg, maintained that only two hundred militia had fought at La Maroma, and both admitted that eight Lipans had joined in the initial action. Langberg's October 25 letter to *El Bejareño* in San Antonio confirmed that three Lipans had initiated the conflict by taunting and then skirmishing with Texans, one of the rare points of agreement between Texan and Mexican accounts. According to Don Manuel's great-grandfather, when the Lipans ran out of ammunition they withdrew from the battleground, blaming the Mexican commander for their lack of bullets and powder. According to tradition, because they were angry at the Mexicans, no Lipans followed the Texans or attacked Callahan again. However, under the cover of darkness, they returned to the battle site to look for spent rounds they could melt and reuse as bullets.[23]

At ten on the morning of October 4, supplies and ammunition replenished, Menchaca hastily marched toward Piedras Negras. In the meantime, Tomás Talamantes, a political leader at Múzquiz, notified Langberg of the situation, basing his report on information sent by Menchaca. It was the first time that Langberg learned that armed Texans had crossed into Mexico. The report was alarming and the situation grave. Receiving Talamantes's communiqué, Langberg notified Vidaurri that because of the crisis on the border he was countermarching, and he left Monclova immediately with veteran troops and 130 militia from nearby pueblos (see map 12.1). Candela furnished fifty of these, but other communities, like Villa de Abasolo, had no one to send. Colonel Leal, in Múzquiz, mobilized approximately five hundred militia and also marched to reinforce Menchaca at Piedras Negras. Talamantes meanwhile reported that Captain Felipe Torralva was marching from Múzquiz to Piedras Negras with Wild Cat and fifty Seminoles and a few Maroons. Many of the latter still did not mobilize; fearing a Texan attack, they stayed home to protect their families and property.[24]

Meanwhile, at Fort Duncan, a Texan, probably Varnell, warned Captain Burbank about the possible catastrophe. Alarm spread throughout the garrison and the panic continued until the rangers returned to Piedras Negras. Mexican and Texan forces prepared for the next clash, while Callahan wrote two letters. To Pease, he summarized events concerning the crossing of the Rio Grande and described the Rio Escondido skirmish and withdrawal to Piedras Negras. Callahan tersely told Pease, "Every inducement was held out to us by the Mexicans on the west bank of the river, to march against the Indian camp . . . three leagues west of the town of San Fernando." Justifying his actions was Callahan's main objective in this communication. In a second letter, he addressed the people of Texas. His described the events, commended his rangers, and recounted his message to Mexican authorities that he came to whip the Indians, not fight Mexicans. He also angrily accused the Mexicans of harboring and supporting Lipans, who habitually plundered and murdered Texans, and he declared that if he had known that the Mexicans supported the Indians, he never would have crossed the Rio Grande. Next, remarking that he and his rangers remained determined to fight, he appealed to Texans to join them. Both notes were delivered by Lieutenant Kyle, who stopped in San Antonio en route to Austin. Texas newspapers published the letters or at least excerpts; even the Spanish-language newspaper, *El Bejareño*, felt obligated to print them, spreading the story all over the state. Even Henry joined the public relations campaign, penning a summary that read in part: "It affords me the pleasure to state that we whipped them, four to one." Reporting the rangers were in Piedras Negras and expecting an attack and would remain until reinforced, Henry issued his own appeal to his fellow Texans to join them. Focusing on Mexican protection of the Lipans, like Callahan, Henry requested reinforcements to engage in a broader conflict.[25]

According to the *Picayune* correspondent, Burbank at Fort Duncan feared only a few rangers had survived an intolerable "butchery" at the Rio Escondido, so he provided protection by aiming several cannons at the ferry crossing. Having expected the Texans to cross the river to safety, Burbank was frustrated by Callahan's refusal to evacuate under the cover of his artillery. Callahan believed his call for reinforcements was the best solution; however, Burbank fretted that a throng of new Texas volunteers would result in a general war. At sunrise on October 4, the few residents remaining in Piedras Negras fled. Meanwhile, seeking to soothe the Texans, the alcalde "professed friendship" and blamed a misunderstanding for the fight at Rio Escondido. Callahan explained to the alcalde that he had no intention of further clashes with the Mexicans; nevertheless, if attacked his rangers would defend themselves and the town might be destroyed. Callahan demanded the pueblo's surrender, threatening to sack it if refused. McDowell described the chaos, claiming terrified citizens waved a white flag, unconditionally surrendering the town. Meanwhile, local men delivered a "military museum" of firearms, including a six-pounder and a double-barreled cannon. Also, the alcalde gave the keys of the garrison to Callahan; however, his sincerity was doubted when several armed men were discovered hiding in there.[26]

Now in control of Piedras Negras, Callahan issued strict orders against plundering and harming the residents. The rangers demanded coffee and food, but by all Texan accounts, they followed orders and did not confiscate personal property, and Sansom recalled that the villagers were cooperative and offered food and forage. According to McDowell, locals claimed ninety Mexican soldiers were killed at Rio Escondido. Expecting an attack, the rangers fortified the streets with timbers and dozens of two-wheeled carts while onlookers across the river in Eagle Pass watched. Sansom recalled: "Preparations were being made for another fight, breast works were soon thrown up of whatever could be found at the moment and all the men stood to their arms." At Fort Duncan, Burbank watched anxiously as the rangers strengthened their positions. Eagle Pass resident Frederick Groos noted that some Texans occupied a few strongly built stone houses. While the rangers prepared to fight, they also transferred their wounded across the Rio Grande. Colquhoun remarked that these men were well tended at Fort Duncan, and McDowell wrote that he and Callahan visited them and spent the night at Eagle Pass, though others dispute this, maintaining that Callahan did not return to Texas until the very last day of his expedition.[27]

October 5 began quietly as the rangers continued to fortify and moved their horses to safety below the high riverbank near the ferry dock. Langberg and Menchaca later claimed that the Texans were looting houses that morning, so what actually occurred is uncertain. Menchaca also maintained he attacked but was repulsed by cannons firing all manner of projectiles, while Burbank wrote that he saw the rangers repel a Mexican attack. However, Langberg complained to Vidaurri that Menchaca did not attack, and Callahan insisted the first Mexican attack came on October 6. It is reasonable to assume that Menchaca probed the Texan positions while he waited for Leal, who was several hours away. Much time was spent exchanging communiques and trying to comprehend what the enemy was contemplating. At midday, Menchaca received a letter from Henry in response to a query from Patiño about Texan motives for invading. In it, Henry insisted that their mission was solely to punish the Lipans and affirmed their friendship for the Mexican people. He wrote that they had the support of the Texas state government and the United States Army, and they intended to stay until the Indians surrendered. Worried about the army's strength and intentions, Menchaca sent a message to Burbank at Fort Duncan asking for his perspective. He also criticized Burbank for failing to keep the rangers from crossing the river in full view of his post. Menchaca requested a reply in Spanish and included the location of his headquarters, but Burbank chose not to respond, increasing Menchaca's suspicions concerning the intentions of the army and Texans.[28]

That night a scout led by Pvt. Colin McRhea reported that Leal's five hundred men had joined Menchaca, along with Torralva's fifty Seminoles and a few Maroons. However, Menchaca and Leal realized that Fort Duncan's four large cannons could devastate their troops and worrisome news came from Leal's scouts, who reported that two companies from Fort Duncan had crossed the Rio Grande each night, providing protection for the *filibusteros* until daybreak. Uncertain of Burbank's intentions, the Mexican commanders decided the best option was to test the Texans' defense on October 6. After an initial exchange of fire, Leal and Menchaca altered their tactics as Mexican soldiers probed for the weakest area before launching a frontal assault. Anticipating the attack, Callahan ordered his men to hold their fire until they could see the enemy. Protected by a parapet of stolen sacks of sugar, flour, and corn, the Texans punished the attackers with small arms fire, supplemented with grapeshot from the commandeered six-pounder. After a short fight, the Mexicans retired.[29]

By late in the afternoon on October 6, Leal and Menchaca completed an investment of the Texans and gave every indication another assault was imminent. Callahan had decided his position was untenable and began sending men and horses across the Rio Grande to Eagle Pass. But ferrying troops in the one available skiff was slow. Faced with a combined force of seven hundred Mexicans, desperation seized some of the young, inexperienced rangers. Callahan asked Burbank for assistance, but the captain, smarting from Callahan's earlier refusal of aid, declined to help and later wrote that he left Callahan to "fight his way out as best he could." According to him, a few Texans then deserted, crossing the river even though it was fifteen feet above normal. Sansom recalled that Aaron Burleson, Ed's younger brother, swam the Rio Grande to deliver the appeal to Burbank and returned in the skiff with his response. Callahan found it impossible to decipher, so Judge X. B. Saunders, claiming he could read anything written in English, read the note, which declined to render aid. To make matters worse, the skiff slipped its mooring ropes, creating further panic until it landed on the Texas side of the river and was retrieved. Sansom wrote that Fort Duncan officers were ordered not to help, but some did so in disguise. McDowell claimed Capt. John G. Walker, in civilian clothes, rowed the ferry, hauling rangers to safety. At some point on October 6, army assistant surgeon George Wood and Eagle Pass resident Edmund Wallace appeared in Piedras Negras. Their motives and what aid they provided are unknown.[30]

Menchaca finally spurred Burbank into action. He sent a threatening note to Fort Duncan that described the Texans as "American dogs," according to Sumpter. This rankled Burbank, so he ordered a battery of artillery aimed at Piedras Negras, causing Menchaca and Leal to withdraw. Burbank thus provided the cover needed for a final extraction of the Texans. Or so they hoped, but by now chaos and desperation prevailed. Texans and Mexicans alike were frazzled as almost no one had slept for three days. What happened next mesmerized observers. The *Picayune* writer described the scene: "The Mexicans, with very faint *vivas*, answered by the Texans by loud and derisive cheering, made a show of charging into the town, but at that moment dense volumes of smoke were seen issuing from every house, and in the twinkling of any eye the entire village was in flames. . . ." Callahan had ordered the burning of some homes to force a Mexican withdrawal and provide cover for the retreating Texans. Simpson Tom torched the first house. However, the Seminoles and Maroons, using a traditional tactic, also launched fire-tipped arrows into the town. When flames and smoke engulfed Piedras Negras, Leal and Menchaca stopped their assaults. In sum, the inferno halted all fighting, forcing the Mexicans to retreat and allowing the Texans to ford the Rio Grande. Eyewitnesses differed on how much of Piedras Negras burned. Ricketts and Burbank said the inferno easily consumed the straw huts. Eagle Pass resident Groos claimed only twenty huts burned, but John Newton, who lived in Piedras Negras, estimated the flames destroyed one hundred houses. Sumpter remembered that the town rapidly and thoroughly burned, and that the spectacle cast a stupendous orange glow. The *Picayune* correspondent was even more dramatic: "The flames of the village . . . mounting into the heavens, illuminated the river and surrounding country with the brightness of day."[31]

Images of escaping Texans, illuminated by shooting flames in the dark night, transfixed people on both banks. Rangers swam or were ferried over the river in an uncoordinated manner. Capt. James B. Ricketts described the panic-stricken Texans fleeing across the river in flatboats and the skiff, noting that some crossed in such haste they left their mounts. Once in Texas, they tethered their horses out of sight and organized themselves on the riverbank behind a makeshift breastwork of sacks of flour, corn, and sugar. The extraction of the remaining ninety required nearly twenty round-trips, five men at a time, and according to Sansom, Callahan rode in the final ferry during the early hours of October 7 (see map 13.2). They left many horses on the Mexican side of the river. In an effort to rescue them, Sansom, McDowell, Solomon Tanner, Francis M. Martin, and others recrossed and captured a few, but thirty escaped. All in all, the Callahan Expedition lost approximately forty horses, one pack mule, and twenty-one weapons. By sunrise on October 7, no Texan, except the dead, remained in Mexico.[32]

At daybreak, the residents of Piedras Negras congregated in silence. Their homes were gone, their possessions, food, and livelihoods lost in the fire. The people of Eagle Pass responded with some aid but seemed to be paralyzed by the enormity of the destruction of the neighboring village. While the Texans camped three miles outside Eagle Pass, Callahan wrote to Pease. His decision to use fire to cover his retreat did not receive the universal endorsement of his men. The *Picayune* correspondent wrote, "The burning of Piedras

Negras . . . was an unfortunate and illy judged act, which many Texans, amongst others Captain Benton and Lieutenant King, loudly condemned." Thus, even a brother-in-law censured Callahan. Sumpter lamented that the rangers had also stolen a lot from Piedra Negras, including jewelry. By the end of the day, people in the area begin to stir as Langberg and four hundred Mexican troops entered Piedras Negras (see map 12.2), too late to fight except with words. Langberg placed the entire blame on the Texans, caustically commenting that they "had burned the town, leaving it in ruins." He had departed Monclova on October 4 and the following day entered Múzquiz, where he collected more men and organized the locals in case of other Texan attacks. Langberg wrote to Vidaurri about his movements, adding, "I will punish with death any captured filibuster." Unbeknownst to the colonel, Vidaurri had already rejected any order to execute the Texans, stating that it was repulsive to the border towns' honor and the magnanimous character of Mexicans.[33]

Langberg also assessed the military situation at Piedras Negras, concluding that Burbank had provided material support beyond pointing cannons at Mexican forces. Burbank received a scathing message from Langberg inquiring why he had exhibited such "unwarranted conduct." The colonel called the rangers a "mob of thieves" and accused Burbank of sending fifty riflemen across the Rio Grande each night to support the bandits. Langberg said he had no doubt of the army's involvement as Henry had told Patiño as much; furthermore, Langberg claimed, the army actually protected the Lipans. He warned Burbank that if the Texans attacked again, he would punish them as pirates, meaning he would execute any armed ranger that he captured. Incensed, Burbank denied knowing about the crossing into Mexico, and as a representative of the U.S. government he declared his disapproval of the crossing. He also denied sending men across the river each night, emphasizing that his country's policy forbid such acts. However, Burbank admitted aiming cannons at Piedras Negras because he understood the Texans had been nearly devastated, while the Mexican forces had not clearly signaled their intentions and could have planned to invade. Burbank also made clear Henry did not have the authority to speak for the army, and he denied protecting the Lipans. In closing, Burbank professed a peaceful friendship toward Mexico and hoped the incident would not disrupt relations between their two countries.[34]

Hearing rumors of Texan reinforcements, Langberg ordered auxiliary troops to muster at San Fernando, where he planned to organize companies for another fight. He may have sent two letters to Vidaurri on October 8. But only one appeared in the *Boletín Oficial* on October 19; in it, Langberg remarked that Piedras Negras was a smoldering ruin, Burbank had supported the rangers, a larger Texan force would return, his forces were consolidating at San Fernando, and he needed artillery and cavalry. Absent from the published note but included in the unpublished one was criticism of Menchaca and Leal and an admission that the alliance with the Lipans failed. Interestingly, the published letter is not in Vidaurri's correspondence at the Archivos General del Estado de Nuevo León, but the second missive is. It may be that Langberg sent only one October 8 communiqué, which Vidaurri abstracted for publication, omitting the controversial parts.[35]

When the rangers occupied Piedras Negras, the few remaining residents abandoned their village. Just days earlier, many had crossed the swollen Rio Grande to Eagle Pass, while others fled to the countryside. Most of the approximately five hundred residents escaped the fighting and fire; however, their problems were only just beginning. Witnessing their desperation, on October 8 Burbank wrote to his superiors in San Antonio suggesting provisions be sent to Piedras Negras. Refugees in Eagle Pass fared somewhat better as the townspeople provided shelter and food. However, Mexican armed forces, intent upon defeating the rangers, showed little concern for their displaced countrymen. With the antagonists separated once more by the river, the local populace began to return home, but emotions remained on edge along the border.[36]

In Austin, Governor Pease composed a mixed reaction to Callahan's October 4 report. Using Lieutenant Kyle, on October 10 Pease sent a sealed message to Callahan. In it, he praised the bravery and skill of the rangers, and he endorsed pursuing the Indians across the Rio Grande to punish them and recover stolen property. Nevertheless, the governor admonished Callahan for occupying Piedras Negras and told him he should have returned to Texas after the fight at Rio Escondido, adding sharply, "I trust that you have already done so." He blamed Callahan for the expedition's failure and expressed the hope that no ranger had committed unwarranted acts toward Mexicans and thus invited recriminations. This rebuke troubled Callahan until his death. In closing, he announced a mustering-out of the rangers at the expiration of their three-month service and he requested that they report to John D. Pitts, Callahan's business partner in San Marcos, officially ending the Callahan Expedition.[37]

Callahan left Eagle Pass with his men on October 8. Reading Black of Encina recalled seeing rangers riding to San Antonio over several days, most of them on October 10 and 11. Texans were left feeling vulnerable by the withdrawal, with many fearing a retaliatory invasion by Mexico. In Encina, families fled and schools closed. However, in Burbank's last communiqué on October 16 to Smith, he wrote, "The excitement last week has subsided," but he added that if the rangers returned, they would be "resisted by the Mexican authorities with their entire force." Meanwhile, Callahan and his men were lauded in the local and national press. Most articles and editorials endorsed Callahan, and some proposed similar raids, such was their great satisfaction with the campaign. But a backlash was already beginning. Both Mexican and American officials would jump into the fray with their own interpretations, sparking a debate that has persisted into the twenty-first century.[38]

CHAPTER 16

The Callahan Expedition, 1855, Repercussions

"A vast deal of magniloquent indignation"

Juan Almonte, Mexican minister to the United States, was a seasoned observer of Texas politics and kept himself informed of events by reading the *National Intelligencer.* At the first hint of hostility toward Mexico, Almonte would protest to Secretary of State William L. Marcy, so of course the fighting near Piedras Negras prompted a response. Their exchange is one of several that established popular and official interpretations of the Callahan Expedition. The controversial episode was debated in ever-widening circles, from the Texas legislature to the U.S. Army, the federal government, and the corridors of international diplomacy. Meanwhile, there were practical matters to be tended in the aftermath of the failed campaign.[1]

The bodies of four Texans lay on the battleground near the Rio Escondido until late October 1855. Capt. Nathaniel Benton acknowledged that Langberg promised to arrange their return, and he later wrote that he had the "melancholy pleasure" to report that Willis H. Jones, William H. Clopton, Augustus Schmidt, and Hal K. Holland were buried on October 27. Weeks of exposure made identification impossible, so they lay in a common grave. Benton claimed the rangers' skulls bore evidence of scalping, and he credited Charles B. Reed, X. B. Saunders, and Ludovic Colquhoun for the retrieval and burial. By now, the wounded rangers were healing, and many had left Fort Duncan's infirmary for home. Polk Kyle's wound was minor, so his brother William took him to San Marcos on his way to deliver a letter to

Governor Elisha M. Pease. Eustace Benton was the most seriously wounded and remained under Dr. James G. Barbee's care until October 29, when he was discharged with his father and left for San Antonio. Henry B. King mended at Eagle Pass for three weeks. Barbee received a total of $67.50 for twenty days extra service.[2]

Due to the loss of horses at Rio Escondido and Piedras Negras, about forty rangers were without mounts for the journey home. Several rode double while others borrowed a horse, and a few even rode pack mules. Many arrived in San Antonio destitute, so William E. Jones lent them money until they mustered out. Benton's and William R. Henry's companies rendezvoused on October 15 at the Leona River, where James Hughes Callahan mustered them out and recorded the value of lost weapons, horses, equipment, and pack animals. On October 18, John D. Pitts received orders from Pease to discharge Callahan's company, and he did so the next day in San Marcos. Pease's instructions included a request for muster rolls and a list of expenses incurred during the expedition. On November 5, Pease appealed to the legislature for an appropriation to cover the costs of the Callahan Expedition and requested authority to send an application to the federal government for reimbursement, which would include the expenses of other companies called into service during 1854 and 1855. On November 22, he submitted to the legislature an itemized estimate of the Callahan company's expenses, and he reminded the legislators of their obligation to the Benton and Henry companies. Pease provided a muster roll for Benton, but he reported that Henry's roster had not been received. He also requested reimbursement for mounts and weapons lost by all three commands. Guadalupe County Senator Henry E. McCulloch led the effort to reimburse the expenses, which was approved by the legislature on December 17.[3]

Not tarrying more than a day, Pease asked Pitts to summon the discharged rangers to San Marcos and disburse the authorized payments. The governor also offered to pay Pitts $100 for this service. Pitts placed an announcement in the *Texas State Gazette* that told Callahan's men to assemble on January 7, 1856. By regulation, their pay included three cents per day for clothing, eight cents for forage and subsistence, thirteen cents for the use of their horses, and five cents per mile traveled to the muster. When Pitts concluded the reimbursements, the cost of the Callahan Expedition to Texas came to $22,437.27. Callahan's totals were $16,813.54, with $8,824.94 for pay, $5,750.60 for supplies, and $2,238 for lost property. Benton's expenses were $2,509.83, including $1,574.83 in pay and $935 for lost property, while Henry's costs were $1,823.90 in pay and $1,290 for lost property, totaling $3,113.90. Benton's men received their disbursements from Pitts on January 8, and Henry's Rangers were paid the next day. Executor J. O. P. Bond received the funds due to Holland's estate, while William E. Jones signed for his son, Willis. Pvt. Marion F. Gholson, accused of deserting at Rio Escondido, claimed he served one month and signed for his payment. Five Benton Rangers and a like number of Henry's men were absent, but each submitted a power of attorney for a representative to receive their money. Callahan's company was also paid on January 8 or 9, with power of attorney writs submitted for at least eight men. Another supposed deserter, Valerious B. Sanders, signed for his pay and compensation for a rifle he lost at Rio Escondido.[4]

There is no record that anyone received the funds payable to Clopton and Schmidt in January 1856 at San Marcos, but in November 1855 William E. Jones, administrator of his son Willis' estate, had applied to oversee the estate of Clopton, which the Comal County Probate Court approved. Jones returned to the court three months later with $62 for Clopton's service, and in September 1856 he requested that the remaining asset, a 160-acre land patent, be sold at public auction, and the court agreed. However, in November the proceedings took a strange twist when Jones "presented a title bond executed by W. H. Clopton" for the sale of the grant to Willis H. Jones and asked for the transfer of Clopton's property to Jones's estate. Meanwhile, to ensure that Clopton had owned the land, Jones petitioned the legislature, which passed "an Act for the relief of the heirs of William H. Clopton." This bill required the General Land Office to issue a title for Clopton's 160 acres located on Curry Creek. Clopton's land thus went into the estate of Jones's son, Willis. William G. Sansom, who had served in Henry's company, bought the land for $266. The submission of "loss of property" affidavits also complicated the final settlement of expenses for the Callahan Expedition: there were twenty-eight from Callahan's Rangers, eleven from Benton's, and fifteen from Henry's. Compensation for a lost six-shooter, rifle, or shotgun was around $25. Reimbursements for lost horses and mules were based on their value at the time of mustering; $100 was the average paid. Pitts reimbursed most of Callahan's men on April 3, 1856. A. Moritz signed as the administrator of Schmidt's estate. Samuel G. Smith of Prairie Lea had died on November 20, 1855, and his administrator received $210, including $85 for a lost horse, $35 for a six-shooter, and $90 for pay. Luther Blassingame got $72 for the mount he lost at Piedras Negras. These transactions settled the state's obligation to the veterans of the Callahan Expedition.[5]

Considering border protection to be a federal expense, the Texas legislature demanded reimbursement for the cost of deploying ranger companies, and this became a protracted debate interrupted by the Civil War. On March 3, 1859, Congress agreed to compensate Texas for the ranger companies formed from 1854 through 1858, and on June 21, 1860, it appropriated funds. Texas sent its documentation, but in 1861 the Treasury Department's auditors submitted a list of deficiencies. The process resumed in 1871 when the Texas secretary of state went to Washington, D.C., and lobbied for reimbursement. The next year, the War Department presented an extensive list of questionable expenses and vouchers. By now the Texas claim totaled almost $510,000, including the cost of the Callahan Expedition. The year 1878 began promisingly when the Senate reviewed Texas's requests, Federal auditors submitted further analyses, Texas officials provided additional documentation, and congressional committees met, but again no legislation resulted. Congress reconsidered the claims in 1880, 1889, and 1890 with no result. Texas officials persisted, and in 1905 the War Department concluded that the Treasury had not reimbursed Texas, but again no payment was made. However, on May 30, 1908, the House approved Senate bill 5581, providing pensions for surviving Texas volunteers who served between 1855 and 1860, including several from the Callahan Expedition. Apparently, Congress would not deprive elderly citizens of their just reward, but it felt no compunction about wrangling over repayment to a state.[6]

The state of Texas settled its accounts with Callahan's Rangers quickly and efficiently. But public reaction to the affair was not so easily dispelled, especially when Callahan himself stirred the pot. His quiet demeanor belied his impulsiveness when angry, and he felt humiliated by the events at Rio Escondido. The Mexican officials' deceit reinforced his already low opinion of their character. In his October 13 report to Pease, Callahan vented his fury and laid the blame for the dishonor on the duplicity of Mexicans and the Mexican authorities in particular. The letter was widely published, and many Texans shared his sentiments. He then refused to let the matter be forgotten. Recounting grievances committed by Indians in Mexico and the lack of effective action by the United States, Texas, and Mexico, Bexar County citizens appointed Callahan and Jones and four other local prominent men—J. A. Wilcox, John Sutherland, Asa Mitchell, and Samuel A. Maverick—as a committee to raise a regiment for an expedition into Mexico. They designated the junction of Cibolo and Santa Clara Creeks as the rendezvous on November 15, 1855. This appeal was published in the *San Antonio Herald* on

October 16 and received further widespread distribution via broadsides plastered throughout the region. Initial enthusiasm ran high, and the *Galveston News* noted that volunteers were plentiful and had established a camp near San Antonio. Other Texas newspapers also encouraged the endeavor.[7]

The discharge of the Callahan Expedition and lack of confidence in the army caused great apprehension on the border. Near Eagle Pass, fear of Mexican retaliation spawned havoc as schools closed and families fled toward San Antonio. Residents in Uvalde and Medina Counties appealed to Pease for protection, as did citizens in San Antonio. On November 10, twenty-eight of Callahan's Rio Blanco neighbors sent a petition to their state senator, Henry E. McCulloch, pleading for the formation of another ranger company. McCulloch and Representative John R. King, older brother of Callahan's brother-in-law Henry B. King, introduced a bill authorizing a regiment, but the legislation languished.[8]

While the regiment envisioned by the committee at San Antonio never materialized, other independent commands did take the field. Ex-Callahan and Henry ranger, William Tom Jr., at the behest of a vigilance committee, enrolled fifty-four men into a company. Tom's command appeared after an October 17 advisory letter was issued by Texas Adjutant General James S. Gillett, its recruitment facilitated by a McCulloch broadside asking men to come with weapons and provisions to Seguin and San Antonio on October 15 and 16. McCulloch mustered them and advised Gillett of their movement toward Eagle Pass, adding that he trusted the governor would approve. The *Neu Braunfelser Zeitung* and the *San Antonio Herald* claimed the volunteers were well-armed and mounted. Tom's company disbanded on November 15. Another Bexar County citizen, William G. Tobin, enrolled twenty-two men on October 12, 1855. Neither he nor Tom reported any fight with Indians. A third company was captained by Levi English, whose forty-seven volunteers had mustered in August 1855. In late September, English's men chased Indians that had stolen horses, the only action they saw before mustering out on November 13, 1855. The muster of three companies, totaling 123 rangers, alleviated somewhat the anxieties felt by local communities.[9]

Texas newspapers published many commentaries concerning the Callahan Expedition. Callahan was generally praised, a view the *San Antonio Herald* typified by commending him for his "gallant conduct, in attempting to give peace to our frontier and protect the lives and property of our citizens." However, Pease, Gen. Persifor F. Smith, and other officials on both sides of the Rio Grande became the targets of scorn. Pease was criticized for his inability to protect the people, and Smith was rebuked for his inaction and hostile attitude toward Texans' pleas for help. The *Texas State Times* editor endorsed the Bexar proposal to organize another expedition, and the *San Antonio Herald* sided with McCulloch and the unofficial musters of rangers, claiming they were the "spontaneous expression of popular will, based upon the right of self-defense." The *Neu Braunfelser Zeitung* demanded an end to Indian raids yet disparaged Callahan for having entered Mexico illegally, being legitimately defeated, and leaving border settlements more vulnerable. The writer noted that Jones had promoted the expedition, but he had lost a son, and his Curry's Creek settlement continued to be the hardest hit by raiders. On the other hand, the *San Antonio Zeitung*, an abolitionist paper, offered unqualified support for the rangers and clamored for the ranger regiment. During subsequent weeks, papers continued to criticize the principal figures; however, the implications of the burning of Piedras Negras and the idea of a full-scale filibuster sobered Texans. As previously mentioned, McCulloch and King proposed legislation for a frontier regiment, but this measure failed. By the year's end, the clamor for a volunteer force dissipated. For Callahan, failing to organize a regiment brought an extra measure of disappointment.[10]

The Callahan Expedition captivated the nation; the press, particularly the *New York Times*, *New Orleans Picayune*, and *National Intelligencer*, provided comprehensive coverage and accounts by Callahan, Emilio Langberg, and Santiago Vidaurri. Often these articles became preambles for editorials mimicking the views of Texas newspapers that supported the Callahan Expedition. "The Rubicon has been crossed and American blood has again flowed on the soil of Mexico," announced the *National Intelligencer*. However, more cautious statements anticipated an international crisis. Over several editions, the *National Intelligencer* informed its readers that Pease supported Callahan, who had no authority to enter Mexico, while the federal government had directed Smith to stop incursions into Mexico. Feeling the need to defend a fellow Texan, a Seguin resident, surely Henry E. McCulloch, wrote to the *National Intelligencer*, summarizing the atrocities committed by Indians, the complicity of Mexican authorities, and the failures of Pease and Smith that made the Callahan Expedition necessary. Not surprisingly, northern papers were less laudatory than southern, with the *North American and United States Gazette* publishing the harshest criticism, wondering "How any military man, with the commonest judgment, could have undertaken such an expedition right into the interior of Mexico." In

Georgia, Callahan's native state, there was more empathy in the press as Georgians understood his motivation: to protect Anglos from Indians. Callahan's attempt mirrored a policy they had advocated from the early 1800s. Overall, readers in the United States, including Mexican diplomats, enjoyed a diversity of viewpoints, and by early November, Callahan's exploits were widely known.[11]

The October headlines and Capt. Sidney Burbank's letters to Smith initiated a flurry of correspondence between federal and state officials. Pease ensured the companies in the Callahan Expedition mustered out, and despite being besieged by petitions and newspaper editorials, he refused to call out additional companies. Instead, on October 17 Pease insisted Smith and federal authorities would provide frontier protection and proposed that Smith should muster three ranger companies to report to the army. Smith responded that he had no intention of using volunteers because they were more of a menace than a help, adding that a mounted army regiment had been assigned to Texas. Smith claimed he could not draw upon existing army mounted units in Texas, blaming Texans for border unrest, but he had authorized frontier commanders to requisition other troops. Smith, for example, was determined to close Paso de Águila, so he had three companies of the Fifth Infantry occupy the Texas side. Additional troops marched from Fort McIntosh at Laredo and Ringgold Barracks at Rio Grande City with orders to hamper any ranger expeditions as well as to stop Indians or Mexicans from crossing the border. Smith was also correct about a new mounted regiment, thanks to Secretary of War Jefferson Davis. The Second United States Cavalry left Jefferson Barracks, Missouri, on October 27, 1855, for the Texas frontier. By January 1856, half of this regiment was stationed at Fort Mason (see map frontispiece).[12]

While federal authorities and the northern press might be hostile, Central Texas residents regarded Callahan as a hero. Pease criticized the occupation and destruction of Piedras Negras, but he publicly recognized the merit of Callahan crossing the Rio Grande and claimed his men routed the enemy at Rio Escondido. Pease was more unrelenting in denouncing Smith and the federal government and how their inaction forced him to call out the rangers in 1854 and 1855. He admitted Indian raids would probably continue, but he emphasized that filibusters must end and discouraged residents from supporting such proposals, including the regiment advocated by Callahan and others. Local papers commended the governor's message, especially his defense of Callahan. Smith agreed with Pease that raids across the border had to stop, but he differed with the governor by assigning part of the blame to Texans. For Smith, border security was the top priority, with protecting settlements coming second, and he reminded his commanders about federal neutrality laws. He supported Burbank's handling of the Callahan Expedition and blamed both Mexican and Texan authorities for allowing raids across the Rio Grande to occur, for which he assigned the greatest blame to the Mexican government. At the same time, he was perplexed by Texans' adulation of Callahan and believed criminal prosecution of him would be futile. As Texans called for new rangers, Smith also feared he lacked the manpower to block expeditions into Mexico. Pease and others believed a viable solution lay with a ranger regiment under army authority, but Smith remained steadfast in refusing: "I will not buy the promise of good conduct of such men." By late November Texans stopped rattling their sabers, allowing Smith to turn his attention to Mexico.[13]

When Langberg arrived in Piedras Negras late on October 7, 1855, he had discontinued all cross-border commerce and forbidden non-Mexicans to cross the river, ending the collection of customs duties. When the financial consequences of the ban became clear, trade was restored, but the embargo of foreigners continued until October 30. Hearing of Tobin's and Tom's ranger companies and Callahan's demands for a new expedition, Langberg posted 1,500 troops along the Rio Grande and sent two spies to San Antonio, while Lieutenant Colonel Manuel Menchaca dispatched patrols to scout the roads to Encina. While Seminoles joined Langberg, Maroons stayed at home to defend their families. When Mexican civilians were ordered away from the border back to San Fernando, Lipan families moved into the mountains. On October 22, Langberg heard that Texans were near the Rio Grande, so he ordered his militia to mobilize at Nava while Múzquiz's militia countermarched toward Piedras Negras. Tom's company, in the Sabinal River valley, had caused the alarm. A few men, including George W. Brackenridge, rode to Fort Duncan and even crossed the Rio Grande into Piedras Negras. However, no organized Texas force materialized, and Langberg learned that Texans had not rallied to Callahan's call for a ranger regiment. As in Texas, by late November tensions on the Mexican side of the border began to subside.[14]

Like Callahan, Langberg was embarrassed and determined to present his perspective. He wrote letters on October 10 and 25 to Xavier B. Debray, editor of *El Bejareño*. He boasted it was his idea to lure the Texans into an ambuscade and ridiculed the timidity of Menchaca and Lieutenant Colonel Manuel Leal. He went on to criticize the professionalism of Captain Burbank and rejected any notion of Mexico collaborating with Lipans. Continuing to feel impugned, Langberg wrote again. He castigated Henry for kidnapping Mexican ferrymen and taking their skiffs and claimed Texans lied when they asserted that the Piedras Negras alcalde had promised assistance. Finally, he complained that Mexico had also endured raids from Lipans and other Indians living in Texas, and the United States had made no effort to stop them. The *San Antonio Herald* responded with a list of insulting comments that accused Langberg of being an embezzler and murderer. By now, Langberg's plan for peon and slave exchanges and convivial dinners with army officers had become distant memories. Even Smith felt compelled to lecture Langberg. The general blamed Coahuila authorities, including the colonel, for enticing Indians to settle in Mexico. Reciting a litany of horse and property thefts in 1855, Smith claimed Mexican authorities benefited by receiving stolen goods and refusing to return them when Texans, who provided documentation of their ownership, attempted to reclaim property. Smith even justified the Callahan Expedition. Langberg may have wanted to continue this debate, but events in Mexico intervened. Impressed by the colonel's military record, President Ignacio Comonfort promoted him to brigadier general and made him his chief-of-staff, leaving Vidaurri to deal with relations between Mexico, Texas, and the United States.[15]

At the time of the Callahan Expedition, Vidaurri was the dominant political leader in northern Mexico, and he was quick to capitalize on the event. However, the *Picayune* lampooned the declarations of Mexican officials like Vidaurri: "They take very high ground, and make out a case of grievous national outrage; and utter a vast deal of magniloquent indignation." Initially, Viduarri assumed the incursion resulted from bandits chasing Indians, or slave owners trying to recover slaves, or filibusters, or even his conservative Mexican foes. However, learning about Piedras Negras's destruction, he took advantage of a political opportunity. As a first step, he sent troops for Langberg to use to secure the border, then set about establishing his authority over his rival, Juan José de la Garza, in Tamaulipas. Vidaurri asked Garza to cooperate as a patriot. Garza did not reply. Accusing him of treason, Vidaurri exploited Garza's intransigence to consolidate his support from the liberals in Mexico City. He communicated regularly with officials there to allay suspicions he intended to create an independent republic, while his pronouncements appeared in Monterrey's *Boletín Oficial* and Mexico City's *El Siglo Diez y Nueve*. In letters to the interim president, Juan Álvarez,

Vidaurri denounced Callahan's violation of Mexican territory. Álvarez readily professed his confidence in Vidaurri, and Comonfort, who followed Álvarez as president, echoed the sentiment. Liberals in southern Mexico considered Vidaurri's actions as proof that he supported the central government and deserved their trust. Central officials also accepted his control of northern Mexico. Thus, the Callahan Expedition temporarily reduced the political opposition to Vidaurri. Historian Edward Moseley asserts this episode propelled Vidaurri to recognition as the most powerful political leader in northern Mexico.[16]

While using the Callahan Expedition to secure his political base in Mexico, Vidaurri also indicated to U.S. authorities that he was willing to try new strategies to control raids by Indians residing in Mexico. Secretary of State Marcy and the American minister to Mexico, James Gadsden, assured Vidaurri that the Callahan incident did not reflect U.S. policy. Additionally, communications from Smith, Burbank, and Captain Isaac Lynde emphasized that the army would enforce neutrality laws, preventing hostile crossings of the border. In his letters to American officials, Vidaurri's message remained consistent—regardless of provocation, Texans had no right to invade Mexico, and American armed forces must prevent such incursions, but at the same time he would prevent Indian raids originating from Mexican territory.[17]

Rather than recovering runaway slaves, the Callahan Expedition dashed any hopes of reclaiming those who had escaped to Mexico. In November 1855, the *Picayune*'s Brownsville correspondent wrote that even though Vidaurri had been willing to return slaves, "at present all thought of such an agreement is given up." Vidaurri did reconsider Texas slave owners' request for an extradition treaty, which he felt would bolster trade revenues and his quest for modern armaments. In a November 1855 letter to Hamilton P. Bee, a member of the Texas legislature from Laredo, Vidaurri inquired about the status of a treaty Bee had proposed, an offer that also sought justice for Piedras Negras inhabitants. Bee finally replied in January 1856, asserting that the legislature had more pressing issues. Obviously, the urgency of reclaiming runaway slaves had faded, either from a loss of trust among Texans for northern Mexican officials or from their realization of the potential cost of solving that issue. Either way, the Callahan Expedition was a key influence on those discussions.[18]

By early 1856, Vidaurri's trade policy with Texas and the United States was showing signs of success, and his growing revenue resulted in renewed suspicion about him in Mexico. An anonymous source even claimed Vidaurri remained interested in establishing a Republic of the Sierra Madre. When Vidaurri proclaimed the union of Coahuila and Nuevo León, President Comonfort overruled the decree and in May 1856 sent Langberg with 4,000 troops to confront Vidaurri. This led Vidaurri to begin an investigation of Langberg's actions during the Callahan Expedition, resulting in claims that he had confiscated property improperly and had even invited Callahan into Mexico. Of course, Vidaurri could not punish Langberg, whose career had become linked to the liberal leaders in Mexico City.[19]

While Vidaurri worked to develop his political base, an interesting diplomatic exchange concerning the Callahan Expedition involved the U.S. consul in Monterrey, Stephen D. Mullowny. He had a medical degree from Jefferson Medical College, served in the army during the Mexican War, and by 1849 lived in Austin. He actively promoted a southern railroad through Mexico, and he became the American consul at Monterrey in 1855. At the same time, he was the inspector of the medical corps in Vidaurri's army, and later he was accused of supporting Texas filibusters and trying to establish the Republic of the Sierra Madre. Mullowny's attitude, like that of other U.S. diplomats, was that Callahan acted in response to Mexican negligence in controlling Indian raids. His first official report, on October 10, 1855, declared that the Texans crossed over to attack the Lipans. Mullowny conferred with Vidaurri, emphasizing Callahan's raid was not the result of official policy, and he wrote to U.S. Army commanders asking them to stop incursions from Texas. Of particular concern to him was the disruption in border trade as a consequence of the Callahan Expedition.[20]

While Mullowny as consul handled the situation locally, Minister Gadsden addressed the broader impact of the Callahan Expedition. He insisted the incursion was not endorsed by American policy and became angered by the anti-American sentiment in the Mexican press. Writing to the Mexican Minister of Foreign Affairs, Miguel M. Arrioja, he berated Mexico for not addressing the complaints made by Texans. In Gadsden's view, the blame lay entirely with the Mexican government for creating a situation Callahan justifiably attempted to rectify. Arrioja did not reply, but of course he had a very different perspective. He had concluded that Henry led the attacks in Mexico while Callahan, in pursuit of Lipans, had never crossed the Rio Grande. Moreover, he believed that Henry and Mullowny were conspiring with Vidaurri and had loaned him $40,000 to fund the seizure of Coahuila. When Vidaurri succeeded without the help of Henry's force, he refused to repay the $40,000. The Texans then sought retribution by invading at Piedras Negras. Arrioja's view of events was distorted, but it reflected the liberals' suspicion of Vidaurri and contained elements similar to Langberg's repatriation proposal and the plan crafted by Hanson Alsbury that Bennett Riddells took to Vidaurri. Though incorrect, Arrioja's conclusion implies that information about these clandestine negotiations had reached Mexico City. After Gadsden complained about the ineptitude of Mexican diplomats, Arrioja was replaced. Eager to put the Callahan Expedition behind him, Gadsden suggested to the new minister of foreign affairs that Mexico and the United States should start anew. When he was rebuffed, Gadsden advised Marcy that withholding $3,000,000 that the United States owed as part of the Treaty of Guadalupe Hidalgo might force Mexico back in line. Indeed, the money was held up, a consequence partially attributable to the Callahan Expedition.[21]

Marcy also heard from the Mexican minister to the United States, Juan Almonte, who was extraordinarily sensitive to real or imagined incursions from Texas into Mexico. During September, Almonte had complained several times after reading reports of armed Texans near the border, including Henry's August incursion. On November 5 when Washington papers blared the news about Callahan, he confronted Marcy, and when he got no reply, he revisited the matter in January. He asked how a governor had the authority to sanction an invasion, noted Henry's claim of Pease's authorization, and declared that Burbank was also complicit and deserved punishment. On January 23, 1856, Marcy responded that Pease justified but did not authorize the expedition, which circumstances warranted, and Mexican officials invited the Texans across the Rio Grande to punish the Lipans. Marcy even appended Smith's October 10 letter defending the expedition and argued that Mexico had not fulfilled its treaty obligation to prevent raids and thus bore substantial blame for the debacle. Almonte angrily accused Marcy of duplicity and promised that Mexican border units would increase their vigilance. In a February 4 letter, Marcy proposed that both governments allow border crossings in order to punish raiders. Concerning the burning of Piedras Negras, he described it as a laudable maneuver in covering a retreat, given that Mexican officials had lured the Texans over the Rio Grande to annihilate them. Furthermore, Burbank deserved no reproach for saving his countrymen, the United States had the right to enlist militia to restrain Indians, and Callahan did not violate the federal neutrality act. Marcy's positions were consistent with those of Mullowny and Gadsden, so Almonte merely sent his note to Mexico City for a response. With this, the immediate diplomatic consequences of the Callahan Expedition ended.[22]

While the issue of culpability was being debated, those of loss and compensation were of greater concern to Piedras Negras residents. Callahan had repeatedly warned his men and those led by Benton and Henry against molesting citizens or property. The only items Callahan and his men admitting confiscating were provisions and weapons. However, Jesse Sumpter, the Eagle Pass saloon owner said he watched the rangers haul loot across the river. He also claimed some rangers were adorned in jewelry, and that he saw a Texan steal a silver-mounted saddle. The 1877 Claims Commission proved unable to determine the amount of theft after four local witnesses—Edmund W. Wallace, Edward T. Moore, Frederick Groos, and John Newton—gave conflicting testimony about pillage. It was not until after the American Civil War that Piedras Negras residents submitted claims for damages and losses. In 1868 Mexico and the United States established an adjustment process, which was extended in 1871, 1876, and 1877 to settle all petitions relative to border incursions. Mexico presented 193 claims for Piedras Negras in amounts ranging from $3,790 to $256,597, with a total of nearly $11,000,000. However, five weeks after the destruction of Piedras Negras, its council, at Langberg's request, had presented a list of losses in which eighty-three claimants stated they had lost property valued at a total of 1,562.50 pesos ($81 U.S.). Unaware of the existence of this list, the 1877 commissioners judged each claim and concluded many were not valid. They also uncovered a scheme, concocted by two Americans and one Mexican, where claimants were persuaded to submit inflated claims in exchange for a portion of the awards. Twenty-two years after the Callahan Expedition, a final report was submitted on February 2, 1877, which President Ulysses S. Grant gave to the Senate. Just 40 percent of the cases were resolved, which included $50,000 for Piedras Negras claimants.[23]

Texans on the southwest frontier anticipated that the Callahan Expedition would halt the Indian raids and, according to newspaper reports and army records, they were right. There was a precipitous decline in raids, from 114 in 1855 to 11 in 1856, while the number of skirmishes between Indians and cavalrymen increased from two to nine. Moreover, most attacks were west of the Callahan defensive line, while few were in the Rio Blanco, Medina River, Eagle Pass, and San Antonio areas. When Indian activity was detected along the Rio Blanco in February 1856, Callahan was eager to call up his rangers again, but Pease and Smith, unwilling to risk another fiasco, curtailed any action by him. Pease asked Smith to send mounted troops to the Blanco, and Smith ordered a detachment of the Second U.S. Cavalry, to the Guadalupe River valley. On March 8, these troopers fought Indians southwest of the Rio Blanco. Pease informed Callahan that federal troops had been mobilized but added that Callahan could organize a scout company of ten to fifteen men but could not conduct "offensive warfare." Callahan did not need such a company; with each passing month, it became more evident that he had succeeded in 1855, at least in the short term. Later actions by the United States and Mexico ensured what happened in the long term. By January 1856, one-half of the Second Cavalry bivouacked at Fort Mason and the other half were garrisoned at posts farther west. Based on monthly reports, cavalry patrols intensified along a line from Fort Mason to Fort Lancaster to Fort Clark. Most of the incidents during 1856 involved units of the Second Cavalry fighting Indians, sometimes Lipans. Texans, on reading accounts of the success of the troopers, became less anxious about Indians and had more confidence in the army, which by 1856 was protecting Callahan's Rio Blanco valley.[24]

In northern Mexico, Vidaurri kept his commitment to wage war against the Lipans. His campaign began the day Langberg viewed the smoldering ruins of Piedras Negras and proposed reevaluating the Lipan alliance. Vidaurri then told Mullowny he would implement a "better system of warfare" against the Lipans. Historian James D. Nichols has concluded that the pragmatic Vidaurri decided to sacrifice the Lipans in order to maintain his power in the north, mollify Texans, and restore bilateral trade. In February 1856, with the Lipans continuing to raid in Coahuila and Texas, Mexican authorities decide to meet violence with equal brutality. Colonel Juan Zuazua captured seventy-four Lipan men, women, and children, placing all under escort for a trip to Saltillo. They were joined by another group of almost one hundred taken prisoner by Captain Miguel Patiño and Lieutenant Pablo Espinoza. When the men attempted to escape and the women began killing the children, enraged Mexican troops massacred their prisoners. Vidaurri reported this to the Mexican minister of war and the commander of Fort McIntosh, citing it as an example the Americans should follow. Texans interpreted the Mexican campaign against the Lipans as vindicating Callahan. The surviving Lipans fled into western Coahuila, joined the Mescaleros in New Mexico, or crossed into Texas where, harassed by the army, many settled in the Big Bend area. After the Civil War, Lipans resumed their raiding in Texas and reestablished a symbiotic relationship with San Fernando's inhabitants. Col. Ranald Mackenzie's 1873 raid was another serious blow, and the 1877–78 campaign by General Jeromino Treviño was particularly effective. By the end of the nineteenth century, about one hundred Lipans remained in northern Coahuila. In the twenty-first century, remnants still reside in Mexico, while others have scattered into the southwestern United States. Lipans residing in Coahuila today believe their extermination by Langberg and Vidaurri began when they did not participate in the defense of Piedras Negras.[25]

The Mexican leaders who attacked both Callahan and later the Lipans did not gain any permanent benefit from their machinations. Langberg's fortunes fluctuated as political factions came and went in Mexico. When President Comonfort lost power, Langberg was without a command. He eventually allied with Maximilian, whom the French installed as the emperor of Mexico, and was assigned to Sonora. In September 1865, his forces were defeated, and he died in uncertain circumstances. He may have been shot as he surrendered, though some describe a gruesome hanging. Vidaurri consolidated his power in northern Mexico, but the new president, Benito Juarez, grew distrustful. Vidaurri's army was defeated at the Battle of Ahualulco de los Pinos, but his fortunes revived through his cotton trade with the Confederacy. After the French invaded, Vidaurri supported Maximilian, who gave him important government appointments. In 1867, when Juarez expelled the French, Vidaurri was arrested and summarily executed, leaving his reputation in tatters. Only the subordinate Mexican commanders apparently died peacefully. Espinoza became a colonel and replaced Langberg as commander of the frontier forces before retiring to his hacienda, where he died in 1885. Menchaca commanded a garrison for several years, then in 1866 fought the French at Matamoros. He survived into his eighties, receiving an annual pension of 500 pesos. Leal's experience as a garrison commander prompted him in 1859 to make a proposal to Vidaurri to invite unhappy Tejanos living in San Antonio to join him at Resurrección, a new village near Piedras Negras. The town was organized but the project failed. As for Patiño, there are no records for him after 1856.[26]

The U.S. Army officers involved in the Callahan Expedition fared better than their Mexican counterparts. Burbank remained at Fort Duncan until 1859, when he was ordered to Kentucky to direct a recruiting station. He was reassigned to command Alton military prison in 1862, but after several prisoners escaped, he was transferred, saw action at Chancellorsville, and was brevetted to brigadier general for bravery at Gettysburg. Returned to recruiting duty in Kentucky, he later chaired the Examining Board of Candidates for Army Appointments and superintended the Freedmen's Bureau in that state. He retired in 1870 and died twelve years later. Smith was sent to Kansas in 1856 to cope with the violence over slavery there, then was assigned to Utah, where conflict had erupted between the army and Mormon settlers. Before he could leave Kansas, he died on May 17, 1858. This was not unexpected. Chronic diarrhea and obesity had debilitated him so that he could hardly walk, and some officers questioned his ability to command; it is also reasonable to question whether his condition affected his performance while defending the Texas frontier.[27]

And what about Callahan's Rangers? At the conclusion of the Callahan Expedition, the 140 men returned to their individual destinies. Most of them had migrated to Texas during the previous decade and were the sons of local ranchers and farmers or were single men who worked as ranch or field hands. They were described as neophytes by the editor of the *Texan Mercury* in 1855, but modern writers have used worse epithets. Fort Duncan historian Richard A. Thompson declared that they were "mercenaries, cutthroats [and] rabble, undisciplined and unscrupulous." Gary C. Anderson accused them of strip-searching "as many Mexican women as possible." Both scholars indulged in hyperbole as no documents support Anderson's accusation, and Thompson's words are similarly unfounded. A more measured opinion came from the proprietor of the *San Antonio Zeitung*, C. D. Adolph Douai, an abolitionist and reformer, who declared it inaccurate to classify Callahan's Rangers as vagabonds and scoundrels, for in reality they were mostly farmers' sons. This perspective, which modern commentators would do well to remember, is supported by the fact that most of them returned to farming and ranching after they returned home, and many did well. Some, however, had more interesting lives.[28]

Only a few of Callahan's men served again as rangers, and even fewer ventured again into foreign territory. William Tom Jr., after organizing his own ranger company in October 1855, was killed in 1859 in a shoot-out on Seguin's market square. In 1856 Ed Burleson Jr. went to buy cattle in Mexico and was arrested there with D. C. Burleson and Polk R. Kyle, but he later served as quartermaster for John S. Ford's Rangers and subsequently commanded his own company. Though opposed to secession, he became a major in the First Texas Cavalry but retired to his Hays County farm before the war ended. Under the postwar provisional governor, Andrew J. Hamilton, Burleson was the agent responsible for confiscating Confederate property in Travis County. In later years, he became a farmer, dying on May 12, 1877. Kyle, after his second adventure in Mexico, joined Col. Henry E. McCulloch's First Texas Mounted Riflemen during the Civil War, serving in the company commanded by Capt. William A. Pitts, a fellow veteran of the Callahan Expedition. Kyle later became a moderately wealthy cattleman before he died in Fisher County in 1916. Pitts prospered as well in the cattle business before his death in 1913, when he was buried in the Confederate section of the Texas State Cemetery.[29]

Among Callahan Expedition veterans, Henry remained the most involved in foreign adventurism. Even while serving as Bexar County sheriff from 1856 to 1858, Henry again offered to assist Vidaurri, but he was rejected and finally threatened with a lawsuit for his part in the expedition. Henry then went to Nicaragua to join ill-fated filibusterer William A. Walker, and he later served in William G. Tobin's ranger company on the Mexican border in 1859–1860. In March 1862, determined to have his own command, he was in San Antonio preparing to take a company from William C. Adams, a wealthy Bandera County rancher. Adams's company had been stationed at Fort Davis since June 1861 and on March 13 he was ordered to San Antonio. Two days later, in front of the Plaza House, Henry challenged Adams to a gunfight. Adams, faster on the draw, shot and killed him. Coincidentally, Robert Augustine, another Callahan Ranger who went to Nicaragua to fight for Walker, allegedly killed several men before a mob hanged him in San Antonio's main plaza in September 1861.[30]

Burleson and Pitts were not the only Callahan Rangers to become Confederate officers. Kyle's cousin Zachariah P. Bugg became a lieutenant in the Twenty-Third Texas Cavalry and after the war married a relative of John D. Pitts; a farmer of meager means, Bugg died in 1887. Henry W. Bridges became a captain in the Sixth Texas Cavalry and then a major and lieutenant colonel until he was mortally wounded in Mississippi in 1864. Nathaniel Benton and his son, Benjamin Eustace Benton, returned to Seguin, and three months later Nathaniel married his second wife, Jane E. Harris, a sister of Callahan ranger John W. Harris. After she died in 1862, he became the lieutenant colonel of the Thirty-Sixth Texas Cavalry and lost his right arm in combat. He died in 1872 at Seguin after serving as a judge for Guadalupe County. The younger Benton, blinded in one eye by a bullet lodged in his head since the fight on the Rio Escondido, served as a lieutenant in McCulloch's First Texas Mounted Riflemen. After the war he moved to Arkansas, where he married and settled at Pine Bluff. He farmed and then sold cottonseed oil before his death in 1914. Many other veterans of the Callahan Expedition served in the Confederate ranks, and some of them also died in service. A few, like John W. Sansom, fought for the Union.[31]

Many veterans of the Callahan Expedition later served in public offices. Polk R. Kyle's brother William lived in Llano County by 1880 and was the county surveyor. Samuel B. Patton was the first judge for Blanco County, and S. J. P. McDowell was Caldwell County's district and county clerk for many years. At least nine became sheriffs: Bugg, Henry, Fabian L. Hicks, Francis M. Martin, Robert R. Page, James M. Patton, Sansom, D. A. T. Walton, and Peter W. Williams. Benjamin F. Patton served as a deputy sheriff. Pease, the governor who authorized the muster of Callahan's Rangers, left office in 1857 but was appointed to another term as governor by federal officials during Reconstruction.[32]

Callahan himself worried about federal prosecution after his 1855 campaign. National newspapers demanded legal action for his violation of neutrality laws. Meanwhile, his supporters defended him. "Rather than arrest, he deserves a vote of thanks," a Sutherland Springs resident wrote to the *Picayune.* Texas papers condoned Callahan's decision while condemning out-of-state newspapers and Washington bureaucrats. While the debate continued, Callahan returned to the business that led him to raise a ranger company. He and his partners in the Pittsburg Land Company hosted their October 25 barbecue promoting land sales in the Horace Eggleston Survey, and they sold numerous lots. They considered the Callahan Expedition a success since it removed a significant impediment to the growth of their business—Indian raids. As for Callahan being arrested or prosecuted, his death in 1856 would make that impossible while it embroiled some of his loyal rangers in what became known as the Blassingame-Callahan affair.[33]

CHAPTER 17

The Callahan Expedition, 1855, Historical Perspective

"Use my creative imagination only to fill in the gaps"

Kenneth W. Porter was a noted professor at the University of Oregon in the 1960s. Trained at Harvard University, he is best known for his publications about African Americans, particularly Black cowboys and Seminoles and Maroons in Mexico and southwest Texas. He was quick to criticize academics who neglected to cite his work and often wrote caustic letters to offenders. He sent such a missive on October 7, 1964, to Ralph A. Smith, a history professor at Abilene Christian College. Smith was widely published on Mexicans, Indians, and Texans along the Rio Grande. He knew the archives well in Chihuahua, Coahuila, and Nuevo León because he spent several summers there, transcribing newspapers and documents. Porter's letter claimed that while Smith's recent essay cited Mexican publications, it was actually "based almost entirely, although without any acknowledgment whatsoever," on Porter's article, "The Seminole in Mexico, 1850–1861." In truth, Smith's work extensively cited Mexican primary sources that were not those used by Porter, which were the Músquiz Records and Luis Alberto Guajardo Papers. This highlights two problems with the scholarship concerning the Callahan Expedition. First, historians have been remiss in not citing key records. Second, Porter's defense of his reputation, as represented by his determination to be cited, made his erroneous conclusions about James Hughes Callahan the foundation for other historians. Callahan's character was sullied by Porter's claims that he owned escaped slaves in Mexico and was a slaver himself, and his expedition came to be associated with slave hunting and filibustering, but none of this is correct.[1]

Any new study of the Callahan Expedition must use primary sources to reveal the many factors that created this complex event. From records of social and political shifts in Mexico, Texas, and the United States, to the individuals involved, all material needs to be reexamined in order to present a fair and thorough interpretation. The loss of vital correspondence has created voids that have led to unsupported arguments, but, using an array of diverse sources, this study refutes erroneous conclusions made by previous scholars. Official records, personal accounts, and newspapers support this revised interpretation of the Callahan Expedition. It was a business strategy, not an effort to nab escaped slaves. Callahan and his Pittsburg Land Company partners needed to stop Indian raids in order to encourage buyers to invest in their Rio Blanco land development project.

The Callahan Expedition was well covered in newspapers, and several participants wrote in diaries or gave accounts of their experiences years later. Most of the latter focus on the skirmish at Rio Escondido and the destruction of Piedras Negras as the Texans retreated across the Rio Grande. Much of the correspondence between Gov. Elisha M. Pease and Callahan has been used in analyzing the expedition, but the September 1, 1855, letter from Callahan to Pease, in which the former declared he would punish the Lipans living in Mexico for raiding the Texas frontier, has been neglected. While newspaper accounts of the Callahan Expedition have been included in prior analyses, more have surfaced that facilitate a substantial modification of prior viewpoints.[2]

Callahan prepared three reports, two for Pease and one for Texas citizens. San Antonio newspapers published two narratives from William R. Henry, and William O. Kyle couriered a letter to his brother-in-law, Ed Burleson Jr. Ludovic Colquhoun produced a synopsis for the *San Antonio Texan*; he may have been at the Rio Escondido fight, and he did join Callahan at Piedras Negras. Two correspondents for the *San Antonio Texan* and *New Orleans Picayune* prepared eyewitness reports near the end of the expedition. Capt. Sidney Burbank, commanding at Fort Duncan, sent two reports to Gen. Persifor F. Smith. Decades later, Eagle Pass resident Jesse Sumpter and Texas Rangers John W. Sansom, Samuel J. P. McDowell, John W. Harris, Fabian L. Hicks, William A. Pitts, John Campbell, and David A. T. Walton (figure 17.1) recorded their recollections, though the last five have received no attention from historians. McDowell based his on a diary he kept during

Fig. 17.1. Callahan Ranger Reunion, D.A.T. Walton Collection. Courtesy of Bryan Wildenthal Memorial Library, Sul Ross State University, Alpine, Texas.

the event, so his memoir is doubtless the most reliable available. The United States-Mexico Claims Commission recorded the depositions of five participants: Burbank and Capt. James B. Ricketts of Fort Duncan, and Eagle Pass residents Edmund W. Wallace, Edward T. Moore, and Frederick Groos. In total, there are twenty-four accounts by participants and observers from the United States.[3]

In the past, historians have relied heavily on Sumpter and McDowell, and occasionally they consulted a narrative by Sansom but neglected his second and more thorough memoir. The backgrounds and experiences of eyewitnesses may influence their perspective, so it is valuable to know more about them. Sumpter arrived in Eagle Pass as an army infantryman and remained after his 1852 discharge. He bought the hotel and bar where he worked, served as a sheriff and customs inspector, and became a rancher and merchant. At the time of the Callahan Expedition, he was a deputy sheriff and later expressed antislavery and pro-Unionist sentiments. McDowell, a Texas newcomer, resided in Lockhart at the time he joined Capt. Nathaniel Benton's company. After hearing Senator Sam Houston describe the glory and beauty of Texas, McDowell had moved from Tennessee in 1853. Like many young male immigrants to Texas, he was eager to become a ranger. Sansom came to Texas in 1838 with his family, which in 1852 moved to Curry's Creek, so he was familiar with many of Callahan's recruits. He wrote the most complete narrative of the Callahan Expedition, and, next to McDowell's, his is the most balanced from the Anglo point of view. Of course, since all three wrote long after the campaign, their memoirs reflect the influence of subsequent events.[4]

Accounts left by Campbell, Harris, Hicks, Pitts, and Walton—buried in remote archives, obscure publications, and newspapers—provide additional details about the Callahan Expedition. Campbell, his two brothers, and a sister resided near the Curry's Creek settlement. The Campbell family had arrived in Gonzales County in 1839 and the siblings were orphaned in 1848, so their sister's marriage brought the Campbell brothers to Curry's Creek. The Harris family moved to Guadalupe County from the Cumberland River Valley of Tennessee in 1851. Harris helped his father on a farm near Seguin. When Callahan asked for reinforcements, Harris enlisted with his future brother-in-law, Benton, expecting to fight Indians. Hicks, a twenty-seven-year-old North Carolina native, joined Henry's company when he arrived in San Antonio. As an overseer in Mississippi, he had watched caravans leave for Texas and decided to take the journey. Pitts, born in Washington County, Georgia, in October 1830, came to Texas in 1846 with his father. The family in 1847 settled at Stringtown in Hays County, near the home of John D. Pitts, William's uncle. In 1850, young Pitts joined Henry E. McCulloch's ranger company and fought in several Indian skirmishes. Eighteen-year-old Walton joined Callahan during the July 1855 muster on the Blanco. Like Harris, his family was new to Texas, moving in 1847 from Mississippi to Guadalupe County, where he carried mail between Bexar and Brazoria Counties.[5]

What is common among these Anglo chroniclers is at the time of the Callahan Expedition they were young, impressionable men. Most had little or no prior experience in fighting Indians or Mexicans. Like many recruited to face the hardships and hazards of patrols and combats, they retained vivid impressions, which appear in their narratives and conversations many years later. Campbell described his recollections to a reporter in 1908. In the 1890s, Hicks told his story to author Andrew J. Sowell and left another recollection recorded by his daughter. Pitts, an adjutant in the Callahan Expedition, was interviewed many years later by a journalist who published their conversation in a Houston paper. Sansom's narrative appeared serially in a magazine in 1911. Some of these accounts did not reach a broad audience until later. Sumpter dictated his memoir in 1906–1907, but it was not published until

1969. Walton several times described the Callahan Expedition in conversations with reporters and written notes, but his descriptions remain among his papers at Sul Ross State University. Nonetheless, these sources provide a valuable inside perspective on Callahan and his campaign.

Mexican accounts are almost equally prolific, although they are a mixture of first- and secondhand reports. Manuel Menchaca left a full report of the Rio Escondido skirmish. Upon his arrival at Piedras Negras, Manuel Leal outlined actions there and also described what he had been told about the Rio Escondido fight. From Múzquiz, Tomás Talamantes relayed to Coahuila and Nuevo León information about the same clash, although he was not there. Emilio Langberg did not arrive until after the fighting ceased; nevertheless, his several reports, based on what he was told, extensively describe events from the beginning of the raid until Callahan left Mexico. Mexican newspapers published four of his reports, and he also wrote two letters to *El Bejareño* and other newspapers in Texas. Langberg also sent Santiago Vidaurri a report that has not been addressed in previous studies. In total, Langberg wrote seven accounts. Finally, Piedras Negras resident John Newton, a Seminole, testified to the Claims Commission about the fighting in his town. There are thus eleven accounts of the Callahan Expedition from the Mexican perspective.[6]

The backgrounds of the Mexican participants should also be considered. Langberg's career, already recounted here, is well documented in extant Mexican and Texan newspapers, the Mexican army archives, and in a 1995 publication. But other Mexican officers involved in the Callahan Expedition are less well known, despite figuring prominently in archival records and representing extensive military experience along the Rio Grande. Menchaca, as a nineteen-year-old Coahuila resident, joined a Mexican army in 1810 to fight for independence and advanced to sergeant. He entered the officer corps in 1821 as a second lieutenant, became a lieutenant in 1831, and was a lieutenant colonel by 1839. He fought the Spanish, Texans, Indians, Mexicans, and the U.S. Army in a career that spanned four decades. Retired in 1851, he became a "*Capitan de Colonia,*" commanding auxiliary troops at Piedras Negras. Leal, born in San Antonio about 1813, was one of many disillusioned Tejanos who left Texas by 1840. He joined Juan Seguin's company for Adrian Woll's campaign in 1842, and afterward commanded a squadron of garrison troops in Coahuila. Recalled to active service in 1845, he earned commendations in combat during the war with the United States. By 1847, Leal resumed garrison command, supervising the relocation of Seminoles and Maroons and battling Comanches and filibusterers on the Rio Grande. Promoted to lieutenant colonel, Leal, like Menchaca, was a garrison commander in 1855. They provide relevant, although not unbiased, perspective on the Callahan Expedition.[7]

John Newton was not the only Indian whose testimony was recorded. In the *Reports of the Committee of Investigation Sent in 1873 by the Mexican Government,* one Maroon summarized his impression of the events at Piedras Negras. During the 1930s, anthropologist Morris E. Opler collected oral histories from the Lipans; one, Percy Bigmouth, provided a brief description of the Lipans' role at the Rio Escondido skirmish. Throughout the 1940s and 1950s Porter interviewed Seminole descendants, and anthropologist José Medina González Dávila is now documenting the Lipans' oral tradition, including the Rio Escondido fight. Finally, while historians in the past have consulted Mexican archives, much new material has been discovered, particularly for the period encompassing the combat at Rio Escondido and Piedras Negras. Some of this material corroborates oral histories provided by the descendants of Indians involved with the Callahan Expedition, enhancing their testimony.[8]

One area of uncertainty that remains is the degree to which Lipans were involved in the skirmish at Rio Escondido. Although there is a discrepancy among eyewitness estimates of the numbers on both sides, in fact, there were 111 Texans and about 200 Mexican militiamen at the skirmish. The Texans also estimated that a significant force of Lipans allied with the Mexicans. Langberg eventually conceded that six or seven were with Menchaca at the Rio Escondido, and in fact he told Menchaca to retain several Lipans after ordering their families to the mountains. Lipan oral histories describe active involvement in the fighting. Anthropologist Dávila asserts that eight ranchería families lived in the area and could have provided up to eighty fighters. Based on the Lipan population reported in the *El Boletín Oficial* and other sources, upward of one hundred could have fought. While it is probable that many did not join the fight, these observations and those of the rangers refute Langberg's assertion of only six or seven Lipans being present.[9]

Much of the reason for denigrating the participation of the Lipans at Rio Escondido was the subsequent effort to remove them from northern Mexico. Although he blasted the Texans as filibusterers, Vidaurri had concerns about Lipan raids. Revealingly, he told Langberg that thefts and murders by Lipans in Texas could have been the real motive for the invasion. Significantly, he admitted to President Juan Álvarez that Lipan attacks in Texas had definitely led to Callahan's incursion, and he declared they must be repressed or eliminated. After the expedition, Vidaurri directed Langberg to warn the Lipans that their continued raiding would be met with efforts to exterminate them. In an era of political turmoil, Lipans became expendable. It is not surprising they decided to ally with Menchaca and his militia in the Rio Escondido skirmish considering that in previous years Lipans and Mexican authorities had established a symbiotic relationship. They realized that the Texans were intent on their destruction, or at least on preventing their horse-stealing raids in Texas. One Lipan descendant has even suggested that the Lipans lured the Texans into the Rio Escondido ambush. But the alliance ended there. Neither Mexicans nor Texans acknowledged any Lipans fighting at Piedras Negras; however, fifty Seminoles and a few Maroons were among the Mexican auxiliaries arriving there on October 6, 1855.[10]

Some participants and observers on both sides of the Rio Grande condemned the Callahan Expedition as a filibuster. Vidaurri used the claim that he had defeated a filibuster to consolidate his leadership in northern Mexico. The accepted definition of a filibuster is that it is a private endeavor. The Callahan Expedition was always a government-sanctioned mission; Pease authorized Callahan to trail the Indians "wherever they may be found." Moreover, Pease was aware of Callahan's intent to enter Mexico in pursuit of Lipans and later endorsed this decision. Furthermore, U.S. minister James Gadsden and Secretary of State William L. Marcy robustly defended Callahan's crossing of the Rio Grande, both claiming that his actions were legitimate under existing treaties. Legalities aside, Callahan never declared territorial ambition to be his goal. Notwithstanding the presence of William R. Henry, who joined other filibustering efforts, the Callahan Expedition does not fit the criteria for a nineteenth-century filibuster.[11]

The contentions that Callahan collaborated with a "cabal of slave hunters," as Susan Miller asserted, or that he "was offered a share in any Negros he might capture," as Porter wrote, are without any source documentation, yet became a popular interpretation in the mid-twentieth century. Some historians accepted Sumpter's claim that Callahan owned "most of the Black Seminole Negros." If they checked tax rolls, censuses, and deeds, they would have seen that Callahan owned only two slaves, each for one year, and leased three, also only for one year, none of whom were Seminoles or Maroons. Furthermore, some historians concluded there was a link between the San Antonio Committee and Callahan. The movement to reclaim slaves from

Mexico was certainly active at the time of the Callahan Expedition, and Bennett Riddells did meet Callahan in San Antonio in mid-September, but Callahan was interested only in his claim that he could negotiate a Rio Grande crossing. This seemed to be fulfilled at Piedras Negras when Callahan received a letter of authorization, ostensibly from Langberg. A brief reference to Riddells does not seem sufficient to conclude, as Porter did, that slavers "promised Callahan a share in any Black Seminoles he might capture." Porter provided no source citation to support his assertion, while Callahan's relationship with Hanson Alsbury seriously undermines it. Alsbury crossed paths with Callahan when his brother's wife filed suit for divorce in order to marry Callahan. The two families had since been separated by years of hostility, and it is doubtful that either man would have sought out the other. An understanding of the individuals involved also makes Ron Tyler's assumption that San Antonians persuaded Callahan to recover their runaway slaves seem dubious.[12]

An explanation for labeling the Callahan Expedition as a slave-hunting campaign may be the misinterpretation of a phrase in the San Antonio Committee's letter on August 25, 1855: "Our future steps and actions will depend entirely upon the information you give us, in the meantime we shall prepare to act swiftly." This translated as "Nuestras futuras providencias y medidas dependerán enteramente del informe que vd. se sirva darnos, preparándonos entre tanto de obrar con prontitud." Some historians understood this to be a threat by the committee to raid Mexico and forcibly reclaim Texas slaves. However, an equally valid interpretation is that the Texans were preparing to receive any returned slaves in an efficient manner once an agreement was signed. This is consistent with the Texans' belief that Riddells's exchange agreement with Vidaurri was imminent, given Langberg's commitment to return escaped Texas slaves. Neither interpretation implicates Callahan in slave hunting.[13]

On several occasions Porter erroneously implied an association between Callahan and the notoriously dishonest Indian agent and slave hunter Marcellus Duval. Porter again cited no sources in asserting that Duval "apparently promised Callahan a share in any Black Seminole he might capture." Smith made the same association, also without documentation. No primary source connects Callahan with Duval. Subsequent scholars who accepted without verification the assertions of Porter have been complicit in creating a false history of Callahan and his expedition. Some go even further. John Gesick wrote, "James Callahan, a famous Texas Ranger, was also a member of the knights of the Golden Circle, a pro-Southern group that promoted secession and slavery." The Knights of the Golden Circle was founded by George W. L. Bickley, who did not organize "castles" for his "knights" in the South until 1859. Historian David C. Keehn also claimed that Callahan was a knight in his study, but it was not until 1860 that castles were established in Texas. Callahan could not have joined any Golden Circle castle; he died in 1856.[14]

Bringing further skepticism to the work of Porter is a letter from Texas historian Ike Moore. Writing in 1942, Moore dismisses any association between Callahan and slave hunting:

> My dear Mr. Porter, I do not think that negro hunting was the chief purpose of the Callahan expedition. There is account after account of depredations committed by the Lipan Indians operating from Mexico in 1854 and 1855, and I do not believe that a purely negro-recovery expedition could have attracted sufficient recruits. . . . It seems to me that the negro phase of the question was chiefly brought out by Olmsted. . . . I have documentary proof of this, which is another story I shall have to write someday.

Moore sent Porter copies of newspaper articles concerning the Callahan Expedition and Indian raids, but Porter never cited any of them.[15]

Porter and Smith's narratives each added a strange episode to the story of the Callahan Expedition. The former asserted: "Another slaving party, it is said, slipped across the river in advance and struck out for Nacimiento [the Maroons' home village]. . . . This first party is said to have fallen into a Seminole ambush. Word of this debacle reached the Mexican authorities before Callahan crossed over." A second Porter publication presented the same information, but neither provided citations. An article by Smith declared, "South of the river plans called for Callahan to draw off mamelukes [Maroons] from their families, leaving women and children to be seized by Henry; but Seminoles and Masgogos [Maroons] ambushed Henry's party." Like Porter, Smith cited no sources. The only mention of this episode is a report from General Smith, who cites an anonymous letter that has not been found in any archive and is not corroborated by any other contemporary source. Unless a credible historical source appears, claims of an ambush near the Maroons' village at that time should be considered false.[16]

It is not clear why Porter and Smith failed to ground their assertions in fact. Both were established scholars, well versed in collecting primary sources and using them to prepare well-written narratives with conventional citations. This is easily established by double-checking the sources they cited for other portions of their publications. They certainly did not collaborate; Porter's letter to Smith accusing him of using his published material without attribution is ample proof. It is also obvious both men had profound empathy for the Maroons and Seminoles, and perhaps that sensibility clouded their judgment. Porter harshly criticized Callahan. In his first draft of a chapter on filibusters, his poetic hyperbole is evident: "In October 1855, the frequent call of 'Wolf! Wolf!' was justified by the sudden appearance of the animal, eyes red, fangs bared, and jaws slavering." Porter was referring to the Callahan Expedition, likening it to a filibustering wolf invading Mexico. Porter's response to prominent Western Americana historian Harry E. Chrisman offers more insight. When writing about Wild Cat, a Seminole leader, Porter noted, "I should adhere to the facts as far as they are known and use my creative imagination only to fill in the gaps." It seems Porter employed his "creative imagination" in writing about the Callahan Expedition, and Smith and others incorporated Porter's perspectives into their works.[17]

Additional insight comes via another scholar familiar with Porter's work. In the early 1940s, Porter interviewed descendants of the Maroons during visits to Brackettville, Texas, and Nacimiento, in Coahuila, Mexico. Fifty years later, historian and archaeologist Shirley Boteler Mock explored the remembrances and experiences of that community in her own book, *Dreaming with the Ancestors*. She examined Porter's work, visiting his archives in the Schomburg Center for Research in Black Culture. She observed: "Porter's notes, provided on file cards, reveal that he blended together conversations from his informants in Mexico and Texas. He did this, as he admits, to enhance readability, though his subjects had differing interpretations of historical events. After interviewing his informants . . . he wrote down the conversations he remembered, trying to provide a sense of the informants' personality and the use of English. I soon determined that this method provides a particular bias to the interviews. . . ." Porter's phrase "Wolf! Wolf!" is a good example of what Mock describes. In another case, a poem about Wild Cat and the Seminoles claiming to have set fire to Piedras Negras was a blended record he created after a conversation with Seminole descendants in Nacimiento. When it came to Seminoles and Maroons, Porter inclined toward a literary style of history that championed the cause of his protagonists, more so than the source-driven analysis expected today.[18]

Remarks concerning William R. Henry's role in the Callahan Expedition do need to be addressed: he was a known troublemaker and interested in retrieving slaves. McDowell noted that some of his comrades were reluctant to associate with Henry and implied there was a debate about a distasteful subject. In fact, Callahan reminded his men that Indians were the sole target of the mission, and he reinforced Pease's admonition not to harass Mexicans or destroy property. Most of his rangers had no vested interest in slaves, and if reclamation was the goal, many would not have felt compelled to take part, a view expressed by Moore. The agreement concerning an exchange of peons and slaves brokered between Vidaurri, Langberg, and the San Antonio committee did not involve Callahan. In fact, the *New Orleans Courier* published a November 6 letter from Laredo that claimed, "Callahan broke up a good understanding with Vidaurri. [Vidaurri] would have cheerfully helped the Texans to get back runaway negros." If Henry wanted to help the committee, Callahan made that impossible. As Riddells told Vidaurri, Callahan's only goal was to pursue Lipans.[19]

It has been suggested that Callahan's August 31, 1855, note admonishing Ed Burleson Jr. about secrecy alluded to their intended recapture of slaves. In fact, Callahan simply wanted to notify Governor Pease of his border crossing before the plan became widely known, which he did the next day. Burleson did, however, create some confusion with a baffling statement to the editor of the *Texas State Times* in November 1855. Commenting upon the recent return of an escaped slave by Mexican authorities, he wrote, "We can guess why they did it." Tyler suggests this comment refers to slave reclamation by the Callahan Expedition. But the return of the captured slave to Texas also coincided with Vidaurri's letter to Hamilton P. Bee and the proposal to the Texas government about a repatriation agreement. Burleson's remark likely focuses on the fact that Vidaurri chose to return the slave as part of his ongoing effort to curry favor in Texas.[20]

Some incorrect conclusions drawn by historians about the Callahan Expedition can be attributed to misinformation from participants. Burleson in a letter to Pease on September 8, 1855, described a skirmish in Texas between Callahan's Rangers and a party of Seminoles and Maroons, leading historians Kevin Mulroy and Tyler to assume that Callahan chased them into Mexico. In correspondence with Tyler, Porter concluded it was unlikely Maroons were in Texas then, and Tyler later decided that Burleson might have concocted the incident to create support for recovering slaves. Since raids into Texas by

Seminoles and Maroons were infrequent, and no other account corroborates this event, it does seem that Burleson's report was a fabrication, probably to broaden support for the Callahan Expedition but not necessarily for chasing slaves. Misrepresentations also came from Langberg. In an April 1856 letter to his sister he boasted, "In the month of November, I had the total fortune of beating an American filibuster party from Texas, which attacked Coahuila for revenge against the Indians." He cited the wrong location since the Rio Escondido fight did not occur at "Cedrito Pass and along the San Antonio River," as he claimed, but was near the village of La Maroma. More than that, he took credit for an incident at which he was not even present.[21]

Langberg was right that Callahan's only purpose was to chastise Indian raiders. The preponderance of evidence indicates that the Callahan Expedition had the sole objective of retaliating against the raids on the Texas frontier communities by Lipans residing in Mexico. Furthermore, Callahan's crossing at Piedras Negras was a business decision. Preventing further raids enhanced the value of the property owned by the Pittsburg Land Company and helped to ensure the success of its real estate venture in the Rio Blanco valley. This is supported by the fact that Callahan acted within the terms of official orders that focused on Indians. After months of Indian depredations and public demands for action, Pease authorized a company of rangers with Callahan in command. Of course, while Callahan and his partner, William E. Jones, who spearheaded demands for action, had the success of their real estate venture as a motive, their efforts benefitted many others. Once granted gubernatorial permission to follow the Indians "wherever they may be found," Callahan sought assurance that Lipans were indeed responsible for the theft of Texan property. On two occasions he sent a scout across the Rio Grande, who returned with proof that stolen horses were being held at a Lipan ranchería. Callahan believed he also got official permission from Langberg to cross the Rio Grande. The evidence clearly shows that the goal of the Callahan Expedition was to retaliate against Indian raids.[22]

To declare that Callahan's Expedition was undertaken solely to chastise the Lipans, and not to seize land or chase slaves, and that Callahan operated within official bounds is not to say that he did not make a terrible mistake. By late August 1855, Callahan had confirmed that the Lipans had stolen horses corralled near San Fernando and El Remolino, and the murder of Reverend John McGhee's son by Indians near Seguin only steeled his determination to strike. This resolve magnified his weakest characteristic—impulsiveness—and caused Callahan to ignore danger signs that appeared as the mission headed toward catastrophe. With no international political or diplomatic background, Callahan little comprehended the complexity of cross-border politics. He naively accepted Riddells's commitment to provide approval for his entry into Mexico and, with no appreciation of the fear created by the threat of filibusters in Nuevo León and Coahuila, he totally misread the situation. Henry had experience with border dynamics, and had received sharp rebukes from authorities in Mexico, but he did not warn Callahan about the sensitivity of the situation. However, considering Henry's reputation, Callahan might have ignored anything he proposed. Langberg claimed he instructed his officers that if any Texans crossed the river, they should be allowed to proceed until he was able to position a superior force to defeat them. Assurances of safe passage by Mexican officials made sense to Callahan as they reinforced the promise by Riddells that the rangers would be given permission to enter Mexico. Moreover, Callahan and Menchaca agreed that Piedras Negras authorities offered to help the Texans. In light of these events, Callahan's assertion that Mexican officials duped him has merit. But the fact remains that his impulsiveness, and lack of political savvy, gave them the opportunity to entrap him, which fueled his indignation and the desire for revenge that he later expressed.[23]

Concerning Callahan's decision to cross into Mexico, Fort Duncan historian Richard A. Thompson asserted that "the 'invasion' by such a force was ludicrous," and from his perspective 150 years later, that assessment may be valid. However, attacking Lipans in Mexico appeared to Callahan no different than his 1854 victory over Apaches in northern Sonora. This affected his judgment, creating an unrealistic expectation that he could repeat the same feat. He believed that he would be allowed to attack the Lipans without interference from Mexican forces, which was indicated by his leisurely march toward San Fernando and his failure to post scouts despite being warned twice by Mexicans about ambushes. Callahan's behavior seems justifiable, if perhaps not prudent, given the information he had. But his decision to hold Piedras Negras, and not instantly retreat across the Rio Grande, must be questioned. Even though some said the river levels made crossing hazardous, staying in Mexico was reckless. Early on October 4, Burbank expected the rangers to evacuate and positioned his artillery to support the Texans. With cannons apparently providing protection, and expecting reinforcements from Texas, Callahan was lulled into a false sense of security. McDowell claimed that Callahan's anger, coupled with the belief that more Texans were coming, influenced his decision to remain in Piedras Negras.

Sansom blamed the delay on Callahan's pride. Whatever the motivation, it was a grave error in judgment.[24]

While Callahan has been criticized for his incursion into Mexico, ironically the officer who stopped him, Langberg, endured an even more negative official investigation. In December 1855, President Ignacio Comonfort promoted Langberg to brigadier general and made him secretary of his cabinet. In the spring of 1856, Vidaurri declared Coahuila and Nuevo León to be a single state, which Comonfort invalidated and sent Langberg with 4,000 troops to Saltillo to undermine Vidaurri. To discredit Langberg, Vidaurri instituted a series of inquiries to determine if he had collaborated with the Texans and abused his fellow Mexicans. The orders from Vidaurri implied Langberg was a traitor, setting the tone for depositions. Forty-four individuals testified, including Menchaca, Alcalde Francisco Maldonado of Piedras Negras, Captain Miguel Patiño, and others who fought on the Rio Escondido or with Langberg.[25]

The testimony concerning Langberg was damning. Almost all the deponents swore that he arbitrarily arrested men, confiscated property, promised payments he never made, and acted like a despot. Several confirmed his orders to Menchaca to withdraw and harass any Texans until he arrived with a superior force. Menchaca asserted that he disobeyed these orders after he and Patiño concluded it was best to confront the Texans near La Maroma. A few claimed that Henry told them later that Langberg gave the Texans permission to enter Mexico with the intention of misleading them. This offer, according to Menchaca, Patiño, and Maldonado, was supported by a letter in English and a map of the route to San Fernando in Spanish found on the Rio Escondido battleground. Moreover, they asserted Langberg confiscated this material, implying an attempt to conceal his collaboration. Menchaca also reported seeing Langberg talking to Callahan at Eagle Pass in September. Maldonado and Menchaca, supported by two others, made another startling assertion. They claimed that on October 8, 1855, Burbank, a "mayor Calajú," and an interpreter met Langberg in Piedras Negras. Called to the meeting, Menchaca recalled Calajú saying in Spanish, "Well, what road are we supposed to take when there is only one," implying that the road to San Fernando had been pointed out to the Texans. Menchaca asserted that evening's events left "not the slightest doubt regarding [Langberg's] antinational conduct."[26]

Menchaca and Maldonado certainly had reason to impeach Langberg; he had removed Maldonado as alcalde and maligned Menchaca's conduct at Rio Escondido. Historian James Nichols concluded that "mayor Calajú" was Callahan, but Menchaca recalling that Calajú spoke Spanish casts doubt on that assertion. Moreover, Menchaca's claim that he saw Langberg talking with Callahan in Eagle Pass was impossible since the former left Piedras Negras on September 2 and the latter did not approach the Rio Grande until later that month (see maps 12.2 and 13.2). Nevertheless, the report of a letter and map found on the Rio Escondido battleground would support Callahan's claim that he received a letter from Langberg granting permission to enter Mexico. However, he wrote that this letter was in Spanish, which he could not read. It seems relevant to note Manuel Leal's failure to testify. He had told Vidaurri to ignore the malicious rumors about Langberg as they were untrue, suggesting that he supported Langberg. His absence may indicate that only men wanting to defame Langberg became deponents. Several said they had heard the Texans were intent on chastising Lipans and Langberg connived with them. Five claimed that Langberg was collaborating with Henry for the return of escaped slaves, but they could only cite rumor concerning his motive or connection with the invading Texans. This second- and third-hand information is questionable, though it does suggest Mexicans were aware of the San Antonio Committee's letter and Langberg's favorable view of it. It is also important to note that Henry's August 1855 foray, which ended with his expulsion, increased his notoriety in northern Mexico. This event occurred near Guerrero and conceivably influenced the three deponents from there to claim that Henry and Callahan were intent on reclaiming slaves. Mexican historian Alejandro González Milea has questioned the Guerrero deponents' claims, arguing that because they were important landowners, they may have resented Langberg's demands on their wealth. If so, their assertions remain suspect. That being said, it is also certain that various persons who came into contact with Langberg considered him entirely capable of deceit to promote his own interests.[27]

Interestingly, little attention has been paid to the role of the U.S. Army in the Callahan Expedition. Eyewitnesses at Eagle Pass and Piedras Negras agree that on October 7, 1855, Burbank trained cannons on the Mexican forces to facilitate the Texans' final withdrawal across the Rio Grande. Four American and three Mexican accounts verify Burbank also offered artillery cover during what he anticipated to be Callahan's abandonment of Piedras Negras on the morning of October 4. The army therefore officially supported Callahan's retreat from Piedras Negras, just as individual officers did throughout the campaign. The first time was on October 1 and 2, when many Texans crossed the flooding Rio Grande in full view of Fort Duncan. Burbank told General Smith that he had no knowledge of this, but several sources, including Callahan, contradict him. Sansom recalled, "Naturally, the officers of the military forces . . . became fully aware of Callaghan's movements and intentions." Moreover, Lt. William M. Davant drowned while helping rangers cross into Mexico downstream from Fort Duncan. Dr. George K. Wood, Fort Duncan's assistant surgeon, was in Piedras Negras at the time of the final fighting. Later, Capt. John G. Walker, in civilian clothes, rowed a skiff to rescue rangers. Mexican officials believed that soldiers crossed into Piedras Negras to reinforce the Texans, but most Anglo sources deny this. Contradictory accounts aside, the evidence indicates that Fort Duncan's garrison assisted in the Callahan Expedition's initial river crossing and their transit back across the Rio Grande, and possibly during the fighting at Piedras Negras as well.[28]

There are four missing documents that if found could dispel some of the controversies about the Callahan Expedition. Callahan wrote to Pease, "While in the act of crossing . . . a paper was brought to me written in Spanish . . . informing the United States officers at Eagle Pass that I was permitted to pass into Mexico in pursuit of the Indians." Callahan later said he placed it in his hat, which he lost with the paper on the field of battle. Langberg confirmed its existence, but it has never been found. A tantalizing lead emerged when a Mexican farmer testified that where the Callahan Rangers had fought, he found a letter in English and a map annotated in Spanish, allegedly prepared by Langberg. Unfortunately for historians, Callahan said the letter he lost was written in Spanish, so the provenance of his permit to enter Mexico remains unknown.[29]

A second missing letter appeared in a report by General Smith on the Callahan incursion. This communication from Laredo has no known author and has not been found in any archive. Furthermore, no one else on the border in the fall of 1855 ever reported the incident it recounts, nor did any newspaper. The writer claimed that "a party of Texan volunteers had crossed the river above [Laredo], intending to attack the Indians; that they had been led into an ambuscade of the Seminoles, and many of them had been killed, and the remainder had fled back to recross the Rio Grande." Smith said the letter was written a week before Callahan crossed the Rio Grande, and he concluded that this incident revealed Callahan's plan and permitted Mexicans to prepare an ambuscade, a perspective not supported by any Mexican document. Smith's October 10 report is the only time this occurrence was mentioned. The incident and letter subsequently disappeared from the dialogue, yet the general's report has confused some scholars, including perhaps Porter and Smith, who concluded that Callahan was involved. In fact, his Texans at this time were slogging through mud and rain shortly after leaving Fort Inge.[30]

The third letter, from the San Antonio Committee to Langberg on August 25, 1855, has been much discussed, but the original version in English has not been found. At the direction of Vidaurri, the *Boletín Oficial* published this missive and Langberg's reply. Spanish translations of both documents currently reside in the Archivo General del Estado de Nuevo León, but English versions do not. Langberg apparently never sent the English drafts to Monterrey, while his reply to the committee was delivered but has also never been found. Examining the August 25 letter, particularly the signatures, or Langberg's reply would clarify the names of committee members. Related to this is an August 30 missive in which Langberg told Vidaurri that Texans planned to cross the Rio Grande at Las Moras in order to chase Lipans. This forecast exactly what Callahan originally planned. Langberg claimed the notice arrived in correspondence from Texas, but he never identified the source. This has vanished as well but if found would settle the question of whether it, rather than the August 25 communication from the committee, caused Vidaurri and Langberg to worry about an invasion from Texas.[31]

Without the English draft of the August 25 letter from the San Antonio Committee, or Langberg's reply, several key figures in the debate concerning the Callahan Expedition remain unidentified. The document was translated into Spanish by "George A. Gisher." Tyler supposed he was George A. Fisher, a well-respected translator. However, this Fisher left Texas for Panama and California in 1850 and, according to the *Weekly Telegram*, did not return until August 1856. On August 30, Langberg wrote to the committee that a "Señor Fisk" presented their letter to him. This was James Nathaniel Fisk, a prominent San Antonian with a history of collaboration with members of the committee. In 1854, Fisk, with George Martin and John S. McClelland, offered a reward of $1,000 for any person arrested for or convicted of stealing slaves. Interestingly, a New Braunfels article in the *New Orleans Picayune* on November 22, 1855, declared that in "late August, a Mr. F——, of this vicinity, crossed over into Mexico in pursuit of about forty (40) runaway negroes belonging to another individual." This person met with Langberg and Vidaurri and offered money for their help. With an agreement contingent on the approval of the Texas government, "Mr. F——" returned to

Texas and placed the documents "in the hands of a gentleman in San Antonio for translation who soon after died." The story is remarkably similar to Riddells's narrative and Alsbury's proposal to Vidaurri, and Onesimus Evans of the committee died October 6, 1855. Of note, there is no known connection between Fisk and Callahan, which reinforces Callahan's lack of ties to the committee.[32]

Sumpter introduced Colonel Alambejar much later into the Callahan Expedition story. While several historians have used his account to argue slave hunting was Callahan's objective, and to claim that extensive plundering occurred, most fail to question the identity of Alambejar. In the early 1970s, Porter and Tyler concluded that Alambejar was Langberg. If so, Sumpter's recollection about Langberg's whereabouts differs from extant newspaper articles and Mexican official records (see map 12.2). Perhaps eighty-year-old Sumpter's memory faltered; even Eagle Pass historian Ben E. Pingenot agreed with Porter about the "perils of relying too heavily" on Sumpter's tales. Unless an incident Sumpter recounts can be verified by another source, his version of events in the Callahan Expedition should be used cautiously.[33]

Some historians have been complicit in producing an inaccurate history of the Callahan Expedition. Their failure to explore all primary materials, and their fabrication of details, have generated erroneous assumptions. For example, slave reclamation has often been presented as a motive for the incursion. General Smith and Frederick Law Olmsted were contemporaries who associated the Callahan Expedition with slave hunting. The avowed abolitionist Olmsted was not in Texas in 1855 and his views surely influenced his distant interpretation. Smith, just days after the fight at Piedras Negras, decided that Lipan raids prompted the campaign, as did other army officers and U.S. officials. Vidaurri, Langberg, and Mexican authorities agreed, and during the fall of 1855 the consensus was that Callahan entered Mexico to retaliate against Lipan raids. In the 1940s, Porter reconsidered the Callahan Expedition. Despite his argument of slave reclamation as its goal being refuted by a fellow historian, Ike Moore, Porter published his work without citing any sources and became influential with many historians, who failed to test his assumptions. Independently, Smith, a Texas borderlands historian, repeated his claims, also with no source documentation. Their unsubstantiated opinions became historical facts.

New evidence uncovered in this study adds some fascinating details to the story of the Callahan Expedition. Despite the denials of the Fort Duncan commander, Captain Burbank, the army actively supported the incursion, especially by transporting rangers to and from Mexico. Moreover, it was Callahan's good fortune that Vidaurri's orders to Langberg meant no large organized force was present to meet the invading Texans, a facet of this episode that historians have failed to explore. Additionally, records and recollections presented here validate that the Lipans were active participants in the Rio Escondido fighting. They were present to a greater extent than Mexican officials admitted, but not to the degree claimed by the Callahan Rangers. Finally, the relationship between Vidaurri, Langberg, and the San Antonio Committee needs to be more fully explored. This would include updated biographies of Vidaurri and Langberg, with more analysis of the 1856 investigation of the latter. Such works could supplement scholarship now emerging on the Lipans, Seminoles, and Maroons in northern Mexico, as well as runaway slaves who may have joined them.

Back in Texas at the close of 1855, Callahan's pride was shattered. Redemption lay with a second invasion whose success would vindicate the disappointing outcome of the first. Blinded by resentment, he had acted on impulse and engaged in the futile formation of a new regiment, this time one not sanctioned by the government. Realizing that such an approach was a bona fide filibuster, fellow Texans and neighbors refused to reinforce him, and legislative support also never materialized. Simultaneously, opinion of the events at Piedras Negras shifted against him. Time had not yet shown that the Callahan Expedition, organized to stop Indian raids and thus protect the Pittsburg Land Company's investment, had greatly reduced depredations in the Rio Blanco valley. Callahan, with the full responsibility for the evident shortcomings of his campaign on his shoulders, resumed the life of a private citizen but was a changed man, having become sullen and resentful.

CHAPTER 18

The Blassingame–Callahan Affair, 1856

"Oh, Lord"

Three men rode slowly west along a narrow road toward a log cabin. All around, bluebonnets and Indian paintbrush blanketed the Rio Blanco valley, but the horsemen were in a somber mood and paid little attention to the beauty surrounding them. The day was Tuesday, April 8, 1856. A woman squinted around the southeast corner of the small dogtrot cabin; her cotton dress and apron flapped in the light breeze as she watched the riders approaching at a leisurely pace. They were James Hughes Callahan, Eli C. "Clem" Hinds, and William S. "Maulheel" Johnson. Within minutes, they formed a line parallel to the east side of the cabin near the corner fence post, ten yards from her. Now standing in the south door, Mary Blassingame waited. The rider on the right, Callahan, held the reins in his left hand, cradling the saddle horn while his right hand rested on his thigh. In a mild tone, he asked if her husband was home. She answered, "Yes." Suddenly the stillness was shattered by three quick shots, with a fourth coming seconds later. Callahan and Johnson were killed on the spot. Hinds was wounded and clung to the saddle as his horse bolted. Hearing gunfire, Johnson's son, Thomas, who had been a short distance to the south, rode up to tend his dying father. Angrily he fired his rifle and six-shooter at the cabin, emptying both weapons. After his fusillade, silence descended again.[1]

As news of the killing of Callahan and Johnson swept through the Rio Blanco and Little Blanco valleys, peacekeeping officials took charge, arresting Mary, her husband, Woodson Blassingame, and their son, Calvin. The Blassingames were held at Middletown, whence Calvin, fearing for their safety, requested help from acquaintances in Hays County. None came.

Seven days after Callahan and Johnson were killed, a mob forcibly took Woodson and Calvin from their temporary jail and shot and killed them. This event, which took place in the Anglo enclave of the Little Blanco, was condemned in predominately German Comal County, thus dividing the region along ethnic lines. Extralegal justice was not uncommon in Texas but, incensed by vigilantism so close to their homes, the German community protected Mary and eventually exonerated her through legal channels. Ultimately, twenty-six men were indicted for the Blassingame murders, and their fates would be debated in the district courts for the next eleven years.[2]

The incident, known locally as the Blassingame–Callahan affair, has been called one of the "saddest and darkest days" for the Blanco River community. While newspapers commented on the event and published letters by Mary and Calvin, it has largely been ignored by scholars. Several decades later, locals John W. Speer, John C. Goar, and W. R. Russell wrote secondary accounts based on the oral tradition among individuals who had lived on the Blanco and Little Blanco at the time. In the 1920s, Louis W. Kemp and Paul Morgan penned commentaries. With the advent of the internet, new versions appeared, but none cited primary, or even secondary, sources. However, more primary documents have been located. These include sworn statements by Hinds, Thomas S. Johnson, and John M. Watson (first witness on the scene), as well as other court documents, including justice of the peace inquiries, indictments, depositions, minutes, and warrants. In addition, a *San Antonio Texan* correspondent summarized the testimony of several witnesses at Mary's habeas corpus hearing. Likewise, the *Neu Braunfelser Zeitung* provided the German community's perspective. Previously ignored letters from Catherine Callahan, oldest daughter of Sarah Medissa and James, are considered here as well. Even James Wilson Nichols left a comment based on his conversations with Callahan's relatives. Lastly, oral traditions from the Callahan, Blassingame, and Hinds families provide yet another frame of reference. These additional sources offer a unique opportunity to reexamine the Blassingame–Callahan affair.[3]

Since Callahan had arranged for his real estate advertisements to reappear on September 22, he obviously anticipated returning home by late October 1855. His livestock, 131 head of cattle and 100 hogs, roaming around his homestead, required attention. However, the events on the Rio Escondido and in Piedras Negras continued to intrude. A trip to Austin with Nathaniel Benton in late November no doubt had awkward moments, and in January 1856, Callahan and John D. Pitts settled accounts with the Callahan

Rangers. However, all was not gloomy. Sarah conceived in December 1855, when she passed her thirty-third birthday, and, unlike the previous year, the Callahans had Christmas together. Yet, sadly, tragedy continued to plague them. Sarah's older sister, Mahala, died on January 26, 1856. She had married Henry B. King in May 1838, and the Kings and Callahans had been neighbors in Seguin. James and Henry had been together in several dangerous undertakings, most recently when King was a lieutenant for Benton during the Callahan Expedition.[4]

Among Callahans' new neighbors were the Blassingames, who settled on land he had sold them on February 1, 1854. The tract was about a quarter mile square, containing 175 acres, and lay near the western boundary of Callahan's homestead, with a 1,300-foot river frontage on the north side (see map 9.2). At that time, Woodson had still lived in Arkansas, so he asked his son Thomas and son-in-law William K. Holmes to purchase the land. Through them, Blassingame gave Callahan $160 and signed a 10 percent note for the balance of $160 due on January 1, 1855, secured by a $1,000 bond. Thomas and his brother Luther had worked as farm and ranch hands in Hays and surrounding counties and were also chain men in the survey crews of Andrew M. Lindsey and William E. Jones. It was during a survey that they heard about Callahan's emerging settlement on the Rio Blanco. Luther later mustered there when he joined the Callahan Expedition. Holmes lived six miles south, near the communities of Twin Sisters and Middletown. Thomas and Luther, along with other relatives, encouraged Woodson and Mary and the rest of their family to move to Texas. Once in possession of the land, Thomas and Luther built a dogtrot log cabin near a spring-fed brook, later named Blassingame Creek.[5]

The Blassingames' arrival on the Rio Blanco marked the end of a long trek similar to that of the Callahans. Woodson, born in 1798, was one of several children of Thomas and Molly Ann Blassingame, who by 1800 lived in Union District, South Carolina. A few years later, Thomas relocated to Warren County, Kentucky, where he died in 1804. The first documented presence of Woodson is in the 1807 legal proceedings of his grandfather James McIlroy's "deed of gift" to the Blassingame siblings. Woodson married Mary (maiden name unknown) no later than early 1825 since their first child, Katherine, was born on December 3, 1825, and by 1830 he was farming in Perry County, Alabama. By 1850, what had become a large family of thirteen was scattered across three states. During 1843 in Bibb County, Alabama, Katherine married William Henderson Fikes, and her sister Mary wed Uriel

Crout, with whom she settled in Union County, Arkansas. Brothers Calvin and George moved to Arkansas with Mary, as did their sister Jane Caroline, who married Reuben Richard Dillard in 1849. Woodson by 1845 settled in Hempstead County, Arkansas, where in 1850 Mary managed their younger children—Luther, Henry, and Sarah—and three orphans from the extended Blassingame family—William, Columbus, and Nancy. By now son Thomas and daughter Frances had moved to Texas, where in 1854 Frances married William K. Holmes in Hays County.[6]

Woodson never had much financial success. In August 1837, he acquired five adjacent tracts totaling 364.7 acres from the federal government; four lay in Perry County, Alabama, and the fifth in Bibb County. In April 1838, he sold one parcel plus eighteen cattle and three horses; seven years later, he sold thirty-five acres to Fikes, his son-in-law. In Alabama, his interactions with neighbors and merchants tended to end in litigation. He lost an eighty-dollar promissory note for money owed him by Joshua Motes, so he sued Motes in order to collect; they settled out of court. The partnership of Wooley and Edwards sued Woodson twice for nonpayment of debts. He lost both suits and, when he still did not pay the debts, the court ordered all his land to be sold. The Blassingames relocated to Arkansas before the final hearings, and it was six years before Woodson acquired land there. In 1851 he owned forty acres, one slave, one horse, and one mule. By 1853 he had increased his land holdings to 240 acres but sold it for $1,000. It is uncertain where the Blassingames lived next, although intriguingly one year after Woodson bought the Rio Blanco property from Callahan, he also acquired a forty-acre plot in Howard County, Arkansas, again from the federal government.[7]

The Blassingames were eventually persuaded by their children Thomas, Luther, and Frances to move to the Rio Blanco in 1855. On July 5, William E. Jones wrote to Gov. Elisha M. Pease that Indians had visited "the farms of Mr. Hines and Mr. Blasengame." His son Calvin remained in Hays County and did not move to the Blanco until later that year. Woodson and Calvin signed a November 10, 1855, petition from the residents of Pittsburg, on the Rio Blanco, to Henry E. McCulloch requesting the formation of a regiment of rangers to protect the frontier, a project in which Callahan was closely involved. During February 1856, Woodson, along with numerous neighbors, attempted to convince Comal County commissioners to construct a road beginning at New Braunfels, passing through Pittsburg, and terminating at Fredericksburg. By 1856 the Blassingames seemed to have found a home in the new community of Pittsburg. But on April 8, 1856, life suddenly became uncertain for them as Woodson, Mary, Calvin, and their three wards waited apprehensively in their cabin just a mile west of Callahan's house (see map 9.2).[8]

Mary implied the conflict between the Blassingames and Callahan began when the latter hired Calvin as an extra hand. According to the oral tradition of the Callahan and Blassingame families, Callahan became dissatisfied with Calvin's work and in March 1856 fired him, which angered the Blassingame family, setting the stage for the fateful confrontation. On the morning of April 8, Callahan and his two eldest sons were branding cattle when neighbor "Maulheel" Johnson arrived to tell Callahan about an inflammatory comment Woodson Blassingame had recently made to him and "Clem" Hinds. To this day there is no concrete evidence as to exactly what Woodson said, although something insulting regarding either the Callahan Expedition or the Callahan women seems most likely. Whatever it was, Callahan wanted confirmation. He rode across the river to Hinds' home to ask if Johnson could have misunderstood Blassingame. Hinds acknowledged that Blassingame had indeed made such a statement. After verifying it, Callahan was so disturbed about the comment that he quit working his cattle and prepared to ride to the Blassingames' cabin.[9]

Blassingame's statement became a controversial subject for newspapers and historians. Mary wrote in her May 8, 1855, letter that her husband had said that the Callahan Expedition was "more for plunder than anything else." Wesley Hughes Callahan testified at Mary's habeas corpus hearing on April 28 that his father accused Woodson "of speaking against his family." Many years later Catherine Callahan, who was present when Calvin Blassingame visited the Callahan house on April 8, agreed with her brother Wesley. Considering Callahan's chagrin at the outcome of his campaign, the rebuke from Pease, and the threat of federal indictment, he would have been in no mood to tolerate insults. Most contemporary Texas newspaper accounts did not mention the specifics of Blassingame's insult other than to say that the words reflected upon the character of Callahan, but there were exceptions. The *Huntsville Item* characterized the comments as "slanders." The *Neu Braunfelser Zeitung* oddly declared that "Blasingame . . . was confronted . . . for speaking with Mrs. Callahan in the night-time." George W. Kendall, neighbor and *New Orleans Picayune* correspondent, wrote that "Blessingate [*sic*] and his son had reported something against the character of Mrs. Callahan."[10]

This claim by Kendall that Sarah had been insulted was repeated by others and created a questionable foundation on which some commentators posed theories concerning the origins of the affair. Speer believed that the Blassingame slur was related to the Callahan Expedition, but he raised the possibility Woodson had made other offensive allegations about Callahan's family. Russell supported this possibility, and Morgan, writing in the *Frontier Times*, went so far as to claim that Woodson's remark concerned the Callahan women. Goar, a mere boy in 1855 whose father was a Callahan neighbor, wrote in 1929 that a Blassingame son had "started a slanderous report concerning some of Callahan's folks," claiming Watson as his source. Kemp identified Sarah as the target of the slander. Although none of these theories were supported by documents, their existence sensationalized the story, and Blassingame's attack on Callahan acquired a more salacious slant. As late as 1987, a spicy entry appeared in the *Blanco County News*: "On his return from an expedition in April, 1856, [Callahan] was informed that his neighbor, Woodson Blassingame, aged 60, had started a rumor concerning Mrs. Callahan." Taking it one step further, Don Watson, a descendant of John M. Watson, posited the theory that Sarah was having an affair with Calvin or Luther Blassingame. This is pure speculation and not supported by any evidence. Thus, evolving interpretations have obscured any understanding of what drove Callahan to visit the Blassingame cabin. However, a memoir by James W. Nichols perhaps provides a relevant perspective. Nichols recalled that "gossip had been running high for a few days," so Callahan decided to talk to the Blassingames to stop it. Nichols suggested that women's gossip having gotten out of hand is what caused the men to become involved. Except for his deposition, Hinds never commented on the event other than to say, "Rumors can kill."[11]

The previously accepted sequence of events leading up to the shooting is challenged by recently discovered records. A key point is the timing of Calvin's visit to the Callahan house on April 8: was it before Callahan had been told about Woodson's insult, or after? The Callahan and Blassingame families left divergent recollections as to the time of the visit and the nature of the conversation. According to the letters written by Calvin twenty-four hours after the killing and by Mary on May 8, Calvin visited the Callahans' home sometime between noon and 1 p.m. By this time, Callahan had returned home with his two sons after being told of Woodson's remarks. Calvin wrote that a shouting match ensued, with Callahan saying he would "have satisfaction or loose his [Callahan's] life." He claimed that Callahan expected Woodson to meet him halfway between their houses, and Calvin also believed that if Woodson did not, Callahan intended to attack him at his own house. Mary's narrative matched the substance of Calvin's letter but, writing weeks later and recalling what Calvin told her, she added to the story. She wrote that Callahan made it clear his dispute was with Woodson and not his sons, and he declared that the charges made by Woodson were so severe that he would rather die than live with them. Mary reiterated that Callahan claimed he could "whip a cavayard of them" and that he would "either kill, or be killed." In her habeas corpus hearing, she said a Callahan son corroborated what Calvin told her. She also said Callahan fired his six-shooter that day. As with much about this affair, Mary's version conflicts with others; but, with her son and husband dead, she certainly had an incentive to defend their memory.[12]

According to the Callahans, April 8 unfolded quite differently. Nine-year-old Catherine's account also placed Calvin at the Callahan home, but it was early in the day, before her father became aware of Woodson's remarks. She recalled that Calvin came to borrow Callahan's shotgun, which he willingly loaned. Calvin left with the weapon as Callahan and his sons went to hunt cows. She never said their conversation was angry. Twelve-year-old Wesley, who testified at Mary's habeas corpus hearing, said Calvin stopped at the Callahans' home on his way to the blacksmith shop with a plow. While Wesley corroborated some points Mary had written, he characterized the tone of the conversation as friendly, and he recalled no threats to harm the Blassingames. After Calvin left, Hinds and Johnson and his son Thomas arrived at the Callahan home, and Wesley admitted that his father fired his revolver before riding to the Blassingame cabin. According to Nichols, the four men—Callahan, Hinds, and the Johnsons—"set out on a cow hunt. It was necessary in those days to carry their arms with them on the account of Indians." Nichols justified the practice of test-firing weapons when traveling into areas known to be the targets of Indian raids. While Calvin Blassingame obviously visited the Callahans' cabin on April 8, the contradictory descriptions of what occurred can never be reconciled. It remains unknown whether Callahan knew about Woodson's inflammatory comment before the visit and in fact had the heated conversation Calvin described, or if he still knew nothing of the comment and had a pleasant conversation and loaned Calvin a gun. Mary of course was not there, so any description she gave of that event came from others. Regardless of the timing and facts of

Calvin's visit, other evidence indicates that Callahan was upset and ready to confront Woodson Blassingame.[13]

The other men rode with Callahan because he invited them to witness his conversation with Woodson, and he solicited their advice about the best way to settle the matter. Hinds in his deposition recalled that Johnson counseled Callahan "to be as mild as possible, not to get angry but to settle it as easy as possible." Hinds concurred and recalled that Callahan agreed. With this understanding, the men departed with a peaceful plan. By mid-afternoon, Callahan, Hinds, and the Johnsons were riding toward the Blassingame residence. According to Callahan and Hinds family lore, Wesley accompanied them. Thomas Johnson later swore that talking to Woodson was not their sole objective; they also drove a small herd of horses, intending to deliver them to the Reverend Samuel Johnson, who lived about a mile past the Blassingames. While they waited for Woodson at the halfway point, Callahan complained about feeling ill so Thomas Johnson offered to drive the horses and left the group. The three men and Wesley continued to wait, and Callahan and others may have test-fired their six-shooters. Deciding Woodson did not intend to appear, Callahan, Hinds, and the elder Johnson rode toward the Blassingames' cabin, but not until after Callahan instructed Wesley to return home. Reluctantly, Wesley turned for home but, unseen by the others, he hid in a motte of oak trees. He could not see the Blassingame cabin, but he could hear what took place.[14]

How exactly the event unfolded at the Blassingame cabin has been difficult to clarify. Callahan family lore and the recollections of locals, including neighbor George W. Kendall, placed the blame on Calvin and Woodson Blassingame. On this point, the Blassingame letters are vague. Mary never stated who fired the first shot, and Calvin claimed the firing "quickly commenced" and that shots were fired into the house. With the discovery of the depositions of Hinds, Watson, and Thomas Johnson, along with the *San Antonio Texan*'s account of the testimony at Mary's habeas corpus hearing, several contradictions can be resolved. In truth, Woodson and Calvin fired the first four shots, mortally wounding Callahan and Maulheel Johnson (figure 18.1).[15]

Mary recalled, "When I went to the door, Callahan asked me if my husband and Calvin were at home. I answered in the affirmative. About that time the firing commenced, and J. H. Callahan and Maulheel Johnson were killed, and Clem Hinds wounded." Various Texas papers published her words, which provides no indication of who shot first. Calvin was more

Fig. 18.1. Killing of Callahan and Johnson at the Blassingame cabin, April 8, 1856. Author's collection.

specific. He wrote that an argument erupted as soon as the three men rode up to the cabin and "fire after fire was heard. Blasingame was shot at several times; several balls were shot into the house." Calvin wrote that young children in the house were under fire, as was his mother. He wanted to blame the visitors for starting the fight, but the depositions of Thomas Johnson and Hinds made it clear who fired first. Johnson described what he saw from his position twenty-five yards from the cabin and to the left of his father, Hinds, and Callahan, when he arrived after delivering the horses (figure 18.1). As soon as Callahan asked to speak to Woodson, two guns were fired from the north room, killing Callahan, mortally wounding the elder Johnson, and badly wounding Hinds. Thomas stated that Callahan and his father never fired. Hinds agreed with this, recalling that the shots from the north room began as soon as Callahan asked "in a mild tone if Mr. Blassingame was at home." Hinds added that they were "in quick succession as fast as one, two, three" and "altogether unexpected." The first hit Callahan, the second hit Maulheel Johnson, and the "third shot struck me," Hinds swore. With the first blast, Hinds' horse reared and turned slightly so that the third load of buckshot only broke Hinds's right arm and wounded him in the neck. The horse then ran toward Callahan's house, taking Hinds out of harm's way.[16]

Wesley Callahan, the only other person close by, heard the attack from his position east of the cabin. He recalled that as soon as the three men reached the Blassingames' house, shots exploded. He watched as Hinds's horse, rearing and pitching, carried the wounded man toward the Callahan home. Interestingly, at Mary's habeas corpus hearing, attorneys never interviewed Wesley. This raises questions about the district court officials, who seemed more interested in who killed the Blassingames. Also, at Mary's hearing her son-in-law William Holmes supported Calvin's account as given in his April 8 letter, though Holmes did not witness the episode. Too, Holmes testified that he saw "ball holes in the house." He appears to have based his testimony on Calvin's letter and discussions among the Blassingame and Holmes families. Fifteen-year-old William Blassingame's testimony at the hearing raised new points. He claimed that he and the other two Blassingame wards were present in the south room of the dogtrot log cabin, and from its doorway Mary spoke to Callahan (figure 18.2). William stated, "We had but two double barrel shot guns on the place." According to Catherine Callahan's account of Calvin's April 8 visit, one of those weapons had been borrowed that morning from her father. Concurring with all accounts, William recounted that firing began as soon as Mary spoke. He said that "firing was all around," but claimed that he did not see anyone inside shoot a weapon, although he admitted that Calvin had a "shotgun, powder bag, and shot." He added, "Mother did not fire any gun, nor did she have anything to shoot with, neither powder or shot." His testimony bears remarkable

Fig. 18.2. South room of the reconstructed Blassingame cabin, 2010. Author's collection.

similarity to Calvin's statement penned three weeks earlier, suggesting he was familiar with Calvin's letter.[17]

The two Blassingames with shotguns did not waste their loads. The first blast pelted Callahan's chest, and a solitary pellet lodged in his neck. As blood soaked his shirt, Callahan looked toward Hinds and cried out, "I am mortally wounded!" He fell to the ground and quickly bled to death as his riderless mount galloped in the direction of home. "The second shot struck Wm. S. Johnson, who exclaimed, 'O Lord,'" Hinds swore in his affidavit. Thomas Johnson, who rode up seconds later, rushed to his father, lowered the wounded man to the ground, and dragged him to safety some distance from the cabin. He was "shot all to pieces," Thomas remembered, and "coughed two gasps and expired." Thomas caressed his father's head before exploding with rage. In the creek below the house, he found his horse and rifle and climbed the bank only to see Calvin running through the house with a shotgun and ammunition. He said that he fired the rifle once and emptied his six-shooter toward the cabin. Because he was 200 yards southeast of the structure, the bullets hit no one, but they may have made the holes that Holmes said he later saw.[18]

Kendall in the *Picayune* summarized what Callahan's neighbors understood had happened: "As they rode up to the house they saw Mrs. B., when Capt. Callahan asked her if her husband was home. She replied he was not, and as they turned their horses to ride away they were fired upon by unseen persons in the house, who fired through the cracks between the logs." While Kendall's comment was not totally supported by depositions, to Texans, firing on three men as they turned to leave was cowardly and nothing less than murder, which was also the conclusion of an inquest's jury. Furthermore, the locals believed, as Speer later wrote, "In the death of Callahan the country lost one of its most watchful and fearless defenders."[19]

Watson saw the wounded Hinds on his runaway mount and followed him to the Callahan home, where he and Sarah Medissa dressed Hinds' wounds and heard the first report of the tragic episode. Later, Watson and Hugh McLaurin, another Callahan neighbor, returned to the shooting site in a wagon to collect the two dead men. A "Mr. Bassham," probably Philip Basson, assisted with this somber task. Watson subsequently swore Callahan had eight chest wounds on his right side and had "bled very freely." He also testified Johnson appeared to have seven fatal buckshot wounds to his neck and chest. Thus, Watson's deposition documented the cause of both deaths as shotgun blasts at close range. At the Callahan residence, the bodies of

Callahan and Johnson were undressed, washed, and examined. Meanwhile, a shocked Sarah and her children wept at the sudden loss of their husband and father. They soon thereafter buried him in an unmarked grave beside his deceased son in the Blanco Cemetery in the nascent village of Pittsburg.[20]

Callahan's violent demise was reported in local and national newspapers. "We have heard of a most painful tragedy at Pittsburg, on . . . the Blanco," stated the *Texas State Gazette.* The *Texas State Times* lamented, "Our whole community is shrouded in the deepest gloom, and unfeigned sorrow is expressed by all save those who perpetrated the cold-blooded and cowardly deed." The *San Antonio Herald* noted Callahan's death was "deeply regretted by his neighbors and friends and a large circle of acquaintances." *El Bejareño* agreed that Callahan was "*bien conocido como uno de los Tejanos mas antiguos y valientes.*" German-speaking residents read the news in the *Neu Braunfelser Zeitung.* Further afield, details of Callahan's murder appeared in the *Picayune, New York Times, Baltimore Sun*, and *National Intelligencer.* Thus, citizens far and wide read about the death of the legendary Texan. Writing to the *Picayune* on April 12, Kendall captured the sentiments of Callahan's family, neighbors, and fellow Texas Rangers: "Capt. Callahan, the gallant ranger, quiet and fearless gentleman, has been dastardly murdered. . . . We lost one of our most efficient citizens, a wife her husband and protector, a number of little children their father and support. . . . Had he served his country less faithfully, he might have left his family less dependent."[21]

Callahan had been killed by a neighbor on land he had sold to him. The irony percolated along the Texas frontier from family to acquaintances and finally to people who had merely read his name in newspapers. Callahan had avoided the Goliad massacre by the munificence of a Mexican colonel. As a Republic of Texas Ranger, he survived Mexican invasions and Indian clashes. In fighting with horse thieves and other outlaws, he never suffered a wound. During Michael Erskine's long cattle drive, he emerged unscathed from hand-to-hand combat with raiding Indians. At the Rio Escondido and in Piedras Negras, he rode away unharmed, having lost only his hat and a six-shooter. But after being admonished by friends to remain peaceful, Callahan was murdered by a concealed, frightened farmer armed with a shotgun that perhaps had been borrowed earlier that same day from Callahan.

New records do help with one simple but important fact about Callahan's death: the date. Some have recorded the date as April 7, as stated by Calvin Blassingame, and not April 8, as declared by Mary Blassingame. However, the depositions of Watson, Hinds, and Thomas Johnson, given one week after the occasion, support Mary—Callahan died on April 8, 1856. Callahan's mother-in-law, Sarah Hembree Day, also recorded this date in her prayer journal. Paradoxically, news articles published in April and May 1856 did not report a date for Callahan's death, with one exception—the April 16 *Neu Braunfelser Zeitung* correctly stated the day of his murder: "On Tuesday last week," or April 8. Even in 1934, when Callahan was reinterred in the Texas State Cemetery at Austin, his date of death was incorrectly inscribed on the tombstone as April 7, 1857. To correct the historical record, James Hughes Callahan died on April 8, 1856.[22]

There is no doubt as to the whereabouts of Thomas Johnson when the shooting began: near the fence in front of the Blassingame cabin (figure 18.1). New records establish that the time of his arrival at that spot should be revised. Mary and Calvin's letters both noted that he "rode up to the fence," and historians interpreted this to mean that he arrived with his father, Callahan, and Hinds. However, Hinds swore the younger Johnson arrived after the Blassingames had mortally wounded the elder Johnson. In Thomas's deposition, he clarified the events: "I did not go all the way from Callahan's to the house of the Blassingames." He instead drove horses to the Reverend Johnson's farm one mile west of the Blassingame cabin, then, returning east, "crossed the stream and went to Mr. Blassingames. I was some twenty-five yards from the house when Callahan, Johnson and Hinds were shot." Not being with the trio of older men may have saved his life. His location south of the cabin obscured him from the shooters until he rushed forward to retrieve his dying father, then emptied his rifle and revolver in a futile expression of anger and grief.[23]

Another dispute has been about who fired first. Both Mary and Calvin described the gunfire, but neither identified a shooter. Hinds and the younger Johnson in their depositions provide clear recollections of shots coming from the Blassingame cabin, with Hinds specifically saying they came from the north room (figure 18.1). Furthermore, Hinds emphasized that neither he, nor Callahan, nor Maulheel Johnson ever drew their six-shooters. Thomas did not deny firing at the Blassingame cabin, but he did so only after the initial volley killed his father and Callahan. According to his deposition, while he was emptying his rifle and pistol, Mary emerged "clapping her hands as if rejoicing." Again, this may be the source of the bullet holes that Holmes claimed to have counted, and no other physical evidence of Callahan, Hinds, and Maulheel Johnson firing at the Blassingame cabin was ever discussed. Based on all written accounts by the survivors and Watson, and the Callahan family, it is certain that Callahan, Maulheel Johnson, and Hinds never fired any shots at the Blassingames.[24]

In the first decade of the twentieth century, Catherine Callahan wrote her recollection of the day her father died. Considering the location of her brother Wesley during the shooting, her recall must have been shaped by his experience as well as what Hinds and the younger Johnson later told her family. Family lore passed down from son James Sanford Callahan closely matched what Catherine recalled. Both corroborate that Callahan, Hinds, and Maulheel Johnson never fired their guns. However, Catherine attributed a startling action to Mary when she told *Hunter's Magazine* writer W. R. Russell that "Capt. Callahan crawled off about 40 yards, when the old lady (if she was ever a lady) took a shotgun, walked up to him and shot him twice, killing him instantly." This is easily refuted. Although Watson and Thomas Johnson reported that Mary's demeanor at the sight of the dead men was one of satisfaction, and Watson even noted that she remarked how she wished she "had shot them" days earlier, she was never seen armed. Watson's examination of Callahan's wounds also did not reveal anything other than the result of a single shotgun blast. It would be sadly ironic if Callahan was shot with his own gun. If that is what happened, then Calvin fired the fatal shot, having borrowed it that morning. Interestingly, both of the shotguns used to kill Callahan and Johnson disappeared. Callahan and Woodson Blassingame owned shotguns, but none appear in either man's probate inventory. It is believable that Luther and Thomas, Calvin's brothers, took them.[25]

Newly discovered records bring clarity to the murders of Callahan and Johnson, but they also raise questions. Because he was on the scene soon after the shooting and the first person to examine the bodies, Watson was considered a primary witness, and subsequent chroniclers of the event, especially Speer and Goar, based their accounts on his version. His influence can even be seen in recent online accounts written by a descendant. Watson's recently recovered deposition substantively contributes to new perspectives presented in this study. Yet, his inaction may have contributed to the deaths of the Blassingames. As a young schoolteacher, Watson certainly did not anticipate becoming a central figure in a grim tragedy. Born on December 29, 1829, he was living in Dyer County, Tennessee, in 1850 when his mother died, and when his father remarried, they all moved to Caldwell County, Texas. John came to the Blanco River valley in late 1853, and in 1854 he taught at the first school in the area. Living near the Callahans and

Blassingames, he was drawn into the affair when he spotted the wounded Hinds on his fleeing horse. Decades later, Speer claimed that Robert L. Page, a veteran of the Callahan Expedition, accompanied him to retrieve the bodies of Callahan and Johnson. However, according to Watson's deposition, it was Hugh McLaurin, not Page, who accompanied him. Establishing McLaurin's presence with Watson is significant for addressing lingering questions.[26]

On April 9, 1856, authorities arrested Woodson, Calvin, and Mary Blassingame for the murder of Callahan and Johnson and the attempted murder of Hinds. The details of the arrest and the tumultuous days that followed are obscured by a variety of unsubstantiated reports published at the time, and others written since. Watson testified that he visited the Blassingame cabin late on April 8 with McLaurin and "Mr. Bassham" to collect the bodies. Subsequently, he admitted that while there he advised the Blassingames to flee to Mexico as he was doubtful of their safety. The trio refused, believing they would have a fair trial with an impartial jury. As a result, they spent the night of April 8 in their cabin. Mary merely noted the family "remained at home until the next day, when they, together with myself were arrested." The *San Antonio Herald* claimed local citizens arrested the Blassingames, but the *Neu Braunfelser Zeitung* reported they were taken into custody by justice of the peace George Lang. Later the *Zeitung* alleged that Deputy Sheriff Richard M. Hokit arrested the Blassingames, guarded them in their home overnight, and then moved them to Lang's house. Years later, Speer wrote that Watson made the arrest. About the same time, James W. Nichols recalled in his memoirs that the local community congregated to arrest the family. Catherine Callahan declared, "John M. Watson arrested the Blassengames alone." The facts are further muddied by a *Frontier Times* article in which Goar stated that Hokit and a group of local men were responsible. Thus, details of the arrest remain a mystery.[27]

According to Mary's May 8 letter, the Blassingames were confined at Lang's home in Middletown (see map 9.2) because the nearest jail was thirty miles away at New Braunfels. But the decision to hold them there was questioned from the outset. The *Neu Braunfelser Zeitung* was critical of Lang because he held the prisoners in an unsecured building rather than transporting them to the county jail, regardless of the distance. Further criticism came much later from Goar: "There was no jail, so the prisoners were placed in a cow lot." Clearly, the facility housing the Blassingames provided no safeguards for the prisoners, or even barriers preventing their escape. Several twentieth-century accounts have stated the Blassingames were held at Twin

Sisters, a village on the Little Blanco River about six miles south of the Callahan cabin. However, Lang's home was on the south bank of the Little Blanco River, three miles upstream at the new hamlet of Middletown. Both Twin Sisters and Middletown were in Twin Sisters precinct, so chroniclers confused the fact that Lang was the justice for Twin Sisters precinct but lived in Middletown.[28]

The Blassingames made no attempt to escape, but Calvin's letter, actually written the day of their incarceration, reflected their panic. Four days later, civil authorities were also concerned. Lang and Hokit posted a guard of twenty-six men around the temporary jail after purportedly being warned by Watson that Callahan's local veneration might lead to retaliation. Mary also confirmed the guard's presence. Writing to "Friends and Fellow Citizens of San Marcos and String Town," Calvin appealed for help and admitted his fear that they would be murdered in revenge. He sent his letter to a peculiar assortment of men whose identities can be established. All but one lived in Hays County, which was not unexpected since several Blassingame family members, including Calvin, had resided there. The men included W. T. Claunch, John D. Pitts, Joseph Bird, J. S. Owens, A. R. Scallons, James L. Malone, G. H. Swisher, Philip F. Prator, S. R. McKie, Thomas G. (Cicero) McGehee, H. W. Davis, J. W. Hill, Clement R. Johns, J. L. Driskill, George C. Prator, and Samuel R. Kone. A "Mr. Cox," might have been the Reverend Josiah Cox who lived on the Rio Blanco, but a "Mr. Mathis" could not be identified. Calvin may have been unaware that many of the recipients of his letter were Callahan associates. Pitts was his partner in the Pittsburg Land Company. Claunch, Owens, Driskill, and the Prators were neighbors of Andrew M. Lindsey, another associate in the Pittsburg Land Company. Ed Burleson Jr. enrolled Charles McGehee, Thomas McGehee's brother, into the Callahan Expedition. His neighbors included Kone, Swisher, and McKie. Kone had wed Pitts's daughter, Rebecca, while Malone had married another Pitts girl, Eliza. Former Republic of Texas congressman Johns lived near Pitts and had married the sister of Thomas Durham, Callahan's friend. Lastly, Davis and Pitts had a long-term friendship. Calvin thus appealed to men whose relationships with Callahan would have trumped any claim he could make, and no help came.[29]

As word of Callahan's murder spread, hostility toward the Blassingames intensified. It reached a peak about midnight on April 13, 1856, when, according to the *San Antonio Herald*, "a hundred or more citizens took the prisoners from custody of the guards." Minutes later, Woodson was shot and

Calvin was killed attempting to escape. According to the paper, Mary was unhurt but witnessed the lynching. The killing of the Blassingame men may not have come as a surprise to people living in the Guadalupe River Basin. The *Picayune* published a letter by Kendall, who had predicted the day before that "[Callahan's] host of warm personal friends will be apt to take vengeance into their own hands, and for once I can't say I should be sorry to see it done." The account published in the April 19 *Texas State Gazette* set the tone for articles that followed. It claimed that 50 to 100 men dispersed all the guards but two and forced themselves into Lang's house. They dragged out Woodson and Calvin "by their heels" and shot them, forty to fifty times according to some reports. A distressed Mary watched and later asserted that the killers choked her and said that "her life depended on her silence." Accounts of the event written much later were usually consistent with the newspaper reports. However, a discrepancy arises in how the Blassingames were shot. Speer, Catherine Callahan, and a Watson descendant reported that the prisoners were shot as soon as the mob overpowered the guards. Goar claimed Woodson and Calvin were ordered to run and shot as they attempted to flee. Father and son were buried near their home in what today is the Sauer Cemetery.[30]

Many accounts of what transpired late in the evening of April 13 contain inaccuracies. Only three facts remain consistent throughout—assailants killed Woodson and Calvin, they were slain just before midnight, and Mary survived. Her letter reported what occurred inside Lang's house, but she did not describe the fracas outside. Nor did she identify the vigilantes. Sometime after nightfall, "everything defensive was taken out by one of the guards," Mary wrote. That included knives, chains, stools, and fireplace pokers. Woodson pled fruitlessly with a guard to leave a few items that could be used for self-defense. Soon the only sentry inside the house left in response to a call from outside. Mary described what happened next: "After a few minutes of whispering near the door, the door was again opened and three men made their appearance; two remained just outside the door and one came in and went to the fire." Grabbing a burning log, the man circled the Blassingames' bed, ordering the trio to leave the house. Mary began screaming, begging him to spare their lives and calling to Lang for help. Because she clung to her husband, the intruder failed to haul Woodson away by grabbing his feet. Giving up, he returned to the door and, Mary recalled, "asked the other two men why they did not come in as they had promised." All three then entered the house. They struggled with Woodson and Mary, ultimately dragging him outside and returning for Calvin. "My husband never spoke, but my son called on them not to murder him," Mary wrote. Although she does not describe how, Mary escaped, crossed the nearby Little Blanco River, and hid in a thicket. "I had got a short distance from the house, when I heard six or eight guns fire," she recounted. The next morning, Ed Burleson Jr. found Mary and took her back to Lang's house.[31]

Three men and six or eight shots were the two key points in Mary's version. Over the years, writers have ignored both. Kendall wrote on April 23 from his ranch near Middletown: "As I predicted in my last [letter], the numerous friends of the murdered men took the law into their own hands, and shot the murderers without giving them the benefit of a judge or jury." In subsequent reports the number of assailants grew, reaching 50 and then 100. These numbers appeared in the *San Antonio Herald* and the *Neu Braunfelser Zeitung*, while the *Texas State Gazette* merely declared that a number of citizens participated. By early May 1856, the reports had been embellished further. Texans read in the *Standard* that a mob rushed into the house and fired forty to fifty shots at Woodson and Calvin, whose bodies thus had numerous wounds. None of the early accounts resembled Mary's description of the attack. This was not surprising since her letter was published after the initial reports were printed, but later publications also claimed that a mob of fifty to one hundred shot the Blassingames, inflicting many wounds. Inexplicably, historians ignored both Mary's version and the minutes of the coroner's inquest, which recorded that "one ball" killed Woodson while Calvin suffered five bullet wounds. Clearly, only a small number of men fired a few shots during the lynching.[32]

How did the tale of a large mob originate? Deputy Sheriff Hokit's detailed report to the Comal County judge declares that one hundred men were reported in the vicinity. The April 25 and May 9 *Neu Braunfelser Zeitung* summarized Hokit's report, and it became the accepted source for the number of assailants. Responsibility for the Blassingames' safety resided with Hokit and Lang. With Woodson, Calvin, and Mary at his home, Lang scheduled a hearing for Monday morning, April 14, to provide time for the Blassingames to retain a lawyer. After daybreak on April 13, Hokit heard that vigilantes intended to seize the prisoners, so he solicited help in the area and posted the round-the-clock guard of twenty-six men. Late in the evening, according to him, the lookouts claimed one hundred men had gathered who, the guards believed, intended to kill the prisoners. Hokit saddled his horse and left, declaring he needed to find reinforcements. Reconsidering his plan, he tried to return to Lang's house but found fifty to one hundred armed strangers in his way. He and a watchman then withdrew, believing the prisoners' safety was impossible to maintain. Hearing of the mob, Lang convinced Hokit to go with him to save the prisoners. As they approached the house with a small group of guards, screams and a door crashing pierced the silence, followed by guns firing. Hokit and Lang found Woodson's body ten yards from the door and Calvin's sixty yards beyond. Hokit's description became the primary source for the story of a large mob firing numerous shots and killing the Blassingames. Following the lead of the *Neu Braunfelser Zeitung*, Texas newsmen cobbled together stories perpetuating Hokit's version, a self-serving, fallacious account that has colored historical viewpoints ever since.[33]

At a coroner's inquest on April 14, 1856, local authorities concluded the Blassingames died after unknown men had taken them from their guards' custody and shot them. As justice of the peace, Lang presided over the inquiry and wrote that the Blassingames "came to their deaths by being shot—with a gun or pistol . . . by a party of white men unknown to the jury." The jury consisted of W. G. Sansom, J. C. Martin, F. W. Martin, Joel Cherry, W. C. McKinney, and foreman R. B. Goar. John W. Harmon, another justice of the peace, also signed the decree. All lived within a few miles of Middletown or Twin Sisters, and some would find themselves further tangled in the Blassingame–Callahan affair. The murders of Callahan and Johnson and lynching of the Blassingames cast a pall upon the vicinity, caused reputations to suffer, and left a palpable tension between the Anglo and German communities. The first clash would soon erupt.[34]

At dawn on April 14, 1856, Burleson, one of several men searching for Mary, found her hiding in a thicket near Lang's house. Why he was present is uncertain. Two of his brothers-in-law, Felix Kyle and J. C. Stevenson, lived nearby on the Rio Blanco, five miles east of the Callahan home. Strangely enough, William O. Kyle, Felix's brother, was also at Lang's house. He and Burleson lived in Hays County and had served together as officers in the Callahan Expedition. Burleson and Kyle might have been in the area visiting family, or they had attended Callahan's funeral and decided to stay a few days. Intriguingly, they could have been among the guards posted for the Blassingames who initially refused to be intimidated by the assailants. Their participation as prosecution witnesses in later proceedings lends credence to this hypothesis.[35]

Nevertheless, with Mary reincarcerated, another remarkable judicial hearing ensued. Hours after being found, she was brought before Harmon and Lang and charged with being an accessory in the murders of Callahan and Johnson. After the coroner's inquest on the death of the Blassingame men, she demanded a jury hearing for the charges brought against her. Not having fired a gun, she believed that she was innocent and probably thought the jurors would agree. For whatever reason, she did not understand where the jurors' sympathy lay and how precarious her situation was. The justices of the peace called Watson as the first witness. After the arrest of the Blassingames, Watson had ridden to Caldwell County and returned several hours before their deaths, bringing a warning that Callahan's acquaintances might try to harm them. His testimony focused upon the Callahan and Johnson death scene. Lethal wounds, the bodies' positions and condition, and Mary's behavior comprised the substance of his statement. The most damning incrimination of her was his recollection of her saying, "I ought to have shot them." Watson also described Mary as agitated, and his testimony did not support her defense. Thomas Johnson's testimony also focused on her demeanor. He could see her in the south doorway when Callahan and Johnson were killed (figure 18.1). Damningly, he said, "I saw one female whom I took to be Mrs. Blassingame the defendant clapping her hands as if rejoicing." However, he admitted, "I saw no weapon in Mrs. Blassingame's hands." Unable to attend due to his injuries, Hinds sent a written statement certified by James M. Pruitt, another Comal County justice of the peace. He also described the shooting scene, confirming that Mary stood in the south doorway during the confrontation.[36]

Jury foreman McKinney read the verdict aloud: "We the jury find the defendant Mary Blassingame guilty of the charge of being accessory to the murder of James H. Callahan and W. S. Johnson." Other jurors included Jack and James Cherry, John W. Sansom, J. B. Green, and J. C. Martin. These men also lived near Middletown or Curry's Creek and interestingly had four relatives who had served on the coroner's jury that morning. Moreover, foreman McKinney and juror Martin had actually been on the coroner's jury. Harmon and Lang agreed with the verdict. Several people posted bonds of $100 each, promising to attend the Comal County district court term and provide evidence "on behalf of the State in the case of the *State v. Mary Blassingame*." Prominent among them were Watson, Thomas Johnson, and Wesley Callahan. John W. Nichols, Augustus Pharr, and Eli S. Hankins,

Callahan's brothers-in-law, could testify about his character, as could William J. Trainer. Robert L. Page, the younger brother of Watson's stepmother, had served as a private in the Callahan Expedition, but how he might contribute is unknown. How local residents Elizabeth McCoy and J. B. Green fitted into roles as witnesses is also a mystery. Most likely McCoy's testimony related to Hinds, her son-in-law. In sum, Callahan associates were eager to testify against Mary in the district court.[37]

By noon of April 14, Lang and Harmon ordered the defendant transferred to the Comal County jail to await the next grand jury, which everyone seemed confident would indict her. Hokit escorted Mary to New Braunfels, where Sheriff George Ullrich took her into custody on April 16. The first hint that matters were shifting in her favor came within a few weeks. The editor of the *Neu Braunfelser Zeitung* on May 9 criticized the absence of adequate counsel for Mary at the inquest conducted by Harmon and Lang. The German-language paper added that Lang had no expertise to record an inquest report. At her district court appearance, Mary was accompanied by M. A. Dooley, an experienced lawyer hired by prominent Germans in New Braunfels as her defense counsel. Mary's destiny now resided in the hands of the longtime legal advocate for the German community. Dooley had battled fearlessly for their land rights, served as Comal County's first chief justice in 1846, and in 1853 became the state representative for Comal and Gillespie Counties. Mary had a good lawyer to defend her, while there were serious questions about the competency of the prosecutor. Frank Egan had secured his license in 1851 and won the office of district attorney over his law partner in an acrimonious race in which he carried Comal County by a large margin. Rancor percolated in Bexar County in 1855, with the *San Antonio Herald*, in an editorial entitled "The Little Persecuting Attorney," criticizing Egan for being vain and incompetent.[38]

On the bench for Mary's trial, Thomas Jefferson Devine embodied the very best of the Texas judicial system. The Nova Scotia-born son of an exiled Irish rebel, Devine graduated from Transylvania University in Kentucky. He set up a legal practice in San Antonio and within a few months became the city attorney and later the district attorney. In 1851 he was elected as judge of the Fourth Judicial District. The *San Antonio Ledger* observed, "Judge Devine's presiding upon the bench is characterized with dignity and firmness mingled with gentlemanly courtesy that is calculated to command the respect of the bar and of the people." He demanded strict adherence to decorum and was known to fine those who deviated from his standards. Devine gaveled the Fourth District Court into session on Monday, April 28, 1856.[39]

After a swift and uneventful buggy ride, Sheriff Ullrich ushered Mary into Devine's courtroom in the Bexar County courthouse—known as the "Bat Cave." The minutes for her hearing are brief, and a *San Antonio Texan* summary provides the sole insight into the testimony. Although it is not certain, the newspaper accounts suggest an intriguing situation: the prosecutor and defense attorney colluded before the hearing. Egan summoned three witnesses—Watson, Wesley Callahan, and William J. Trainer. Egan presented the testimony taken at Lang's inquest, and then the court reporter read the depositions of Thomas Johnson and Eli Hinds. Inexplicably, neither of them was asked to attend. The *San Antonio Texan* noted that Watson was questioned only about the placement and condition of the two bodies. In contrast, Dooley subpoenaed new witnesses and effectively cross-examined Wesley, whose testimony favored Mary. He recalled Calvin's April 8 visit, describing the conversation as "at first friendly, but afterwards excited." Furthermore, Wesley said his father accused Calvin and Woodson of slandering the Callahans and pledged to settle the matter that evening or the next day by visiting the Blassingames' cabin. Calvin denied Callahan's charges and refused his demands. When Callahan told Calvin to have his father meet him halfway, Calvin replied that he could not since he was plowing. After Calvin left, Hinds and the Johnsons arrived "all armed with six shooters, and Tom Johnson with a rifle also." Wesley admitted that his father "fired off his six shooter and reloaded it" at the midpoint. Dooley's cross-examination insinuated that Callahan, Hinds, and Maulheel Johnson intended to harm the Blassingames, and yet Egan did not have Hinds or Thomas Johnson offer a rebuttal.[40]

Dooley's defense witnesses provided some interesting information. Some implied that the Blassingame cabin was shot at, and Mary's son-in-law William Holmes described the damage to the structure, although William Blassingame, her ward, could not identify a specific shooter. Both William and Holmes swore the Blassingames had just two double-barreled shotguns to defend themselves, so Mary never held a weapon. An astonishing new detail came from Holmes, who said "that there was a previous misunderstanding between the Johnsons and Blassingames." Trainer and Jesse Greene likewise testified that they knew antagonism existed between Maulheel Johnson and Woodson Blassingame. None of these three witnesses explained the disagreement, but their testimony suggests ill feelings toward Blassingame were widespread. These new facts raised the possibility that Maulheel Johnson had used Callahan to seek revenge on Blassingame. As a new settler, Blassingame did not seem to appreciate the possible repercussions of his frank opinions and other harmful comments. James W. Nichols suggested in his memoirs written four decades later that he paid the ultimate price for spreading gossip. After hearing the witnesses, Devine dismissed the charges against Mary. The *San Antonio Texan* merely noted, "There being no evidence adduced, implicating the defendant, Mrs. Mary Blasingame, she was acquitted and discharged." Mary's reaction was more expressive: "I was liberated by his honor Judge Devine, there being no ground for my detention." Exhausted, she left the courthouse a free woman.[41]

In reporting the Blassingame–Callahan affair, two San Antonio newspapers published opposing opinions reflecting how differently the Anglo and German communities reacted to the tragedy. The *San Antonio Texan* editor wrote, "In regard to the affair by which [Callahan] and Johnson lost their lives we have not a word of comment; but we consider the murder of the old man Blassingame and son as a bloody stain on the escutcheon of Western Texas." On the other hand, the editor of the *San Antonio Herald* wrote: "Where peaceful and quiet citizens meet and hear the facts in a case, they are a competent tribunal to pass sentence, as though they had been legally empanelled as a jury. . . . We are no advocate of mob law, but we do contend that the peace and safety of community, aye justice, often demands a resort to it." The first writer expressed well the German-Texan notions of righteousness, while many Anglo-Texans agreed with the second opinion. District Attorney Egan owed his victory in a close race to the strong support of German voters in Comal County, and leaders in the German community wanted to bring the Blassingame killers to justice. In 1856 Egan was reelected for a second term, again with a large majority in Comal County.[42]

While judicial officials prepared for the next round of legal battles, the Blassingame and Holmes families left the Rio Blanco and Little Blanco valleys. Mary and her children went to Union Parish, Louisiana, settling near her daughter, Mary Crout, who lived in Union County, Arkansas. They remained there for months before relocating to Leon County, Texas. By moving away, Mary's daughter and son-in-law, Frances and William Holmes, lost their exemption grant for their property on the Little Blanco. The Holmes family also moved to Leon County and by 1860 lived next to the surviving Blassingames. Mary's legacy in this affair is her May 8, 1856, letter to the *Texas State Gazette*. In view of the press attention given to her family and the rumors that were circulating, it is reasonable she would want to justify the actions taken by her husband and son. While self-serving, the language and style of the letter suggests it was written with legal guidance. It read in part, "To lay all the facts before an enlightened community . . . You will therefore, confer a great favor upon a distressed widow." Then the captivating word *cavayard* appears. *Cavayard*, a Texan corruption of the Spanish word *cavallado*, meaning a herd of horses, was not commonly used except by early Texas settlers, and it is doubtful Mary had ever heard it. But Dooley would have, so he must have contributed to her letter, and possibly wrote the missive based upon Mary's oral testimony and recollections. Nevertheless, Mary signed the letter, and it became her legacy to Texas history.[43]

The Blassingames did not have a clear title to their Rio Blanco property, so Callahan's probate judge ordered its transfer after Augustus Pharr and Luther Blassingame swore Callahan had received the last payment on January 21, 1856. Callahan's executor, E. C. Pettus, provided the title's release and the Comal County clerk filed it on September 30, 1856. On the same day, Luther, Thomas, and George W. Blassingame signed the same deed over to brothers Charles and Henry Mayrhofen, who three weeks earlier had paid Mary $1,000. Thus, she earned a profit of $680 on the land. When probate proceedings for Woodson Blassingame's estate commenced on June 29, 1856, the judge appointed Thomas as administrator and ordered an inventory by Josiah Cox, John Lindemann, and R. B. Goar, who had served as jury foreman for the coroner's inquest in Woodson's death. Blassingame's estate was appraised at $1,650, but the evaluators later added $140 when the corn crop matured. Besides the land, he owned kitchen furniture valued at $200; "implements of husband," $50; five milk cows, $100; a pair of oxen and a horse, $60; and twenty hogs, $2 each. In August 1857, the court finalized his probate. After settling claims and costs, it was worth $1,228.30. Mary received half and the children, including the wards, the remainder, or $55.83 each. Blassingame's estate was typical for a yeoman farmer on the Texas frontier.[44]

Beyond the outrage of the murders of Callahan and Johnson, and the lynching of Calvin and Woodson Blassingame, the Blassingame–Callahan affair exposed deep cultural fissures in the upper Guadalupe River Basin. The Rio Blanco area lost its appeal as word of the violence deterred new settlers, ironically undermining the development efforts of the surviving partners in the Pittsburg Land Company. Further afield, it added to the tensions between Anglo and German communities as both sought to establish themselves. Reflecting on the tension engendered by the affair, Speer remarked, "The year 1856 closed darkly on the settlers of Blanco. The murder of Callahan and Johnson . . . put the whole country in a high state of excitement and the population was on the eve of dividing into desperate contending parties or factions. . . ." Sadly, much of this was because Callahan had established such a high reputation among neighbors and associates. In the meantime, as District Attorney Egan knew, there was still justice left undone.[45]

CHAPTER 19

Blassingame–Callahan Affair Repercussions, 1856–1860

"Made an assault with a six-shooter"

On the second Monday in March 1859, Comal County District Clerk Gustav Dreiss prepared the documents for the next term. Sheriff George Ullrich had asked him to send a warrant to Hardy F. Stockman, sheriff of adjacent Blanco County, asking him to apprehend an indicted fugitive in the case of the *State of Texas v. George Lang et al.* James Waddel, one of thirteen guards implicated in the murders of Woodson and Calvin Blassingame, remained at large and was proving difficult to find. Blanco County District Clerk J. B. Tennison forwarded the writ to Stockman, but he was reluctant to act. Blanco County residents had tired of the continued persecution of the men who had guarded the Blassingames. Deputy Benjamin F. Patton wrote "Came to hand May 3 1859 not executed for want of time" on the summons and returned it to Comal County. Ironically, while James Hughes Callahan's failed expedition into Mexico caused little disturbance within Central Texas, his murder and the violence that accompanied it created conflict for years afterward.[1]

Central Texas became the backdrop for a long-running legal drama because the Anglo- and German-Texan communities had differing concepts of justice. The arrests and trials of men accused of killing the Blassingames provide insight into how county judicial systems reflected the diversity of the Guadalupe River Basin in antebellum Texas. Beginning in 1845, German emigrants arrived, becoming a majority in Comal County and a third of the population in Guadalupe County. For many, legal injustice in Germany had been an incentive to leave, and in Texas they wanted to ensure the judicial system was trustworthy. Meanwhile, Anglos, who outnumbered foreign settlers in Guadalupe, Caldwell, and Blanco Counties, also preferred an efficient judicial system, but their experience on the frontier taught them to be occasionally tolerant of extralegal solutions. The events that followed the murder of the Blassingames exposed these differing views. Established a mere two decades earlier and incorporating elements from its Spanish predecessor, the Texas legal system was open to change. Most criminal proceedings followed English common law; but after annexation by the United States, federal law prevailed over state law, prompting the legislature to rewrite many civil and criminal statutes. The latter remained the jurisdiction of district courts, but while each judge served several counties, each county directed its own sessions. While in theory this promoted uniformity, in practice the application of laws in antebellum Texas took place unevenly within a populace dominated by Anglos imbued with a tendency toward Jacksonian independence.[2]

Conditions in Texas worked against rather than for judicial uniformity and efficiency. During the ten years as a republic, many counties deferred construction of courthouses and jails. Furthermore, individualistic Texians often had little reverence for authority. In 1837, at the first district court session in Shelby County, Judge Robert "Three-Legged Willie" Williamson drew a pistol to cow a defendant who threatened him with a Bowie knife. According to historian Wayne Gard, vigilantism flourished. In 1841 when Neches River settler Thomas Yocum defied an order to leave the county, vigilantes fatally shot him. The Regulator–Moderator War engendered the most notorious vigilante activity during the Republic, when many East Texians lost their lives fighting over fraudulent land titles. Vigilantism continued after annexation and South-Central Texas was not immune. Judge Thomas J. Devine rescued his brother, the mayor of San Antonio, from vigilantes after he killed a member of the American Party. During the spring of 1857, the *San Antonio Ledger* noted that vigilantes hung seven horse thieves near the San Antonio River. That same year, New Englander George S. Denison wrote to his sister from San Antonio that "a Vigilance Committee was formed . . . [and] five men were killed. Since then ten or a dozen have been hung & a great many bad men driven away." Also, in 1857, five men freed from the Karnes County jail were found hanging from live oak trees, while in the Nueces Valley cattle rustlers were lynched. Southwest of San Antonio in September 1857, the *Western Texan* reported a gang hauled "a man named Anderson . . . from his family in the middle of the night" and hanged him.[3]

Grady McWhiney has proposed that much of this extra-legal violence can be attributed to the "Cracker Culture" of the South, which he defined as an extension of the Celtic mores of its Scots-Irish settlers that included a willingness to settle matters themselves when institutional authorities failed. Many of these people came to Texas and brought a proclivity for vigilantism with them. While later generations often denounced them as chaotic and merciless, historian John Ross has discovered that they were not always reactionary. He argues that, on occasion, vigilantes would treat the victim with some formality, employ a type of court proceeding before a final judgment, and even be merciful. Josiah Gregg concluded that mob law was "dangerous," but at times the honest men in a community had to "take execution of the law into their hands" to prevent "rascals" from ruling. It should also be noted that in Texas, Anglos were not the only vigilantes. Antonio Rodriguez murdered a pregnant Carmen Bustamante during June 1855 near Laredo, resulting in a mass meeting of Tejanos that condemned and hanged him. Nonetheless, vigilantism was most often led by Anglos, many of whom were Scots-Irish, who thought that the judicial system would fail or had failed. And, as Gregg noted, their community condoned such activity.[4]

By 1855 a substantial swath of counties in the Colorado and Guadalupe river basins provided a home to German immigrants, who strongly favored institutional justice over the extralegal. For many of them, oppressive politics and limited economic opportunities at home, along with positive reports from travelers and German immigrants in Texas, had led them to the frontier. Germans migrated to the United States, and Texas, in three waves. The first, during the 1820s, was a consequence of the German government becoming more authoritarian. During this phase, more than one hundred German men joined the Texians to fight in the Texas Revolution, and many remained to help establish the Republic of Texas. Germany in the late 1830s and early 1840s was characterized by the collapse of the industrial revolution, agricultural famines, and a suppression of political liberalism. This created the second wave of emigration, which included thousands brought to Texas by Henri Castro, who also recruited Alsatians and Swiss, and the *Adelsverein* (a company formed in Germany to encourage emigration to Texas), whose villages included New Braunfels. Discord in Germany between conservatives and liberals escalated into violence in 1848, forcing more to leave for America in a third exodus. Having briefly established constitutional government and believing justice was worth fighting for, Germans known as the Forty-Eighters pursued their vision in a new country. Many of them who came to Texas became productive citizens; several occupied political positions in Comal County, and they used their authority to pursue justice, including punishing those who killed the Blassingames.[5]

Two men involved in the Blassingame case exemplified the second migration into Comal County. Ullrich was appointed sheriff in June 1855 and served until August 1856, and he was elected for another term from August 1858 through July 1860. He had originally migrated from Lindenau, Germany, and first settled in Colorado County, Texas. He joined the *Adelsverein*, became a founder of New Braunfels, and led wagon trains of German immigrants from the Texas coast to Comal County. New Braunfels in 1847 became a city, and the citizens elected him as an alderman. Ullrich well understood his community's commitment to justice, and he issued arrest warrants for the men implicated in the Blassingame murders. Julius von Bose, who had several degrees from Leipzig University, had disembarked in Texas in July 1845 and settled in Seguin, where he married, and later moved to New Braunfels. As Comal County sheriff from August 1856 to August 1858, he delivered arrest warrants and subpoenas for defendants and witnesses and searched widely for the men indicted in the Blassingame case. He knew Callahan and many others associated with the affair, including Augustus Pharr, Callahan's brother-in-law. More important, he knew the law and tried to enforce it.[6]

Publicly there were few conflicts between Anglos and Germans in Central Texas prior to the Blassingame case. Neither the *San Antonio Zeitung* nor the *Neu Braunfelser Zeitung* reported overt tension, while positive stories about Germans appeared in San Antonio, Austin, and Seguin newspapers. Moreover, both German- and English-language newspapers supported the Callahan Expedition. None criticized Callahan; instead, the *Neu Braunfelser Zeitung* blamed William E. Jones. Anglos and Germans interacted in business and politics but tended to socialize among themselves, when German-Texans expressed an overt haughtiness toward their Anglo-Texan neighbors. They did disagree over slavery. Most Germans believed it should be illegal, but only through state action—a view expressed by the editor of the *Neu Braunfelser Zeitung*. However, the *San Antonio Zeitung*'s editor, a more outspoken abolitionist, was threatened by vigilantes. Otherwise, Germans avoided commenting about political issues. That stoicism was disrupted by the frustration that attended efforts to secure justice in the Blassingame–Callahan affair.[7]

In the months before Callahan's death, any suspicion that the Anglos had about German justice had been enhanced by a murder trial that captivated the populace of Comal County and the surrounding area. When a German named Christof Moeschen died, unanswered questions led authorities to suspect foul play, and contradictions in statements by his wife, daughter, and son-in-law added to the sensationalism. A coroner's jury examined the body and decided Moeschen had been murdered. The victim's wife, daughter, and son-in-law were arrested and questioned by Ullrich. At the inquest, the daughter confessed to killing her father, claiming he brutalized her mother, husband, and her. The fall 1855 grand jury indicted all three for murder. At the March 1856 district court trial, M. A. Dooley represented the defendants, while District Attorney Frank Egan prosecuted, and Judge Thomas J. Devine presided. Egan told the jury that Moeschen's wife convinced her daughter to hold a lantern while she (the wife) struck Moeschen repeatedly with an ax while he slept. The son-in-law witnessed the attack and helped conceal the murder. After a long deliberation, the trial jury unexpectedly convicted the trio for second-degree murder and sentenced them to nine years in prison. Devine lamented that the jury did not sentence them to "hang by the neck." This leniency by a Comal County jury, composed of Germans, did not go unnoticed by Anglos, who refused to allow the Blassingames to be tried by a similar jury.[8]

Although District Attorney Egan was criticized for the Moeschen trial, he saw a chance for redemption with the Blassingame case. He composed a statement to that grand jury, claiming numerous vigilantes "made an assault . . . with . . . a six shooter," shooting Woodson once, mortally wounding him in the breast, and Calvin five times in the back. He accused twenty-three men of murder, and the Comal County grand jury issued that number of indictments on September 5, 1856, four months after Devine dismissed all charges against Mary Blassingame. The names of the indicted men clearly indicated that Egan and the grand jury believed the Blassingames had been killed by the men guarding them. Egan called only three witnesses before the grand jury: Felix Kyle, Ed Burleson Jr., and William O. Kyle. The latter two were officers in the Callahan Expedition, and Felix was married to Burleson's sister. On April 13, all three volunteered to guard the Blassingames, and by various accounts they are believed to have refused to participate in the lynching. It was Burleson who found Mary the next morning and safely returned her to custody. With their brief but focused testimony, Egan secured the indictments he wanted.[9]

Egan's argument for indictment contained a mysterious contradiction. In the first half, he described the killer as a single individual with twenty-two accomplices, and in the second he said another person or persons not among the guards shot the Blassingames. Egan's indictment listed the following men: "James Campbell, John W. Sansom, Christian Speiser, Robert Cherry, John Tenney, J. Sansom (unknown to the jurors), Hugh McLarin, George Lang, Marion Martin, John Hoyt, James Martin, John Green, William Babb Sr., William Babb Jr., George Weaver, George McCrockling, James Waddel, Joseph Williams, Benjamin Bassan, R. M. Hoket (unknown to the jurors), Chancey Stevenson, William Campbell, and Solomon Tanner." Except for Speiser and Lang, all were Anglos. The grand jury that issued the indictments included: "[Gustav] B. [V.] Hoffmann (foreman), [J. C. Wilhelm] Ludewig, [Heinrich] J. Englehardt, Carl [Friedrich] Griesenbeck, [Johann] Gabriel Remmler, Thomas Schwab Jr., Joseph Landa, [Johann] Carl Schaefer, Christian Hanz, Carl Steubing, Jacob Jung, Christian Loeffler, Heinrich Scholl, Heinrich Startz, Emil von Stein, Adam Kunz, [George] Andreas Pape, William Bishop, and Gustav Gotthardt." With the exception of William Bishop, all were German immigrants. This was not unusual, as by Texas law the county commissioners selected men for grand jury service, and in 1856 German-Texans dominated Comal County.[10]

The jurors' backgrounds provide some insight into their decision to indict. Fifteen had migrated from central and western states of the German Confederation; two were Prussians, Hoffmann and von Stein; Landa came from the German-speaking part of Poland; and Bishop was the solitary Anglo. Eleven came from Hessen, Württemberg, and Nassau. All three had large populations of tradesmen, craftsmen, and professionals, and they were hotbeds of liberalism in despotic conservative states. For these eleven, the Blassingame murders were uncomfortably reminiscent of a system of so-called justice they had hoped not to experience again. The grand jury also included eight founders of New Braunfels, and none of the jurors had been in Texas less than seven years. By any measure, they were established in the community and familiar with Texas law. They were also conscious of differences that separated them from the Anglos. They had done well financially. Most were farmers and ranchers, but Ludewig was a gunsmith, Kunz and Scholl were cabinetmakers, Gotthardt cut stone, and Landa had a store. Most were active in politics. Grand jury foreman Hoffmann served as the first mayor of New Braunfels, von Stein was a city marshal, Remmler became county treasurer, and Ludewig was a city treasurer. The jurors represented a good sample of successful Comal County Germans.[11]

While backgrounds are germane, the previous legal experiences of the grand jurors are equally relevant. With the exception of Bishop, every member of the grand jury participated in at least one district court proceeding before fall 1856. In antebellum Texas, district judges could bestow citizenship on an immigrant who had lived in the United States for five years, declared an intention to become a citizen, and was known to have good moral character. Eleven jurors had received their American citizenship in the district court of Comal County. Three were defendants or plaintiffs in civil cases in the same court: Gotthardt, Hoffmann, and Landa. Three had been in the courtroom as criminal defendants: Gotthardt, Englehardt, and Kunz. Nine had served on at least one petit jury, and most had served several times. Eleven had been grand jurors on one to five previous occasions. Clearly, most of the grand jurors were well versed in the workings and processes in a Texas district court, and many had previously voted for indictments.[12]

District court minutes indicate that the Germans who dominated grand juries in Comal County from annexation through the spring of 1856 did not vary much in their indictments from the Anglos on grand juries in nearby counties. Over this decade, eighty-eight individuals were indicted. Germans in Comal County assaulted each other about as often as Anglos in Guadalupe and Caldwell Counties. There were more livestock thefts in Guadalupe County than in Comal County, but there were more cattle in Guadalupe County. Germans regarded civic duty seriously and used laws to enforce participation. In Guadalupe and Caldwell Counties, men also always worked on county roads when assigned or authorities overlooked infractions. Similarly, either Anglos had more of a penchant for gambling than Germans or Comal County authorities ignored card playing. Lawmen in Guadalupe and Caldwell Counties were either more tolerant of adultery and fornication or Anglos were less likely to engage in such activities than Germans. This may be why Comal County had twice as many divorces as Guadalupe and Caldwell. Once indicted, Anglos and Germans seemed to have been convicted equally, about 10 percent of the time. With such similarities, the angry divisions over the Blassingame case became even more striking.[13]

However, it is relevant to emphasize key perspectives on justice that German immigrants brought to Texas. The evolution of German liberalism in the early nineteenth century came with distinctive complexities and contradictions. German liberals were concerned about maintaining freedom for all under a legitimately strong government, while limiting the participation of the lower classes. This elitist approach reflected their simultaneous wariness of concentrating power in a bureaucracy on the one extreme and unrestrained mob rule on the other. German-Texans were wary of Anglo-Texan bureaucracy, and at the same time abhorred mob action. Both were elements in the Blassingame–Callahan affair.[14]

The news of the indictment of twenty-three men for murder or being an accessory to murder stunned the inhabitants of the Rio Blanco area. Of the twenty-three indicted, ten were jailed in New Braunfels. On September 24, 1856, nineteen days after the indictments, the chief justice of Texas, John Hemphill, held a habeas corpus hearing in Devine's district court in New Braunfels. The *Texas State Gazette* notified its readers that fifteen indicted in the Blassingame affair received writs of habeas corpus. Hemphill rarely conducted such hearings. It is not certain why he did, but he had served with Callahan as a Texas Ranger and may have been persuaded to hold the hearing by Jones, at the time the coeditor of Austin's *Texas State Times*. Jones and Hemphill's relationship stretched back to the Republic, when both men served on the Texas Supreme Court. Jones's interest extended beyond being a business partner and friend of Callahan: several of the indicted men were his Curry's Creek neighbors and he was their lawyer. Days later, on October 10, Hemphill wrote to the district clerk in New Braunfels, "Enclosed I transmit you the Recognizance of Hoyt and his sureties. You will please show this to the Sheriff who is ordered to forthwith discharge the said Hoyt from Custody." Other releases included Lang, the Middletown justice of the peace in whose house the Blassingames were confined. John W. Hoyt and Francis M. Martin posted bonds of $1,000; Lang had to guarantee $2,500 because Egan claimed he shot and killed Woodson Blassingame.[15]

When assembling guards to protect the Blassingames, Lang had summoned men from Middletown, Twin Sisters, Curry's Creek, and Pittsburg. Hence, they lived in the immediate neighborhood and shared similar backgrounds. They and their neighbors previously cooperated in petitioning county authorities for a new road through their area and asked state officials for permission to form a ranger company to provide protection. In fact, men enrolling at the same time in John W. Sansom's Ranger company at Middletown became the nucleus of the guards. For many, volunteering to guard the Blassingames was a normal civic responsibility. All but two were Anglos, the majority in that area, and many were closely related or would be before their ordeal ended. Frontier families tended to move together, marriage partners were found locally, and social activities involved neighbors and relatives. The Sansoms, Martins, Babbs, Campbells, and Lang and his brother-in-law were all kinfolk. Such relationships created peer pressure to join the guards, but others may have joined because of their connection to Callahan. Hugh McLaurin was a friend and neighbor, Joseph Williams undoubtedly knew Callahan in Prairie Lea, and seven of the guards had participated in the Callahan Expedition.[16]

Lang actually was of German ancestry and previously lived in New Braunfels. The *Neu Braunfelser Zeitung* reported, "Mr. Lang is known to us as the consort of the widow Madam Blessing." Following the death of her husband, Rosine Speiser Blessing married Lang on April 10, 1853. The couple sold their New Braunfels lots in 1854 and bought land on the Little Blanco River near Middletown, where Lang was elected justice of the peace. From 1853 until 1862, the Langs owned this property. However, a neighbor said that in September 1857 the Langs moved from Middletown to San Antonio. Except for his brother-in-law Christian Speiser, Lang had no prior connection with any of the other twenty-one accused men and none with Callahan, but his enlistment in Sansom's April 1856 ranger company formed at Middletown a few days after the Blassingames' deaths is intriguing. Lang took advantage of the rangers' presence and asked for their help. Speiser was a twenty-year-old native of Württemberg, Germany, and a new arrival, having obtained a 160-acre grant on the Little Blanco in 1855. So, by family connection he found himself a Blassingame guard and accused of being an accomplice to murder.[17]

Lang was one of three men considered by Egan to be ringleaders in the killing of the Blassingames. The person identified by the *Neu Braunfelser Zeitung* as the one who had arrested the Blassingames, "Hoket," was Egan's second primary suspect. Actually, Georgian Richard M. Hokit straddled the German and Anglo communities by marrying German immigrant Theresa Meyer in 1849. Hokit had fought in the Mexican War, which brought him to Texas. In 1856, the Hokits were newcomers to Middletown and became close friends of the Sansoms. Carrying out his duties as a deputy sheriff led thirty-five-year-old Hokit to be regarded by Egan as a principal leader in the Blassingame murders. Information about Hoyt—Egan's third primary suspect—before the Civil War is sparse. He migrated to Texas in the mid-1850s but why he was in the Little Blanco River valley in the spring of 1856 is unknown. The only mention of him in Comal County records is his participation as a petit juror in the 1856 fall term—on the same day he was indicted by the grand jury for murdering the Blassingames. No connection to Callahan appears in any records, so it seems simply a quirk of fate that he ended up guarding the Blassingames and came to be considered by Egan as a leader in their murders.[18]

Unlike the three suspected ringleaders, the four men of the Sansom family did have ties to Callahan and possible motives for killing the Blassingames. Convicted of stealing horses, William G. Sansom had been, on October 4, 1849, the first convict sent to the Texas prison at Huntsville. After serving eleven months, he received a pardon and in 1850 moved his family to Curry's Creek. He and his son, John W. Sansom, served in the Callahan Expedition. Both were also at Middletown in April 1856, because at the time John was organizing the aforementioned ranger company, in which his father was a private. William G. Sansom's daughter, Dicy Ann, married twenty-two-year-old Francis Marion Martin in 1855 and settled with him on a 160-acre farm on the Little Blanco close to Middletown and near his older brother, James Claxton Martin, who also had a land grant. Both men had left Missouri in the early 1850s for Texas, and the younger Martin was a member of Callahan's company during the Callahan Expedition. His farm was near Lang, so his close proximity, respect for Callahan, and the involvement of his in-laws, the Sansoms, led him to join the Blassingame guards, as did his brother. Interestingly, Francis Martin was appointed overseer of the road between Middletown and Fredericksburg at the end of 1856, while he was under indictment in Comal County.[19]

Other indicted guards also had ties to Callahan. In 1855, Joel Cherry moved his family from Bastrop County to a farm on the Little Blanco between Middletown and Twin Sisters, and the following year, his seventeen-year-old son Robert Washington Cherry received a grant for 160 adjacent acres. Two of the four Cherry boys undertook ranger duties: Noah in the Callahan Expedition and James with Sansom's Rangers. Living near Lang, Robert W. Cherry responded to his call for guards. McLaurin and Callahan were friends at Prairie Lea, and McLaurin followed Callahan to the Rio Blanco. His stepson, Robert L. Page, rode with Callahan in his 1855 expedition. McLaurin accompanied John M. Watson to retrieve the bodies of Callahan and Johnson from the Blassingames' cabin and volunteered to guard the reputed killers of his friend. Notwithstanding his indictment, McLaurin succeeded

Lang as justice of the peace. Egan's indictment included "John Tenney," but that should have read John L. Tinney, the son of DeWitt colonist Ambrose Tinney. A Missourian born in 1830, Tinney married Martha Ann, the oldest daughter of William N. Trainer. Attracted by Callahan's description of the Rio Blanco valley, Trainer moved to the area in 1855 and Tinney and his wife settled nearby. Tinney's mother and Eli C. Hinds's mother-in-law were sisters from the well-known John McCoy family. Thus, Tinney became a guard at the request of his father-in-law, Trainer, Callahan's friend, or because of family ties to Hinds.[20]

Caldwell County resident Solomon Tanner and his three siblings—Isaac, Malinda, and Samuel—inherited a twenty-acre farm and several lots in Lockhart when their father died in 1852. Solomon and Isaac moved to the Little Blanco by the mid-1850s, after participating in the Callahan Expedition. Isaac owned land a mile from Lang's cabin, and Solomon helped him with a horse herd. The brothers moved to the area because their stepmother had married William R. Huckobey, whose grant was nearby. Only twenty-one years old, Solomon volunteered to guard the Blassingames. Eighteen-year-old James Mifflen Campbell and his brother, twenty-four-year-old William Carter Campbell, were also caught up in the Blassingame affair, and a third brother, John, had a tangential role. Their parents had arrived in Gonzales in 1839 and settled close to the Tinney family. In 1848, the Campbell siblings, like the Tanners, were orphaned. A sister married W. A. Blackwell, who moved near Middletown in 1854, and this brought James, William, and John to the area. William served in the Callahan Expedition and signed a petition to the Comal County commissioners asking for a road to be built, and James was one of many who sent a petition to Henry E. McCulloch asking for a ranger company to be mustered.[21]

Some of the guards had simply joined their friends or relatives. Tennessee native John Marion Green, his parents, and siblings left Mississippi for Texas in 1856, settling on a 160-acre grant near Middletown. Green was twenty when he responded to Lang's call, joining William H. Babb and his son William M. Originally Missourians, the Babbs came from Arkansas, and once in the Rio Blanco area they became active in civic tasks. With their father, the two oldest Babb sons, William M. and James M., signed the petition for a ranger company and endorsed the road petition sent to the Comal County commissioners. According to historian J. M. Franks, William H. Babb "had a heart as big as a beef steer, and was always ready to help a friend." He and his son guarded the Blassingames because of their willingness to perform a civic duty. About one year after his indictment, Green married William H. Babb's daughter.[22]

A few of the indicted men left little evidence of any ties to the area. Nothing is known of George W. L. Weaver except that he joined Sansom's company, and George McCrockling is a mystery. He was not a member of the Jesse L. McCrocklin family on the Rio Blanco, but John A. McCrocklin served in the Callahan Expedition, so perhaps there was an error in documentation. Benjamin Bassan does not appear in local records. However, Watson swore "Mr. Bassham" accompanied him and McLaurin to collect the bodies of Callahan and Johnson, and Philip Basson lived near the Callahan home; perhaps these were the same person. The identity of James Waddel is also a riddle. Even if Sheriff Stockman had searched for Waddel, finding the fugitive was impossible without a correct name. In 1856, Joseph Williams had a farm near Middletown and like many of his neighbors signed the road petition. He likely knew Callahan at Prairie Lea since in 1850 a thirty-five-year-old Joseph Williams owned 250 acres there and lived with the town blacksmith, Edward Evans. Chancey Stevenson is a conundrum. He was in Comal County before Callahan's death since he was indicted for assault and battery, and he married Martha Ann Miller there six weeks after Callahan died. Stevenson went to New Braunfels for his marriage license, and justice of the peace John S. Hodges in Curry's Creek performed the service and sent the record to the county clerk. A local rancher, James Henderson, who was also involved in the assault incident, paid Stevenson's bail and employed him to wrangle cattle on his 3,500 acres on the Guadalupe River, eight miles south of Middletown. All this indicates that Stevenson was well known in the western part of the county, and no doubt his proximity to Lang was the reason he was asked to guard the Blassingames, in spite of the earlier assault indictment.[23]

Comal County District Clerk Alexander Rossy issued arrest warrants for the twenty-three guards within twenty-four hours of their indictment on September 5, 1856, and Sheriff Julius von Bose arrested ten men—James M. Campbell, Robert W. Cherry, Hoyt, Lang, Francis M. Martin, McLaurin, Tinney, Speiser, and William G. and John W. Sansom. These were the prisoners who were freed on bonds by Hemphill. More problematic for Bose and his successor, George Ullrich, was the capture of the other thirteen defendants. By the spring of 1857, when the district court met, William H. and William M. Babb, Bassan, William C. Campbell, Green, Hokit, James

C. Martin, McCrockling, Stevenson, Tanner, Weaver, Williams, and Waddel had not been arrested. For the spring term, Sheriff Bose recorded on each fugitive's arrest warrant "not found this 2nd day of March 1857." Migration allowed some to disappear or even reinvent themselves, and the closing of ranks within the Anglo community quashed information regarding their whereabouts. For example, James Martin moved to Comanche County, where he was elected sheriff, which made his capture especially difficult. For the spring term, upon hearing that Tanner was in Hays County, Bose sent a warrant to that county's sheriff, who returned it with a notation that Tanner was "not found." However, Tanner remained visibly active, returning to Blanco County in May 1858 to marry Cynthia George and one year later joining forty-two others in signing a petition requesting a ranger company. He openly farmed and raised horses in Blanco County until the Civil War. Like others, locating Tanner was easy, but arresting him proved impossible.[24]

Receiving information that the Babbs and Green had fled to Dallas County, Sheriff Bose requested their delivery to the district court of Comal County for the September 1857 term. On June 23, 1857, Dallas County Deputy Sheriff W. M. Moore returned the unserved warrants to the Comal County district clerk, claiming the three men had gone to Missouri. Whether this was true or not, it is probable that when the Comal County district court met in March 1857, they were close by, because Green married William H. Babb's daughter, Elizabeth, there on March 15, 1857. In this case, the Anglo community on the Rio Blanco and Little Blanco maintained a discreet silence, thwarting Bose. Ullrich pursued at least one defendant into 1859. Someone told him that Waddel lived in Blanco County. On March 9, 1859, the Comal County district clerk dispatched a warrant that was returned by Blanco County Deputy Sheriff Benjamin F. Patton with the notation "not executed for want of time." Patton had served in the Callahan Expedition, his father was a friend of Callahan and joined the same campaign, and his sister married into the Sansom family. He and other Blanco County officials chose not to cooperate in bringing those accused of the Blassingame murders to trial. By the beginning of the Civil War, authorities made no progress in the capture or prosecution of the thirteen fugitives. Ten years later, the district judge and attorney dismissed all indictments against them.[25]

Not so fortunate were the ten men who had been arrested and released on bail in the fall of 1856. On March 4, 1857, Judge Devine opened the proceedings in *Texas v. George Lang et al.* The ten defendants were divided into two groups. Hoyt, Lang, and Francis Martin appeared in the courtroom, where their attorney requested a change of venue, claiming his clients could not obtain a fair trial in Comal County and submitting affidavits from James Henderson, John S. Hodges, and James W. Moore supporting the move. Being farmers and ranchers with substantial land and livestock, these were men with influence in the community. It is almost certain Jones was the attorney, and of course he was also quite prominent. In any case, Devine moved the case to neighboring Guadalupe County. Martin's new bond of $300 was secured by Hodges and Jones, and W. A. Blackwell, another well-to-do farmer and Tanner's brother-in-law, joined Hodges for Hoyt's similar bond. Lang's bail was set at $1,000 and former New Braunfels city clerk and Middletown cofounder Conrad Seabaugh, along with his fellow Bexar County stock raiser George Judson, signed as sureties. In later bond hearings, other well-connected, affluent men pledged Lang's bail.[26]

Two days later, James Campbell, Cherry, McLaurin, John and William Sansom, Speiser, and Tinney also requested changes of venue. Henderson, Hodges, and Moore again submitted sworn statements claiming a fair trial in Comal County was impossible. Devine also moved their trials to Guadalupe County and set a bond of $250 for each. Prominent Anglos once more paid their bail: Hodges and Blackwell for Campbell; Henderson and L. C. Sims, a moderately wealthy Caldwell County farmer, for Cherry; Henderson and William W. Montgomery, another Caldwell County farmer with moderate wealth, for McLaurin; Hodges and Jones for John Sansom; Hodges and Henderson for William Sansom; John Schuhmacher, a New Braunfels landlord and Comal County farmer, for Speiser; and Sims and Griffin Tinney, a Caldwell County farmer and younger brother, for Tinney. Jones probably was the defense attorney for these seven men. Negotiations conceivably took place between the defense counsel, the district attorney, and the judge before the court met as no party objected to the venue change, which was good for the defendants since the juror pool in Guadalupe County was dominated by Anglos who were more likely to support them. There were also many friends and relatives of Callahan still living in Guadalupe County.[27]

Judge Alexander Watkins Terrell presided over the district court in Guadalupe County, while the prosecutor was District Attorney George W. Jones and later Alonso D. "Derastus" McGinnis. Barely of legal age for the bench, thirty-year-old Terrell had defeated an older, better known opponent in the September 1857 election. Presiding over *Texas v. George Lang et al.* in the November 1857 session was his first big trial. Jones, the district attorney, had oratory skills that were almost equal to Terrell's. He was a colorful character who fought against gambling and illegal liquor trafficking, despite his predilection for alcohol. His reputation was untarnished by his killing of a Bastrop lawyer during a bitter altercation in June 1855. When Jones decided not to pursue a second term in 1858, McGinnis, a twenty-six-year-old Bastrop resident, entered the contest as a dark horse Democratic candidate against the party's nominee and unexpectedly won. His debating skills and prior service for the Democratic Party provided the margin for victory. Thus, beginning in the fall of 1858, McGinnis prosecuted *Texas v. George Lang et al.*[28]

On November 9, 1857, when Terrell brought his court to order, procedural motions were addressed. Prosecution witnesses Ed Burleson Jr., Felix Kyle, and Mary Blassingame reaffirmed their pledges to appear. Mary came supported by the endorsement of A. R. Scanlon and Dorsey Wilson, ranchers in Hays County. William A. Blackwell, John Campbell, and James M. Pruitt, Little Blanco ranchers and farmers, posted more bonds for the defendants; Campbell, a private in the Callahan Expedition, was the brother of defendant James Campbell and fugitive William Campbell. Each man promised to appear at the next session and to be present until they were discharged. In a motion by the defense attorney, the court ordered Robert L. Page to appear at the next term. Page was reluctant to testify; a veteran of the Callahan Expedition and the stepson of defendant Hugh McLaurin, he had just married into fugitive John Green's family. Moreover, in a few months he would become the first sheriff of Blanco County. With these arrangements made, Judge Terrell continued the case until the next session.[29]

According to docket records, Jones and Cornelius Reich were the defendants' attorneys. Considering that many of them lived near him, and his close relationship with Callahan, it is understandable why Jones chose to defend these men. Twenty-five-year-old Reich joined Jones since he resided in Seguin and, being on-site, he could handle filings between the terms, which multiplied as they secured continuances. Reich had arrived in Texas in the early 1850s, opened a practice and land office in Fredericksburg, moved to Seguin in 1856, and immediately outpolled Andrew Neill to become the mayor. The new term brought a change on the bench when Devine and Terrell voluntarily switched courts, an option district judges sometimes used. On May 24, 1858, Devine opened the court in Guadalupe County and approved a motion by District Attorney Jones for thirty-six jurors to appear the next week. Blanco County Sheriff Robert L. Page posted bond. Signaling fresh evidence, Jones subpoenaed two new prosecution witnesses, Houston

Tom and his brother William Tom Jr., veterans of the Callahan Expedition whose father fought in the War of 1812 and Texas Revolution. Both were very well acquainted with Callahan, his extended family, and many of the defendants. Once more the defense counsel asked for a continuance and Devine postponed the case to the fall 1858 term, releasing the thirty-six jurors. An unexpected freeze welcomed Judge Terrell in November 1858, and McGinnis appeared for the first time as district attorney. Once again thirty-six jurors were summoned. However, Mary Blassingame did not appear, resulting in another delay and a forfeiture of her bond. The freezing weather must have provided Mary with a suitable excuse, since in the following term the court reversed the forfeiture of her bond.[30]

On the first day of the May 1859 term, Judge Terrell ordered "a Special venire . . . for forty legally qualified Jurors" as he pushed to resolve the Blassingame case. Zachariah P. Bugg, Hays County sheriff, veteran of the Callahan Expedition, and defense witness, appeared. After just two days of testimony and deliberation, rulings in the two-year-old case began. Jones, as the attorney for Francis M. Martin, James Campbell, John W. Sansom, Speiser, and Cherry, had asked that their trial be separated from the other defendants, and Terrell had concurred. Their jury, led by foreman and wealthy Seguin merchant G. B. Hollamon, returned a not guilty verdict. Although acquitted, Speiser had to give a new bond and promised to appear again as a defense witness. Callahan and Hollamon had jointly leased two slaves in January 1855 and, being merchants in the area, traded with each other. How this relationship may have swayed Hollamon's decision, or ultimately that of the jury, is unknown. Unfortunately, court records do not identify the men who served as petit jurors with him. Callahan friends and colleagues E. C. Pettus and Ben McCulloch had been called for jury service but were disqualified, as was William Tom Jr., and thus only a handful of the men who remained in the pool had lived in the Seguin area when Callahan did. While jurors might have read about Callahan in the newspapers, most had no direct links to him. The only apparent biases were Hollaman's influence and the Anglo proclivity for vigilantism.[31]

On the following day, May 19, McGinnis approached the bench with a motion of *nole prosegui* for W. G. Sansom and John Tinney. With the district attorney unwilling to prosecute, Terrell dismissed the cases against both defendants. Consequently, charges remained for three men—Lang, McLaurin, and Hoyt. After Terrell overruled a defense motion for a continuance, McLaurin pled not guilty. McGinnis presented the evidence, and defense attorneys rebutted. On May 24, after four days of deliberation, jury foreman John F. Tiner, a Guadalupe County farmer, announced a deadlock. This jury was dismissed, and two days later McGinnis tried Hoyt before other jurors. After one day of considering the evidence, jury foreman and local farmer J. H. Rice declared that his colleagues could not agree. Following that jury's dismissal, Terrell ordered all three cases to remain on the trial docket. With two hung juries and one non-conviction, all parties accepted the impossibility of finding an impartial panel of peers in Guadalupe County. Terrell arranged a change of venue to Caldwell County and ordered the witnesses and accused to appear in the October 1859 district court. In addition to Burleson, Kyle, and Mary Blassingame, Sheriff Ullrich and Middletown merchant Otto Wuppermann became prosecution witnesses. Cofounder of Middletown, Wupperman had sold two lots to Lang on April 10, 1856, and lived across the river from him. McGinnis also filed a motion for the bond forfeiture of a subpoenaed prosecution witness, O. O. Searcy. The Caldwell County doctor had failed to appear in court, as had Seguin merchant Thomas D. Johnston, who faced contempt charges for not responding to a summons for jury duty. Both men had been friends of Callahan, which may explain their absence.[32]

On Friday, November 4, 1859, the Caldwell County district clerk announced *Texas v. George Lang et al.* First came defendants Hoyt and Lang since Terrell had separated their case from McLaurin's. Judge Terrell accepted as securities for their bonds Thomas Durham, James Malone, and E. Ben George. Malone, a well-known rancher and farmer, lived in Hays County; it was to Malone that Calvin Blassingame had vainly appealed for help in his letter. Durham, a Hays County merchant and longtime friend of Callahan, had supplied rations to the Callahan Expedition, in which his son served. George, a Callahan colleague, lived near defendant Lang, and his daughter had recently married fugitive Solomon Tanner. Terrell honored a request from the defense counsel for a subpoena for Felix Kyle, brother of prosecution witness William O. Kyle. In order to locate him, proceedings were again delayed until the spring term of 1860. On November 5 McLaurin pled not guilty to the Blassingame murders, and Terrell swore in twelve Caldwell County jurors: William Jourdon, J. G. Wiley, J. Saffield, Joseph Laney, G. G. Haynes, Holloway Ellison, J. G. Blanks [Blenk], J. P. Jennings, Thomas Warren, J. F. Miller, Alexander Williams, and Charles Proctor. With the exception of Ellison, all resided near Lockhart, eight miles northwest of Callahan's old home at Prairie Lea. While Ellison and Eli C. Hinds were former neighbors, seven of the twelve had settled in the county since 1850 and may never have known Callahan. With one possible exception, none had a German surname. By all appearances, Terrell empaneled as close to an impartial jury as possible, albeit an Anglo one. After testimony, they retired to consider a verdict. Hours later, they reported that "they could not agree." Terrell dismissed them and ordered McLaurin's case continued until the spring term.[33]

Judge Terrell did not convene the district court in Caldwell County in the spring of 1860, and that summer brought new elections for officers. McGinnis placed his name on the ballot for district attorney along with four others. However, within two months three candidates withdrew, leaving McGinnis and one opponent, Thomas E. Sneed. Twenty-eight-year-old Sneed had been the mayor of Austin and an alderman on that city's council. His father, attorney Sebron Sneed, along with law partner Williamson Oldham, held considerable sway with lawyers and politicians, including Terrell. Furthermore, Oldham and Sebron Sneed led the Travis County Democratic Party. Needless to say, the elder Sneed's influence was far-reaching and somehow, he convinced the three contenders to drop out. Not surprisingly, Sneed defeated McGinnis. On October 22, 1860, Terrell gaveled the court into session and Sneed conveyed his intent to resolve *Texas v. George Lang et al.* by asking for a special panel of forty-four jurors for Wednesday October 31. On that date, the district clerk scribbled in the court's minutes, "On this day came the District Attorney Thomas E. Sneed and dismisses the Prosecution. Whereupon it is ordered adjudged and decreed by the court that the Defendants go hence without day." For Lang, Hoyt, and McLaurin, the Blassingame case was finally over.[34]

Why did Sneed dismiss the case? Only a week earlier his request for a jury pool of forty-four men had signaled that he wanted a trial. Three plausible explanations deserve consideration. First, the impact of the national political crisis cannot be overestimated. Just four days before the dismissal, the *San Antonio Ledger* and the *Texas State Gazette* endorsed secession; Sneed and Terrell surely knew Texans did not need more conflict. A second reason was more personal: the trial could potentially affect Sneed's upcoming wedding into the Burleson-Kyle family. Burleson Jr. and the Kyles had been prosecution witnesses throughout, and two more witnesses with ties to the Kyle family had been subpoenaed for the defense. Third, the Anglos closed ranks, making a judicial resolution appear impossible. For whatever reason, Sneed motioned to dismiss the case, and Terrell agreed. The trials of the ten Blassingame guards who had been arrested had ended. What started with a German-Texan grand jury was ended by an Anglo-Texan district attorney and district judge in a county dominated by Anglo-Texans. While thirteen fugitives remained at large, the Blassingame trials truly appeared to be closed.[35]

The three alleged ringleaders in the Blassingame murders subsequently lived relatively successful lives. Lang and his wife, Rosine, moved to San Antonio, where he worked as a butcher until 1861, when he moved to Fort Leavenworth, Kansas, because of his Unionist views. After the war, Rosine joined him and in 1885 they settled in Los Angeles, where he was a prosperous butcher and cattleman. In 1898, while driving cattle to Canada, Lang died in Alberta, where he was buried. Rosine's brother, Speiser, moved to New Braunfels and worked as a butcher. During the Civil War, he joined the First Texas Cavalry, USA. In 1867 he married and settled in San Antonio, operated a butcher shop on Alamo Plaza, and invested in land until his death in 1892. Hoyt remained in Caldwell County, and in 1861 he joined the First Texas Mounted Riflemen and later the Thirty-Sixth Texas Cavalry, from which he deserted in February 1864. By 1867 he was in Brownsville, where he was a postmaster, bookkeeper, real estate broker, oil company agent, and land investor. He died in 1914. Richard and Theresa Hokit moved to Parker County, but by 1870 they lived in Guadalupe County. In the mid-1870s, they settled on a small farm in Uvalde County near the Sansoms and Martins. During these years Hokit said he was a trader, Methodist minister, and farmer, but he also claimed to be a doctor. He died in 1891.[36]

William G. Sansom and his son, John W. Sansom, continued living on their Curry Creek farm. In April 1856, soon after the Blassingame murders, John had been elected as captain of a ranger company at Middletown. One month earlier, Callahan, E. Ben George, and others had asked Pease to authorize the formation of a company. The governor demurred but suggested that the area's residents could organize a patrol. Hokit was Sansom's lieutenant, Solomon Tanner was sergeant, and the privates included William Sansom, Lang, Francis M. Martin, and George W. L. Weaver. Half of the company, therefore, was indicted by the grand jury for the murder of the Blassingames. How they participated in guarding the Blassingames or in their demise is hard to determine. It is conceivable that they were already gathering near Lang's house in anticipation of joining the patrol and took the opportunity to serve as guards for the Blassingames.[37]

The Sansoms remained active in their community until the Civil War erupted. Persistent Indian raids caused John to form another ranger company in 1859. He married Victoria Helen Patton, daughter of fellow Callahan expedition veteran Samuel Patton. Appointed as sheriff of Kendall County, John found that his Unionist sympathies created problems and in 1862, while leading German Unionists to Mexico, he escaped the Nueces River massacre by Confederate forces. Crossing the Rio Grande, he enlisted in Union units throughout the rest of conflict. The Sansom families later followed in-law Francis M. Martin to Uvalde, where they opened a hotel in the mid-1880s. William Sansom died and was buried there in 1903. John served several more times as a ranger captain and was a successful rancher, hotel proprietor, and Texas historian. He died in 1920 at San Antonio. By 1860, Francis Martin and his wife, Dicy Ann, managed a hotel in Lampasas. During the Civil War he served in the Fifteenth Texas Cavalry until he was injured. For the rest of the war, he was the Lampasas County sheriff. Afterward, the Martins ranched and owned a hotel in Uvalde County. At some point he became a doctor before he died in 1907. His brother, James C. Martin, was determined to avoid arrest, so he sold his land to rancher Neill Robinson and moved to Comanche County, where in 1858 he was elected sheriff. During the war, he served in the home guards in Erath and Comanche Counties. When the war ended, he returned to his farm at Carlton, now in Hamilton County, where he died in 1884.[38]

Three of the men arrested and tried together had very different experiences during the Civil War. McLaurin returned to his ranch near the Rio Blanco. In 1861 he entered a cattle and horse raising partnership with relatives, but the war contributed to the venture's failure. Fearful of McLaurin's testimony in a Blanco County court, horse rustlers ambushed and killed him about 1866. Cherry briefly returned to his Little Blanco River farm. During the war, he was in the Sixth Texas Infantry, which fought at Arkansas Post, Chickamauga, Chattanooga, and Atlanta. Cherry was captured at Atlanta, ending the conflict as a Camp Douglas prisoner of war. Released in June 1865, he returned to farming in Blanco and Lee Counties and died in 1907. Tinney and his wife boarded in Caldwell County during the Blassingame trials and remained there until 1861, when they returned to the Rio Blanco area. He joined the Third Texas Infantry, the same regiment in which Augustus Pharr and Callahan's son Wesley Hughes served. After being hospitalized while in the service, Tinney returned to Caldwell County to farm, dying in 1867.[39]

Others had more colorful destinies. In 1860 Solomon Tanner lived on 160 acres in Blanco County, where he raised beef cattle, had a dairy, and joined Ed Burleson Jr.'s ranger company. During the war, he enlisted in the Third Texas Infantry and was sent on detached service in August 1862, transporting wool until December 1863, when he was declared absent without leave. He is believed to have hidden in Blanco County. In the fall of 1866, a Comal County grand jury indicted him for assault and battery, but he was never arrested. By then he was in Caldwell County, living on a small farm, but soon returned to Blanco County, where his horses were stolen in an 1870 Indian raid. Tanner lost his desire for ranching and became a peddler in San Antonio. By 1875, he had moved to Brown County, where he operated an inn, and in 1877 he became Brownwood's first mayor. He died in 1891.[40]

William C. Campbell was never arrested, had no ties to the area, and lived with his brother-in-law, so he was free to relocate to Shelby County, where he married and operated a sawmill. In 1862 he joined Madison's Regiment, Texas Cavalry, but he returned to Guadalupe County in 1864. He soon moved to Parker County, 200 miles north of New Braunfels, where he farmed until his death in 1909. His younger brother, James M. Campbell, was not so lucky. After being arrested and tried for killing the Blassingames, he stayed in Blanco County until the war, when he joined the Seventh Texas Cavalry. He was hospitalized for most of 1862, captured during an October 1863 skirmish at Camp Pratt, Louisiana, and exchanged in December. By 1866 he was farming in Blanco County, where he married Maria Paulina Lindemann, whose sister had married R. B. Goar, the foreman of the Blassingame inquest. James and Paulina were living on his Little Blanco River farm when he died in 1894.[41]

Livestock sustained many Texans during and after the Civil War, including many of the men involved in the Blassingame murders. By 1860 the livestock-raising Babb clan had settled in Hamilton County, but John M. Green, who had married into the family, was not with them. He died of typhoid fever on May 24, 1860, in Blanco County. The older son, William M. Babb, rode in the Thirtieth Texas Cavalry, and afterward the family moved to Bosque, Coryell, and Coleman Counties. Their frequent moves were due to William M., his brother, and cousins being accused of robbery and murder. However, they eventually must have restored the family reputation; in 1877 the *Galveston News* noted, "Mr. William Babb [is] a prominent stock-raiser." The family prospered, with the younger Babb owning nearly 1,100 cattle and, at one time, almost 1,500 horses. He died in 1911 in Concho County; his father, William H. Babb, had passed thirty years earlier, in 1881. Of the remaining six men indicted for killing the Blassingames, nothing has been found and little can be surmised, except for Chancey Stevenson. During the late 1850s and 1860s, he was absent from census and tax rolls, and he avoided arrest on the charge of assault and battery that was dismissed in 1866. By 1860 James Henderson, the man who employed him and posted his bond during the trials, had moved his ranching operation to San Saba County, and Stevenson probably continued working for Henderson.[42]

The regional turmoil generated by the deaths of Callahan and Johnson, followed by the demise of their killers, the Blassingames, seemed to be ending as the Civil War loomed on the national horizon. But those seeking justice in the German-Texan community of New Braunfels persisted, and the effort to bring to justice the vigilantes who killed the Blassingames bifurcated in 1857 when three new suspects were brought to trial. Thus, a district courtroom continued to provide the stage for this judicial drama. Surprisingly, the new defendants were Callahan's brothers-in-law, as the long arm of the law reached deep within his extended family.

CHAPTER 20

Blassingame–Callahan Affair Repercussions, 1857–1867

"Disturbed by impolite conduct"

With the fall harvest done and ranching tasks on the wane, people in the Rio Blanco valley gathered to renew their Christian faith. In the third week of October 1857, worshippers arrived to attend the Reverend Samuel Johnson's camp meeting, erecting tents on the Rio Blanco near Pittsburg. After sunset on the second night, with most of the campgoers participating in the service, there was an unexpected intrusion. Comal County Sheriff Julius von Bose and Luther and Thomas Blassingame burst into the campground, weapons drawn, to arrest Augustus Pharr. When one of the Blassingames fired his double-barreled shotgun, men and women scattered, running helter-skelter. Amazingly, only Thomas Blassingame was wounded. In the melee, Pharr escaped, and the next morning, a Sunday, the worshippers disassembled their tents and left for home.[1]

While the case of *Texas v. George Lang et al.* was still winding its way through the Guadalupe and Caldwell County courts, District Attorney Frank Egan began criminal proceedings against three additional men for the killing of Woodson and Calvin Blassingame, all three of whom were brothers-in-law of James Hughes Callahan. In this case, there would be no change of venue; the trials remained in Comal County. However, none of the new defendants lived in Comal County, and while cooperation from all officials was expected, these indictments would test a different set of loyalties. The new case—*Texas v. Augustus Fahr [*sic*], John Nichols, and Eli Hankins*—began in the fall of 1857 and continued through the Civil

War and Reconstruction, during years of turmoil in which unique influences shaped the proceedings.

Egan had lost his opportunity to prosecute when the indicted Blassingame guards had convinced Judge Thomas J. Devine to change their venue from Comal County to Guadalupe County. Not content with twenty-three indictments, Egan considered other options. In September 1857, in the district court at New Braunfels, he convinced a new grand jury to issue three more indictments. On the day after the killing of Woodson and Calvin Blassingame in April 1856, several men had posted $100 bonds, promising to testify against Mary Blassingame. All lived near Middletown—except three. Mary claimed in her May 8, 1856, letter that three men had entered George W. Lang's house and forcibly removed her husband and son. Statements to the first grand jury by Ed Burleson Jr. and Felix and William O. Kyle must have also implicated three men. Egan had argued that Lang, John W. Hoyt, and Hugh McLaurin led in killing the Blassingames, but now he had three other suspects in mind.[2]

On September 7, 1857, thirteen Comal County men selected for grand jury service strolled into Johannes Schumacher's house, which served as the courthouse. This group appeared similar to the one that indicted the Blassingame guards, but there were differences. Gustav V. Hoffmann and J. C. Wilhelm Ludewig had participated in the 1856 grand jury that issued the twenty-three original indictments. Immigrants from the liberal bastion of the Duchy of Nassau had dominated that grand jury, but there were only two from there on the 1857 grand jury—Wilhelm Seekatz and Friedrich W. Kalteyer. Four jurors—Ludewig, Eduard von Hartz, Heinrich Meine, and Heinrich Huffmeyer—emigrated from Hanover, and five came from Prussia—Robert Bechem, Hoffmann, Theodore Diesselhorst, Hermann Heffter, and Eugen Voelker. Of the two remaining jurors, Ludwig Donop came from North Rhine-Westphalia and Joseph Baetz from Hesse. These origins suggest a more conservative panel than the one in 1856. They would have been more inclined to abhor mob action and accept the authority of Egan. All of the thirteen had come to the United States before 1850, and except for Kalteyer had been in Texas since their arrival. He had moved to Texas after first settling in Louisiana. They thus resembled the 1856 jurors in having ample time to understand Texans and their justice system. Unlike their 1856 counterparts, only one-half of the German-Texan jurors in 1857 were farmers; the rest lived in New Braunfels. This is remarkable as the ratio of farmers to townsmen in Comal County was almost five to one, but it is unclear if this affected their decision to indict. Another disparity between the two grand juries was the number of Anglo-Texan members. In the six juries before fall 1856 and the four after fall 1857, there was only one Anglo Texan. However, the September 1857 grand jury had two Anglo Texans. Nevertheless, German Texans dominated every grand jury, and it took only a two-thirds vote to indict someone.[3]

The Anglo Texans on the 1857 grand jury were Alex Ferguson and Richard B. Goar. Ferguson, a Scotsman, was well connected with the German community in Comal County and had been in New Braunfels since 1845, when he and his brother moved their mercantile business there from St. Thomas in the Caribbean. Goar came to Texas from North Carolina and by 1850 was living in New Braunfels. He married the daughter of Prussian-born John Lindemann Sr., an early member of the community. For some years, Goar operated a New Braunfels store, but lured by the attractions of the Rio Blanco he moved and settled three miles southeast of Callahan, with whom he became friends. As foreman of the inquest jury into the Blassingames' deaths, Goar was intimately familiar with the case. Two other Anglos were summoned, John S. Hodges and Eli C. Hinds, but did not appear. Hinds, who had been wounded at the time Callahan was killed, would have not been impartial. Hodges, a longtime resident of Gonzales County, settled in Comal County during the early 1850s, built a mill on Curry Creek, and owned considerable land and livestock. His farm adjoined the homestead of William E. Jones, Callahan's partner in the Pittsburg Land Company. Hodges had, along with James Henderson and James W. Moore, convinced Judge Devine to change the venue of *Texas v. George Lang et al.* to Guadalupe County due to the biases of Comal County citizens. Had Hodges and Hinds participated in the grand jury they might have thwarted Egan's goal to indict three more men. However, their absence paved the way for the final stage of the Blassingame–Callahan affair.[4]

Egan explained to the 1857 grand jury that he first became aware of three additional suspects after Lang's inquest revealed their presence in Middletown when the Blassingames were murdered. He became suspicious when the three men promised to testify against Mary Blassingame. The testimony of the Kyles and Burleson Jr. at the 1856 grand jury hearing had also raised the possibility of other participants, so Egan had phrased his 1856 indictment in a manner suggesting he thought another unknown person had shot and killed the Blassingames. Then the 1857 jurors heard testimony from Burleson Jr., the Kyles, Mary Blassingame, her son Luther, and her son-in-law

William K. Holmes. Egan reinforced his argument by providing statements from Lang's wife Rosine, William A. Blackwell, "Dr. Davis," and "Mr. Huckley." Rosine wanted to help her husband, whose case was then in the Guadalupe County court, and she had been present in Middletown when the Blassingames were killed. Blackwell, who resided near Curry's Creek settlement, had earlier pledged securities for his brother-in-law, James M. Campbell, and Hoyt, but what he gave as testimony is unknown. "Huckley" was William R. Huckobey of Middletown; although his role in the Blassingame murders was in doubt, he had married the widowed stepmother of fugitive Solomon Tanner. On September 10, 1857, grand jury foreman Kalteyer announced three indictments. Innocent or not, Pharr was indicted for the Blassingame murders, while Eli S. Hankins and John W. Nichols were accused of aiding Pharr.[5]

That day, Comal County district clerk Alexander Rossy sent an arrest warrant to Sheriff Bose for Pharr, and on October 14 he sent a writ to Guadalupe County Sheriff John M. Tom for the arrest of Nichols. Just days later a warrant for the arrest of Hankins went to Caldwell County Sheriff Samuel H. Henderson. When Bose could not find Pharr in Comal County, Rossy sent another writ on November 4 to Sheriff Tom. Egan was determined to try the new defendants, and this must have influenced Bose. At the insistence of the two surviving Blassingame brothers, he decided to confront Pharr, who lived on the Rio Blanco. He did not anticipate the consequences.[6]

When Callahan moved to the Rio Blanco valley in 1853, several relatives and friends followed. At the time of his death, James Milford Day and his family, including Sarah Hembree Day, were neighbors, while the Pharrs were in the process of selling their Guadalupe County homestead and relocating to the Blanco. The community created by the extended Day family and others like them was underpinned by a religious culture typical across Texas. Local men built a campground on the south bank of the river near Pittsburg in October 1857, beginning with an open-sided, square arbor. The Reverend Johnson convened the congregation on the evening of October 16. He and his wife, Hannah, had arrived in Texas from Tennessee in 1848 and in 1856 settled on 100 acres three miles west of Pittsburg, where he began leading Sunday services. His neighbors knew him as a "faithful, kind, and obliging" minister. However, on Saturday night, October 17, his Christian spirit faced a new ordeal.[7]

Johnson wrote a poignant narrative, published in the *Texas Christian Advocate*, describing the intrusion by Sheriff Bose and the two Blassingames:

> On Saturday night we had a good time. . . . A pious sister was called on to pray, and while at prayer, a tremendous alarm was raised inside of the encampment. . . . A cry of distress, an outcry for assistance, violent scuffling, followed by the discharge of a pistol, a double barrel shot gun, and the cry of murder, all in rapid succession, threw the congregation into the utmost surprise and consternation. The more so, because it is not common here for our congregations to be disturbed by impolite conduct, much less by acts of violence, and this had all transpired in a few yards of the arbor.

In several additional paragraphs, Johnson continued to describe "the facts as nearly as we could ascertain them, as they occurred." At first the startled congregation thought Indians had attacked but soon realized that Bose and two other men had interrupted the services to apprehend Pharr, who was at his tent taking care of his children while his wife, Meeky, was praying. After gunshots and finding a wounded man bleeding on the ground near the arbor, what had happened became clear. Two days earlier, Bose and the Blassingames had ridden thirty-five miles to hide in the Rio Blanco valley and wait for the meeting. At first, they seized and choked Pharr, who managed to escape. During their pursuit an unknown person fired a pistol, wounding Thomas in the back and causing temporary paralysis. At the sound of the pistol shot, Luther fired both barrels of his shotgun without hitting Pharr. Congregants managed to carry Thomas a half mile to the local physician. Pharr returned to his tent, Bose left the valley, and the camp meeting broke up. Clearly, Bose and the Blassingame brothers badly bungled their effort to arrest Pharr.[8]

News of the disturbance was published widely, with the first report appearing in the *Texas State Gazette* on October 24, 1857. Electrifying accounts surfaced in New Orleans, and the *Southern Intelligencer* and *Galveston Weekly News* went beyond publishing a narrative of the event. They declared that "The sheriff is in every respect reprehensible for the time, place and manner of attempting to arrest Pharr." He was unarmed, at a religious meeting, and gave Bose no reason to assume he would resist arrest. Moreover, Bose had promised not to involve the Blassingames in any arrest. The articles included the Reverend Johnson's view that Bose had invaded a church of God. Furthermore, Johnson asserted Bose had planned the attack since he had spent two days before the meeting secretly observing Pharr, whom he knew after having patrolled roads with him in Guadalupe County. Johnson also wrote that Pharr had remained at home since the indictment, so Bose could have arrested him there. Even at the camp meeting, an unarmed Pharr was an easy target in his tent with the children, while his wife participated in the service.[9]

Despite having put up a fierce struggle to escape, it seems that Pharr was not perturbed by the attempted arrest. He returned to his family tent and spent the night, and the following day he and James Milford Day entertained Mrs. Otto Wuppermann and Carl von Iwonski. The main error of judgment made by Bose was to involve the Blassingames. Reverend Johnson declared that Bose had "promised never to bring them [the Blassingame brothers] into the valley again." The sheriff defended his decision, arguing he could not convince any other Anglo Texan to help him. Rather than seeking the help of German-Texans, Bose accepted the offered assistance of the Blassingame brothers. Even though Johnson could not discern where the shot came from that hit Thomas Blassingame, the wounded man was graciously treated at a local physician's house while, according to Johnson, a chastened Bose returned to New Braunfels that night.[10]

The *Neu Braunfelser Zeitung* carried an extensive account reflecting Bose's view of what transpired at the camp meeting. The condescending editorial mirrored the law-abiding attitudes of the German community. There was resentment toward the people of Pittsburg for not enforcing the arrest warrant, and instead aiding the indicted Pharr, who the newspaper implied was guilty. With the encouragement of the newspaper, Bose wrote Gov. Elisha M. Pease asking for help and giving his version of the episode. After reminding the governor of the Blassingames' murders, Bose noted that a grand jury had recently indicted other men, one of whom the Blassingame brothers reported lived on the Rio Blanco at Pittsburg. Thomas and Luther Blassingame begged Bose to join them and arrest the man, but upon arriving at Pharr's house they found many men there so they decided it was safer to apprehend him at the camp meeting, believing the congregants would help in the arrest. Instead, the people helped rescue Pharr, who escaped. In the melee, Thomas was shot, Luther left for parts unknown, and Bose stole away to New Braunfels, outwitting two men who pursued him. Bose declared that if such things were allowed, sheriffs could not enforce the law, and he asked Pease for assistance.[11]

Governor Pease had little enthusiasm for intervening in the conflict on the Rio Blanco. Sheriff Bose never received a reply, nor did law enforcement aid arrive. Pease had experienced the rage of the locals after the Callahan

Expedition, and he realized state interference might provoke more bloodshed. Bose's attempt to arrest Pharr reveals his underestimation of Anglo-Texan attitudes about the limits of government, especially considering the strong familial ties and community bonds, as well as the religious setting. Bose allowed himself to be coerced by the Blassingame brothers and his own idealistic conception of justice. Although highly educated and not a Texas newcomer, he let his zealousness cloud his judgment. He believed a ride to Pharr's hometown would result in an uncomplicated arrest and when that did not happen, he naively interrupted a religious service, thinking worshippers would help clamp handcuffs on their friend and neighbor. In his defense, there were enormous expectations placed on him by the German community and Egan. The intensity of this pressure precipitated a poorly planned and executed operation.[12]

In truth, the Blassingames were very persuasive. Thomas and Luther remained in Hays County after the death of their father and brother, and further exacerbated the situation after the indictments of Pharr, Nichols, and Hankins. The slowness of court proceedings converted their grief into a need for retribution and—according to the *Southern Intelligencer, Neu Braunfelser Zeitung*, and Bose—the Blassingames forced Pharr's attempted arrest. While he had promised not to involve the Blassingame brothers, Bose considered he was mitigating the potential for a more violent revenge by them. But all three men underestimated how their actions at the camp meeting could lead to violence. The *Texas State Gazette, Neu Braunfelser Zeitung*, and Bose claimed that an unknown person shot Thomas, and the individual was never identified. James Milford Day, a veteran of several frontier campaigns, was present at the revival and may have wounded Blassingame. This would not be the first time the extended Day family looked out for each other. Naturally, the aftermath reverberated throughout the area, especially after Johnson sent his vivid letter to the *Texas Christian Advocate.* The incident escalated tensions between Rio Blanco inhabitants and officials at New Braunfels, and the former gained some useful distance when Blanco County was created in 1858. Blanco County Sheriff Hardy F. Stockman in 1859 did not execute a Comal County arrest warrant for James Waddel, one of the twenty-three indicted in 1856 for the Blassingame murders.[13]

After the debacle at the camp meeting and with Pharr still at large, Egan focused his attention on Nichols and Hankins. Apprehending Hankins proved every bit as exasperating as trying to arrest Pharr but capturing Nichols was easy. In the last week of April 1858, judges Alexander W. Terrell and

Devine agreed to exchange benches for the term. Sheriff Tom of Guadalupe County arrested Nichols on April 27, 1858, on the warrant sent from Comal County. According to the *Neu Braunfelser Zeitung*, Nichols spent just two days in the Comal County jail before the court met. The Nichols and Tom families had been neighbors for several years and it is certain that Sheriff Tom made sure Nichols was only briefly in custody before he appeared in the courtroom. Judge Terrell conducted a *habeas corpus* hearing and, after concluding there was sufficient evidence to justify a trial, set Nichols's bail at $5,000. His two brothers, Solomon G. and James W. Nichols, along with neighbor and real estate business partner John M. Anderson, provided the security bond. An unshackled Nichols rode home to Guadalupe County but was required to return in six months.[14]

By late April 1858, no Texas sheriff had arrested Pharr or Hankins. Their whereabouts, as far as Comal County officials were concerned, remained a mystery. After Sheriff Bose failed to arrest him, Pharr felt secure living in Blanco County. Its first sheriff, Robert L. Page, had served in the Callahan Expedition and appeared as a defense witness for the guards indicted for killing the Blassingames. His successor, Stockman, was a former Texas Ranger and Mexican War veteran who had lived for six years near Prairie Lea and therefore knew Callahan, Hankins, and Pharr. Hankins may have been hiding in plain sight, too, as he was a friend of Caldwell County Sheriff Henderson. Freedman Manuel Hardeman would later claim both men socialized with the same friends. Henderson's successor, Harrison M. Daugherty, lived in Prairie Lea and served on road patrols with Hankins, Callahan, and William S. "Maulheel" Johnson. Moreover, Hankins and Daugherty were Master Masons at Prairie Lea Lodge No. 114, and Nathaniel Daugherty, the sheriff's younger brother, was in Nathaniel Benton's company during the Callahan Expedition. Finally, Harrison Daugherty and Hankins were deacons in the Shiloh Baptist Church at Prairie Lea. Thus, Sheriff Daugherty knew Callahan and had an enduring relationship with Hankins.[15]

Before the district court met again, both Judge Devine and District Attorney Egan faced reelection. In the August balloting, both triumphed, Egan by again defeating his old law partner. In the second week of November 1858, they returned to New Braunfels for the fall term. In the case of *Texas v. Fahr et al.*, defendant Nichols subpoenaed his brother-in-law James M. Day, of Blanco County, to testify on his behalf. Sheriff Stockman received the summons on November 5 and read it to Day three days later. But neither Nichols nor Day appeared in court, so Devine continued *Texas v. Fahr et al.* until the spring 1859 session. Before that term began, George Ullrich, now Comal County sheriff, heard that Pharr was in Fort Bend County, so he told the district clerk to send a warrant to Sheriff Thomas J. Smith, who replied on April 20, 1859, that he could not locate Pharr. The district court convened during the last week of April 1859. Nichols's attorney, S. N. Elliott, had previously requested summonses for witnesses Day and Polly Moore of Fort Bend County. While the Comal County district clerk issued the writs on April 8, 1859, Sheriff Stockman returned his notice, claiming that he did not have "time to give proper notice," and Sheriff Smith returned the Moore writ with the notation "not found in my county." Nichols appeared in court but faced a continuance with none of his witnesses present. Defense attorney Elliott once again requested summonses for Moore and Day and added William A. Blackwell to the list of witnesses. Nichols alleged that Mary Blassingame told Moore that she did not know any of the men who killed her husband and son. Day had declared, according to Nichols, that Nichols was at his house, seven miles from where the Blassingames were killed. Blackwell planned to swear that the murders took place about midnight on April 13, 1856. Devine issued the writs for the witnesses and ordered the case continued.[16]

In preparation for the 1859 fall term, Elliott subpoenaed Hinds and Day, with the district clerk issuing both summonses on August 23. Sheriff Stockman claimed the writs did not arrive until October 4. He served Hinds that day but declared that Day was not in the county. By now Day had accepted one subpoena and allegedly was not present in Blanco County when several others arrived. Why Day refused to appear in court as a defense witness for his brother-in-law is unclear. One possibility is that his absence provided a reason for continuances in Nichols' case, so perhaps Elliott orchestrated this or at least depended upon it occurring. As the fall 1859 court term approached, Egan seemed intent on ensuring all the defendants were present. Comal County authorities believed Hankins remained in Caldwell County despite Sheriff Henderson's inability to locate him. So, the Comal County district clerk sent yet another arrest warrant for Hankins to Caldwell County's new sheriff, Daugherty, who received it on September 8. But Egan never got the chance to discover if Daugherty would be more cooperative. Illness prevented Egan from carrying out his duties, and Judge Devine assigned Christopher C. Upson as a temporary district attorney. Egan spent his last weeks at his father's home in Greensburg, Pennsylvania, where he died on November 17, 1859. Consequently, Upson's appointment continued.

A native of New York, he had migrated to Texas in 1854, established a legal practice in Castroville, and ran for state senator in 1859 but lost, whereupon he joined Egan as a law partner.[17]

Judge Devine commenced the fall court term on October 31, 1859. Two weeks earlier, the district clerk had sent a summons for another defense witness for Nichols, "Dr. Reed" of Guadalupe County, but Sheriff Tom said he could not find him. Another order was delivered to Sheriff Stockman of Blanco County to "attach the body of James M. Day" and bring him to the next term. By now Comal County officials knew Day lived in Blanco County and, suspecting he had no intention of appearing in court, they wanted him seized and conveyed to New Braunfels. Not unexpectedly, two days before court commenced, a Blanco County deputy sheriff swore he could not locate the elusive Day. When Devine turned his attention to criminal cases, Nichols appeared, but his subpoenaed defense witnesses—Reed, Day, and Hinds—did not. Moreover, Caldwell County Deputy Sheriff Daugherty, the sheriff's brother, returned an unexecuted arrest warrant asserting Hankins was not in his county. Even prosecution witness Mary Blassingame failed to appear. Upson was granted permission to force her presence. With no recourse, Devine agreed to another continuance and issued various decrees ordering county officials to locate the defendants and witnesses and arrange for all to attend the next term.[18]

In spring 1860, Devine exchanged benches with sixty-six-year-old Milford Phillips Norton of the Fourteenth Judicial District. Norton had had an illustrious legal career in Maine before establishing his practice in Texas. His health was poor, which accounts for his accepting Devine's offer to serve in a local court rather than travel. Norton dedicated the new limestone courthouse in New Braunfels and William E. Jones spoke at the ceremony. With all civil cases adjudicated, Judge Norton and District Attorney Upson concentrated on the criminal cases and continued most. However, with Nichols in court, Upson unexpectedly declared his case *nolle prosequi* and Norton ordered the case dismissed. Nichols left the Comal County courtroom a free man. His unconditional release must have thrilled him and dismayed his fellow defendants, Pharr and Hankins, who clearly missed an opportunity to end their trials. The reason for the dismissal remains unclear. Norton's health was fragile—he died one month later on June 8—but since the decision not to prosecute originated with Upson, the more probable deciding factor lies with his desire to close out many cases held over by Egan. The *San Antonio Ledger* observed that Upson had dismissed several Bexar County cases that Egan had opened. Upson may also have considered the trials of the 1856 defendants, none of whom had been convicted. Furthermore, Upson had decided not to seek election, which freed him from voter approbation. When Jones spoke at the courthouse dedication, he undoubtedly lobbied both Norton and Upson to dismiss the charge against Nichols, and this may have been the final push for Upson.[19]

When Malcolm (Mack) G. Anderson, Egan's ex-partner who had lost twice to him in previous elections, heard that Upson chose not to seek the district attorney's office, he declared for the position. In the 1860 race, four local attorneys competed against Anderson, but he won a plurality. The *San Antonio Ledger* described him as "shrewd and attentive to business," and in the fall of 1860 he assumed the responsibility for prosecuting Pharr and Hankins. But no matter how competent he was, he proved no match for the legal disruptions of the Civil War, into which Texas was rushing headlong. In October 1860, visiting District Judge Edmund J. Davis convened the fall term at New Braunfels. A Floridian, Davis had migrated to Texas in 1848 and served as a district attorney. A staunch Unionist, he would gain fame by fighting for the Union during the Civil War and being a controversial Republican governor for Texas during Reconstruction. However, it was business as usual in October 1860, with Davis issuing numerous summonses and, except for two cases that went to a jury trial, continuing every criminal case on the docket, including *Texas v. Augustus Fahr and Eli Hankins*. The mood in Texas had not improved when Judge Devine convened the Comal County district court on May 1, 1861. With the war officially begun, Devine rushed through the docket in one day and continued most of the civil and all the criminal cases. He then hurried to tend his new duties as judge of the Western District of Texas, Confederate States of America.[20]

In spite of his Unionist views, twenty-five-year-old Thomas H. Stribling won the August 1861 election and succeeded Devine. An Alabama native, he had been in Texas since 1837 and in 1850 lived with the Andrew Neill family; he later was a neighbor of James M. Day before he moved to San Antonio to practice law. Stribling was licensed to practice in William E. Jones's court and undoubtedly met Callahan. In court on October 28 for the fall 1861 term, Stribling and Anderson rapidly disposed of civil and criminal cases, dismissing some and continuing others, including *Texas v. Fahr and Hankins*. After that, the war forced most cases to languish. In fact, by the spring of 1865, the Comal County district court had met for only four of six wartime sessions, and Stribling and Anderson never took up an old case.

The court considered only new cases, seventeen civil and twelve criminal, indicating that it operated at a minimal level.[21]

In the statewide ballot for secession, Blanco County voted 170 to 86 against disunion. Regardless of this division, the withdrawal of the U.S. Army exposed settlers to Indian raids, and so several locals—including Jones, Blackwell, and John Lawhon—enlisted men from the region in minuteman companies for defense. In July 1862 at San Antonio, Pharr and several other Blanco County men joined Company I of the Third Texas Infantry, as did John Tinney, a former defendant in the killing of the Blassingames. Pharr's nephew and Callahan's son Wesley joined the same unit in October. John M. Watson, the first man on the scene at the Blassingame cabin after the murders of Callahan and Johnson, was a lieutenant in Company I. Quite possibly there was a tense moment for Pharr when Company I camped for the first time near Company K, which was under the command of Capt. Julius von Bose. The former sheriff and the fugitive now served in the same regiment.[22]

The Third Texas's service was typical for units that remained mostly within Texas. As the *Texas State Gazette* reported in July 1862, Luckett's regiment was responsible for protecting cotton exports at Brownsville, where the Confederacy traded directly with Mexico and Europe. In late 1862, Company I was at Camp Madena, which was east of Ringgold Barracks on the Rio Grande, but it went to Fort Brown at Brownsville before January 1863 and remained there until going in May to Alleytown, a hub of the Mexican cotton trade. Orders in late summer sent the men to Camp Lubbock near Houston, and afterward, the company marched to the Texas coast in late 1863 and bivouacked at Camps Velasco and Sabine. When Union Maj. Gen. Nathaniel P. Banks launched his Red River Campaign in the spring of 1864, the Third Texas joined the fray in Arkansas, enduring bloody fighting at Camden and Jenkins' Ferry. The regiment remained near Little Rock until December 1864, when they were ordered to Shreveport. The cold, wet tramp became a hellish ordeal. One of the men who fell ill was Pharr, who required hospitalization until March 1865. The following month, Company I was back in Texas at Camp Hempstead north of Houston, where those who had not already deserted surrendered in June. Pharr, however, had already gone home to Blanco County.[23]

Hankins chose to navigate the war in a different way. Perhaps because of his opposition to slavery, he did not join a military unit. In light of their dependence on slaves and cotton, it was no surprise when 70 percent of

Caldwell County voters endorsed secession, which left him in an awkward situation. He effectively dispelled assertions of disloyalty by hauling cotton to Mexico. Beginning in 1861, Hankins made four trips annually from Prairie Lea to Mexico. Outbound, he packed wagons with cotton; on his return, he carried coffee, sugar, and other popular items. In exchange for transportation permits, Hankins, like other teamsters, brought back rifles, powder, percussion caps, and other war matériel in the return cargo. Three well-traveled, rutted roads led from the Texas interior to the Rio Grande. The first originated at Alleytown, west of Houston, passed through Goliad, and traveled on to a major hub at the King Ranch. Smaller trails fed into this congested station, where wagons were organized into long trains for the trek to Brownsville. Laredo and Eagle Pass served as termini for the second and third tracks, with San Antonio as a transshipment hub. Traversing these two trails, teamsters passed through the upper portion of the Trans-Nueces chaparral, confronting not only dehydration and extreme weather conditions but also bandits. In the spring of 1863, the *Houston Telegraph* predicted some 20,000 teams would start for Mexico, and though this figure was an exaggeration, the magnitude of traffic along these roads was considerable. With Prairie Lea easily accessible to the routes to Brownsville, Laredo, and Eagle Pass, Hankins likely traversed each.[24]

While many drivers used oxen to pull their wagons, Hankins chose Missouri mules for their endurance in long hauls. Because he managed more than one wagon and team, he hired or borrowed slaves as drivers. In one recollection, he described how he kept his mules warm when the weather changed: "In the winter a blue-norther blew in on a hot afternoon. The mules would be wet with sweat, and to prevent them from freezing, the drivers would whip the mules into a fast run and keep it up until the mules kept warm." Four trips a year took a toll on his health, and Hankins' descendants claimed that they shortened his life. The desert-like environment presented one barrier, while ever-changing regulations were another. Confederate and Mexican officials halted shipments, added taxes, changed rules, or even confiscated some of his cargo. Persistent turmoil in Mexican politics, complicated by a French invasion of Mexico, kept Hankins and his fellow teamsters speculating as to who or what they would encounter at the border. After Union troops occupied the lower Rio Grande in 1863, greater confusion reigned. Always thousands of speculators flooded Brownsville, Laredo, and Eagle Pass, where unsavory characters also lurked. All sales were transacted in specie, and traders went to great lengths to protect their wealth from ubiquitous thieves. Hankins's granddaughter remembered being told that he hid his money in different places each night; sacks of flour or sugar were favorite spots. While robbers coveted his gold, Indians prized his mules, and on the trail their attacks remained a constant threat. His safe return home after each trip was a celebration as neighbors eagerly anticipated the delivery of goods otherwise absent in Texas. His son remembered, "People would arrive at the Hankins's place on the San Marcos River several days before their return and wait to buy coffee and sugar." Hankins profited as a result of these arduous and dangerous trips. "He always had more money than he paid for the goods—evidently gold," recalled his son.[25]

After the war, Hankins and Pharr settled on their farms—Hankins in Caldwell County and Pharr in Blanco County. They may have ignored the Comal County indictments, but local officials did not. The charges still remained on the docket, while politics delayed a resolution. When Reconstruction began, President Andrew Johnson appointed Unionist Andrew J. Hamilton as provisional governor for Texas. Hamilton appointed many officials, but in some jurisdictions, he did not remove incumbents. President Johnson's Reconstruction plan thus allowed conservative Democrats to retain power in many southern states, including Texas. In the June 1866 elections, Elisha M. Pease, endorsed by the Unionists, lost the governorship to James W. Throckmorton, a pre-secession Unionist but former Confederate officer supported by the conservatives. National indignation turned passionate when the legislature failed to approve the Thirteenth Amendment and refused to provide political and civil rights to blacks. Republicans in Congress seethed. With the national elections of 1866, they gained sufficient control of both houses to override any veto. The First Reconstruction Act in March 1867 required new state constitutions and unobstructed voting by freedmen, and it extended the power of military commanders to remove officeholders. The generals in charge of Texas manipulated local and state offices. The political turmoil rippled down to the local level, where the turnover of judges, district attorneys, and sheriffs was high and partisan animosities complicated many trials, including those for Pharr and Hankins.[26]

The Comal County district court had a new judge in the spring of 1865 after Stribling left the country in 1864 due to threats to his life. Bexar County attorney John H. Duncan resigned from the Confederate army in May 1864 to be appointed in his place. He convened the district court in New Braunfels on the last day of April 1865 and, after reviewing the docket, announced a continuance in *Texas v. Fahr and Hankins,* at the request of District Attorney

Anderson. It was the last appearance of both Duncan and Anderson in the Comal County district court. Despite Anderson's declaration of allegiance to the Republican Party in an attempt to continue in office, both men were replaced by Governor Hamilton in the summer of 1865. Stribling resumed his old position as judge of the Fourth Judicial District, and when the court convened in October 1865 a newly appointed district attorney, Almon O. Cooley, stood before him. A Democrat, Cooley had publicly professed support for the Union during the war. While the citizens of Gillespie County elected him to the Texas Senate in 1863, he never swore an oath against the United States, and so Hamilton appointed him as a district attorney. In both the fall 1865 and spring 1866 sessions, a backlog of citizenship applications and civil cases, including divorces, occupied the court on most days. Cooley prosecuted only new indictments, and all prior criminal cases, including *Texas v. Fahr and Hankins*, were continued.[27]

Cooley gave up his office and ran for state senator during the June 1866 elections. In the meantime, Unionist Theophilus G. Anderson of San Antonio, Malcolm's brother, won the 1866 race for the district attorney position. Perhaps most important for Pharr and Hankins, Anderson was married to Mecca Isabelle Sneed, the sister of Thomas E. Sneed, who had dropped the cases against the final three guards accused of murdering the Blassingame men. In early November 1866, Anderson joined Stribling in New Braunfels for court. Judge Stribling again ordered the case against Pharr and Hankins to be continued due to the absence of the defendants. Shortly afterward, recently elected Comal County Sheriff Wilhelm Schmidt sent arrest warrants to the sheriffs of Blanco and Caldwell Counties for Pharr and Hankins. He did not know that the two fugitives held political positions with the support of their sheriffs. In June 1866, Blanco County voters had elected Andrew J. Kercheville as sheriff and Pharr as tax assessor and collector. The former, a son-in-law of Callahan's colleague Jesse L. McCrocklin, had settled in 1854 on the Blanco and was a Mexican War veteran and prewar Blanco County tax collector. He ignored the writ and did not arrest Pharr. In Caldwell County, Marion M. Hudson won the race for sheriff in 1866. He did not arrest Hankins, who had been appointed by Governor Hamilton as a Caldwell County constable.[28]

The Texas legislature on October 11, 1866, passed an act that inadvertently hastened a final resolution of *Texas v. Fahr and Hankins*. When Stribling won his 1866 bid for reelection, William P. Bacon was also elected judge of the Eleventh Judicial District. Bacon had served in the Union army and decided to remain in El Paso after the war, where he joined the Republicans and participated in the 1866 Constitutional Convention. Intent on eliminating both Stribling and Bacon, who were believed to be Radical Republicans, the legislators gerrymandered the judicial districts. When the ordinance went into effect on December 31, 1866, Stribling and Anderson no longer had jobs. Comal County now fell under the jurisdiction of moderate Republicans Judge George Henry Noonan and District Attorney John R. Shook. Thus, when the district court convened on March 4, 1867, at New Braunfels, Noonan presided and Shook prosecuted. Nine days earlier, Hankins had yielded to pressure from Sheriff Hudson and agreed to appear. He and his friend and neighbor John MacKey each pledged a $500 surety. Noonan took up the criminal docket on the morning of March 6; of the twenty-two pending cases, he continued eighteen to the next session, dismissed two, and approved a change of venue, while a jury found one defendant guilty. *Texas v. Fahr and Hankins* was one of the cases continued. Hankins failed to appear.[29]

Coinciding with the spring 1867 court term, the Republican-dominated Congress took control of Reconstruction. In Texas, Unionists and Republicans had complained of injustice, freedman disenfranchisement, and incompetent, arrogant ex-Confederate judges. Stribling led public meetings and spoke in other forums to highlight the crisis as the debate turned vitriolic. Gen. Phillip H. Sheridan, commander of Military District Number Five, issued several decrees including Special Order No. 65, published on June 10, 1867, which reestablished the pre-October 11, 1866, judicial districts and reinstated Bacon and Stribling as judges. A later decree expanded this declaration to include Anderson. Thus, at the fall 1867 term in New Braunfels, Stribling presided, with Anderson prosecuting. Undoubtedly the two men arrived in sullen moods. It took three days to address the civil cases, but on September 5 the court reviewed the criminal docket. Stribling and Anderson dismissed six long-standing cases, one of which was *Texas v. Fahr and Hankins*. Another was *Texas v. George Lang et al.* for the ten defendants who had never been arrested. And so, as easily as that, Judge Stribling's gavel ended the legal course of the Blassingame–Callahan affair.[30]

After over eleven years, eleven sheriffs, seven judges, and eight district attorneys, the trials of men indicted for killing the Blassingames ended. The State of Texas never convicted anyone, although two grand juries indicted twenty-six. Woodson and Calvin Blassingame had been shot dead, but the killer remained unknown, and rumors continued to circulate about the killing of Callahan and Johnson. What prompted Stribling and Anderson to dismiss the last indictments? Two inferences seem reasonable. First, Anderson's familial attachments with Sneed, Burleson Jr., and the Kyles may have influenced him. Perhaps he did not want to continue prosecuting cases related to those that his brother-in-law Sneed had dismissed, and in which the others may have played a role. Another motivation may have been that witnesses became more difficult to find, and some died, including crucial prosecution witness Mary Blassingame in 1866. Whatever the reason, it was over.

Although a single case among many, *Texas v. Fahr and Hankins* illustrates how Texas justice, particularly in the Guadalupe River Basin, evolved before, during, and after the Civil War. Moreover, along with *Texas v. George Lang et al.*, it reveals how Anglo-Texans and German-Texans deployed the judicial system to satisfy their notions of justice. Certainly, the slaying of Callahan and Johnson and the murders of the Blassingames aroused intense emotions. After the Blassingames were killed, District Attorney Egan, acting on behalf of the German majority in Comal County, sought to punish the vigilantes. In contrast, some Anglos viewed their deaths as a justifiable response to their assassination of Callahan and Johnson, and they feared a jury dominated by Germans would convict the indicted men. Therefore, the Anglo community did its utmost to undermine the judicial process. Even though Comal County sheriffs persisted, thirteen indicted guards were never arrested, and eleven years later their cases were dismissed. The arrested guards requested a change of venue so they could be tried in an Anglo county, and they sought a succession of delays. After multiple hung juries, the district attorney decided not to prosecute the remainder. These failed prosecutions also illustrate how influential family ties may have been to the outcome of the cases.

Having been outmaneuvered by the change of venue for the indicted guards, Egan and the German-Texans indicted Callahan's three brothers-in-law in Comal County, but for naught. Two were never arrested because various sheriffs ignored warrants, and when Sheriff Bose tried to apprehend a fugitive, his inept plan backfired. Moreover, key witnesses failed to appear in court, and the case was continued term after term. Then, with a visiting judge and a new district attorney, defense attorney Elliott, through skill or connections, managed to have the case for John W. Nichols dismissed. After a period of inactivity during the Civil War, politics shaped the justice system during Reconstruction. Judge Stribling and District Attorney Anderson found themselves back in the Fourth District courtroom after the legislature eliminated their positions, and they simply agreed to dismiss the case against

Pharr and Hankins, ten years after they had been indicted. There was no new evidence or admission of guilt or innocence, just a decision made by a judge and a district attorney.

While the trials continued, the Blassingame family adjusted to their violently altered lives. Mary Blassingame's grown sons and married daughters lived close by and supported her, but she also gained an income from three minor children, the offspring of her relative William Blassingame. William's estate provided a measure of wealth to any person named custodian of his minor children. Mary became their guardian, and she also received funds for each child from her husband's estate. She settled on a farm in Leon County, where she died on February 12, 1866, after an illness. After the altercation at the camp meeting, Luther Blassingame moved to Leon County near his mother and siblings, where he eked out a meager living. During the Civil War he became a sergeant in the Twenty-Sixth Texas Cavalry, was demoted and jailed after he deserted, then transferred to Capt. W. H. D. Carrington's company on the Rio Grande. He last appeared in the census for 1870, when he was a thirty-three-year-old widowed farmer with two minor children living in Liberty County. His brother Thomas survived his gunshot wound at the camp meeting and continued to live in Hays County, working at odd jobs. He joined a Leon County company in the Fifth Texas Infantry, which fought in Virginia as part of Hood's Texas Brigade. Blassingame descendants believe he died in Virginia.[31]

The Blassingame victims' families also struggled to adjust. Amy, Maulheel Johnson's widow, received $369.15 from her husband's estate and one year later sold their farm for $500 and left for parts unknown. Her son, Thomas S. Johnson, gave every indication he intended to stay in the Rio Blanco area; he bought twenty-three town lots and a farm lot in Pittsburg and served three months in John S. Hodges's Texas Ranger company in 1858. But as a lieutenant in the Eighteenth Texas Cavalry, he was captured at Arkansas Post in January 1863, held at Camp Chase and Fort Delaware until he was exchanged in April 1863, then killed in the fighting at Chattanooga in November 1863.[32]

The wounds Hinds sustained when Callahan and Johnson died caused him pain in his neck and left lung for the rest of his life. He and his wife stayed on their Rio Blanco farm, then increased the size of their holdings in June 1859 by purchasing another 232 acres from Callahan's estate, on which Hinds built the first stone house in the area. When Blanco County was created in 1858, Hinds became a county commissioner and was elected again in 1864. A horse and cattle rancher, he added 400 sheep to his herds in 1859. Hinds may have had Unionist sympathies since Hamilton appointed him as a county commissioner, an office he also won in 1870 and 1872. He paid taxes on as much as $5,000 in real and personal property before he died on February 6, 1879; family tradition contends that he died from an infection of the wounds inflicted by the Blassingames.[33]

And there were, of course, Callahan's associates and family. His death in 1856 created problems that required immediate solutions, apart from the tangled efforts to try his killers and then the men who murdered them. The Pittsburg Land Company suffered a serious blow in the loss of its onsite agent. Furthermore, the murders tarnished the reputation of the Rio Blanco area and drove a wedge between the German and Anglo communities. The four remaining partners also had to address the issue of Callahan's probate, to balance his considerable wealth against his outstanding debts, and to provide for his widow and children. As for Sarah Medissa Day, their concerns paled in comparison to her predicament. Facing life on the Texas frontier without a husband, she had to cope with poor health and being pregnant with her sixth child. Given the legal disruption of her extended family, her future and that of her children looked bleak indeed. While many scholars would long debate the impact of the Callahan Expedition, the murder of Callahan and the repercussions that followed left deeper scars on his community and family.

CHAPTER 21

Probate, 1856–1873

"Estate of James H. Callahan, deceased"

Sarah Medissa Callahan watched the sun clear the horizon on the morning of September 24, 1856. Relatives and neighbors would soon arrive for the final day of the auction settling her husband's estate, bringing an end to any happiness she had known. The sale of his livestock had intensified her grief; now she had to endure yet another day listening to the auctioneer's chatter. It would prove more than she could bear.

The settlement of James Hughes Callahan's estate offers some insight into probates of the Civil War era in Texas. While he was a prosperous middle-class rancher, the administration of his estate reveals the vulnerability of widows, as Sarah and her children relied upon an executor. Callahan's probate also illustrates how the Civil War and Reconstruction changed the lives of common folk, the role credit played on the Texas frontier, and the prominence of litigation in the lives of people in the Guadalupe River Basin during this time. Probate judges had key roles in overseeing executors, ensuring the management of assets for the benefit of heirs and creditors. Over seventeen years it is not surprising that six men served as probate judges for the Callahan estate. The estate had three different executors, and how they were paid may help explain why many cases continued for years. It is not hard to imagine that nineteenth-century estates could be shorn of assets by unscrupulous executors, but the Callahan heirs were fortunate in this regard. The disposition of Callahan's estate also affected his partners in the Pittsburg Land Company, as his death led to the demise of that venture. Later, when the state of Texas created Blanco County, part of Callahan's share of the company lands provided for the founding of the City of Blanco.

Sarah requested to be appointed as her husband's executor ten days before the May 26, 1856, session of the Comal County probate court. She attended the session although she was pregnant and the sixty-mile round-trip from her home to the county seat was arduous. Family history also contends she was in poor health. Hearing no objections, Comal County chief justice Walter A. Andross approved Sarah's request. She signed a bond of $8,000, providing securities endorsed by two guarantors, and Andross selected her neighbors Eli C. Hinds, William N. Trainer, and Josiah Cox to appraise the estate. In truth, Sarah did not serve long. William E. Jones filed Callahan's last will with the Comal County clerk on June 21, 1856. Callahan had stipulated that Sarah was to use their land and personal property during her lifetime, after which the remainder was to be equally divided among their children. He also asked that Edward C. Pettus and Thomas H. Duggan be appointed executors and that they provide everything necessary for the comfort of his family, especially the children's education. Significantly, Callahan specified that his estate was not to be submitted to a probate court other than having his will recorded. Moreover, he granted Sarah authority to select any place to live if she chose not to remain on their homestead, and he gave the executors powers to carry out his wishes without orders from the probate court. On July 28, 1856, John W. Nichols swore the will was authentic and affirmed that he and Augustus Pharr had witnessed Callahan's signature on April 20, 1854. Duggan declined his executor's role, so the duty fell to Pettus, who posted a $20,000 bond with John D. Pitts and Duggan as securities. Andross then appointed new appraisers—Hinds, Thomas Durham, and James Milford Day. It remains unclear why he named new appraisers and ignored Callahan's request that his will not be probated, and why Duggan declined to serve as an executor. Nevertheless, Sarah and her children now depended on Pettus.[1]

Pettus by 1856 was a prosperous community leader and cotton plantation owner who had encountered Callahan several times. Born September 19, 1812, in Virginia, Pettus had arrived in Texas as a boy with his father, one of Stephen F. Austin's Old Three Hundred. In 1831 Pettus got his own league of land on the San Marcos River in DeWitt's Colony, three miles upriver from the future site of Prairie Lea. In 1835, he fought at Bexar and on January 8, 1836, James W. Fannin instructed him to drive ox carts and rendezvous at Copano Bay with troops, including the Georgia Battalion, arriving by sea and here Pettus saw Callahan for the first time. On January 23, 1844, he married Frances Malvina Murphee and beginning in 1848 they lived on his San

Marcos River plantation near Prairie Lea, where he and Callahan became close friends.[2]

On August 25, 1856, Theodore Koester, Comal County's new chief justice, listened as the three appraisers presented an inventory of Callahan's estate, assets typical of a middle-class land developer, rancher, and farmer on the Texas frontier during that era. Included were 1,000 acres in the Williams Survey (worth $5,000), 310 acres in the Eggleston Survey ($1,000), 640 acres in the Redfield Survey ($350), and a town lot in Velasco ($10). His livestock—120 head of cattle, 100 hogs, 3 horses, and 2 mules—had a total value of $1,540. There was also a wagon with a yoke of oxen ($220), a two-horse buggy and harness ($130), tools ($35), household and kitchen furniture ($225), a rifle and a six-shooter ($50), and a saddle ($15). Together with $575 in cash, Callahan's estate had a value of $9,150. Missing in the inventory was the shotgun that Callahan loaned to Calvin Blassingame. And, although Callahan had purchased the Velasco lot in June 1839 and paid taxes on it through 1855, none of his executors found this deed, one of several missing documents.[3]

Other estate assets included payments due, illustrating the vital role of credit on a cash-poor frontier. Pharr owed $1,100 for land in the Williams Survey that he purchased on January 21, 1856. More notes from John C. McKibbin, Bruce Campbell, W. D. Hammonds, James R. Roberts, and Leroy T. Roberts totaled about $300, and small debts by five other men added up to $41. Of funds due to the Pittsburg Land Company, Callahan's portion was almost $110. For lots sold by the company at its barbecue on October 25, 1855, twenty-two mortgages were listed; Callahan had the copies of the notes, indicating that he kept the company's records. Importantly, and mistakenly, the appraisers did not list any debts owed by Callahan. They did note that he owned one-fifth of the Pittsburg Land Company but included no estimate of the company's holdings in acreage or value. The estate also possessed two corn crops, a few acres of millet, "two old board shanties or sheds," and a dairy on the San Marcos River near Prairie Lea. The appraisers told the probate court that they found other claims but could not determine if these represented separate or community property, or whether Callahan owned the property at all.[4]

The true value of the land in Callahan's estate is not clear. The appraisers' tabulations are contradictory, so the exact amount Callahan owned at his death was uncertain. The market would determine the land's value, as well as that of the stock grazing on it. Pettus petitioned the court to permit the sale of Callahan's cattle with the exception of sixteen milk cows and calves to be used by Sarah and her children. Additionally, he requested permission to auction two mares, two mare mules, and the two-horse buggy with its harness. Pettus remarked that Callahan's will gave the executor discretion concerning the best interests of Sarah and the children. Koester fixed the first year's support allowance for them at $500 plus the corn crop. He approved Pettus's proposal for selling livestock but ordered the property set aside for the family was to include the 310-acre homestead, furniture, tools, a yoke of oxen, twenty hogs, three horses, two mules, and the buggy with harness. Koester instructed Pettus to sell the remaining property at auction. In August 1856, Sarah was thirty-three years old and in the last month of her pregnancy, and, according to Pettus, it was at her insistence that a yearly allowance was set aside for her and the children.[5]

On September 25, 1856, the day after the last auction and five months since her husband's murder, Sarah died (figure 21.1). About two weeks earlier, she had delivered a son who was stillborn or died at birth. His death had a lasting impression upon the surviving siblings, according to family tradition. For them, September was another heart-breaking month in a tragic year. Family and friends buried Sarah beside her infant son, her husband, and William Milford Callahan, the son who had died a year earlier. In the year since the Blanco Cemetery was platted, four Callahans had been buried there. Sarah's great-grandson Papa Phillips always said she died of heartache, and Blanco historian John W. Speer made the same claim in the late 1800s. W. R. Russell, who knew the Callahans, claimed that she "pined away," meaning her health failed due to grief. After enduring the deaths of two children and her husband, as well as that of her sister Mahala King in January 1856, the sale of the estate was too much to bear.[6]

Speer wrote that "the year 1856 closed darkly on the settlers on [the] Blanco because of the murder of Callahan and Johnson, the death of Mrs. Callahan and her infant, and the breaking up of the Callahan family." Meanwhile,

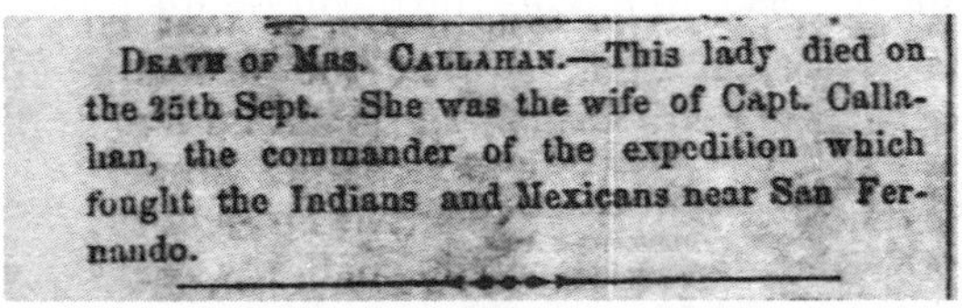

DEATH OF MRS. CALLAHAN.—This lady died on the 25th Sept. She was the wife of Capt. Callahan, the commander of the expedition which fought the Indians and Mexicans near San Fernando.

Fig. 21.1. Death notice of Sarah Medissa Callahan, *Texas State Times*, October 4, 1856. Author's collection.

Wesley Hughes (age thirteen), James Sanford (twelve), Josiah Asbury (ten), Armesida Catherine (eight), and Mahala Caroline (two) faced the prospect of depending on others and possible separation. At the next probate session, four days after Sarah's death, Pettus asked to be appointed as the guardian of all five children, and Koester approved. Pettus then asked permission to sell personal property from the Callahans' estate. Koester required all purchases to be made in cash or credit with good security and also authorized Pettus to rent their homestead. Luther Blassingame had petitioned for a clear title to the 175 acres his father purchased from Callahan in February 1854. After he and Pharr swore that Callahan had received the final payment in January 1856, Koester ordered the title released to the Woodson Blassingame estate. Lastly, Pettus submitted a record of livestock sales recently conducted at the Callahan residence. John S. Hodges and James M. Pruitt bought 142 head of cattle, Trainer 3 cows and 3 yearlings, and Durham one mare mule. These sales earned a total of $1,007—all on twelve-month notes.[7]

On December 8, 1856, Pettus began auctioning the remaining livestock and household assets at the Callahan homestead. The sale lasted three days and yielded $1,828; he received $51 in cash and accepted twelve-month notes for the balance. The list of sold items filled seven pages in the probate ledger, and some are exceptionally revealing. The Callahans enjoyed a high level of comfort. They had enough sheets, blankets, and pillows for four beds, with spare sets. Sarah's kitchen was well equipped with skillets, pots, pans, ovens, and a waffle iron. And with the cutlery, place settings, tablecloths, and glasses she had, she could serve her family and many guests. While a coffeepot was not unusual, five tea kettles revealed the family also drank tea. The two churns must have been busy every day, since they owned sixteen milk cows. Seeds and two and one-half barrels of salt reveal Sarah's plan to pickle and can vegetables. There was an ample supply of beans. Carding tools allowed her to weave cloth, and with her quilting set she could make bed covers with remnants left over from sewing clothes. She owned yards of calico, gingham, muslin, edging, and lace. Washtubs and a barrel of soap indicated that she had a clean home. The furniture included a rocking chair, sitting chairs, kitchen table, cupboard, dining table, a bookcase and books, three brass candleholders, and two lanterns. Sarah also had many sets of curtains. Not everyone on the Texas frontier lived so well; for example, the Blassingames owned a fraction of what the Callahans had owned.[8]

Callahan also possessed an extensive collection of tools and equipment. He had saws, squares, trowels, a bench screw, and a foot auger to build and maintain his house, barns, and other outbuildings. The large quantity of nails, boards, planks, and shingles served the same purpose. His farming implements included plows, crowbars, axes, hoes, a grindstone, and a wheelbarrow. He had quit smoking but chewed tobacco—his estate included thirty and one-half plugs. He and Sarah even had a buggy for traveling. The estate inventory listed a few garments (hat, shoes, boots), but no other clothes (men's or women's) appeared. It also mentioned no slaves, indicating the leased female slave and her daughter had been returned to their owner.[9]

After the September auction, nine chickens, two guinea hens, over a hundred hogs, two steers, and a pair of oxen were found, and Pettus sold them in December. From the earlier inventory, he also auctioned two horses, a mule, the saddle and wagon, fifty-six bushels of corn, and another yoke of oxen. Days later, Eli S. Hankins, Callahan's brother-in-law, bought a cow and a calf, and other men carted off the boards and planks, a stack of fodder, and forage. Lastly, Pettus reported he had rented out the homestead with several acres under cultivation and a number of planted rows of peach scions. The sales totaled 262 transactions, and many items were bought by Sarah's mother, Sarah Hembree Day, and her in-laws. Family members purchased or rented 27 percent of the estate, which included much of the furniture and a lease on the homestead. The remainder was purchased by neighbors. In order of the number of items bought, Hodges, Pruitt, Rev. Samuel Johnson, Samuel Durham, J. L. Anderson, and J. C. Stephenson together acquired 47 percent of the assets, while Trainer, Hinds, Joseph Burleson, Edward Burleson Jr., Thomas Durham, Robert L. Page, and six others took home the rest.[10]

Pettus reminded Koester that on October 25, 1855, the Pittsburg Land Company partners had sold town lots in the Eggleston Survey, for which purchasers had asked the court for clear titles to the land they bought. Koester did so while instructing Pettus to collect all monies due. The executor continued to dispose of the estate's personal property, but he did not sell real estate from either the Williams or Eggleston Surveys. Pettus had collected a considerable sum, mostly on credit, at his auctions. With proper financial management, the estate appeared well-suited for supporting the Callahan children until they all were twenty-one years old.[11]

Callahan's estate began to unravel by May 1857. Pettus filed an account of the sale of the remaining cattle and lumber, which netted $208 in notes but no cash. By now, he had sold all of Callahan's livestock and other personal property except a mare, rifle, and six-shooter. From his efforts, the estate generated $728 in cash and $3,659 in notes, with most due by December 1857. Unless the notes were paid on time, or Pettus sold land, Callahan's heirs would face a cash flow crisis in 1858. Adding more confusion, Pettus told the court that considerable acreage listed in the estate inventory had in fact already been sold. Since the deeds had been found in Callahan's house, the appraisers assumed he still owned the land but Callahan had sold most of the Llano River tracts without keeping copies of the transactions. To complicate matters, Pettus requested the court rescind the land sale between Callahan and Pharr. The estate held a promissory note from Pharr for $1,100 for a parcel in the Williams Survey, which Pharr could not pay since the buyer of his homestead in Guadalupe County had defaulted. Canceling the Pharr sale added 500 acres to the estate but decreased the amount due on credit to $2,559 at a time when cash, not land, was needed. So Pettus requested authority to sell land in either the Williams or Eggleston Surveys to raise funds to support the children and pay the estate's debts. Koester agreed. The executor also joined the Pittsburg Land Company partners in requesting partition of the remaining undivided interest in the Eggleston Survey. By now, they were annoyed by a partnership with an estate, particularly with an executor intent on protecting the interest of the heirs. To settle matters, Koester appointed three commissioners to identify Callahan's share of the jointly owned property.[12]

On June 9, 1857, commissioners Hinds, Trainer, and John M. Watson filed their report on the Eggleston Survey. The partners along with Pettus filed a petition expressing satisfaction with their partition proposal. Koester agreed. Thus, within fifteen months of Callahan's death, the Pittsburg Land Company rid itself of the complications of his probate. Callahan's estate was assigned 22 lots (almost 22 acres) in Pittsburg Township and 403 acres of the Eggleston Survey, located on the Rio Blanco opposite the town of Pittsburg. Thus, Callahan's estate received 14.9 percent of the Eggleston Survey; Chandler, 14.6 percent; Pitts, 14.4 percent; Jones, 26.2 percent; and Lindsey, 29.9 percent. The commissioners excluded Callahan's homesite and acreage set aside for Pittsburg in the division, and they also noted the earlier partnership sold 553 acres. No one explained why Callahan, Chandler and Pitts got substantially less than Jones or Lindsey.[13]

Before the Pittsburg Land Company partners finalized the partition of the Eggleston Survey, they sold two farm lots, to James M. Day for $26 and Sarah Hembree Day for $50. At the time, James and his wife, Susan, were living in the Callahan house, and Sarah lived with them. These two purchases made it clear that they intended to settle in Pittsburg. Immediately after the partition, the surviving partners sold other portions of their divided interest, mainly to relatives. By all appearances, they arranged these sales before the partition. These transactions also indicate they had difficulty attracting buyers and were resorting to relatives to sustain their venture. At the end of the June 1857 probate session, Callahan's estate still owned 713 acres and 22 Pittsburg lots in the Eggleston Survey, 1,500 acres in the Williams Survey, $728 in cash, and $2,559 in notes, along with an unspecified amount due from James M. Day and L. M. Nunn.[14]

By the spring of 1857, creditors began making claims against Callahan's estate. William R. Connor of Houston County asked the probate court to execute a deed for a 450-acre parcel on the Llano River. Koester authorized Pettus to deliver a deed for the land, except for one tract that Callahan had reserved. Next, Pettus reported his attempt to sell part of Callahan's share of the Eggleston Survey in order to support his children and pay the Fowler heirs, a debt the executor had not previously itemized. Callahan and the other Pittsburg Land Company partners still owed about $4,300 to them. On July 7, 1857, Pettus stood on the Comal County courthouse steps for seven hours waiting for bidders. None appeared. Needing funds for the children, Pettus asked for the estate to provide him $75 per month to cover his expenses for them; this totaled $675 for the previous nine months. Koester also allowed him a one-time payment of $150 for time and travel. Concerned that expenses exceeded the cash in the estate, Koester also gave Pettus three months to report all claims against and due the estate. The imbalance between income and debts in the Callahan estate had become alarming.[15]

The next four months were frustrating for Pettus. In October 1857, he reported the estate possessed just $86.50 in cash, though the recent sale of a horse netted $160 on a six-month note. With the homestead lease expiring in December, Koester authorized Pettus to negotiate another agreement, but the renter had to sign a contract with securities. On the Monday after Christmas, Pettus complained about having insufficient time, so Koester granted him another month. When the Comal County probate court convened in January 1858, he filed another report and presented a rental contract for the Callahan homestead signed by Joseph Burleson. This stipulated that the estate would receive one-third of the crops harvested. As he had before, Koester ordered Pettus to obtain funds to pay creditors and support the children, a goal Pettus still found elusive.[16]

The April 1858 probate session proved to be a watershed. Seven days earlier, Pettus had prevailed in a Comal County district court suit against Hodges, Pruitt, and Jones. Pettus sued to collect on notes signed by Hodges and Pruitt when they bought livestock and personal property at the 1856 auction. They had made no payments, and Jones was their surety. Jones, however, was Pettus's attorney, so Judge Thomas J. Devine dismissed him as a defendant before ruling in favor of Pettus, awarding $550 from Hodges and $661 from Pruitt. Pruitt and Hodges epitomized the kind of buyers the Pittsburg Land Company partners had sought. Both were well-known and respected in the Guadalupe River Basin and were business partners, owning land separately and jointly in the Curry's Creek area. Hodges had a gristmill that also housed the post office, was an active Mason, and led a Texas Ranger company. Jointly their wealth was almost $20,000. With a writ against Pruitt and Hodges, Pettus asked sheriffs to locate any assets owned by them. Hodges eventually paid $597 to Jones in April 1859. When the Blanco County sheriff got a writ from Comal County, Pruitt paid $90 to Jones, Pettus's attorney, who told the sheriff not to execute a seizure. By the end of 1860 Pruitt still owed the Callahan estate $571 and had serious financial problems. He had borrowed money in Guadalupe, Comal, and Caldwell Counties, and when he failed to repay, his creditors sued him. These debts hastened his departure from Texas.[17]

Moments after Koester pounded the probate court into session in July 1858, Pettus filed a fascinating request. He reported that in February 1858, the legislature had created Blanco County and local citizens wanted the county seat located within Callahan's 403 acres of the Eggleston Survey. Pettus later delivered a deed for a 128-acre parcel of land to Blanco County authorities. Thus, Callahan's estate provided the land that became the City of Blanco, the first county seat of Blanco County. While Callahan would have been pleased with the seat on his property, he might have been displeased that his Pittsburg Land Company partners failed to donate their share. In the same session, Pettus also appealed for an order to sell land in the Eggleston Survey to pay a $1,240 judgment in the District Court of Guadalupe County. An event that Callahan observed would bring him "grief until my dying day" came back to haunt his estate. Collin Johnson, the owner of Humphrey, the slave Callahan killed in 1855, sued for loss of property, and Pettus was ordered to reimburse him a significant amount of money from the cash-poor estate.[18]

In October 1858, newly elected chief justice Friedrich H. Heffter was on the probate court bench when Pettus filed two petitions: to resign as executor and to withdraw as trustee and guardian of the Callahan children. He also filed his final financial report. Pettus never revealed why he withdrew. However, the care of eleven children, six of his own and five Callahan heirs, must have been a tremendous burden for him and his wife, who was pregnant. As an executor, Pettus had to travel to tend Callahan's property and to New Braunfels for hearings. Raising funds from the estate was onerous, as was Pettus's relationship with the Pittsburg Land Company. Two surviving partners had taken more than their fair share of the Eggleston Survey, and a breaking point may have come when Callahan's estate had to donate all of the acreage for the new Blanco County seat. In addition, Pettus may not have been well; he died in 1863 at the age of fifty-two.[19]

Pettus' replacement as executor perhaps reveals more about his departure. On December 1, 1858, Heffter announced William E. Jones had filed to be the executor of Callahan's estate. According to Pettus's reports, it included $2,500 in debts, plus unspecified amounts due from James M. Day and Nunn, an unknown amount of cash, 713 acres and twenty-two Pittsburg lots in the Eggleston Survey and 1,500 acres in the Williams Survey. Jones took the administrator's oath and provided a $20,000 bond, and Heffter ordered him to raise funds to pay Pettus for his time and expenses. Jones also petitioned the court for an appointment as guardian. Because of their ages, Wesley Hughes and James Sanford Callahan had the right to select their custodian. Appearing in court, they "declared themselves satisfied to have Wm. E. Jones as their guardian," and when nobody objected, Heffter agreed. The next day, Jones submitted a petition declaring the estate's debts amounted to $3,000: $1,100 to the Fowler heirs (one-fifth of the Pittsburg Land Company's obligation), $1,380 to Collin Johnson, $320 to the Pittsburg Land Company, and $200 to Pettus. He asked permission to sell real estate, excluding the homestead, within the Eggleston Survey from the steps of the Blanco County courthouse. Heffter approved the auction but instructed Jones to take care of the children before applying any proceeds elsewhere.[20]

On February 7, 1859, Jones reported that Robert Silliman had obtained the 201 acres bought by James M. Day and paid Callahan's estate the outstanding balance of Day's note, an amount seemingly sufficient to support the children. Moreover, Jones said Charles Mayrhofen bought 150 acres in the Eggleston Survey for $843.75, a transaction Heffter made contingent upon the buyer providing a "note with good and sufficient security." Jones had done what Pettus could not—sell land on the courthouse steps. However, the unscrupulous Mayrhofen failed to deliver a proper note so Jones sold the property for $840 to Frederick Muenzler, who submitted a note with security. In December, Jones summarized the expenditures for the Callahan orphans for the past year and also payments on the estate's debts. Paying the Fowler heirs was a priority since liquidation of this liability would benefit both the Pittsburg Land Company and Callahan's estate. In November, Jones had sent $1,013.20 to Pitts, which paid Callahan's part of that debt. Jones later indicated the other partners had paid the Fowler heirs as well.[21]

In April 1860, Jones claimed the uncollected assets of Callahan's estate totaled $1,350, while its unpaid debts were $1,300. He again sought authorization to sell land in the Eggleston Survey, not including the homestead. Heffter ruled that any sale had to be endorsed by the court and that the proceeds were for the "support and education of the children." Next, Jones told the court that Callahan's sister Margaret Callahan Rounsavall Alley, who lived in Walker County, Georgia, wanted to raise the two girls, Catherine and Caroline, paying for all but "clothing and schooling." Saying they would benefit from "the advantages of an older settled country," Jones asked for Heffter's consent. Furthermore, Jones explained that Pruitt, who had defaulted on his debt to Callahan's estate, and his wife intended to travel to Georgia and had offered to transport both girls. Heffter agreed and authorized Jones to raise funds for their travel expenses. En route to Georgia, the Pruitts were in Cass County, Texas, when an 1860 census taker enumerated their household plus three, not two, Callahans—Catherine, Caroline, and Josiah. The boy definitely went to Georgia with the girls, as Catherine confirmed in an affidavit she signed decades later. Jones never explained Josiah's inclusion in the group, nor did he inform the probate court. Pruitt and his wife, Sarah (née Rounsavall), had both been born in Georgia, and they simply dropped off the Callahan siblings on their way to see relatives. In 1860 Callahan's sister Margaret and her second husband, Marcus Napoleon Bonaparte Jonathan Hampton Alley, resided on a farm near Pond Springs in Walker County, Georgia. Another sister, Nancy Callahan Hamilton, and her husband and six children lived next door. None expected war would soon come to their valley.[22]

In December 1861, Jones submitted his most comprehensive tally of the Callahan estate's finances to date. The estate had $319.53 in cash, plus $43.50 due for that year's corn and wheat crops. Uncollected notes for prior years included $303.26 for crops and $270 for homestead rent. These amounts did not include uncollected debts. For example, Pruitt had yet to pay the $150 he owed. On the other hand, according to Hays County probate records, Pitts' estate paid $312.92 to Callahan's estate, yet this does not appear in any document submitted by Jones. Furthermore, he did not address land holdings or amounts owed by the estate to creditors. Among the creditors was Johnson, who had not been paid his $1,380. While Jones covered expenses for the Callahan orphans from his own pocket, he also paid himself, charging a 5 percent commission on all disbursements and monies received.[23]

During the Civil War, Heffter opened his probate court only nineteen times out of forty-one scheduled sessions, hearing mostly new cases and ignoring most pre-1862 estates. Jones, a Unionist, stayed at home. After the war, he relocated to San Antonio, became an editor for the *San Antonio Express*, supported the Republicans, and ran for a seat on the Texas Supreme Court; he lost. In this hectic period, Jones sent his law partner, Hermann Seele, to deliver an accounting of Callahan's estate after a lull of almost five years. During August 1866, Seele appeared in court before the new judge, Georg Klappenbach. The judge read Jones's report of December 1861, which the Comal County clerk had endorsed almost five years before his successor entered it into the probate ledger. Neither clerk explained the delay. Klappenbach also reviewed an account of disbursements and receipts for the war years. By Jones's calculations, the estate had $257.03 in cash, and his explanatory remarks revealed the difficulty of wartime finances. Thomas Durham owed $120 and James M. Day $189 in unpaid rent for the homestead. Jones noted that Day's 1861 rent had been paid in Confederate money, which was now useless. Durham also owed $99.88 for crops raised on the homestead. Finally, Jones reported he had paid the "State Taxes" for the last five years, though he provided no receipts. He had used payments from Muenzler, who in the end paid Callahan's estate a total of $762.62, to pay the last money owed the Fowler heirs and to make payments on the debt to Johnson. Despite all these difficulties, the estate's cash flow remained positive, it never defaulted on a debt, and Jones never had to auction any of the estate's land.[24]

By May 1867 Jones was again concerned about the Callahan estate cash flow. According to his calculations, the estate owed approximately $1,405 but had assets of only $1,035. Receipts minus disbursements since August 1866 show that he had spent $83.54 of his own money. The probate minutes also indicate Jones had received payments for most of the collectible debts owed to the estate. Thus, any future funds would have to be raised from the sale of property. This prompted him to ask the court for an order to sell the estate's remaining holdings in the Eggleston Survey, except the homestead, to pay unpaid debts and the expenses for Catherine and Caroline Callahan, who remained under his guardianship, to come to Texas. Klappenbach agreed but again stipulated all sales were to be in cash or on a twelve-month note with a security. He barred Jones from selling any Pittsburg plots reserved for schools, a cemetery, and springs. Thus, Jones and the judge continued to protect the homestead, the town, and the 1,500 acres in the Williams Survey (see map 9.2).[25]

During the summer of 1867, Jones auctioned tracts by personal solicitations or from the steps of the Blanco County courthouse, attracting eager buyers. Louis Capt purchased 404 acres and Robert P. Harrison 127 acres of the Eggleston Survey. Capt paid $850, but in the Harrison sale, the Callahan estate earned one-fifth ($55) of the proceeds, a puzzling entry considering the Pittsburg Land Company partnership dissolved in 1857. Five other individuals signed twelve-month notes for fourteen lots in Pittsburg. With potential proceeds of $973.75 from these sales, Callahan's estate had a positive balance of $890.21. Fifteen months passed before Jones sent his next statement in August 1868, when he admitted he made mistakes in the sale of Pittsburg lots. Five did not belong to Callahan, implying they were owned by his former partners, who received the proceeds. This is odd since Pitts died in 1861 and Lindsey in 1865, so the only two surviving partners were Chandler and Jones. Intriguingly, Callahan's estate owned the remaining nine lots sold by Jones, but the purchasers failed to comply with the sale conditions and the transactions were voided. Consequently, Jones asked to sell the estate's other twenty-two lots in Pittsburg, even though neither he nor Pettus had ever successfully done so. Jones also disclosed he had again leased the Callahan homestead and insinuated the man expressed interest in purchasing it. Jones's next statement, in February 1869, brought more good news. He reported selling twenty-two town lots in Pittsburg, for which he had secured $52.80 in cash.[26]

Jones did not present another statement to the probate court until September 1870, when he requested a partition of the 1,500 acres in the Williams Survey and appointment of appraisers for the estate. He also asked District Judge George Noonan to issue summons to the three oldest children: Wesley H., James S., and Catherine. Jones was beginning the estate's final dissolution to address changes in the laws and his personal life. The 1869

Texas Constitution gave district courts, not county courts, jurisdiction over probate, and the Twelfth Legislature made substantial modifications in the regulations for executors. Too, Gov. Edmund J. Davis had appointed Jones as a district judge, forcing him to abandon his role as an executor. But matters were complex. Wesley had married Lovina Pinrod Lawhon Rawls and resided near Jones on Curry Creek in Kendall County, while James had wed Sarah Elizabeth Neill and lived nearby. Catherine and Caroline reportedly returned to Texas in 1867, but no one knew the whereabouts of Josiah.[27]

After Jones was appointed to the Thirty-Second Judicial District, he moved his family to Georgetown, seat of Williamson County. His circuit included Williamson, Burnet, and Llano Counties. The April 1871 term in Burnet lasted two weeks, and Jones left for Llano on April 14. On Tuesday morning, April 18, he was on the bench when he was "stricken with paralysis, and after an illness of only four hours, departed this life." The legal community hailed him as "our esteemed brother, as a statesman, jurist, and judge, as worthy of the respect and admiration of the present and all future members of the bar." The homage befitted a man of his stature in law and civic service. Always on the move, he had accomplished more than most men of his generation.[28]

Jones's death left the Callahan estate unsettled. Judge I. N. Everett of the Twenty-Sixth Judicial District approved James S. Callahan's request to become the executor on February 5, 1872. James supplied a $3,600 bond, which Blanco County citizens Pharr (his uncle), Capt, and C. L. Pruitt signed as sureties. His first task was to assess the estate, but with both the previous executors deceased, this proved difficult. He visited William Kenner Jones, Jones's son and co-executor of the Jones estate. In June 1873 James reported he had collected $160.50 from Jones's estate and $16 from another, and he paid $25 in attorney fees for the 1860 Lindsey settlement. Commissions, stamps for bonds, travel, and clerk's fees totaled almost $72. A substantial sum, $76.63, went to pay overdue property taxes for the land in the Williams and Eggleston Surveys. After all that, the Callahan estate possessed $3.11 in cash and 1,500 acres along the Rio Blanco. Everett approved James's report and ordered publication of a final settlement. With no objection, on October 10, 1873, Everett closed the Callahan estate and James divided the land among the surviving heirs. The documents submitted during the seventeen-year span of the probate provide an imperfect picture of the estate's total worth, but it was approximately $13,000. Disbursements amounted to about $6,800. Several notes were never paid; these totaled about $2,900.

When the estate closed, its residual worth was about $3,300, with most of that in the Williams Survey.[29]

Pettus, Jones, and young Callahan fulfilled all their duties in collecting debts, paying creditors, and supporting the estate's minor heirs. Jones also made sure that the Pittsburg Land Company partners, including himself, received their money. In the end, the estate owed no one. Disposing of personal property was easy, but selling the real estate was more challenging. Most difficult was the collection of debts. Sufficient assets existed to pay bills, but collecting the cash took time, especially during the war. In 1873, the surviving heirs still got substantial acreage. Jones made money as the executor of Callahan's estate for fifteen years—seven years after the oldest son, Wesley, became a legal adult. But criticism of him may be misplaced; he was still guardian of a Callahan minor at the time he died, and there may have been other circumstances bearing on the estate and its administration that are unknown today.

The Callahan probate reveals how nineteenth-century Texans used the courts in financial matters. Executors, creditors, and liability holders all sought relief in a courtroom because courts were the best venues for enforcing payment of unpaid obligations. Pettus and Jones frequently engaged in litigation as both plaintiff and defendant in administering the Callahan estate. Again, it must be admitted that lawyers benefited from these proceedings. During the Callahan probate, several attorneys, including Jones, received significant sums from the estate for various services. The experiences of widows and orphans in this system cannot be analyzed like an estate's fiscal holdings. Their lives could easily become little more than a brief entry in a probate report. Sarah Medissa Day, who endured the deaths of three of her family, had to place her future and that of her surviving children in the hands of an executor she hardly knew. Although Pettus and Jones were diligent in managing assets for the Callahan children, they could not shield them from such events as being sent to Georgia to live with an aunt they had never met. Yet, after the deaths of James Hughes Callahan and Sarah Medissa Callahan, the future of their legacy in the Guadalupe River Basin lay with the orphans.

CHAPTER 22

Orphans, September 1856–April 1926

"Loved and respected"

On a hot day with little breeze, a cortege trudged from the Callahan homestead to the cemetery in Pittsburg. It was the fourth time in twelve months that a Callahan had been interred there. At the front, a shrouded Sarah Medissa Day Callahan lay in her wooden coffin. Her five children—Wesley Hughes, James Sanford, Josiah Asbury, Armesida Catherine, and Mahala Caroline—trailed behind, with family, friends, and neighbors following. At the cemetery, the minister read the Holy Scripture, announcing Sarah had lived a Christian life. After the last hymn and prayer, many mourners returned home, yet the Callahan children lingered, uncertain of their fate. In the end, none of them would expand upon their father's legacy in the Guadalupe River Basin.[1]

Wesley, James, Josiah, Catherine, and Caroline initially lived with Edmund C. Pettus, their court-appointed legal guardian, at his plantation on the San Marcos River, three miles from Prairie Lea. The children had friends in the area, and ten cousins close in age within a few miles. In addition, there were six Pettus children, four of whom were the same ages as the Callahan siblings. The probate judge authorized Pettus to receive $75 per month from the Callahan estate for the maintenance of the orphans, and furthermore, he possessed considerable assets. In 1857 and 1858 the four oldest Callahans went to the local school with the older Pettus children. Later, Catherine's sound education was evident in her clear, firm script and facility for arithmetic.[2]

When William E. Jones became their guardian in the fall of 1858, the orphans returned to the Curry's Creek community in Blanco County. In the Jones home, they joined the six Jones boys, who were about their ages. Jones's homestead, according to Frederick L. Olmsted, was a picturesque place where, in addition to farming and ranching, he operated a shingle mill and general store. It is easy to understand how Wesley, James, and Josiah fit into the household. William Kenner Jones described their childhood of wrangling livestock, working the crops, stacking plows, making oxen yokes, repairing wagons, thrashing wheat, and hunting. But Catherine and Caroline must have bonded with Jones's wife, Keziah, a "feisty and determined" woman. From her the girls learned to spin and weave homegrown cotton and to make straw hats from sotol. Children in Curry's Creek attended classes in the local schoolhouse and the elder Jones, an advocate for education, also kept a library at his home. Occasionally, religious services took place in the schoolhouse. While living with the Jones family, the Callahan orphans enjoyed a well-rounded frontier lifestyle.[3]

In the summer of 1860, Jones told the probate judge that Catherine and Caroline would benefit from the "advantages of an older settled country." A sister of James Hughes Callahan had offered to take the two if Jones provided their transportation to her Georgia home. He did not tell the judge that Josiah went with his sisters, a detail that was confirmed by Catherine years later. There were in fact two of Callahan's sisters living in Walker County, Georgia. After her husband died, Margaret, James's oldest sister, relocated near her sister Nancy in Pond Springs, where she married Marcus Napoleon Bonaparte Jonathan Hampton Alley, a widowed lawyer. Nancy, Callahan's second oldest sister, had married Alexander C. Hamilton, a farmer, in 1835, about the time her brother left Georgia to fight in the Texas Revolution. The Callahan orphans arrived in Walker County by January 1861. Pond Springs lay in the central part of the county, on the western side of a valley divided by Chickamauga Creek. A typical town in the Georgia Piedmont, it had about sixty-five families by 1860 and, unlike most of Georgia with its cotton economy, local farmers planted corn and wheat as their principal cash crops.[4]

Jones described North Georgia as "older settled country," but the Callahan orphans found it to be quite the opposite. By the time they arrived, most Georgia counties favored secession, but Walker County was in turmoil and its citizens flew the United States flag at the courthouse after Georgia seceded. However, the county contributed two companies to the Thirty-Ninth Georgia Infantry, which included two Callahan cousins—Archibald

Newton Hamilton and Harvey Alley. In 1862 the wheat and corn harvests were dismal, stored corn ran out, milk cows went dry, and the locals teetered on the verge of starvation. By the middle of 1863 open resistance by bands of deserters and Unionists grew in northwestern Georgia. The bloody Battle of Chickamauga in September 1863, which included skirmishes in Pond Springs, left Walker County scarred. In October 1863 Union General Philip H. Sheridan's men killed livestock, looted larders, and drove away horses and mules, and in December young Hamilton became one of thirty-six who deserted his company. With wounded soldiers returning, dances gave way to hospital visits and schools closed. By 1864, refugees were leaving Walker County and the next year all order disappeared. When young Alley came home in the summer of 1865, he scarcely recognized his hometown.[5]

Josiah may have fallen victim to the war. He is listed in his father's 1854 will, the 1856 guardianship request made by Pettus, and the 1860 Cass County census when he was en route to Georgia with his sisters. He was fourteen when the war began, but there is no clear evidence that he joined the Confederate army. However, the roster of the Thirty-Ninth Georgia Infantry lists a J. Callahan of an unknown age who enlisted on August 3, 1862, and received $44 on January 21, 1863. This was the regiment that Josiah's cousins joined. Catherine's 1926 obituary claimed that all three of her brothers fought in the Civil War. Moreover, in all post–Civil War probate records for the Callahan estate, Josiah's name never appears. In a 1916 affidavit to the Kimble County clerk, Catherine left the most complete, yet still perplexing, perspective on Josiah's fate. She declared that "J. A. Callahan was last heard from about the time of the ending of the civil war. What become of him has never been known. He was unmarried."[6]

Few records show where the two Callahan girls were during the war, but reasonable inferences can be made. According to a 1931 newspaper, Catherine tended wounded Confederate soldiers in Walker County, so it is plausible that Caroline helped her. The sisters' aunt Nancy Hamilton appears on the 1862 and 1863 Walker County salt list. In August 1863 her husband joined the Tenth Cavalry Battalion, Georgia State Guards, in Walton County, and in 1867 he is listed on the Clarke County "Oath and Registration" ledger. Thus, Nancy and her family left Walker County before the war ended. Their other aunt Margaret also appears on the 1862 salt list, but she died in 1863. Her husband remained in Walker County even after his unit, the Sixth Cavalry Battalion, Georgia State Guards, was activated. Caroline and Catherine resided with one or both of their aunts during the first half of the war, but postwar documents indicate they spent the last two years with Marcus Alley's children in Walker County.[7]

In the aftermath of the Civil War, Georgia was in pandemonium and many left the state. Nancy and Alexander Hamilton's daughter married into the Carlock family and, after an 1865 revenge killing of the Carlock patriarch, both the Hamiltons and Carlocks relocated to Marion County, Tennessee. Meanwhile, Catherine and Caroline moved with Alley to Talladega County, Alabama. In 1870, sixteen-year-old Caroline was a housekeeper living in Coleta with George J. and Celia Mason. Her inability to read or write, recorded in the census, reveals the impact of the war on her schooling. Widower William Carlock married the Hamilton's second child, Mary Ann. This link between the Hamilton and Carlocks provided ample opportunity for Caroline to become acquainted with John W. Carlock, William's oldest son from his first marriage. In 1870, while Caroline was in Talladega County, twenty-year-old John taught school in Boone County, Arkansas. On August 10, 1871, Caroline and John married in Yell County. According to her sister Catherine and Blanco County records, the newlyweds moved to Texas, where Caroline died in childbirth on October 14, 1872. Six months later, John sold his six-month-old daughter Sarah's inherited interest in the Callahan estate and left Texas. Sarah died sometime between June 23, 1874, and September 3, 1877, but the circumstances of her death are unknown.[8]

The census taker for Millerville, Alabama, in 1870 listed Catherine as a housekeeper for Alley. By the end of the next year, Catherine joined Caroline and her husband in Blanco County, where they reunited with their brothers, Wesley and James. Subsequent records place Catherine in Blanco County for the next two decades. She had ties to Sara Harriett Pharr, the daughter of her maternal aunt Meekness Amanda "Meeky" Pharr and her husband, Augustus. After he died in March 1876, Meeky owned a boardinghouse, where Catherine may have stayed until about 1888. The 1880 census, however, records her living in Guadalupe County with another maternal aunt, Hepzibah Clemons Brill, and her husband, Solomon. Catherine lived somewhat independently. She paid taxes on the Blanco County land she inherited, which indicates she had income, and like her father she invested in land. In 1873 when the Callahan estate closed, she received an interest in 1,500 acres. From 1873 to 1893, Catherine bought and sold Blanco County land in the Williams, Eggleston, and Starrock surveys and in Johnson City, earning several thousand dollars. She also leased property and earned money selling her Johnson Day inheritance in Kimble County. By 1894, Catherine moved to Georgetown, where she worked as a seamstress and a clerk who sold fabrics and other sundries. She lived successively with grocery merchant Henry Y. Allen, widow Rosell Whittenberg, Reverend and Mrs. William B. Gilleland, and lastly, newly widowed cousin Sara.[9]

Catherine actively preserved her father's history. From 1907 through 1912 she corresponded with Texas historian James T. DeShields, Callahan Expedition member John W. Sansom, and W. R. Russell, a resident of Harper in Gillespie County. The letters focused on his days in the Texas Revolution, his Georgia roots, and the Callahan Expedition. On a more emotional level, the correspondence conveys what Catherine knew about her father's death, his sword, and family photographs. Her details appeared in a narrative constructed in the 1930s by Texas historian Harbert Davenport and have been integrated into various sections of this work. But two of her treasures have been lost. Her father posed for an 1854 or 1855 photograph; one copy was destroyed when Wesley's only child's house burned in the early 1900s, and James Sanford lost the second. Catherine had her father's sword in her possession, and even showed Sansom a photograph of it, but since her death it has disappeared. In 1926, Catherine's health deteriorated, and she died on April 4, 1926, at the age of seventy-seven. Her cousin Sara hosted the funeral at her house and bought a plot for Catherine in the Georgetown Independent Order of Odd Fellows cemetery. John N. Renfro, pastor of the Methodist church, and J. H. Sandstrom, pastor of the Swedish Methodist church, officiated; Catherine clearly remained a Methodist all her life. The obituary in the *Williamson County Sun* declared: "Miss Kate Callahan . . . was loved and respected by all who have known her"; the thirty pallbearers at her funeral suggest the esteem in which the community held her. Today, a simple granite tombstone marks her grave.[10]

After Catherine, Caroline, and Josiah left for Georgia in 1860, Wesley and his brother James remained with Jones and his family in the Curry's Creek settlement, which continued to suffer Indian raids. Jones and others complained to the governor, resulting in formation of a company of thirty-five rangers, including sixteen-year-old Wesley Callahan, led by Captain John W. Sansom. They patrolled from September through November, but they saw little action except when a few men chased a band of Indians who had killed cows and murdered a Kerrville settler.[11]

On April 17, 1861, New Braunfels attorney Hermann Seele visited the Jones residence and spoke with "three young fellows" going to San Antonio to join the Confederate army. It is believed that two of these men were Wesley and James, as two days later in San Antonio both enlisted in Company D, First Texas Mounted Riflemen. Henry E. McCulloch, an old friend of their father, was the commanding officer and the regiment's major, Ed Burleson Jr., had served in the Callahan Expedition. In the *Texas State Gazette*, McCulloch proclaimed, "Gentlemen will be found in the regiment," and greenhorns, gamblers, drunkards, and slackers were not accepted. McCulloch ordered each enlistee to ride a mature, sturdy horse equipped with a Texas saddle, blanket, and a curb-bit bridle with a single rein. Each man also had to have a canteen, durable sleeping blanket, at least one six-shooter, and either a rifle or a shotgun. Wesley's and James's horses were appraised at $50 to $80, their gear was worth $10 to $30, and they were willing to fight, so they must have met McCulloch's standards. Their comrades included a cousin, William Day, and John W. Hoyt, who had been indicted for the Blassingame murders. The brothers were present when the last federal garrison in Texas surrendered at San Lucas Springs on May 9, and then their unit was posted at Fort Chadbourne and Fort Mason as McCulloch's regiment guarded the Texas frontier. Company D patrolled in a westward arc north and south of Fort Chadbourne. In a skirmish with Comanches on June 23 one private was killed. By April 1862, each of the ten companies in the regiment had dwindled to about forty men due to death, illness, and furloughs. When the regiment disbanded that month, Wesley and James, like many soldiers in Company D, returned to civilian life.[12]

Wesley left Jones's ranch again in October 1862 to join Company I of the Third Texas Infantry. His uncle Augustus Pharr and several other Blanco County men had enlisted in the same company in June. Wesley served with Company I until September 1863, when he received an interesting new assignment. At Sabine Pass on September 8, Lieutenant Richard W. Dowling, First Texas Artillery, and perhaps sixty men repulsed a federal invasion, capturing 350 prisoners and two gunboats, the USS *Clifton* and USS *Sachem*. The Third Texas Infantry was camped a few days' march from Sabine Pass, and orders from Gen. J. Bankhead Magruder sent Wesley and several others to serve in the Texas Marine Department, aboard the renamed CSS *Clifton*. Capt. James R. Marmion reported to Magruder that its crew numbered 122, including Wesley. Assigning Texas soldiers to naval duty upset local army commanders, who lobbied to have the troops released from marine service. They succeeded, and Wesley reappeared briefly on the rolls of Company I in January and February 1864. He then disappeared from Confederate records;

descendants believe he left the army sometime in 1864 due to deteriorating health.[13]

On April 24, 1867, twenty-three-year-old Wesley married thirty-eight-year-old Lovina Pinrod Lawhon Rawls in Kendall County. She lived on her late second husband's property on Curry Creek. In Cherokee County, Lovina had married her first husband, Jesse Lawhon, on October 24, 1850, and they moved to the Curry's Creek settlement, where Jones hired Jesse as his overseer. Jesse and Lovina had two surviving children before Indians killed him on May 26, 1855. Lovina then married the elderly Reverend Daniel Rawls on January 12, 1858. Rawls had a large tract on Curry Creek that was worked by slaves, and marrying him appealed to Lovina despite a fifty-year age difference. Rawls had come to Texas with Stephen F. Austin's Old Three Hundred and fought in the Texas Revolution before settling on Curry Creek, where he built a cotton gin. He and Lovina had one child, Maria Smith Rawls, to whom he left his estate, valued at $21,175, when he died in 1862. He named Lovina as executor until Maria became an adult.[14]

When Wesley returned from the Civil War in 1864, Lovina was managing a large parcel of land and a livestock herd. Despite their age difference, marriage seemed mutually beneficial. Their only child, Alzada Clara Callahan, was born on July 18, 1868, and by 1870, they reported 14 horses, 3 mules, 20 milk cows, 4 oxen, 180 head of cattle, 85 sheep, 16 hogs, 250 bushels of corn, 3 bales of cotton, and 540 pounds of butter. During 1866, 1867, and 1868 Indian raids plagued the area. Jones wrote to the *San Antonio Ledger,* describing the raids, tallying the losses, and claiming it was "dangerous to travel" in the area. One night in October 1868 Wesley became concerned about Lovina's $500 horse he had imported from Spain. He tied it to a porch post and slept by it with two dogs to alert him. During the night, an Indian decoyed the dogs while another cut the tether, riding off on the mare. Wesley slept through the theft and was embarrassed when neighbors woke him early the next morning.[15]

Indian raids continued until 1870, when Jones and J. W. Hermann appealed to the governor, claiming their region's losses totaled almost $17,000. They were not alone, so the Adjutant General responded by authorizing the muster of fifteen companies. John W. Sansom of Curry's Creek organized Company C, enlisting fifty-eight men including Wesley H. Callahan. The rangers were sworn into service on August 25, 1870, and camped at Camp Verde, ten miles south of Kerrville. On September 11, Sansom dispatched four patrols; Wesley was in an eleven-man group that rode forty-five miles west to the divide between the Medina and Frio Rivers. No one found Indians. On October 4, Sansom organized and dispatched two large patrols. Wesley did not accompany either group. A cough had plagued him for a month, and after consulting the company's medical officer, he decided to return home. At sundown on October 6, the doctor gave Wesley a dose of medicine and he went to sleep expecting to leave in the morning. Instead, he was found dead. Sansom, in a letter printed in the *San Antonio Express*, declared that Wesley was a "good citizen" and reminded readers that he was the son of James Hughes Callahan, "well known in this State, for his military service in the days of the 'Republic'; and later for valuable services rendered on our frontier." Sansom later wrote that influenza was common during the fall of 1870, and Lovina's oldest son, John William Lawhon, recalled Wesley's weakness from his war service made him more susceptible. His gravesite is unknown; however, there are unmarked graves in the Jones Cemetery. In 2008, descendants of Curry Creek pioneers who placed a marker for Jesse Lawhon suspected the adjacent graves belonged to Rawls and Wesley. Lovina received $37.25 from the state for Wesley's service and never filed a probate. She never remarried, moved with her daughter Alzada to Oxford in Llano County, and died on December 21, 1891.[16]

Unlike Wesley, James did not return to Jones's ranch in April 1862 but went to Caldwell County, where he stayed for seven months. In November he joined Company E, commanded by his uncle Henry B. King, in the First Texas Cavalry, Arizona Brigade, at San Antonio. James's subsequent service is poorly documented, but some sources do support a story he often told later. Union soldiers captured him and a fellow soldier; both were bound and held prisoner in the back room of a house while their captors gambled, drank, and bragged about killing the captives the next morning. Alarmed, the prisoners broke their bonds, burst into the front room, and scattered the inebriated Union soldiers. The pair remained free for a day before being recaptured and sent to a federal prison. The March and April 1863 muster rolls for Company E record that Callahan had been absent on a medical furlough in Caldwell County since January. In September, Gen. Nathaniel P. Banks dispatched forces. One failed to take Sabine Pass and a second marched across south Louisiana into Texas. Banks then landed troops on the Gulf Coast from Brownsville to Matagorda Bay, some of whom occupied Mustang Island. General Magruder responded by ordering furloughed men to return to service. In Caldwell County, James responded to the call by joining the Eighth Texas Infantry or the Twenty-Fourth Battalion. Sent to the

Aransas Pass area, Confederates led by Maj. George O. Dunaway were captured on Mustang Island. James was almost certainly with this detachment as Dunaway was also imprisoned in New Orleans and both were exchanged on July 23, 1864, at Red River Landing. James then returned to Company E and remained with it until March 1865, when James, like many Texas Confederates, left for Caldwell County.[17]

James settled at Prairie Lea with Eli S. and Caroline Hankins, his uncle and aunt, but it was not family ties that lured him there. He went there to marry Sarah Elizabeth Neill. While the Callahan orphans had been with Pettus, James and Sarah began a friendship that had blossomed into romance, and they married on January 24, 1866. Sarah, like James, descended from Texas pioneers with a colorful history. Her mother, Lourahama, had come to Texas in 1825 with her parents, Francis and Sarah Elizabeth Berry, and settled near Gonzales. She married Anson G. Neal on July 25, 1838. A veteran of the Texas Revolution, Neal owned land but preferred adventure, fighting in the Federalist War along the Rio Grande in 1840 and against Indians in 1841. He joined the ill-fated 1841 Santa Fé Expedition and was left ill in El Paso. Neal's absences continued as he served with Capt. John Grumbles, whom he deserted in May 1847. He joined John S. Ford's expedition to El Paso in 1849, and in May 1850 he was in Austin. Lourahama last saw Neal in 1840, though she gave birth to a second son, Milton, in 1843. Neal was generally thought to have died and Lourahama entered into a common-law marriage with Samuel Clinton Neill about 1844 after Neill's wife died. The couple formally married on June 2, 1847, and their daughter, Sarah, was born on January 28, 1848. Samuel and Lourahama had been married for a few months when Neal appeared and filed for divorce. He claimed that in April 1839 Lourahama had "voluntarily left his bed and board and that since that time has lived in [illegible] adultery with other men . . . [and] given birth to children got in adultery." Lourahama was convicted of adultery, the Neal marriage was dissolved, and she remained married to Neill.[18]

Sarah's father was the son of James Clinton Neill, who allegedly fired the cannon in Gonzales to start the Texas Revolution. The elder Neill, a veteran of the Battle of Horseshoe Bend, moved to Austin's Colony in 1831, attended the 1833 Consultation, led the artillery during the Siege of Bexar in 1835, and commanded the Alamo until mid-February 1836. Neill headed the rear guard as Sam Houston's army retreated in the Runaway Scrape. At San Jacinto, Neill commanded the artillery; however, a wound the previous day prevented his participation in that epic battle. His son, Samuel, served in ranger companies before settling in Washington County and marrying his first wife, who died in 1844. He soon met Lourahama and the couple lived together in Gonzales County, and had four children, before he died in 1856. Sarah was the oldest. Lourahama brought to their marriage a tract from her father's survey on Plum Creek in neighboring Caldwell County. After Samuel's death, she managed her land, raised cattle, and moved to Prairie Lea.[19]

Sarah was eighteen when she married James, then twenty-one. Their marriage began under a cloud of suspicion when James and his cousin James Milford Day Jr. were arrested in Lockhart on February 23, 1866, and accused of stealing twenty oxen and two horses. At their arraignment Callahan and Day posted three bonds totaling $2,000, with sureties signed by Eli S. Hankins, Wesley H. Callahan, Lourahama Neill, George Lockhart, and J. A. Glenn. On March 29, 1866, the Caldwell County grand jury indicted both young men. Neither Callahan nor Day appeared when the court convened, and the judge ruled they had forfeited their bonds and that the guarantors were liable. The district attorney until April 1871 regularly requested warrants for Callahan and Day, which were sent to the sheriffs in Caldwell, Hays, Guadalupe, and Blanco Counties. In spring 1871, District Judge Henry Maney agreed to dismiss the three theft charges. Maney, was a personal friend of Jones, had been with James Hughes Callahan during the 1854 cattle drive, and served in the 1855 Callahan Expedition. These friendships persisted across generations, often facilitating circumvention of proper legal channels. Nevertheless, the civil cases for the forfeiture of their bonds proceeded. In the fall of 1866, Callahan, Day, and their sureties asked for a nonjury trial, which they were not granted, but during the spring of 1867 Lourahama was released from her surety commitment. Two of the civil cases then disappeared from the record, but one for $500 continued into January 1871. Once more, Maney dismissed the case but the district attorney objected so the case was restored to the docket. When no defendant appeared at the next term, Maney ruled the state could recover $500 plus legal fees. After six years, James was free of any criminal charges, but he faced the possibility that his assets could be seized.[20]

While his court case continued, James and Sarah moved to Blanco County in 1867 and by 1870 settled next to his brother Wesley in neighboring Kendall County. He worked for Wesley until his brother's death. At the time, increased livestock thefts in the Blanco County region prompted the legislature to authorize minutemen companies. So on March 7, 1873, James joined the company of Lt. S. B. Gray and was elected second sergeant. He earned $88, but $30 was deducted for the Winchester carbine he kept. Meanwhile, James continued settling his father's estate. The resolution of accounts proceeded easily; however, dividing real estate among the family proved difficult. At the closing of the estate in 1873, only James and Catherine of the Callahan orphans remained alive. On June 18, they sold part of their holdings in the Eggleston Survey for $1,500. However, a problem arose due to eight men having purchased various amounts of estate lands. All parties sought relief in the Blanco County district court and on June 23, 1874, the judge ordered a distribution. Both James and Catherine retained a significant amount of the Williams and Eggleston leagues. For several years, Blanco County tax rolls listed her as the owner of 190 acres in the Williams Survey and 145 in the Eggleston Survey. She and James also jointly owned a farm lot in the township of Pittsburg that they donated to the Methodist Church in 1888.[21]

By mid-1874, James had earned $1,750 from selling part of his inheritance and purchased 160 acres one-half mile south of the Blassingame cabin. In August 1874, however, the civil case for bond forfeiture caught up when the district court ordered him to pay $819.40, a debt he could not afford, so the sheriff seized 132 acres he owned in the Williams Survey. James's financial situation worsened, so on December 21, 1876, he sold the last parcel of his inherited land, earning $1,000. He certainly needed the money because by 1878 he and Sarah had six surviving children. Looking further afield, in 1878 they sold the homestead, making a $50 profit, and moved to Stephens County, two hundred miles north. Stephens was a new county, organized in 1876, and the Callahans settled near Crystal Falls. All the men there in the 1880 census declared they were farmers or stock raisers except Callahan and one other man, who were laborers. Stephens County was no more forgiving than Blanco County. Papa Phillips, his grandson, claimed James found it difficult to make ends meet, and in the midst of a trying time, Sarah delivered another girl and their oldest son died.[22]

By 1885 the Callahans had moved once more, settling in Wapanucka, Chickasaw Nation, Indian Territory. There rapid changes were underway. The demand for land by Anglos escalated, but the Indian nations balked, a standoff the Dawes Commission tried to resolve. A resolution in favor of the Anglos came with statehood for Oklahoma in 1907. Meanwhile, Sarah

Fig. 22.1. Sarah E. Neill Callahan, ca. 1890. Author's collection.

worked as the laundress at the Chickasaw Indian Academy for fifteen years. She was remembered as a "kind lady who would ride side saddle for miles to help someone who was sick." In a photograph taken in Oklahoma, the stresses of survival seem etched on her forty-year-old face (figure 22.1), and the resemblance to her mother, Lourahama, is remarkable. Sarah died on February 15, 1900. James's quest for financial security ended when Sarah died. He stopped working and moved back and forth between Comanche, Mills, and Brown Counties in Texas, and Coal, Johnston, and Atoka Counties in Oklahoma, living with one child and then the next (figure 22.2). He last appeared in official records on March 13, 1918, when he signed an

Fig. 22.2. James Sanford Callahan, ca. 1890. Author's collection.

affidavit in Johnston County. By most accounts, he died in Oklahoma during the 1918–1919 Spanish flu epidemic.[23]

The death of James Hughes Callahan, followed closely by the demise of his wife, Sarah Medissa, brought an end to their legacy in the Guadalupe River Basin. Their children had a less precarious existence than most orphans because of their parents' wealth and connections. The executors of the Callahan estate ensured their financial support and also tried to tend to their other needs. But the Civil War intervened in their destinies, as it did for most of their generation. Josiah's disappearance and Wesley's death were directly related to military service. Arguably, James's legal problems and financial struggles resulted from the chaos of Reconstruction. And if the Callahan girls had not been sent to North Georgia, where they also witnessed the impact of the war, Catherine and Caroline might have married into local families and indirectly sustained the family name in the Guadalupe River Basin. Instead, none of the Callahan siblings had their father's impact.

CHAPTER 23

Destinies, 1856–2012

"This is it"

The morning was a chilly 41 degrees, but the sun broke through the clouds later, warming the January day to 64; the year was 1931. Thurlow B. Weed had chosen an ideal day for his solemn duty. Driving his hearse into the Blanco City Cemetery, he spotted "two aged pioneers of Blanco County," Joe A. Speer and Thomas Durham III, waiting for him. Walking to a "small mound of rocks," Speer exclaimed, "This is it," and Durham agreed. Retrieving his shovel, Weed began to excavate the graves of James Hughes Callahan, Sarah Medissa Day Callahan, William Milford Callahan, and likely another Callahan child who had not lived long enough to have a name.[1]

With the 1936 Texas Centennial approaching, Weed had been authorized by Louis W. Kemp to collect the remains, as he had funds from the legislature to designate historic sites with markers, commission statues of notable Texans, create the San Jacinto Foundation and Park, and arrange for the remains of prominent Texans to be reburied in the Texas State Cemetery. When Edward Burleson Sr. died in 1851, future governor Andrew J. Hamilton had provided a portion of his Austin farm for Burleson's burial. Three years later the legislature purchased twenty more adjacent acres and designated it as the Texas State Cemetery. The Texas Centennial provided a perfect opportunity for Kemp to raise its profile by reinterring renowned Texans there. In addition to the Callahans, those whose remains were moved at this time included others who were influential in the settlement of the Guadalupe River Basin and had crossed paths with the Callahans. Interestingly,

Callahan was the only Pittsburg Land Company partner buried in the Texas State Cemetery.[2]

After Callahan disappeared from the Guadalupe River Basin, his family and comrades endured years of conflict. While Caldwell, Comal, Gonzales, and Guadalupe Counties voted to leave the Union and sent hundreds of men to the Confederate army, Blanco County voted against secession and became a haven for deserters and draft dodgers. The title of James W. Nichols's memoir, *Now You Hear My Horn*, meant anyone who harassed him about his Unionism would receive a blast from his shotgun. A wartime feud led to Hugh McLaurin's assassination in 1866. Some, like John W. Sansom, went to Mexico. Otto Wuppermann, the founder of Middletown, and his wife became so disillusioned that they sailed to Germany and never returned. After the war came emancipation and the emergence of African Americans as freedmen who could own land, vote, and hold office. In Guadalupe County support for freedmen's rights divided along ethnic lines, with Anglos in opposition and Germans in accord. Henry Maney took advantage of the German alliance with freedmen to be elected as a county judge even after being impeached from his district court judgeship.[3]

The demographic profile of the region also changed in other ways. After a smallpox epidemic and the exodus to Mexico, virtually no Lipans lived in Texas. Hostile campaigns by Santiago Vidaurri in 1856 and American and Mexican armies in the 1870s further reduced their number. By the close of the nineteenth century, a few lived on Mescalero reservations in the United States, while only two hundred survived in Mexico. Meanwhile, the Tonkawas relocated to the Indian Territory and were almost exterminated by other Indians during the Civil War. While Indians faded from the Guadalupe River Basin, Tejanos began to increase by the turn of the century, when they far outnumbered African Americans. Germans remained a strong component of the regional populace, although by the beginning of the twenty-first century they had been mostly assimilated.[4]

In the mid-1850s Sarah Hembree Day's extended family totaled nearly fifty in the Guadalupe River Basin, where familial bonds were strong. But in 1855, human connections in the area began to unravel. The Callahans' young son William was the first in a succession of deaths that included Mahala J. Day King, James Hughes, and Sarah Medissa, all within a twelve-month period. Sarah Hembree Day died in 1858. The date of her death is uncertain, but family tradition places her grave in the Prairie Lea Cemetery. The morning after the disastrous camp meeting on the Rio Blanco in the fall of 1857,

James Milford Day, his wife, Margaret, and their seven children packed a wagon and drove to the Callahan homestead. By 1860, Day had 700 acres, 3 horses, 165 cattle, and 40 bushels of wheat, for a personal worth of $3,700, and he received an annual pension of $100 to $200 from the state. The war and personal events reduced his status. Through 1865 he leased the Callahan place and his family lived safely in Blanco, away from Indians and bushwhackers. Day never joined an army, perhaps because of beliefs or health, but his third marriage proved contentious. Margaret died about 1863 and he married Nancy Ellen McCoy Cloud, a widow with three children who was the older sister of Eli C. Hinds's wife. They moved to Guadalupe County in 1865 and bought land. This did not solve their marital problems, so on October 8, 1866, they signed a separation agreement. The turmoil caused Day to resume gambling, and he sold the Guadalupe County land and moved to Blanco County in 1867.[5]

During Reconstruction, Day's possessions diminished to a couple of horses and a handful of cattle, two Blanco lots, and ninety acres in Kimble County. For several years about one-fourth of his worth was cash, indicating he hoarded money rather than investing in land or livestock. He deliberately continued to withdraw from society, but Nancy may have had empathy for him; they were living together again in 1870. Day continued his meager lifestyle throughout the 1870s, and Nancy again left. Nevertheless, they still did not divorce, and their relationship became more complex when his oldest son wed her oldest daughter. With his health deteriorating, in 1884 Day (figure 23.1) sold his Blanco lots and settled with a son in Gillespie County. He visited Blanco and in 1887 wrote a letter on stationery from his sister's boardinghouse asking state officials when he would get his next pension check. The federal government began paying pensions to Mexican War veterans, so he got more money. He spent his last years at his son's remote west Texas ranch, where he died on October 23, 1894, and was interred in the Klein Branch Cemetery. Nancy died a few days later in Blanco.[6]

Day's sister, Meekness Amanda, affectionately called Meeky, stayed in Blanco with her six children when her husband, Augustus Pharr, joined the Third Texas Infantry in June 1862. Meeky and other women spun and wove cloth, and the Confederate government contracted with them to make clothes for soldiers. Illness compelled Pharr in the winter of 1865 to return home. While he still had a murder charge pending in Comal County, he and Meeky resumed their life together, and she had four more children. For support, they relied on open-range ranching, buying only lots in Blanco.

Fig. 23.1. James Milford Day, ca. 1890. James Wilson Nichols Family photo file. Courtesy of the Daughters of the Republic of Texas Collection, Texas A&M University–San Antonio.

After an experiment in raising sheep, they abandoned that venture and by 1874 sold 320 acres they held in Gillespie County, earning $300. Pharr also made money in politics. In 1866 he was elected as the Blanco County tax assessor-collector, but his political career was almost cut short. Under the Reconstruction Acts of 1867, nearly four hundred Texas county officials were removed, including Pharr. The man appointed to replace him refused to serve, so Pharr remained in office until 1869. While serving as assessor-collector, Pharr built a five-room clapboard house one block east of the courthouse.[7]

Pharr's wartime service affected his health, and a steady decrease of his cattle herd and the sale of town lots by 1874 indicated he was consolidating assets. He died in Blanco in March 1876. Meeky had married daughters nearby and three younger children at home, but the two oldest sons left soon after their father's death. Meeky sold her horse and the last thirty head of cattle to start a boardinghouse, Traveler's Home. Her sturdy house near the courthouse and stage depot was suited for this. She did well; a newspaper in 1879 claimed she lived "in comfortable circumstances" and headed "a good family." In 1884, she received a windfall of $1,695 when her late husband's half of his mother's league of land in Zavala County sold. She left Blanco in 1888 and leased her house until she sold it in 1894 for $300. She settled in Marble Falls, thirty-five miles north of Blanco, and according to family tradition she died there in November 1896.[8]

Meeky's sister Mahala died forty years before her in 1856. Mahala's husband, Henry B. King, unable to cope with their young children, sent four to his brother and kept the two oldest boys. He revealed in a letter a decade later that losing Mahala was overwhelming. He sold his homestead in Guadalupe County, earning $1,825, but borrowed money from Edmund C. Pettus to buy another parcel nearby. By 1858 he settled in Prairie Lea, bought and sold town lots, and served as secretary of the Shiloh Baptist Church. He believed his April 1859 marriage to Eliza Jane Culberson, a widow from Bexar County, would rekindle a happy family life. In the spring of 1861, that changed. He wrote his last minutes for the church in March, and later claimed that on April 10, 1861, Eliza abandoned him, refusing "to perform the part and duty of a wife."[9]

Henry must have viewed going to war as an escape from his troubled life. He enrolled in the Fourth Texas Infantry, went to Virginia, and worked for the brigade commissary. His tasks irritated his shoulder, so he requested a medical discharge that was granted on July 25, 1862. Collecting $113.13 in back pay, he returned to Seguin and decided to form his own company. Recruiting was difficult, though his son John did enlist, and by November 24, 1862, Henry and the few men he had gathered were in the Second Texas Cavalry of the Arizona Brigade and stationed at Camp Colorado on the Texas frontier. In early 1863, a reorganization placed Henry's company in the First Texas Cavalry of the Arizona Brigade, commanded by Col. Peter Hardeman from Prairie Lea. Henry and his men rendezvoused at Camp Goodrich, near Victoria, then bivouacked at Camp Bankhead in Indian Territory until April 1864. The regiment then went to Arkansas, where it fought at Poison Springs, at Massard Prairie near Fort Smith, and at the Second Battle of Cabin Creek. The Texans killed and captured many Union soldiers, collecting weapons, supplies, horses, mules, and cattle. In the spring of 1865, with Confederate forces in disarray, Henry again requested a medical discharge. Considering his age (forty-seven) and past ill health, a regimental surgeon endorsed his request, which was approved.[10]

Before his discharge, Henry returned to Caldwell County once on furlough. On April 16, 1864, he asked the district court there for a divorce from Eliza, stating that she "continued to live separate and apart." By March 1865 she countersued, accusing him of abandonment and asking the court to award her their town lots in Prairie Lea. In September 1865 the judge combined both cases and the jury granted a divorce, giving Eliza the lots and bringing an end to what had become a hostile relationship. How and when they met may have contributed to the unhappiness. Eliza had inherited land and money when her first husband died. She had been appointed as his executor and allowed Henry to become her coexecutor, an unusual arrangement since husbands usually did this role. The estate closed in the fall of 1860, six months before Henry claimed she abandoned him, suggesting a connection.[11]

Nineteen months after his divorce, Henry was a clerk in a Galveston grocery. There he wrote two heart-wrenching letters, one to his brother John R. King and the other to his sister-in-law, Ruth Eliza King. To John, Henry lamented, "My heart has been full of trouble and sometimes it feels like it will burst. . . . Still I try to live for my children, they are all I have." He added, "I was once a happy man. I had a Sweet little home with happy little faces to meet me and a kind wife to cheer me—but how it is now all Scattered Some in heaven Some on earth & without a home & myself without friends. <u>Oh</u> what <u>Sad</u> thoughts." To Eliza, Henry wrote much the same. Recalling happier times with Mahala and their children, Henry remarked that Eliza was lucky to have her family. He added an odd request: "I come plain to the point—is there any fast or slow [illegible] gal or widow what has got plenty of Dollars that wants to marry if So I am the boy if She is the gal." Whether this was a jest is hard to say. Henry closed with "Bud is well and learning very fast," indicating that despite his depression he still cared for Henry "Bud" King, his youngest child. In 1868 he paid taxes in DeWitt County on two horses valued at $125. He faced a setback in November of that year when the administrator of Pettus's estate won a judgment against him for $2,634.44, for failing to repay $1,300 of $1,700 he borrowed from Pettus in 1858. The judge ordered the sale of the last acres that Henry had, which may have been too much to bear. He died on December 11, 1868, in DeWitt County, and according to family tradition he lies in the Cuero Cemetery.[12]

At the end of the Civil War Eli S. Hankins crossed the San Marcos River and parked his cotton wagon for the last time in his yard at Prairie Lea. He and his wife, Elizabeth Caroline Day Hankins, had lost three children, but they had five who survived. To support them, he remained on the 109 acres at Prairie Lea that he had bought from the Callahans, buying only seventy additional acres in 1881. Eli had not protected his headright in Gonzales, so in 1885 he sued, won, and immediately sold that property. Before and during the war he raised cattle, keeping a herd that reached 190 head, but afterward he sold most, keeping enough for beef and milking, and grew corn for food and fodder, a pattern that continued into the 1880s. He dabbled in raising sheep and hogs and cotton but in 1874 he became a miller. There were five mills in the county, including one owned by Joseph W. Tennison on Callahan Creek at Prairie Lea. Eli purchased one-half interest in this mill and four years later bought the remaining half.[13]

Elizabeth and Eli Hankins were active in the Prairie Lea community. In 1856 they joined the Shiloh Baptist Church, and in 1858 he was ordained a deacon, which he remained for almost thirty years. When the congregation built its first building in 1870, Eli collected funds, disbursed payments, and signed the deed. The Hankins supported the Grange at Prairie Lea, with a son and son-in-law participating at the state level. The Hankins children first attended a school in Prairie Lea that the Callahans helped establish, but the youngest boy was among those photographed in front of the new two-story clapboard schoolhouse in 1881. Becoming a constable and justice of the peace involved Eli in the legal turmoil that engulfed Prairie Lea throughout Reconstruction. Prairie Lea had more than its share of violence, intimidation, and conflict between the black and white communities, and Eli endorsed a letter to the governor asking for troops to be sent there. When his term expired in 1871, he was appointed as his precinct's cattle and hide inspector.[14]

While the Hankins's business thrived, Eli's health deteriorated, and he died on November 2, 1887. His children claimed that he never fully recovered from the brutal labor and exposure he endured while hauling cotton during the war. Usually the Shiloh Baptist Church minutes were succinct and not personal, but when Eli died, they noted that: "He was ordained to the Deacons in 1857 and labored in that office with credit unto himself and the cause til his death. Though ready for his coming Lord, death came upon him in an unexpected moment while standing upon his feet he fell asleep in Jesus." After Eli's death Elizabeth managed the family business. Her photograph, probably made about the time Eli died, reveals a proud, confident

Fig. 23.2. Elizabeth C. Day Hankins, obituary photo, *San Antonio Express*, March 15, 1911. Author's collection.

woman whose slight smile suggests a likable disposition (figure 23.2). She sold sixty acres, generating $1,000 to provide a financial base. Tax rolls indicate her main focus was the mill, though she kept milk cows and raised hogs. Her two daughters living in Prairie Lea died, so for a year Elizabeth fostered an infant granddaughter. Her other children moved away, leaving Elizabeth alone to manage the mill. She died on March 2, 1911, at the age of eighty, after being ill for six weeks. Her obituary noted that she had been a member of the Shiloh Baptist Church for fifty-five years, and that she "bore her suffering with the fortitude that characterized her." The $14,580 value of her mill is a testament to her business acumen.[15]

After the judge dismissed the murder charges against John W. Nichols in the spring of 1860, he and his wife, the former Mary M. Day, returned to their home on San Geronimo Creek, three miles east of Seguin. Living nearby was Mary's sister, the former Hepzibah Clemons Day, and her husband, Solomon W. Brill. Their lives paralleled each other. By 1860, the Brills and Nichols each had five children, and the families on their small homesteads together had nearly 700 head of livestock, 500 pounds of butter, and 100 pounds of cheese, but raised no cash crops. Open-range ranching provided their main income. Only the oldest boy in each family joined the Confederate army. Their fathers did not volunteer for the local home guards, though John later said the Confederate government hired him to haul cotton to the Rio Grande. The war's chaos halved both families' livestock and total wealth. Both tried to regrow their herds but by the early 1870s resorted to growing cotton to earn money, an undertaking they had rejected since 1838.[16]

Wartime disruptions also led to legal problems for the Brills and Nicholses. In May 1863, Judge Alexander W. Terrell appointed as temporary district attorney the irascible Andrew J. Neill, who convinced the grand jury to issue thirty-nine indictments, including several against men that he felt had wronged him. These included Solomon Brill, John Nichols, and their friend Thomas Hicklin, a wealthy rancher. Hicklin and Neill kept the court in bedlam. Nichols was hauling cotton to the Rio Grande, but once home he became indignant, beat Neill with a chair, and was arraigned for assault and battery. Brill, Nichols, and Hicklin were found not guilty or the charges were dismissed. During the late 1860s, Brill and his son were indicted six times for livestock thefts and accused a dozen times of not submitting cowhides to the county court as required. Only Solomon was convicted on one count and sent to jail for eight days; all other charges were dropped. Then the Brills became pawns in a political dispute. Democrats regained most state offices in 1874, but German Texans and freedmen in Guadalupe County continued to elect Republicans to local offices. One was Brill's son-in-law James F. McKee, the county judge. Another was Sheriff John F. Gordon, an early Seguin settler and friend of the Brills and McKees. The local Democrats were led by John Ireland, a former Confederate officer and conservative leader in the Constitutional Convention of 1866. After Reconstruction, he became an associate justice of the Texas Supreme Court. From 1874 to 1876, Gordon was removed three times by the district judge but was reelected each time. He petitioned the Supreme Court, which rebuked the judge, infuriating Ireland. During this conflict, Solomon and his son, McKee, and Gordon's nephew were indicted eight times for stealing cattle or failing to send cowhides to the county court. The editor of the *Galveston Daily News* sarcastically noted that this was for the "relief of Mr. John Ireland, who had been trying to get out and keep out of office this sheriff Gordon for several years." Eventually, all defendants were found not guilty or the charges were dismissed.[17]

The Nicholses also lost lawsuits for not paying debts, and three parcels of their land were sold on the courthouse steps. Seguin attorney S. N. Elliott sued John for not paying his fees in the Blassingame murder case. The district court ruled in Elliott's favor, and he obtained a lien on John's cotton. The sheriff could not find the cotton, so John got the charges dropped. In another case, Sarah Hembree Day's family fought among themselves. Henry B. King used money from the sale of his homestead to buy property on Geronimo Creek that was later sold to the Nicholses, who lost it in a lawsuit. The King children, believing they still owned the land, sued their uncle John and won in the district court. Into the 1880s the Nicholses, like the Brills, lived on small farms, owning a few horses and cows, churning a pound of butter and gathering a dozen eggs each day, and annually harvesting bushels of corn, wheat, peas, beans, and peaches. They quit free-range ranching and sold their last cotton in 1873. During these years, the Brills' wealth averaged about $1,400 each year, while for the Nicholses it was $2,000. By 1882 the Brills had reduced their homestead to 80 acres, while the Nicholses sold parcels until they owned 200 acres.[18]

Fittingly, given how intertwined their lives had been, John Nichols died at the age of seventy-six on December 29, 1882, ten days after the death of eighty-one-year-old Solomon Brill. Solomon was buried in the Holland-Brill Cemetery located on his homestead. Descendants believe John is also interred there. In anticipation of his demise, John and his wife, Mary, divided their homestead and John prepared his will. It is uncertain when Mary left their farm, but she did not pay any taxes after 1882 because the settlement of three lawsuits had resulted in a total loss of her property. In 1900 Mary, who was eighty-one years old, lived in Victoria County with her daughter. No record documents when she died or where she is buried. Solomon left no will and his estate was not probated as Hepzibah continued to occupy their 80-acre farm alone for over a decade, tending a horse or two and a few cattle. Most of her children moved elsewhere in Texas, and about 1900 she went to Fayette County to live with a daughter. On March 19, 1916, ninety-three-year-old Hepzibah died in Harris County. Newspapers noted that she was survived by three daughters, eighteen grandchildren, and thirty-six great-grandchildren. Her probate revealed she still had the 80-acre farm, the last part of Guadalupe County owned by a child of Sarah Hembree Day. She was buried beside her husband.[19]

Apart from James Hughes and Sarah Medissa Day Callahan, Sarah Hembree Day's extended family contributed to locally developing the frontier of Texas. It is noteworthy that both men and women help to stake out and protect the fragile Texas frontier around Seguin during the Republic of Texas and they left a legacy of churches, roads, government, schools, and two towns. To be sure, they were mostly good people, and they worked hard as farmers, ranchers, businessmen, and even local politicians. It should be noted that the daughters of Sarah Hembree Day were strong; four survived their husbands, and two supported themselves by operating businesses. This was in addition to what all six accomplished by raising their families, often in the absence of husbands away on business, military service, or other duties. But among the Day family, James and his wife, Sarah, were the pioneers who pushed the Texas frontier west up the Guadalupe River Basin and helped to defend it. And that is why historian Louis W. Kemp decided they should be in the Texas State Cemetery (figures 23.3, 23.4).

Fig. 23.3. The Callahans' tombstone (*front*). Texas State Cemetery, Austin. Author's collection.

Fig. 23.4. The Callahans' tombstone (*back*). Texas State Cemetery, Austin. Author's collection.

Kemp contacted Sarah Harriett Ford of Georgetown, having concluded that she was the closest living Callahan relative. Sarah was the daughter of Meeky and Augustus Pharr, and it was her cousin Catherine Callahan who kept the Callahan family bible. Sarah agreed to allow James to be reinterred but insisted Sarah and their son William be reburied with him. Kemp agreed and, after obtaining $250 from the legislature, he contracted with the Waxahachie Marble and Granite Company for a tombstone. The funds also paid Thurlow Weed, an Austin funeral home owner, to exhume and rebury the Callahans in the Republic Hill section of the state cemetery. Weed placed the "moulded bones" he found under a "pile of weather beaten rocks" in one casket. Exhumation occurred on Thursday, January 22, 1931, and the reburial took place on Saturday. Reverend Daniel N. Crieder of the Austin

Presbyterian Church gave an invocation, and Victor B. Gilbert, legislative representative for Callahan County, read a eulogy. During the Texas Centennial many reburials occurred in the Texas State Cemetery, but James and Sarah are unique as the only parents with a child reburied with them. In fact, it is almost certain that two are interred with them. William Milford Callahan died on September 6, 1855, and was the first burial in the Blanco Cemetery. However, Sarah shortly before her death delivered a boy who died at birth or soon after, a child who was not recorded in the family Bible but who was remembered by Callahan descendants. He was buried beside his father and brother, next to where his mother was interred days later. James, Sarah, William, and the unnamed son were buried for almost seventy-five years before they were disinterred. No one told Kemp there were four Callahans, and Joe A. Speer and Thomas Durham III, born after the Callahans' deaths, had no knowledge of a fourth child. Experts say that unless a person is specifically trained, they will not recognize infant remains. Little wonder that Weed believed that he exhumed only three bodies when in fact he collected the remains of four.[20]

Like other episodes in the lives of the Callahans, inaccuracies on their tombstone in the Texas State Cemetery are hard to explain. Official correspondence indicates that Sarah copied dates from Catherine's Bible to another one, then shared the transcribed records with Kemp. At one point, Kemp asked if it was possible in the process that incorrect dates were recorded. He even presented Ford with copies of 1856 newspaper articles documenting that the Callahans died in 1856, but she insisted the year was 1857. Compounding the errors, Kemp used the date of April 7 for Callahan's death, probably based upon Calvin Blassingame's letter. Moreover, his research on the Georgia Battalion led him to conclude Callahan was born in Marion, Georgia, which also was etched onto the tombstone. Subsequent research has confirmed that James was born in Jefferson, in Jackson County, Georgia; he was killed on April 8, 1856, and Sarah died the same year. In 1996, local historian Curtis Chubb notified the Texas State Cemetery of the errors and asked whether a bronze plaque or stone marker could be set beside the original monument to correct them. Gerron Hite, the cemetery preservation coordinator, maintained the tombstone was itself a historic artifact that could not "be changed or altered." Thus, correcting the record about the lives of the Callahans will remain the purview of publications such as this.[21]

In 1858, the Texas legislature named a new county in honor of James Hughes Callahan, just two years after he died and three years since the

Callahan Expedition had made him a figure of greater historical importance. The topography of Callahan County transitions from the Cross Timbers in the east to the Llano Estacado in the west. As if reflecting Callahan himself, farming transitions to ranching in Callahan County. In the southern part, the Llano Estacado tapers to a series of elongated hills, with periodic gaps, that extend southeast almost 140 miles. Named the Callahan Divide, this feature separates the two largest internal watersheds in Texas, the Brazos River to the north and the Colorado River to the south. Considering the Callahans' development instincts and their role in the westward movement of the Texas frontier, Callahan County and the Callahan Divide are aptly named.[22]

Appendix

San Antonio Committee on Slave Recovery, Letter to Emilio Langberg (translation), Siglo Diez y Nueve, November 12, 1855, Boletín Oficial, October 24, 1855

San Antonio, August 25, 1855—

Dear Colonel—
We, the ones that have signed below, who have heard the news of your achievement in revolutionizing the State of Cohahuila, of which you currently command, and we who hold great esteem for you and for your good feelings toward both borders, address this communication to you.

We would like to know what can be done about retrieving the black fugitives in Mexico that belong to Texan citizens.

This business is of utter importance to Texas, and we send the carrier of this missive with the objective of obtaining your opinion on this essential matter, and we hope that you will be kind enough to answer the following questions.

1. Can something be done about this business, and when.
2. The number of blacks that can be recovered.
3. The amount that should be paid for each black transported to the other side of Rio Grande, and in what place.
4. The manner in which the payment should be made.

We do not involve ourselves in this business because of personal interests, but to recover and return the black fugitives to their owners, thus securing the owners' future properties by discouraging their properties from emigrating from our country, which was the reason for their detainment.

All returned blacks will be treated according to our laws, giving all proprietors time to claim their properties.

Our future decisions and actions depend entirely on the report that you give us; in the meantime we will prepare to act with promptness.

With respect, yours faithfully—B. Lacoste, O. Evans, M. B. Knot, Janbpusk, M. S. M. Geellam, G. Martin, A. Milshell, T. S. Hcevill, M. Killeo, H. Debray

I certify, on my word of honor, that I have tried to translate this letter word for word.
Piedras-Negras, August 31, 1855—George A. Gisher

Notes

ABBREVIATIONS

ACSH	Archivo de Cancelados, Sección de Historias
ADAH	Alabama Department of Archives and History
AGEC	Archivos General del Estado de Coahuila
AGENL	Archivos General del Estado de Nuevo León
AHC	Austin History Center
AMM	Archivo del Municipio Monclova
BHMFP	Ben and Henry Eustace McCulloch Family Papers
BIA	Bureau of Indian Affairs
BRBML	Beinecke Rare Book and Manuscript Library
BWML	Bryan Wildenthal Memorial Library, Sul Ross State University
CAH	Dolph Briscoe Center for American History
CC	County Clerk
CCM	Commissioners Court Minutes
CR	Church Records
DATWC	D. A. T. Walton Collection
DAM	Dirección de Archivo Militar
DBBL	Daniel Baugh Brooks Letters
DC	District Clerk
DCFR	District Court Final Records
DCM	District Court Minutes
DCR	District Court Records
DHC	Davenport, Harbert, Collection
DHP	Davenport, Harbert, Papers
DP	Dancy, Jon Winfield Scott, Papers
DRTL	Daughters of the Republic of Texas Library
EBP	Burleson, Edward, Jr., Papers
EMPP	Elisha Marshall Pease Papers
Exp.	Expediente (File)
FCMO	Fondo Colonias Militares de Oriente
FSXIX	Fondo Siglo XIX

FU	Furman University
GSA	Georgia Archives
GSG	Georgia Surveyor General
HAAP	Harvey Alexander Adams Papers
HBTO	*Handbook of Texas Online*
HOC	History of Coahuila
JBDL	James B. Dukes Library
JSFP	John Salmon Ford Papers
JTDSP	J. T. DeShields Papers
JWNP	Nichols Papers
KC	Kemp, L. W., Collection
KWPP	Kenneth Wiggins Porter Papers
LFP	Lindsey Family Papers
LV	Library of Virginia
M	Microfilm
MEOP	Morris Edward Opler Papers
MMR	Músquiz, Mexico, Records
MR	Muster Roll
MSBP	Miles S. Bennet Papers
NAB	National Archives Building, Washington, D.C.
NACP	National Archives, College Park, Md.
NARA–SW	National Archives and Records Administration–Southwest Region, Fort Worth, Tex.
NCSA	North Carolina State Archives
NGPP	Niles–Graham–Pease Papers
NOP	*New Orleans Picayune*
NYPL	New York Public Library
NYTimes	*New York Times*
OM	Operaciones Militares
OR	*War of the Rebellion: Official Records of the Union and Confederate Armies*
PCFH	Phillips–Callahan Family History
PL	Probate Ledger
PM	Probate Minutes
PR	Probate Record
PWAP	Pitts, William A., Papers
RTMR	Republic of Texas Military Roll
SA	Saltillo Archives
SBHLA	Southern Baptist Historical Library and Archives
SCDHA	South Carolina Department of History and Archives
SDPJ	Sarah Day Prayer Journal
SEDENA	Secretaría de la Defensa Nacional
SGM	Secretaría de Guerra y Marina
SM	Sección Militar
SR	Service Records
SWHQ	*Southwestern Historical Quarterly*
TA	Texas Agency
TAC	Tax Assessor-Collector

TAGD	Texas Adjutant General's Department
TGLO	Texas General Land Office
TNSLA	Tennessee State Library and Archives
TR	Tax Roll
TRMR	Texas Ranger Muster Rolls
TRR	Texas Ranger Records
TSG	*Texas State Gazette*
TSLA	Texas State Library and Archives
TSSR	Texas Secretary of State Registers
TST	*Texas State Times*
TTR	*Telegraph and Texas Register*
VF	Vertical File
VSCE	Vidaurri, Santiago, Correspondencia Extranjeros
VSCP	Vidaurri, Santiago, Correspondencia Particular
WC	Wuppermann Collection
WMP	Washington Daniel Miller Papers

INTRODUCTION

1. For a comprehensive biography on James Clinton Neill, see C. Richard King, *James Clinton Neill.* Neill's life is summarized in chapter 22.

CHAPTER 1

1. Kate Callahan to J. T. DeShields, Sept. 15, 1907, Box 9, Folder 434, J. T. DeShields Papers (hereafter JTDSP), Daughters of the Republic of Texas Library (hereafter DRTL); *Texas State Gazette* (hereafter TSG), May 24, 1856; L. W. Kemp to Waxahachie Marble and Granite Company, Dec. 9, 1930, Box 2R245, L. W. Kemp Collection (hereafter KC), Dolph Briscoe Center for American History (hereafter CAH); Henry Beckman, telephone conversation with author, Aug. 2011. Beckman worked for the Waxahachie Marble and Granite Company; he described the sandblasting technique.

2. *Columbus Enquirer*, Nov. 29, 1855; *New Orleans Picayune* (hereafter *NOP*), Apr. 27, 1856; *Southern Banner*, May 1, 8, 1856; Callahan to DeShields, Sept. 15, 1907, Box 9, Folder 434, JTDSP, DRTL.

3. Muir, "State Cemetery."

4. Callahan to DeShields, Sept. 15, 1907, Box 9, Folder 434, Kate Callahan to J. W. Sansom, Sept. 15, 1907, Box 11, Folder 579, JTDSP, DRTL.

5. Wall, *Davie County,* frontispiece (map), 6–7, 38–39, 61, 73–77, 288–92; Callahan, *Callahan*, 6, 9; Kenneth Whitehead, married a Callahan descendant, telephone conversations and e-mails with author, various dates 2009–13, 2018; Ben F. Callahan, Callahan descendant, telephone conversations and e-mails with author, various dates 2009–12, 2018; Patty Callahan Walker, Callahan descendant, interviews, telephone conversations, and e-mails with author, various dates 2011–13; Estates Records, John K. Kellahan, 1765, Rowan County, North Carolina State Archives (hereafter NCSA); Tax Lists, 1782, File Box G.A. 46.1, Tax Lists, 1785, 1797, File Box CR.086.928.4, Rutherford County, NCSA; Marriage Bonds, Edward Callahan, Mary Nickels, Oct. 25, 1768, Rowan County, File Box MB.085, NCSA; Court of Pleas and Quarter Sessions, 1779–1798, July Term, 1782, Jan. Term, April Term, 1783, Rutherford County, C.086.30001, NCSA; Deeds, vol. A–D, 170–71, Rutherford County, NCSA; E. Bowen, *Story,* 7, 10–11, 14, 22–23, 36–37, 60; Coleman, *History*, 75, 79 (map), 81, 85; Georgia Surveyor General (hereafter

GSG), Colonial and Headright Plat Book G, 1784–85, p. 101, M51/20, Georgia Archives (hereafter GSA), Morrow, Ga.; Wilkes County, Deeds, bk. GG, 1790–93, pp. 132–33, M43/31, GSA; Elrod, *Historical Notes*, 18, 20, 23, 30, 32 (Ga. map–1796), 33–38; Jackson County, Deeds, bk. B, 1799–1801, p. 158, M171/5, GSA; Jackson County Tax Digest, 1799, Kelough's district, M61/25, 1804, Gaitright's district, M166/55, 1810, Smith's district, M166/5, GSA; Minutes, 1796–1802, p. 114, Inferior Court, Jackson County, Jefferson, Ga.; Wills, vol. C, 3, 146, 336, Reel (hereafter R) 179, vol. E, 134, 271, R180, Maury County, Tennessee State Library and Archives (hereafter TNSLA); Probate Records (hereafter PR), Loose Records, B-1128, B-1961, Maury County, TNSLA.

6. Coleman, *History*, 110, 123; E. Bowen, *Story*, 110, 118; G. Smith, *History*, 38, 15, 43–49, 55, 68–70, 113–14.

7. Jackson County Tax Digest, 1804–10, Dept. of Revenue, p. 68, M166/5, GSA; Jackson County, Deeds, bk. G, 75, 1812–22, M161/1, Deeds, bk. L, 125, 128, 1838–43, M161/3 GSA; Jackson County Tax Digest, 1809, Thomas's district, M166/5, 1820–34, May's district, M171/B 20, 24, and Riden's district, M171/14, Dept. of Revenue, GSA; Minutes, 1796–1802, p. 50, Inferior Court, Jackson County, Jefferson, Ga.; GSG, Walton County Land Lottery Records, districts 3–4, p. 182, M285/100, GSA; GSG, Monroe County Land Lottery Records, district 10, p. 210, M285/90, GSA; Walton County, Deeds, bk. H, 125, 128, 1828–30, M122/32, GSA; Upson County, Deeds, bk. A, 218–19, 1825–30, M145/3, GSA.

8. U.S. Census, 1850, 1860, Jackson County, Ga.; *Southern Banner*, Sept. 19, 1844, May 1, 8, 1856; Estates, Chambers County, Josiah T. Callahan, Box 5, Folder 9, S2005.0795, Alabama Department of Archives and History (hereafter ADAH); Callahan Family, Family Folders, Vertical File (hereafter VF), GSA; Pitts and Champ, *Collin County*, 2:45–46; Callahan to Sansom, Sept. 15, 1907, Box 11, Folder 579, JTDSP, DRTL; Marriages, bk. ABC, pp. 162, 182, 296, 351, 356, 379, 1805–61, Jackson County, GSA; U.S. Census, 1820, 1840, 1850, 1860, 1870, 1880, Jackson County, Ga.; Jackson County, Deeds, bk. M, 1843, pp. 86, 87, M161/4, GSA; *Southern Watchman*, Aug. 29, 1858, June 3, 11, 1874; Jarrett, "Reminiscence," 5–7; PR, bk. C, 271–73, Probate Court, Jackson County, Jefferson, Ga.; Rounsavall and Rounsavill, *Richard Rounsaveil*, 2:315; U.S. Census, 1830, DeKalb County, 1840, Walton County, 1850, 1860, Walker County, Ga.

9. Marriages, bk. B, 76, Probate Court, Troup County, La Grange, Ga.; U.S. Census, 1840, 1850, Chambers County, Ala.; William Jackson Callahan Papers, 1890–1936, MS 63, Box 1, Folders 1, 11, Archives and Manuscripts Department, Pitts Theology Library, Emory University; Marriages, bk. 5, pp. 340, 789, Probate Court, Chambers County, Lafayette, Ala.; U.S. Census, 1850, 1860, 1870, Chambers County, Ala.; U.S. Census, 1880, Collin County, Tex.; SR, Wesley S. Callahan, 49th Alabama Infantry, Confederate, RG109, M331, R424, NAB; Callahan Family, Family Folders, VF, GSA; Estates, Chambers County, Josiah T. Callahan, Box 5, Folder 9, S2005.0795, ADAH; see note 5 for communications with Whitehead; Tommy Miller, Callahan descendant, James Callahan's children, telephone conversation with author, July 2011.

10. Coulter, *Georgia*, 108–9, 155–56; U.S. Census, 1850, 1860, 1870, Jackson County, Ga.; Estates, Josiah T. Callahan, Box 5, Folder 9, S2005.0795, Chambers County, ADAH.

11. Superior Court Minutes, 1796–1851, Clerk of Courts, Jackson County, Ga.; Inferior Court Minutes, 1799–1843, Jackson County, M168/16, 168/17, 168/18, GSA; *Southern Watchman*, June 3, 1874.

12. Coleman, *History*, 92–93, 100 (map), 103, 106–8, 119, 130–34; Cadle, *Land Surveying*, 7 (map), 76.

13. Graham, *Land Lottery*, 1, 3–4, 31, 39, 53–55, 85; Cadle, *Land Surveying*, 168–78; *Milledgeville Intelligencer*, Nov. 22, 1808; *Georgia Journal*, Mar. 22, 1815, Mar. 24, 1818, Jan. 30, 1827, Jan. 5, 1832; *Federal Union*, Jan. 12, 1832; *Southern Recorder*, Feb. 15, 1820; Jackson County, Lottery List, 1827, 1832, M171/24, Walton County Land Lottery Records, District 2, p. 124, M285/100, GSA.

14. *Augusta Chronicle*, July 30, 1813, July 31, 1824, Sept. 9, Nov. 11, Dec. 27, 1826, Feb. 7, 1827, Sept. 19, 1829, Feb. 27, Dec. 4, 1830; Thaxton, Thaxton, and Thaxton, *Indian Depredation*, 201–24, 361–66, 409–19; Cadle, *Land Surveying*, 161, 204, 206–7, 223, 253, 257–64, 268, 276, 279.

15. Coleman, *History*, 118 (map), 181; Gibson and Jung, *Historical Census*, n.p., table 25; Carey, *Parties*, 5–6, 35, 86; U.S. Census, 1820, 1830, 1840, 1850, Jackson County, Ga.; *Census for 1820*, p. 116; *Abstract of the Returns*, 23; *Return of the Whole Number of Persons*, 55; Jackson County Tax Digest, 1804–10, M166/5, 1820–34, M171/B 20, 24, Riden's District, M171/14, Dept. of Revenue, GSA; *Athenian*, Mar. 9, Apr. 6, 1827, Jan. 25, Apr. 18, June 3, 1828, Feb. 17, May 5, Oct. 27, Dec. 8, 1829, Mar. 9, July 20, Oct. 5, Dec. 21, 1830, Apr. 12, May 10, Aug. 16, 1831.

16. Kilpatrick, "Beginnings," 5, 7, 9; *Macon Telegraph*, Nov. 23, 1841; Elrod, *Historical Notes*, 138, 145–47; G. J. N. Wilson, *Early History*, 19, 112, 255; U.S. Census, 1870, Chambers County, Ala.; U.S. Census, 1870, Jackson County, Ga.; Chambers, *Early History*, 12.

17. G. Smith, *History*, 24, 27, 34, 40, 75, 111, 160, 513; E. Bowen, *Story*, 24, 118–19, 125; "The History of the Antioch Methodist Church, Jackson County, Nicholson, Ga.," VF, Pitts Theology Library, Emory University; Marriages, bk. ABC, 182, 1805–61, Jackson County, GSA; William Jackson Callahan Papers, 1890–1936, MS 63, Box 1, Folders 1, 11, Pitts Theology Library, Emory University; *Southern Watchman*, June 3, 1874. Reverend James Glenn married John Callahan and Nancy Lay. Several descendants of James Callahan became Methodist ministers and missionaries.

18. Hitz, "Georgia Militia Districts," 283–90; Cadle, *Land Surveying*, 496–98, 503; Carey, *Parties, Slavery, and the Union*, 126, 128; Longstreet, *Georgia Scenes*, 131–37.

19. Carey, *Parties*, 8–9; Coleman, *History*, 53–54, 116–17, 165; Spencer King, *Georgia Voices*, 148, 155, 157. Also see McWhiney, *Cracker Culture*.

20. Carey, *Parties*, 10; Longstreet, *Georgia Scenes*, 4–21, 97–105, 120–37, 152–64, 182–98; James Hughes Callahan, Box 4, Folder 14, Nichols Papers (hereafter JWNP), DRTL; *Southern Watchman*, June 3, 1874.

CHAPTER 2

1. Arrivals, June 22, 1836, New Orleans Passenger Lists, 1820–1945, RG 36, M259, R14, NAB; *Daily Advocate*, Oct. 26, 1855; Ornish, *Ehrenberg*, 212, 241, 282–83, 334, 355.

2. Campbell, *Gone*, 99–107, 108–13, 116–31, 119 (map); de la Teja et al., *Texas*, 160–64, 169–76, 181–84, 189–98; J. Jackson, *Almonte's Texas*, 9, 36; Jenkins, *Recollections*, 155; Barker, "Austin, Stephen Fuller"; Lukes, "DeWitt, Green"; Roell, "De León, Martín."

3. *Southern Banner*, May 15, 1832, Aug. 16, Nov. 15, 1834; *Macon Telegraph*, July 17, 1834; *Columbus Enquirer*, Sept. 25, 1835.

4. *Macon Telegraph*, Nov. 5, 12, 1835; *Southern Banner*, Nov. 5, 12, 1835; *Southern Recorder*, Nov. 13, 17, 1835; *Federal Union*, Nov. 6, 1835; Jenkins, *Papers*, 4:112–113;

Houston, *Thomas H. Crosby*, 4–6; Elliott, "Georgia and the Texas Revolution," 236–37, 239, 243, 315–18 and "Alabama and the Texas Revolution," 316; R. Davis, "Goliad," 25–27; J. Scarborough, "Georgia Battalion," 511–12; Cutrer, "McLeod, Hugh."

5. *Macon Telegraph*, Nov. 26, 1835; *Federal Union*, Nov. 20, 1835; *Macon Messenger*, Nov. 26, Dec. 10, 1835; R. Davis, "Goliad," 28–29; Elliott, "Georgia and the Texas Revolution," 241–42; J. Scarborough, "Georgia Battalion," 512–13; Jenkins, *Papers*, 4:112–13; S. T. Brown's letter in D. Baker, *Texas Scrap-Book*, 244; Hazlewood, "Troutman, Joanna."

6. R. Davis "Goliad," 29; *Telegraph and Texas Register* (hereafter TTR), Jan. 30, 1836; Elliott, "Alabama and the Texas Revolution," 318; "Ticknor's Company," 413–14; Elliott, "Georgia and the Texas Revolution," 242; Spellman, *Forgotten*, 18; *Mobile Commercial Register and Patriot*, Dec. 5, 1835, *Macon Messenger*, Dec. 10, 1835; Gray, *From Virginia*, 200; Lloyd, *Lloyd's Steamboat Directory*, 74–75; Davenport, "Notes from an Unfinished Study."

7. *Mobile Commercial Register and Patriot*, Dec. 5, 1835; *Dallas Morning News*, Jan. 22, 1936; Edward L. Miller, *New Orleans*, 1–5, 19–37, 72, 74, 77, 86, 129; *South-Western American*, June 8, 1853; *New Orleans Bee*, Dec. 3, 4 , 5, 6, 7, 8, 9, 11, 12, 1835; *Commercial Bulletin*, Dec. 12, 1835; *Macon Telegraph*, Nov. 19, 26, 1835; *Columbus Enquirer*, Nov. 20, 27, 1835; *Southern Recorder*, Nov. 24, 1835; *Federal Union*, Nov. 27, 1835; *Georgia Citizen*, Apr. 23, 1853; D. Baker, *Texas Scrap-Book*, 160, 244; J. Scarborough, "Georgia Battalion," 513; R. Davis, "Goliad," 29; Elliott, "Georgia and the Texas Revolution," 242; Jenkins, *Papers*, 3:112–13; Gammel, *Laws*, 2:42; Davenport, "Notes from an Unfinished Study"; Nathaniel Hoyt, Republic Claims, Archives and Information Services Division, Texas State Library and Archives (hereafter TSLA).

8. *Commercial Bulletin*, Dec. 2, 8, 12, 1835; *Spectator*, Nov. 19, 1835; *Federal Union*, Nov. 27, 1835; *Mobile Commercial Register and Patriot*, Dec. 5, 1835; *New Orleans Bee*, December 8, 12, 1835, January 4, 1836; *TTR*, January 16, 1836, October 28, November 14, 1837, September 11, 1839; *Macon Telegraph*, Nov. 26, 1835, January 21, 1836; Roller, "Capt. John Sowers Brooks," 162, 169–171; Schooners *Pennsylvania, America, Comanche*, and *Santiago*, Republic Claims, TSLA; D. B. Brooks to Robert Brooks, January 18, 1836, Daniel Baugh Brooks Letters (hereafter DBBL), 1836, 1938, CAH; R. Davis, "Goliad," 29; Elliott, "Georgia and the Texas Revolution," 242.

9. *Georgia Citizen*, Apr. 23, 1853; *South-Western American*, June 8, 1853; Jenkins, *Papers*, 3:305–306, 322–323; Odintz, "Bullock, Uriah Irwin"; Davenport, "Notes from an Unfinished Study"; Davenport, "Men of Goliad," 1–41.

10. Wharton, *Remember*, 21–28; G. Brown, *Hesitant*, 3–8, 23, 39–40, 51–55, 59, 66, 70–74; Hartmann, "Fannin, James Walker, Jr."; George R. Gilmer to J. W. Fannin, Executive Secretary's Letters Books, 1829–31, 2:77, GSA; R. Davis, "Goliad," 26–27; U.S. Census, 1830, Bibb County, Ga.; U.S. Census, 1820, 1830, Clarke County, Ga.; *Macon Telegraph*, June 11, 1831, Oct. 31, 1833, May 29, Nov. 6, 1834, Jan. 22, 1839; Roell, "Ward, William"; McCabe, *Gwinnett County, Georgia*, 551–52; Wilson, *Early History*, 298–99; *Augusta Chronicle*, Feb. 7, 1829.

11. Roller, "Capt. John Sowers Brooks," 172, 174, 177; Brooks to Brooks, Jan. 8, 1836, DBBL, CAH; *South-Western American*, June 8, 1853; *Georgia Citizen*, Apr. 23, 1853; D. W. C. Baker, *Texas Scrap-Book*, 160; R. Davis, "Goliad," 30, 34.

12. Davenport, "Notes from an Unfinished Study"; *Georgia Citizen*, Apr. 23, 1853; *South-Western American*, June 8, 1853; Isaac Ticknor, Republic Claims, TSLA; *New Orleans Bee*, Dec. 29, 1835, Jan. 6, 1836; *Mobile Commercial Register and Patriot*, Dec. 21,

30, 1835; John O. Allen, N. R. Allen, James B. Grice, E. J. D. Grinolds, John Barton, John Bright, Box 2R245, KC, CAH; *Macon Telegraph*, Nov. 12, 1835; "Biographies of Fannin's men," Davenport (Harbert) Collection (hereafter DHC), TSLA; Louis W. Kemp, "Veteran Biographies," Herzstein Library, San Jacinto; last and first names, Winn's company Muster Roll (hereafter MR), Land Grant Search, TGLO; New Orleans Passenger List, 1820–1945, RG 36, M259, R14, NAB; W. Speer and Brown, *Encyclopedia of the New West* 408–9; T. Miller, "Fannin's Men," 532; Gammel, *Laws*, 3:681, 4:1183; S. Crosby to the Texas legislature, petition, Nov. 19, 1857, Davenport, Harbert Papers (hereafter DHP), CAH; *TSG*, Nov. 23, 1850, June 18, 1853; Literary Effort: "Sabina Brown's Mournful Story," DHC, TSLA: Mona Macy, Winters family descendant, e-mail to author, 2010; Mrs. W. C. Jones Sr. to Harriett Smither, Jan. 27, 1936, DHP, CAH; Robert Casey, Brooks family researcher, e-mail, 2010; Casey and Casey, *Brooks Family History*, 7–212–14, 7–418–20; J. Brown, *History of Texas*, 1:628.

13. Huson, *Refugio*, 276–79; Davenport, "Men of Goliad," 9–10; R. Davis, "Goliad," 34–35; *Georgia Citizen*, Apr. 23, 1853; *South-Western American*, June 8, 1853; Gulick et al., *Papers*, 1: 302, 311, 313–16, 323–24; *Southern Recorder*, May 3, 1836; J. Fannin to John R. Foster & E. C. Pettus, Jan. 8, 1836, Samuel Erson Asbury Papers: 1872–1960, Cushing Memorial Library, Texas A&M University, College Station, Tex.; Roller, "Capt. John Sowers Brooks," 191; Jenkins, *Papers*, 3:445, and 4:103–106, 114, 165–66, 255–57. Kemp, "Veteran Biographies," Herzstein Library, San Jacinto; Pettus, Edward.

14. Huson, *Refugio*, 279; Davenport, "Men of Goliad," 10; *TTR*, Jan. 9, 1836; R. Davis, "Goliad," 35; *Georgia Citizen*, Apr. 23, 1853; *South-Western American*, June 8, 1853; Roller, "Capt. John Sowers Brooks," 191; Jenkins, *Papers*, 4:279–83; *Southern Recorder*, May 3, 1836; Hardin, "Plácido Benavides," 63–64.

15. Huson, *Refugio*, 282–85; Davenport, "Men of Goliad," 17–19, 21–22; R. Davis, "Goliad," 35–36, 39–41; *Georgia Citizen*, Apr. 23, 1853; *South-Western American*, June 8, 1853; Roller, "Capt. John Sowers Brooks," 178–80, 183, 188, 191, 193–94; Jenkins, *Papers*, 4:350–51, 371, 391–92, 398–400, 419, 429–30, 443–44, 5:47–48; Hendrix, "Johnson, Francis White"; Stuart Reid, *Secret War*, acknowledgements, 4–5, 124–27; Yeager, "Letter from Old Goliad," 325; O'Connor, *Presidio La Bahia*, 163–64; Daniel Baugh Brooks to Robert Brooks, Mar. 10, 1836, privately held.

16. Brooks to Brooks, Mar. 10, 1836, privately held; Burr H. Duval to William P. Duval, Mar. 9, 1836, Burr H. Duval Papers, 1836, undated, CAH; O'Connor, *Presidio La Bahia*, 126, 163–64; Yeager, "Letter from Old Goliad," 325; *Kentucky Gazette*, June 2, 1836; Roller, "Capt. John Sowers Brooks," 180–82, 185–90; James Hughes Callahan, Box 4, Folder 14, JWNP, DRTL; Davenport, "Notes from an Unfinished Study"; Huson, *Refugio*, 284–85; Barnard, *Journal*, 13–15; Davenport, "Men of Goliad," 19; Jenkins, *Papers*, 4: 429, 338–99; Grinolds, E. J. D., Box 2R245, KC, CAH.

17. Huson, *Refugio*, 286–88; Gulick et al., *Papers*, 1:341–42; Barnard, *Journal*, 13; Davenport, "Men of Goliad," 19–20; Hardin, "Plácido Benavides," 65; Santos, *Santa Anna's Campaign*, 16–17, 27, 66–68, 163 (map); Herring, *Urrea*, 13–14, 17, 23–25, 27–29, 39–41; Archivo de Cancelados, Sección de Historias (hereafter ACSH), Urrea, José, General, Exp. D/111/4/4031, DAM, SEDENA; de la Peña, *With Santa Anna*, 68; Castañeda, *Mexican Side*, 220–23; Filisola, *Memoirs*, 151, 189–90; Exp. XI/481.3/1898, DAM, SEDENA; Roller, "Capt. John Sowers Brooks," 193; F. Johnson, *History*, 1:420.

18. Barnard, *Journal*, 15–16; R. Davis, "Goliad," 43; Huson, *Refugio*, 289, 293–95; Davenport, "Notes from an Unfinished Study"; Elliott, "Georgia and the Texas Revolution," 245; F. Johnson, *History*, 1:427–28; Oberste, *Texas Irish Empresarisos*, 198–99; Davenport,

"Men of Goliad," 12, 23; "Refugio and the Texas Revolution: A Study in Contradiction," DHC, TSLA; Bonham, *Merchant*, 65; D. Baker, *Texas Scrap-Book*, 242; Ayers, "Lewis Ayers," 272–73 (Lewis Ayers); *Georgia Citizen*, Apr. 23, 1853 (Lewis M. H. Washington, Bullock's Company); *San Antonio Daily Express*, Nov. 10, 1889 (Henry Scott, Refugio Mission); *Texas Almanac* (1860), 71–72 (E. N. Hill, Refugio Mission); Jenkins, *Papers*, 7:40 (Samuel G. Hardaway, Bullock's Company); *Dallas Morning News*, Sept. 13, 1931 (Andrew Jackson Hitchcock, Wadsworth Company); *South-Western American*, June 8, 1853 (Samuel T. Brown, Bullock's Company); Foote, *Texas and Texans*, 248–249 (L. T. Pease, Bullock's Company); *Kentucky Gazette*, June 2, 1836 (Benjamin Bradford, Wyatt's Company); Literary Effort: "Sabina Brown's Mournful Story of the War at the Mission," DHC, TSLA; *Macon Telegraph*, May 12, 1836 (Richard Rutledge, Wadsworth Company); Gulick et al., eds., *Papers*, 4:237–238 (Joseph W. Andrews, Bullock's Company); Uriah I. Bullock to Charles Cotton, Mar. 31, 1836, Archives RG 4–2–46, [DOC 2012], GSA; Castañeda, *Mexican Side*, 225. Noted here is the person and cited source; hereafter only the source is cited.

19. Huson, *Refugio*, 293–295, 300–301; Ayers, "Lewis Ayers," 273; *Georgia Citizen*, Apr. 23, 1853; Foote, *Texas and Texans*, 248–249; Chapter[s] from unidentified library effort, DHC, TSLA; Oberste, *Texas Irish Empresarisos*, 199; *San Antonio Daily Express*, Nov. 10, 1889; *Texas Almanac* (1860), 71–72; Jenkins, *Papers*, 7:39–45; *Dallas Morning News*, Sept. 13, 1931; *Kentucky Gazette*, June 2, 1836; Literary Effort: "Sabina Brown's Mournful Story," DHC, TSLA; Bullock to Cotton, Mar. 31, 1836, Archives RG 4–2–46, [DOC 2012], GSA; Bonham, *Merchant*, 47, 65–66; R. Davis, "Goliad," 42, 45; *South-Western American*, June 8, 1853; *Macon Telegraph*, May 12, 1836; Davenport, "Notes from an Unfinished Study"; Castañeda, *Mexican Side*, 225; W. Dunn, "The Founding of Nuestra Senora," 174, 177, 183–84. Benjamin Bradford, acting commander of Wyatt's company, joined Ward with twenty-two men.

20. Davenport, "Notes from an Unfinished Study"; Chapter[s] from unidentified library effort, DHC, TSLA; Ayers, "Lewis Ayers," 273; *Georgia Citizen*, Apr. 23, 1853; R. Davis, "Goliad," 43; Castañeda, *Mexican Side*, 225–26; Exp. XI/481.3/1902, DAM, SEDENA; Filisola, *Memoirs*, 193; Elliott, "Georgia and the Texas Revolution," 246; Huson, *Refugio*, 298–99; *Dallas Morning News*, Sept. 13, 1931; *South-Western American*, June 8, 1853; Jenkins, *Papers*, 7:40; *Macon Telegraph*, May 12, 1836.

21. Castañeda, *Mexican Side*, 226–27; Exp. XI/481.3/1902, DAM, SEDENA; Oberste, *Texas Irish Empresarisos*, 201–2, 207–8; R. Davis, "Goliad," 43–45; *Texas Almanac* (1860), 72; Ayers, "Lewis Ayers," 273; Elliott, "Georgia and the Texas Revolution," 246; Huson, *Refugio*, 302–3; Jenkins, *Papers*, 7:40; *Macon Telegraph*, May 12, June 12, 1836; *Georgia Citizen*, Apr. 23, 1853; *Texas Almanac* (1860), 72; *San Antonio Daily Express*, Nov. 10, 1889; Foote, *Texas and Texans*, 249–50; Gulick et al., eds., *Papers*, 4:237–38; Chapter[s] from unidentified library effort, DHC, TSLA; Literary Effort: "Sabina Brown's Mournful Story," DHC, TSLA; *Federal Union*, June 2, 1836.

22. Castañeda, *Mexican Side*, 226–27; Exp. XI/481.3/1902, DAM, SEDENA; Huson, *Refugio*, 303–7; Literary Effort: "Sabina Brown's Mournful Story," DHC, TSLA; Chapter[s] from unidentified library effort, DHC, TSLA; Jenkins, *Papers*, 7:40; *Macon Telegraph*, May 12, 1836; *Georgia Citizen*, Apr. 23, 1853; *Texas Almanac* (1860), 72; *San Antonio Daily Express*, Nov. 10, 1889; Foote, *Texas and Texans*, 250–51; Gulick et al., eds., *Papers*, 4:237–38; *Kentucky Gazette*, June 2, 1836; Filisola, *Memoirs*, 195; *South-Western American*, June 8, 1853; Davenport, "Notes from an Unfinished Study."

23. Castañeda, *Mexican Side*, 227; Exp. XI/481.3/1902, DAM, SEDENA; Oberste, *Texas Irish Empresarisos*, 203; Elliott, "Georgia and the Texas Revolution," 246; R. Davis, "Goliad," 45; Huson, *Refugio*, 306–7; Bullock to Cotton, Mar. 31, 1836, Archives Records Group 4–2–46, [DOC 2012], GSA; Dimmick, *Analysis*, 31n9; Perry Davis, Republic Claims, TSLA.

24. Exp. XI/481.3/1902, DAM, SEDENA; Oberste, *History*, 204–5; R. Davis, "Goliad," 45; Huson, *Refugio*, 307–8; Literary Effort: "Sabina Brown's Mournful Story," DHC, TSLA; *Texas Almanac* (1860), 72; *San Antonio Daily Express*, Nov. 10, 1889; Gulick et al., eds., *Papers*, 4:239–40; Foote, *Texas and Texans*, 252; *Dallas Morning News*, Sept. 13, 1931; *Kentucky Gazette*, June 2, 1836.

25. Castañeda, *Mexican Side*, 227; Ayers, "Lewis Ayers," 273–75; *Texas Almanac* (1860), 72; *San Antonio Daily Express*, Nov. 10, 1889; Literary Effort: "Sabina Brown's Mournful Story," DHC, TSLA; Chapter[s] from unidentified library effort, DHC, TSLA; Huson, *Refugio*, 308–9, 312; Davenport, "Notes from an Unfinished Study."

26. Castañeda, *Mexican Side*, 227; Filisola, *Memoirs*, 194–96; Dimmick, *Analysis*, 35; Ayers, "Lewis Ayers," 275; Huson, *Refugio*, 309–11; Davenport, "Notes from an Unfinished Study"; Harbert Davenport to Harriet Smither, Jan. 10, 1929, DHP, CAH; Oberste, *Texas Irish Empresarisos*, 211; Ornish, *Ehrenberg*, 288; *Commercial Advertiser*, May 30, 1836; Harbert Davenport to Dora Bonham, Jan. 10, 1929, Bonham (Dora Dieterich) Papers, CAH.

27. Huson, *Refugio*, 364–65; R. Davis, "Goliad," 48; Castañeda, *Mexican Side*, 227; *Macon Telegraph*, May 12, 1836; *Georgia Citizen*, Apr. 23, 1853; *South-Western American*, June 8, 1853; Jenkins, *Papers*, 7:40–41; *Kentucky Gazette*, June 2, 1836; *Dallas Morning News*, Sept. 13, 1931; Perry Davis, Republic Claims, TSLA. The seven men were David J. Holt, Hugh Rogers, Monroe Bullock, Robert H. Dickinson, Richard Rutledge, O. H. Perry Davis, and Henry G. Hudson. All survived.

28. Huson, *Refugio*, 365–67; Oberste, *Texas Irish Empresarisos*, 206–7; R. Davis, "Goliad," 48; Castañeda, *Mexican Side*, 236–38; *Georgia Citizen*, Apr. 23, 1853; *South-Western American*, June 8, 1853; Jenkins, *Papers*, 7:40–41; Gulick, *Papers*, 4:239–40; Davenport, "Notes from an Unfinished Study." The thirteen men who left the Georgia Battalion during its retreat were Amos D. Kenyon, Allen Ingram, M. K. Moses, George Rounds, Joseph W. Andrews, Samuel T. Hardaway, L. T. Pease, James P. Trezevant, Charles F. Heck, B. F. Bradford, Joel D. Rains, John Bright, and Martin Moran. Hardaway slept in a canebrake the night of March 21, 1836.

29. Castañeda, *Mexican Side*, 228–39; Exp. XI/481.3/1903, DAM, SEDENA; de la Peña, *With Santa Anna*, 76–77; Dimmick, *Analysis*, 65.

30. *Georgia Citizen*, Apr. 23, 1853; *South-Western American*, June 8, 1853; Castañeda, *Mexican Side*, 239; Exp. XI/481.3/1903, DAM, SEDENA.

31. Castañeda, *Mexican Side*, 16–19, 52–62, 236, 241, 243–45; Huson, *Refugio*, 369; Elliott, "Georgia and the Texas Revolution," 248; Davenport, "The Men of Goliad," 32; Gulick, *Papers*, 4:239–40; *Georgia Citizen*, Apr. 23, 1853; Santos, *Santa Anna's Campaign*, 89–90; de la Portilla, *Diary*, 3–4; Filisola, *Memoirs*, 197–204; de la Peña, *With Santa Anna*, 83–95; Dimmick, *Analysis*, 113; Herring, *Urrea*, 51, 53; Santa Anna, *Manifiesto*, 47–48; Barnard, *Journal*, 30–31; *South-Western American*, June 8, 1853.

32. Santos, *Santa Anna's Campaign*, 89–90; Nance, "Abel Morgan," 216–20; Davenport, "Men of Goliad," 37–38; R. Davis, "Goliad," 50–52; *South-Western American*, June 8, 1853; Barnard, *Journal*, 31–35; Foote, *Texas and Texans*, 2:242; de la Teja et al., *Texas*, 211;

de la Peña, *With Santa Anna*, 86; Roell, "Shackelford, Jack"; Davenport, "Notes from an Unfinished Study"; Robert Casey, Brooks family researcher, e-mail, 2010; Casey and Casey, *Brooks Family History*, 7–212–14, 7–418–20; *Georgia Telegraph*, Apr. 16, Nov. 22, Dec. 24, 1835, Dec. 11, 1838; Mrs. L. W. to H. Davenport, Mar. 24, 1943, DHP, CAH; John M. Powers, John Aldridge, John M. Bryson, George Eubanks, Land Grant Search, TGLO; Aldridge, *Records*, 118–20; Beth Klein, Aldridge family descendant, e-mail, 2010; Beall, Josias, B., Box 2R245, KC, CAH; Cummins, *Georgia Bealls*, 23, 52–53, 66; Beall History and Family Papers, privately held; *Augusta (Ga.) Chronicle*, June 16, 1827; Hays, *Georgia Military Affairs*, 6:212, M269/14, GSA; Houston, *Thomas H. Crosby*, 2–3; T. Miller, "Fannin's Men," 526; Ely, *Descendants*, 71–72; *Columbus* [*Ga.*] *Enquirer*, Feb. 2, 1833, Feb. 12, 1836; John Eubanks to Thomas S. Gordon, Esq., July 23, 1839, DHP, CAH; Marie Lee-Walker and Craig Lee, John Anderson Lee descendants, father of Green Lee, e-mails, 2010; Huxford, *Pioneers*, 210–11; John Nobles, Lewis Sanders Nobles descendant, father of Watkins Nobles, e-mail, 2010; *TTR*, Jan. 30, 1836; David Robinson, Patrick Osborn descendant, e-mail, 2010; *Macon Telegraph*, July 23, 1835; Central Georgia Genealogical Society, *First Hundred and Ten Years*, 188.

33. J. Brown, *History*, 1:628; Castañeda, *Mexican Side*, 245–48; Ornish, *Ehrenberg*, 316; *South-Western American*, June 8, 1853; Hamilton, *Goliad Survivor*, 64; Barnard, *Journal*, 34; O'Connor, *Presidio La Bahia*, 269–274; SR: Alavez Telesoforo—Republic of Mexico, DHC, TSLA; E. Owens, *Story of Her Life*, 10; Coalson, "Alavez, Francita"; Last and first name (table 2.3), Discharge dates, Republic Claims, TSLA; *Dallas Morning News*, Sept. 13, 1931; W. N. Rowell and H. Davenport letters, 1936, DHC, TSLA; S. Moore, *Savage Frontier*, 2:154, 182, 277, 290, 306–7, 310, 341, 344, 3:12, 37, 131, 135, 166–67, 189–90, 211, 224, 226, 275, 314, 362; Spurlin, *Texas Volunteers*, 237, 242.

34. *South-Western American*, June 8, 1853; Castañeda, *Mexican Side*, 263, 281; Gen. Vicente Filisola to the commander of the Texas army, May 27, 1836, Thomas Jefferson Rusk Papers, 1824–59, CAH; James H. Callahan, J. C. P. Kennymore, James H. Barnwell, William L. Wilkinson, Republic Claims, TSLA.

35. Castañeda, *Mexican Side*, 227; Davenport, "Men of Goliad," 12, 23; Gulick, *Papers*, 4:238; Foote, *Texas and Texans*, 249; *Dallas Morning News*, Sept. 13, 1931; *South-Western American*, June 8, 1853; *Kentucky Gazette*, June 2, 1836.

36. Roller, "Capt. John Sowers Brooks," 172; Brooks to Brooks, Jan. 8, 1836, DBBL, CAH; last name of each man, Winn's company, Virtual Vault, General Name File, GSA; Georgia Military Affairs, vol. 6, M 269/14, GSA; Georgia Military Records Book, 1799–1839, GSA.

37. Castañeda, *Mexican Side*, 226–27; Davenport, "Notes from an Unfinished Study"; *Kentucky Gazette*, June 2, 1836; *Macon Telegraph*, May 12, 26, 1836; *San Antonio Daily Express*, Nov. 10, 1889; *Dallas Morning News*, Sept. 13, 1931; *Georgia Citizen*, Apr. 23, 1853; *South-Western American*, June 8, 1853; Foote, *Texas and Texans*, 252; Literary Effort: "Sabina Brown's Mournful Story," DHC, TSLA; Dimmick, *Analysis*, 31; *Federal Union*, June 2, 1836.

38. Ayers, "Lewis Ayers," 273; *Dallas Morning News*, Sept. 13, 1931; Literary Effort: "Sabina Brown's Mournful Story," DHC, TSLA; Bullock to Cotton, Mar. 31, 1836, Archives RG 4–2–46, [DOC 2012], GSA; Davenport, "Notes from an Unfinished Study"; *Kentucky Gazette*, June 2, 1836; *Macon Telegraph*, May 26, 1836; *South-Western American*, June 8, 1853.

39. Davenport, "Notes from an Unfinished Study."

40. Graham, *Land Lottery*, 159; Brooks to Brooks, Mar. 10, 1836, privately held; Roller, "Capt. John Sowers Brooks," 182–85; R. Davis, "Goliad," 26–27; Casey and Casey, *Brooks Family History*, 7–212–7–213; *Macon Telegraph*, Nov. 12, Dec. 10, 24, 1835; Basil Lamar, affidavit May 5, 1860, Land Grand Search, TGLO; Steen, "Analysis," pt. 1 (1937): 309, 329, 332, pt. 3 (1938): 328–29, 337; last and first name, Winn's company muster roll, Land Grant Search, TGLO; Miller, *Bounty and Donation*, ix, 24–34, 885–86; *Southern Recorder*, June 1, 1837; *Federal Union*, June 29, 1858; *Georgia Weekly Telegraph and Journal & Messenger*, May 20, 1873.

41. *Macon Telegraph*, Dec. 3, 10, 17, 24, 31, 1835, and Jan. 7, 21, 28, Feb. 4, 11, 18, Mar. 3, 10, Apr. 28, May 26, 1836; *Southern Banner*, Dec. 3, 10, 31, 1835, Jan. 14, 28, Feb. 18, 25, Apr. 21, 1836; *Federal Union*, May 12, 1836; *Macon Messenger*, Jan. 14, 21, June 2, 1836; *Columbus Enquirer*, May 13, 1836.

42. *Macon Telegraph*, June 9, 23, 1836; Arrivals, June 22, 1836, New Orleans Passenger Lists, 1820–1945, RG36, M259, R14, NAB; Gulick et al., *Papers*, 1:396–99; *New Orleans Bee*, June 23, 1836.

43. Arrivals, June 22, 1836, New Orleans Passenger Lists, 1820–1945, RG36, M259, R14, NAB.

44. Nixon, "Field, Joseph E."; Ornish, *Ehrenberg*, xviii, xix, 364; *Dallas Morning News*, Sept. 13, 1931; *New Orleans Bee*, June 23, 1836; *Mobile Commercial Register and Patriot*, June 30, 1836; *Austin City Gazette*, Feb. 17, 1841; *Galveston News*, May 5, 1881.

45. *Columbus Enquirer*, Mar. 9, 1837; *Acts of the Assembly of Georgia*, 327–28; Gammel, *Laws*, 4:444–45, 9:435, 27:39–41, 29:182–83; E. M. Pease to H. V. Johnson, Aug. 8, 1856, Box 301–25, Folder 33, Records of the first two terms, Texas Governor Elisha Marshall Pease (hereafter EMPP), TSLA; William F. Fannin to Elisha M. Pease, Dec. 27, 1857, Texas Governor Hardin Richard Runnels Papers, TSLA; Herschel V. Johnson to S. A. Briscoe, Nov. 15, 1855, Georgian Battalion Pay Vouchers—1855, TSLA; H. H. Waters to H. Percy Brewster, Feb. 20, 1858, Executive Secretary's Letters Books, vol. 2, Apr. 27, 1852–July 19, 1858, GSA; *TSG*, July 26, Aug. 9, 1856; "Veterans Who Fell at Refugio," DHC, TSLA; Davenport, "Men of Goliad," 1; *General Laws* (Tex. 33rd Leg.), 112; R. Davis, "Goliad," 55; *Albany News*, June 2, 30, 1976; *Journals* (Tex. Sen. 2nd Called Sess. 33rd Leg.), 225–26; Hazlewood, "Joanna Troutman"; News Items, 441.

CHAPTER 3

1. "[W]e came back to South Carolina Anderson Co[unty in] June 1828": Sarah Day Prayer Journal (hereafter SDPJ), n.p.

2. David Embray, 1749, Lists of tithables, taxable property, 1748–1818, Lunenburg County Court Records, Library of Virginia (hereafter LV); David Hembree, Granville Proprietary Land Office, Surveys, Warrants, etc., North Carolina Secretary of State, NCSA; David Hembree to David Alley, 1761, Registration of Deeds, County Court, 1752–64, pt. 1, p. 51, Orange County, CR.073.301.3, NCSA; Wheeler, *John Sallis*, 15–22; Anthony Steel agt. [*v.*] David Hembrie [Embree] & et al., Aug. Term, 1764, CR.073.301.3, Feb. Term, 1765, CR.073.301.4, William Ursury agt. [*v.*] David Embre, Feb. Term, Aug. Term, 1765, CR.073.301.4, Robert Carmichael agt. [*v.*] David Embre & Jacob Womack, May Term, 1765, CR.073.301.3, Court of Pleas and Quarter Sessions, Orange County, NCSA; Deeds 8:248, Craven County, County Plats Book 27:248, Ninety-Six District, South Carolina Department of History and Archives (hereafter SCDHA); U.S. Census, 1790, 1800, Pendleton District, S.C.; Edgar, *South Carolina*, 182–83, 212–16, 242–44,

246, 257; L. Owens, *Taproot*, 1, 4–18, 24 (map)–26, 32–45; Klein, *Unification*, 42–45, 48, 51–60, 64–65, 74–77, 83–87, 152, 247–48, 254; Conveyances, bk. I–J, 329–33, C944, bk. N, 83–84, C945, Anderson County [Pendleton District], SCDHA; David Hembree, PR, Packet 332, C1125, Anderson County Estate Papers, 1790–1878, SCDHA.

3. U.S. Census, 1790, 1800, 1810, Pendleton District, S.C.; Job Felton, Wills, bk. B, 1807–26, pp. 63–64, M46/10, Oglethorpe County, GSA; Descendants of David Hembree, VF, Anderson County Museum, Anderson, S.C.; James Hembree, Anderson County Estate Papers, 1790–1878, Packet 1187, C1150, SCDHA; Vaughn, *Lebanon Baptist Church*, 9; U.S. Census, 1790, 1800, Anderson County, S.C. James Hembree's will lists his children: Amariah (b. May 7, 1781, d. May 11, 1855), John (b. March 1783, d. ca. 1853), Hepzibah (b. ca. 1786, d. ca. 1849), Winnie (b. ca 1787, d. ca. 1870), Didama (b. ca. 1788, d. 1860), James (b. 1791, d. January 20, 1867), Mahala (b. 1793, d. ca. 1860), Sarah (b. August 6, 1795, d. 1858), and Mary Polly (b. September 29, 1796, d. May 31, 1867).

4. Ford, *Southern Radicalism*, 19–21, 24, 30–31, 33–35; Klein, *Unification*, 282–83, 285, 294–96, 300–301; Feb. Term, 1800, July Term, 1801, Mountain Creek Baptist Church, M1798–1981, Special Collections and Archives, James B. Dukes Library (hereafter JBDL), Furman University (hereafter FU); Vaughn, *Lebanon Baptist Church*, 9; Hopewell Baptist Church, M Scrapbooks, 1803–1987, M history, 1803–1981, Salem Baptist Church, M1805–1901, Hopewell Baptist, Anderson Co., box 27, Lebanon Baptist, Anderson Co., box 33, Salem Baptist, Anderson Co., box 47, South Carolina Baptist Church Files, JBDL, FU; Garrett, *Saluda*, 149–52, 158.

5. *Pendleton Messenger*, Oct. 9, 1822; Garrett, *Saluda*, 17, 19, 21, 23–24, 28–29, 32, 37, 40, 43–46, 49–53, 342–43; Oct. Term, 1838, Salem Baptist Church (Anderson County), M1837–1942, JBDL, FU.

6. Memorials and Petitions to Practice Thomsonian Medicine, Legislative Papers, 1782–1866, Series S165005, SCDHA (Hembree's petition is no. 04251); Flannery, "Early Botanical Medical Movement," 442, 445–46; *Journal of the House of Representatives of the State of South Carolina* (1842), 45, 59, 94, 130 and (1844), 86, 113, 138; *Journal of the Senate of the State of South Carolina*, 28, 72, 98, 94, 100; Conveyances, bk. I–J, 332, C944, bk. M, 595–96, C945, bk. O, 535, C946, bk. Q, 399–400, C947, bk. U, 749–40, C949, bk. V, 386–87, bk. W, 31, 465–66, C950, Anderson County, SCDHA; U.S. Census, 1820, Pendleton District, S.C.; U.S. Census, 1840, 1850, Anderson County, S.C.; Vaughn, *Lebanon Baptist Church*, 9; Garrett, *Saluda*, 260; *Charleston Courier*, Aug. 28, 1849.

7. James Hembree, PR, Packet 1187, C1150, Anderson County Estate Papers, 1790–1878, SCDHA; Garrett, *Saluda*, 97, 260.

8. "Sally Day was bornd August 6th 1795," SDPJ; Registry, St. John's Church Collection, M229, Church Records (hereafter CR), Maryland State Archives; Poland, *From Frontier to Suburbia*, xv (map), 5 (map), 25–29, 39–48, 51–59; Loudoun County, Tithables, 1758–99, R99, LV; U.S. Census, 1790, 1800, Fairfield County, S.C.; U.S. Census, 1800, Pendleton District, S.C.; Minutes, July Term, 1804, Big Creek Baptist Church (Anderson County), M1801–1936, JBDL, FU; Tax Returns, 1792, pp. 9, 10, Fairfield County, D22, SCDHA; L. Ford, *Southern Radicalism*, 44, 74–78; Edward Day, PR, Packet 176, C1120, Anderson County Estate Papers, 1790–1878, SCDHA.

9. Poland, *From Frontier*, 25–61; Loudoun County, Tithables, 1758–99, R99, LV; U.S. Census, 1790, Fairfield County, S.C.; U.S. Census, 1800, 1810, 1820, Pendleton District, S.C.; State Grants, 4:316, 21:5, 42:384, Camden District, SCDHA; Deeds, bk. K, 83–84,

255–56, R1, Fairfield County, SCDHA; Conveyances, bk. H, 448–49, C943, bk. I & J, C944, bk. M, C945, Anderson County, SCDHA; Minutes, Big Creek Baptist Church (Anderson County), M1801–1936, JBDL, FU; Abraham Mayfield, Packet 427, Estate Papers, Anderson County [District], C1128, SCDHA.

10. Deeds, bk. K, 108–9, Fairfield County, C300, SCDHA; Conveyances, bk. M, 354–56, Anderson County (Pendleton District), C945, SCDHA; U.S. Census, 1800, Pendleton District, S.C.; Ballard Day, Packet 171, C1120, Estate Papers, Anderson County, 1790–1878, SCDHA; Klein, *Unification*, 270–72, 277, 281, 289–91, 301; L. Ford, *Southern Radicalism*, 5–6, 19, 22–24, 32, 52–53, 73; Minutes, Big Creek Baptist Church (Anderson County), M1801–1936, Minutes, Bethel Association, M1802–45, JBDL, FU. Ballard and Sylvia's children were Alfred (born ca. 1793), Johnson (July 19, 1794), Ballard Jr. (ca. 1795), Middleton (ca. 1797), Hezekiah (ca. 1801), Oswald (ca. 1802), Meekness (ca. 1804), and Emma Cordie (1813).

11. Conveyances, bk. M, 374–75, 589–90, C945, Anderson County, SCDHA; Ballard Day, Packet 171, C1120, Estate Papers, Anderson County, 1790–1878, SCDHA; U.S. Census, 1800, 1810, 1820, Pendleton District, S.C.; U.S. Census, 1830, Tishomingo County, Miss.; Ballard Day, Packet 171, C1120, Estate Papers, Anderson County, 1790–1878, SCDHA.

12. "At nineteen years old," "1816 Sylvia M. Day was bornd," "But being sadly opposed," SDPJ.; Garrett, *Saluda*, 97, 260; SR, Johnson Day, Compiled Military Service Files, South Carolina, War of 1812, RG94, M602, R055, NAB; U.S. Census, 1790, 1800, 1810, Pendleton District, S.C.; Conveyances, bk. N, 51–52, C945, bk. O, 346–47, bk. P, 244–45, C946, Anderson County, SCDHA; Minutes, Big Creek Baptist Church (Anderson County), M1801–1936, Salem Baptist Church Minutes (Anderson County), M1805–1900, 1908–81, JBDL, FU; Marriage and Death Records, Pate Family Bible; Conveyances, bk. P, 477, 499, C946, Anderson County, SCDHA.

13. Conveyances, bk. P, 477, 499, C946, Anderson County, SCDHA; "in the year 1822," SDPJ; L. Ford, *Southern Radicalism*, 14–15; Edgar, *South Carolina*, 273–74; *National Intelligencer*, Sept. 28, 1821.

14. Lambert, *Tuscaloosa County*, 1:1, 5, 7, 12, 21–22, 109; Letter to wife, Apr. 20, June 2, 1821, William H. Ely letters, MSS.0484, W. S. Hoole Special Collections Library, University of Alabama; "Salley M was born 1822 dec 18th," "In January [1823] we came Back," "In October [1823] we came back," SDPJ; Coker Baptist, Sardis Baptist, M377, CR, Special Collections, Samford University Library; U.S. Census, 1820, 1830, Hall County, Ga.; Conveyances, bk. T, 224, C949, Anderson County, SCDHA.

15. Edgar, *South Carolina*, 275; L. Ford, *Southern Radicalism*, 73; *Charleston Courier*, July 16, 31, Aug. 8, 11, 18, 1824, Sept. 6, 10, 1825, June 6, 15, Aug. 22, 23, Sept. 7, Dec. 14, 1826, May 30, Dec. 8, 1827, Aug. 19, Dec. 20, 1828, Oct. 5, 13, 17, Dec. 7, 9, 1829, June 19, 1830, Aug. 20, 1831; *State Gazette*, Aug. 8, Sept. 13, 1828; "Hepzibah C. Day was bornd February 6th 1825," SDPJ; Mills, *Statistics of South Carolina*, 645–46, 677.

16. Neal's Creek Baptist Church (Anderson County), box 39, Mount Tabor Baptist Church (Anderson County), box 38, CR, JBDL, FU; Garrett, *Saluda*, 261; "June 1828 it was pleased God," SDPJ.

17. U.S. Census, 1830, Lancaster County, S.C.; "Elizabeth C Day Was bornd Oct 9th 1830," "the year 1830," "Meeky A. was bornd," SDPJ; *Charleston Courier*, May 28, 1827, May 1, Aug. 12, 1828.

18. Edgar, *South Carolina*, 276–77, 626; Conveyances, bk. U, 249, 315, Anderson County [Pendleton District], C949, SCDHA; "wee left South Carolina 1st January

1833," SDPJ; Henrietta S. Fitzhugh Diary, 72–73, 83, Special Collections Research Center, Swem Library, College of William and Mary; "Returns of the Fifth Census," U.S. Congress, House, 22nd Cong., 1st sess., 1832, H. Doc. 269, p. 28; Tax List, 1828, 1832, 1833, Hardeman County, vol. 1836, R74, TNSLA; Hardeman County Historical Commission, *Historical Sketches*, 6–7.

19. Tax Lists, 1834, 1835, 1836, Hardeman County, vol. 1836, R74, TNSLA; "Mill Creek Baptist Church," 36–37, 39–40, 42–45, Record Bk. 1824–57, CR, TNSLA; Hardeman County Historical Commission, *Historical Sketches*, maps (frontispiece), 14, 21; Wills, Hardeman County, 1:510, R34, TNSLA; "History of BHBA"; "in March wee three joined," SDPJ.

20. "Mill Creek Baptist Church," TS, 36–37, 39–40, 42–45, Record Bk. 1824–57, CR, TNSLA.

21. F. Wilson and Baumgartner, "Tennessee-Texas Land Company," 97–100; McLean, *Papers*, 10:204; Hardeman, *Wilderness*, 69–70, 121–22, 125–28, 130, 132–34, 151–52, 306–7; *National Banner and Nashville Whig*, Feb. 25, Apr. 2, July 9, Nov. 10, 1834, Jan. 26, May 6, June 12, Aug. 28, Sept. 28, Oct. 2, 7, 21, 23, Nov. 13, 27, Dec. 28, 1835, Jan. 12, Feb. 22, Mar. 25, Apr. 1, 8, May 9, 20, June 29, 1836.

22. "in March wee three joined," SDPJ; "Mill Creek Baptist Church," TS, 36–37, Record Bk. 1824–57, CR, TNSLA; Adam Miller, "Hopefield (Crittenden County)"; Kellar, "Journey Through the South," 355; J. W. Nichols, *Now You Hear*, 4–5, 12; 1835 Arkansas map, Burr, *New Universal Atlas*, 40.

23. J. W. Nichols, *Now You Hear*, xi, 5–6, 12, 166–67; George Washington Nichols family, Nichols Family Papers Collection, privately held by Billie Jo Nichols Bennett.

24. Longnecker, "Road Divided," 205–7 (map), 212–15, 217, 218–19; J. W. Nichols, *Now You Hear*, 5, 12; Burr, *New Universal Atlas*, 40; Parker, "Mirabeau B. Lamar's Texas Journal," 205; *TTR*, Oct. 26, 1835.

25. Parker, "Mirabeau B. Lamar's Texas Journal," 207–8; Handbook of Texas Online, "Gaines Ferry"; J. W. Nichols, *Now You Hear*, 12.

CHAPTER 4

1. *TTR*, Mar. 14, 1837; *Texas Republican*, Mar. 14, 1835; J. W. Nichols, *Now You Hear*, 12.

2. "Old San Antonio Road," *HBTO*, http://www.tshaonline.org/handbook/online/articles/ex004, last modified Nov. 27, 2017; Parker, *Trip to the West*, 149–50; Lundy, *Life*, 115; McCroskey, "San Augustine, TX (San Augustine County)"; Covington, "Runaway Scrape"; Francis Richards, Land Grant Search, TGLO; San Augustine County, Map 77414, Maps, TGLO; J. W. Nichols, *Now You Hear*, 12; *Twentieth Century History*, 2:402.

3. J. W. Nichols, *Now You Hear*, 12–13; *Twentieth Century History*, 2:402; *Commercial Advertiser*, Feb. 24, 1837; *NOP*, Mar. 8, 1837; Tax Roll (hereafter TR), 1837, Tax Assessor-Collector (hereafter TAC), Nacogdoches County, TSLA; A. McDonald, "Nacogdoches, TX."

4. Jordan, "Pioneer Evaluation," 239–40; Lundy, *Life*, 119–21; Christian, "Washington-On-The-Brazos, TX"; Clay and Kleiner, "Colorado River"; Leffler, "La Grange, TX."

5. *NOP*, Sept. 14, 18, 19, 21, 25, 29, Oct. 6, 7, 1837; Reminiscences, MS, 42, 50–51, Harvey Alexander Adams Papers (hereafter HAAP), 1840–43, 1849, 1889, CAH; Rather,

"De Witt's Colony," 101, 120, 158–61, 192 (map); TR, 1837, TAC, Gonzales County, TSLA; *TTR*, Aug. 5, 1837; J. W. Nichols, *Now You Hear*, 13.

6. J. W. Nichols, *Now You Hear*, 13–14.

7. Gonzales County, 1837, 1838, box 2–9/44, Department of State, Republic of Texas Election Returns, TSLA; TR, 1837–38, TAC, Gonzales County, TSLA; Johnson Day, Justice of Peace Oath, Deeds, bk. A, 70, Gonzales County, CC; Rather, "De Witt's Colony," 102, 163–67; Commissioners Court Minutes (hereafter CCM), bk. A, 1, Gonzales County, CC; District Court Minutes (hereafter DCM), bk. 1, p. 1, Gonzales County, District Clerk (hereafter DC), Gonzales, Texas; *TTR*, Feb. 24, May 16, June 8, 1838; Gammel, *Laws*, 1:1381, 1427–28; Marriages, vol. A, 18, Gonzales County, CC; Jenkins and Kesselus, *Edward Burleson*, xi–xiv.

8. Smithwick, *Evolution*, 32, 109, 291; Johnson Day, Probate Ledger (hereafter PL), 1838, Gonzales County, CC; Hogan, *Texas Republic*, 25–28, 30–35, 45–47; *TTR*, May 2, Oct. 18, 1837, Jan. 6, 20, July 31, 1838; Gonzales County Historical Commission, *History*, 124–25.

9. J. W. Nichols, *Now You Hear*, 14, 23; Gammel, *Laws*, 1:1041–42, 1293–95; Marriages, vol. A, 1–22, Gonzales County, CC; TR, 1838–39, TAC, Gonzales County; "King Family Bible (transcript)," 47.

10. William G. Kishbaugh, "Henry B. King–Texas Ranger, 1818–68," 2002, DeWitt Colony Biographies, Sons of DeWitt Colony Texas website http://www.sonsofdewitt colony.org/; U.S. Census, 1820, Steward County, Tenn.; Circuit Court Minutes, Mar. 15, 1837, July 18, 1837, vol. 2, Stewart County, R1, TNSLA.

11. Marriages, vol. A, 1–15, Gonzales County, CC; Marriage bond, William W. Alsbury and Sarah Medissa Day, Gonzales County, 1838, Apr. 10, Folder 1, Nichols-Day Collection, DRTL; Gammel, *Laws*, 1:1293–95; Johnson Day, PL, 1838, Gonzales County, CC; K. Miller, "Alsbury, Thomas"; Allsbury or Alsbury, Thomas, Harvey, Charles G., and Horace A., Land Grant Search, TGLO; Captain Thomas Alsbury Jr. (Biography by Delbert W. Whitaker), Alsbury Collection, Brazoria County Museum of History; Bugbee, "Old Three Hundred," 110; Deposition of William W. Alsbury, 9 Oct. 1832, Correspondence and Ledger Entries, 1826–36, Despatches from U.S. Consuls in Matamoros, Mexico, 1826–1906, Records of the Department of State, RG59, M281, National Archives, College Park (hereafter NACP); Paróquias Católicas. (Catholic Church parishes). Marriages. Tamaulipas, Mexico; Barker, *Austin Papers*, 477.

12. Diary entries, July 29, 1838, and Aug. 4, 1838, Jon Winfield Scott Dancy Papers (hereafter DP) (1832–56), CAH; *Twentieth Century History* 2:402; *Day v. Alsbury*, District Court Final Records (hereafter DCFR), bk. A, 456, Gonzales County, DC; Johnson Day's birth and death, Nichols Family Papers; Johnson Day's death, Otho Benjamin Phillips to Tommy McDonald, Phillips-Callahan Family History (hereafter PCFH), 1955–77; Johnson Day's death, Michael Gonzales Papers of James Milford Day; Rather, "De Witt's Colony," 192 (map); Pat Mosher, Gonzales County archivist, e-mail, 2009.

13. Gammel, *Laws*, 1:1213–14, 2:284–306; PM, bk. A, 33, Gonzales County, CC; Johnson Day Estate, PR, Gonzales County, CC.

14. Johnson Day Estate, PR, Gonzales County, CC.

15. Gammel, *Laws*, 1:1213; Johnson Day Estate, PR, Gonzales County, CC; Johnson Day, Land Grant Search, TGLO.

16. First Minute Book of Seguin, 1, Call No. 2–231/971, TSLA; Deeds, vol. A, 113–14, 263–65, bk. E, 130, Gonzales County, CC; Neilson, "Mathew Caldwell," 478–502; Gesick, *Under*, 4, 46; Sowell, *Texas Indian Fighters*, 409–12; Humphries Branch, Joseph

Martin, Land Grant Search, TGLO; Guadalupe County, Map 3607, Maps, TGLO; Weinert, *Authentic History*, 54.

17. First Minute Book of Seguin, 2–3, Call No. 2–231/971, TSLA; Gesick, *Under*, 47–48; *Seguin Enterprise*, Apr. 1, 1938; Deeds, bk. B, 276, Gonzales County, CC; Gonzales County Historical Commission, *History*, 285–86; Miles Dikes, Land Grant Search, TGLO.

18. CCM, bk. 1, pp. 2–5, Gonzales County, CC; *Seguin Enterprise*, Apr. 1, July 31, 1896; First Minute Book of Seguin, 68, 73, 77–80, 84, Call No. 2–231/971, TSLA; *TTR*, May 1, 1839; de la Teja, "Juan N. Seguín," 213–28.

19. First Minute Book of Seguin, 35, 44, Call No. 2–231/971, TSLA; Deeds, bk. A, 20–21, bk. G. T., 140–41, Guadalupe County, CC; Deeds, bk. D, 406–7, Gonzales County, CC; Gesick, *Under*, 32 (map), 60, 62, 68; *Seguin Enterprise*, July 31, 1896; Old Ranger Station, Floyd McKee Papers and Photographs, privately held; "Feb 7th [1846]," SDPJ; Sarah Day's House, Gonzales Papers; Jarmon, "Old Ranger Station," privately held; Seth Eastman, *Sketchbook*, 41; Gesick and Seguin-Guadalupe County Heritage Museum, *Seguin*, 23; Guadalupe Regional Foundation, *Evolution*, panel 1; James Hughes Callahan, box 4, folder 14, JWNP, DRTL; Floyd McKee, e-mails, telephone conversations, 2010–18; Weinert, *Authentic History*, 95. Sarah's descendants have hearth bricks, the wood mantle, and walnut log rafters.

20. Boswell, *Her Act*, 33–44; Malone, *Women*, 53.

21. TR, 1840–46, TAC, Gonzales County, TSLA; Rather, "De Witt's Colony," 179; Sarah DeWitt, Land Grant Search, TGLO; Lukes, "DeWitt, Green"; J. W. Nichols, *Now You Hear*, xii; Marriages, bk. A, 23, Gonzales County, CC; DCM, bk. A, 50–51, Gonzales County, DC.

22. J. W. Nichols, *Now You Hear*, 41, 93; *Seguin Enterprise*, July 31, 1896; James Nicholson to My Dear Wife, June 27, 1839, Nicholson-McDowall Family Papers, 1825–91, 1907–15, 1927–31; Entries on last page and back fly page, SDPJ; Hogan, *Texas Republic*, 31–38, 46–47.

23. Henson, *Anglo-American Women*, 27, 28; entries on last page and back fly page, SDPJ; Jarmon, "Old Ranger Station," privately held.

24. "Entries on the fly page," "November 1844," SDPJ; Sowell, *Texas Indian Fighters*, 425; Weinert, *Authentic History*, 19; Brawner, *150 Years of Methodism*, chap. entitled "Women of the Church."

25. DCM, bk. 1, p. 19, Gonzales County, DC; DCFR, *Day v. Russell*, Nov. 1839, 1838–44, bk. A, 29–31, Gonzales County, DC; First Minute Book of Seguin, 3, Call No. 2–231/971, TSLA; Malone, *Women*, 23; "The Battle of Salado," transcript, p. 3, Miles S. Bennet Papers (hereafter MSBP), 1838–1900, CAH; Sowell, *Texas Indian Fighters*, 410; de la Teja et al., *Texas*, 236–38; S. Moore, *Savage Frontier*, 2:2–15, 73–80; Winfrey and Day, *Indian Papers*, 1:28–42.

26. S. Moore, *Savage Frontier*, 2:10–11, 14–18; Nance, *After San Jacinto*, 115–20; Campbell, *Gone*, 166–67.

27. *TTR*, June 16, July 21, Sept. 1, 15, Oct. 6, Nov. 3, 10, 14, 17, 24, Dec. 12, 29, 1838; Wilbarger, *Indian Depredations*, 1–2, 80–81; S. Moore, *Savage Frontier*, 2:96–97; Sowell, *Texas Indian Fighters*, 339–42.

28. Gammel, *Laws*, 2:44; S. Moore, *Savage Frontier*, 2:134, 179, 185, 193; Gulick et al., *Papers*, 2:402–3; Caldwell, Mathew, Gonzales Rangers, 1839, Oversize 401–717, Folder 8, Republic of Texas Military Rolls (hereafter RTMR), Texas Adjutant General's Depart-

ment (hereafter TAGD), TSLA; First Minute Book of Seguin, 3, 62–63, 68, 72, 74, 82, Call No. 2–231/971, TSLA.

29. Nance, *After San Jacinto*, 122–26; S. Moore, *Savage Frontier,* 2:185–90; Sowell, *Rangers*, 187, 189; Sowell, *Texas Indian Fighters*, 417, 419; *TTR*, May 1, 1839; Jenkins, *Recollections*, 84–85; J. W. Nichols, *Now You Hear*, 33; Pierce, *Texas*, 60–83.

30. J. W. Nichols, *Now You Hear*, 32–33; S. Moore, *Savage Frontier,* 2:190–93; Nance, *After San Jacinto*, 128; Sowell, *Rangers*, 186–87.

31. Sowell, *Rangers*, 189–90; Sowell, *Texas Indian Fighters*, 417; Nance, *After San Jacinto*, 128–29; D. N. Poore, David Reynolds, James M. Day, Thomas Nichols, John W. Nichols, Republic Claims, TSLA; J. W. Nichols, *Now You Hear*, 34–35; S. Moore, *Savage Frontier,* 2:193–96; Gammel, *Laws*, 3:1063, 4:1466.

32. *TTR*, May 1, 1839; S. Moore, *Savage Frontier,* 2:198–99; J. Brown, *Indian Wars*, 64–65; Sowell, *Rangers*, 190.

33. *TTR*, May 1, 21, 1839; Nance, *After San Jacinto*, 129; J. Brown, *Indian Wars*, 64–65; "Neill, Andrew," *HBTO*, http://www.tshaonline.org/handbook/online/articles/fne09, accessed June 15, 2010.

34. J. W. Nichols, *Now You Hear*, 35–38; Wilbarger, *Indian Depredations*, 156–57; Sowell, *Rangers*, 188. Nichols was mistaken since James Hughes Callahan had not arrived in Seguin.

35. J. W. Nichols, *Now You Hear*, 54; Wilbarger, *Indian Depredations*, 157–67; Caldwell, Mathew, Gonzales Rangers, 1839, Oversize 401–717, Folder 8, RTMR, TAGD, TSLA.

36. *TTR*, May 21, 1839; Hardin, "Texana, TX"; CCM, bk. 1, pp. 6–7, Gonzales County, CC; DCM, bk. 1, pp. 1–31, Gonzales County, DC; DCFR, 1838–44, bk. A, 2–77, 93–99, Gonzales County, DC.

37. DCM, bk. 1, 1–31, Gonzales County, DC; DCFR, 1838–44, bk. A, 14–15, 29–31, 69–73, 93–99, bk. B, 163, Gonzales County, DC; Deeds, bk. B, p. 163, Gonzales County, CC; Ben McCulloch, box 4, folder 17, JWNP, DRTL.

CHAPTER 5

1. *TTR*, June 23, 1841; Smither, *Journals*, 3:422–23; *Austin City Gazette*, July 28, 1841.

2. de la Teja et al., *Texas*, 16 (map); P. Abbott and Woodruff, *Balcones Escarpment*, preface.

3. La Vere, *Texas Indians*, 134–39, 169 (map); F. Smith, *Dominance*, 27, 29 (map), 34, 97–98, 104–5, 137, 162–63, 165; S. Moore, *Savage Frontier,* 2:290–94, 307–9, 314 (map), 324, 327, 329–34, 341–45, 348 (map); Wilbarger, *Indian Depredations*, 19–20; Appendix to the Journals of the House of Representatives: Fifth Congress, 125–31; TTR, Dec. 1, 18, 25, 1839; Lackman, "Howard, George Thomas,"

4. *TTR*, Jan. 31, Mar. 3, Apr. 7, 22, 28, 1840; Winfrey and Day, *Indian Papers* 1:101–2, 105–6; Brice, *Comanche Raid*, 21–26; S. Moore, *Savage Frontier,* 3:1–3, 22–27, 36–40; Weinert, *Authentic History*, 15; Gesick, *Under*, 51.

5. J. W. Nichols, *Now You Hear*, 38–40, 47–48; *Texas Sentinel*, Apr. 29, July 25, 1840; *TTR*, Apr. 22, 1849; *Brazos Courier*, Mar. 31, Apr. 7, 28, 1840; Sowell, *Rangers*, 201–2; Maverick and Maverick, *Memoirs*, 26–30, 41–42.

6. Brice, *Comanche Raid*, 28–33; S. Moore, *Savage Frontier,* 3:78–80, 82, 85–90; *TTR*, Sept. 2, 9, 15, 1840. Numerous historians have written about the 1840 Comanche Raid; a short list includes Utley, *Lone Star*, 28–32; Wilkins, *Legend Begins*, 83–85; Jenkins and Kesselus, *Edward Burleson*, 244–60. Participants left written accounts; a few are Linn,

Fifty Years, 338–44; J. W. Nichols, *Now You Hear*, 54–75; Brazos, *Life*, 53–58; Morrell, *Flower*, 124–31; Jenkins, *Recollections*, 60–68; Lee, *Three Years Among the Camanches* (1859), 25–26; W. D. Miller (*TTR*, Sept. 9, 1840). The story presented here emphasizes the role of Seguin's men.

7. Brice, *Comanche Raid*, 29, 33–37; S. Moore, *Savage Frontier*, 3:80–85, 90–94, 97, 100–102.

8. Brice, *Comanche Raid*, 37–42; 44, 48; S. Moore, *Savage Frontier*, 3:102–5, 108–18, 122–23; *TTR*, Sept. 9, Oct. 20, 1840; J. W. Nichols, *Now You Hear*, 61; H. E. McCulloch to M. P. Woodhouse, Aug. 16, 1840, Woodhouse Papers, box 2–23, folder 904, TSLA.

9. *TTR*, Nov. 14, 1840; *Brazos Courier*, Nov. 17, 1840; Brice, *Comanche Raid*, 46–47; S. Moore, *Savage Frontier*, 3:122, 125; J. W. Nichols, *Now You Hear*, 71–72; Brazos, *Life*, 58; Jenkins, *Recollections*, 68; Manns, "Great Plains Saddle," 40–42.

10. Brice, *Comanche Raid*, 31, 44–45, 49, 53, 56, 64–65; S. Moore, *Savage Frontier*, 3:87, 119–21,128, 145, 153–54, 157; J. W. Nichols, *Now You Hear*, 65–67; Jenkins, *Recollections*, 66; *TTR*, Dec. 23, 1840; Brazos, *Life*, 58; F. Smith, *Dominance*, 176;

11. Brazos, *Life*, 56; Brice, *Comanche Raid*, 42, 63; S. Moore, *Savage Frontier*, 3:22–24, 157–58; J. W. Nichols, *Now You Hear*, 64; Koury, *Arms*, 27, 29–46; *TTR*, Nov. 18, Dec. 10, 1840; Baumgartner, "History of the Alsey Silvanus Miller Homestead," Records Center and Archives, Gonzales County, Tex.

12. Caldwell, Mathew, Gonzales Rangers 1840, Oversize 401–717, folder 8, RTMR, TAGD, TSLA; Howard, George T., Army of the Republic Military Rolls, July 1–Dec. 1, 1840, Oversize 401–715, folder 6, RTMR, TAGD, TSLA; S. Moore, *Savage Frontier*, 3:137, 140, 143.

13. James H. Callahan, chap. 15, box 4, folder 17, JWNP, DRTL; Carey, *Parties*, 38, 40, 43; *TTR*, Mar. 28, 1837; *Charleston Courier*, May 1, 1837; McComb, *Galveston*, 6–8, 9 (map), 27, 39–44; J. De Cordova, *Texas*, 236.

14. Lubbock, *Six Decades*, 44–46, 49, 57; Hogan, *Texas Republic*, 40–1, 92, 129; Bollaert, *Texas*, 17; *TTR*, June 8, 1837; Holley, *Texas Diary, 1835–1838*, 36–38; Deeds, bk. A, 248, bk. C, 342–44, Gonzales County, CC; Deeds, bk. C, 330, Brazoria County, CC; James Callahan, Land Grant Search, TGLO; Lavaca County, Map 5012, Maps, TGLO.

15. Nackman, "Making of the Texan Citizen Soldier," 232, 241, 246–48, 250–51; Collins, *Texas Devils*, 3, 7; Weiss, "Texas Rangers Revisited," 621–26; J. Ford, *Rip Ford's Texas*, 81; John C. Caperton, "Sketch of Colonel John C. Hays, Texas Ranger," MS, Hays Collection, box 2R35, p. 10, CAH.

16. *TTR*, Sept. 2, 1840; S. Moore, *Savage Frontier*, 3:137–45; Caldwell, Mathew, Gonzales Rangers, Nov. 16, 1840, Oversize 401–717, folder 8, RTMR, TAGD, TSLA; Mathew Caldwell, George T. Howard, James Callahan, A. C. Acklin, Tillman Berry, Jeremiah Roberts, John Hemphill, Republic Claims, TSLA; Ford Memoirs 2:235–37, J. Ford Papers (hereafter JSFP), TSLA; Jenkins, *Recollections*, 187–91; First, last name, Gonzales Rangers, Republic Claims, TSLA.

17. *Austin City Gazette*, Aug. 26, 1840; *TTR*, Sept. 2, Dec. 2, 1840; *Brazos Courier*, Sept. 15, Nov. 17, 1840; S. Moore, *Savage Frontier*, 3:141–42, 188; Ford Memoirs 2:235–36, JSFP, TSLA; Gulick et al., *Papers*, 4, pt. 1:231; Jenkins, *Recollections*, 187–90; Sowell, *Texas Indian Fighters*, 809.

18. *Brazos Courier*, Nov. 17, 1840; *Baltimore Sun*, Nov. 28, 1840; S. Moore, *Savage Frontier*, 3:142–43; Ford Memoirs 2:236–37, JSFP, TSLA; Sowell, *Texas Indian Fighters*, 809; Jenkins, *Recollections*, 191.

19. S. Moore, *Savage Frontier,* 3:14–44; Ford Memoirs 2:237, JSFP, TSLA; Mathew Caldwell, John Hemphill, Republic Claims, TSLA; Caldwell, Mathew, Gonzales Rangers 1840, Oversize 401–717, folder 8, RTMR, TAGD, TSLA; *National Intelligencer*, Dec. 18, 1840; Gulick et al., *Papers*, 4, pt. 1:231.

20. F. Smith, *Dominance*, 176–77, 180, 245; La Vere, *Texas Indians*, 215; James H. Callahan, box 4, folder 14, JWNP, DRTL.

21. James H. Callahan, box 4, folder 14, JWNP, DRTL; Deeds, bk. B, 394, Gonzales County, CC;

22. Nance, *After San Jacinto*, 281, 288–89, 328, 336, 400–403; *Brazos Courier*, Mar. 3, Apr. 7, Sept. 15, Dec. 10, 1840; Gammel, *Laws*, 2:646–48; S. Moore, *Savage Frontier,* 3:172–73, 177–79, 181, 183–94, 210–44, 255–73, 279–89; *TTR*, Dec. 16, 23, 1840, Feb. 10, 17, 24, Mar. 24, Apr. 28, May 27, June 9, July 14, Aug. 4, Dec. 4, 1841; *Journals of the House of Representatives of the Republic of Texas: Fifth Congress, First Session*, 636.

23. Citizens of Gonzales County, Defense of the Frontier petition, Memorials and Petitions, TSLA; J. W. Nichols, *Now You Hear*, 24–26; Carrier, *One Zumwalt Family*, 127; Simon Cockrell or Cockrill, Republic Claims, TSLA; Wallace L. McKeehan, "Children of David and Mary Ann Zumwalt Burket," Sons of DeWitt Colony, http://www.sonsofdewittcolony.org/davidburketgrand.htm, accessed Mar. 24, 2018; Mary Ann Roseanna Green Rae to Margaret Mahala Green Braud/Woodrome, Jan. 1927, Zumwalt Family Papers, privately held

24. J. W. Nichols, *Now You Hear*, 23–31; Gelo, "'Comanche Land,'" 280.

25. *Autobiography of Henry Eustace McCulloch,* TS, 1, 24–25, McCulloch, Ben, and Henry Eustace McCulloch Family Papers (hereafter BHMFP), CAH; Kemp, Veteran Biographies, Herzstein Library; First and last name, McCulloch Rangers, Land Grant Search, TGLO; First and last name, McCulloch Rangers, Republic Claims, TSLA; S. Moore, *Savage Frontier,* 1:90–91, 168, 184, 216, 2:9–10, 179, 185, 193, 3:106–7, 140; *Muster Rolls of the Texas Revolution*, 25, 56, 130, 133, 152, 165, 188, 209; Hines, *Life of Eli Clemmons Hinds*, n.p.; *Twentieth Century History*, 2:401–2; Rather, "De Witt's Colony," 163–72.

26. *Autobiography of Henry Eustace McCulloch*, TS, 24–25, BHMFP, 1798–1961, CAH; Wilbarger, *Indian Depredations*, 289; Brown, *Indian Wars*, 84–85.

27. Brown, *Indian Wars*, 84–85; Hines, *Life of Eli Clemmons Hinds*, n.p.; *Twentieth Century History of Southwest Texas* 2:401–2; J. W. Nichols, *Now You Hear*, 64; Rather, "De Witt's Colony," 165; McKeehan, "The DeWitt Colony Alamo Defenders." Sons of DeWitt Colony, http://www.sonsofdewittcolony.org/gonreliefframe.htm.

28. *Autobiography of Henry Eustace McCulloch*, TS, 25, BHMFP, CAH; Ben McCulloch, James H. Callahan, Johnson Day, Wilson Randell [Randle], Sion D. Green, Land Grant Search, TGLO; Kimble County, Map 3765, Maps, TGLO; W. D. Miller to Sam Houston, July 10, 1841, box 1878/3–2, folder 25, Washington Daniel Miller Papers (hereafter WMP), TSLA.

29. Gonzales County Minute Men (James H. Callahan), Oversize 401–721, folder 2, RTMR, TAGD, TSLA; Kemp, Veteran Biographies, Herzstein Library; First and last name, Gonzales Rangers, Land Grant Search, TGLO; *Muster Rolls of the Texas Revolution*, 9, 50, 56, 72, 84, 86, 88, 98, 130, 133, 175, 187–88, 195, 207, 209, 229, 256; S. Moore, *Savage Frontier,* 1:168, 184, 2:179, 193, 198, 230, 3:106–7, 140; Marriages, bk. A, 42–43, Gonzales County, CC; First and last name, Gonzales Rangers, Republic Claims, TSLA; Rather, "De Witt's Colony," 163–72; *Texian Advocate*, Mar. 2, 1849; Sowell, *Rangers*, 107,

414; *San Luis (Tex.) Advocate*, Sept. 28, 1840; U.S. Census, 1850, Gonzales County, Tex.; Sowell, History, vi.

30. See note 29; Nichols brothers, Nichols Family Papers, privately held; U.S. Census, 1850, 1860, Guadalupe County, Tex.; U.S. Census, 1850, Gonzales County, Tex.; Brazos, *Life*, 7; Fretz, Brief History, 327–28.

31. Deeds, bk. A, 173, 205, 286, 306, bk. B, 15–19, 30, 312, 427, 465, bk. C, 2–3, 10–11, 46, 503, 506, 519–21, 582–84, 591–92, bk. D, 7, 10–11, 197–99, 280–81, Gonzales County, CC; First Minute Book of Seguin, 3, Call No. 2–231/971, TSLA; TR, 1840, 1841, 1842, TAC, Gonzales County, TSLA; Gonzales County Minute Men (James H. Callahan), Oversize 401–721, folder 2, RTMR, TAGD, TSLA.

32. Gonzales County Minute Men (James H. Callahan), Oversize 401–721, folder 2, RTMR, TAGD, TSLA; Loomis, *Texan-Santa Fé*, 215; *Daily Bulletin*, Dec. 10, 1841.

33. Smither, *Journals*, 3:422; Caperton, "Sketch of Colonel John C. Hays, Texas Ranger," MS, Hays Collection, box 2R35, pp. 15–18, CAH; Greer, *Colonel Jack Hays*, 1, 10, 15–22, 29; Weiss, "Hays, John Coffee"; Sowell, *Texas Indian Fighters*, 331–36.

34. Greer, *Colonel Jack Hays*, 49–51; Caperton, "Sketch of Colonel John C. Hays, Texas Ranger," MS, Hays Collection, box 2R35, pp. 1–10, 13–15, CAH; *Austin City Gazette*, July 7, 1841; Smither, *Journals*. 3:422–23; Hays, John C.—Company of Spies, Oversize 401–718, folder 22, RTMR, TAGD, TSLA; Perez, Antonio—Spy Company, Oversize 401–719, folder 33, RTMR, TAGD, TSLA; Sowell, *Rangers*, 197–98; Gonzales County Minute Men (James H. Callahan), Oversize 401–721, folder 2, RTMR, TAGD, TSLA; McCulloch to Woodhouse, July 22, 1841, Woodhouse Papers, box 2–23, folder 904, TSLA.

35. Smither, *Journals*, 3:423–24; Diary entry, 181, DP, CAH; *Austin City Gazette*, July 28, 1841; Real County, Map 66992, Edwards County, Map 66811, Maps, TGLO; Sowell, *Rangers*, 197–99.

36. Gonzales County Minute Men (James H. Callahan), Oversize 401–721, folder 2, RTMR, TAGD, TSLA; *Daily Bulletin*, Dec. 10, 1841; "Devil's Backbone (Comal County)," *HBTO*, http://www.tshaonline.org/handbook/online/articles/rjd10, accessed June 12, 2010; "great horse country," West Papers, privately held; *San Antonio Light*, June 6, 1915; *Daily Bulletin*, Dec. 10, 1841; searched last names of individuals owning land along the Llano River, Kimble County, Land Grant Search, TGLO; Kimble County, Map 3765, TGLO. The parcels surveyed were James Hughes Callahan, Ira Fuller, Sion D. Green, Wilson Randell [Randle], Edward Miles (two surveys), Benjamin Duncan, Abraham Roberts, Johnson Day heirs, E. D. Kelly, Ezekiel Haines (five surveys), David Dougherty, Sara Jones, E. Tibble, James Dufner, Joseph Dufner, Isaac Mitchell, Harriet M. McIlvail, Josiah Munce, Ulrich Durst, E. Ruhl, George Kimble (five surveys), and John Lee Witter.

37. *Daily Bulletin*, Dec. 10, 1841; F. Smith, *Dominance*, 105, 135, 141.

38. Hogan, *Texas Republic*, 267–90; DCM, bk. A, 10–11, 22, 28, 34–36, 38, 40–41, 44, 46, 50, 55, 68, 96, 102, 104, 107, 109, 131, 146–49, 151–54, 156, 204, 230–32, 250–51, Gonzales County, DC; CCM, 1838–45, pp. 2, 9, 15–17, Gonzales County, CC. Entries for county surveyor Arthur Swift and attorney Andrew Neill were too numerous to cite.

39. Miller to Houston, July 10, 1841, box 1878/3–2, folder 25, WMP, TSLA; *TTR*, Mar. 24, Nov. 24, Dec. 4, 15, 1841; Nance, *After San Jacinto*, 422–23.

40. Gonzales County Minute Men (James H. Callahan), Oversize 401–721, folder 2, RTMR, TAGD, TSLA; S. Moore, *Savage Frontier*, 3:358; Gammel, *Laws*, 2:574–75; *TTR*, Dec. 15, 22, 1841.

41. *TTR*, Nov. 24, Dec. 15, 22, 1841; Nance, *After San Jacinto*, 521; Utley, *Lone Star Justice*, 34.

CHAPTER 6

1. S. Moore, *Savage Frontier*, 4:57–59; Nance, *Attack*, 304, 307, 311, 320–21, 323, 337, 342–45.

2. Ramos, *Beyond*, 178–83; Nance, *After San Jacinto*, see chaps. 10–14; Nance, *Attack*, 4–8; Vigness, "Arista, Mariano."

3. *TTR*, June 16, July 21, Aug. 18, Dec. 8, 22, 1841; *NOP*, Nov. 30, Dec. 6, 8, 21, 1841; Ramos, *Beyond*, 181–82; Loomis, *Texan-Santa Fé*, 3–8, 14–15, 31 (map), 43 (map), 70 (map), 80–90, 93 (map), 112–13, 115 (map), 129 (map), 133 (map), 203, 215, 243.

4. Campbell, *Gone*, 176–78; Arista, no. 100, Nov. 27, 1841, no. 1, Dec. 29, 1841, Proclamation, Jan. 9, 1842, Orders to Vásquez and Valera, Jan. 10, 1842, Operaciones Militares (hereafter OM), 1839, 1841, 1842, Exp. XI/481.3/1728, DAM, SEDENA; "Vasquez, Rafael," *HBTO*, http://www.tshaonline.org/handbook/online/articles/fva22.

5. Arista, Feb. 21, 1842, La fuerza que marcha a Bejar, Vásquez, Mar. 18, 1842, OM, 1839, 1841, 1842, Exp. XI/481.3/1728, DAM, SEDENA; *TTR*, Feb. 23, Mar. 9, 1842; Miller to Houston, Feb. 9, Mar. 2, 1842, WMP, TSLA; Seguin, *Personal*, 22–23; Nance, *Attack*, 9–12; S. Moore, *Savage Frontier*, 4:4–6; Maverick and Maverick, *Memoirs*, 54.

6. Sowell, "Incidents Connected with the Early Settlers of Guadalupe County, Texas," 24, TZ 976.41 G93S, Littlefield Fund, unpublished, CAH; *Weekly Texian*, Mar. 9, 1842; Bexar Committee of Safety to Col. Andrew J. Neill and citizens of Seguin, Gon[zales] County, San Antonio, Feb. 27, 1842, box 2–9/8, folder 8, General Correspondence, Department of State, Republic of Texas, TSLA; Green, *Samuel Maverick* 151–52; Miller to Houston, Mar. 6, 1842, WMP, TSLA; Nance, *Attack*, 14–18; *TTR*, Mar. 16, Apr. 6, 1842; Maverick and Maverick, *Memoirs*, 54–56.

7. Creed Taylor Narrative, Vásquez Invasion, box 1, folder 52, JTDSP, DRTL; Brown, *History*, 212; Nance, *Attack*, 16–23; S. Moore, *Savage Frontier* 2:29, 71, 131, 179, 184–85, 193, 230, *3:*106–8, 138–39, 222, 337, 4:9–10; *TTR*, Mar. 16, 1842; Greer, *Colonel Jack Hays*, 63; Maverick and Maverick, *Memoirs*, 56; Miller to Houston, Mar. 7, 1842, WMP, TSLA; TR, 1841–43, TAC, Gonzales County, TSLA; *Muster Rolls of the Texas Revolution*, 84, 88, 130, 222; Vásquez Campaign (commander James H. Callahan) [Mar. 1–Apr. 1,] 1842, Oversize 401–714, Folder 6, RTMR, TAGD, TSLA; Baker, *Texas Scrap-Book*, 627; First and last name, Vásquez Campaign (commander James H. Callahan), Land Grand Search, TGLO and Republic Claims, TSLA; Mortality Schedule, U.S. Census, 1850, DeWitt County, Tex.; *Texas Democrat*, June 24, 1845; U.S. Census, 1850, Lavaca County, Tex.; *TSG*, Aug. 7, 1852.

8. Ráfael Vásquez report, Mar. 14, 1842, OM, 1839, 1841, 1842, Exp. XI/481.3/1728, DAM, SEDENA; Creed Taylor Narrative, Vásquez Invasion, box 1, folder 52, JTDSP, DRTL; Brown, *History*, 212–13; Nance, *Attack*, 24–33; *TTr*, Mar. 16, 30, Apr. 6, 1842; Miller to Houston, Mar. 9, 10, 1842, WMP, TSLA; S. Moore, *Savage Frontier*, 4:11–14; Hall, "Taylor, Creed"; Green, *Samuel Maverick*, 155; Jenkins, *Recollections*, 220.

9. "March Seguin," and "On the Eighth," SDPJ; Maverick and Maverick, *Memoirs*, 57–59; *TTR*, Mar. 16, 30, 1842; *NOP*, Mar. 16, 1842; Ráfael Vásquez report, Mar. 14, 1842, OM, 1839, 1841, 1842, Exp. XI/481.3/1728, DAM, SEDENA; Scrapbook, Mr. Valentine Bennet, Cuero, Tex., MSBP, CAH; Nance, *Attack*, 35–36, 47–51; S. Moore, *Savage Frontier*, 4:14; Miller to Houston, Mar. 13, 1842, WMP, TSLA.

10. "[T]he 11th Got to Gonzales": SDPJ; Maverick and Maverick, *Memoirs*, 59–60; Creed Taylor Narrative, Vásquez Invasion, box 1, folder 52, JTDSP, DRTL; Nance, *Attack*, 36.

11. *TTR*, Mar. 16, 30, 1842; Arista report Mar. 19, 1842, OM, 1839, 1841, 1842, Exp. XI/481.3/1728, DAM, SEDENA; Nance, *Attack*, 39–44.

12. *TTR*, Mar. 16, Apr. 20, May 4, 1842; *NOP*, Mar. 16, 17, 25, 29, 31, 1842; Nance, *Attack*, 57–63, 70–74, 83, 92–93, 98, 100–101, 114, 146–50; S. Moore, *Savage Frontier*, 4:16; Scrapbook, Mr. Valentine Bennet, Cuero, Tex., MSBP, CAH; Vásquez Campaign (commander James H. Callahan) [Mar. 1–Apr. 1,] 1842, Oversize 401–714, folder 6, Campaigns of 1842, RTMR, TAGD, TSLA; Miller to Houston, Mar. 16, 17, 1842, WMP, TSLA; Louis P. Cooke, Republic Claims, TSLA; Mar. 30, 31, 1842; Diary entries, 117, DP, CAH; Creed Taylor Narrative, Vásquez Invasion, box 1, folder 52, JTDSP, DRTL; Robert E. Cunningham, "Somervell, Alexander."

13. J. W. Nichols, *Now You Hear*, 89–90; "May the 21," SDPJ; Mariano Arista to Adrian Woll, Apr. 2, 1842, Arista, May 27, 1842, OM, 1839, 1841, 1842, Exp. XI/481.3/1728, DAM, SEDENA.

14. Payroll, Vasquez Campaign (commander James H. Callahan) [Mar. 1–Apr. 1,] 1842, Oversize 401–714, folder 6, Campaigns of 1842, RTMR, TAGD, TSLA; Gonzales County Minute Men (James H. Callahan), Oversize 401–721, folder 2, RTMR, TAGD, TAGD, TSLA; Maverick and Maverick, *Memoirs*, 58.

15. Brown, *History*, 212; Nance, *Attack*, 28.

16. Entries on last page and back fly page, SDPJ; *TTR*, Apr. 20, May 4, June 29, July 20, Aug. 17, Sept. 7, 14, 1842; *Clarksville Standard*, Sept. 3, 1842; Creed Taylor Narrative, Vásquez Invasion, box 1, folder 52, JTDSP, DRTL.

17. Mariano Arista, May 28, 1842, Isidro Reyes, May 29, 1842, Partes de los Generales Mariano Arista y Isidro Reyes, OM, 1842, Exp. XI/481.3/1739, Adrián Woll, Regimental Strength, Rio Grande, Aug. 31, 1842, OM, 1842, Exp. XI/481.3/1731, DAM, SEDENA; Woll, *Expedicion*, 4–9; Nance, *Attack*, 299, 304–11, 306 (map), 306n28; *TTR*, May 11, Aug. 17, 1842; Green, *Samuel Maverick*, 386; *Journals of the House of Representatives of the Seventh Congress of the Republic of Texas*, 18–20; J. W. Nichols, *Now You Hear*, 91; Nance, "Woll, Adrian."

18. Woll Report, Sept. 12, copied by Reyes, Sept. 20, Casualty report, Bejar Prisoners, Juan Fernandez, Sept. 11, copied by Reyes, Sept. 20, OM, 1842, Exp. XI/481.3/1735, DAM, SEDENA; Woll, *Expedicion*, 6–10, 13, 18, 20–21, 24–28, 32–33; Nance, *Attack*, 313–24, 326–28, 332; *Journals of the House of Representatives of the Seventh Congress of the Republic of Texas*, 20–21; *TTR*, Sept. 21, 28, 1842.

19. Nance, *Attack*, 335–36, 348; *Journals of the House of Representatives of the Seventh Congress of the Republic of Texas*, 21–22; Manuscript of the Mexican War by James Ramsay, 7, 9, MSBP, CAH; *TTR*, Sept. 21, Nov. 2, Dec. 21, 1842; S. Moore, *Savage Frontier*, 1:84, 76, 160, *2*:35, 85, 203, 278, 308, 344, *3*:106, 138, 4:61–65; TR, 1841–42, TAC Gonzales County; U.S. Census 1850, Gonzales, Guadalupe, Caldwell Counties, Tex.; First, last names, Land Grant Search, TGLO, and Republic Claims, TSLA; Brown, *History*, 223; *Muster Rolls of the Texas Revolution*, 69, 213, 254; Loomis, *Texan-Santa Fé*, 214.

20. J. W. Nichols, *Now You Hear*, 93; Sowell, *Rangers*, 220.

21. Loomis, *Texan-Santa Fé*, 131–32, 142; Scrapbook, Mr. Valentine Bennet, Cuero, Tex., undated newspaper articles, MSBP, CAH; *Houston Daily Post*, Oct. 14, Nov. 26, Dec. 5, 1897; Urwitz, "Valentine Bennet," 145–56; Nance, *Attack*, 336–38, 343; Manuscript of the Mexican War by James Ramsay, 6–7, MSBP, CAH; J. W. Nichols, *Now You*

Hear, 91, 93; Morrell, *Flower*, 163–64; Sowell, *Life*, 58; "Expedition Against the Southwest in 1842 and 1843," MS, 4, HAAP, CAH; *TTR*, Sept. 21, Nov. 2, 1842; *Journals of the House of Representatives of the Seventh Congress of the Republic of Texas*, 22–23.

22. Scrapbook, Mr. Valentine Bennet, Cuero, Tex., undated newspaper articles, MSBP, CAH; *Houston Daily Post*, Dec. 5, 1897; J. W. Nichols, *Now You Hear*, 93, 95; Nance, *Attack*, 343–45, 352–54; *TTR*, Sept. 21, 28, Oct. 5, Nov. 2, 1842; Woll, *Expedicion*, 31–32; de la Teja, *Revolution Remembered*, 99, 179; Manuscript of the Mexican War by James Ramsay, 8, MSBP, CAH; Morrell, *Flower*, 163–64.

23. Nance, *Attack*, 338, 343, 347–49; Manuscript of the Mexican War by James Ramsay, 10–12, MSBP, CAH; *TTR*, Sept. 21, 28, Oct. 5, Nov. 2, 1842; Biographical Note, Peck Papers, CAH.

24. Nance, *Attack*, 349–50; J. W. Nichols, *Now You Hear*, 96; Utley, *Lone Star*, 311n12; *TTR*, Nov. 2, 1842.

25. Brazos, *Life*, 71; Nance, *Attack*, 349–51, 354–59; Scrapbook, Mr. Valentine Bennet, Cuero, Tex., undated newspaper articles, MSBP, CAH; *Houston Daily Post*, Dec. 5, 26, 1897; J. W. Nichols, *Now You Hear*, 98; Woll, *Expedicion*, 35, 39–41; *Journals of the House of Representatives of the Seventh Congress of the Republic of Texas*, 16–18; Morrell, *Flower*, 167–68; *TTR*, Oct. 5, Nov. 2, 1842.

26. J. W. Nichols, *Now You Hear*, 98–99, 102; Woll, *Expedicion*, 41–42; Nance, *Attack*, 359–62; Brown, *History*, 224–25; *TTR*, Oct. 12, Nov. 2, 1842; Morrell, *Flower*, 169–70; Brazos, *Life*, 72; Scrapbook, Mr. Valentine Bennet, Cuero, Tex., undated newspaper articles, MSBP, CAH; *Houston Daily Post*, Dec. 26, 1897.

27. *Texas Democrat*, May 26, 1846 (Dawson participant account, Joseph C. Robinson); *TTR*, Sept. 28, Oct. 22, 26, Nov. 2, 16, 1842, May 3, 1843; Woll, *Expedicion*, 36–37, 42, 47; Nance, *Attack*, 363, 366–68, 375–76; Morrell, *Flower*, 170–72; J. W. Nichols, *Now You Hear*, 103–4, 108; Brown, *History*, 226–27; Sowell, "Incidents Connected with the Early Settlers of Guadalupe County," 37, CAH; Davis, "Dawson, Nicholas Mosby"; Brazos, *Life*, 71–72.

28. Brazos, *Life*, 72; *TTR*, Sept. 21, 28, Oct. 26, Nov. 2, 1842, May 3, 1843; Nance, *Attack*, 376, 382–87, 389–99, 406; Woll, *Expedicion*, 48–50; J. W. Nichols, *Now You Hear*, 109, 113; Smithwick, *Evolution*, 253.

29. Woll, *Expedicion*, 9, 46–47, 53, 55–56; Nance, *Attack*, 352–53, 362, 373, 378–80, 389–99, 406; J. W. Nichols, *Now You Hear*, 113; *Galveston Civilian*, Jan. 28, 1843; *TTR*, Sept. 28, Oct. 26, Nov. 2, 1842.

30. Woll, *Expedicion*, 18, 46; Wilkins, *Legend Begins*, 67; Woll's Invasion, Creed Taylor narrative, JTDSP, DRTL.

31. Sowell, *Rangers*, 225; *Seguin Enterprise*, Feb. 5, 1937; *Seguin Bulletin*, Mar. 22, 1934; J. W. Nichols, *Now You Hear*, 117–19; Gonzales County Historical Commission, *History*, 530–31.

32. Nance, *Attack*, 407; "Expedition Against the Southwest in 1842 and 1843," MS, 1, HAAP, CAH; McCutchan, *Mier*, 199, 201.

33. TR, 1842–46, TAC, Gonzales County; TR, 1846–52, TAC, Guadalupe County, TSLA; Ramos, *Beyond*, 191–95; Nance, *Attack*, 10, 53–54; de la Teja, "Juan N. Seguín," 226; Deeds, bk. C, 53–56, bk. D, 586–88, bk. E, 134–39, Guadalupe County, CC; D. McDonald, *José Antonio Navarro*, 15, 70–77, 90–91, 111–12, 128–31, 148–58, 173–74, 193, 200; J. W. Nichols, *Now You Hear*, 82–83.

34. Sowell, *Rangers*, 193; J. W. Nichols, *Now You Hear*, 82–84; Lee, *Three Years Among the Camanches* (1859), 51, 58; D. McDonald, *José Antonio Navarro*, 158.

35. J. W. Nichols, *Now You Hear*, 84; Lee, *Three Years Among the Camanches* (1859), 52–53; Sowell, *Rangers*, 193; Sowell, "Incidents Connected with the Early Settlers of Guadalupe County," 39, CAH.

36. Sowell, "Incidents Connected with the Early Settlers of Guadalupe County," 40, CAH; Lee, *Three Years Among the Camanches* (1859), 54–58; J. W. Nichols, *Now You Hear*, 84–85; Sowell, *Rangers*, 193; *Clarksville Standard*, June 22, 1843; *TTR*, May 10, 1843.

37. J. W. Nichols, *Now You Hear*, 82–86; Lee, *Three Years Among the Camanches* (1859), 49–70; Sowell, "Incidents Connected with the Early Settlers of Guadalupe County," 38–39, CAH; S. Moore, *Savage Frontier*, 3:334–36; "History of John C. Hays," pt. 1, 1933, pp. 224–28, box 2Q401, Affleck Papers, CAH; *Clarksville Standard*, June 22, 1843; *TTR*, May 10, 1843; Gary Clayton Anderson, foreword to Lee, *Three Years Among the Comanches* (1991), xx; Thurman, "Nelson Lee and the Green Corn Dance," 239–43; TR, 1842–43, TAC, Gonzales County, TSLA; Nelson Lee, Republic Claims, TSLA.

38. de la Teja, *Texas*, 234–36; J. W. Nichols, *Now You Hear*, 88; Lee, *Three Years Among the Camanches* (1859), 41, 45, 59, 64; Ramos, *Beyond*, 167–98; Nance, *Attack*, 10, 326.

39. Morrell, *Flower*, 181; TR, 1841–45, TAC, Gonzales County, TSLA; TR, 1846–55, TAC, Guadalupe County, TSLA; District Court Index, 1841–46, Gonzales County, DC; District Court Index, 1846–55, Guadalupe County, Tex., DC; Gonzales County Minute Men (James H. Callahan), Oversize 401–721, folder 2, RTMR, TAGD, TAGD, TSLA; Scrapbook, Mr. Valentine Bennet, Cuero, Tex., undated newspaper articles, MSBP, CAH; *Houston Daily Post*, Dec. 5, 1897; James Hughes Callahan, box 4, folder 14, JWNP, DRTL; "To the Honorable Congress of the Republic," Dec. 1841, Memorials and Petitions, TSLA; Solms-Braunfels, *Voyage*, 175.

40. James Hughes Callahan, box 4, folder 14, JWNP, DRTL; Henry E. McCulloch to *Blanco News*, Feb. 12, 1885, Blanco County, VF, Institute of Texan Cultures.

CHAPTER 7

1. First Minute Book of Seguin, 14, Call No. 2–231/971, TSLA; DCFR, bk. A, 455–56, Gonzales County, DC.

2. Stuntz, *Hers, His, and Theirs*, 32–34, 92–94, 101–5,116–17; Carroll, *Homesteads*, 78–80, 99–100; Boswell, *Her Act*, 17–22, 26; Larson, "History of Divorce," 2–5, 30–32; Pruitt, "'But a Mournful Remedy,'" 26–27.

3. Boswell, *Her Act*, 17–18; Townes, "Sketch," I, 29–30, 35–53; Gammel, *Laws*, 1:1437, 2:482–86; Larson, "History of Divorce," 32–34; Pruitt, "'But a Mournful Remedy,'" 22.

4. Pruitt, "'But a Mournful Remedy,'" Abstract, 5–8, 8 (map), 33, 35–36, 62–64, 66, 148–52; Boswell, *Her Act*, 6, 12–30, Appendices B, C; Sager, "States of Suffering," 15, 235, 238, 240; Larson, "History of Divorce," 5–6; DCM, bk. 1, 111–12, 117, 132, 146–47, 158, 200, 202, 226, 236, 242–43, 250, bk. A, 4, Gonzales County, DC; DCFR, bk. A, 140–42, 455–58, 486–91, 564–67, bk. B, 299–31, 340–42, Gonzales County, DC.

5. DCM, bk. 1, 4, 18, 47, 111–12, 146–47, 158, 200, 202, 226, 236, 242–43, 250, bk. A, 4–8, 122, Gonzales County, DC; DCR, *Smothers v. Smothers*, Cause 180, Gonzales County, DC; DCFR, bk. A, 140–44, 340–42, 482–92, 564–67, bk. B, 4, 89–92, 191–93, 291–94, 299–31, 486–92, Gonzales County, DC; Smothers (Smithers) Family History, privately held; Sager, "States of Suffering," 8–9, 233–34.

6. DCM, bk. 1, 18, 47, 111–12, 119, 132–33, 136–37, 146–47, 154, 158, 165, 200, 202, 226, 236, 242–43, 250, bk. A, 4–8, Gonzales County, DC; DCFR, bk. A, 140–44, 288–334, 140–44, 455–58, 486–92, 564–67, B, 191–93, 299–31, 340–42, Gonzales County, DC;

DCR, *Smothers v. Smothers*, Cause 180, Gonzales County, DC; Morris, *Becoming Southern*, 57; Gonzales County Historical Commission, *History*, 226, 446.

7. Lathrop, "Texas vs. Louisiana," 96–97; DCM, bk. 1, 146–47, Gonzales County, DC; DCFR, bk. A, 486–92, 564–67, Gonzales County, DC; PR, Richardson Perry, Case 290 loose leafs, Washington County, CC; Marriages, bk. 1, p. 8, Washington County, CC; Rather, "De Witt's Colony," 164; Dikes Family History, privately held; Benjamin Power, Land Grant Search, TGLO; Wooster, "West, Claiborne"; Sons of the Republic of Texas, *Sons*, 147–48; First Minute Book of Seguin, 2–3, Call No. 2–231/971, TSLA.

8. DCM, bk. 1, 119, 132–33, 146–47, Gonzales County, DC; DCFR, bk. A, 455–58, Gonzales County, DC; Gammel, *Laws*, 2:483–86; William Allsbury or Alsbury, Land Grant Search, TGLO.

9. Marriages, bk. A, 1–15, Gonzales County, CC; Johnson Day's birth and death, Nichols Family Papers; Johnson Day Estate, PR, Alsbury and Slade account, Gonzales County, CC; Charles Larabee, Land Grant Search, TGLO; *Daily Texan*, December 18, 1841; William Alsbury, Charles Larabee, Republic Claims, TSLA; Caldwell Gonzales Rangers, Nov. 16, 1840, Oversize 401–717, folder 8, RTMR, TAGD, TSLA; James Campbell Estate, PR, Gonzales County, CC; Loomis, *Texan-Santa Fé*, 112–15, 125, 128–33, 177, 200, 203, 274; *TTR*, Jan. 1, 1839, Dec. 8, 1841, May 11, Aug. 3, 10, 17, 24, 1842; *Weekly Texan*, Dec. 15, 1841; *Colorado Gazette*, June 4, 1842; Relaciones de los prisoneros . . . Santa Fe, New Mexico, Puestos en Libertad, 1842, Exp. XI/481.3/1737, DAM, SEDENA (Santa Fe prisoners released from Santiago Prison, June 16; Alsbury was number eleven); *NOP*, Aug. 19, 1842; TR, 1842, TAC, Galveston County, TSLA.

10. Medissa Allsbury petition, Dec. 14, 1842, Memorials and Petitions, Records of the Legislature, TSLA; *Journals of the Senate of the Seventh Congress of the Republic of Texas*, 124–25; *Journals of the House of Representatives of the Seventh Congress of the Republic of Texas*, 242; Bejar Prisoners, Juan Fernandez, Sept. 11, copied by Reyes, Sept. 20, OM, 1842, Exp. XI/481.3/1731, DAM, SEDENA.

11. DCM, bk. 1, 119, 132–33, 146–47, Gonzales County, DC; DCFR, bk. A, 455–58, bk. B, 89–92, 291–94, Gonzales County, DC; Nance, *Attack*, 502, 505; Wilkins, *Legend Begins*, 152; S. Moore, *Savage Frontier*, 4:64, 103; *TTR*, July 5, 1843; *Galveston Weekly News*, Nov. 15, 1845; *Galveston Civilian and Gazette*, May 5, 1848; Spurlin, *Texas Veterans*, 1, 5; *Clarksville Standard*, Nov. 21, 1846; PM, bk. 2, 400–409, bk. 3, 2–4, 191, 203–6, 230, Galveston County, CC; Probate Returns, bk. 1, 54–56, Galveston County, CC.

12. Marriages, bk. A, 45, Gonzales County, CC; "November four days waiting," SDPJ; James Hughes Callahan, box 4, folder 14, JWNP, DRTL.

13. Boswell, *Her Act*, 3–4, 31; Carroll, *Homesteads*, xi–xx, 80–81, 90–91, 98; Riley, *Building and Breaking*, 5, 7, 11–12, 16, 23–24, 27, 49, 51–53; Smith and Hindus, "Premarital Pregnancy," 537–70; Gammel, *Laws*, 2:483–86; Gonzales County Minute Men (James H. Callahan), Oversize 401–721, folder 2, RTMR, TAGD, TSLA; D'Emilio and Freedman, *Intimate Matters*, 73; James Hughes Callahan and Sarah Medissa Day marriage, PCFH.

14. Deeds, bk. B, 394, C, 8, Gonzales County, CC; Weinert, *Authentic History*, 58.

15. Marriages, bk. A, 16–17, Gonzales County, CC; Marriages, bk. A, 5, Guadalupe County, CC.

16. Floyd McKee (Brill descendant), e-mail to author, June 2014; Sarah Medissa Day, PCFH; Mildred Hankins Norris to Lola H. Cloninger, Jan. 24, 1983, TS, Eli Hankins and Elizabeth Hankins Family Papers, privately held.

17. Marriages, bk. A, 53, Gonzales County, CC; Jody McKee and Floyd McKee, "New McKee Family History," 60, privately held; Doherty, *Settlers*, 2:731–50; *Seguin Enterprise*, Feb. 6, 1937; Solomon Brill, Charles Harrison, Republic Claims, TSLA; Wilson, "Kentucky Volunteers in the Texas Revolution," 20; Brazos, *Life*, 21–22.

18. *TTR*, Sept. 20, 27, Oct. 18, Dec. 17, 1836, Feb. 14, 28, 1837; Brazos, *Life*, 22–23; *Muster Rolls of the Texas Revolution*, 158–59, 167 (Brill is spelled Bule and Bull); Solomon Brill, Juan Seguin, Republic Claims, TSLA; Seguin, *Personal*, 15–16; Nance, *After San Jacinto*, 29, 32; S. Moore, *Savage Frontier*, 1:209, 242–43; de la Teja, *Revolution Remembered*, 159–69; *Seguin Enterprise*, Feb. 6, 1937, Aug. 10, 1945; *Seguin Bulletin*, Mar. 22, 1934, Guadalupe County Scrapbook, box 3L226, CAH; *TTR*, Mar. 28, 1837.

19. Solomon Brill, Land Grant Search, TGLO; Deeds, bk. C, 222–23, Guadalupe County, CC; Sowell, *Rangers*, 225; *Seguin Enterprise*, Feb. 5, 1937; *Seguin Bulletin*, Mar. 22, 1934, Guadalupe County Scrapbook, box 3L226, CAH; TR, 1842–45, TAC, Gonzales County, TSLA; TR, 1846–50, TAC, Guadalupe County, TSLA.

20. Marriages, bk. A, 4, Guadalupe County, CC; "February seventh [1847]," SDPJ; Levi Hinds Estate, PM, bk. A, 60, 70, bk. E, 238, Brazoria County, CC, Angleton, Tex.; *TSG*, June 12, 1852; Rather, "De Witt's Colony," 102–4, 154, 170; James Hinds, Shelton Hinds, Republic Claims, TSLA; James Hinds, Gerren or Garen Hinds, Thomas S. Hinds, Levy or Levi Hinds, Clement or Clemmons Hinds, Land Grant Search, TGLO. Melinda Hinds married John Hankins on March 7, 1817. Ruth Ann was born in 1825.

21. James Hinds, James, Gerren or Garen Hinds, Thomas S. Hinds, Levy or Levi Hinds, Clement or Clemmons Hinds, Land Grant Search, TGLO; Hines, *Eli Clemmons Hinds*, n.p.; PM, bk. A, 70, Brazoria County, CC; Eli Hankins, Guardianship Records, Probate 94, Gonzales County, CC; PM, bk. A, 206, Gonzales County, CC; Caldwell County, Map 77227, TGLO; *Twentieth Century History*, 401–3; S. Moore, *Savage Frontier*, 3:106, 4:64, 81, 129, 133–35; Wilkins, *Legend Begins*, 137; *Clarksville Standard*, June 15, 1843; *TTR*, July 12, 1843.

22. PM, bk. E, 200, 238–41, Brazoria County, CC; Eli Hankins, Guardianship Records, Probate 94, Gonzales County, CC; James Hinds, PR, Gonzales County, CC; PM, bk. A, 206, 231, 333, 338, 434, bk. B, 66–67, 92, Gonzales County, CC; Caldwell County, Map 77227, TGLO; Deeds, bk. E, 174, G., 832–33, Gonzales County, CC; Gonzales County, Map 1841, TGLO; Eli Hankins or Hankens, Land Grant Search, TGLO. Ruth Ann Hankins Ward, Eli's sister, received $300 for her portion of Levi Hinds's estate.

23. Marriages, bk. A, 23, Guadalupe County, CC; "July the 3 1849," SDPJ; Marriages, bk. C, 1818–25, pp. 108–9, Circuit Clerk, Warren County, Vicksburg, Miss.; Pharr, *Pharrs and Farrs*, 249, 265–69; Weir, "Bailey, James Briton"; First Census of Austin's Colony, 1826, Call No. TZ312.764 T312F, CAH; McCormick, *Scotch-Irish in Ireland and in America*, 163; Samuel Pharr, Land Grant Search, TGLO; James Bailey, VF, Brazoria County Historical Museum.

24. Hallstein, "Brazoria, TX"; Hallstein, "Bailey's Prairie, TX"; Probate Will Record, bk. A. 188–89, 198–200, 204–20, 578–79, Brazoria County, CC; Holley, *Texas*, 114; "Milburn, David H.," *HBTO*, http://www.tshaonline.org/handbook/online/articles/fmi06; First Census of Austin's Colony, 1826, Call No. TZ312.764 T312F, CAH; David Milburn, VF, Brazoria County Historical Museum; *Texas Gazette*, Sept. 25, Oct. 24, 1829, Mar. 13, 15, 17, 1830; *Texas Gazette and Brazoria Commercial Advertiser*, July 23, 1832; *Constitutional Advocate and Texas Public Advertiser*, Sept. 5, 1832, June 15, 1833, Feb. 22, 1834; *Texas*

Republican, June 13, 27, July 18, Sept. 6, 19, Oct. 3, 10, 17, 24, 31, Nov. 14, 1835; David Milburn, Republic Claims, TSLA.

25. Deeds, bk. C. 1–3, Brazoria County, CC; Probate Will Record, bk. A, 198–200, Brazoria County, CC; Ammon Underwood, "Journal," 149–51; Elizabeth Milborn and Milburn, Land Grant Search, TGLO; Nance, *Attack*, 409, 445, 465–68, 485, 488–92, 514, 521–22, 557–62, 567, 576, 634–35; Augustus Pharr, Republic Claims, TSLA. Millburn's estate was worth almost $40,000, or $1.2 million in 2019 dollars.

26. Marriages, bk. A, 173, 190, 199, Brazoria County, CC; J. Bryan, "Rector, Claiborne"; TR, 1840–48, TAC, Brazoria County, TSLA; Pharr, *Pharrs and Farrs*, 249, 265–66; Deeds, bk. D, 408–9, Brazoria County, CC; Morgan Rector Family, John Sutherland Menefee Papers, CAH; Claiborne Rector, Republic Claims, TSLA; Claibourn and Claiborne Rector, Grant Search, TGLO; Elizabeth Milbourn and Milborn, Land Grant Search, TGLO; TR, 1848, TAC, Guadalupe County, TSLA; Marriages, bk. A, 23, Guadalupe County, CC.

27. Martha Hannah Nichols Day's death, Nichols Family Papers; Martha Hannah Nichols Day's death and Care of Children, Gonzales Papers; Spurlin, *Texas Veterans*, 171–72, 239–40; *Texas Democrat*, Sept. 23, Nov. 4, 1846; SR, James Milford Day, Henry E. McCulloch, Mexican War, RG94, M278, R10, NAB; J. W. Nichols, *Now You Hear*, 130; "November 13 [1846]," SDPJ; *Texas Democrat*, Mar. 20, 1847.

28. *Texas Democrat*, Mar. 20, Apr. 3, 10, July 24, 1847; *Texas Presbyterian*, Mar. 13, 1847; *Democratic Telegraph and Texas Register*, Mar. 15, 22, 29, Apr. 5, 1847; J. W. Nichols, *Now You Hear*, 132–38; James M. Day Mexican War service, Gonzales Papers; Marriages, bk. A2, 5, Guadalupe County, CC; "July 4, [1847]," SDPJ.

29. *Seguin Enterprise*, Feb. 11, 1987; U.S. Census, 1850, 1860, 1870, Guadalupe County, Tex.; U.S. Census, 1880, Wilson County, Tex.; James and Susan Day's children, Gonzales Papers; James and Susan Day's children, Nichols Family Papers.

30. J. W. Nichols, *Now You Hear*, 121.

CHAPTER 8

1. Campbell, *Gone*, 182–86, 194–98, 198 (map), 210–12, 227–30; T. Smith, *U.S. Army*, 17–19; 27–37; 41, 50–52, 72–74, 156–57; Jordan, *German Seed*, 44–52.

2. Gammel, *Laws*, 2:1320, 1339, 3:53–54, 1139–40; Petition for the Creation of the County of Plum Creek, Dec. 16, 1847, Memorials and Petitions, TSLA.

3. DeBow, *Statistical View*, 40, 82, 308–13; *TSG*, Aug. 25, 1849; U.S. Census, 1850, Caldwell, Gonzales, Guadalupe Counties, Tex.; Nonpopulation Census Schedules, Tex., 1850–80, Bureau of the Census, MT1134, R10, R21, NAB; Campbell and Lowe, *Wealth*, 16 (map), 85–87; Lowe and Campbell, *Planters*, 29, 32, 39–40, 44, 93.

4. *Ledger and Texan*, Jan. 1, 1854; Eastman, *Sketchbook*, 40–42; Hardinge, *Views of Texas*, 33.

5. TR, 1840–45, TAC, Gonzales County, TSLA; TR, 1846–54, TAC, Guadalupe County, TSLA; TR, 1848–54, TAC, Caldwell County, TSLA; TR, 1854, TAC, Comal County, TSLA; *TSG*, Oct. 12, 1850; *TTR*, Apr. 12, 1843; *Democratic Telegraph and Texas Register*, Oct. 21, Dec. 9, 1847; J. W. Nichols, *Now You Hear*, 11, 17, 49.

6. Jordan, *North American*, 211–18; *Texas v. Solomon Brill*, Case 85, District Court Records (hereafter DCR), Guadalupe County, DC; Caldwell, Guadalupe Counties, Nonpopulation Census Schedules, Tex., 1850–80, MT1134, R10, R21, NAB; DeBow, *Statistical View*, 310–13.

7. Deeds, bk. C, 463–64, bk. D, 197–98, Gonzales County, CC; *Weekly Journal*, July 9, 1852; Jordan and Greiner, "Texas Travel Diary," 351, 357; "History of Prairie Lea," 47; Ruthven, *Proceedings*, 2:276; Sofge, "San Marcos River Valley," 13, 16–19; CCM, bk. 1, 15, Caldwell County, CC; Deeds, bk. B, 684–85, bk. C, 39–40, Guadalupe County, CC; Deeds, bk. B, 43–44, 224–25, bk. D, 373–74, Caldwell County, CC; Minutes, Oct. 12, 1852, bk. 1, p. 32, Shiloh Baptist Church, no. 5330, Southern Baptist Historical Library and Archives (hereafter SBHLA), Nashville; *TSG*, Oct. 18, 1851, Feb. 12, 1853; TR, 1850–54, TAC, Caldwell County, TSLA; U.S. Census, 1850, Caldwell, Guadalupe Counties, Tex.

8. *TTR*, Oct. 4, 11, 18, 25, 1843; *Galveston Civilian and Gazette*, Oct. 21, 28, 1843; *Gonzales Inquirer*, Oct. 1, 15, 22, 29, 1853; *Texan Mercury*, Oct. 1, 8, 15, 22, 29, 1853, Jan. 21, 1854; PL, bk. H, 1–8, Comal County, CC, New Braunfels, Tex.; Louis Hipp Estate, PR, bk. B, 23–115, Guadalupe County, CC.

9. Roemer, *Texas*, 87; M. Jackson, *Lone Star*, 27, 137–39; C. Jones, *Texas Roots*, 117–20, 201–3; Henson, *Anglo-American Women*, 19–21; *Democratic Telegraph and Texas Register*, July 13, 1848, Feb. 21, 1950.

10. Coltharp, "'Hog-Killing Good Time,'" 183–85; Jackson, *Lone Star*, 27–28, 102–3, 141; C. Jones, *Texas Roots*, 113–14, 119, 140–42, 196, 199, 202–3, 215–16, 223; Lowe and Campbell, *Planters*, 16, 22; Caldwell, Guadalupe Counties, Nonpopulation Census Schedules, Tex., 1850–80, Bureau of the Census, MT1134, R10, R21, NAB; Eastman, *Sketchbook*, 40–42.

11. Jarmon, "Old Ranger Station," privately held; Carrington, *Women*, 45; *Texas Ranger*, Apr. 27, 1854; *Democratic Telegraph and Texas Register*, Feb. 7, 1848; McLean, *Papers*, 9:269; "Sewing for Mr. Williams" and "Washing for Mr. Towner," SDPJ.

12. Campbell, *Gone*, 219; Billy M. Jones, "Health Seekers," 287; *Galveston Civilian and Gazette*, July 20, 1844; *TTR*, May 10, 1843, July 31, 1844, June 21, 1849; Morrell, *Flower*, 136; *Western Texan*, Jan. 12, 1849; *Texian Advocate*, Apr. 17, 1851; Comments on health and sickness, July 3, 1849, June 13, 1852, SDPJ; Elise Tipps Wuppermann, "The Diary of Elise Tipps Wuppermann," Wuppermann Collection (hereafter WC), privately held; PR, bk. A, 209, Guadalupe County, CC.

13. "March 29, [1846]," "June 18th 1853," SDPJ; Wuppermann, "Diary of Elise Tipps Wuppermann," WC; Gish, *Diary*, xii–xix, 76, 100, 170, 172–75, 183, 189, 191, 220, 222, 228, 252, 277, 279–80, 291, 293, 300, 313, 325, 336.

14. Nixon, *Medical Story*, 280–83, 314, 358, 368, 472; Hogan, *Texas Republic*, 232–33; Campbell, *Gone*, 220; *TTR*, Apr. 25, 1851; *Texian Advocate*, Mar. 6, 1852; *Gonzales Inquirer*, Sept. 3, 1853.

15. Hogan, *Texas Republic*, 191–98; "November four, [1844]," SDPJ; Phelan, *History*, 24–25, 33, 38–44, 116–22, 194, 212–15, 238–39, 295, 299; Weinert, *Methodism*, 1–7, 9–10, 12–14, 21, 23, 69, 81; DeVilbiss, *Reminiscences*, 40, 99, 115, 136; H. G. Horton, "Old Seguin Church," 165–66; Brawner, *150 Years of Methodism*, n.p.

16. "September 1843," "June the 22, [1845]," "October 13, [1848]," "March the 16, 1851," "August the 6, 1853," SDPJ.

17. "November 1844," "April the 1 [1845]," "June the 8, 1848, October [1849]," SDPJ; Phelan, *History*, 298–99.

18. "Sept[ember] 12 [1850]," "Newyear Day 1852," "May the 16 [1852]," "August the 5th 1852," "April 17 [1853]," SDPJ; Weinert, *Authentic History*, 60; Brawner, *150 Years Faith Celebration*, n.p.

19. Deeds, bk. B, 684–85, Guadalupe County, CC; *TSG*, Sept. 22, 1849, Oct. 1, 1851; *Gonzales Inquirer*, Sept. 1, 1853; Minutes, Oct. 12, 1852, p. 32, Shiloh Baptist Church, no. 5330, SBHLA; Phelan, *History*, 302.

20. Campbell, *Gone*, 207, 228; Hogan, *Texas Republic*, 41–42; Gammel, *Laws*, 1:1379–81, 2:272–74, 280–82, 345–46, 842–45, 3:1373–75, 1560–61; Phelan, *History*, 280; Morrell, *Flower*, 22, 91; *Texas Presbyterian*, Feb. 6, Mar. 13, 1847; *Democratic Telegraph and Texas Register*, May 6, June 21, July 8, 1846, Sept. 6, 13, Oct. 4, 1849, Feb. 28, 1850; *Texas Democrat*, Apr. 8, 1848; *TTR*, Apr. 22, 1851; *TSG*, Dec. 22, 1849, Jan. 12, 1850, Jan. 8, Sept. 24, Nov. 29, 1853; *Texan Mercury*, Oct. 22, Dec. 3, 10, 1853; *Gonzales Inquirer*, Nov. 12, 1853; DCM, bk. AB, 399–40, Guadalupe County, DC; DCM, bk. A, p. 369–72, Caldwell County, DC.

21. *Galveston Civilian and Gazette*, June 10, 1851; *TSG*, June 1, 22, Sept. 7, Oct. 26, Nov. 2, 1850, May 22, 1852, Aug. 3, Sept. 10, Nov. 29, Dec. 6, 1853; *Texan Mercury*, Oct. 1, 1852, Oct. 15, Dec. 3, 10, 1853; *Gonzales Inquirer*, Aug. 17, Oct. 15, 1853; *San Antonio Ledger*, May 27, 1852; Deeds, bk. F, 429, Guadalupe County, CC; James Hughes Callahan, box 4, folder 14, JWNP, DRT.

22. Campbell, *Gone*, 228, 230; Evans, *Story*, 18–19, 23–32, 34–39, 48–52, 60–62, 65–68, 70; Gammel, *Laws*, 2:600–604; *Texas National Register*, Oct. 2, 1845; *TTR*, Feb. 17, 1841, July 29, 1840, Oct. 25, 1843, Jan. 7, Mar. 18, 1846; *Texas Democrat*, Nov. 25, 1846; *Weekly News*, Apr. 11, 1844; Morgan Rector Family, Menefee Papers, 1813–1934, CAH; "February the 4th [1846]," SDPJ.

23. Gammel, *Laws*, 3:351–53, 682–83, 1461–65, 4:257; Deeds, bk. C, 522–23; 601–2, Guadalupe County, CC; *San Antonio Ledger*, Aug. 19, 1852; *TTR*, Jan. 28, 1853; Moellering, "History," 103, 105–6; *Gonzales Inquirer*, June 18, 1853; *Texan Mercury*, Dec. 31, 1853, Feb. 4, May 27, July 8, 1854; Evans, *Texas Schools*, 61–63.

24. Deeds, bk. B, 224–25, Caldwell County, CC; Stock, "Prairie Lea, TX"; *Galveston Journal*, July 9, 1852; *TSG*, Feb. 26, 1853. *San Antonio Ledger*, Aug. 19, 1852.

25. Matovina, *Tejano*, ix, 52; Jordan, "Century," 389 (map); F. Smith, *Dominance*, 163 (map), 187–89, 206–7, 215–217; Winfrey and Day, *Indian Papers*, 1:164–65, 3:124–25.

26. *Texas Democrat*, June 2, 1849; Crimm, "Fernando de León," 103–27; Biesele, *German Settlements*, 117, 118n17; Deeds, bk. E, 58–60, Comal County, CC; Amberson, McAllen, and McAllen, *I Would Rather Sleep*, xi–xii, 2–5. *Democratic Telegraph and Texas Register*, Dec. 7, 1846; *TSG*, Sept. 1, Dec. 8, 1849, May 6, Aug. 10, 1850, Mar. 29, July 12, Oct. 4, 1851, Mar. 11, May 29, June 19, 1852, Aug. 13, 1853; Collins, *Texas Devils*, 56–63; Nance, *Attack*, 10, 384.

27. Matovina, *Tejano*, 57–58; Marriage Index, 1846–53, Guadalupe County, CC; U.S. Census, 1850, 1860, Caldwell, Guadalupe Counties, Tex.; District Court Index, 1846–53, Guadalupe County, DC; Marriage Index, 1848–53, Caldwell County, CC; *Gonzales Inquirer*, Sept. 19, 1853; *Texan Mercury*, Dec. 24, 1853; "To the Honorable Congress of the Republic," Dec. 1841, Petition to form Guadalupe County, Memorials and Petitions, TSLA; Solms-Braunfels, *Voyage*, 175; James Hughes Callahan, box 4, folder 14, JWNP, DRT; J. W. Nichols, *Now You Hear*, 82–83; Guadalupe County, 1849, box 2–12/502, Secretary of State, Election Returns, TSLA; *Texian Advocate*, Aug. 7, 1851; "Committee of Twenty, Seguin," privately held.

28. *Texas National Register*, May 1, 1845; U.S. Census, 1850, Guadalupe, Caldwell Counties, Tex.; TR, 1850–51, TAC, Caldwell County, TSLA; Brister, "Adelsverein."

29. de la Teja, Marks, and Tyler, *Texas*, 160, 233–34; Campbell, *Laws*, 52–60; Campbell, *Empire*, 19, 56–57; U.S. Census, 1850, 1860, Guadalupe, Caldwell Counties, Tex.; TR, 1839, 1845, TAC, Gonzales County, TSLA.

30. "Remembrances of Eli Skaggs Hankins," Mildred N. Pinson (granddaughter), Sept. 15, 1987, Eli and Elizabeth Hankins Papers; Gretchen, *Slave Transactions*, 99, 144–45, 194, 248, 254; Engledow, "Record of Bills of Sale," 6; Bahlmann, Bahlmann, and Bahlmann, "Slave Transactions Gonzales County," Records Center and Archives, Gonzales County, Tex.; TR, 1851, 1856–57, TAC, Guadalupe County, TSLA; PR, bk. E, 278, Guadalupe County, CC; Deeds, bk. B, 171, bk. D, 544, bk. E, 278, Guadalupe County, CC; PM, bk. D, 26–27, Guadalupe County, CC; DCM, bk. C, 103, 110, 280, Guadalupe County, DC; DCR, *Collin Johnson v. J. H. Callahan and G. B. Hollamon,* Civil Case 590, Guadalupe County, DC; Deeds, bk. C, 406, Caldwell County, CC; U.S. Census, Slave Schedules, 1860, Guadalupe County, Tex.; Randolph Campbell e-mail to author, definition of a slave owner, February 24, 2015.

31. Guadalupe, Caldwell Counties, 1849, box 2–12/502, Secretary of State, Election Returns, TSLA; *Texas Democrat*, Apr. 7, 1849.

32. CCM, bk. A, 1–7, Guadalupe County, CC; Gonzales County, 1841, box 2–9/45, Republic of Texas, Department of State, Election Returns, TSLA; Guadalupe County, 1846, box 2–12/496, Caldwell County, 1852, box 2–12/512, Secretary of State, Election Returns, TSLA; CCM, bk. A, 81, 90, 101–9, Caldwell County, CC.

33. CCM, bk 1, p. 24, Gonzales County, CC; CCM, bk A, 1–7, 18–19, 24, 27, 34, 46–47, 50, 53, 62, 89, 91, 96, 105, 125, 127–31, 148, 166, Guadalupe County, CC; CCM, bk. A, 1–2, 6, 8, 15, 17, 21, 32, 34, 39, 43, 54–55, 64–65, 74, 88, 90–92, 95, Caldwell County, CC.

34. CCM, bk. A, 58, Guadalupe County, CC; *Texas Democrat*, Apr. 22, 1848; Gammel, *Laws*, 2:323–25.

35. Gammel, *Laws*, 1:1258–71, 2:1476–83; DCM, bk 1, pp. 43, 128, 153, 179–86, 223, 230, 247, bk A, 3, 7, Gonzales County DC; DCM, bk A, 2, 4–5, 8, 12, 18, 43, 50, 94, 118–19, 124, 126, 129–30, 139, 158, 163, 199–200, 205–6, 225, 230, 238, 273, bk AB, 2, 18, 54, 94, 99, 133, Guadalupe County, DC.

36. Hogan, *Texas Republic*, 260; DCM, bk 1, 141, 143, 155, 157, 164, 169, 171, 190, 232–33, 253, bk A, 16, 49, 55–56, 89, Gonzales County, DC; DCM, bk A, 3–4, 11–12, 22, 29–31, 51, 59, 65,162, 210 258–59, bk AB, 5, 28, 30, 71–72, 109, 11, 150, 168, 205–14, Guadalupe County, DC; DCM, bk A-1, 7, 13, 32, 40, 58–59, 53–54, 75–76, 83–85, 96–97, 127–28, 184–85, 195–98, Caldwell County, DC.

37. Gammel, *Laws*, 1:228–29, 2:106–8, 3:219–32; DCM, A, 9–11, 45–51, 109, 122–27, 160–62, 177–87, 224–25, bk. AB, 6–10, 13, 23–27, 37–47, 75, 77, 118, 127–31 153, 171, 225–27, 229, 240–41, 263 Guadalupe County, DC; DCM, A-1, 5–9, 23–26, 43–48, bk. A, 187, Caldwell County, DC; DCM, bk. 1, 129–32, 142–46, 154–61, 194–200, 216–22, 240, bk. A, 56–63, 84–85, 106–12, 119, 136, 145, 155, Gonzales County, DC; *Seguin Enterprise*, July 31, 1896.

38. DCM, bk. A, 9–11, 29, 35, 43, 75, 83–84, 120, 195, 227–28, 272, bk. AB, 208, Guadalupe County, DC; DCR, Cases 6, 22, 24, 47, 101, 102, 137, 255, Guadalupe County, DC; DCM, bk. A-1, 216–17, 231, Caldwell County, DC; DCM, bk. 1, 209, 227–28, Gonzales County, DC; DCR, bk. B2, 161–65, Gonzales County, DC; Hartley, *Reports of Cases Argued and Decided*, vol. 4:31–34.

39. DCM, bk. A, 4–5, 31, 51, 61–62, 89–90, bk. AB, 54, 72, 111, 117, 121, 151, 157, 160, 163, 168, 230–35, 262, 304–6, 314, 353, bk. C, 1–2, 56–57, 76, Guadalupe County, DC; DCR, Cases 4, 25, 37, 85, 97, 98, 113, 114, 115, Guadalupe County, DC.

40. Hartley and Hartley, *Reports of Cases Argued and Decided*, 13:40; DCR, Case 85, Guadalupe County, DC; Solomon Brill, Application for Pardon, Clemency Records, Secretary of State, box 2–9, folder 315, TSLA.

41. *Galveston Journal*, July 15, 1853.

42. Morris, *Becoming Southern*; xvi–xviii, 11–14, 23, 43; *Texian Advocate*, Aug. 7, 1851.

CHAPTER 9

1. Patrick Jack, Land Grant Search, TGLO.

2. Bishop, *Lots of Land*, 121–22; James Callahan, Land Grant Search, TGLO.

3. Weber, *Spanish Frontier*, 143–46, 166–67; de la Teja, Marks, and Tyler, *Texas*, 158–62, 176; T. Miller, *Public Lands*, 17–18.

4. Campbell, *Gone*, 167–68; T. Miller, *Public Lands*, 28–31, 45–52; Brooks to Brooks, Mar. 10, 1836, letter, privately held; Bishop, *Lots of Land*, 114–16; T. Miller, *Bounty and Donation*, 24–34.

5. T. Miller, *Public Lands*, 30–31; T. Miller, *Bounty and Donation*, 42–46; Bishop, *Lots of Land*, 118–19; Elgin Williams, *Animating Pursuits*, chaps. 1 and 2.

6. T. Miller, *Bounty and Donation*, 54; Lusk, PR, Fort Bend County, CC; TR, 1850–55, Bexar, Guadalupe Counties, TSLA; *New Orleans Daily Delta*, Nov. 28, 1845; *Niles Weekly Register*, March 18, 1837.

7. Johnson Day (Heirs), Kimble County, Land Grant Search, TGLO; "Paid to Mr. Calliahan six dollars," SDPJ.

8. *Matagorda Bulletin*, Mar. 7, 1838; Williams, *Animating Pursuits*, 203; Deeds, bk. B, 276, bk. E, 86, Gonzales County, CC; Deeds, bk. A, 20, bk. B, 101, bk. E, 540, bk. F, 150, 323, Guadalupe County, CC; Deeds, bk. E, 646, Comal County, CC; "June the 18 1853," SDPJ; General Land Office Records, "Military Warrant, Faribault Land Office, Minnesota," Bureau of Land Management, U.S. Department of the Interior, https://glorecords.blm.gov/search/default.aspx (searched Day, Johnson).

9. Solomon Brill, Land Grant Search, TGLO; A. Crawford, Land Grant Search, TGLO; Ira Bisbee, Land Grant Search, TGLO; Deeds, bk. D2, p. 20, Bexar County, CC; Ira Bisbee, Republic Claims, TSLA; J. Sydnor, Land Grant Search, TGLO; Sarah Cloud, Land Grant Search, TGLO; Wyatt, *Families*, 1:98–99.

10. TR, 1857, 1861, 1864, 1867, 1870, 1873, 1877, 1881, TAC, Guadalupe County, TSLA; Deeds, bk. C, 222, bk. D, 540, bk. E, 45, bk. F, 258, bk. N, 17, 524, bk. O, 19, bk. 15, p. 61, Guadalupe County, CC; Deeds, bk. A, 472, Kimble County, CC; Deeds, bk. D2, 20, Bexar County, CC.

11. Deeds, bk. E, 174, bk. G, 219, K2, 414–15, Gonzales County, CC; Deeds, bk. A, 93, bk. B, 387, bk. G, 32, Caldwell County, CC; E. (Eli) Hankins, Land Grant Search, TGLO; TR, 1846–48, TAC, Gonzales County; TR, 1848–88, TAC, Caldwell County, TSLA.

12. Deeds, bk. C, 352, bk. F, 701, bk. G, 105, Caldwell County, CC; TR, 1854–61, TAC, Caldwell County, TSLA; Caldwell County, Nonpopulation Census Schedules, Texas, 1850–80, MT1134, R10, R21, NAB.

13. Elizabeth Milbourn, Augustus Pharr, Land Grant Search, TGLO; Deeds, bk. M, 163, Gillespie County, CC; Deeds, bk. D, 408, bk. H, 367, Brazoria County, CC; Deeds, bk. E, 407, Guadalupe County, CC; Deeds, bk. C, 636, bk. D, 308, 754, bk. E, 407, 812, bk. G, 185, Guadalupe County, CC; TR, 1848–58, TAC, Guadalupe County, TSLA; PL, bk. H, 1–8, 220–21, Comal County, CC.

14. H. (Henry) King, Land Grant Search, TGLO; Deeds, bk. A, 279, bk. B, 30, 278, 398, bk. D, 291, 381, bk. E, 65, bk. F, 171, Gonzales County, CC; Deeds, bk. A, 12, 26, 30,

57, 73, 76, bk. B, 55, 59, 70, 303, 556, bk. C, 297, 303, 556, bk. D, 83, 312, 631, 780, bk. E, 112, 256, 598, bk. F, 47, 310, 314, 524, 746, 765, bk. G, 186, 475, 489, Guadalupe County, CC; TR, 1845–54, TAC, Guadalupe County, TSLA.

15. John W. Nichols, Thomas Jackson, Land Grant Search, TGLO: Deeds, bk. N, 598, Gonzales County, CC; Deeds, bk. G, 551, Guadalupe County, CC.

16. Deeds, bk. A, 202, 266, 278, 298, bk. B, 286, 2, 312, bk. C, 604, bk. D, 125, 202, 404, 407, bk. E, 259, bk. F, 31, Gonzales County, CC; Deeds, bk. A, 107, 139, bk. B, 15, 62–63, 348, 655, 716, 774, bk. C, 136, 568–71, bk. D, 381, 397, 822, bk. E, 56, 562, 566, 571, bk. F, 226, 306, 388–89, 438, 441, 499, bk. G, 159, 348, 387, bk. H, 117, 119, 138–39, 257, bk. I, 258, bk. J, 345–46, 397–99, 441, 471, bk. N, 219, bk. S, 183, Guadalupe County, CC; TR, 1845–54, TAC, Guadalupe County, TSLA.

17. James M. Day, Morgan Hamilton, M. T. Johnson, Land Grant Search, TGLO; *South-Western American*, Nov. 15, 1851; Gammel, *Laws*, 3:1047; Deeds, bk. B, 297, 400, bk. C, 299, 581, bk. D, 53, 156, 406–7, bk. F, 92, Gonzales County, CC; TR, 1845, TAC, Gonzales County, TSLA; Marriages, bk. A, 5, Guadalupe County, CC; Deeds, bk. GT, 300, 434, bk. A1, 20, 28, bk. B1, 9, 173, bk. B, 73, 228, bk. C, 322, 327, bk. D, 66, 245, 453–54, 458, 563, bk. F, 422, 429, bk. I, 202, bk. N, 129, Guadalupe County, CC; Deeds, bk. E, 645, Comal County, CC; TR, 1846–54, TAC, Guadalupe County, TSLA.

18. James H. Callahan, chap. 15, box 4, folder 17, JWNP, DRT; Gammel, *Laws*, 1:925–26, 951–54, 982–83, 1094, 1134, 1324, 1367–68; T. Miller, *Bounty and Donation*, 24–27, 38, 40, 42–43, 887; James Callahan, Land Grant Search, TGLO; Lavaca County, Map 5012, TGLO; Deeds, bk. C, 343–44, bk. F, 170–71, Gonzales County, CC; Deeds, bk. A, 29–30, Lavaca County, CC.

19. T. Miller, *Public Lands*, 30–31; James Callahan, Land Grant Search, TGLO; *TTR*, Aug. 23, 1849; U.S. Census, 1850, 1860, 1870, 1880, New Orleans; "Family of Erastus H. Harris & Adelaide Harriet McGaughy," privately held; Day, *Jacob De Cordova*, 26–27, 56–57, 68, 80–92, 123, 129–30; *TTR*, June 3, 1846; De Cordova, *Texas*, 300; Ribb, "Colony of Kent."

20. Deeds, bk. D, 403–4, Brazoria County, CC; Deeds, bk. 1, 519–21, bk. 2, 566–67, bk. 3, 15–17, 196–97, bk. 7, Kimble County, CC; Deeds, bk. A, 59–60, Guadalupe County, CC; Deeds, bk. B, 403–4, Gillespie County, CC; Deeds, bk. O2, pp. 77–78, bk. F2, pp. 224–25, Bexar County, CC; TR, 1838, TAC, Brazoria County, TSLA; Davenport, "Notes from an Unfinished Study"; Gulick et al., *Papers*, 1:392; Groneman, "Kimble, George C."; Gonzales County Historical Commission, *History*, 446; George Kimble and Kimbill, Ira Fuller, Henry Redfield, James Callahan, Sion Green, Land Grant Search, TGLO; McKinney, "Redfield, Henry Prentice." Sion D. Green was in Isaac Ticknor's company and was captured and with Urrea's troops on their retreat to Mexico. W. D. Redd claimed that in late May 1836, he talked with Green, who said he planned to continue with the Mexican army to Matamoros. Redd accused Green of being a traitor. It is not known how Sion Green made his way to Brazoria two years later.

21. *Autobiography of Henry Eustace McCulloch*, TS, 25, BHMFP, CAH; DCM, bk. 1, p. 241, Gonzales County, DC; DCR, Case 224, Gonzales County, DC; Deeds, bk. O2, pp. 77–79, 347–48, bk. F2, pp. 224–25, bk. P1, pp. 338–39, Bexar County, CC; Deeds, bk. 3, pp. 196–97, 200–201, 267–68, bk. 18, pp. 519–21, Kimble County, CC.

22. Deeds, bk. O2, pp. 347–48, bk. P1, pp. 338–39, Bexar County, CC; Deeds, bk. 3, pp. 200–201, 267–68, bk. 18, pp. 519–21, Kimble County, CC; Deeds, bk. B, 194, 247, Guadalupe County, CC; Deeds, bk. B, 405, bk. F, 186, Gillespie County, CC; Fisher, *It Occurred*, 26–27, 189.

23. Deeds, bk. A, 240–42, 280–81, bk. B, 394–95, bk. C, 8, 343, 349–50, 463–64, bk. D, 197–98, bk. E, 201–2, bk. F, 170, 407–8, Gonzales County, CC; Deeds, bk. A, 10–12, 23–24, 34–35, 57–60, bk. B. 16–17, 67–68, 81–82, 147–48, 682–84, bk. C, 50–51, 225–26, 639–40, bk. D, 72–73, 602, Guadalupe County, CC; Deeds, bk. A, 29, Lavaca County, CC; Deeds, bk. C, 330, Brazoria County, CC; CCM, bk. A, 3, Guadalupe County, CC; Sofge, "San Marcos River," 16–17; Deeds, bk. A, 615–16, 675, bk. B, 89, 224–25, 684–85, bk. C, 42, 70–71, 302, 352, 648, bk. D, 315, 323–24, 338, Caldwell County, CC; *TSG*, Sept. 22, 1849, Oct. 1, 1851; *Gonzales Inquirer*, Sept. 1, 1853; TR, 1848, 1852, TAC, Caldwell County, TSLA.

24. Campbell, *Gone*, 207–11; de la Teja, Marks, and Tyler, *Texas*, 245; TR, 1843–45, TAC, Gonzales County, TSLA; TR, 1846–53, TAC, Guadalupe County, TSLA; TR, 1848–53, TAC, Caldwell County, TSLA; Day, *Jacob De Cordova*, 1–8, 12, 18, 22–24, 27–30, 36–40, 43 72–76, 142; *South-Western American*, Sept. 2, 1850, Dec. 6, 1851, Dec. 15, 1852, *Neu Braunfelser Zeitung*, Dec. 17, 1852; Deeds, bk. B, 588–93, Guadalupe County, CC; Antonio Esnaurrizar, Land Grant Search, TGLO.

25. *Texas Sentinel*, Mar. 18, 1841; *Texas Gazette*, Apr. 24, 1852; Gammel, *Laws*, 2:1073–75, 3:1550–52.

26. J. Moursund, *Blanco County History*, 1–8, 10, 15, 24–28, 31, 34; "the spurs on a man riding a horse," West Papers, privately held.

27. Biesele, *German Settlements*, 111, 117–19, 139–40, 145, 152, 154–57; *Texas Democrat*, Feb. 10, 1849; Curry's Creek, Kendalia Scrapbooks, Kendalia Public Library; Jasinski, "Curry's Creek Settlement"; TR, 1850–53, TAC, Comal County, TSLA; Jennette, *Biographical Directory*, 151; *San Antonio Express*, Sept. 21, 1996.

28. Deeds, bk. E, 760–61, Comal County, CC; Deeds, bk. 3, pp. 678–79, bk. 5, pp. 344–45, Kendall County, CC; TR, 1850–54, TAC, Comal County, TSLA; William E. Jones, Land Grant Search, TGLO; Guadalupe County, Map 7729, Hays County, Map 73176, Comal County, Map 3430, Blanco County, Map 6675, Kendall County, Map 73203, Maps, TGLO; Deeds, bk. C, 302–3, 353–54, 608–9, bk. D, 338–39, Caldwell County, CC; Deeds, bk. D, 602–3, Guadalupe County, CC.

29. Garver, "Benjamin Rush Milam," 177–79; Milam's Register of Families, Milam's Colony Records, TGLO; Gonzales County Historical Commission, *History*, 296; Marriage Bonds, Number 29, Gonzales County, CC; Horace Eggleston, Benjamin Williams, Republic Claims, TSLA; Horace Eggleston, Benjamin Williams, Land Grant Search, TGLO; *TTR*, May 2, 1837.

30. *TTR*, May 2, 1837, Nov. 6, 1839, Oct. 28, 1840, Feb. 10, Sept. 9, 1841; Deeds, bk. A, 469–71, bk. B, 23, bk. D, 24–25, 99–102, 345–47, Comal County, CC; Deeds, bk. A, 337–38, bk. B, 412, 740, Fort Bend County, CC; Deeds, bk. 55, pp. 438–42, Blanco County, CC; Deeds, bk. A, 351–56, Travis County, CC; Partition of Dean's Half of Williams Survey, Sept. 5, 1859, Estate of Jabez Dean, dec., Case 137, PR, Washington County, CC; Mary Whatley Clarke, *Swenson Saga and the SMS Ranches*, 17–24, 43–51, 85–86, 101–9; Biographical notes, William S. Pierson Collection, 1795–1906, CAH; Cutrer, "Handy, Robert Eden."

31. Jabez Dean, Land Grant Search, TGLO; U.S. Census, 1840, Davidson County, Tenn.; Arrivals, July 5, 1840, New Orleans Passenger Lists, 1820–1902, RG85, M259, R21, NAB; Jabez Dean, Republic Claims, TSLA; Charter, Nashville Texas Emigrant Society, Bransford Family Papers, II-H-6, box 1, folder 1, TNSLA; TR, 1850, TAC, Comal County, TSLA; Deeds, bk. B, 184–85, bk. H, 504–6, Washington County, CC; Deeds, bk. A, 323, Fort Bend County, CC; Deeds, bk. C, 87–89, Fayette County, CC; Deeds,

bk. A, 490–91, bk. C, 126–27, Lavaca County, CC; Deeds, bk. G, 98–100, Matagorda County, CC; U.S. Census, 1850, Washington County, Tex.

32. J. Moursund, *Blanco County History*, 87; J. Speer, *History of Blanco County*, 1; *South-Western American*, July 9, 1853; *TSG*, Oct. 8, 1853; *San Antonio Light*, June 6, 1915.

33. *San Antonio Light*, June 6, 1915; Callahan homestead, Rio Blanco, West Papers, privately held. The Callahans' clapboard house survived until the mid-1950s when a flood washed it away.

34. *San Antonio Light*, June 6, 1915; J. Moursund, *Blanco County History*, 88–90; TR, 1853, 1854, TAC, Comal County, TSLA; Hugh McLaurin, William N. Trainer, Land Grant Search, TGLO.

35. Hines, *Eli Clemmons Hinds*, n.p.; Deeds, bk. D, 194, Comal County, CC; Deeds, bk. 1, pp. 266–68, Blanco County, CC; *Blanco County News*, Mar. 26, 2008; Marriages, bk. A, 51, Gonzales County, CC; Gonzales County Historical Commission, *History*, F405–7; Clemmons Hinds, John McCoy, Land Grant Search, TGLO; Eli C. Hinds, John McCoy, Elizabeth McCoy, Republic Claims, TSLA; S. Moore, *Savage Frontier*, 3:222, 4:64, 81, 92; *Galveston Daily News*, Feb. 20, 1879.

36. Deeds, bk. D, 207, Comal County, CC; Janelle Holmes, interviews, telephone conversations, and e-mails with author, various dates, 2009–10, 2018. Janelle Holmes's husband is a descendant of Woodson and Mary Blassingame.

CHAPTER 10

1. Diary entry, Apr. 20, 1854, DP, CAH; PM, bk. B, 154–55, Comal County, CC.

2. Dary, *Cowboy*, 37–42, 72–74; J. Jackson, *Mesteños*, 7, 92, 445, 536; Thonhoff, "Texas and the American Revolution," 514–15.

3. Goetzmann, *Army Exploration*, 114 (map), 194; *Democratic Telegraph and Texas Register*, Sept. 6, 1849; Bieber, "Southwestern Trails," 349, 353–56; Neighbors, "Expedition," 33–59.

4. *Daily Alta California*, July 13, 1850, May 1, 1851, Dec. 16, 1852, Jan. 1, 1853; DeBow, *Seventh Census: 1850*; Kennedy, *Preliminary Report*, 2; *Daily Placer Times and Transcript*, Aug. 5, 1852, Jan. 1, 19, 1853; *Daily Missouri Republican*, July 27, 1853; Erskine, *Diary*, 17–18; Bell, "Log," pt. 1, 209.

5. J. Jackson, *Mesteños*, 78–85; Beatie, *Saddles*, 48, 50, 54–55, 58, 219; Dary, *Cowboy*, 13–14, 31–33, 64, 77, 85–86, 115–16, 154–55, 204–5, 243–48; J. W. Nichols, *Now You Hear*, 71–72; *Washington American*, Nov. 8, 1855 (Hope saddle); *San Antonio Herald*, May 8, 1855 (Childress saddle); *Western Texan*, Feb. 16, May 11, 1854; *TSG*, Mar. 21, Apr. 15, 1854; *Gonzales Inquirer*, Apr. 8, 1854; *Texan Mercury*, Apr. 22, 1854.

6. Dary, *Cowboy*, 5–7, 31–35, 72, 137–40, 148–55; J. Jackson, *Mesteños*, 10–12, 594–99.

7. The Diary and Letters of Michael Erskine, 2–11,18–30, 35, Andrew Nelson Erskine Papers, 1845–62, CAH; "Erskines and Ehringhauses," 9–11, 18, 94–97, 99, 102, 110, 116–18, privately held; TR, 1841–48, TAC, Gonzales County, TSLA; TR, 1849–1854, TAC, Guadalupe County, TSLA; Deeds, bk. GT, 32–33, 241–42, 294–96, 318–19, bk. C, 94–99, Guadalupe County, CC; Guadalupe County, 1847, box 2-12/486, Republic of Texas, Department of State, Election Returns, TSLA; Muckelroy, "History of El Capote Ranch," 3–4; J. Baume, Land Grant Search, TGLO; Biographical Material, Baume Will (1834), El Capote Ranch Records, Southwest Collection/Special Collections Library, Texas Tech University; Michael Erskine Estate, PR, Guadalupe County, CC.

8. James Campbell, Land Grant Search, TGLO; Clarkson, "Belle," 272, 275–76; U.S. Census, 1850, Bexar County, Tex.; *Texan Mercury*, Apr. 8, 1854; *San Antonio Herald*, May 15, 1855; Bell, "Log," pt. 2, p. 297, pt. 3, pp. 47, 57; *Sacramento Daily Union*, May 13, July 3, 1853.

9. U.S. Census, 1850, Bexar County, Tex.; James, *Frontier*, 17–23, 28, 32, 92; *Galveston Daily News*, Nov. 30, 1877; Pease, "Sweet, James R."; *TSG*, Sept. 28, 1850, Sept. 16, 1854; *Ledger and Texan*, Jan. 4, July 7, Aug. 4, 1855, July 2, Sept. 3, 1857; Bexar, Victoria Counties, Nonpopulation Census Schedules for Texas, 1850–80, MT1134, R10, R21, NAB; Joseph Beck, Land Grant Search, TGLO; *Alamo Star*, June 17, 1854; Cutrer, "Pyron, Charles Lynn"; *Western Texan*, Sept. 23, Oct. 14, 1852; *Houston Telegraph*, Sept. 2, 1869; Marrin and Sheppard, *Paradise*, 14, 24–25, 54; *Clarksville Standard*, Jan. 15, 1853, Jan. 21, 1854; *Twentieth Century History of Southwest Texas*, 139.

10. J. Evetts Haley edited Bell's diary, "Log of the Texas–California Cattle Trail," publishing it in three installments in the *Southwestern Historical Quarterly* in 1932. In 1852, Tennessean James G. Bell (b. ca. 1830) came to Texas and settled in San Antonio, where his father opened a jewelry store.

11. *TSG*, Apr. 29, May 27, 1854; "Erskines and Ehringhauses," 118, 124, 131, 136; Erskine, *Diary*, 27, 29; Huson, *Refugio* 2:227–29.

12. Erskine, *Diary*, 43–44; Bell, "Log," pt. 1, pp. 208–13; *Texan Mercury*, Apr. 29, 1854; Woodhouse, *From Texas*, xxi–xxii, 23; U.S. Census, 1850, Bexar County, Tex.

13. Erskine, *Diary*, 44–47; Bell, "Log," pt. 1, pp. 212–14; Eccleston, *Overland*, 72 (map); Stillman, *Wanderings*, 118, 120–21; J. Reid, *Tramp*, 88–89; *Daily Alta California*, Aug. 16, 1854.

14. Erskine, *Diary*, 46–53; Bell, "Log," pt. 1, pp. 212, 215–17, 219–20, 222, 226–27; J. Smith, "Camp Hudson"; *Daily Alta California*, Aug. 16, 1854.

15. Erskine, *Diary*, 48, 50, 53; Bell, "Log," pt. 1, pp. 214–15, 217–23, 225, 227; Austerman, *Sharps Rifles*, 39, 53–55.

16. Erskine, *Diary*, 53–54; *Clarksville Standard*, Sept. 2, 1854.

17. Erskine, *Diary*, 55–56; Bell, "Log," pt. 1, p. 228; Austerman, *Sharps Rifles*, 54; *TSG*, July 29, Aug. 5, 1854.

18. Erskine, *Diary*, 54–57; Bell, "Log," pt. 1, pp. 228-231; J. Reid, *Tramp*, 125; Woodhouse, *From Texas*, 47; Eccleston, *Overland*, 121.

19. Erskine, *Diary*, 56–57, 61; Bell, "Log," pt. 1, pp. 230–33; Sowell, *Texas Indian Fighters*, 685; J. Reid, *Tramp*, 166, 168–69; Kohout, "Magoffin, James Wiley."

20. Erskine, *Diary*, 61; Bell, "Log of the Texas–California Cattle Trail," pt. 2, pp. 290–91, 294.

21. Erskine, *Diary*, 61–67, 75–76; Bell, "Log," pt. 2, pp. 290–91, 294, 298, 304–6; Bartlett, *Personal Narrative*, 1:247, 251–52, 254–55, 2:330–32; Faulk, "Bartlett, John Russell."

22. J. Reid, *Tramp*, 182–83; Durivage, "Through Mexico," 203, 205–9; A. B. Clarke, *Travels*, 61; Erskine, *Diary*, 76–78; Bell, "Log," pt. 2, pp. 305–7.

23. Erskine, *Diary*, 76–78; Bell, "Log," pt. 2, pp. 307–8; Clarke, *Travels*, 63; Durivage, "Through Mexico," 207–8; Sowell, *Texas Indian Fighters*, 685–90; Baylor, "Gen. Baylor," 359–62.

24. Sowell, *Texas Indian Fighters*, 687–90; Baylor, "Gen. Baylor," 360–62.

25. Erskine, *Diary*, 78–79; Sowell, *Texas Indian Fighters*, 690; Baylor, "Gen. Baylor," 362; *Daily Placer Times and Transcript*, Nov. 7, 1854.

26. Erskine, *Diary*, 79–81; Bell, "Log," pt. 2, pp. 310–16, pt. 3, pp. 47–48; Bartlett, *Personal Narrative*, 2:329, 298–99; Martin, "From Texas," 143–44; A. Clarke, *Travels*,

67–68; Durivage, "Through Mexico to California," 209–12; Eccleston, *Overland*, 202; J. Reid, *Tramp*, 185–87.

27. Erskine, *Diary*, 81–82, 84; Bell, "Log of the Texas–California Cattle Trail," pt. 3, pp. 48–52; Durivage, "Through Mexico," 213–20; A. Clarke, *Travels*, 68–69, 71–74; Eccleston, *Overland*, 204–7, 209–22; J. Reid, *Tramp*, 227–30; Martin, "From Texas," 144.

28. Erskine, *Diary*, 84–89; Bell, "Log," pt. 3, pp. 51–56; Martin, "From Texas," 201–3.

29. Erskine, *Diary*, 89–91; Bell, "Log," pt. 3, pp. 56–59. Not all careless weeds (*Amaranthus palmeri*) are poisonous, some more so during certain growth stages.

30. Erskine, *Diary*, 91–93; *Sacramento Daily Union*, Nov. 9, 1854.

31. "From Texas to the Gold Mines," 273; Durivage, "Through Mexico," 229–33; Woodhouse, *From Texas*, 167–74; Martin, "From Texas," *Daily Alta California*, Oct. 7, 11, Nov. 7, 1854; Hill, *History*, 63, 94–96, 101, 104, 107–11, 113–14, 121, 127, 130, 135–39; Erskine, *Diary*, 93–94; U.S. Congress, Senate, 30th Cong., 1849, 1st sess., S. Ex. Doc. 7, p. 106.

32. Erskine, *Diary*, 93–94.

33. Ibid., 35, 47, 67–72, 79, 81, 89–94.

34. *Sacramento Daily Union*, May 5, Sept. 4, 6, 18, Dec. 13, 18, 1854; Hoover and Kyle, *Historic Spots*, 224; *TSG*, March 28, May 27, July 29, Aug. 5, Nov. 4, Dec. 2, 1854; *Daily Placer Times and Transcript*, Aug. 26, 1854; Erskine, *Diary*, 43–45, 65, 77, 79, 93–94; Bell, "Log," pt. 2, pp. 297 307, pt. 3, pp. 47, 57, 59; *Texan Mercury*, Apr. 29, May 13, 20, 1854; *Daily Alta California*, June 16, Aug. 1, Sept. 3, 9, Oct. 7, Nov. 7, 1854; *San Antonio Ledger and Texan*, Mar. 30, May 4, 18, June 1, 8, July 20, 1854; *Western Texan*, Apr. 13, 20, May 18, July 20, Oct. 19, 1854; *Nacogdoches Chronicle*, Mar. 28, 1854; *Daily Placer Times and Transcript*, July 17, Sept. 27, Nov. 7, 24, Dec. 18, 1854; *California Farmer and Journal of Useful Sciences*, Nov. 30, 1854; *Texas State Times* (hereafter *TST*), Feb. 17, 1855; *Alamo Star*, May 20, 1854; *Texas Planter*, Nov. 8, 1854; *Clarksville Standard*, Sept. 23, 1854; *Galveston Weekly News*, Nov.7, 1854; *NOP*, Oct. 29, 1854; *Los Angles Star*, July 21, 1854: *Neu Braunfelser Zeitung*, May 5, 1854.

35. Erskine, *Diary*, 27, 43–46, 50–51, 56–68, 78–79, 89, 91–94, 97, 101, 127, 129, 133, 136, 138, 156; U.S. Census, 1850, Guadalupe County, Tex.; *Clarksville Standard*, Sept. 2, 1854; Sowell, *Texas Indian Fighters*, 683, 686; U.S. Census, 1860, Caldwell, Comal Counties, Tex.; *Ledger and Texan*, July 10, 1856; *Daily Union*, Dec. 6, 1854; U.S. Census, 1870, Mariposa County, Calif.; TR, 1876–70, TAC, Guadalupe County, TSLA. *TSG*, Dec. 2, 1854. In 1870, James G. Bell was a jeweler in Mariposa County, California. John Box Roberts returned to Guadalupe County, resumed farming, married again in 1869, and died in 1872.

36. Erskine, *Diary*, 54, 94, 115; Bell, "Log," pt. 3, pp. 60–64; *Daily Alta California*, Dec. 1, 2, 1854; Westfall, *Girl*, 2, 10, 23, 39–44, 53–54; "Across," 250–51; *Diario de la Marina*, Dec. 24, 1854. A lighter is a type of flat-bottomed barge used to transfer goods and passengers to and from moored ships.

37. *Diario de la Marina*, Dec. 27, 1854; *NOP*, Dec. 30, 1854, Jan. 2, 1855; *New Orleans Bee*, Jan. 4, 1855; DCR, *Collin Johnson vs. J. H. Callahan and G. B. Hollamon,* Civil Case 590, Guadalupe County, DC.

38. Erskine, *Diary*, 103, 111, 113; James, *Frontier*, 25; *TSG*, Oct. 28, 1854.

39. Erskine, *Diary*, 38–40, 99–134, 138–57; Michael Erskine at Capote, chap. 8, Andrew Nelson Erskine Papers, CAH.

40. SR, A. N. Erskine, T. Igg Johnston [Johnson], 4th Texas Infantry, Confederate, Civil War, RG109, M323, R0286, R0288, NAB; Michael Erskine at Capote, chap. 8, Andrew Nelson Erskine Papers, CAH; *Tri-Weekly News*, July 31, 1872; *San Antonio Express*, Feb. 28, 1923; Promissory Notes, 1872–83, Deeds, 1844–77, El Capote Ranch Records, Southwest Collection/Special Collections Library, Texas Tech University; Muckelroy, "History of El Capote Ranch," 15–16.

41. *Memorial and Genealogical Record*, 475–76; SR, Henry Maney, 4th Mounted Volunteers, Sibley's Brigade, Confederate, RG109, M323, R0029, NAB; *House Journal of the 10th Legislature*, app.1; *Cases Argued and Decided*, 38:305–29; *Journal of the Reconstruction Convention*, 520; *Houston Telegraph*, Apr. 4, May 16, June 27, Dec. 5, 1872, Mar. 6, 20, July 17, Aug. 14, 21, 1873; *Galveston Daily News*, Mar. 27, Apr. 2, 9, 15, May 29, 1879; *San Antonio Light*, July 13, 1920.

CHAPTER 11

1. Horace Eggleston, Milam's Register of Families, Milam's Colony Records, Land Grant Search, TGLO; Gonzales County Historical Commission, *History*, 296; Horace Eggleston, Republic Claims, TSLA; Deeds, bk. 59, pp. 60–70, Blanco County, CC; Deeds, bk. D, 109–10, 346, 433–36, 463–65, bk. E, 258–59, Comal County, CC; Deeds, bk. A, 352–54, bk. B, 117–18, Travis County, CC; DCM, bk. B, 360–61, bk. E, 258–59, Comal County, DC; DCR, *Heirs of Joseph Fowler v. Jabez Dean*, Civil Case 170, Comal County, DC; Deeds, bk. 1, 399–400, Kendall County, CC.

2. DCR, *Johnson v. Callahan and Hollamon*, Civil Case 590, Guadalupe County, DC; Campbell, *Empire*, 82–92; Campbell, "Slave Hiring," 111, 114.

3. U.S. Census, 1850, 1860, Cooper County, Mo.; U.S. Census, 1850, 1860, Guadalupe County, Tex.; U.S. Census, 1850, 1860, Slave Inhabitants, Guadalupe County, Tex.; TR, 1855–65, TAC, Guadalupe County, TSLA; PR, Cases 807, 812, Guadalupe County, CC; DCR, *Johnson v. Callahan and Hollamon*, Civil Case 590, Guadalupe County, DC; *Seguin Mercury*, Dec. 22, 1858; Weinert, *Authentic History*, 16, 69.

4. *San Antonio Light*, June 6, 1915 (description of Devil's Backbone in 1853); DuCoin, *Lawmen*, 31, 34, 47–48; F. W. Schweppe, "Curry's Creek," Kendalia Scrapbooks, Kendalia Public Library; TR, 1852–55, TAC, Comal County, TSLA.

5. *TSG*, Feb. 3, 1855; Blanco County, Map 66715, Maps, TGLO; "Soils of Texas," 168–69, Map L-74; West Papers, privately held; Brune, *Springs*, 1:76–79, 129–30; "Curry Creek," *HBTO*, http://www.tshaonline.org/handbook/online/articles/rbcns; Loflin and Loflin, *Grasses*, 39, 51.

6. La Vere, *Texas Indians*, 141 (map), 169 (map); J. Moursund, *Blanco County History*, 1–8; *TSG*, June 12, 1852; Benjamin Williams, Horace Eggleston, Noel Mixon, Jesse McCrocklin, Land Grant Search, TGLO; S. Moore, *Savage Frontier*, 1:3–7, 2:329–36, 3:143; J. W. Nichols, *Now You Hear*, 24–29, 31; Callahan in the Rio Blanco Valley, West Papers, privately held; Biesele, *German Settlements*, 139–52, 186–87.

7. Deeds, bk. D, 194, 207, Comal County, CC; Hines, *Eli Clemmons Hinds*, np; Deeds, bk. 1, pp. 266–68, Blanco County, CC; *Blanco County News*, Mar. 26, 2008; TR, 1853–55, TAC, Comal County, TSLA; J. Moursund, *Blanco County Families*, 41–42.

8. TR, 1852–56, TAC, Comal County, TSLA; J. Speer, *History of Blanco County*, 1–4; J. Moursund, *Blanco County Families*, 32, 41–43, 72–73, 162–63, 238–41, 254, 281–83, 289–91, 293, 332–33, 416–19, 440–41, 454; J. Moursund, *Blanco County History*, 87–96; William Trainer, William Johnson, Hugh McLaurin, Jesse McCrocklin, Samuel

Johnson, John M. Watson, Robert Page, John Lindemann (Lindeman), Land Grant Search, TGLO; *San Antonio Light*, June 6, 1915.

9. TR, 1852–56, TAC, Comal County, TSLA; J. Speer, *History of Blanco County*, 1; J. Moursund, *Blanco County Families*, 20–21, 59–62, 216, 275, 292–93, 415, 436–37, 482–83; J. Moursund, *Blanco County History*, 89–91, 94–95; Joel and James Cherry, William McKinney, Isaac Tanner, J. McKibbin, Francis, M. and James C. Martin, Land Grant Search, TGLO; *Western Texan*, Mar. 23, 1854.

10. TR, 1852–56, TAC, Comal County, TSLA; J. Speer, *History of Blanco County*, 3–4; J. Moursund, *Blanco County Families*, 244–45, 251–52, 353–53, 373–74, 428–30; J. Moursund, *Blanco County History*, 83, 88–96; Jonas, *Kendalia*, 2:2–9, 18–25; William E. Jones, John Sansom, James Campbell, William Clopton, S. B. Patton, Land Grant Search, TGLO.

11. J. Speer, *History of Blanco County*, 3–4; Jonas, *Kendalia*, 2:8, 14.

12. Wuppermann, "Diary of Elise Tips Wuppermann," WC, privately held; J. Speer, *History of Blanco County*, 3–4; Jonas, *Kendalia*, 2:8, 14; DCR, *Johnson v. Callahan and Hollamon*, Civil Case 590, Guadalupe County, DC; *TSG*, Feb. 24, Mar. 10, 24, Apr. 7, 28, 1855; *Neu Braunfelser Zeitung*, Mar. 2, Mar. 9, 16, 23, 30, Apr. 6, 13, 1855; TR, 1855, TAC, Comal County, TSLA.

13. DCR, *Johnson v. Callahan and Hollamon*, Civil Case 590, Guadalupe County, DC; *Neu Braunfelser Zeitung*, Apr. 18, 1855; Olmsted, *Journey*, 501; *TST*, May 5, 1855; *Blanco Courier*, Mar. 8, 1911; *TSG*, May 12, 1855.

14. *TST*, Feb. 10, 1856; James Hughes Callahan, box 4, folder 14, JWNP, DRTL.

15. Campbell, *Empire*, 96–114; Campbell, *Laws*, 56–86; DCR, *Johnson v. Callahan and Hollamon*, Civil Case 590, Guadalupe County, DC; DCM, vols. A-1, A, Caldwell County, DC; DCM, vols. A–C, Comal County, DC; DCM, vols. A, AB, C, Guadalupe County, DC; *Gonzales Inquirer*, May 11, 1854; *TSG*, Mar. 28, Apr. 22, Aug. 12, Sept. 9, Oct. 7, 1854, Feb. 24, Mar. 3, 17, June 9, 1855, Mar. 15, 1856; *Texas Ranger*, July 13, 1854; *Texas Planter*, Aug. 23, 1854; *Galveston Weekly News*, Sept. 5, Nov. 7, 1854, May 29, June 12, 1855, Mar. 25, 1856; *Western Texan*, Sept. 7, 1854; *TST*, Feb. 17, Apr. 21, May 5, Sept. 15, Nov. 3, 1855, Feb. 10, Mar. 15, 1856; *Texas Sun*, Mar. 5, 1855; *Ledger and Texan*, July 19, Nov. 17, 1855; *Galveston Civilian and Gazette*, Mar. 21, 1856; *Weekly Telegram*, May 7, 1856.

16. *Weekly Statesman*, Nov. 5, 1885; *Representative Men and Old Families*, 1:9; *Texas Legal Directory*, 57; Marten, "Hamilton, Andrew Jackson"; SR, Frederick W. Chandler, McCulloch's Co. 1st Texas Mounted Volunteers, Mexican War, RG94, M616, R6, NAB; Civil Docket and Process Record, 1843–51, Fayette County, DC; Civil Docket Journal, 1839–54, Bastrop County, DC; Bar Docket, vols. 2–5, Travis County, DC; V. L. Brooks, *History of the First Baptist Church*, 14; Deed Index, CC, Fayette, Travis, Bexar, Williamson Counties; F. W. or Frederick Chandler, Land Grant Search, TGLO; DCR, *Heirs of Fowler v. Dean*, Civil Case 170, Comal County, DC; DCM, bk. B, 351–52, Comal County, DC.

17. *Memorial and Genealogical Record*, 168–69; Trimble and Lindsey letters, Galveston, 1837, folder 5, Period as Surveyor of Bexar County, folders 7, 10, Period as Surveyor of Fayette County, folder 12, Statement of William Lindsey and Estate, 1838, 1866, Papers Involving Land Transactions, folder 18, Biographical material, box1981/160–1, Lindsey Family Materials, folder 11, A. M. Lindsey Diary, 1852, Diary, 1855, folder 29, Business Diaries, folder 1, box 1981/160–2, Lindsey Family Papers (hereafter LFP), TSLA; Deed Index, Hays County, CC; William Lindsey, Land Grant Search, TGLO; Stovall et al.,

Clear Springs, 71, 82–86, 89; Galveston, Trimble and Lindsey Map, Maps, TGLO; PR, bk. B, 188–92, Hays County, CC.

18. Talbot, *Stringtown*, 6–11; Gracy, "Pitts, John Drayton"; Stovall et al., *Clear Springs*, 83–84, 86; *Southern Recorder*, Apr. 7, 1831; Pitts, John Drayton, General Name File, GSA; U.S. Census, 1820, 1830, Washington, County, Ga.; U.S. Census, 1840, Stewart County, Ga.; *Journal of the House of Representatives* (2nd Leg., State of Tex.), 7; D. Pitts, Mar. 20, 1848, Bonds and oaths of county and State officials, box 2–9/872, Secretary of State, TSLA; Deeds, bk. A, 342, Hays County, CC; TR, 1847–61, TAC, Hays County, TSLA; Denman, "Office of Adjutant General," 311, 322; Ruthven, *Proceedings*, 2:315; *Democratic Telegraph and Texas Register*, Feb. 17, Mar. 2, 1848; *TSG*, Nov. 29, Oct. 8, 1853, Dec. 5, 1857; *Texan Mercury*, Oct. 15, 1853.

19. DuCoin, *Lawmen*, 3–9, 24, 24n28, 31, 236–39; Abbett, "William Early Jones," 1–3; Marriages, bk. 1, p. 7, bk. 2, p. 267, Probate Court, Jackson County, Ga.; Elrod, *Historical Notes*, 45, 56; Col. Russell Jones Sr., File II Names, Virtual Vault, GSA; G. J. N. Wilson, *Early History*, 286; A. H. Jones, Republic Claims, TSLA; Jenkins, *Papers*, 2:384–85; Jones, William E., Jackson County, 1831, General Name File, Virtual Vault, GSA; Inferior Court Minutes, 1822–43, pp. 246–47, Jackson County, M168/18, GSA; Sverdlik "Augusta Chronicle"; *TSG*, June 12, 1852.

20. DuCoin, *Lawmen*, 9–12; Jackson Rowark, Land Grant Search, TGLO; TR, 1841, TAC, Gonzales County, TSLA; Russell Jones Jr., PR 121, Gonzales County, CC; Sophia Jones to Dr. James Cunningham, Feb. 3, 1841, Letitia Smith to Cunningham, July 10, 1841, James Cunningham Papers, TSLA; Abbett, "William Early Jones," 5; Smither, *Journals*, 3:1.

21. Abbett, "William Early Jones," 6–18, 20–26; DCM, bk. B, 41–43, Bexar County, DC; Winkler, "Bexar and Dawson Prisoners," 294–311, 313–17, 320–24; Bejar Prisoners, Juan Fernandez, Sept. 11, copied by Reyes, Sept. 20, OM (1842), Exp. XI/481.3/1731, DAM, SEDENA; Nance, "Brigadier General Adrian Woll's Report," 531; Fred Riley Jones, "San Antonio Prisoners," 8–13; Lander, "General Waddy Thompson," 33–34: *Augusta Chronicle*, Apr. 26, 1843; *TTR*, May 24, 1843; *Clarksville Standard*, May 18, June 8, Sept. 21, Oct. 28, 1843; *Weekly Citizen*, Dec. 9, 1843.

22. Abbett, "William Early Jones," 30–37, 39–41; Winkler, "Bexar and Dawson Prisoners," 310–11; *TTR*, Feb. 7, 14, 1844; *Clarksville Standard*, Feb. 24, 1844.

23. Gammel, *Laws*, 1:1139; Dallam, *Opinionst*, 316–436 (*Herbert v. Moore*, p. 375); Paulsen, "Missing Cases of the Republic," 372–415; Paulsen, "Short History," 297–98, 301; Townes, "Development," 30, 43–44; S. S. Cox, "Supreme Court," 271–77.

24. DCM, bk. A, 1–2, Comal County, DC; DCM, bk. A, 1, 3, Guadalupe County, DC; DCM, bk. A, 2–5, Caldwell County, DC; DCM, bk. A, 7, 10, Hays County, DC; DCM, bk. A, 5–6, Williamson County, DC, Georgetown, Tex.; DCM, bk. A, 512, 521, Bastrop County, DC; DCM, bk. B, 77, 79, Bexar County, DC; DCM, bk. C, 1–4, Travis County, CC.

25. DCFR, bk. B, 299–331, Gonzales County, DC; DCR, Civil Case 101, *Callahan v. Patterson*, Guadalupe County, DC; *Weekly Journal*, June 10, 1851; Paulsen, "Missing Cases of the Republic," 377, 379–80, 386–87; DCM, *Jones v. Erskine et al.*, Civil Cases 1113, 1114, bk. D, 59–60, Guadalupe County, DC; James Webb and Duval, *Reports of Cases Argued and Decided*, 1:57–56, 399–411, 2:1–98, 127–29, 269–73, 305–10, 315–23, 340–41, 357–62, 381–97, 449–51, 581–82, 3:31–35, 51–57, 79–93, 111–13, 360–96; Hartley, *Reports of Cases Argued and Decided*, 4:1–5, 10–16, 19–21, 31–34, 55–59, 5:1–2, 103–6, 144–45, 221–26, 231–34, 236–39, 7:24–30, 34–38, 55–86, 87–105, 118–20, 130–34, 193–30,

9:7–12, 21, 22, 24–33, 41–43, 118–20, 131, 143–62. District court terms in which Jones was the district judge are in: DCM, bk. A, bk. B, Comal County, DC; DCM, bks. A, AB, Guadalupe County, DC; DCM, bk. A-1, Caldwell County, DC; DCM, bk. A, Williamson County, DC; DCM, bk. B, Bastrop County, DC; DCM, bk. A, Travis County, DC; DCM, bk. B, Bexar County, DC; DCM, bk. A, Gillespie County, DC; DCM, bks. 1, B, Gonzales County, DC.

26. DCM, bk. A, 68–77, Guadalupe County, DC; DCM, bk. A, 54–64, Comal County, DC; DCR *Jones v. Jones*, Civil Case 35, Guadalupe County, DC; U.S. Census, 1850, Bexar County; *El Bejareño*, Mar. 1, 1856; Marriages, bk. A, 8, Guadalupe County, CC; DuCoin, *Lawmen*, 41, 73, 79, 91, 101, 109, 113, 139; Rector Lineage, Nelson Rector to Lelia Neibert, Dec. 1926, Jones Family Papers, privately held.

27. *TSG*, June 21, 1851; *Galveston News*, July 1, 1851; DuCoin, *Lawmen*, 47; *Gonzales Inquirer*, Oct. 8, 1853; James M. Day, Land Grant Search, TGLO; Deeds, bk. GT, 386, 471, bk. B, 1–2, 69, 112–14, 553–54, bk. C, 36–37, 39, 150–53, 168–70, bk. D, 92, 440–41, 549–50, 593–94, 605, 835–36, bk. F, 147, 154, 157, bk. G, 404, Guadalupe County, CC; U.S. Census, 1860, Guadalupe County; U.S. Census, 1860, Slave Inhabitants, Guadalupe County; DCR, *Jones v. Morrison*, Civil Case 402, *Jones v. Brackenridge*, Civil Case 1402, Guadalupe County, DC. Morrison only paid the first two years' annual annuity to Caroline and failed to pay the $2,500 after Caroline had asked for it. So, Jones sued, repossessing the property, which he sold to George Brackenridge, who in 1865 also defaulted, causing Jones to sue and once more regain the property. Paintings of the Morrison house made in 1853–54 exist, and it is probable the house was built by Jones (Hardinge, *Views of Texas*, 46–51).

28. *Galveston News*, July 1, 1851; *Texas Democrat*, Oct. 7, 14, 1846, Mar. 20, 1847; *Clarksville Standard*, Feb. 3, 1844; W. Speer and Brown *Encyclopedia of the New West*, 579.

29. DCM, bk. B, 350–52, 360–61, bk. E, 258–59, Comal County, DC; July 3, 1855 entry, Diary, 1855, Business Diaries, LFP, TSLA; Deeds, bk. D, 434–36, bk. E, 258–59, 553–55, Comal County, CC; Deeds, bk. 59, pp. 67–70, Blanco County, CC; Deeds, bk. D, 434–36, Comal County, CC; DCR, *Heirs of Fowler v. Dean*, Civil Case 170, Comal County, DC; Deeds, bk. 1, pp. 399–400, Kendall County, CC.

30. Deeds, bk. E, 258–59, 560–61, Comal County, CC; DCM, bk. B, 408–9, Comal County, DC.

31. July 16–24, Aug. 14–17, 1855 entries, Diary, 1855, Business Diaries, LFP, TSLA; Moursund, *Blanco County Families*, 72; TR, 1857–58, TAC, Comal County, TSLA.

32. Deeds, bk. E, 572, Comal County, CC; Wuppermann, "Diary of Elise Tips Wuppermann," WC, privately held; *TST*, Sept. 1, 1855; *TSG*, Sept. 22, 1855.

CHAPTER 12

1. Commentaries on the 1855 Callahan Expedition are extensive; some of the key ones are: Tyler, "Callahan Expedition of 1855," 574–85; Shearer, "Callahan Expedition, 1855," *SWHQ* 54 (1951): 430–51; Mulroy, *Freedom*, 77–81; Collins, *Texas Devils*, 72–88; J. D. Nichols, *Limits of Liberty*, 192–203; J. D. Nichols, "Line of Liberty," 413–33; Medina González Dávila, "La Batalla," 40–41; Wilkins, *Defending*, 45–64; May, *Manifest*, 42–43, 53, 90, 145, 173, 260–61; Porter, *Black Seminoles*, 151–53; S. Miller, *Coacoochee's Bones*, 168–69; Porter, "Seminole in Mexico," 18–20; Utley, *Lone Star*, 94–97; Gesick, "1855 Callahan Raid," 47–64; Tyler, *Santiago Vidaurri*, 22–24; Thompson, *Fort Duncan*, 29–31; Tyler, "Slave Owners," 44–67; Tyler, "Age," 40–48; Moseley, "Public Career," 152–62; Enríquez Terrazas and Rodríguez García, *Coahuila*, 152–54; Porter, *Negro*; R. Smith, "Mame-

lukes," 79–83; Olmsted, *Journey*, 333; Sumpter, *Paso*, 61–69; Tyler, "Fugitive Slaves," 1–12; Anderson, *Conquest*, 268–69; Schwartz, *Across*, 35–36; Cunningham and Hewitt, "'Lovely Land,'" 408–10; T. Smith, *Fort Inge*, 80–81; Chubb, "Revisiting," 417–29; Tyler, "Callahan Expedition."

2. Campbell, *Gone*, 235–37; *TSG*, Apr. 14, June 23, Aug. 5, 1854, Sept. 9, 1855.

3. May, *Manifest*, xi, xv, 1–4, 20–33, 36–38; Collins, *Texas Devils*, 64–67, 93–98; *TSG*, June 23, 1855; *La Patria*, Apr. 10, 1853, Nov. 18, 1854.

4. Medina González Dávila, "'¡Pero es tan sólo un río!,' 56; Emory, *Report* (U.S. and Mex. Boundary Survey), 1:56–58, 68–72; Lane, *I Married*, 5, 16; J. Brooks, "Served," 24–27, 34; Cazneau, *Eagle Pass*, 38, 110; Olmsted, *Journey*, 336; A. Scarborough, *Pass*, 47–48; R. Johnson, *Soldier's Reminiscences*, 63–64; Vizcaya Canales, *Tierra de guerra*, 20–21, 306; Rodríguez García, *Historias de resistencia*, 27–29

5. Vizcaya Canales, *Incursiones de indios*, 28–29; F. Smith, *Dominance*, 192–11, 216 (map), 236–37; Anderson, *Conquest*, 230–31. T. Smith, "U.S. Army Combat Operations," 507; *TSG*, Oct. 27, Aug. 25, 1849; *San Antonio Ledger*, July 20, 1854; Wilkins, *Defending*, 11, 15–19, 22–24, 29, 39–43; Utley, *Lone Star*, 89–94; Collins, *Texas Devils*, 39, 47, 71–72.

6. *San Antonio Ledger*, Mar. 23, May 4, 11, 13, 18, 25, Aug. 17, Sept. 28, 1854; *TSG*, May 18, 27, June 13, July 8, 29, Aug. 26, 1854; Edmond J. Davis, Webb County, to E. M. Pease, Mar. 13, 1854, Pease to Gen. Persifor F. Smith, Mar. 24, Aug. 8, 18, Sept. 28, Nov. 4, 1854, Box 301–23, Folder 4, Burnet County to Pease, Apr. 20, 1854, [Petitioners of Fort Inge] to Pease, Apr. 29, 1854, William E. Jones to Pease, Apr. 30, 1854, Box 301–23, Folder 5, Citizens of Starr, Webb, and Nueces Counties to Pease, July 27, 1854, Box 301–23, Folder 8, EMPP, TSLA; *Western Texan*, Aug. 17, 1854.

7. *TSG*, Oct. 7, Nov. 4, 1854, Jan. 1, Mar. 10, 1855; *TST*, June 2, 16, 1855; Pease to Smith, June 20, 1855, Box 301–24, Folder 19, EMPP, TSLA; Winfrey and Day, *Indian Papers*, 3:219–20; Collins, *Texas Devils*, 73; *NOP*, May 1, 1855.

8. Guerra, "Henry, William R."; Marriages, bk. B, 211–12, Bexar County, CC; J. Ford, *Rip Ford's Texas*, 267; *TSG*, Apr. 21, June 23, Aug. 11, 1855; *San Antonio Ledger and Texan*, Jan. 16, 1851, Jan. 5, 1854, July 21, 28, 1855; *El Bejareño*, July 31, Sept. 1, 1855; *San Antonio Herald*, Aug. 14, 1855, May 29, 1858 (Henry wrote this biography); *TST*, Apr. 7, Aug. 25, Sept. 1, 15, 1855; Emilio Langberg to Villa Rio Grande, Aug. 11, 1855, Saltillo Archives, 1688–1921 (hereafter SA), Vol. 46, Box 2Q323, p. 148, CAH; Olmsted, *Journey*, 256–57.

9. *New York Times* (hereafter *NYTimes*), July 10, Aug. 10, 17, 24, 26, Sept. 15, 19, 1855; *TST*, Apr. 7, 1855; *NOP*, Sept. 25, 1855; U.S. Congress, House, 34th Cong., 1st sess., 1855, H. Ex. Doc. 1, pt. 2, p. 52; *TSG*, Apr. 14, 1855; W. R. Henry to Pease, Sept. 2, 1855, Box 301–24, Folder 22, EMPP, TSLA; Gerónimo Cardona to Ministero de Guerra y Marina, Mar. 4, 1855, OM, 1855, Exp. XI/481.3/5538, DAM, SEDENA.

10. Moseley, "Public Career," 47–162; Medina Peña, *Los bárbaros*, 44–56; Luis Alberto García, interview by author, July 28–29, 2017, Monterrey, Nuevo Léon; Tyler, *Santiago Vidaurri*, 17–30; Enríquez Terrazas and Rodríguez García, *Coahuila*, 197–206; J. D. Nichols, *Limits of Liberty*, 191–93.

11. Cunningham and Hewitt, "Lovely Land," 387–409; Langberg, Emilio, Exp. XI/111/2–400, pp. 17–28, ACSH, DAM, SEDENA; *NYTimes*, Sept. 15, 1855; *TST*, July 14, Sept. 1, 1855; *San Antonio Herald*, May 31, Nov. 6, 1855; *TSG*, July 14, 1855; *San Antonio Texan*, Aug. 9, 1855; *San Antonio Ledger*, Aug. 25, 1855; *El Bejareño*, Sept. 1, 1855; Vidaurri to Múzquiz, Aug. 3, 1855, Miguel Lobos, Aug. 6, 1855, Box 9, Folder 104, Músquiz, Mexico, Records (hereafter MMR), WA MSS S-1482, Western Americana

Collection, Beinecke Rare Book and Manuscript Library (hereafter BRBML), Yale University; Monclova Viejo to Langberg, July 27, 1855, Piedras Negras to Langberg, July 29, 1855, Langberg to Múzquiz, July 29, 1955, R6, Box B, WA MSS S-668, History of Coahuila (hereafter HOC), Western Americana Collection, BRBML, Yale University; Letters to and from various towns in northern Coahuila, C4, F3, F4, F5, F6, Fondo Siglo XIX (hereafter FSXIX), Archivo General del Estado de Coahuila (hereafter AGEC); *El Restaurador de la Libertad,* Aug. 4, Aug. 18, 1855; *Boletín Oficial,* Sept. 25, 1855; Rodríguez García, *Historias de resistencia,* 16–18, 55–95, 119, 123; Vizcaya Canales, *Tierra de guerra,* 186–205, 229–49, 272–96; Enríquez Terrazas and Rodríguez García, *Coahuila,* 137–38.

12. Mulroy, *Freedom,* 6–89, 111; Porter, *Black Seminoles,* 3–110, 124–58; S. Miller, *Coacoochee's Bones,* 1–43, 121–71; Cazneau, *Eagle Pass,* 73–77; Jesus de Coatacovez to Villa Santa Rosa, Aug. 15, Coatacovez to Múzquíz, Aug. 18, 1854, Box 9, Folder 101, MMR, BRBML; Juan Manuel Maldonado, July 24, 1850, Census, July 24, 1850, and Nov. 15, 1850, Vol. 45, 1851–53, Box 2Q323, pp. 21–25, SA, CAH; Serapio Frasgosa to Comisionado General del Gobierno, Mar. 21, 1851, Antonio María Jáuregui to Inspector General, Sept. 27, 1851, C9, F5, FSXIX, AGEC.

13. *Texian Advocate,* Nov. 7, 1850; *Houston Telegraph,* June 28, 1848, Nov. 6, 1850; *Galveston News,* Apr. 15, 1851; *NYTimes,* Nov. 7, 1851; *Texas Ranger,* Mar. 13, 1853; *San Antonio Ledger,* Jan. 6, 1853, Mar. 23, May 18, 1854; El Gobierno de Coahuila to Ministro de Gobernación, Aug. 17, 1854, C7, F7, FSXIX, AGEC; *TST,* Aug. 25, 1855; Cazneau, *Eagle Pass,* 73–77; U.S. Congress, House, 1854, 33rd Cong., 2nd sess., H. Ex. Doc. 15, pp. 6–7.

14. Rodríguez García, *Historias de resistencia,* 31, 53, 68, 71, 92, 184–86; Enríquez Terrazas and Rodríguez García, *Coahuila,* 67, 174; Medina González Dávila, "La Batalla," 41; Miguel Blanco to Gobernador y Comt. general del Departamento de Nuevo León, Aug. 19, 1854, Box 165, Secretaría de Guerra y Marina (hereafter SGM), 1854–55, Archivo General del Estado de Nuevo León (hereafter AGENL); Emilio Langberg to Santiago Vidaurri, Aug. 1, 16, 1855, Vidaurri, Santiago, Correspondencia Particular (hereafter VSCP), AGENL; José Medina González Dávila, e-mail, July 2009; Manuel Ramirez to Múzquiz, Aug. 2, 1854, Box 9, Folder 101, MMR, BRBML; Vizcaya Canales, *Tierra de guerra,* 26, 271–96; Vizcaya Canales, *Incursiones de indios,* 25–28; Medina González Dávila, Lipan interviews, field notes, Don Esteban, 2009, Don Armando, 2010, privately held.

15. Francisco de Castañeda to Antonio María Jáuregui, Aug. 14, 1849, C3, F4, Maldonado to Jáuregui, July 3, 1850, C7, F9, Aug. 14, 1850, C8, F5, Mar. 22, 1851, C12, F5, Apr. 29, 1851, C13, F8, May 23, 1851, C13, F14, June 23, 1851, C14, F2, Sept. 22, 1852, C19, F4, Nov. 24, 1852, C20, F3, Fondo Colonias Militares de Oriente (hereafter FCMO), AGEC; El Ministero de Guerra y Marina to inspector general, Sept. 6, 1850, C9, F2, Feb. 19, 1851, C11, F10, Castañeda to Onefre Díaz, Apr. 23, 1853, C21, F10, FCMO, AGEC; *La Patria,* June 28, 1851 Aug. 27, 1853.

16. Maldonado to Júaregui, Sept. 22, Oct. 21, 1852, C19, F4, Díaz to Castañeda, Mar. 26, Félix Gonzáles, to Castañeda, May 27, 1853, C21, F10, FMCO, AGEC; Minor, *Turning Adversity,* 169–70; Vidaurri to Espinosa, Mar. 11, 1856, F12, E6, Correspondencia, Secretaría de Relaciones Exterior, AGENL; Rodríguez García, *Guerra,* 170–71; El Gobierno de Saltillo to Ministro de Gobernación, Aug. 4, 1854, C7, F7, Aug. 8, 1854, C7, F3, El Gobierno de Coahuila to Ministerio de Guerra, May 7, 1855, C3, F7, La Comandancia General de Gobierno to Castañeda, Aug. 12, 1855, C4, F6, FSXIX, AGEC;

see fourteen letters during August 1854 in Box 7, FSXIX, AGEC; J. D. Nichols, *Limits of Liberty*, 170–88.

17. U.S. Congress, House, 34th Cong, 1st sess., 1855, H. Exec. Doc. 1, pt. 2, pp. 53–54; June 1855 Post reports, Forts Clark, Duncan, Returns from Military Posts, RG393, M617, R213, R335, National Archives and Records Administration–Southwest Region, Fort Worth (hereafter NARA–SW); *TSG*, June 23, July 7, 1855; Britten, *Lipan*, 216; Britten, "Treacherous, Deceitful, or Just Plain Smart?"

18. Stella Lapaz, Percy Bigmouth, and Antonio Apache, Lipan oral history, Box 44, Folder 54, Morris Edward Opler Papers (hereafter MEOP), Division of Rare and Manuscript Collections, Cornell University Library; Britten, *Lipan*, 35–41; 42 (map), 44–50, 53–54, 57 (map), 110 (map), 174, 196, 215–16, 228 (map); Winfrey and Day, *Indian Papers*, 1:164–65; *San Antonio Ledger*, Apr. 20, June 1, 1854; Geo. T. Howard to Manypenny, May 4, June 9, Nov. 20, 1854, Bureau of Indian Affairs (hereafter BIA), Texas Agency (hereafter TA), RG75, M234, R859, NARA–SW; Comisión Pesquisidora, *Reports of the Committee*, 417–18; Rodríguez García, *Historias de resistencia*, 68–71, 92, 184–86; Medina González Dávila, "La Batalla," 41; *NYTimes*, May 11, 1853; Ramirez to Múzquíz, Aug. 2, 1854, Box 9, Folder 101, MMR, BRBML; Vizcaya Canales, *Tierra de guerra*, 26, 271–96; Juan Manuel Maldonado, Jan. 24, 1851, Vol. 45, 1851–53, 2Q323, pp. 134–35, SA, CAH; Medina González Dávila, Lipan interviews, field notes, Don Armando, 2010, privately held.

19. Sumpter, *Paso*, 61; Mulroy, *Freedom*, 69, 75–76; Tyler, "Fugitive Slaves,"4–9; Tyler, "Callahan Expedition," 574–79; Olmsted, *Journey*, 331–32; *TSG*, Nov. 8, 1853, June 2, Sept. 16, 1854; *TST*, June 2, 23, July 28, 1855.

20. Guerrero Presidencia to Comandante de la Rio Grande, Mar. 11, 1851, C10, F2, Manuel Flores to Secretario de Gobierno, Mar. 20, 1851, C3, F8, June 27, 1851, C6, F6, Correspondencia to Villa de Guerrero, Oct. 18, 1851, C9, F10, Nov. 13, 1851, C10, F2, Maldonado to Comisario Municipal de la Villa de Guerrero, Jan. 2, 1855, C1, F1, FSXIX, AGEC.

21. J. Ford, *Rip Ford's Texas*, xvii–xxxvi; Tyler, "Slave Owners," 4; *New York Daily Tribune*, Jan. 1855; Kennedy, *Preliminary Report* (8th Census), 11–12; *TSG*, Jan. 6, 10, 17, Mar. 14, 21, Apr. 4, 22, 29, May 6, May 20, 27, June 24, July 1, 15, 29, Aug. 5, 19, Sept. 2, 9,16, 23, Dec. 2, 1854, Jan. 6, Feb. 10, Mar. 3, 24, 31, Apr. 21, May 5, 12, 26, June 2, 9, 16, Aug. 25, Oct. 6, 20, Dec. 22, 1855; *San Antonio Ledger*, Jan. 19, Mar. 2, 15, 23, Apr. 13, 20, 27, May 18, 25, June 1, July 13, Aug. 17, 1854, July 7, Aug. 18, 1855; *Bastrop Advertiser*, May 27, 1854; *Clarksville Standard*, Aug. 5, Sept. 9, Oct. 21, 1854, Jan. 13, 20, May 12, June 23, 1855; *San Antonio Herald*, Apr. 29, May 22, Sept. 25, Oct. 9, 1855; *TST*, Feb. 11, June 24, Nov. 18, 1854; Feb. 10, 17, 24, Apr. 21, May 5, 19, June 2, 16, 30, July 28, Aug. 11, 18, 25, Sept. 15, 29, Oct. 6, Nov. 3, 17, Dec. 8, 15, 1855; *Gonzales Inquirer*, Feb. 11, 25, 1854; *Texas Ranger*, Sept. 28, Nov. 23, 1854, Aug. 11, 1855; *Indianola Bulletin*, May 24, July 27, 1855; *Texas Planter*, Aug. 23, 1854, June 27, 1855; *San Antonio Sentinel*, July 14, 1855; *Nacogdoches Chronicle*, Mar. 21, 1854; *Western Texan*, Aug. 24, 1854; *Texas Sun*, Sept. 8, 1855; Texas Runaway Slave Project, East Texas Research Center, Stephen F. Austin State University, http://digital.sfasu.edu/cdm/landingpage/collection/RSP.

22. Village and State Communications, 1851–55, C1–C10, FSXIX, AGEC; Miguel Castro to la Secretería de Gobierno del Estado, Jan. 12, 1853, C1, F2, Cuevas to Gobernador del Estado de Coahuila, Apr. 23, 1849, C2, F8, Maldonado to Comisario Municipal, Jan. 2, 1855, C1, F1, Jan. 13, 1855, C1, F4, E8, FSXIX, AGEC. See Fondo Colonias Militares de Oriente, Fondo Siglo XIX, Mascogos y Seminoles en los Siglos XIX y XX, and

Esclavos en el Siglo XIX, AGEC. The MMR (1854–55) and the HOC (1850–57) were also searched.

23. Tyler, *Santiago Vidaurri*, 22–24; Tyler, "Age," 42–43; Moseley, "Public Career," 152–53, 178; *El Siglo Diez y Nueve*, Nov. 12, 1855; J. Ford, *Rip Ford's Texas*, 196–97, 214–15; *NYTimes*, Sept. 15, 1855 (newspaper account of Langberg's proposal); *TST*, June 2, July 28, Oct. 14, Nov. 4, 1854, July 14, Sept. 8, 1855; Cunningham and Hewitt, "Lovely Land," 411–12; *TSG*, June 2, 16, Nov. 2, 9, 16, 1854, Apr. 7, June 2, 9, 1855; *Clarksville Standard*, Nov. 11, 1854; *San Antonio Herald*, June 15, 1855.

24. Hanson Alsbury to Colonel Bennett Riddells, June 29, 1855, Riddells to Vidaurri, Oct. 12, 1855, Box 26, Exp. 484, Vidaurri, Santiago, Correspondencia Extranjeros (hereafter VSCE), AGENL; Tyler, "Age," 43; Luis Alberto García, interview by author, July 28–29, 2017, Monterrey, N.L., México; U.S. Congress, Senate, 31st Cong., 1st sess., 1850, S. Ex. Doc. 44, pp. 137, 200; J. Ford, *Rip Ford's Texas*, 215; *San Antonio Ledger*, July 30, 1852, Jan. 1, 1853; Riddells to I. I. Crittenden, Department of State, Dec. 1, 1852, Despatches from U.S. Consuls in Chihuahua, Mexico, 1830–1906, Records of the Department of State, RG59, M289, R1, NACP; Directing Committee Broadside, signed by Hanson Alsbury, Vidaurri, Santiago, manuscripts, privately held. I appreciate receiving a copy of this broadside from Catalina and Patricia Roell.

25. Denison, "Some Letters," 1145–50, 1157–59; Cazneau, *Eagle Pass*, 32; Stillman, *Wanderings*, 86–89, 180; Olmsted, *Journey*, 148–52, 156–60; T. Smith, *Old Army*, 47–48; T. Smith, *U.S. Army*, 41, 50–58, 74, 156; Winfrey and Day, *Indian Papers*, 3:224–28; William Wright and John Wright, *Recollections*, 10.

26. Sumpter, *Paso*, viii, xxii, 9–11, 17–27, 45–60; Pingenot, "Eagle Pass, TX"; Lane, *I Married*, 19; Richard A. Thompson, *Fort Duncan*, 2, 7–8, 11; Sumpter, "Life," 4–57; Pingenot, "Paso del Águila"; Olmsted, *Journey*, 138, 319–20; Maldonado to inspector general, Apr. 1850, C6, F3, El Ministero de Guerra y Marina to inspector, Aug. 13, 1850, C8, F5, FCMO, AGEC; Cazneau, *Eagle Pass*, 94–97, 110, 118–20, 153–54; Canales Santos, *Piedras Negras*, 81, 86; Wright and Wright, *Recollections*, 32–33; *San Antonio Ledger*, Jan. 6, Sept. 15, Dec. 30, 1853, Mar. 23, June 6, 22, May 18, 1854.

27. Olmsted, *Journey*, 340–45, 349–54.

28. Griffin, "Connecticut Yankee," 8, 18–21, 23–28, 48–50, 75–76, 89–93, 102–3, 115–16, 165–68, 216; Cutrer, "Smith, Persifor Frazer"; R. Johnson, *Soldier's Reminiscences*, 76; MacKinnon, *At Sword's Point*, 469–73; "Fort Duncan," HBTO, http://www.tshaonline.org/handbook/online/articles/qbf17; James L. Bowen, *Massachusetts*, 892–93.

CHAPTER 13

1. *TST*, June 16, 1855; *TSG*, May 19, 1855; Sowell, *Texas Indian Fighters*, 246–48.

2. *TSG*, Mar. 24, May 19, July 11, 1855; *TST*, July 16, 1855; Winfrey and Day, *Indian Papers*, 3:219–21; Pease to Callahan, July 5, 1855, Box 301–24, Folder 20E, EMPP, TSLA.

3. Persifor F. Smith to Adjutant General, May 22, 1855, BIA, TA, RG75, M324, R860, NARA–SW; U.S. Cong., House, 34th Cong., 1st sess., 1855, H. Ex. Doc. 1, pt. 2, pp. 53–54; *TSG*, Mar. 3, 24, Apr. 14, 1855; *San Antonio Texan*, Mar. 22, 1855; Howard to Manypenny, Nov. 20, 1854, BIA, TA, RG75, M234, R859, NARA–SW; *NOP*, Feb. 10, 1855; Britten, *Lipan*, 228 (map); Castañeda to Villa de Guerrero, Mar. 17, 1855, C2, F14, FSXIX, AGEC; Stella Lapaz, Antonio Apache, and Percy Bigmouth, Lipan oral history, Box 44, Folder 54, 14–25–3238, MEOP.

4. *TSG,* Apr. 14, 21, May 12, June 9, 16, 30, July 7, 1855; *NOP,* May 1, 1855; *San Antonio Texan,* Mar. 22, 1855; Medina River Camp to Neighbors, Mar. 18, 1855, BIA, TA, RG75, M234, R860, NARA–SW.

5. *TST,* Feb. 17, June 16, 1855; Sowell, *Rangers,* 78–80; Pease to Smith, June 20, 1855, Box 401–24, Folder 19, EMPP, TSLA; Winfrey and Day, *Indian Papers,* 3:219–20; Pease to Jones, June 20, 1855, Box 81, Niles-Graham-Pease Papers (hereafter NGPP), Austin History Center (hereafter AHC); *Dallas Weekly Herald,* Aug. 4, 1855; *TSG,* June 2, July 7, 1855; *San Antonio Texan,* June 14, 21, July 14, 1855; *NYTimes,* Aug. 8, 1855; *National Intelligencer,* July 26, 1855.

6. *TSG,* Mar. 14, 19, 21, 28, Apr. 16, 22, May 6, 27, June 3, 10, July 1, 8, 29, Aug. 8, Oct. 7, Dec. 2, 9, 1854, Jan. 20, Feb. 3, 10, 17, 24, Mar. 3, 17, 24, 31, Apr. 14, 21, May 12, June 9, 13, July 7, 1855; *San Antonio Ledger,* Apr. 20, 27, May 4, 11, 25, 18, June 1, 8, 10, July 27, Aug. 5, Sept. 21, 28, 30, Nov. 4, Dec. 2, 1854, Jan. 1, Mar. 1, May 1, 1855; *TST,* Mar. 18, 21, Oct. 7, 1854, Feb. 10, 24, Mar. 3, 17, 26, May 10, June 2, 9, 13, 16, July 7 (Jones), 1855; *Tri-Weekly State Times,* Jan. 14, Mar. 14, 28, 1854; *Texan Mercury,* Mar. 2, 10, May 27, June 16, 31, 1854; *Texas Ranger,* Apr. 27, May 11, 1854, Mar. 17, 1855; *Western Texan,* Mar. 23, June 1, July 20, Aug. 17, 1854; *Nacogdoches Chronicle,* May 2, June 13, 1854; *Galveston Weekly News,* Jan. 3, Sept. 5, Nov. 7, Dec. 5, 1854, May 1, 8, 22, 1855; *Nueces Valley,* Mar. 18, 1854; *Gonzales Inquirer,* Mar. 25, 1854; *Alamo Star,* May 13, 27, 1854; *Standard,* June 10, 17,1854; *San Antonio Herald,* Apr. 24, June 5, 16, July 10, 1855; *San Antonio Texan,* Feb. 15, Mar. 22, May 31, June 21, 1855; *El Bejareño,* Sept. 1, 1855; Heitman, *Historical Register,* 2: 401–2; T. Smith, "U.S. Army Combat Operations," 507; Bandera City to Neighbors, Nov. 28, 1854, Medina River Camp to Neighbors, Mar. 18, 1855, BIA, TA, M234, R860, NARA–SW.

7. *Nueces Valley,* Mar. 18, 1854; *San Antonio Ledger,* Apr. 20, 1854; *TSG,* May 27, 1854; *TST,* Feb. 10, Mar. 3, Apr. 7, July 7, 1855; *San Antonio Herald,* July 10, 1855.

8. Vizcaya Canales, *Incursiones de indios,* 1–10, 23–31; Vizcaya Canales, *Tierra de guerra,* 11–36, 207–28, 273–96; Rodríguez García, *Historias de resistencia,* 31–64, 75–86, 102–4, 111–17; Comisión Pesquisidora, *Reports of the Committee,* 318–37; Castañeda, Aug. 18, Cardona, Aug. 24, Gobierno de Estado, Sept. 3, Sept. 5, Prefecto Político de Río Grande, Oct. 10, Gobierno Eclesíastico del Obispado de Monterrey, Oct. 10, La Laguna de Jaco, undated letter, 1854, R4, and fifteen communications among local and state officials, 1854, R5, Box 8, HOC, BRBML; Comisario, entries in municipal ledger, Jan. 7, 17, June 5, 28, July 10, 25, 1854, Manuel Ramírez, Aug. 2, 9, 1854, Folder 101, Sept. 15, Oct. 5, 1854, Folder 102, May 8, 1855, Folder 104, Box 9, MMR, BRBML; forty-eight communications among municipal and state officials in 1854, C1–9, 1855, C1–5, C–7, FSXIX, AGEC; Post Reports, Forts Clark and Duncan, Texas, Returns from Military Posts, RG393, M617, R213, 335, NARA–SW; *TSG,* June 23, July 7, 1855; U.S. Congress, House, 33rd Cong., 2nd sess., 1854, H. Ex. Doc. 15, pp. 3–9.

9. Winfrey and Day, *Indian Papers,* 3:222–23; *TST,* July 7, 1855; *San Antonio Texan,* July 12, 1855; *Neu Braunfelser Zeitung,* Oct. 12, 1855; Jones family in San Antonio, 1855, Candice DuCoin, Jones descendant, e-mail, Dec. 2010.

10. *TST,* Apr. 7, June 16, 30, 1855; Winfrey and Day, *Indian Papers,* 3:219–20; *Galveston Weekly News,* May 8, 1855; *TSG,* May 12, 1855; *NOP,* May 1, 1855.

11. *TST,* July 7, 1855; Winfrey and Day, *Indian Papers,* 3:223–24; *TSG,* Sept. 29, 1855.

12. Pease to Callahan, July 5, 1855, Box 301–24, Folder 20, EMPP, TSLA; *San Antonio Ledger,* July 14, 1855; *TST,* July, 7, 1855; *NYTimes,* July 17, 1855; *NOP,* July 8, 1855.

13. Pease to Callahan, July 25, 1855, Box 301–24, Folder 20. EMPP, TSLA; MR, James H. Callahan, July 20, 1855, Oversize 401–723, Folder 6, TRMR, TSLA.

14. Winfrey and Day, *Indian Papers*, 3:224–29; *TST*, Oct. 10, 1855.

15. MR, Callahan, July 20, 1855, Oversize 401–723, Folder 6, TRMR, TAGD, TSLA; Sansom, "Thrilling," *Hunter's*, 1, no. 5 (Mar. 1911): 8–10, 1 #6 (1911) 4; *Memorial and Genealogical Record*, 370–72; Spurlin, *Texas Veterans*, 18, 197–98; Wilbarger, *Indian Depredations*, 616–20; Marriages, bk. A, p. 20, Hays County, CC; *TST*, Apr. 7, 1855; Althaus, "Kyle, Claiborne."

16. Collins, *Texas Devils*, 75; MR, Callahan, July 20, 1855, Oversize 401–723, Folder 6, TRMR, TAGD, TSLA; MR, William R. Henry, Oct. 10, 1854, Dec. 14, 1854, Oversize 401–723, Folders 9, 18, MR, G. K. Lewis, Jan. 1, 1853, Map-case 401–794, Folder 11, MR, Owen Shaw, Aug. 18, 1852, Oversize 401–795, Folder 31, Map-case 401–795, Folder 17, MR, William Fitzhugh, Oct. 2, 1854, Map-Case 401–793, Folder 6, MR, John G. Walker, 1854, Map-case 401–795, Folder 19, MR, Henry E. McCulloch, Nov. 1850, May, 1851, Map-case 401–794, Folder 13, TRMR, TAGD, TSLA; names on muster rolls, Land Grant Search, TGLO; S. Moore, *Savage Frontier*, 1:159–60, 166, 168, 172–73, 183–84, 189, 192, 195, 205, 216, 231, 236, 263, 273, 276, 282, 285, *2:*28–36, 45–47, 68–71, 102, 107–9, 114, 124–31, 142, 163, 184–85, 189, 193, 206, 215, 220, 230, 260, 269–80, 296–98, 300, 317–21, 330–31, 343–45, *3:*52–53, 58, 106–8, 135, 138–39, 148–49, 160–61, 181, 190–91, 198–99, 206–7, 220, 222, 228–29, 234, 238, 258–63, 265, 270–71, 278, 281, 283, 294, 296, 300, 303–4, 312–13, 318–20, 324, 331, 342, 351; *Journals of the Senate* (State of Tex., 6th Leg.), 42–43; Spurlin, *Texas Veterans*, 21, 138, 171, 197; *Texan Mercury*, Oct. 23, 1853.

17. Wilkins, *Defending*, 47; MR, Callahan, July 20, 1855, Oversize 401–723, Folder 6, TRMR, TAGD, TSLA; Pease to Callahan, July 5, July 25, 1855, EMPP, TSLA; See MRs for Lewis, Shaw, Fitzhugh, Walker, and McCulloch, n16; Kennedy, *Preliminary Report* (8th Census), 131; *Texan Mercury*, Oct. 23, 1853; TR, 1855, TAC, Comal, Caldwell, Guadalupe Counties; *San Antonio Express*, June 14, 1908.

18. Gesick, "1855 Callahan Raid," 55; U.S. Census, 1850, 1860, and Slave Inhabitants, Comal, Guadalupe, Caldwell, Travis, Bexar, Hays, Bastrop Counties, Tex.; TR, 1855–56, TAC, Comal, Guadalupe, Caldwell, Travis, Bexar, Hays, Bastrop Counties, TSLA.

19. Denison, "Some Letters," 1159; *TST*, Oct. 28, 1855; MR, Callahan, July 20, 1855, Oversize 401–723, Folder 6, TRMR, TAGD, TSLA; Walton photo, D. A. T. Walton Collection (hereafter DATWC), Bryan Wildenthal Memorial Library, Sul Ross State University (hereafter BWML); Sowell, *Texas Indian Fighters*, 527; Quartermaster records, Box 401–1153, Folder 24, Texas Ranger Records (hereafter TRR), TAGD, TSLA.

20. Quartermaster records, Box 401–1153, Folder 24, Box 401–1154, Folders 1–4, Oversize 401–1238, Folder 3; TRR, TAGD, TSLA; Burleson deposition, Swenson requisition, Aug. 3, 1855, Unprocessed, NGPP, AHC; MR. Callahan, July 20, 1855, Oversize 401–723, Folder 6, TRMR, TAGD, TSLA; *Medical and Surgical Register*, 1084.

21. *San Antonio Herald*, July 10, 1855; *TSG*, Apr. 14, July 7, 1855; *TST*, July 7, 21, Aug. 4, 1855; *San Antonio Texan*, Mar. 22, Aug. 2, 9, 1855; F. Smith, *Dominance*, 214–19; Britten, *Lipan*, 215–16, 228 (map).

22. Winfrey and Day, *Indian Papers*, 3:230–31; *TST*, July 7, Aug. 4, 1855; *TSG*, July 7, 1855; *Indianola Bulletin*, July 13, 27, 1855; *San Antonio Ledger*, July 14, 1855; Stillman, *Wanderings*, 91–92.; U.S. Census, 1850, Medina County, Tex.

23. Pease to Callahan, July 25, 1855, Callahan to Pease, Aug. 10, 1855, Box 301–24, Folders 20, 21, EMPP, TSLA; *San Antonio Daily Express*, June 25, 1905; *TST*, Aug. 25, 1855; *El Bejareño*, Sept. 1, 1855; Ed Burleson to S. M. Swenson, Aug. 20, 1855, Swenson to

Burleson, undated, 1855, Quartermaster records, Box 401–1153, Folder 24, Box 401–1154, Folders 1–4, Box 401–1238, Folder 4, TRR, TAGD, TSLA; R. Moore, "Swenson, Swante Magnus"; Order No. 7, Callahan to Burleson, Aug. 28, 1855, Box 2B158, Burleson Papers (hereafter EBP), CAH.

24. *San Antonio Daily Express*, June 25, 1905; Sansom, "Thrilling," *Hunter's*, 1, no. 5 (Mar. 1911): 8–10; Winfrey and Day, *Indian Papers*, 3:243; *TST*, Sept. 8, 29, 1855. Jones told the governor this last fight occurred on August 30.

25. Chebahtah and Minor, *Chevato*, 18; Raid and War, Antonio Apache, Box 44, Folder 25, 14–25–3238, MEOP; Lipan raiding, José Medina González Dávila, e-mail, July 2009.

26. *TST*, Sept. 1, 8, 1855; *TSG*, Aug. 25, Sept. 15, 1855; *San Antonio Herald*, Aug. 14, 1855; *El Bejareño*, Aug. 18, Sept. 1, 1855; *San Antonio Zeitung*, Aug. 25, Sept. 8, 22, 1855; *San Antonio Texan*, Aug. 4, 30, 1855; Winfrey and Day, *Indian Papers*, 3:231–33; *Galveston Weekly News*. Aug. 8, 1865.

27. *TSG*, Sept. 16, 1855; *El Bejareño*, Sept. 1, 1855; *San Antonio Texan*, Aug. 30, Sept. 6, 1855; *San Antonio Ledger*, Sept. 8, 1855; *San Antonio Herald*, Sept. 11, 1855. Winfrey and Day, *Indian Papers*, 3:232–33, 243–44; *TST*, Sept. 8, 15, 29, 1855; C. Smith, "Early History," 15–18; Deems, *Annals*, 381–83.

28. Winfrey and Day, *Indian Papers*, 3:228, 231–36; *TST*, Aug. 25, 1855; *TSG*, Sept. 8, 16, 1855.

29. *San Antonio Ledger*, Mar. 31, June 10, 16, Sept. 8, 1853; *TSG*, June 23, Sept. 8, 1855; U.S. Congress, House, 32nd Cong., 2nd Sess., 1852, H. Ex. Doc. 1, pt. 2., p. 4; Pease to Smith, Sept. 5, 1855, Box 301–24, Folder 22, EMPP, TSLA.

30. *El Restaurador de la Libertad*, July 7, 14, 1855; *Boletín Oficial*, July 24, 1855; Comisario Municipal de Guerrero, July 19, C4, F2, July 25, C4, F2, July 29, C4, F3, Santiago Vidaurri letters, July 26, C4, F2, July 27, 1855, C4, F3, FSXIX, AGEC; dozens of administrative communiqués, 1855, C4, F2–3, FSXIX, AGEC; *San Antonio Ledger*, July 21, 1855; Moseley, "Public Career," 111–14, 127; Tyler, "Age," 8–11.

31. Cunningham and Hewitt, "Lovely Land," 408–9; I. Moore, *Life*, 82; *El Bejareño*, Aug. 18, 1855; Langberg to local commanders, July 27, 1855, Ficha 1862, C11, F10, FSXIX, Archivo del Municipio Monclova (hereafter AMM), Monclova; Langberg to Vidaurri, Aug. 1, 16, 1855, Caja 18, Exp. 256, Manuel Leal to Vidaurri, Aug. 1, 1855, Caja 21, Exp. 71, Menchaca to Vidaurri, July 29, 1855, Caja 24, Exp. 830, VSCP, AGENL; dozens of administrative communiqués, 1855, C4, F2–3, FSXIX, AGEC.

32. José Ignacio Fernández, Aug. 10, C4, F5, Langberg, Aug. 11, C4, F5, Aug. 22, C4, F7, Aug. 25, C4, F8, Aug. 27, C4, F9, José Maria Sainz, Aug. 11, C4, F5, Comandancia General de Gobierno, Aug. 12, C4, F6, Luis de la Garza, Aug. 19, 1855, C4, F7, FSXIX, AGEC.

33. Persifor F. Smith to Adjutant General, May 22, 1855, Neighbors to Manypenny, Oct. 8, 1855, Neighbors to Pease, Sept. 20, 1855, BIA, TA, RG75, M324, R860, NARA–SW; *Texas State Times*, Oct. 6, 1855; Manning, *Diplomatic*, Vol. 9, *Mexico*, 193–94; U.S. Congress, House, 42nd Cong., 2nd sess., 1872, H. Ex. Doc. 277, pp. 103–4; James Hughes Callahan, Box 4, Folder 14, JWNP, DRTL; *Picayune*, Nov. 1, 1855; *Texas State Times*, Aug. 25, 1855; Sansom, "Thrilling," *Hunter's* 1, no. 6 (Apr. 1911): 4.

34. Callahan to Burleson, Aug. 31, 1855, Box 2B158, EBP, CAH; Callahan to Pease, Sept. 1, 1855, Box 84, NGPP, AHC; Pease to Callahan, July 5, 1855, Box 301–24, Folder 20, EMPP, TSLA; *Texas State Times*, Sept. 22, 1855; Burleson to Pease, Sept. 8, 1855, Box 301–24, folder 22, EMPP, TSLA.

35. Watson and Phillips, "Family Tree of James Hughes Callahan"; Texas State Cemetery website, accessed Apr. 15, 2009 (searched James Hughes Callahan); "Death of William Milford Callahan," 1977, PCFH, privately held.

36. *TST,* Sept. 1, 1955; Broadside, "Middletown," OWP, privately held.

CHAPTER 14

1. Denison, "Some Letters," 1147, 1149–50; *San Antonio Ledger*, Feb. 9, 1854, Dec. 22, 1855; San Antonio Committee to Colonel Langberg, Aug. 25, 1855, Caja 165, Seccíon Militar (hereafter SM), AGENL.

2. *TSG*, June 20, Sept. 8, 16, 29, 1855; *San Antonio Herald*, Sept. 11, 1855; *San Antonio Ledger,* Sept. 8, 1855; *TST,* Sept. 16, 29, 1855; *Neu Braunfelser Zeitung*, Sept. 14, 1855; *National Intelligencer*, Sept. 25, 1855; *Texas Sun*, Oct. 13, 1855; TR, 1854–55, TAC, Comal County; Winfrey and Day, *Indian Papers*, 3:244–45.

3. *San Antonio Herald*, Sept. 11, 1855; *TSG*, Sept. 16, 22, 29, Oct. 6, 1855; *TST*, Sept. 29, 1855; *Neu Braunfelser Zeitung*, Sept. 14, 1855; *San Antonio Ledger*, Sept. 22, 1855; Winfrey and Day, *Indian Papers*, 3:241–42, 244–45; *El Bejareño*, Sept. 29, 1855; Minton, "Leakey, Texas"; *NYTimes*, Oct. 20, 1855; McCaslin, "Sutherland, John, Jr."

4. *Neu Braunfelser Zeitung*, Sept. 14, 1855; *TST,* Sept. 22, 1855; Camp Near Bandera, Camp Ridley, *Records, 1850–1861,* Box 401–1153, Folder 24, TRR, TAGD, TSLA.

5. *TST,* Sept. 22, 1855; Burleson to Pease, Sept. 8, 1855, Box 301–24, Folder 22, EMPP, TSLA; Menchaca to Villas Militar de la Frontera, Sept. 17, 1855, C5, F3, FSXIX, AGEC.

6. Winfrey and Day, *Indian Papers,* 3:236–42; Pease to Evans et al., Sept. 5, 6, 1855, Box 301–24, Folder 22, EMPP, TSLA; *Neu Braunfelser Zeitung*, Sept. 14, 1855; *TSG,* Sept. 22, 1855; *Galveston News*, Oct. 2, 1855.

7. Winfrey and Day, *Indian Papers,* 3:243–47; *TSG*, Sept. 22, 1855; *TST,* Sept. 22, 29, 1855; *NYTimes*, Oct. 20, 1855.

8. Callahan to Burleson, Sept. 12, 1855, Box 2B158, EBP, CAH; Callahan to Burleson, Sept. 12, 1855, Doss Contract, Callahan to Burleson, rations, Quartermaster Records, 1850–61, Box 401–1153, Folders 4, 24, TRR, TAGD, TSLA.

9. Callahan to Pease, Sept. 1, 1855, Box 84, NGPP, AHC; Callahan to Burleson, Aug. 31, 1855, Box 2B158, EBP, CAH; *TST*, Sept. 22, 1855; Ford, "Callahan's Expedition," 9; Varnell agreement, Quartermaster Records, Oversize 401–1238, Folder 3, TRR, TAGD, TSLA; I. Moore, *Life*, 84.

10. MR, Nathaniel Benton, Sept. 15, 1855, Oversize 401–723, Folder 1, TRMR, TADG, TSLA; Niemeyer, "Benton, Nathaniel"; Moellering, "History," 59–61; Craig W. Smith, "Early History," 15–18; Marriages, Vol. A, p. 115, Guadalupe County, CC; Kishbaugh, "Henry B. King." S. Moore, *Savage Frontier,* 3:363–71; Spurlin, *Texas Volunteers*, 185; SR, Gustavus Fox, Soldiers Who Served in Volunteer Organizations during the Indian Wars, RG94, M629, R12, NAB; *Power of Attorney Records*, 1855–59, Box 401–1185, Folder 1, TRR, TAGD, TSLA; See MRs for Lewis, Shaw, Walker, Fitzhugh, and McCulloch cited in chap. 13, n16; MR, Henry, Dec. 14, 1854–Mar. 31, 1855, Map-Case 401–794, Folder 9, TRMR, TAGD, TSLA.

11. Jack Ellis and C. McConnally to Burleson, Sept. 25, Burleson to Pease, Sept. 25, 1855, Box 2B158, EBP, CAH; Ford, "Callahan's Expedition," 3; J. Brown, *Indian Wars*, 618–19.

12. Cunningham and Hewitt, "Lovely Land," 407–9; *El Restaurador de la Libertad*, Aug. 4, 1855; *San Antonio Herald*, Nov. 6, 1855; *NYTimes*, Sept. 15, 1855; Tyler, "Age,"

41–42; Directing Committee Broadside, signed by Hanson Alsbury, in Vidaurri, Santiago, manuscripts, privately held; Hanson Alsbury to Bennett Riddells, June 29, 1855, Caja 26, Exp. 484, VSCE, AGENL.

13. *El Restaurador de la Libertad*, Aug. 4, 18, 1855; Riddells to Vidaurri, Oct. 12, 1855, Caja 26, Exp. 484, VSCE, AGENL; *El Siglo Diez y Nueve*, Nov. 12, 1855; J. Ford, *Rip Ford's Texas*, 215; *San Antonio Sentinel*, in *NYTimes*, Aug. 30, 1855; Cunningham and Hewitt, "Lovely Land," 408–9; *Boletín Oficial*, Sept. 25, 1855.

14. *El Siglo Diez y Nueve*, Nov. 12, 1855; *Boletín Oficial*, Oct. 24, 1855; *El Bejareño*, Sept. 1, 1855; Langberg to San Antonio Committee, Aug. 31, Langberg to Vidaurri, Aug. 31, 1855, Caja 165, SM, AGENL; J. Ford, "Callahan's Expedition," 4.

15. Tyler, "Callahan Expedition," 578; Porter, *Black Seminoles*, 152–53; Porter, *Negro on the American Frontier*, 441; Tyler, "Fugitive Slaves," 7–8; Tyler, "Slave Owners," 46–50; S. Miller, *Coacoochee's Bones*, 168; Mulroy, *Freedom*, 78–79; *El Siglo Diez y Nueve*, Nov. 12, 1855; *Boletín Oficial*, Oct. 24, 1855; San Antonio Committee to Langberg, Aug. 25, 1855, Caja 165, SM, AGENL; *TSG*, Sept. 16, 1854.

16. U.S. Census, 1850, 1860, 1870, Bexar County, Tex.; U.S. Census, 1850, 1860, Slave Inhabitants, Bexar County, Tex.; TR, 1854–55, TAC, Bexar County, TSLA; Eckel, "Evans, Onesimus"; *San Antonio Ledger*, Sept. 23, 1852, Jan. 6, 13, Feb. 3, July 16, Oct. 23, Dec. 8, 30, 1853, Jan. 5, Apr. 13, Aug. 17, 1854, Aug. 1, 1855; *TSG*, Sept. 16, 1854; *San Antonio Herald*, Oct. 9, 1855; *Western Texan*, Jan. 6, 1853; Pease, "Lacoste, Jean Batiste"; Schoen, "Free Negro," 95–98;

17. *El Siglo Diez y Nueve*, Nov. 12, 1855; *Boletín Oficial*, Oct. 24, 1855; *TSG*, May 25, July 29, Aug. 15, Sept. 16, 1854; George P. Isbell, "Mitchell, Asa"; U.S. Census, 1850, 1860, Bexar, Bastrop, Comal, Guadalupe Counties, Tex.; U.S. Census, 1850, 1860, Slave Inhabitants, Bexar County, Tex.; TR, 1854–55, TAC, Bexar County, TSLA; Thrall, *History*, 31; *San Antonio Ledger*, Jan. 6, 20, Aug. 18, Sept. 8, Oct. 6, Dec. 23, 1853, Jan. 5, Mar. 30, Apr. 6, 13, May 25, Sept. 2, 25, 1854, Apr. 7, 1855; *Texan Mercury*, Mar. 25, 1854; *El Bejareño*, Feb. 17, Oct. 29, 1855; Bailey, "Debray, Xavier Blanchard."

18. Ruthven, *Proceedings*, 2:234.

19. Peterson, *Daughters*, 8; Lowry and McCardle, *History*, 478–79, 482, 556; Hanson Alsbury, Land Grant Search, TGLO; Captain Thomas Alsbury, Jr. (Biography by Delbert W. Whitaker), Alsbury Collection, Brazoria County Museum of History; Spurlin, *Texas Volunteers*, 141; *NOP*, Oct. 31, 1849; U.S. Census, 1850, Bexar County, Tex.; U.S. Census, 1850, Slave Inhabitants, Bexar County, Tex.; TR, 1854–55, TAC, Bexar County, TSLA; *San Antonio Texan*, Feb. 21, 1856; *San Antonio Ledger*, Jan. 6, Apr. 14, July 7, Aug. 18, Sept. 8, Oct. 6, 1853, Feb. 9, Mar. 2, 1854; *El Bejareño*, July 7, 1855; *TSG*, Sept. 16, 1854, Aug. 27, 1856; *Galveston Civilian and Gazette*, May 5, 1857.

20. Moseley, "Public Career," 131–52; Langberg to Villa de Guerrero, Sept. 1, Manuel Fernández to Administración de la Aduana, Sept. 3, 1855, C5, F1, Aniceto Castilla to Monclova, Sept. 18, 1855, C5, F4, FSXIX, AGEC; *El Restaurador de la Libertad*, Sept. 1, 8, 15, 22, 1855; *Boletín Oficial*, Sept. 5, 21, 25, 28, 29, 30, 1855; Álvarez to Vidaurri, Sept. 10, 1855, Caja 7, Exp. 9, VSCP, AGENL.

21. I. Moore, *Life*, 82–83; Langberg to Vidaurri, Sept. 1, 1855, Caja 18, Exp. 256, VSCP, AGENL.

22. Galindo to Langberg, Aug. 28, Langberg to Villa Santa Rosas, Aug. 31, Langberg to Secretaría de Guerra, Monterrey, Sept. 2, 3, Vidaurri to Villas de Salinas, Villaldama, Lampazos, and Alamo, Sept. 3, Langberg to Monterrey, Sept. 12, 1855, Caja 165, SM, AGENL; Langberg to Galindo, Sept. 1, Langberg to Patiño, Sept. 1, Langberg to Vidaurri, Sept. 2,

Sept. 18, 19, 1855, Caja 18, Exp. 256, VSCP, AGENL; Langberg to Villa de Guerrero, Sept. 1, C5, F1, Sept. 4, C5, F1, Sept. 8, C5, F2, Langberg to Secretario de Gobierno del Estado de Coahuila, Sept. 2, 1855, C5, F1, FSXIX, AGEC; Langberg to Múzquiz, Sept. 13, 1855, Box 9, Folder 104, MMR, BRBML; *Boletín Oficial*, Sept. 25, 1855.

23. Langberg to Galindo, Sept. 1, 1855, Caja 18, Exp. 256, VSCP, AGENL; Langberg to Secretaría de Guerra, Sept. 1, Vidaurri to Langberg, Sept. 10, 1855, Caja 165, SM, AGENL; Francisco Castro to Secretario de Gobierno de Coahuila, Sept. 18, C5, F4, Manuel Menchaca to Villas Militar de la Frontera, Sept. 17, C5, F3, Menchaca to Villa de Rosas, Sept. 24, 1855, C5, F1, FSXIX, AGEC.

24. Callahan to Pease, Oct. 4, 1855, Box 84, NGPP, AHC; J. Ford, "Callahan's Expedition," 4; I. Moore, *Life*, 79–80; *San Antonio Ledger*, July 21, 28, 1855; *TSG*, Apr. 21, June 23, Aug. 11, Oct. 13, 1855; *El Bejareño*, July 31, 1855; *San Antonio Herald*, Aug. 14, 1855; *TST*, Aug. 25, Sept. 1, 1855; *NYTimes*, Aug. 10, 17, Sept. 15, 19, 26, 1855; Henry to Pease, Box 310–24, Folder 22, EMPP, TSLA; *San Antonio Daily Express*, July 2, 1905; *National Intelligencer*, Aug. 15, 23, 29, 1855.

25. Alsbury to Riddells, June 29, 1855, Riddells to Vidaurri, Oct. 12, 1855, Caja 26, Exp. 484, VSCE, AGENL; Henry to Pease, Sept. 2, 1855, EMPP, TSLA; Callahan to Burleson, Aug. 31, Sept. 12, 1855, 2B158, EBP, CAH; Callahan to Pease, Sept. 1, Oct. 4, 13, 1855, Box 84, NGPP, AHC; MR, Benton, Sept. 15, 1855, Oversize 401–723, Folder 1, TRMR, TAGD, TSLA; *Galveston Daily News*, Jan. 8, 1893; Walton interviews, Box 1, Folder 11, DATWC, BWML; *San Antonio Ledger*, Sept. 19, 22, 1855; *TSG*, Oct. 20, 1855; Jones family in San Antonio, 1855, Candice DuCoin, e-mail, Dec. 2010.

26. MR, William R. Henry, Sept. 15, 1855, Oversize 401–724, Folder 18, TRMR, TAGD, TSLA; *NYTimes*, Sept. 26, 1855; *San Antonio Daily Express*, July 2, 1905; J. Ford, "Callahan's Expedition," 5; Sansom, "Thrilling," 1, no. 5 (1911): 8–10.

27. See MRs for Lewis, Shaw, Walker, Fitzhugh, and McCulloch cited in chap. 13, n16; MR, Henry, Sept. 15, 1855, Oversize 401–724, Folder 18, Nov. 2, 1854, Dec. 14, 1854, Oversize 401–794, Folder 9, TRMR, TAGD, TSLA; last name, Henry muster roll, Land Grant Search, TGLO; S. Moore, *Savage Frontier*, 3:363–71; Spurlin, *Texas Volunteers*, 153, 155, 176, 183, 185, 219; Soldiers Who Served in Volunteer Organizations during the Indian Wars, RG94, M629, R13, R14, R30, R32, R38, NAB; U.S. Census, 1850, 1860, Slave Inhabitants, Bexar, Comal, Guadalupe, Caldwell, Hays Counties, Tex.; TR, 1854–55, TAC, Bexar, Caldwell, Comal, Guadalupe, Hays Counties, TSLA.

28. Ford, "Callahan's Expedition," 4–5; *San Antonio Daily Express*, July 2, 1905; Sansom, "Thrilling," 1, no. 5 (1911): 8–10.

29. Quartermaster Records, Box 401–1153, Folder 24, Box 401–1154, Folders 1–4, Correspondence, Box 401–1153, Folders 3–6, TRR, TSLA; Ford, "Callahan's Expedition," 5; *San Antonio Texan*, Oct. 25, 1855; Walton Interviews, Box 1, Folder 11, DATWC, BWML; *Victoria Daily Advocate*, Feb. 20, 1915; *San Antonio Daily Express*, July 2, 1905; C. Robinson, *Bad Hand*, 134–36; Sansom, "Thrilling," 1, no. 6 (1911): 4.

30. *TST*, Sept. 1, 15, 1855; *NOP*, Oct. 24, 1855; *San Antonio Texan*, Oct. 25, 1855; Langberg to Villa de Guerrero, Sept. 18, 1855, C5, F4, E2, FSXIX, AGEC; Sansom, "Thrilling," 1, no. 6 (1911): 4; Walton interviews, Box 1, Folder 11, DATWC, BWML; *Seguin Enterprise*, Dec. 22, 1905; J. Ford, "Callahan's Expedition," 5; Callahan to Pease, Oct. 4, 1855, Box 84, NGPP, AHC; *San Antonio Daily Express*, July 2, 1905, June 14, 1908; Sansom, "Thrilling," 1, no. 6 (1911): 4; Sumpter, *Paso*, 36, 61–62; Sumpter, "Life," chap. 4, n.p.; *Boletín Oficial*, Oct. 24, 1855; *Victoria Daily Advocate*, Feb. 20, 1915; *Seguin Enterprise*, Dec. 22, 1905; Sowell, *Texas Indian Fighters*, 527–28.

31. Sumpter, *Paso*, 61–62; Cunningham and Hewitt, "Lovely Land," 408–9; *Boletín Oficial*, Aug. 7, Sept. 25, 1855; *El Bejareño*, Sept. 1, 1855; Langberg to Villa de Guerrero, Sept. 18, 1855, C5, F4, Langberg to Villa de Guerrero, Sept. 25, 1855, C5, F6, FSXIX, AGEC.

32. Langberg to Vidaurri, Sept. 13, Tomás Talamantes et al. Pronouncement, Sept. 20, 1855, Box 9, Folder 104, MMR, BRBML; Langberg to Villa de Guerrero, Sept. 18, C5, F4, Manuel Ramirez to Gobierno del Estado de Nuevo León y Coahuila, Sept. 17, C5, F3, Talamantes, Oct. 1, 1855, C5, F8, FSXIX, AGEC; Langberg to Vidaurri, Sept. 19, 1855, Caja 18, Exp. 256, VSCP, AGENL; *Boletín Oficial*, Sept. 25, 1855.

33. Manuel Leal to Vidaurri, Sept. 17, 20, 1855, Caja 21, Exp. 71, VSCP, AGENL; Langberg to Menchaca, Sept. 28, 1855, "Investigation of Langberg," Caja 122, SM, AGENL (Langberg was responding to Menchaca's Sept. 23 note, which is now lost); Juan de Jesus Muñoz announcement, Sept. 26, 1855, Box 9, Folder 104, MMR, BRBML; Langberg to Villa de Guerrero, Sept. 25, Oct. 2, Oct. 3, 1855, C5, F8, Talamantes to Alcabalas, Oct. 1, 1855 ,C5, F8, FSXIX, AGEC; Langberg to Monclova, Sept. 26, 1855, Ficha 1912, C12, F3, FSXIX, AMM; *Boletín Oficial*, Sept. 25, 1855; J. Ford, "Callahan's Expedition," 4–5; *Galveston Daily News*, Jan. 8, 1893.

34. Menchaca to Villa de Guerrero, Sept. 13, Menchaca to Villas Militar de la Frontera, Sept. 17, C5, F3, Teodoro Herra to Villa de Guerrero, Sept. 28, 1855, C5, F7, FSXIX, AGEC; Langberg to Menchaca, Sept. 28, 1855, "Investigation of Langberg," Caja 122, SM, AGENL; Menchaca to Múzquiz, Sept. 24, 1855, Box 9, Folder 104, MMR, BRBML; Langberg to Vidaurri, Sept. 1, 1855, Caja 18, Exp. 256, VSCP, AGENL.

35. Menchaca to Vidaurri, Sept. 28, 1855, Caja 24, Exp. 830, VSCP, AGENL; Menchaca to Villa de Guerrero, Sept. 30, Menchaca to Villas de Rosa, Morelos, Allende, Nava, Gigedo, and Guerrero, Sept. 30, 1855, C5, F7, FSXIX, AGEC; Antonio Ortega to Múzquiz, Sept. 13, 1855, Box 9, Folder 105, MMR, BRBML.

CHAPTER 15

1. *TST*, Sept. 15, Oct. 6, 1855; *San Antonio Texan*, Oct. 4, 1855; *New Orleans Bee*, Oct. 15, 1855.

2. Sumpter, *Paso*, 62–63; *San Antonio Daily Express*, July 2, 1905, June 14, 1908; *NOP*, Oct. 24, 1855; *Galveston Weekly News*, Oct. 23, 1855; Sansom, "Thrilling," 1, no. 6 (1911): 4; J. Ford, "Callahan's Expedition," 5; Oct. 1855, Fort Duncan, Returns from Military Posts, RG393, M617, R335, NARA–SW; R. W. Johnson, *Soldier's Reminiscences*, 84–85; Hanahan, *Place*, 159–60.

3. *NOP*, Oct. 24, 1855; Callahan to Pease, Oct. 4, 13, 1855, Box 84, NGPP, AHC; *San Antonio Texan*, Oct. 25, 1855; J. Ford, "Callahan's Expedition," 5; *San Antonio Daily Express*, July 2, 1905; Sansom, "Thrilling," 1, no. 6 (1911): 4; U.S. Congress, Senate, 45th Cong., 2nd sess., 1878, S. Ex. Doc. 19, pp. 178–80.

4. *NOP*, Oct. 23, 1855; Comisión Pesquisidora, *Reports of the Committee*, 191–94, 181; *Boletín Oficial*, Sept. 30, Oct 19, 24, 1855; *El Siglo Diez y Nueve*, Nov. 12, 1855; *San Antonio Ledger*, Sept. 22, 1855.

5. *San Antonio Daily Express*, July 2, 1905; Sansom, "Thrilling," 1, no. 6 (1911): 4; Sumpter, *Paso*, 63.

6. Sumpter, *Paso*, 62–63; Callahan to Pease, Oct. 4, 13, 1855, Box 84, NGPP, AHC; J. Ford, "Callahan's Expedition," 5; *Galveston Daily News*, Jan. 8, 1893; *San Antonio Daily Express*, July 2, 1905, June 14, 1980; Sansom, "Thrilling," 1, no. 6 (1911): 4; *San Antonio Texan*, Oct. 25, 1855; *NOP*, Oct. 24, 1855; Ortega a la 1.° autoridad de la Villa de Múzquiz, Oct. 2, 1855, Box 9, Folder 105, MMR, BRBML; *TST*, Oct. 6, 1855.

7. Callahan to Pease, Oct. 13, 1855, Box 84, NGPP, AHC.

8. Menchaca to Villas de Rosa, Morelos, Allende, Nava, Gigedo, and Guerrero, Sept. 30, Menchaca to las villas de Partido, Oct. 1, 1855, C5, F7, FSXIX, AGEC; Menchaca to Patiño, Oct. 1, 1855, R5, Box 8, HOC, BRBML; Langberg to Menchaca, Sept. 28, 1855, "Investigation of Langberg," Caja 122, SM, AGENL; Chebahtah and Minor, *Chevato*, 13, 44 (maps); Susan A. Miller, *Coacoochee's Bones*, 140 (map); Stella Lapaz, Antonio Apache, and Percy Bigmouth, Lipan oral history, Box 44, Folder 54. MEOP; José Medina González Dávila, e-mail, July 2009.

9. *Boletín Oficial,* Oct. 19, 1855; *National Intelligencer,* Nov. 13, 1855; Miguel Davila et al., Oct. 1, Ortega to la Villa de Múzquiz, Oct. 2, Patiño to Juan Rodriguez, Oct. 2, 1855, Box 9, Folder 105, MMR, BRBML.

10. *Boletín Oficial,* Oct. 19, 1855; Langberg to la villa de Guerrero, Oct. 3, Talamantes to Receptor de Alcabalas, Oct. 1, 1855, C5, F8, FSXIX, AGEC; J. Ford, "Callahan's Expedition," 5–6; Sansom, "Thrilling," 1, no. 6 (1911): 4; *San Antonio Ledger*, Oct. 6, Oct. 13, 1855.

11. Callahan to Pease, Oct. 4, 13, 1855, Box 84, NGPP, AHC; *NYTimes,* Oct. 26, 1855; J. Ford, "Callahan's Expedition," 5–6; *San Antonio Daily Express*, July 2, 1905; Sansom, "Thrilling," 1, no. 6 (1911): 4; *San Antonio Texan,* Oct. 25, 1855. The Rio Escondido skirmish coordinates are from DAM, SEDENA (Medina González Dávila, "La Batalla," 41).

12. Chebahtah and Minor, *Chevato,* 13 (map), 20, 44 (map); Walton Interviews, Box 1, Folder 11, DATWC, BWML; Medina González Dávila, field notes, Lipan interviews, Doña Estela, 2009, Doña Socorro and Don Miguel, 2010, privately held; Percy Bigmouth, Lipan oral history, Box 44, Folder 54, MEO; Langberg to Menchaca, Sept. 28, 1855, "Investigation of Langberg," Caja 122, SM, AGENL.

13. *Boletín Oficial,* Oct. 19, 1855; Menchaca to Patiño, Oct. 1, 1855, R6, Box B, HOC, BRBML; *Neu Braunfelser Zeitung*, Oct. 26, 1855; García, *Guerra*, 49–53; J. Nichols, *Limits*, 194, 213; *San Antonio Express*, June 14, 1908; *National Intelligencer,* Nov. 13, 1855.

14. Callahan to Pease, Oct. 4, 1855, Box 84, NGPP, AHC; *NYTimes,* Oct. 26, 1855; *San Antonio Ledger,* Oct. 13, 1855; Sumpter, *Paso*, 63; J. Ford, "Callahan's Expedition," 6; *San Antonio Daily Express*, July 2, 1905, June 14, 1908; Sansom, "Thrilling," 1, no. 6 (1911): 4; *San Antonio Texan,* Oct. 25, 1855.

15. *San Antonio Daily Express*, July 2, 1905, June 14, 1908; Sansom, "Thrilling," 1, no. 6 (1911): 4; *San Antonio Texan,* Oct. 11, 25, 1855; Kyle to Burleson, Oct. 7, 1855, 2B158, EBP, CAH; *NYTimes,* Oct. 26, 1855; Callahan to Pease, Oct. 4, 13, 1855, Box 84, NGPP, AHC; *NOP,* Oct. 24, 1855; J. Ford, "Callahan's Expedition," 6; *Seguin Enterprise*, Dec. 22, 1905; Walton Interviews, Box 1, Folder 11, DATWC, BWML; H. E. McCulloch to *Blanco News,* Feb. 12, 1885, Blanco County, BC-9, VF, Institute of Texan Cultures; Sowell, *Texas Indian Fighters*, 527; TR, 1855, TAC, Bexar County, TSLA; Cutrer, "Colquhoun, Ludovic," Olmsted, *Journey*, 503; *NOP,* Oct. 24, 1855; I. Moore, *Life*, 84–85.

16. *Boletín Oficial,* Oct. 19, 1855; *National Intelligencer,* Nov. 13, 1855.

17. Medina González Dávila, field notes, Lipan interviews, Don Manuel, Don Armando, Doña Socorro, and Don Miguel, 2010, privately held.

18. Callahan to Pease, Oct. 4, 1855, Box 84, NGPP, AHC; *NOP,* Oct. 24, 1855; *National Intelligencer,* Nov. 13, 1855; J. Ford, "Callahan's Expedition," 6–7.

19. *San Antonio Daily Express*, July 2, 1905, June 14, 1908; Sansom, "Thrilling," 1, no. 6 (1911): 4, 17; Kyle to Burleson, Oct. 7, 1855, 2B158, EBP, CAH; Walton Interviews, Box 1, Folder 11, DATWC, BWML; *San Antonio Texan*, Oct. 11, 1855; Sowell, *Texas Indian Fighters,* 527–28; *San Antonio Ledger,* Oct. 13, 1855.

20. Sumpter, *Paso,* 63; Sowell, *Texas Indian Fighters,* 527–28; *San Antonio Daily Express,* July 2, 1905, June 14, 1908; Sansom, "Thrilling," 1, no. 6 (1911): 4, 17; J. Brown, *Indian Wars,* 601.

21. Callahan to Pease, Oct. 4, 1855, Box 84, NGPP, AHC; J. Ford, "Callahan's Expedition," 7; *San Antonio Daily Express,* July 2, 1905; Sansom, "Thrilling," 1, no. 6 (1911): 4, 17; *San Antonio Texan,* Oct. 11, 25, 1855; *NOP,* Oct. 24, 1855; Kyle to Burleson, Oct. 7, 1855, 2B158, EBP, CAH.

22. MR, James H. Callahan, July 20, 1855, Nathaniel Benton, Sept. 15, 1855, Oversize 401–723, Folders 1, 6, William R. Henry, Sept. 15, 1855, Oversize 401–724, Folder 18, TAGD, TRMR, TSLA; *San Antonio Texan,* Oct. 11, 1855; Callahan to Pease, Oct. 4, 1855, Box 84, NGPP, AHC; *TSG,* Oct. 13, 1855; Abbett, "William Early Jones," 3; Winfrey and Day, *Indian Papers,* 3:219–24; *NOP,* Oct. 24, 1855; *San Antonio Zeitung,* Oct. 16, 1855; *Seguin Enterprise,* Feb. 17, 1899; Strom, "Kyle, Texas"; J. Moursund, *Blanco County Families,* 334–37; Odintz, "Patton, Samuel B."; Moellering, "History," 59–60; Pitts Interviews, 1851–1917, Box 3C152, PWAP, CAH.

23. *Boletín Oficial,* Oct. 19, 1855; *National Intelligencer,* Nov. 13, 1855; *TST,* Nov. 17, 1855; Medina González Dávila, field notes, Lipan interviews, Don Manuel, 2010, privately held.

24. *Boletín Oficial,* Oct. 8, 19, 1855; Langberg to Vidaurri, Oct. 8, 1855, Caja 18, Exp. 256, VSCP, AGENL; Pedro Rodriguez to Monclova, Oct. 5, C5, F8, Francisco Castro to Gobierno del Estado de Coahuila, Oct. 8, 1855, C5, F9, FSXIX, AGEC.

25. U.S. Congress, House, 42nd Cong., 2nd sess., 1872, H. Ex. Doc. 277, p. 95; Callahan to Pease, Oct. 4, 1855, Box 84, NGPP, AHC; *TSG,* Oct. 13, 1855; *NYTimes,* Oct. 26, 1855; Kyle to Burleson, Oct. 7, 1855, 2B158, EBP, CAH; *El Bejareño,* Oct. 13, 1855; *National Intelligencer,* Oct. 29, 1855; *Neu Braunfelser Zeitung,* Oct. 12, 1855; *San Antonio Ledger,* Oct. 6, 13, 1855.

26. U.S. Congress, House, 42nd Cong., 2nd sess., 1872, H. Ex. Doc. 277, p. 95; *NYTimes,* Oct. 26, 1855; Callahan to Pease, Oct. 4, 13, 1855, Box 84, NGPP, AHC; J. Ford, "Callahan's Expedition," 7; *NOP,* Oct. 24, 1855.

27. Callahan to Pease, Oct. 13, 1855, Box 84, NGPP, AHC; J. Ford, "Callahan's Expedition," 8; *San Antonio Daily Express,* July 2, 1905; Sansom, "Thrilling," *Hunter's Magazine* 1, no. 7 (1911): 9; U.S. Congress, Senate, 45th Cong., 2nd sess., 1878, S. Ex. Doc. 19, pp. 164, 180; *San Antonio Texan,* Oct. 11, 1855; *NOP,* Oct. 24, 1855; *National Intelligencer,* Nov. 2, 13, 1855, U.S. Congress, House, 42nd Cong., 2nd sess., 1872, H. Ex. Doc. 277, p. 99.

28. *Boletín Oficial,* Oct. 8, 24, 19, 1855; *National Intelligencer,* Nov. 13, 1855; Callahan to Pease, Oct. 13, 1855, Box 84, NGPP, AHC; *San Antonio Texan,* Oct. 11, 25, 1855; Burbank to Asst. Adjt. Gen., Department of Texas, Oct. 8, 1855, Box 401–1153 Folders 3–4, TRR, TAGD, TSLA; *San Antonio Daily Express,* July 2, 1905; Sansom, "Thrilling," 1, no. 7 (1911): 9; Henry to Patiño, Oct. 6, 1855, Menchaca to Fort Duncan, Oct. 5, 1855, Exp. XI/481.3/5538, OM, DAM, SEDENA.

29. *Boletín Oficial,* Oct. 19, 24, 1855; *El Siglo Diez y Nueve,* Nov. 12, 1855; *San Antonio Daily Express,* July 2, 1905; Sansom, "Thrilling," 1, no. 7 (1911): 9.

30. *San Antonio Daily Express,* July 9, 1905; Sansom, "Thrilling," 1, no. 7 (1911): 9; Ford, "Callahan's Expedition," 8; U.S. Congress, Senate, 45th Cong., 2nd sess., 1878, S. Ex. Doc. 19, pp. 165–66.

31. Sumpter, *Paso,* 64–65; *San Antonio Daily Express,* July 2, 9, 1905; Sansom, "Thrilling," 1, no. 7 (1911): 9; Burbank to Asst. Adjt. Gen., Department of Texas, Oct. 8, 1855,

Box 401–1153, Folders 3–4, TRR, TAGD, TSLA; *El Siglo Diez y Nueve*, Nov. 12, 1855; *Boletín Oficial*, Oct. 24, 1855; *San Antonio Ledger*, May 18, 1854; Sowell, *Texas Indian Fighters*, 534; *NOP*, Oct. 24, 1855; Porter, "Lament," 47; U.S. Congress, Senate, 45th Cong., 2nd sess., 1878, S. Ex. Doc. 19, pp. 164–65, 180; *San Antonio Texan*, Oct. 25, 1855; Sumpter, *Paso*, 65; *National Intelligencer*, Nov. 2, 13, 1855.

32. U.S. Congress, Senate, 45th Cong., 2nd sess., 1878, S. Ex. Doc. 19, p. 164; *San Antonio Daily Express*, July 9, 1905; Sansom, "Thrilling," 1, no. 7 (1911): 9; Callahan to Pease, Oct. 13, 1855, Box 84, NGPP, AHC; *TSG*, Oct. 20, 1855; *El Siglo Diez y Nueve*, Nov. 12, 1855; *Boletín Oficial*, Oct. 24, 1855; MR, Callahan, July 20, 1855, Benton, Sept. 15, 1855, Oversize 401–723, Folders 1, 6, Henry, Sept. 15, 1855, Oversize 401–724, Folder 18, TRMR, TAGD, TSLA.

33. *NOP*, Oct. 24, 1855; *National Intelligencer*, Nov. 2, 13, 1855; Callahan to Pease, Oct. 13, 1855, Box 84, NGPP, AHC; Burbank to Asst. Adjt. Gen., Department of Texas, Oct. 8, 1855, Box 401–1153, Folders 3–4, TRR, TAGD, TSLA; Sumpter, *Paso*, 65, 68; J. Ford, "Callahan's Expedition," 8; *Boletín Oficial*, Oct. 19, 1855; Langberg to Vidaurri, Oct. 8, 1855, Caja 18, Exp. 256, VSCP, AGENL; Noticia 160, Múzquiz, Nov. 22, 1855, Box 11, Folder 128, MMR, BRBML.

34. Langberg to Vidaurri, Oct. 8, 1855, Caja 18, Exp. 256, VSCP, AGENL; *Boletín Oficial*, Oct. 19, 24, 1855; *El Siglo Diez y Nueve*, Nov. 12, 1855; *National Intelligencer*, Nov. 13, 1855; Langberg to Commander, Fort Duncan, Oct. 8, Burbank to Langberg, Oct. 8, 1855, Exp. XI/481.3/5538, OM, DAM, SEDENA.

35. *Boletín Oficial*, Oct. 19, 1855; Langberg to Vidaurri, Oct. 8, 1855, Caja 18, Exp. 256, VSCP, AGENL.

36. Sumpter, *Paso*, 62–64; *San Antonio Daily Express*, July 2, 9, 1905; Burbank to Asst. Adjt. Gen., Department of Texas, Oct. 8, 1855, Box 401–1153, Folders 3–4, TRR, TAGD, TSLA.

37. Pease to Callahan, Oct. 10, Box 301–24, Folder 23, EMPP, TSLA.

38. I. Moore, *Life*, 84–85; U.S. Congress, House, 42nd Cong., 2nd sess., 1872, H. Ex. Doc. 277, p. 104.

CHAPTER 16

1. Manning, *Diplomatic*, Vol. 9, *Mexico*, 190–94; J. Jackson, *Almonte's Texas*, 2–9, 12–13, 20–66, 387–402, 430–82.

2. *Galveston News*, Nov. 8, 13, 1855; *San Antonio Herald*, Nov. 6, 13, 1855; *San Antonio Texan*, Nov. 8, 1855; I. Moore, *Life*, 85; Callahan to Pease, Oct. 4, 13, 1855, Box 84, NGPP, AHC; Quartermaster Records, 1855, Box 401–1153, Folder 24, TRR, TAGD, TSLA; *NOP*, Nov. 25, 29, 1855.

3. J. Ford, "Callahan's Expedition," 8–9; *Neu Braunfelser Zeitung*, Nov. 16, 1855; MR, Callahan, July 20, 1855–Oct. 19, 1855, MR, Benton, Sept. 15, 1855–Oct. 15, 1855, Oversize 401–723, Folders 1, 6, MR, Henry, Sept. 15, 1855–Oct. 15, 1855, Oversize 401–724, Folder 18, TRMR, TAGD, TSLA; Pease to John D. Pitts, Oct. 18, 1855, Box 301–24, Folder 23, EMPP, TSLA; Quartermaster Records, 1855, Box 401–1153, Folder 24, TRR, TAGD, TSLA; Pease to Gentlemen of the Senate and House of Representatives, Nov. 22, 1855, Box 301–23, Folder 24, EMPP, TSLA; *Texas Ranger*, Nov. 29, 1855; *TSG*, Nov. 13, 1855, Mar. 8, 1856; *Journal of the Senate* (State of Tex. 6th Leg.), 33–39, 42–43, 226; Gammel, *Laws*, 4:186–87, 224.

4. *TSG*, Dec. 22, 1855, Mar. 18, Apr. 12, 1856; Quartermaster Records, Box 401–1153, Folder 24, Box 401–1154, Folders 1–4, Powers of Attorney Records, Box 401–1185, Fold-

ers 3–22, Oversize Quartermaster Records, Officer Pay Vouchers, Oversize 401–1242, Folders 15–18, Statements, 1855–60, Box 401–1238, Folder 3, Correspondence, 1855, Box 401–1153, Folders 3–4, TRR, TAGD, TSLA; U.S. Congress, Senate, 45th Cong., 2nd sess., 1878, S. Ex. Doc. 19, p. 154.

5. PR, bk. B, 36, 69, 128, 205, 210, bk. E, 146, Comal County, CC; Gammel, *Laws,* 4:120; Deeds, bk. 1, pp. 305–7, 315–16, Kendall County, CC; Statements, 1855–60, Box 401–1238, Folder 3, Correspondence, 1855, Box 401–1153, Folders 3–4, TRR, TAGD, TSLA.

6. *Statutes at Large,* 10:673, 11:434, 35:553; U.S. Congress, House, 42nd Cong., 2nd sess., 1872, H. Ex. Doc. 277, pp. 51–54, 131–38; *Journal of the House of Representatives* (State of Tex., 12th Leg.), 1529–30; U.S. Congress, Senate, 45th Cong., 2nd sess., 1878, S. Ex. Doc. 19, pp. 1–13, 141–56; U.S. Congress, Senate, 59th Cong., 1st sess., 1905–6, S. Doc. 169, pp. 1–33.

7. James Hughes Callahan, Box 14 Folder 14, JWNP, DRTL; Callahan to Pease, Oct. 13, 1855, Box 84, NGPP, AHC; *San Antonio Herald,* Oct. 16, 23, 1855; *Galveston News,* Oct. 23, 1956; Winkler, "Check List," 223.

8. Pease to Smith, Oct. 17, 1855, Box 401–24, Folder 23, EMPP, TSLA; I. Moore, *Life,* 84–85; Winfrey and Day, *Indian Papers,* 3:248–50, 258–60; *San Antonio Herald,* Oct. 23, Nov. 6, 1855; City of Rio Blanco to Henry McCulloch, Nov. 10, 1855, Box 310–24, Folder 24, EMPP, TSLA; *Journal of the Senate* (State of Tex., 6th Leg.), 58; *TST,* Nov. 17, 1855.

9. Long, "Tom, William"; *National Intelligencer,* Nov. 1, 1855; *Neu Braunfelser Zeitung,* Nov. 2, 1855; U.S. Congress, Senate, 45th Cong., 2nd sess., 1878, S. Ex. Doc. 19, p. 19; *San Antonio Herald,* Oct. 23, 1855; *NOP,* Oct. 30, 1855; MR, William G. Tobin, Oct. 12, 1855, Oversize 401–725, Folder 32, MR, Levi English, Aug. 6, 1855, Oversize 401–723, Folder 12, TRMR, TAGD, TSLA; Gillespie, "Tobin, William Gerard"; *Victoria Advocate,* Sept. 29, 1855; Leffler, "English, Levi"; *TSG,* Sept. 16, 1855.

10. *TSG,* Oct. 13, 20, 1855; *San Antonio Herald,* Oct. 9, 23, Nov. 6, 1855; *TST,* Oct. 6, Nov. 17, 1855; *Neu Braunfelser Zeitung,* Oct. 12, 1855; *San Antonio Zeitung,* Oct. 13, 20, 27, Nov. 3, 1855.

11. *National Intelligencer,* Oct. 26, 30, 31, Nov. 1, 13, 1855; *NOP,* Nov. 1, 1855; *NYTimes,* Oct. 18, 22, 26, 29, 31, Nov. 3, 9, 1855, Jan. 28, 1856; *Baltimore Sun,* Oct. 26, 1855; *Georgia Weekly Telegraph,* Oct. 23, 1855; *Southern Watchman,* Nov. 1, 8, 1855; *Southern Banner,* Nov. 22, 1855; *North American and United States Gazette,* Oct. 26, Nov. 8, 1855.

12. Pease to Smith, Oct. 17, 1855, Box 301–24, Folder 23, EMPP, TSLA; U.S. Congress, House, 42nd Cong., 2nd sess., 1872, H. Ex. Doc. 277, pp. 104–7; *NOP,* Oct. 14, 1855; Oct. 1855, Forts Clark, Duncan, McIntosh, Ringgold, Returns from Military Posts, RG393, M617, R213, 335, 681, 1019, NARA–SW; Harold B. Simpson, *Cry Comanche,* 38, 49.

13. *San Antonio Herald,* Oct. 9, Nov. 13, 1855; *TSG,* Oct. 13, 1855; *NOP,* Nov. 2, 22, Dec. 6, 1855; *Seguin Mercury,* Nov. 24, 1855; Pease to Smith, Oct. 13, 1855, Box 301–24, Folder 23, EMPP, TSLA; *San Antonio Texan,* Nov. 15, 1855; *Galveston News,* Nov. 13, 1855; U.S. Congress, House, 42nd Cong., 2nd sess., 1872, H. Ex. Doc. 277, pp. 95–96, 98–107.

14. Langberg to Vidaurri, Oct. 8, 1855, Caja 18, Exp. 256, Langberg to Vidaurri, Nov. 18, 1855, Caja 21, Exp. 703, VSCP, AGENL; *Boletín Oficial,* Oct. 19, 26, 1855; Langberg to La Primera Autoridad de Guerrero, Oct. 25, 1855, C5, F11, Ministero de Gobernación to Gobernador del Estado de Coahuila, Oct. 30, 1855, C5, F12, Comandante de esta Frontera to 1.º Autoridad of pueblos, Nov. 8, 1855, Menchaca to brigada de

operaciones, Nov. 11, 1855, C6, F2, FSXIX, AGEC; message to Langberg, Oct. 22, 1855, Múzquiz, Oct. 22, 1855, Box 9, Folder 105, MMR, BRBML; Juan Galán to Monclova, Oct. 24, 1855, Ficha 1940, C12, F4, FSXIX, AMM.

15. *National Intelligencer,* Nov. 2, 13, 1855; *TST,* Nov. 17, 1855; *San Antonio Herald,* Nov. 6, 1855; Smith to Langberg, Dec. 6, 1855, Box 401–1153, Folders 3–4, TRR, TSLA; Cunningham and Hewitt, "'Lovely Land,'" 412; Langberg, Emilio, Exp. XI/111/2–400, pp. 27–28, 40–48, 292–300, ACSH, DAM, SEDENA.

16. *NOP,* Nov. 6, 21, 1855; *Boletín Oficial,* Oct. 7, 8, 10, 17, 18, 19, 23, 26, 27, Nov. 7, 1855; *National Intelligencer,* Nov. 2, 13, 29, 1855; Mullowny to Marcy, Oct. 10, 1855, Despatches from U.S. Consuls in Monterrey, Mexico, 1849–1906, RG84, M165, R1, NACP; *El Siglo Diez y Nueve,* Nov. 2, 8, 12, 1855; Vidaurri to Álvarez, Oct. 8, 1855, Álvarez to Vidaurri, Oct. 21, 22, 1855, Jan. 23, 1856, Caja 1, Exp. 9, VSCP, AGENL; Moseley, "Public Career," 160–69.

17. Moseley, "Public Career," 155–58; *Boletín Oficial,* Oct. 24, Dec. 9, 1855; Mullowny to Marcy, Oct. 10, 1855, Despatches from U.S. Consuls in Monterrey, Mexico, 1849–1906, RG84, M165, R1, NACP; *El Restaurador de la Libertad,* Nov. 13, 1855, cited by Moseley, "Public Career," 156–57; D. C. Buell to Vidaurri, Oct. 8, 1855, Isaac Lynde to Vidaurri, Oct. 29, 1855, Burbank to Vidaurri, Nov. 9, 1855, Vidaurri to Ruggles, Fort McIntosh, Mar. 31, 1856, Caja 26, Exp. 484, VSCE, AGENL.

18. *NOP,* Nov. 6, 21, 1855; *National Intelligencer,* Nov. 29, 1855; Tyler, "Age," 44; Vidaurri to Bee, Nov. 29, 1855, Bee to Vidaurri, Jan. 20, 1856, Vidaurri, Santiago, manuscripts, privately held.

19. Investigation of Langberg, May–June 1856, Caja 122, SM, AGENL; Investigation of Colonel Langberg, correspondence and affidavits, Mar.–June 1856, Spanish Material from Various Sources Collection, Vol. 46, 1853–1866, Box 2Q323, pp. 128–56, SA, CAH; Unsigned, undated plan from Monterrey for erección de la Republica de Sierra Madre, Exp. XI/481.3/4817, OM, DAM, SEDENA; Langberg, Emilio, Exp. XI/111/2–400, pp. 27–28, 40–48, 292–300, ACSH, DAM, SEDENA; *El Monitor Republicano,* May 21, June 22, 1856; *El Ómnibus,* May 14, June 18, 1856.

20. Mullowny to Marcy, Oct. 10, 1855, Mullowny to Fort McIntosh, Oct. 23, 1855, Despatches from U.S. Consuls in Monterrey, 1849–1906, RG84, M165, R1, NACP; U.S. Congress, Senate, 41st Cong., 3rd sess., 1871, S. Ex. Doc. 36, pp. 574–78; Registry of the U.S. Army, 1798–1914, Adjutant General, 1780s–1917, RG94, M233, R42, NAB; *Texas Democrat,* Feb. 17, 24, June 2, 1849; *South-Western American,* June 18, 1851; Mullowny to Vidaurri, Aug. 25, 1855, Caja 165, SM, Aug. 30–Nov. 11, 1855, AGENL. Mullowny died on June 5, 1856, in Monterrey.

21. *NYTimes,* Oct. 23, 1855; Manning, *Diplomatic,* Vol. 9, *Mexico,* 788, 792–800, 803–12, 814–15; *El Restaurador de la Libertad,* Nov. 13, 1855, cited by Moseley, "Public Career," 156–57; Arrioja to Ministero de la Guerra, Dec. 6, 1855 (letters 1 and 2), Exp. XI/481.3/5538, OM, DAM, SEDENA.

22. Manning, *Diplomatic,* Vol. 9, *Mexico,* 190–94, 197–201, 781–82, 789–92, 816–17, 820–23.

23. *NYTimes,* Oct. 26, 1855; U.S. Congress, House, 42nd Cong., 2nd sess., 1872, H. Ex. Doc. 277, pp. 95, 98–99, 104; Sumpter, *Paso,* 68; "Mexico, 1868, Convention" (July 4, 1868), 581–84; "Mexico, 1871, Convention" (Apr. 19, 1871), 586–87; *Statutes at Large,* 15:679–85, 19:642–44; U.S. Congress, Senate, 44th Cong., 2nd sess., 1877, S. Ex. Doc. 31, pp. 1–16, 78–79, 88–89, 92–93; U.S. Congress, Senate, 45th Cong., 2nd sess., 1878, S. Ex. Doc. 19, pp. 156–89; Piedras Negras Municipal Proceedings, Nov. 15, 1855, Box 2Q323,

44:122–29, SA, CAH; Langberg to La Primera Autoridad de Guerrero, Oct. 12, 1855, C5, F9, FSXIX, AGEC; Pingenot, *Piedras Negras Claims*, TS, n.d., pp. 1–14.

24. *NOP,* Dec. 6, 1855; *Galveston News,* Nov. 13, Dec. 25, 1855, July 22, 1856; *NYTimes,* Dec. 19, 26, 1855; *TST,* Mar. 15, 1856, Jan. 17, 1857; *TSG,* Mar. 8, May 31, Sept. 13, 1856; *Dallas Weekly Herald,* June 28, July 7, Aug. 9, Sept. 27, 1856; *San Antonio Texan,* Feb. 7, 1856; Heitman, *Historical,* 2:401–2; Winfrey and Day, *Indian Papers,* 3:263–64; Pease to Smith, Mar. 4, 1856, Box 301–25, Folder 28, EMPP, TSLA; Simpson, *Cry Comanche,* 19, 28, 30–31, 37–50, 63, 68–69, 74–75, 78–82; Forts Clark, Duncan, Lancaster, Mason, Returns from Military Posts, 1856, RG393, M617, R213, R335, R589, R759, NARA–SW.

25. Langberg to Vidaurri, Oct. 8, 1855, Caja 18, Exp. 256, VSCP, AGENL; Mullowny to Fort McIntosh, Oct. 23, 1855, Despatches from U.S. Consuls in Monterrey, 1849–1906, RG84, M165, R1, NA; J. Nichols, *Limits,* 204–6, 213; Rodríguez García, *Historias de resistencia,* 70–73, 186–88; Espinoza to Commandancia military de la frontera del Río Grande, Mar. 19, 21, Apr. 15, 1856, Archivo del Municipio Guerrero, AGEC; Pablo Espinoza letters, Mar. 20, 22, 1856, Captain Patiño letter, Apr. 25, 1856, R5, Box 8, HOC, BRBML; Juan Zuazua to Vidaurri, Mar. 20, 22, 24, Apr. 19, May 1, 1856, Vidaurri, Santiago, Correspondencia Particular, Museo de Historia Mexicana, Monterrey, N.L., Mexico; Vidaurri to Ruggles, Mar. 31, 1856, Ruggles to Vidaurri, Apr. 18, 1856, Caja 26, Exp. 484, VSCE, AGENL; Comisión Pesquisidora, *Reports of the Committee,* 304, 333, 417–21; Britten, *Lipan,* 217–31, 228 (map); C. Robinson, *Bad Hand,* 134–44; José Medina González Dávila, field notes, Lipan interviews, Don Armando and Doña Socorro, 2010, privately held.

26. Cunningham and Hewitt, "'Lovely Land,'" 410–25; *New York Herald,* Dec. 7, 1865; *El Monitor Republicano,* June 22, 1856, Sept. 13, 1857, July 9, 1867; *La Sociedad,* Oct. 12, 1866; Tyler, *Santiago Vidaurri,* 98–103, 128, 136–43, 153–55; Moseley, "Vidaurri, Santiago," *HBTO*; Langberg, Emilio, Exp. XI/111/2–400, pp. 28–41, Espinoza, Pablo, Exp. D/111/4/2027, pp. 19–21, 58–59, Menchaca, Manuel, Exp. D/111/4/4031, pp. 1–15, 77–88, Leal, Manuel, Caja 869/111/16, p. 141, ACSH, DAM, SEDENA; González Milea, "Entre Arcadia," 48–50.

27. Adjutant General's Office, *Official Army Register* (Jan. 1873), 180; S. Burbank to S. Thomas, Adjutant General, May 21, June 4, 1862, Jan. 22, 1864, RG94, M619, R0077, R0237, NAB; J. L. Bowen, *Massachusetts,* 892–93; Heitman, *Historical Register,* 1:902; MacKinnon, *At Sword's Point, Part 2,* pp. 469–73.

28. *Texan Mercury,* Oct. 23, 1853; Richard A. Thompson, *Fort Duncan,* 30; Gary Clayton Anderson, *Conquest,* 268–69; *San Antonio Zeitung,* Oct. 26, 1855.

29. Handbook of Texas Online, "Burleson, Edward, Jr.," http://www.tshaonline.org/handbook/online/articles/fbu41; SR, Polk Kyle, 1st Texas Cavalry, 8th Texas Cavalry, Confederate, RG109, M323, R003, R0051, NAB; PR, Polk R. Kyle, Case 280, Fisher County, CC, Roby, Tex.; SR, William A. Pitts, 1st Texas Cavalry, Confederate, RG109, M323, R0004, NAB; William A. Pitts, Texas State Cemetery website, accessed Dec. 30, 2018.

30. Tise, *Texas County Sheriffs,* 43; Henry to Vidaurri, Aug. 12, 1856, Vidaurri to Henry, Sept. 8, 1856, Vidaurri, Santiago, Correspondence, 1855–1864, CAH; Henry to Vidaurri, June 13, 1858, Vidaurri to Henry, July 12, 1858, Henry to Vidaurri, Sept. 15, 1860, Caja 26, Exp. 484; VSCE, AGENL; McCaslin, *Fighting,* 82–88; TR, 1859–60, TAC, Uvalde County, TSLA; SR, W. C. Adams, 2nd Texas Cavalry, Confederate, RG109, M323, R0008, NAB; *San Antonio Texan,* June 18, 1857; *Galveston Civilian and Gazette,* Nov. 24,

1857; Robert Augustine, Convict Record Ledgers, Vol. 1998/038–139, p. 17, Huntsville Prison, TSLA; Bliss, *Reminiscences*, xiv–xx, 259–62.

31. Niemeyer, "Benton, Nathaniel"; U.S. Census, 1860, 1870, Guadalupe County, Tex.; U.S. Census, 1870, 1880, 1900, 1910, Jefferson County, Ark.; Marriages, 6:44, CC, Jefferson County, Pine Bluff, Ark.; *Ledger and Texan*, June 1, 1861; SR, Benjamin E. Benton, Z. P. Bugg, 1st Texas Cavalry, Confederate, RG109, M323, R0002, R0116, NAB; SR, Henry W. Bridges, 6th Texas Cavalry, Confederate States, RG109, M323, R0037, NAB.

32. TR, 1881–86, TAC, Llano County, TSLA; TR, 1890–98, TAC, Wilbarger County, TSLA; Tise, *Texas County Sheriffs*, 27, 39, 43, 45, 65, 79, 170, 249, 300, 319; DCR, Arrest Warrants, *Texas v. George Lang et al.*, Criminal Case 82, Comal County, DC; *Lockhart Post-Register*, June 3, 1920; J. Moursund, *Blanco County History*, 550; Griffin, "Connecticut Yankee," 165–68, 216.

33. *National Intelligencer*, Oct. 31, 1855; *NOP*, Nov. 12, 1855, Jan. 11, 1856; *NYTimes*, Dec. 5, 19, 1855; *Dallas Weekly Herald*, Dec. 8, 1855.

CHAPTER 17

1. Kenneth W. Porter to Ralph A. Smith, Oct. 7, 1964, Box 28, Folder 3, Porter Papers (hereafter KWPP), New York Public Library (hereafter NYPL); Porter, *Negro*, xv–xvi, 7, 95, 138, 154, 183, 205, 237, 262, 294, 338, 359, 368, 471, 493; Porter, *Black Seminoles*, 259–60; Porter, "Seminole in Mexico." 1–36; Kenneth Wiggins Porter, Biographical/Historical Information, KWPP, NYPL; Kenneth Wiggins Porter to Joe Austell Small, Aug. 17, 1965, Box 26, Folder 5, KWPP, NYPL; Ralph A. Smith, "Mamelukes," 79–83; Duane K. Hale, "Ralph A. Smith," 177–92; Annette Allene Shelfer, Smith's daughter, telephone conversation, Sept. 2010; TSS, articles copied from Mexican newspapers, Ralph Smith Papers, Callie Faye Milliken Special Collections, Margaret and Herman Brown Library, Abilene Christian University, Abilene, Tex.

2. James H. Callahan to E. M. Pease, Sept. 1, 1855, Box 84, NGPP, AHC.

3. *Clarksville Standard*, Nov. 10, 1855; *TSG*, Oct. 20, 1855; *NYTimes*, Oct. 26, 1855; *San Antonio Texan*, Oct. 11, 25, 1855; *San Antonio Ledger*, Oct. 6, 1855; Kyle to Burleson, Oct. 7, 1855, 2B158, EBP, CAH; *NOP*, Oct. 24, 1855; *National Intelligencer*, Nov. 2, 1855; Burbank to Asst. Adjt. Gen., Department of Texas, Oct. 4, 8, 1855, Box 401–1153, Folders 3–4, TRR, TAGD, TSLA; Sumpter, *Paso*, 61–75; J. Ford, "Callahan's Expedition," 5; *Galveston Daily News*, Jan. 8, 1893; *San Antonio Daily Express*, June 25, July 2, 9, 1905; Sansom, "Thrilling," 1, no. 5 (1911): 8–10, no. 6 (1911): 4, 17, no.7 (1911): 9–10; *Victoria Daily Advocate*, Feb. 20, 1915; *San Antonio Express*, June 14, 1908; Walton Interviews, Box 1, Folder 11, DATWC, BWML: *Seguin Enterprise*, Dec. 22, 1905; Sowell, *Texas Indian Fighters*, 526–28; Pitts Interview, 1851–1917, Box 3C152, PWAP, CAH; U.S. Congress, Senate, 45th Cong., 2nd sess., 1878, S. Ex. Doc. 19, pp. 164–66, 178–80.

4. Sumpter, *Paso*, vii–xiv; Sumpter, "Life," chaps. 1–6.; Glenn, *Capt'n John*, ix–x, 7–17, 26–49; *Lockhart Register*, June 3, 1920; *Fort Worth Star-Telegram*, May 29, 1920.

5. *Seguin Enterprise*, Feb. 5, 1904, Dec. 15, 22, 1905; *Hondo Anvil*, Dec. 9, 1922; Walton Interviews, Box 1, Folder 11, DATWC, BWML; Madray, *History*, 47–49; Tise, *Texas County Sheriffs*, 39, 65; Sowell, *Texas Indian Fighters*, 527–28; Hunter, *Pioneer*, 121–23; Hicks Family History, privately held; Pitts Interviews, 1851–1917, Box 3C152, PWAP, CAH; *Biographical Encyclopedia of Texas*, 81–83; William A. Pitts, Texas State Cemetery website, http:/www.cemetery.state.tx.us/search.asp.; Campbell Family Records, privately held; Isaac Campbell, PR, Gonzales County, CC; *San Antonio Express*, June 14, 1908, Apr. 9, 11, 1911. Harris farmed in Guadalupe Country and died in Medina County,

November 30, 1922. Walton was the sheriff in Bee and Brewster Counties and died in Uvalde County in 1915. During his ranching life, Hicks accumulated 17,000 acres in Bandera County; he died in January 1899. Pitts died in 1913; he is buried in the Texas State Cemetery. Campbell founded Campbellton, Atascosa County; his ranching estate was worth $250,000 when he died in April 1911.

6. *Boletín Oficial,* Oct. 8, 19, 24, 1855; *El Siglo Diez y Nueve,* Nov. 12, 13, 1855; Langberg to Vidaurri, Oct. 8, 1855, Caja 18, Exp. 256, VSCP, AGENL; *TST,* Nov. 17, 1855; *National Intelligencer,* Nov. 13, 1855; U.S. Congress, Senate, 45th Cong., 2nd sess., 1878, S. Ex. Doc. 19, p. 180.

7. Langberg, Emilio, Exp. XI/111/2–400, pp. 1–164, ACSH, DAM, SEDENA; Cunningham and Hewitt, "Lovely Land," 387–425; Menchaca, Manuel, Exp. D/111/4/4031, pp. 1–15, 77–88, Leal, Manuel, Exp. Oja 869/111/16,141, n.p., ACSH, DAM, SEDENA; Seguin, *Personal,* 28.

8. U.S. Congress, Senate, 45th Cong., 2nd sess., 1878, S. Ex. Doc. 19, p. 180; Porter, "Lament," 47; "Filibusters," Box 23/SL, MG 222, Folder 13, KWPP, NYPL; Bigmouth, Lipan oral history, Box 44, Folder 54, MEOP; Interviews of Lipan descendants, e-mail, José Medina González Dávila, July 2009; Medina González Dávila, field notes, Lipan interviews, 2009, 2010, Coahuila, Mex., privately held.

9. Callahan to Pease, Oct. 4, 1855, FP A.1 P, Box 84, NGPP, AHC; *TST,* Nov. 17, 1855; *El Bejareño,* Oct. 25, 1855; Langberg to Menchaca, Sept. 28, 1855, Investigation of Langberg, Caja 122, f. 2, SM, AGENL; Medina González Dávila, field notes, Lipan interviews, Doña Estela, 2009, Don Manuel, 2010, Coahuila, Mex., privately held; Percy Bigmouth, Lipan oral history, Box 44, Folder 54, MEOP; Lipan Population–250, Neighbors to Maypenny, Feb. 4, 1856, BIA, TA, RG75, M234, R860, NARA–SW; *Boletín Oficial,* Nov. 18, 1855 (Lipan population–269).

10. *Boletín Oficial,* Oct. 7, 8, 10, 19, 24, 26, 1855; *TST,* Nov. 17, 1855; Medina González Dávila, field notes, Lipan interviews, Doña Estela, 2009, Coahuila, Mex., privately held; Porter, "Seminole in Mexico," 19; *San Antonio Texan,* Oct. 11, 1855; *El Siglo Diez y Nueve,* Nov. 12, 1855; *NOP,* Nov. 6, 1855; *San Antonio Daily Express,* July 2, 1905; J. Nichols, *Limits of Liberty,* 198, 203–15.

11. *Boletín Oficial,* Oct. 7, 1855; *National Intelligencer,* Oct. 26, 31, 1855; Manning, *Diplomatic,* Vol. 9, *Mexico,* 197–201, 794, 799–802, 816–17; Moseley, "Public Career," 154–56; Collins, *Texas Devils,* 88; Mulroy, *Freedom,* 79; May, *Manifest,* 42–43, 53; Porter, *Black Seminoles,* 151–52; *Journal of the Senate* (State of Tex., 6th Leg.), 36–37.

12. Porter, *Black Seminoles,* 152; Porter, *Negro,* 441; Tyler, "Callahan Expedition of 1855," 579, 583; Tyler, "Slave Owners," 56–59; Ralph A. Smith, "Mamelukes," 80–81; Porter, "Seminole in Mexico," 18–20; S. Miller, *Coacoochee's Bones,* 168; May, *Manifest,* 260–61; Mulroy, *Freedom,* 78–80; Sumpter, *Paso,* 61–62; Callahan to Pease, Oct. 13, 1855, Box 84, NGPP, AHC; Riddells to Vidaurri, Oct. 12, 1855, Caja 26, Exp. 484, VSCE, AGENL; For documentation of Callahan's slave ownership, see chap. 8, n30.

13. San Antonio Committee to Langberg, Aug. 25, 1855, Langberg to San Antonio Committee, Aug. 30, 1855, Caja 165, SM, AGENL; Tyler, "Callahan Expedition of 1855," 577.

14. T. Brown, "Seminole," 65–68; U.S. Congress, House, 32nd Cong., 2nd sess., 1852, H. Ex. Doc. 1, pt. 2, p. 393; Porter, "Seminole in Mexico," 18–19; Porter, *Negro,* 441; Porter, *Black Seminoles,* 152; Lack of association, DuVal and Callahan at KWPP, NYPL, Alice Adamczyk, archivist and researcher, e-mails, May, Oct.–Dec. 2009, this author's searches, December, 2016, KWPP, NYPL; R. Smith, "Mamelukes," 81; Gesick,

"1855 Callahan Raid," 47; Crenshaw, "Knights," 23–26, 37, 41–42; R. Dunn, "KGC in Texas," 549; Keehn, *Knights*, 39; *Dallas Weekly Herald*, Feb. 1, Oct. 17, 1860. Searches for Marcellus Duval were conducted at TSLA, CAH, Travis County CC, Travis County DC, Crawford County (Ark.) Clerk, the libraries of Crawford and Van Buren Counties, Arkansas, and the Ralph Smith Papers, Margaret and Herman Brown Library. Marcellus Duval schemed in the 1840s and 1850s to sell Maroons, and frequent absences while hunting for escaped slaves resulted in his 1853 dismissal.

15. Buder, "Moore, Ike Henry"; Ike Moore to Kenneth Porter, Jan. 19, Feb. 16, 1942, Box 249, Folder 8, KWPP, NYPL; Porter to Moore, Jan. 24, 1942, Moore Papers, privately held. Ike Henry Moore's death in May 1945 prevented his planned commentary on the Callahan Expedition; however, he left a short note and a file.

16. Porter, "Seminole in Mexico," 18–19; Porter, *Negro*, 441; R. Smith, "Mamelukes," 81; Smith to Cooper, Oct. 10, 1855, U.S. Congress, House, 42nd Cong., 2nd sess., 1872, H. Ex. Doc. 277, 100–101. Records searched were MMR and HOC at BRBML at Yale, archives of Mexican villages in the area (AGEC, AGNEL), archives at SEDENA, TSLA, Mexican official publications (*Boletín Oficial*, *El Restaurador de la Libertad*, and *La Patria*), U.S. military correspondence, and Texas newspapers.

17. Filibusters!, Box 23, Folder 13, KWPP, NYPL; Kenneth W. Porter to Harry E. Chrisman, Oct. 19, 1965, Chrisman to Porter, Oct. 23, 1965, Porter to Chrisman, Jan. 2, 1966, Box 14, Folder 7, KWPP, NYPL.

18. Mock, *Dreaming*, 18–21, 337–38; Porter, "Lament," 47; Index cards, 1855 Callahan Expedition, Box 26, folders 4, 5, KWPP, NYPL. During my visits to the Schomburg Center, NYPL, I was stymied by Porter's system of notetaking and index cards. His notes on the Callahan Expedition, with his sources and comments, are found on only five small index cards.

19. Porter, *Black Seminoles*, 153; J. Nichols, *Limits of Liberty*, 199–201; Collins, *Texas Devils*, 79–80; Mulroy, *Freedom*, 79; May, *Manifest*, 260–61; Gesick, "1855 Callahan Raid," 56–57; Tyler, "Callahan Expedition of 1855," 579; Henry to Pease, Sept. 2, 1855, Box 310–24 Folder 22, EMPP, TSLA; *San Antonio Daily Express*, July 2, 1905; J. Ford, "Callahan's Expedition," 4–5; San Antonio Committee to Langberg, Aug. 25, 1855, Langberg to San Antonio Committee, Aug. 30, 1855, Caja 165, SM, AGENL; *Victoria Daily Advocate*, Nov. 20, 1855.

20. Callahan to Burleson, Aug. 31, 1855, Box 2B158, EBP, CAH; Callahan to Pease, Sept. 1, 1855, Box 84, NGPP, AHC; Tyler, "Fugitive Slaves," 57, 59–60; Tyler, "Callahan Expedition of 1855," 584; Luis Alberto García, interview by author, July 2017, Monterrey, N.L.; Vidaurri to Bee, Nov. 29, 1855, Bee to Vidaurri, Jan. 20, 1856, Vidaurri, Santiago, manuscripts, privately held.

21. Tyler, "Callahan Expedition of 1855," 579–80; Mulroy, *Freedom*, 70–71, 76–77, 79; *TST*, Sept. 22, 1855; Burleson to Pease, Sept. 8, 1855, Box 301–24, Folder 22, EMPP, TSLA; Porter to Tyler, Feb. 15, May 26, 1976, Tyler to Porter, Feb. 18, 1976, Box 26, Folder 4, KWPP, NYPL; Molbech, *General Langbergs Haendelser*, 132–36; Cunningham and Hewitt, "Lovely Land," 409–10; T. S. Abbott, *Carta general*.

22. Pease to Callahan, July 5, 1855, Box 301–24, Folder 20, EMPP, TSLA; *NOP*, Oct. 23, Nov. 1, 1855; *TST*, Oct. 6, 1855; Sansom, "Thrilling," 1, no. 6 (1911): 4; *Galveston Daily News*, Jan. 8, 1893; Callahan to Pease, Oct. 4, 13, 1855, Box 84, NGPP, AHC. Numerous newspaper articles on Indian raids were discussed in chaps. 12 and 13; see also maps 13.1,14.1.

23. J. Ford, "Callahan's Expedition," 4–5; James Hughes Callahan, Box 14, Folder 14, JWNP, DRT; H. E. McCulloch to *Blanco News,* Feb. 12, 1885, Blanco, Tex., BC-9, Blanco County, VF, Institute of Texan Cultures; Callahan to Pease, Oct. 4, 13, 1855, Box 84, NGPP, AHC; *National Intelligencer,* Oct. 13, Nov. 5, 1855.

24. Thompson, *Fort Duncan,* 29–31; Baylor, "Gen. Baylor," 21, 359–62; Sansom, "Thrilling," 1, no. 6 (1911): 4, 17; *Galveston Daily News,* Jan. 8, 1893; Burbank to Asst. Adjt. Gen., Department of Texas, Oct. 4, 1855, Box 401–1153, Folders 3–4, TRR, TSLA.

25. Langberg, Emilio, Exp. XI/111/2–400, pp. 28–41, ACSH, DAM, SEDENA; *El Monitor Republicano,* May 21, June 22, 1856; *El Ómnibus,* May 14, June 18, 1856; Investigation of Langberg, caja 122, ff. 3–4, 8, 10, SM, AGENL; Conducta Emilio Langberg, Villas de Rosa, Cuatro Cienegas, Abasolo, Nava, Múzquiz, Allende, Piedras Negras, Morelos, 1856, C4, F6, Sumeria instruido contra Emilio Langberg, Villa de Guerrero, 1856, C4, F8, FSXIX, AGEC; Sumerio instruido contra Emilio Langberg, Vol. 46, pp. 128–56, Box 2Q323, SA, CAH; *TSG,* May 24, 1856.

26. Depositions, Investigation of Langberg, caja 122, ff. 3–4, 8, 10, SM, AGENL; Depositions, Conducta Emilio Langberg, Villas de Rosa, Cuatro Cienegas, Abasolo, Nava, Múzquiz, Allende, Piedras Negras, Morelos, 1856, C4, F6, Depositions, Sumerio instruido contra Emilio Langberg, Villa de Guerrero, 1856, C4, F8, FSXIX, AGEC; Depositions, Sumerio instruido contra Emilio Langberg, Vol. 46, pp. 128–56, Box 2Q323, SA, CAH.

27. J. Nichols, *Limits of Liberty,* 198, 201; Callahan to Pease, Oct. 4, 1855, Box 84, NGPP, AHC; Leal to Vidaurri, Sept. 20, 1855, Caja 21, Exp. 71, VSCP, AGENL; Depositions, Investigation of Langberg, caja 122, ff. 3–4, 8, 10, SM, AGENL; Depositions, Conducta Emilio Langberg, Villas de Rosa, Cuatro Cienegas, Abasolo, Nava, Múzquiz, Allende, Piedras Negras, Morelos, 1856, C4, F6, Depositions, Sumerio instruido contra el Emilio Langberg, Villa de Guerrero, 1856, C4, F8, FSXIX, AGEC; Depositions, Sumerio instruido contra Emilio Langberg, Vol. 46, pp. 128–56, Box 2Q323, SA, CAH; González Milea, "Las ideas de Emilio Langberg," 130–31.

28. Burbank to Asst. Adjt. Gen., Department of Texas, Oct. 4, 8, 1855, Box 401–1153, Folders 3–4, TRR, TSLA; Callahan to Pease, Oct. 4, 1855, Box 84, NGPP, AHC; U.S. Congress, Senate, 45th Cong., 2nd sess., 1878, S. Ex. Doc. 19, pp. 100, 165–66, 180–81; Oct. 1855, R. Johnson, *Soldier's Reminiscences,* 84; *San Antonio Daily Express,* July 2, 9, 1905, June 14, 1908; *Galveston Weekly News,* Oct. 23, 1855; *Boletín Oficial,* Oct. 19, 24, 1855; Sansom, "Thrilling," 1, no. 6 (1911): 4, 17, no. 7 (1911): 9–10; Bound vol. 7, John W. Sansom Memoirs, Collection 882, JTDSP, DRTL; *Galveston Daily News,* Jan. 8, 1893; *San Antonio Texan,* Oct. 25, 1855; *NOP,* Oct. 24, 1855; *TST,* Nov. 17, 1855.

29. Callahan to Pease, Oct. 13, 1855, Box 84, NGPP, AHC; *TST,* Oct. 27, Nov. 24, 1855; *San Antonio Herald,* Oct. 30, 1855; Testimony, Florencio Rodriguez, June 4, 1856, Investigation of Langberg, Caja 122, ff. 11–12, SM, AGENL; J. Nichols, *Limits of Liberty,* 198, 201.

30. Smith to Cooper, Oct. 10, 1855, U.S. Congress, House, 42nd Cong., 2nd sess., 1872, H. Ex. Doc. 277, 100–101; Smith to L. Thomas, Oct. 17, 1855, Box 401–1153, Folders 3–4, TRR, TAGD, TSLA. See n16.

31. *Boletín Oficial,* Oct. 24, 1855; Moseley, "Public Career," 152–56; Tyler, "Age," 41–44; Luis Alberto García, e-mails, Aug. 2009, July 2010; Langberg to Vidaurri, Sept. 1, 1855, Caja 18, Exp. 256, VSCP, AGENL. This second August 30 letter to Langberg, which he referenced in his letter to Vidaurri, was not found in the archives of SEDENA, AGENL, or AGEC.

32. *Boletín Oficial*, Oct. 24, 1855; Tyler, "Callahan Expedition of 1855," 577–78; *Houston Weekly Telegraph*, Aug. 20, 1856; Hazlewood, "Fisher, George"; Tyler, "Slave Owners," 47; W. Speer and Brown, *Encyclopedia of the New West*, 313–14; *NOP*, Nov. 22, 1855.

33. Sumpter, *Paso*, 62; Pingenot, "Sumpter, Jesse"; Tyler to Porter, Dec. 1, 1970, Jan. 6, Feb. 12, Dec. 29, 1971, Porter to Tyler, Dec. 30, 1970, Feb. 8, 1971, Ben E. Pingenot to Porter, Dec. 29, 1971, Box 26, Folder 5, KWPP, NYPL. During my August 31, 2010, visit, the Archivos Militar, SEDENA, staff told me no service file existed for the name "Alambejar."

CHAPTER 18

1. DCR, E. C. Hinds, Thomas S. Johnson depositions, *Texas v. George Lang et al.*, Criminal Case 82, Comal County, DC; Diary entry, Apr. 8, 1856, DP, CAH.

2. *NOP*, Apr. 23, 1856; DCR, *Texas v. Mary Blessingame*, *Texas v. George Lang et al.*, Criminal Case 82, Comal County, DC.

3. *TSG*, Apr. 26, May 24, 1856; J. Speer, *History of Blanco County*, 7–8; Goar, "Bloody Times," 446–47; W. Russell, "Murder of Captain Callahan," 22; P. Morgan, "Henry Bruemmer's Experience," 7; Kemp, "Blanco County Tragedy," 412–16; *Blanco County News*, July 29, 1987; "Callahan–Blassingame Incident," TS; DCR, *Texas v. Mary Blessingame*, Hinds, Johnson, J. M. Watson, depositions, *Texas v. George Lang et al.*, Criminal Case 82, Comal County, DC; *San Antonio Texan*, May 1, 1856; W. R. Russell to J. T. DeShields, Apr. 12, 1911, box 11, folder 575, "Written for the Old Guard," by W. R. Russell, n.d., box 11, folder 575, Kate Callahan to J. T. DeShields, Feb. 26, 1911, box 9, folder 439, JTDSP, DRTL (Kate Callahan described the Blassingame incident in a letter to Russell, which no longer exists. Russell penned the undated article, "Written for the Old Guard," based on Kate's letter.); Death of James Hughes Callahan, box 4, folder 14, JWNP, DRTL; Death of James Hughes Callahan, PCFH; Hines, *Eli Clemmons Hinds*, n.p.; *Neu Braunfelser Zeitung*, Apr. 18, 25, May 9, 1856.

4. TR, 1855, TAC, Comal County, TSLA; Death of James Hughes Callahan, PCFH; *TSG*, Sept. 22, Dec. 22, 1855, Apr. 12, 1856; *National Intelligencer*, Oct. 31, 1855; *NOP*, Dec. 1, 9, 1855, January 11, 1856; *NYTimes*, Dec. 5, 19, 1855; *Dallas Weekly Herald*, Dec. 8, 1855; PM, Callahan estate, Aug., 1856, Probate bk. B, 189, Comal County, CC; Marriage and Death Records, Pate Family Bible, privately held; Kayser, "King–Ranger Cemetery," accessed Dec. 7, 2009.

5. Deeds, bk. D, 207, bk. E, 330, Comal County, CC; Hugh McLarin, Thomas Barbee, Land Grant Search, TGLO; Janelle Holmes, interviews, telephone conversations, e-mails, 2009–10, 2018; MR, Callahan Company, July 20, 1855, Oversize 401–723, Folder 6, TRMR, TAGD, TSLA; Jordan, *Log Cabin*, 25–27. Janelle Holmes's husband is a descendant of Woodson and Mary Blassingame.

6. U.S. Census, 1800, Union District, S.C.; Will bk. A, 1798–1814, p. 88, Deeds, bk. 2, 341–42, Warren County, CC, Bowling Green, Ky.; U.S. Census, 1830, Perry County, 1850, Bibb County, Ala.; Descendants of Woodson Blassingame, privately held; U.S. Census, 1850, Hempstead, Union Counties, Ark.; Minutes, County Court, May 1857, vol. G, 281–83, Leon County, CC, Centerville, Tex.; Marriages, vol. A, 22, Hays County, CC.

7. U.S. Department of the Interior, Bureau of Land Management, General Land Office Records, "Perry and Bibb Counties, Cahaba Land Office, Alabama," "Howard County, Washington Land Office, Arkansas," https://glorecords.blm.gov/search/default

.aspx, accessed Oct. 20–21, 2009 (searched Blasingame [name spelled in records]); Deeds, bk. D, 98–99, bk. F, 47–48, bk. H, 426–27, Perry County, CC, Marion, Ala.; Circuit Court, Minutes, Records bk. 1, pp. 532–35, County Court, Minutes, Records bk. B, 162, 173, 176–77, Bibb County; Deeds, bk. K, 375–76, L, 193–94, Tax Records, 1851–53, Hempstead County Records, Arkansas History Commission.

8. City of Rio Blanco to Henry McCulloch, petition, Nov. 10, 1855, box 301–24, folder 24, EMPP, TSLA; TR, 1855, TAC, Hays County, TSLA; CCM, vol. B, 180–81, Comal County, CC.

9. "James H. Callahan," box 4, folder 14, JWNP, DRTL; J. Speer, *History of Blanco County*, 7; Goar, "Bloody Times," 446; W. Russell, "Murder of Captain Callahan," 22; Janelle Holmes, conversations, e-mails with author, 2009–10, 2018; "Callahan's death," PCFH; *San Antonio Texan,* May 1, 1856; DCR, Hinds deposition, *Texas v. George Lang et al.*, Criminal Case 82, Comal County, DC.

10. *TSG*, Apr. 12, May 24, 1856; *San Antonio Texan,* May 1, 1856; Russell to DeShields, Apr. 12, 1911, "Written for the Old Guard," by Russell, n.d., box 11, folder 575, JTDSP, DRTL; W. R. Russell, "Murder of Captain Callahan," 22; *San Antonio Herald,* Apr. 19, 1856; *El Bejareño,* Apr. 19, 1856; *Huntsville Item,* Apr. 19, 1856; *Neu Braunfelser Zeitung,* Apr. 16, 1856; *NOP*, Apr. 23, 1856.

11. J. Speer, *History of Blanco County*, 7; W. R. Russell, "Murder of Captain Callahan," 22; Paul Morgan, "Henry Bruemmer's Experience," 7; Goar, "Bloody Times," 446–47; Kemp, "Blanco County Tragedy," 412–16; *Blanco County News,* July 29, 1987; "Callahan–Blassingame Incident," TS; James H. Callahan Death, box 4, folder 14, JWNP, DRTL; Hines, *Eli Clemmons Hinds*, n.p.

12. *TSG*, Apr. 26, May 24, 1856; *San Antonio Texan,* May 1, 1856.

13. Russell to DeShields, Apr. 12, 1911, box 11, folder 575, "Written for the Old Guard" by Russell, n.d., box 11, folder 575, JTDSP, DRTL; Death of James Hughes Callahan, PCFH; *San Antonio Texan*, May 1, 1856; Fourth DCM, vol. D, 12, Bexar County DC, Bexar County Records Center Archives; James Hughes Callahan Death, box 4, folder 14, JWNP, DRTL.

14. DCR, Hinds, Johnson depositions, *Texas v. George Lang et al.*, Criminal Case 82, Comal County, DC; Russell to DeShields, Apr. 12, 1911, box 11, folder 575, "Written for the Old Guard," by Russell, n.d., box 11, folder 575, Callahan to DeShields, Feb. 26, 1911, box 9, folder 439, JTDSP, DRTL; Death of James Hughes Callahan, PCFH; Hinds, *Eli Clemmons Hinds*, n.p.

15. J. Speer, *History of Blanco County*, 6–9; W. Russell, "Murder of Captain Callahan," 22; Paul Morgan, "Henry Bruemmer's Experience," 7; Goar, "Bloody Times," 446–47; Kemp, "Blanco County Tragedy," 412–16; *Blanco County News,* July 29, 1987; "Callahan–Blassingame Incident," TS, privately held; *TSG*, Apr. 26, May 24, 1856; DCR, Johnson, Hinds, Watson depositions, *Texas v. George Lang et al.*, Criminal Case 82, Comal County, DC; *San Antonio Texan,* May 1, 1856; *NOP,* Apr. 23, 1855.

16. *TSG*, Apr. 26, May 24, 1856; DCR, Johnson, Hinds depositions, *Texas v. George Lang et al.*, Criminal Case 82, Comal County, DC.

17. Death of James Hughes Callahan, PCFH; DCR, Hinds deposition, *Texas v. George Lang et al.*, Criminal Case 82, Comal County, DC; *San Antonio Texan,* May 1, 1856; *TSG,* Apr. 26, May 24, 1856.

18. DCR, Johnson, Hinds depositions, *Texas v. George Lang et al.*, Criminal Case 82, Comal County, DC.

19. *NOP,* Apr. 23, 1856; *San Antonio Herald,* Apr. 19, 1856; J. Speer, *History of Blanco County,* 9.

20. Goar, "Bloody Times," 447; DCR, Watson deposition, *Texas v. George Lang et al.*, Criminal Case 82, Comal County, DC; TR, 1859, TAC, Blanco County, TSLA; TR, 1855–59, TAC, Comal County, TSLA; J. Speer, *History of Blanco County,* 9.

21. *TSG,* Apr. 12, 1856; *TST,* Apr. 12, 1856; *San Antonio Herald,* Apr. 19, 1856; *El Bejareño,* Apr. 19, 1856; *Neu Braunfelser Zeitung,* Apr. 16, 1856; *NOP,* Apr. 23, 24, 26, 27, 1856; *NYTimes,* May 3, 1856; *Baltimore Sun,* May 15, 1856; *National Intelligencer*, Apr. 29, 1856.

22. TSG, Apr. 26, May 24, 1856; DCR, Johnson, Hinds, Watson depositions, *Texas v. George Lang et al.*, Criminal Case 82, Comal County, DC; Woodall, "Callahan, James Hughes," HBTO, reprinted at Texas State Cemetery website, http://www.cemetery.state.tx.us/search.asp, accessed Oct. 31, 2009; "Callahan Murdered," SDPJ; Neu Braunfelser Zeitung, Apr. 16, 1856. There are dozens of publications citing Callahan's incorrect death date; most are noted in this narrative.

23. DCR, Johnson, Hinds depositions, *Texas v. George Lang et al.*, Criminal Case 82, Comal County, DC; TSG, Apr. 26, May 24, 1856.

24. *TSG,* Apr. 26, May 24, 1856; DCR, Hinds, Johnson depositions, *Texas v. George Lang et al.*, Criminal Case 82, Comal County, DC; *San Antonio Texan,* May 1, 1856; *Blanco County News,* July 29, 1987.

25. Russell to DeShields, Apr. 12, 1911, box 11, folder 575, "Written for the Old Guard," by Russell, n.d., box 11, folder 575, Callahan to DeShields, Feb. 26, 1911, box 9, folder 439, JTDSP, DRTL; J. Speer, *History of Blanco County,* 7; W. Russell, "Murder of Captain Callahan," 22; Death of James Hughes Callahan, PCFH; DCR, Watson, Johnson depositions, *Texas v. George Lang et al.*, Criminal Case 82, Comal County, DC.

26. J. Speer, *History of Blanco County,* 3, 8, 19; DCR, Watson deposition, *Texas v. George Lang et al.*, Criminal Case 82, Comal County, DC; Don Watson, Watson descendant, e-mail, Feb., 2009; U.S. Census, 1850, Dyer County, Tenn.

27. DCR, Watson deposition, *Texas v. George Lang et al.*, Criminal Case 82, Comal County, DC; Goar, "Bloody Times," 447; *TSG,* May 24, 1856; *San Antonio Herald,* Apr. 19, 1856; *NYTimes,* May 3, 1856; *Neu Braunfelser Zeitung,* Apr. 18, 25, May 9, 1856; J. Speer, *History of Blanco County,* 8; James Hughes Callahan Death, box 4, folder 14, JWNP, DRTL; Russell to DeShields , Apr. 12, 1911, box 11, folder 575, "Written for the Old Guard," by Russell, n.d., box 11, folder 575, Callahan to DeShields, Feb. 26, 1911, box 9, folder 349, JTDSP, DRTL; W. R. Russell, "Murder of Captain Callahan," 22; Don Watson, e-mail, Feb. 2009.

28. *Neu Braunfelser Zeitung,* Apr. 25, May 9, 1956; *TSG,* May 24, 1856; Goar, "Bloody Times," 447; Bruhn, "Twin Sisters, TX"; J. Moursund, *Blanco County History,* 89–91, 100–102, 110. Deeds, bk. D, 124–25, Comal County, CC; Elise Tips Wuppermann, "Diary," WC, privately held.

29. *TSG,* Apr. 25, May 24, 1856; *Clarksville Standard,* May 3, 1856; *Neu Braunfelser Zeitung,* May 9, 1956; J. Speer, *History of Blanco County,* 8; U.S. Census, 1850, 1860, Hays County, Tex.; TR, 1855, TAC, Hays County, TSLA; Gifford White, *Texas Scholastics,* 107–9; "1855 School Census, Hays County," 4–10; J. Moursund, *Blanco County Families,* 17, 62, 72–73, 343; *Memorial and Genealogical Record,* 145–46, 156–58, 295–96; Jennette, *Biographical Directory,* 113; MR, Callahan Company, July 20, 1855, Oversize 401–723, Folder 6, TRMR, TAGD, TSLA.

30. *San Antonio Herald,* Apr. 19, 1856; *NOP,* Apr. 23, 26, 27, 1856; *NYTimes,* May 3, 1856; *Neu Braunfelser Zeitung,* Apr. 25, May 9, 1956; *TSG,* Apr. 19, 1856; *Galveston News,* Apr. 16, 1856; *National Intelligencer,* May 5, 1856; J. Speer, *History of Blanco County,* 9; Russell to DeShields, Apr. 12, 1911, "Written for the Old Guard," by Russell, n.d., box 11, folder 575, Callahan to DeShields, Feb. 26, 1911, box 9, folder 439, JTDSP, DRTL; Death of James Hughes Callahan, PCFH; W. R. Russell, "Murder of Captain Callahan," 22; Paul Morgan, "Henry Bruemmer's Experience," 7; Goar, "Bloody Times," 447; "Sauer Family Cemetery," accessed Mar. 25, 2018.

31. *TSG,* May 24, 1856.

32. NOP, May 1, 1856; *San Antonio Herald,* Apr. 19, 1856; TSG, Apr. 19, May 24, 1856; *Neu Braunfelser Zeitung,* Apr. 25, May 9, 1856; *Clarksville Standard,* May 3, 1856; J. Speer, *History of Blanco County,* 9; W. Russell, "Murder of Captain Callahan," 22; Paul Morgan, "Henry Bruemmer's Experience," 7; Goar, "Bloody Times," 446–47; Kemp, "Blanco County Tragedy,"415; Blanco County News, July 29, 1987; "Callahan–Blassingame Incident," TS; DCR, W. G. Sansom et al., inquest, Apr. 14, 1856, *Texas v. George Lang et al.*, Criminal Case 82, Comal County, DC.

33. *Neu Braunfelser Zeitung,* Apr. 25, May 9, 1856.

34. *TSG,* Apr. 19, 1856; DCR, W. G. Sansom et al., Apr. 14, 1856, *Texas v. George Lang et al.*, Criminal Case 82, Comal County, DC; J. Moursund, *Blanco County Families,* 59, 162, 292, 299, 373.

35. *TSG,* May 24, 1856; Winfrey and Day, *Indian Papers* 3:223; J. Moursund, *Blanco County Families,* 111, 416.

36. *Neu Braunfelser Zeitung,* May 9, 1856; *TSG,* May 24, 1856; DCR, *Texas v. Mary Blessingame,* Watson, Johnson, Hinds depositions, *Texas v. George Lang et al.*, Criminal Case 82, Comal County, DC; TR, 1855–56, TAC, Comal County, TSLA; J. Speer, *History of Blanco County,* 19, 29, 43, 70, 72.

37. "We acknowledge counselors . . . ," John M. Watson et al., *Texas v. George Lang et al.*, Criminal Case 82, DCR, Comal County, DC; J. Moursund, *Blanco County Families,* 61, 170–72, 287–88, 292, 373–76, 440–41, 454; *Blanco County News,* June 25, 2008.

38. George Lang, G. Ullrich, Apr. 16, 1856, *Texas v. George Lang et al.*, Criminal Case 82, DCR, Comal County, DC; *Neu Braunfelser Zeitung,* May 9, 1856; *Journal* (House, State of Tex., 5th Leg.), 5; Biesele, "Early Times," 82, 87, 91; *Weekly Journal,* July 9, 1851; *San Antonio Ledger,* Feb. 3, June 16, Oct. 27, 1853, Mar. 30, May 25, Oct. 7, 1854, *San Antonio Herald,* Aug. 21, 1855.

39. *San Antonio Ledger,* June 6, 1854, Apr. 17, Oct. 16, 1858; Y. Russell, "Devine, Thomas Jefferson."

40. *San Antonio Texan,* May 1, 1856; Fourth DCM, vol. D, 12, Bexar County, DC, Bexar County Records Center Archives; Watson et al., Johnson, Hinds depositions, *Texas v. George Lang et al.*, Criminal Case 82, DCR, Comal County, DC.

41. *San Antonio Texan,* May 1, 1856; DCR, Johnson deposition, *Texas v. George Lang et al.*, Criminal Case 82, Comal County, DC; James Hughes Callahan, box 4 folder 14, JWNP, DRTL; Fourth DCM, vol. D, 12, Bexar County, DC, Bexar County Records Center Archives.

42. *San Antonio Texan,* May 1, 1856; *San Antonio Herald,* Apr. 19, 1856; *TSG,* June 14, 1856, May 16, 1857; *San Antonio Ledger,* Jan. 24, Dec. 19, 1857.

43. Janelle Holmes, e-mails, 2009–2010, 2018; U.S. Census, 1860, Leon County, Tex.; Deeds, bk. E, 366, Comal County, CC; *TSG,* May 24, 1856; Ophia D. Smith, "Trip to Texas," 37.

44. Deeds, bk. E, 330–31, 366–67, 439–39, 673–74, Comal County, CC; PM, bk. B, 147, 156–57, 214–16, 306, 381–82, bk. C, 6, 17–20, Comal County, CC; J. Moursund, *Blanco County Families,* 72–73, 161, 281–82.

45. J. Speer, *History of Blanco County*, 9.

CHAPTER 19

1. Haas, *History*, 248, 266; U.S. Census, 1850, 1860, Comal County, Tex.; DCR, Arrest Warrants, *Texas v. George Lang et al.*, Criminal Case 82, Comal County, DC; J. Speer, *History of Blanco County,* 10–11, 19; J. Moursund, *Blanco County History*, 556–57; Tise, *Texas County Sheriffs*, 45.

2. Townes, "Sketch. I," 29–30, 35–53, "Sketch. II," 135–40.

3. D. Robinson, *Judge*, 160–61; Gard, "Vigilantes"; *Trinity Advocate,* May 20, 1857; Cuthbertson, "Regulator-Moderator"; *TSG*, Sept. 27, 1856; Guthrie, *Raw Frontier*, 2:117–18; Denison, "Some Letters," 1163; *Galveston Civilian and Gazette,* Sept. 29, 1857.

4. McWhiney, *Cracker Culture*, xii, xiv, 162, 167, 169; Gregg, *Diary*, 2:85; Ross, "Lynching"; *San Antonio Texan*, June 14, 1855.

5. Biesele, *German Settlements*, 6–20, 42–45, 61 (map), 61–62, 78–88, 101 (map), 119–20, 140–41, 163 (map), 163–164; Tiling, *German Element*, 10, 19, 24–29, 33–36, 43–47, 53–57, 60–72, 73–128, 197–200; Weaver, *Castro's Colony*, 16–19, 20 (map), 49–56, 73–74, 82 (map), 92–93, 96, 109; Seele, *Cypress*, 5–18, 26–28; *Texas Presbyterian*, Mar. 13, 1847; Dunt, *Journey*, 175–82.

6. Fey, *New Braunfels*, 1:574–75; Tise, *Texas County Sheriffs*, 124; Haas, *History,* 51; Julius Bose, VF, Sophienburg Museum and Archives, New Braunfels, Tex.; U.S. Census, 1850, Guadalupe County, Tex. George Ullrich died October 8, 1889, and Julius Bose on April 28, 1905; both in New Braunfels.

7. *TSG,* June 30, 1855; *San Antonio Ledger,* June 22, 1854; Biesele, *German Settlements,* 196–204, 225; Tiling, *German Element,* 130–31; *New York Daily Tribune,* Jan. 20, 1855. Immigrant German-Texans' attitudes, revealed in the *San Antonio Zeitung* and *Neu Braunfelser Zeitung,* in the antebellum and post–Civil War periods have not been well studied nor the two newspapers utilized often by scholars.

8. Seele, *Cypress,* 127–41; *TSG*, Sept. 26, 1855, Mar. 15, 1856; *San Antonio Ledger*, Mar. 15, 1856; DCM, vol. B, 414, 450, Comal County, DC.

9. *San Antonio Ledger,* Dec. 10, 1859; DCR, Indictment, *Texas v. George Lang et al.*, Criminal Case 82, Comal County, DC; DCM, bk. C, 15, Comal County, DC; J. Speer, *History of Blanco County,* 25; John H. Jenkins and Kesselus, *Edward Burleson*, 373.

10. DCR, Indictment, *Texas v. George Lang et al.*, Criminal Case 82, Comal County, DC; *Neu Braunfelser Zeitung*, Sept. 5, 1856; DCM, vol. C, 17–18, Comal County, DC; U.S. Census, 1850, 1860, Comal County, Tex.; CCM, vol. B, 440, Comal County, CC.

11. Fey, *New Braunfels* 1:354–55, 384, 397, 427–29, 493–95, 522, 541–43, 557–58; Geue and Geue, *New Land,* 96, 103, 106, 117, 127, 131, 135, 142, 144, 145; Biesele, *German Settlements,* 15, 20, 133, 194; Landa, *As I Remember*, 13–16; Tiling, *German Element*, 12–13; Taylor, "Furniture."

12. DCM, bk. A, 23, 31, 39, 42, 70–71, 77, 90, 144, 151–52, 155, 160, 171, 173, 189, 191, 193, 197, 221, 225, 248, bk. B, 1, 25, 64, 84, 89, 96, 102, 106, 110, 144, 152–53, 159–60, 174, 178, 189, 201, 217, 227, 242, 244, 274, 277–78, 282, 287, 317, 321, 326, 330, 337, 340, 346, 348, 356, 379, 389, 393, 404, 413, 428, 434–35, 438–39, Comal County, DC. Five men (Schwab, Schaefler, Landa, Remmler, and Hanz) arrived during Republic of Texas. Citizenship records for Loeffler and Starz were not found.

13. DCM, bk. A, B, Comal County, DC; DCM, bk. A, AB, Guadalupe County, DC; DCM, bk. A-1, Caldwell County, DC. The period analyzed was the district court 1846 fall term through the 1856 spring term. See chap. 8, n36, n37.

14. Sheehan, *German Liberalism*, 33, 36, 43–44, 47, 55.

15. *TST*, Sept. 27, Oct. 4, 11, 1856; *TSG*, Sept. 27, 1856; *Neu Braunfelser Zeitung*, Oct. 3, 1856; *San Antonio Ledger*, Aug. 2, 1856; John Hemphill to A. Rossy, Oct. 10, 1856, *Texas v. George Lang et al.*, Criminal Case 82, Comal County, DC; Cutrer, "Hemphill, John."

16. DCR, Indictment, *Texas v. George Lang et al.*, Criminal Case 82, Comal County, DC.

17. TR, 1853–58, TAC, Comal County, TSLA; TR, 1858–63, TAC, Blanco County, TSLA; *Neu Braunfelser Zeitung*, Apr. 16, 1856; Marriages, bk. A, 301b, Comal County, CC; Deeds, bk. D, 124–25, 134–35, bk. E, 85, Comal County, CC; U.S. Census, 1860, Bexar, Comal Counties, Tex.; MR, John W. Sansom, Apr. 16, 1856, box 401–725, folder 29, TRMR, TAGD, TSLA; Christian Speiser, biographical information, private collection; Elise Tips Wuppermann, "Diary," WC, privately held.

18. DCR, Indictment, *Texas v. George Lang et al.*, Criminal Case 82, Comal County, DC; *Neu Braunfelser Zeitung*, May 9, 1856; *TST*, Oct. 4, 1856; Marriages, bk. A, 144, Comal County, CC; Haas, *History* , 64; DCM, bk. C, 16, 18, Comal County, DC; TR, 1852–60, TAC, Bexar, Blanco, Comal, Caldwell Counties, TSLA; U.S. Census, 1850, 1860, Bexar, Comal, Caldwell Counties, Tex.; Carmen Thompson-Gibson, Hoyt descendant, e-mail, Jan. 2017.

19. Convict Ledger, Texas Prison Museum; Blanco County, Map 4886, Kendall County, Map 6687, Maps, TGLO; Lich, "Sansom, John William"; DCM, bk. E, 248–49, Fayette County, DC; U.S. Census, 1850, Jasper County, Mo.; TR, 1856–57, TAC, Comal County, TSLA; Marriages, bk. B, 140, Comal County, CC; J. Moursund, *Blanco County Families*, 299; J. Moursund, *Blanco County History*, 101; CCM, vol. B, 355, Comal County, CC; MR, Sansom, Apr. 16, 1856, box 401–725, folder 29, TRMR, TAGD, TSLA; James C. Martin, Francis M. Martin, Land Grant Search, TGLO; Martin Family History, oral tradition, privately held.

20. J. Moursund, *Blanco County Families*, 59–62, 293, 438, 440–41; TR, 1855–57, TAC, Comal County, TSLA; DCR, Indictment, *Texas v. George Lang et al.*, Criminal Case 82, Comal County, DC; U.S. Census, 1850, Bastrop, Caldwell Counties, Tex.; MR, Benton, Sept. 15, 1855, Oversize 401–723, folder 1, MR, Sansom, Apr. 16, 1856, box 401–725, folder 29, TRMR, TAGD, TSLA; TR, 1848, TAC, Caldwell County, TSLA; Blanco County, Map 4886, Maps, TGLO; Marriages, bk. A, 15–16, 48–49, Caldwell County, CC; Probate bk. A, 97, Caldwell County, CC; Blanco County News, *Heritage*, 618; CCM, vol. B, 304, Comal County, CC; McKeehan, "Tinney," accessed Mar. 24, 2018; Hines, *Eli Clemmons Hinds*, n.p.

21. U.S. Census, 1850, Caldwell County, Tex.; Probate bk. A, 151, 333, 347, 351, 357, Caldwell County, CC; *San Antonio Ledger*, May 27, 1852: MR, Callahan, July 20, 1855, Oversize 401–723, folder 6, TRMR, TAGD, TSLA; Isaac Campbell Family, Family Records, LoRetta Hughes, Saginaw, Tex.; W. A. Blackwell, Isaac Campbell, W. R. Huckabe [Huckobey], Land Grant Search, TGLO; Isaac Campbell, PR, Gonzales County, CC; TR, 1856, TAC, Comal County, TSLA; City of Rio Blanco, Nov. 10, to Henry McCulloch, petition, box 301–24, folder 24, EMPP, TSLA; CCM, vol. B, 180–81, Comal County, CC; Kendall County, Map 6687, Maps, TGLO; Goar, "Bloody Times," 447.

22. U.S. Census, 1850, Lauderdale County, Miss., and Hot Springs County, Ark.; TR, 1856–57, TAC, Comal County, TSLA; Blanco County, Map 4886, Maps, TGLO; J.

Moursund, *Blanco County Families*, 170–71; Cathy Morgan, "Family Tree," accessed Mar. 25, 2018; City of Rio Blanco, Nov. 10, to Henry McCulloch, petition, box 301–24, folder 24, EMPP, TSLA; CCM, vol. B, 180–81, Comal County, CC; Franks, *Seventy Years*, 13.

23. MR, Sansom, Apr. 16, 1856, box 401–725, folder 29, MR, Callahan, July 20, 1855, Oversize 401–723, folder 6, TRMR, TAGD, TSLA; DCR, Indictment, Watson deposition, Arrest Warrants, *Texas v. George Lang et al.*, Criminal Case 82, Comal County, DC; TR, 1855–57, TAC, Comal County, TSLA; J. Moursund, *Blanco County Families*, 289–91; Blanco County, Map 4886, Maps, TGLO; Clara Watkins, *Kerr County*, 33; CCM, vol. B, 180–81, Comal County, CC; TR, 1848–49, TAC, Caldwell County, TSLA; DCM, bk. B, 120, 203, 214, 395, 434, Comal County, DC; DCR, *Texas v. Chancey Stevenson,* Criminal Case 73, Comal County, DC; U.S. Census, 1850, 1860, Comal, Caldwell Counties, Tex.; Marriages, vol. C, 17, Comal County, CC. There is one intriguing possibility: thirty-five miles west of Middletown, a Mr. Waddell taught school during 1858–59 at Center Point, Kerr County, Texas.

24. DCR, Arrest Warrants, Hemphill to Rossy, Oct. 10, 1856, *Texas v. George Lang et al.*, Criminal Case 82, Comal County, DC; DCM, bk. C, 15, Comal County, DC; *TST,* Oct. 4, 1856; Tise, *Texas County Sheriffs*, 124, 126; J. Speer, *History of Blanco County*, 12; Tanner, Blanco County, 1860, Agriculture, Nonpopulation Census Schedules for Texas, 1850–80, Bureau of the Census, RG29, T1134, R47, NAB; Winfrey and Day, *Indian Papers* 5:351–53; Blanco County News, *Heritage*, 7–8; Solomon Tanner Marriage, Tanner Family biographical information, privately held.

25. DCR, Arrest Warrants, *Texas v. George Lang et al.*, Criminal Case 82, Comal County, DC; Cathy Morgan, "Family Tree," accessed Mar. 25, 2018; DCM, vol. D, 101, Comal County, DC.

26. DCM, bk. C, 36–38, 41–42, 49–52, Comal County, DC; *Neu Braunfelser* Zeitung, Mar. 13, 1857; Haas, *New Braunfels and Comal County*, 98; U.S. Census, 1850, Comal, Hays Counties, Tex.; TR, 1855–56, TAC, Hays, Comal Counties, TSLA; U.S. Census, 1860, Bexar County, Tex.; J. Moursund, *Blanco County Families,* 20–21.

27. DCM, bk. C, 49–52, Comal County, DC; TR, 1855–56, TAC, Comal, Caldwell Counties, TSLA.

28. DCM, vol. C, 330, Guadalupe County, DC; F. Johnson, *History,* 1:1063–64; Gould, *Alexander Watkins Terrell,* 3–14, 18–27, 56–60, 66–74, 78–84, 105–7, 124–29, 159–61; Cutrer, "Jones, George Washington"; *TSG,* Mar. 14, 28, May 16, 23, June 6, 13, Oct. 10, 1857, June 5, 1858, Sept. 17, 1859; *TST*, June 30, 1855; *Southern Intelligencer*, Dec. 7, 1857, Mar. 31, June 16, Aug. 11, 1858; *Galveston Civilian and Gazette*, Aug. 17, 1858.

29. DCR, *Texas v. George Lang et al.*, Criminal Case 321, Guadalupe County, DC; *San Antonio Ledger*, Nov. 14, 1857; DCM, vol. C, 331, 340, 344, Guadalupe County, DC; U.S. Census, 1860, Hays County, Tex.; MR, Callahan, July 20, 1855, Oversize 401–723, folder 6, TRMR, TAGD, TSLA; J. Moursund, *Blanco County Families*, 332; Cathy Morgan, "Ancestor Chart," 139.

30. Criminal Docket bk., 30, 44, 58, 66, Guadalupe County, DC; DCM, vol. C, 380, 416, 418–20, vol. D, 112–13, Guadalupe County, DC; Tise, *Texas County Sheriffs,* 45; MR, Callahan, July 20, 1855, Oversize 401–723, folder 6, TRMR, TAGD, TSLA; *Seguin Mercury,* Nov. 24, 1855; *Houston Weekly Telegraph*, Nov. 10, 24, 1858; DCR, *Texas v. George Lang et al.*, Criminal Case 321, Guadalupe County, DC; Long, "Tom, John Files."

31. DCM, vol. D, 72–73, 98–99, 101, 123–26, Guadalupe County, DC; *Seguin Mercury,* Dec. 22, 1858; Weinert, *Authentic History,* 16, 69; MR, Callahan, July 20, 1855,

Oversize 401–723, folder 6, TRMR, TAGD, TSLA; DCR, *Collin Johnson v. J. H. Callahan and G. B. Hollamon,* Civil Case 590, Guadalupe County, DC.

32. DCM, vol. D, 100–110, 123–24, Guadalupe County, DC; U.S. Census, 1850, 1860, Caldwell, Comal, Guadalupe Counties, Tex.; Deeds, bk. E, 163–64, 246–47, Comal County, CC; Elise Tips Wuppermann, "Diary," WC, privately held; Weinert, *Authentic History,* 14, 20; DCR, *Texas v. George Lang et al.,* Criminal Case 321, Guadalupe County, DC.

33. DCM, vol. B, 231–33, Caldwell County, DC; U.S. Census, 1850, 1860, Comal, Hays, Caldwell Counties, Tex.; J. Moursund, *Blanco County Families,* 110–11.

34. *TSG,* May 12, June 30, Aug. 11, 18, 1860; Wilder, "Sneed, Thomas Eskridge"; Koch, "Sneed, Sebron Graham"; Cutrer, "Oldham, Williamson Simpson"; *Biographical Encyclopedia,* 239; DCM, vol. B, 249, 253, 277, Caldwell County, DC.

35. *TSG,* Oct. 27, 1860; *San Antonio Ledger,* Oct. 27, 1860; *Biographical Encyclopedia,* 239; J. Speer, *History of Blanco County,* 25; *Memorial and Genealogical Record,* 275–76.

36. TR, 1860–62, 1892–93, TAC, Bexar County, TSLA; Lang, Geo. W., 1863 (p. 97), 1885 (p. 175), City Directory, Leavenworth, Kansas State Historical Society; Lange, G. W., butcher, p. 251, 1888, *Los Angeles City Directory,* accessed Nov. 28, 2016; Lang biographical information, privately held; Christian Speiser biographical information, privately held; SR, Christian Speiser, 1st Texas Cavalry, USA, RG109, M393, R2, NAB; *San Antonio Light,* Jan. 24, 1885; TR, 1860, TAC, Caldwell County, TSLA; SR, John W. Hoyt, 1st Texas Mounted Riflemen, 36th Texas Cavalry, Confederate, RG109, M227, R18, NAB; Record of Appointment of Postmasters, Sept. 30, 1971, Texas, RG28, M841, R121, R124; NAB; Carmen Thompson, Hoyt descendant, e-mail, Jan. 2017; TR, 1869, 1871–74, 1877, 1887–88, 1890–93, TAC, Cameron County, TSLA; *Brownsville Herald,* Mar. 18, 1893, May 26, 1897, Feb. 1, 1902, Nov. 14, 16, 1906, Aug. 28, 1908, Mar. 24, 1914; U.S. Census, 1860, Parker County, Tex.; TR, 1867–71, TAC, Guadalupe County, TR, 1877–89, TAC, Uvalde County, TSLA.

37. Winfrey and Day, *Indian Papers* 3:263–264; MR, Sansom, Apr. 16, 1856, box 401–725, folder 16, TRMR, TAGD, TSLA; DCR, Indictment, *Texas v. George Lang et al.*, Criminal Case 82, Comal County, DC.

38. MR. Sansom, Aug. 31–Nov. 30, 1859, box 401–725, folder 16, TRMR, TAGD, TSLA; Glenn, *Capt'n John, x,* 110; Tise, *Texas County Sheriffs,* 126, 300, 319; *Twentieth Century History,* 1:208–10; SR, John W. Sansom, 1st Texas Cavalry, USA, RG94, M402, R0007, NAB; U. S. Census, 1870, 1880, Kendall County, Tex.; U. S. Census, 1870, 1880, 1900, Uvalde County, Tex.; U.S. Census, 1910, 1920, Bexar County, Tex.; J. Moursund, *Blanco County Families,* 299; SR, Francis M. Martin, 15th Texas Cavalry, Confederate, RG109, M227, R23, NAB; U.S. Census, 1860, Comanche, Lampasas Counties, Tex.; James C. Martin, Erath County, Co. B, 1862, Cunningham's Company, 1864, Texas State Troops, TAGD, TSLA; TR, 1884, TAC, Hamilton County, TSLA.

39. Blanco County, Texas, 1860, Agriculture, Nonpopulation Census Schedules for Texas, 1850–80, Bureau of the Census, RG29, T1134, R47, NAB; TR, 1860–63, 1866, 1871, 1877, 1879, 1881–87, 1897–1903, TAC, Blanco County, TSLA; Blanco County News, *Heritage of Blanco,* 618; *Blanco County News,* Nov. 1, 2013; SR, Robert W. Cherry, 6th Texas Infantry Regiment, Confederate, RG 109, M227, R7, NAB; Death Indexes, 1903–40, Vital Statistics Unit, Texas Department of State Health Services; TR, 1901, TAC, Lee County, TSLA; TR, 1860–67, TAC, Caldwell County, TSLA; J. Moursund, *Blanco County Families,* 438; SR, John Tinney, 3rd Texas Infantry, Confederate, RG109, M227, R36, M323, R0279, NAB; Probate bk. C, 182, Caldwell County, CC.

40. Blanco County, 1860, Agriculture, Nonpopulation Census Schedules for Texas, 1850–80, RG29, Bureau of the Census, T1134, R47, NAB; MR, Ed Burleson, Jan. 30, 1860, Oversize 401–723, folder 5, TRMR, TAGD, TSLA; SR, Solomon Tanner, 3th Texas Infantry, Confederate, RG109, M227, R36, NAB; Winfrey and Day, *Indian Papers* 4:327, 5:351–53; DCM, bk. D, 56, 76, 90, bk. E, 177, 228, Comal County, DC; TR, 1866–67, TAC, Caldwell County, TSLA; TR, 1875–91, TAC, Brown County, TSLA; *Galveston Daily News*, Dec. 15, 1876; *Weekly Statesman*, Nov. 15, 1883; Mayor Tanner, Tanner Family biographical information, privately held.

41. *History of Texas* (Chicago: Lewis, 1895), 301–2; Isaac Campbell Family, private collection; SR, William C. Campbell, Madison's Texas Cavalry Regiment, Confederate, RG109, M323, R0197, NAB; TR, 1866–70, 1873, 1876, 1886–87, 1894, 1897, TAC, Parker County, TSLA; Blanco County, 1860, 1880, Agriculture, Nonpopulation Census Schedules for Texas, 1850–80, Bureau of the Census, RG29, T1134, R47, NAB; SR, James Campbell, 7th Texas Cavalry, Confederate, RG109, M323, R045, NAB; TR, 1860, 1873–94, TAC, Blanco County, TSLA; Blanco County News, *Heritage,* 593.

42. Blanco County, Mortality Schedules, Non-population Census Schedules for Texas, 1850–80, Bureau of the Census, RG29, T1134, R53, NAB; Franks, *Seventy Years*, 13; SR, William M. Babb, 30th Texas Cavalry, Confederate, RG109, M227, R002, M 323, R0150, NAB; TR, 1861–68, TAC, Hamilton County, TSLA; TR, 1871–76, TAC, Bosque County, TSLA; TR, 1875–78, TAC, Coryell County, TSLA; TR, 1880–86, TAC, Coleman County, TSLA; *Galveston News,* Feb. 12, 1877, June 19, Dec. 22, 1878; *San Antonio Express*, Oct. 24, 1911; Babb Family Collection, privately held; DCM, bk. D, 51, Comal County, DC; DCR, *Texas v. Stevenson,* Criminal Case 73, Comal County, DC; U.S. Census, 1860, San Saba County, Tex.; TR, 1861, TAC, San Saba County, TSLA.

CHAPTER 20

1. *TSG,* Oct. 24, 1857; *Texas Christian Advocate*, Nov. 12, 1857; J. Speer, *History of Blanco County,* 12–13.

2. DCM, bk. C, 36–38, 49–52, Comal County, DC; DCR, Watson et al., *Texas v. George Lang et al.*, Criminal Case 82, Comal County, DC; *TSG*, May 24, 1856.

3. Haas, *History*, 99–101; U.S. Census, 1850, 1860, Comal County, Tex.; Geue and Geue, *New Land,* 89, 97, 99, 100, 110, 117, 120, 141–42, 149; DCM, vol. A., 54, vol. B, 4, 13, 28–29, 59, 61, 68, 119–20, 189, 256, 309, 317–18, 345–46, 355, 381–82, vol. C, 17, 21, 57, 60–61, 140, 194, 234, 269, Comal County, DC; Seele, *Cypress,* 42, 86; Kalteyer, "Kalteyer, George Henry"; TR, 1855–58, TAC, Comal County, TSLA; Fey, *New Braunfels* 1:140, 382–83.

4. U.S. Census, 1850, Comal County, Tex.; Alexander Ferguson, Land Grant Search, TGLO; Biesele, *German Settlements*, 125, 146, 166–67; J. Moursund, *Blanco County Families*, 162–63, 281–82; DCR, W. G. Sansom et al., *Texas v. George Lang et al.*, Criminal Case 82, Comal County, DC; DCM, vol. A., 67, B, 157, vol. C, 36–38, 60, Comal County, DC; TR, 1854–57, TAC, Comal County, TSLA; Kendall County, Map 6687, Maps, TGLO; Jasinski, "Curry's Creek Settlement."

5. DCM, vol. C, 82, Comal County, DC; DCR, *State of Texas v. Augustus Fahr, John Nichols, and Eli Hankins*, Criminal Case 90, Comal County, DC; DCR, Watson et al., *Texas v. George Lang et al.*, Criminal Case 82, Comal County, DC; J. Moursund, *Blanco County Families*, 20–21, 219; TR, 1856–58, TAC, Comal County; Blanco County, Map 4886, Maps, TGLO; W. Blackwell, W. Huckabe [Huckobey], Land Grant Search, TGLO; U.S. Census, 1860, Comanche County, Tex.; Goar, "Bloody Times," 447. In

1858, the William R. Huckobey family moved to Comanche County and lived near their friend James C. Martin, a fugitive in the first set of indicted men.

6. DCR, *Texas v. Fahr, Nichols, and Hankins*, Criminal Case 90, Comal County, DC.

7. Deeds, bk. D, 754, bk. E. 407, 812, bk. F, 277, 422–23, Guadalupe County, CC; Deeds, bk. E, 645–46, Comal County, CC; June 18, 1855, entry, SDPJ; J. Speer, *History of Blanco County*, 9, 16; *Southern Intelligencer*, Oct. 21, 1857; *Galveston Weekly News*, Oct. 27, 1857; *Texas Christian Advocate,* Nov. 12, 1857, Dec. 30, 1882; *Memorial and Genealogical Record,* 373; Blanco County, Map 4886, Maps, TGLO; J. Moursund, *Blanco County Families,* 238–41.

8. *Texas Christian Advocate*, Nov. 12, 1857.

9. *TSG,* Oct. 24, 1957; *Southern Intelligencer*, Oct. 21, 1857; *Galveston Weekly News,* Oct. 27, 1857; *NOP*, Oct. 31, 1857; *Texas Christian Advocate*, Nov. 12, 1857.

10. *Texas Christian Advocate*, Nov. 12, 1857; Elise Tips Wuppermann, "Diary," WC, privately held; McGuire, *Iwonski*, 11–14, 17–20, 32–33.

11. *Neu Braunfelser Zeitung*, Oct. 23, 1857; Julius Bose to E.M. Pease, Oct. 20, 1857, EMPP, TSLA.

12. CCM, vol. A, 47, Guadalupe County, CC; Julius Bose, VF, Sophienburg Museum and Archives; *Neu Braunfelser Zeitung,* Oct. 23, 1857; Bose to Pease, Oct. 20, 1857, EMPP, TSLA.

13. Bose to Pease, Oct. 20, 1857, EMPP, TSLA; *Neu Braunfelser Zeitung,* Oct. 23, 1857; *Southern Intelligencer* Oct. 21, 1858; *Texas Christian Advocate*, Nov. 12, 1857; *TSG,* Oct. 24, 1857; Janelle Holmes, e-mails, 2009–10, 2018; DCR, Arrest Warrants, *Texas v. George Lang et al.*, Criminal Case 82, Comal County, DC.

14. DCM, vol. C, 135, 141, Comal County, DC; DCR, *Texas v. Fahr, Nichols, and Hankins*, Criminal Case 90, Comal County, DC; *Neu Braunfelser Zeitung*, May 7, 1858; Long, "Tom, John Files"; Tise, *Texas County Sheriffs*, 220.

15. Tise, *Texas County Sheriffs,* 45, 79; TR, 1848–60, TAC, Caldwell County, TSLA; *Austin Republican,* Oct. 20, 1868; MR, Callahan, July 20, 1855, MR, Benton, Sept. 15, 1855, Oversize 401–723, Folders 1, 6, TRMR, TAGD, TSLA; Spurlin, *Texas Veterans*, 108, 121; Sofge, "San Marcos River Valley Settlement," 16–19; CCM, vol. A, 39, 42, 46, 55, 64, 74, 95, 96A, 102, Caldwell County, CC; Ruthven, *Proceedings*, 2:276; Sowell, *Texas Indian Fighters*, 381: Minutes, bk. 2, p. 2, Shiloh Baptist Church, 5330, SBHLA.

16. *San Antonio Ledger*, Nov. 6, 1858; DCR, *Texas v. Fahr, Nichols, and Hankins*, Criminal Case 90, Comal County, DC; *Weekly Journal*, Aug. 13, 1852; DCM, vol. C, 179, 219, 230, Comal County, DC; *TSG,* May 7, 1859; DCR, *S. N. Elliott v. John W. Nichols*, Civil Case 1432, Guadalupe County, DC.

17. DCR, *Texas v. Fahr, Nichols, and Hankins*, Criminal Case 90, Comal County, DC; Tise, *Texas County Sheriffs*, 79; *San Antonio Ledger,* Oct. 1, Dec. 10, 1859, July 13, Aug. 17, Nov. 26, 1959, Mar. 17, 1860; *TSG,* May 16, 1857.

18. DCM, vol. C, 252–55, Comal County, DC; DCR, *Texas v. Fahr, Nichols, and Hankins*, Criminal Case 90, Comal County, DC.

19. *San Antonio Ledger*, Mar. 31, June 5,1860; Huson, "Norton, Milford Phillips"; *TSG,* May 12, 1860; DCM, vol. C, 285–89, 304–5, Comal County, DC; *Neu Braunfelser Zeitung*, May 4, 1860.

20. *TSG*, Sept. 28, 1850, May 23, 1857, Oct. 13, 1860; *San Antonio Ledger,* May 5, 1853, Feb. 9, 1854, May 12, June 25, Sept. 15, 22, Oct. 29, 1860; DCM, vol. C, 317–26, 330–35, Comal County, DC; Moneyhon, "Davis, Edmund Jackson"; Y. Russell, "Devine, Thomas Jefferson."

21. Norvell, "Reconstruction Courts," 156; M. Moursund, *Stribling*, 51; U.S. Census, 1850, Guadalupe County, Tex.; *El Bejareño,* Feb. 7, Dec. 22, 1855; *San Antonio Ledger,* Feb. 28, 1857, Mar. 31, Apr. 4, July 18, 1860, June 22, 1861; *TSG*, Oct. 12, 1861; Thomas H. Stribling, Register of Elected and Appointed State and County Officials, 1860–65, pp. 37–38, TSLA; DCM, vol. C, 340–70, Comal County, DC.

22. J. Speer, *History of Blanco County,* 31–33; J. W. Nichols, *Now You Hear,* 143–47, 168–70; MR, William A. Blackwell, William E. Jones, John W. Lawhon, Texas State Troops, TAGD, TSLA; SR, Augustus Pharr, W. H. Callahan, John M. Watson, John Tinney, Julius Bose, 3rd Texas Infantry, Confederate, RG109, M227, R4, R6, R29, R38, NAB.

23. Regimental Summary, 3rd Texas Infantry, Confederate, RG109, M323, R273, NAB; *TSG*, July 12, 1862; *Houston Tri-Weekly Telegraph,* July 6, Oct. 14, 1863; *Houston Daily Telegraph,* May 4, 18, 1864; McGowen, *Horse Sweat,* 105; Bose letters published in *Neu Braunfelser Zeitung*, Apr. 4, 11, July 4, 1862, Feb. 14, Mar. 13, July 3, Dec. 4, 1863, June 10, 1864, Jan. 13, 1865, in Haas, *History,* 165–69.

24. Mildred N. Pinson (granddaughter), "Remembrances of Eli Skaggs Hankins," Sept. 15, 1987, Eli and Elizabeth Hankins Papers, privately held; *Clarksville Standard,* Jan. 26, 1861; *Galveston Weekly News,* Oct. 22, 1861; Tyler, *Santiago Vidaurri*, 42, 98–101, 104, 114; Tyler, "Cotton on the Border," 73–74, 461–62; Delaney, "Matamoros," 473–75, 477–80, 484 *Houston Tri-Weekly Telegraph*, Oct. 17, Nov. 28, Dec. 3, 1862; May 11, 1863, Nov. 18, Dec. 9, 1864, Apr. 26, 1865.

25. Delaney, "Matamoros," 474–75; Mildred N. Pinson (granddaughter), "Remembrances of Eli Skaggs Hankins," Sept. 15, 1987, Eli and Elizabeth Hankins Papers, privately held; *Houston Tri-Weekly Telegraph*, Jan. 12, Apr. 22, May 11, Aug. 21, Nov. 16, 1863; *Houston Daily Telegraph*, Feb. 26, Mar. 4, 9, Apr. 11, 18, May 23, July 4, Aug. 17, 19, Oct. 26, 1864; Tyler, "Cotton on the Border," 472–73; Tyler, *Santiago Vidaurri*, 148–49.

26. Campbell, *Gone*, 268, 270–76; J. Marten, "Hamilton, Andrew Jackson"; Norvell, "Reconstruction Courts," 142–43; D. Minor, "Throckmorton, James Webb."

27. DCM, bk. C, 374, 379, Comal County, DC; Campbell, *Gone*, 270–74; *Houston Tri-Weekly Telegraph*, Apr. 28, May 1, 3, 5, Oct. 9, Nov. 15, 1865, Apr. 2, 1866; 4th Judicial John H. Duncan, Aug. 1864, June 1865, A. O. Cooley, June 1865, District Courts, R4, Texas Secretary of State Registers (hereafter TSSR), TSLA; DCM, vol. C, 384–96, vol. D, 3–32, Comal County, DC; Jasinski, "Cooley, Albert O. [A.O.]."

28. 4th Judicial District, Thomas H. Stribling, T. G. Anderson, June 1866, R4, TSSR, TSLA; Marriages, vol. 2, p. 81, Travis County, CC; Gammel, *Laws*, 5:944–45; Campbell, "District Judges," 364–66; *Flake's Bulletin,* Aug. 7, 22, Oct. 1866, Nov. 16, 1867; *Southern Intelligencer*, July 5, 1866; DCM, vol. D, 51, Comal County, DC; DCR, *Texas v. Fahr, Nichols, and Hankins*, Criminal Case 90, Comal County, DC; Tise, *Texas County Sheriffs*, 45, 79, 124; William Schmidt, June 1866, Comal County, Andrew J. Kercheville, and Augustus Pharr, June 1866, Blanco County, Eli S. Hankins, Aug. 1865, Marion M. Hudson, June 1866, Caldwell County, R3, R4, TSSR, TSLA; J. Moursund, *Blanco County Families*, 254–55; 340; *San Antonio Express*, Mar. 7, 1913; *Weekly Statesman*, May 29, 1884. In 1867, General Order No. 195 removed Marion Hudson (d. 1884) as sheriff. In 1869, Kercheville (1821–1913) was removed as Blanco County sheriff by the U.S. Army.

29. Gammel, *Laws,* 5:944–45; El Paso County, R VR-4, Voter Registration, 1867, TSLA; William P. Bacon, George H. Noonan, June 1866, R4, TSSR, TSLA; Campbell, "District Judges," 364–66; U.S. Congress, Senate, 40th Cong., 1st sess., 1876, S. Exec.

Doc. 14, pp. 218–20; *Constitution as Amended,* 22; SR, William P. Bacon, 5th New York Cavalry, United States, RG 109, M 551, R4, NAB; *Twentieth Century History,* 1:436–38; U.S. Census, 1860, 1870, Medina County, Tex.; U.S. Census, 1860, Atascosa County, Tex.; *Galveston News,* Mar. 27, 30, Apr. 19, 28, May 5, 1867; DCM, vol. D, 72, 75–77, 83–84, Comal County, DC; DCR, *Texas v. Fahr, Nichols, and Hankins,* Criminal Case 90, Comal County, DC.

30. Campbell, "District Judges," 366–68; *Dallas Weekly Herald,* Mar. 23, May 4, June 1, 1867; *Flake's Bulletin,* May 22, June 19, 1867; *NOP,* June 12, 1867; *Galveston News,* June 13, 1867; *San Antonio Express,* June 19, July 9, Sept. 9, Nov. 25, 1867; DCM, bk. D, 101–2, Comal County, DC.

31. Minutes, County Court, bk. J, 281–82, bk. K, 81, Leon County, CC; Janelle Holmes, interviews, telephone conversations, and e-mails with author, 2009–10, 2018. U.S. Census, 1860, Leon County, Tex.; U.S. Census, 1870, Liberty County, Tex.; TR, 1859–60, Leon County, TSLA; SR, Luther Blasingame [Blassingame], 26th Texas Cavalry, Confederate, RG109, M323, R131, NAB; TR, 1856, 1859–60, TAC, Hays County, TSLA; SR, Thomas Blasingame, [Blassingame] Whaley's Company, Company C, 5th Texas Infantry, Confederate, RG109, M323, R292, R441, NAB; U.S. Census, 1860, Van Zandt County, Tex.; *Houston Weekly Telegraph,* Dec. 15, 1863. The Thomas Blassingame in this narrative is not Thomas M. Blassingame who appears in the muster rolls of the 26th Texas Cavalry. Thomas M. Blassingame was younger (seventeen), enrolled in Van Zandt County, appeared on the 1860 U.S. census for Van Zandt County in the W. B. Blassingame family, and died in a Houston hospital on April 6, 1862.

32. PR, Estate of William S. Johnson, dec., bk. B, 151–52, Comal County, CC; PM, bk. C, 5–6, Comal County, CC; Deeds, bk. E, 567–68, 688–89, Comal County, CC; John S. Hodges to Governor Runnels, Mar. 18, 1858, box 301–27, folder 4, Records, Texas Gov. Hardin Richard Runnels, TSLA; TR, 1859–78, TAC, Blanco County, TSLA; SR, Thomas S. Johnson, 18th Texas Cavalry, Confederate, RG109, M323, R0101, NAB. After Thomas S. Johnson's death, either his brother Rufus or his mother paid the annual property tax on his lots in Pittsburg.

33. Deeds, bk. E, 576–79, Comal County, CC; Deeds, bk. 1, pp. 269–70, Blanco County, CC; E. C. Hinds, Blanco County, 1858, 1864, 1870, 1872, TSSR, TSLA; Hines, *Eli Clemmons Hinds,* n.p.; J. Moursund, *Blanco County History,* 552–53; U.S. Census, 1870, Blanco County, Tex.; E. C. Hinds, Wills, bk. A, 13–15, Blanco County, CC; Blanco County, 1860, Agriculture, Nonpopulation Census Schedules for Texas, 1850–80, RG29, T1134, R47, NAB. Catherine Hinds, Clem's wife, died May 15, 1907.

CHAPTER 21

1. PM, bk. B, 145, 154–57, Comal County, CC; CCM, vol. B, 170, Comal County, CC.

2. Kemp, "Pettus, Edward Cratic"; Fannin to Foster & Pettus, Jan. 8, 1836, Box 25, Folder 65, Asbury Papers, Cushing Memorial Library, Texas A&M University; 1st Division (John York), Dec. 5, 1835, Oversize 401, folder 714, RTMR, TAGD, TSLA; Marriages, bk. A, 95, Fayette County, CC; TR, 1848–56, TAC, Guadalupe County, TSLA; U.S. Census, Slave Inhabitants, 1850, Guadalupe County, Tex.; CCM, vol. 1, pp. 39, 122, Guadalupe County, CC.

3. PM, bk. B, 187–89, Comal County, CC; PL, bk. H, 1–8, 34, Comal County, CC; Fey, *New Braunfels,* 1:410–15; Deeds, bk. C, 306–7, Brazoria County, CC.

4. PL, bk. H, 1–8, 220–21, Comal County, CC; Deeds, bk. E, 572–76, 645–46, 660–61, 688–89, Comal County, CC; TR, 1855–56, TAC, Comal County, TSLA; J. Moursund, *Blanco County Families*, 292, 357–60, 440–41.

5. Deeds, bk. D, 99–102, 194, 207, 346–47, 434–36, bk. E, 258–60, 330, bk. F, 8, 60–61, Comal County, CC; Deeds, vol. 55, pp. 438–41, Travis County, CC; Deeds, bk. 1, pp. 269–70, Blanco County, CC; PM, bk. B, 187–89, Comal County, CC; *Southern Intelligencer*, Aug. 27, 1856; *TSG*, Sept. 13, 27, 1856. The Pittsburg Land Company possessed about 3,140 undivided acres at the time of Callahan's death.

6. *Galveston Weekly News*, Oct. 14, 1856; *TST*, Oct. 4, 1856; "1856 death of Callahan boy," "Death of Sarah Medissa Callahan," PCFH, privately held; J. Speer, *History of Blanco County*, 10; "Old Guard" transcript, W. R. Russell to J. T. DeShields, Jan. 22, 1912, box 11, folder 575, JTDSP, DRTL; Marriage and Death Records, Pate Family Bible, privately held.

7. PM, bk. B, 214–16, Comal County, CC; Deeds, bk. E, 330–31, Comal County, CC; PL, bk. H, 7–8, Comal County, CC; J. Moursund, *Blanco County Families*, 88–92, 95, 97, 100.

8. PL, bk. H, 132–40, Comal County, CC.

9. PL, bk. H, 1–8, 34 132–40, Comal County, CC; PM, bk. B, 187–89, Comal County, CC.

10. PL, bk. H, 132–40, Comal County, CC; J. Moursund, *Blanco County Families*, 4, 20–21, 23, 32, 109–10, 238–41, 332–34, 416–19, 440–41; J. Moursund, *Blanco County History*, 87–93, 95–97, 99–100, 110–11; TR, 1855, 1857, 1859, TAC, Comal County, TSLA; Haas, *History*, 77, 131.

11. PM, bk. B, 187–89, 256, Comal County, CC.

12. PL, bk. H, 1–8, 132–40, 217–18, Comal County, CC; PM, bk. B, 313–15, 318–21, Comal County, CC; DCM, *Augustus Pharr et al. v. Ezra Keyser*, Civil Cause 1321, bk. C, 43–44, Gonzales County, DC.

13. PM, bk. B, 338, Comal County, CC; PM, bk. B, 50, 189–91, Hays County, CC; PR, Estate of Wm. E. Jones, deceased, Case 57, Williamson County, CC; PL, bk. H, 223–27, Comal County, CC; Deeds, bk. E, 576–79, Comal County, CC. Lindsey died in 1866 and Jones in 1871; their estates listed no land in Blanco County. Pitts died on February 5, 1861; his probate listed 575 acres and numerous Pittsburg lots in the Eggleston Survey.

14. Deeds, bk. E, 579–80, 645–46, 661, Comal County, CC.

15. PM, bk. C, 7–9, Comal County, CC; Deeds, vol. 3, pp. 198–205, 267–68, Kimble County, CC; Deeds, bk. D, 433–36, Comal County, CC; Deeds, bk.1, pp. 392–94, Kendall County, CC.

16. PM, bk. C, 29–30, 52, 61–62, Comal County, CC; J. Moursund, *Blanco County History*, 93, 100, 114; J. Moursund, *Blanco County Families*, 416–19.

17. PM, bk. C, 61–62, Comal County, CC; DCM, bk. C, 136–37, Comal County, DC; DCR, *Edward Pettus v. Johns S. Hodges*, Civil Case 242, *Edward Pettus v. James M. Pruitt,* Civil Cases 243, 244, Comal County, DC; Deeds, bk. E, 256–57, 416. Comal County, CC; TR, 1855–57, TAC, Comal County, TSLA; TR, 1859–60, TAC, Blanco County, TSLA; J. Moursund, *Blanco County History*, 90–92, 95, 114; Hodges and Pruitt, Biographical Information, Kendalia Scrapbooks, vols. 1, 2, Kendalia Public Library; Execution Docket, vol. [unlabeled], Civil Cases 242, 243, 244, 288, Comal County, CC.

18. PM, bk. C, 85–86, 125, 144–45, Comal County, CC; Gammel, *Laws*, 4:1070–72; *Blanco Courier*, Mar. 8, 1911; *TSG,* May 12, 1855; DCR, *Collin Johnson v. E. C. Pettus excu.*

of J. H. Callahan dec. and Geo. B. Hollamon, Civil Case 590, Guadalupe County, DC; James Hughes Callahan, box 14, folder 14, JWNP, DRTL.

19. Geue and Geue, *New Land*, 100; *Neu Braunfelser Zeitung*, Feb. 1, 1894; PM, bk. C, 167, Comal County, CC; U.S. Census, 1850, Guadalupe County, Tex.; PR, bk. C. 233, Guadalupe County, CC. Pettus's estate was valued at $34,822.67; he is buried in the Pettus–Stanfield Cemetery, Guadalupe County.

20. PM, bk. C, 168–69, 172–73, Comal County, CC; Gammel, *Laws*, 3:285–87; *Neu Braunfelser Zeitung*, Nov. 5, 12, 19, 26, 1958.

21. PM, bk. C, 9, 206, 212–14, 265–66, 287, bk. E, 26–28, Comal County, CC; Fey, *New Braunfels* 1:465–69; Deeds, bk. D, 433–36, bk. E, 330–31, 674–75, Comal County, CC; PL, bk. B, 214–16, bk. C, 80, 261, bk. I, 383–84, Comal County, CC; J. Moursund, *Blanco County Families*, 307–8, 325.

22. PM, bk. C, 236–37, Comal County, CC; U.S. Census, 1860, Cass County, Tex.; Deeds, vol. 21, p. 3, Kimble County, CC; U.S. Census, 1860, Chattooga, Walker Counties, Ga; Karen Pruitt Schooler, Pruitt descendant, e-mail, Dec. 2010; Rounsavall and Rounsavill, *Richard Rounsaveil*, 2:498. James Pruitt settled in Mississippi, where he died in 1888.

23. PM, bk. C, 265–66, bk. D, 116, Comal County, CC; PL, bk. I, 346–47, Comal County, CC; PM, bk. B, 108, Hays County, CC.

24. PM, bk. D, 116–342, Comal County, CC; PL, bk. I, 342–44, 346, Comal CC; Donecker, "San Antonio Express-News"; *San Antonio Express*, Sept. 27, 1865, May 24, 1866, Jan. 3, 1867; *Flake's Bulletin*, Dec. 27, 1865, Apr. 17, Nov. 11, 1866; *Southern Intelligencer*, June 14, 1866; Abbett, "William Early Jones," 67–75; Seele, *Cypress, xi–xiii*; Georg Klappenbach, Comal County, 1865, TSSR, TSLA; DCM, vol. A, 102, vol. B, 111, Comal County, DC.

25. PL, bk. I, 383–84, Comal County, CC; PM, bk. E, 26–28, Comal County, CC.

26. PM, bk. E, 41–42, 81, 93–94, Comal County, CC. PL, bk. I, 434–35, Comal County, CC.

27. *Journal of the Reconstruction Convention*, 112, 467; Gammel, *Laws*, 3:222, 240–41, 282–84, 315–16, 333–35, 348–50, 354–55, 358, 370; W. E. Jones, 32nd District Judge, 1870, TSSR, TSLA; *Flake's Bulletin*, Aug. 6, 1870; Campbell, *Gone*, 277–83; PM, bk. E, 26, 140–41, Comal County, CC; Deed bk. 1, p. 42, Kendall County, CC; Marriages, bk. C–D, 139, Caldwell County, CC.

28. Abbett, "William Early Jones," 92; DuCoin, *Lawmen*, 38; *San Antonio Express*, Apr. 25, 1871; *Austin Daily Journal*, Apr. 23, 1871; *Houston Telegraph*, Apr. 26, 1871.

29. PM, bk. C, 350–51, bk. E, 200, 211, 219, 233, 266, 280–81, Comal County, CC; PL, bk. [no letter], 49–50, 94–96, Comal County, CC; PR, Estate of Wm. E. Jones, deceased, Case 57, Williamson County, CC; DuCoin, *Lawmen*, 73–82; *Neu Braunfelser Zeitung*, July 19, 26, Aug. 2, 1873.

CHAPTER 22

1. Diary entry, Sept. 27, 1856, DP, CAH; "Burial of Sarah Medissa Callahan," PCFH, privately held.

2. TR, 1855–56, TAC, Guadalupe, Caldwell Counties, TSLA; Gifford White, *Texas Scholastics*, preface, 65–66, 59–72; Evans, *Story*, 60–69.

3. PM, bk. C, 169–70, Comal CC; DuCoin, *Lawmen*, 31–39, 41n16, 45 (map), 46–47, 50, 62n2, 73, 79–89, 91, 101, 109, 113, 139; Olmsted, *Journey*, 212–13; Marriages, bk. A, 13, Guadalupe County, CC.

4. PM, bk. C, 237–39, Comal County, CC; Deeds, vol. 21, p. 3, Kimble County, CC; U.S. Census, 1850, 1860, Walker County, Ga.; Alley, *Alley Ancestors*, AR-10, NC-7; Callahan, Josiah T., box 5, folder 9, RS2005.0795, Estates, Chambers County, Ala., ADAH; Sartain, *History*, 1:4, 7, 12, 16–21, 41–42, 44, 204–6; Kennedy, *Population* (1860), 73; *Southern Recorder*, Apr. 1, 1856.

5. *Southern Banner*, Jan. 30, 1861; T. Conn Bryan, *Confederate*, 1–11, 130–131,137–40, 142–55, 188–90, 222, 224–25, 227; SR, Harry [H. C.] Alley, Newton Hamilton, 39th Georgia Infantry, Confederate, RG109, M226, R1, R26, NAB; *Macon Telegraph*, Dec. 1, 1862, Oct. 7, 1863, Dec. 15, 1864; *Southern Confederacy*, May 1, Mar. 21, 1863; *Southern Watchman*, Dec. 21, 1864; Sartain, *Walker County*, 1:58, 120, 123, 151–54; Kilpatrick, "Beginnings," 14–15.

6. U.S. Census, 1850, Caldwell County, Tex.; PM, bk. B, 154–55, bk. E, 26–28, 140–41, Comal County, CC; U.S. Census, 1860, Cass County, Tex.; *Williamson County Sun*, Apr. 9, 1926; SR, J. Callahan, 39th Georgia Infantry, Confederate, RG109, M226, R10, NAB; Deeds, vol. 21, p. 3, Kimble County, CC.

7. *Williamson County Sun*, Jan. 30, 1931; SR, Alexander Hamilton, 10th Battalion, M. N. Alley, 6th Battalion, Georgia State Guards, Confederate, RG109, M266, R43, NAB; Families Supplied with Salt, 1862–64, Commissary General's Department, M Drawer 73, box 4, p. 862, GSA; Reconstruction, Registration Oath Books, District 27, vol. 161, p. 496, Clarke County, M 296/55, GSA.

8. U.S. Census, 1870, Marion County, Tenn.; Sartain, *Walker County*, 1:121, 540; U.S. Census, 1870, Talladega, Clay Counties, Ala.; General Land Office Records, Bureau of Land Management, U.S. Department of the Interior, "Huntsville Land Office, Ala.," https://glorecords.blm.gov/search/default.aspx (searched George Mason); U.S. Census, 1850, 1860, Walker County, Ga.; Carlock, *Carlock Family*, 437–38; Marriages, bk. A, 270, 386, Circuit and County Clerk's Office, Yell County, Ark.; Deeds, vol. 21, p. 3, Kimble County, CC; Deeds, vol. 1, pp. 81–82, vol. 2, pp. 27–34, Blanco County, CC.

9. *Williamson County Sun*, Apr. 9, 1926, Jan. 30, 1931, Feb. 27, 1920, Apr. 14, 1933; U.S. Census, 1870, Clay County, Ala.; Deeds, vol. 2, pp. 496–97, vol. 21, p. 3, Kimble County, CC; Deeds, vol. 1, pp. 81–82, 264, 584–86, vol. 2, pp. 27–34, vol. 5, pp. 32–33, vol. 7, pp. 80–81, vol. 9, pp. 432–34, vol. 13, pp. 234–35, 398, vol. 14, pp. 256–57, 529–31, vol. 24, p. 214, Blanco County, CC; TR, 1876–90, TAC, Blanco County, TSLA; U.S. Census, 1880, Guadalupe, Blanco Counties, Tex.; U.S. Census, 1900, 1910, 1920, Williamson County, Tex.

10. Russell to DeShields, Dec. ?, 1910, Feb. 11, Apr. 12, 25, 1911, Jan. 22, 1912, "Written for the Old Guard," by W. R. Russell, n.d., Collection 882, box 11, folder 575, Callahan to DeShields, Sept. 15, 1907, June 9, Aug. 18, 1910, Feb. 26, 1911, Collection 882, box 9, folder 439, Sansom to DeShields, Esq., Aug. 14, Sept. 11, Dec. 5, 1907, Callahan to Sansom, Sept. 15, 1907, box 11, folder 579, JTDSP, DRTL; *Williamson County Sun*, Apr. 9, 1926; Deeds, bk. 227, p. 402, Williamson County, CC.

11. MR, John W. Sansom, Aug. 31–Nov. 30, 1859, box 401–725, folders 16, 29, TRMR, TAGD, TSLA; *San Antonio Ledger and Texan*, Aug. 3, Sept. 10, 17, Oct. 8, Nov. 5, 12, 26, Dec. 24, 1859; *TSG*, Oct. 1, Nov. 26, 1859; Blanco County to His Excellency H. R. Runnels, June 29, 1859, William E. Jones to His Exy. Gov. Runnels, Sept. 3, 1859, Richard Hardin Runnels Records, TSLA.

12. Gish, *Diary*, 389; SR, Wesley, James Callahan, 1st Texas Mounted Riflemen, Confederate, RG109, M227, R6, NAB; Cutrer, *Ben McCulloch*, 179–86, 188; D. Smith,

Frontier, 30–36, 44; Henry McCulloch to Charles E. Jones, Jan. 22, 1889, Military Correspondence, 1852–89, box 3G37, BHMFP, CAH; *Dallas Weekly Herald*, Apr. 3, 1861; *Galveston Weekly News*, Apr. 23, July 18, 1861; *TSG*, Apr. 6, 1881; McGowen, *Horse Sweat*, 10–36, 50–51; Ordnance Returns, San Antonio, Fort Chadbourne, Fort Mason, 1861, box 401–843, folders 19, 25, 36–37, Quartermaster Records, Texas State Troops, TAGD, TSLA.

13. SR, Wesley Callahan, Augustus Pharr, James R, Marmion, 3rd Texas Infantry, Confederate, RG109, M323, R2, R27–78, NAB; *Houston Telegraph*, Sept. 14, 16, 18, 1863; Cotham, "'Nothing but Disaster,'" 138–44; *War of the Rebellion: Official Records* (hereafter *OR*), ser. 1, vol. 36, pt. 2, pp. 218–20, 281, 318–21; Marmion, *Texas Soldier & Marine*, n.p.

14. Marriages, Deeds, bk. 1, p. 442, Kendall County, CC; Marriages, bk. A, 149, Cherokee County, CC; Jesse and Lovina Lawhon's children, Description of Daniel Rawls, Lawhon Papers, privately held; Marriage and Birth Records, Alzada Callahan Bible, privately held; *TST*, July 16, 1855; *TSG*, May 19, 1855; Marriages, bk. C, 101, Comal County, CC; Kendall County, Map 66887, Maps, TGLO; Deeds, bk. 1, pp. 80–82, 625–27, bk. 2, pp. 121–25, Kendall County, CC; "Rawls, Daniel," *HBTO*, http://www.tshaonline.org/handbook/online/articles/fra48; U.S. Census, 1850, St. Mary Parish, La.

15. TR, 1864–65, TAC, Kendall County, TSLA; CCM, bk. 1, pp. 79, 93, Kendall County, CC; Marriage and Birth Records, Alzada Callahan Bible, privately held; Marriages, bk. 1, p. 119, Marriages, Reverse Index, vol. 1, Kendall County, CC; Kendall County, 1870, Agriculture, Nonpopulation Census Schedules for Texas, 1850–80, RG29, T1134, R10, NAB; *Dallas Weekly Herald*, June 30, 1866, Apr. 13, 1867 (Jones's letter, *San Antonio Ledger*), July 4, 1868; *Flake's Bulletin*, June 26, 1866, Sept. 19, 1867; *Southern Intelligencer*, Aug. 9, 1866.

16. Winfrey and Day, *Indian Papers*, 4:324–326; General Orders no. 3 and 7, vol. 401–984, Sansom reports to Adjutant General, box 401–1156, folders 15–17, Letterpress Book, Paymaster, vol. 401–1104, Correspondence, Frontier Forces Records, TAGD, TSLA; MR, John W. Sansom, Company C, Oversize 401–742, folder 3, Frontier Forces Military Rolls, TAGD, TSLA; Callahan, Wesley, call no. 401–133, Texas Adjutant General Service Records, http://www.tsl.state.tx.us/arc/service/viewdetails.php?id=3163, accessed May 2, 2011; Glenn, *Capt'n John*, 72; *San Antonio Express*, Nov. 20, 1870; John William Lawhon's comment on Wesley Callahan's health, Lawhon Papers; DuCoin, *Lawmen*, 53–54, 63; TR, 1871–80, TAC, Kendall County, TSLA; Marriage and Birth Records, Alzada Callahan Bible, privately held; Linda Howard, e-mails, 2009, 2011.

17. SR, James S. Callahan, Henry B. King, Hardeman's Cavalry, Confederate, RG109, M323, R195, NAB; "Capture of James Sanford Callahan," PCFH, privately held; SR, James S. Callahan, 24th Battalion Infantry (State Troops), Confederate, RG109, M323, R417, NAB; James Callahan, G. O. Dunaway, Selected Records of the War Department Relating to Confederate Prisoners of War, RG109, M598, R3, NAB; SR, James S. Callahan, William H. Maltby, 8th Texas Infantry, Confederate, RG109, M323, R322, and M323, R325, NAB; Townsend, *Yankee Invasion*, 9, 16–17, 26–31, 48, 150n25; Fitzhugh, "Saluria, Fort Esperanza, and Military Operations," 80–98; *Houston Telegraph*, Dec. 9, 12, 1863; *TSG*, Sept. 16, 1863; *Tri-Weekly Telegraph*, Sept. 16, Oct. 20, 38, Dec. 15, 1863; *OR*, ser. 1, 20:680–684; vol. 26, pt. 1, pp. 416–23, 438, 733–34, pt. 2, pp. 255, 275–76, 297, 347–48, 357–58, 366, 433, 442–44, 476–78, 498–99, 508–9, 512, 519.

18. Marriages, bk. C–D, 139, Caldwell County, CC; *TSG*, Apr. 23, 1853; Stulting, "Pioneer Woman," 5–7; Francis Berry, Anson Neal, Republic Claims, TSLA; Gonzales

County Historical Commission, *History*, 250; TR, 1838–52, TAC, Gonzales County, TSLA; Marriages, bk. A, 27, Gonzales County, CC; Nance, *After San Jacinto*, 226, 234, 248, 308, 336, 357; Moore, *Savage Frontier*, 3:227–28; *Democratic Telegraph and Texas Register*, Nov. 30, 21, 1846; Loomis, *Texan–Santa Fé*, 243; DCFR, bk. A, 175, Gonzales County, CC; *TTR*, Jan. 26, 1842; *Tri-Weekly Times*, Nov. 16, 1853; SR, Anson G. Neal, Grumble's Co., 1st Texas Mounted Volunteers, Mexican War, RG94, M616, R27, NAB; Second son Milton, Common-law marriage, Berry and Neill biographical information, privately held; Births and Deaths, James Sanford Callahan Family Bible, privately held; DCM, bk. MII, 39, 60, bk. B, 7, 21, 49, 78, 126, Gonzales County, DC; DCR, *Neal v. Neal*, Final 122, Gonzales County, DC; Deeds, bk. A, 176, bk. F, 242–43, Gonzales County, CC.

19. King, *James Clinton Neill*, 15, 18–21, 32–33, 37, 44, 52–53, 61, 71–75, 77–79, 97, 100, 106, 110, 115, 151, 156, 178, 200–206; Jenkins, *Recollections*, 155; Austin's Register of Families, Archives and Records, TGLO; Marriages, vol. 1, p. 6, Washington County, CC; S. Moore, *Savage Frontier*, 1:24; Gonzales County Historical Commission, *History*, 427–28; Births and Deaths, James Sanford Callahan Family Bible, privately held; Deeds, bk. A, 46–48, bk. F, 242–43, Gonzales County, CC; Deeds, bk. D, 409–10, Caldwell County, CC; PM, vol. A-2, pp. 200–201, 263, 191–92, vol. B, 117, 122, Caldwell County, CC;

20. Marriages, bk. C–D, 139, Caldwell County, CC; DCM, bk. B, 421, 434–36, 497–99, 514–15, 572–73, B supplement, 58, 81, 213, 114, 238–39, bk. C, 6, 23–24, 58, 75, 106, 124, 159, 169–71, 277–78, 285, 359, Caldwell County, DC.

21. U.S. Census, 1870, Kendall County, Tex.; PM, bk. E, 280–81, Comal County, CC; PL, bk. [no letter], 94–96, Comal County, CC; *Galveston Tri-Weekly News*, Jan. 22, 31, Feb. 3, 22, Mar. 19, May 28, 1873; *San Antonio Express*, July 13, 17, Aug. 6, 19, 1873; Ordnance Stores Issued No. 1, 1870–76, vol. 401–1072, Minute Men (1872–77) Records, MR, S. B. Gray, Apr. 1–Oct. 1, 1873, Oversize 401–743, folder 3, Company A (Blanco County), Minute Men (1872–77) Military Rolls, TAGD, TSLA; Gammel, *Laws*, 7:36–37, 631; J. Moursund, *Blanco County Families*, 168–69; DCM, bk. A, 32–39, vol. 9, p. 529, Blanco County, DC; Deeds, vol. 1, pp. 81–82, 615–17 584–86, vol. 2, pp. 27–33, Transcribed Deed, vol. 17–18, pp. 622–24, Blanco County, CC; TR, 1874, 1876, 1877, TAC, Blanco County, TSLA.

22. Deeds, vol. 3, pp. 239–42, vol. 9, p. 529, vol. 29, pp. 528–29, Blanco County, CC. Births and Deaths, James Sanford Callahan Family Bible, privately held; *Dallas Weekly Herald*, June 1, 1878; Charles G. Davis, "Crystal Falls, TX"; "James Sanford Callahan making a living," PCFH, privately held. Papa Phillips always told the story of James Sanford meeting Sam Bass. I believe this occurred in 1878 at Bass's hideout near Crystal Falls. The children were: Mary Rue, born Mar. 1, 1870; Willie Katherine, Sept. 30, 1871; Anna Bolden, Mar. 8, 1873; Headley Hughes, June 6, 1875 (died 1884); Mollie Caloma, Mar. 28, 1877; James Sanford Jr., Apr. 1, 1878; Carrie May, May 3, 1881

23. Births and Deaths, James Sanford Callahan Family Bible, privately held; U.S. Census, 1900, Indian Territory; Moore Cemetery, VF, Coal County Genealogical Society, Coalgate, Okla.; Muriel H. Wright, "Wapanucka Academy," 402; Namoi Mobbs (granddaughter of James Sanford Callahan) Oral History, privately held; Photograph of Rachel Beatrice Phillips, PCFH, privately held; U.S. Census, 1910, Comanche, Mills, Brown Counties, Tex.; *Comanche Chief*, Aug. 18, 1977. Papa Phillips mailed a photo of his first child, Rachel Beatrice, born June 20, 1917. Thus, Callahan was alive in the summer of 1917. Rachel Beatrice is my mother.

CHAPTER 23

1. *Abilene Reporter Morning News*, Jan. 25, 1931; *San Antonio Light*, Jan. 22, 1931; L. W. Kemp to Thurlow B. Weed, Jan. 6, 1931, General biographical notebooks, Burl–Chi, Box 2R220, KC, CAH.

2. Gilchrist, "Kemp, Louis Wiltz"; Muir, "State Cemetery"; Gammel, *Laws*, 3:1556–57; Deeds, bk. G, 101–2, Travis County, CC.

3. Biesele, *German Settlements*, 208–28; J. Moursund, *Blanco County History*, 196–250; Gonzales County Historical Commission, *History*, 36–43; Moellering, "History," 114–50; J. W. Nichols, *Now You Hear*, 169; Elise Tips Wuppermann, "Diary," WC, privately held; *San Antonio Ledger*, May 25, 1867.

4. Britten, *Lipan*, 210, 214, 227, 235–39; Patterson and Allen, *Tickanwa-tic*, accessed Dec. 22, 2016.

5. Aug. 6, 1857, entry, SDPJ (On this date, her sixty-second birthday, Sarah wrote her last entry); James Milford Day and Martha Hannah Nichols, Nichols Family Papers Collection, privately held; James Milford Day and Margaret Susan Hudson Family, Gonzales Papers, privately held Gammel, *Laws*, 5:1466; Blanco County, 1860, Agriculture, Nonpopulation Census Schedules for Texas, 1850–80, RG29, T1134, R47, NAB; J. Speer, *History of Blanco County*, 28–29, 31–32, 34–35; Hines, *Eli Clemmons Hinds*, n.p.; Deeds, bk. I, 525–26, bk. J, 118–19, 157–58, Guadalupe County, CC; DCM, bk. E, 198, 277–78, 290–300, 337, 417, 470, Guadalupe County, DC.

6. TR, 1861–84, TAC, Blanco County, TSLA; U.S. Census, 1870, 1880, Blanco, Kimble, Gillespie Counties, Tex.; James M. Day to Thomas H. Miller, June 25, 1887, Pension Claim File, Republic Claims, TSLA; James M. Day, Index to Mexican War Pension Files, 1887–1926, v. 4, RG15, MT317, R4, NAB; James Milford Day biography, Gonzales Papers, privately held.

7. Pharr and Day ancestry records, privately held; *Weekly State Gazette*, July 20, Oct. 19, 1864; J. Speer, *History of Blanco County*, 29–30, 32; TR, 1862–63, 1865–74, TAC, Blanco County, TSLA; Deeds, bk. M, 163, Gillespie County, CC; Blanco County, 1866, Election Returns, Secretary of State, TSLA; *Flake's Bulletin*, Nov. 14, 1867, May 29, 1869; Blanco County News, *Heritage*, 51–52.

8. TR, 1872–94, TAC, Blanco County, TSLA; Pharr and Day ancestry records, privately held; U.S. Census, 1870, 1880, Blanco County; *Galveston Daily News*, July 8, 1879; Deeds (Transcribed), bks. 13–14, pp. 174–77, Blanco County, CC; PM (Transcribed), bk. A–C, 120–24, Blanco County, CC.

9. Deeds, bk. F, 746, 765–66, bk. G, 186, 438, 475, 439, 559, Guadalupe County, CC; Deeds, bk. G, 214, 260–61, bk. H, 111–12, 328–29, 339–40, Caldwell County, CC; Minutes, bk. 1, pp. 87–90, bk. 2, pp. 1–25, Shiloh Baptist Church, 5330, SBHLA; Marriages, bk. C, 44, Caldwell County, CC; DCR, *Henry B. King v. Eliza Jane King*, Civil Case 974, Caldwell County, DC; Mahala and Henry King children, Pate Family Bible, privately held. In 1856,

10. SR, Henry B. King, 4th Texas Infantry, Confederate, RG109, M323, R0288, NAB; SR, Henry B. King, John M. King, Hardeman's Cavalry, Confederate, RG109, M323, R0195, NAB; *OR*, ser. 1, vol. 26, pt. 2, pp. 26, 73, 84–85, 106–8, 378–79, vol. 34, pt. 1, pp. 785, 845–49, vol. 41, pt. 1, pp. 31–36, 788–93, pt. 3, pp. 966–67; Hardeman, *Wilderness*, 120–22, 151–52, 243–44, 250, 258–59.

11. DCR, *King v. King*, Case 974, Caldwell County, DC; DCM, vol. B, 387, 392–93, Caldwell County, DC; *Daily Ledger and Texan*, Sept. 4, 1860; PM, bk. D, 353–54, 377, Bexar County, CC; PR, F. S. Culberson, vol. E., 133, 145, Bexar County, CC.

12. DCM, vol. B, 479, Caldwell County, DC; H. B. King to John R. King, Dec. 16, 1866, H. B. King to Eliza, n.d., H. B. King Death, King Family Papers, privately held; William Kishbaugh Jr., telephone conversation, Dec. 2016; TR, 1868, TAC, DeWitt County, TSLA; "King Family Bible (transcript)," 46; Deeds, bk. G, 559, Guadalupe County, CC; DCR, *Thomas L. Stanfield v. H. B. King*, Civil Case 1573, Guadalupe County, DC; DCM, bk. E, 61, 114, 258, 273, 360, 394–95, Guadalupe County, DC.

13. Hankins Bible, Hankins Paper, privately held; U.S. Census, 1870, 1880, Caldwell County, Tex.; *Twentieth Century History*, 401–3; TR, 1856–80, TAC, Caldwell County, TSLA; Deeds, bk. Q, 623–26, bk. S, 631, bk. W, 66, bk. X, 151, 396–97, bk. 10, p. 12, Caldwell County, CC; Caldwell County, 1870, 1880, Agriculture, Nonpopulation Census Schedules for Texas, 1850–80, RG29, T1134, R16, R7, NAB;

14. Minutes, bk. 1, pp. 79–80, 82, 89, 161–65, bk. 2, pp. 68, 146–47, Shiloh Baptist Church, 5330, SBHLA; Deeds, bk. B, 224–25, bk. P, 25–26, Caldwell County, CC; *Lockhart Register*, June 25, 1881; *Dallas Morning News*, June 27, 1887; Sofge, "San Marcos River Valley Settlement," 19, 21; Deviney, *Link*, 6, 25–26; Caldwell County, 1865, 1867, Election Returns, Secretary of State, TSLA; *Flake's Bulletin*, Jan. 3, 11, Apr. 10, Nov. 14, 1867, Mar. 5, 10, 31, 1869; *Southern Intelligencer*, Dec. 20, 1866; Cattle and Hide Inspector, Bonds and Oaths, Secretary of State, TSLA.

15. Minutes, bk. 1, pp. 161–65, 167–73, bk. 2, pp. 68–69. 147–48, Shiloh Baptist Church, 5330, SBHLA; *Lockhart Post*, Mar. 9, 1911; Mildred Hankins Norris to Lola H. Cloninger, Jan. 24, 1983, Hankins Papers, privately held; TR, 1890, 1895, 1900, 1905, 1910, TAC, Caldwell County, TSLA; "Wenona's Autobiography," 1–6, privately held; Deeds, bk. 10, pp. 12–13, bk. 50, pp. 537–39, 566–73, Caldwell County, CC; Hankins Bible, Hankins Papers, privately held; *Twentieth Century History*, 2:401, 403.

16. DCM, bk. C, 288, Comal County, DC; TR, 1856–61, TAC, Guadalupe County, TSLA; Guadalupe County, 1860, Agriculture, Nonpopulation Census Schedules for Texas, 1850–80, RG29, T1134, R4, NAB; John Walker Nichols Family, Nichols Family Papers Collection, privately held; Jody McKee and Floyd McKee, "New McKee Family History," 60–61, privately held; A. J. Nichols, "From a Real Pioneer," 16; SR, H. J. Brill, Border's Regiment, J. A. Nichols, McCord's Frontier Regiment, Confederate, RG109, M323, R0186, R0205, NAB; TR, 1865–73, TAC, Guadalupe County; Deeds, bk. I, 514–15, bk. J, 354, 397–98, bk. O, 432–36, Guadalupe County, CC.

17. DCM, bk. D, 248, 363–66, 368–70, 372–85, 392, 394–95, 398–401, 407–8, 410–13, 425–29, bk. E, 28–40, Guadalupe County, DC; DCR, *Texas v. John W. Nichols*, Criminal Cases 446, 464, 498, 536, *Texas v. S. W. Brill*, Criminal Cases 445, 474, Guadalupe County, DC; DCM, bk. E, 149, 169, 171, 201, 208, 214, 222, 279, 291, bk. F, 211, 387, 392, 446–47, 536, 540, 552–53, 565, 590–91, 668, bk. G, 178, 196–203, 205–12, 215, 218–19, 263–65, 286–87, 300, 308–9, 322, 324, 328–31, 335, 363, 433–35, 440, 456–57, 461–62, 465, 483, 485–86, 494–96, 499, 564, bk. H, 30–32, 227, 537, 583, Guadalupe County, DC; DCR, *Texas v. H. Johnson Brill*, Criminal Case 982, *Texas v. H. J. Brill*, Criminal Cases 1041–42, 1078–80, *Texas v. Solomon Brill, Johns[on] Brill, and Wm. S. Gordon*, Criminal Case 1310, *Texas v. James F. McKee and Solomon Brill*, Criminal Case 1344, *Texas v. H. Johnson Brill and James F. McKee*, Criminal Case 1345, *Texas v. H. Johnson Brill and S. W. Brill*, Criminal Cases 1346, 1396, *Texas v. Johns[on] Brill*, Criminal Case 1552, *Texas v. John F. Gordon*, Criminal Case 1391, Guadalupe County, DC; Tise, *Texas County Sheriffs*, 220; *Galveston Daily News*, June 23, 1875; Aragorn Storm Miller, "McKee, James F."; Elliott, "Ireland, John."

18. Deeds, bk. I, 514–15, bk. J, 354, 397–98, bk. O, 432–36, bk. K, 394, bk. L, 125, bk. N, 219, bk. O, 19–20, Guadalupe County, CC; DCM, bk. E, 69–70, 76, 87, 92, 288, bk. F, 25, 57, 63, 554, 586, bk. G, 5–6, bk. H, 18–19, 584–85, Guadalupe County, DC; DCR, *Texas v. John W. Nichols*, Criminal Case 856, *S. N. Elliott v. John W. Nichols*, Civil Case 1432, *R. A. F. Reid et al. v. John. W. Nichols et al.*, Civil Case 2248, Guadalupe County, DC; Mortgages, bk. A, 189, bk. B, 59, 254, Guadalupe County, CC; TR, 1873–82, TAC, Guadalupe County, TSLA; Guadalupe County, 1880, Agriculture, Non-population Census Schedules for Texas, 1850–80, RG29, T1134, R26, NAB.

19. Jody McKee and Floyd McKee, "New McKee Family History," 59, privately held; Descendants of John Walker Nichols, Nichols Family Papers Collection, privately held; *Seguin Enterprise*, Feb. 5, 1937; Brill Family Records, privately held; Deeds, bk. S, 183–84, Guadalupe County, CC; TR, 1882, TAC, Guadalupe County, TSLA; U.S. Census, 1900, Victoria County, Tex.; PR, bk. G, 236–38, PM, bk. D, 217–18, Guadalupe County, CC; DCR, *J. B. Dibrell. v. John. W. Nichols et al.*, Civil Case 1869, *John W. Nichols and Mary Nichols v. J. B. Dibrell*, Civil Case 2646, *R. A. F. Reid et al. v. John. W. Nichols et al.*, Civil Case 2248, Guadalupe County, DC; DCM, bk. H, 18–19, Guadalupe County, DC; TR, 1882–1906, TAC, Guadalupe County, TSLA; U.S. Census, 1900, Fayette County, Tex.; U.S. Census, 1910, Harris County, Tex.; PM, bk. L, 22–24, Guadalupe County, CC; *Galveston Daily News*, Mar. 21, 1916; *San Antonio Light*, Mar. 21, 1916.

20. L. W. Kemp to Mrs. W. E. Ford, Oct. 27, 1930, Mrs. W. E. Ford to L. W. Kemp, Oct. 28, 1930, L. W. Kemp to Waxahachie Marble & Granite Co., Dec. 9, 1930, Thurlow B. Weed to L. W. Kemp, Jan. 14, 1931, Callahan, James Hughes, Fannin notes, A–F, box 2R245, KC, CAH; *General Laws* (State of Texas, 41st Leg., 5th Called Sess.), 266–67; *Williamson County Sun*, Jan. 30, 1931; "Callahan's Body Taken to Austin," 247–48; Cisco, Tex., newspaper article, Jan. 25, 1931, Callahan, James Hughes, Biographical File, CAH; *San Antonio Light*, Jan. 22, 1931 (best account of reburial); *Abilene Morning Reporter*, Jan. 25, 1931; *Blanco County News*, Jan. 22, 1931 (gives exhumation date as Wednesday, Jan. 21, 1931); *Galveston Weekly News*, Oct. 14, 1856; *TST*, Oct. 4, 1856; "1856 death of Callahan boy," PCFH, privately held; Will Erwin, senior historian, Texas State Cemetery, telephone conversation, Apr. 17, 2017; Baker, Dupras, and Tocheri, *Osteology*, 1, 3, 5, 11; Lisa Bright, osteologist, Michigan State University, fetal bone development, e-mail to author, July 26, 2018.

21. Kemp to Ford, Nov. 30, 1929, Dec. 3, 1930, Kemp to Waxahachie Marble & Granite Co., Dec. 8, 1930, letters, Fannin Notes, C–D, box 2R245, KC, CAH; Curtis Chubb to Harry Bradley, Mar. 1, 20, 28, 1996, May 13, 1997, Gerron S. Hite to Curtis Chubb, July 14, 1998, Sarah Medissa and James Hughes Callahan File, Texas State Cemetery, Texas Historical Commission, Austin.

22. Gammel, *Laws*, 4:961.

Bibliography

ARCHIVES AND MANUSCRIPTS

Alabama Department of Archives and History, Montgomery
  Chambers County, Estates
Anderson County Museum, Anderson, S.C., Vertical File
Archivo del Municipio Monclova, Coahuila, Mexico
  Fondo Siglo XIX
Archivo General del Estado de Coahuila, Saltillo, Mexico
  Archivo del Municipio Guerrero
  Fondo Colonias Militares de Oriente
  Fondo Siglo XIX
Archivo General del Estado de Nuevo León, Monterrey, Mexico
  Seccíon Militar
  Secretaría de Guerra y Marina
  Secretaría de Relaciones Exterior
  Vidaurri, Santiago, Correspondencia Extranjeros; Correspondencia Particular
Arkansas History Commission, Little Rock
  Hempstead County Records, Deeds; Tax Records
Austin History Center, Austin Public Library, Austin, Tex.
  Niles-Graham-Pease Papers
Bastrop County, Bastrop, Tex.
  District Clerk, Civil Docket Journal; District Court Minutes
Bexar County Records Center Archives, San Antonio, Tex.
  District Clerk, Fourth District Court Minutes
Bexar County, San Antonio
  County Clerk, Deeds; Deed Index; Marriages; Probate Records; Probate Minutes
  District Clerk, District Court Minutes
Bibb County, Centerville, Ala.
  Circuit Court, Minutes
  County Court, Minutes
Blanco County, Johnson City, Tex.
  County Clerk, Deeds; Probate Minutes

Brazoria County, Angleton, Tex.
    County Clerk, Deeds; Marriages; Probate Minutes; Probate Will Record
Brazoria County Museum of History, Angleton, Tex.
    Alsbury Collection
    Vertical File
Caldwell County, Lockhart, Tex.
    County Clerk, Commissioners Court Minutes; Deeds; Marriages; Marriage Index; Probate Book
    District Clerk, District Court Minutes
Chambers County, Lafayette, Ala.
    Probate Court, Marriages
Cherokee County, Rusk, Tex.
    County Clerk, Marriages
Coal County Genealogical Society, Coalgate, Okla., Vertical File
College of William and Mary, Swem Library, Williamsburg, Va.
    Fitzhugh, Henrietta S., Diary
Comal County, New Braunfels, Tex.
    County Clerk, Commissioners Court Minutes; Deeds; Execution Docket; Probate Minutes; Probate Ledger; Probate Records
    District Clerk, District Court Minutes; District Court Records
Cornell University Library, Division of Rare and Manuscript Collections, Ithaca, N.Y.
    Opler, Morris Edward, Papers
Daughters of the Republic of Texas Library, Alamo, San Antonio, Tex.
    DeShields, J. T., Papers
    Nichols, James Wilson, Papers
    Nichols–Day Collection
    Sansom, John W., Memoirs
Dolph Briscoe Center for American History, University of Texas at Austin
    Adams, Harvey Alexander, Papers, ca. 1840–43, 1849, 1889
    Affleck, I. D., Papers, ca. 1890, 1933
    Bennet, Miles S., Papers
    Biographical File
    Bonham, Dora Dieterich, Papers
    Brooks, Daniel Baugh, Letters
    Burleson, Edward, Jr., Papers
    Dancy, Jon Winfield Scott, Papers, 1832–56
    Davenport, Harbert, Papers
    Duval, Burr H., Papers
    Erskine, Andrew Nelson, Papers
    First Census of Austin's Colony
    Guadalupe County Scrapbook
    Hays, John C., Collection
    Kemp, L. W., Collection
    Littlefield Fund
    McCulloch, Ben, and Henry Eustace McCulloch Family Papers, 1798–1961
    Menefee, John Sutherland, Papers, 1813–1934
    Peck, Benjamin B., and William D. W. Peck Papers, 1845–61, 1892

Pierson, William S., Collection, 1795–1906
Pitts, William A., Papers
Rusk, Thomas Jefferson, Papers, 1824–59
Saltillo Archives
Emory University, Pitts Theology Library, Atlanta, Ga.
Antioch Methodist Church, Vertical File
Callahan, William Jackson, Papers
Fayette County, La Grange, Tex.
County Clerk, Deeds; Deed Index; Marriages
District Clerk, Civil Docket and Process Record; District Court Minutes
Fisher County, Roby, Tex.
County Clerk, Probate Records
Fort Bend County, Richmond, Tex.
County Clerk, Deeds; Probate Records
Furman University, James B. Dukes Library, Greenville, S.C.
Bethel Association
Big Creek Baptist Church (Anderson County)
Hopewell Baptist Church
Mount Tabor Baptist Church (Anderson County)
Mountain Creek Baptist Church
Neal's Creek Baptist Church (Anderson County)
Salem Baptist Church (Anderson County)
S.C. Baptist Church Files
Galveston County, Galveston, Tex.
County Clerk, Probate Minutes; Probate Returns
Gillespie County, Fredericksburg, Tex.
County Clerk, Deeds
District Clerk, District Court Minutes
Georgia Archives, Morrow
Clarke County, Registration Oath Books
Commissary General's Department, Families Supplied with Salt
Executive Secretary's Letters Books
Georgia Military Affairs
Georgia Military Records Book
Georgia Surveyor General, Colonial and Headright Plat
Jackson County, Deeds; Inferior Court Minutes; Marriages; Lottery List; Superior Court Minutes; Tax Digests
Monroe County, Land Lottery Records
Oglethorpe County, Wills
Upson County, Deeds
Virtual Vault, General Name File; File II Names
Vertical File, Family Folders
Walton County, Deeds; Land Lottery Records
Wilkes County, Deeds
Gonzales County, Gonzales, Tex.
County Clerk, Commissioners Court Minutes; Deeds; Guardianship Records; Oaths; Marriages; Marriage Bonds; Probate Ledger; Probate Minutes; Probate Records

District Clerk, District Court Minutes; District Court Records; District Court Final Records; District Court Index
Gonzales County Records Center and Archives, Gonzales, Tex.
Bahlmann, Kathy, Jeffrey Bahlmann, and Victoria Bahlmann, "Slave Transactions, Gonzales County, Texas, 1839–1865" (unpublished survey)
Baumgartner, Dorcas Huff, "History of the Alsey Silvanus Miller Homestead and Surrounding Area, 1700–1992" (manuscript)
Guadalupe County, Seguin, Tex.
County Clerk, Commissioners Court Minutes; Brands and Marks; Deeds; Index of Deeds; Marriages; Marriage Index; Mortgages; Probate Minutes; Probate Records
District Clerk, Criminal Docket; District Court Index; District Court Minutes; District Court Records
Hays County, San Marcos, Tex.
County Clerk, Deeds; Deed Index; Marriages; Probate Records; Probate Minutes
District Clerk, District Court Minutes
Institute of Texan Cultures, San Antonio, Tex.
Vertical File, Blanco County
Jackson County, Jefferson, Ga.
Clerk of the Court, Superior Court Minutes
Inferior Court, Minutes
Probate Court, Marriages; Probate Records
Jefferson County, Pine Bluff, Ark.
County Clerk, Marriages
Kansas State Historical Society, Topeka
City Directory, Leavenworth
Kendalia Public Library, Kendalia, Tex.
Kendalia Scrapbooks
Kendall County, Boerne, Tex.
County Clerk, Commissioners Court Minutes; Deeds; Marriages, Reverse Index
Kimble County, Junction, Tex.
County Clerk, Deeds
Lavaca County, Hallettsville, Tex.
County Clerk, Deeds
Leon County, Centerville, Tex.
County Court, Minutes
Library of Virginia, Richmond
Loudoun County, Tithables
Lunenburg County, Court Records; Lists of Tithables and Taxable Property
Margaret and Herman Brown Library, Abilene Christian University, Abilene, Tex.
Callie Faye Milliken Special Collections; Smith, Ralph Papers
Maryland State Archives, Annapolis
Church Records, St. John's Church Collection, Registry
Matagorda County, Bay City, Tex.
County Clerk, Deeds
Museo de Historia Mexicana, Monterrey, N.L., Mexico
Vidaurri, Santiago, Correspondencia Particular
National Archives and Records Administration–Southwest Region, Fort Worth, Tex.

Bureau of Indian Affairs, Texas Agency
Returns from Military Posts
National Archives Building, Washington, D.C.
Adjutant General
Bureau of the Census, Nonpopulation Census Schedules Texas
Confederate Service Records
Index to Mexican War Pension Files
Mexican War Service Records
New Orleans Passenger Lists, Arrivals
Record of Appointment of Postmasters
Selected Records of the War Department Relating to Confederate Prisoners of War
Soldiers Who Served in Volunteer Organizations during the Indian Wars, Service Records
United States, Texas, Service Records
War of 1812, Service Records, Compiled Military Service Files, South Carolina
National Archives, College Park, Md.
Records of the Department of State, Despatches from U.S. Consuls in Chihuahua, Mexico; Despatches from U.S. Consuls in Matamoros, Mexico; Despatches from U.S. Consuls in Monterrey, Mexico
New York Public Library, Schomburg Center for Research in Black Culture
Porter, Kenneth Wiggins, Papers
North Carolina State Archives, Raleigh
North Carolina Secretary of State, Granville Proprietary Land Office
Orange County, County Court; Registration of Deeds; Court of Pleas and Quarter Sessions
Rowan County, Estate Records; Marriage Bonds
Rutherford County, Court of Pleas and Quarter Sessions; Deeds; Tax Lists
Paróquias Católicas (Catholic Church parishes), Marriages, Tamaulipas, Mexico
Perry County, Marion, Ala.
County Clerk, Deeds
Samford University Library, Birmingham, Ala.
Church Records, Coker Baptist; Sardis Baptist
Secretaría de la Defensa Nacional, Mexico City
Dirección de Archivo Militar, Archivo de Cancelados, Sección de Historias; Diario de la Operaciones Militares (1839, 1841, 1842); Puestos en Libertad, 1842
Secretaría de Relaciones Exterior, Mexico City
Correspondencia
Shiloh Baptist Church, Prairie Lea, Tex.
Sophienburg Museum and Archives, New Braunfels, Tex.
Vertical File
South Carolina Department of History and Archives, Columbia
Anderson County, Conveyances; Estate Papers
Camden District, State Grants
Craven County, Deeds
Fairfield County, Deeds; Tax Returns
Legislative Papers, Memorials and Petitions to Practice Thomsonian Medicine
Ninety-Six District, County Plats Book
Oglethorpe County, Wills

Southern Baptist Historical Library and Archives, Nashville
Sul Ross State University, Bryan Wildenthal Memorial Library, Alpine, Tex.
Walton, D. A. T., Collection
Tennessee State Library and Archives, Nashville
Bransford Family Papers
Church Records Collection, Record Book, Mill Creek Baptist Church
Hardeman County, Tax List; Wills
Maury County, Probate Records; Wills
Stewart County, Circuit Court, Minutes
Texas A&M University, Cushing Memorial Library, College Station
Asbury, Samuel Erson, Papers
Texas Department of State Health Services, Vital Statistics Unit, Austin
Death Indexes
Texas General Land Office, Austin
Archives and Records, Austin's Register of Families
Maps
Milam's Colony Records, Milam's Register of Families
Texas Historical Commission, Austin
Texas Prison Museum, Texas State Penitentiary, Huntsville
Convict Ledger
Texas State Library and Archives, Archives and Information Services Division, Austin
Cunningham, James, Papers
Davenport, Harbert, Collection
First Minute Book of Seguin
Ford, John Salmon, Papers
Huntsville Prison, Convict Ledgers
Lindsey Family Papers
Memorials and Petitions, Citizens of Gonzales County, Defense of the Frontier petition; Medissa Allsbury petition; Petition for Creation of County of Plum Creek; To the Honorable Congress of the Republic
Miller, Washington Daniel, Papers
Nicholson–McDowall Family Papers
Pease, Elisha Marshall, Papers; Records
Register of Elected and Appointed State and County Officials
Republic of Texas, Department of State, Election Returns; General Correspondence
Runnels, Hardin Richard, Records
Secretary of State, Bonds and Oaths of County and State Officials; Clemency Records; Election Returns; Registers
Tax Assessor-Collector, Tax Roll
Texas Adjutant General's Department, Texas State Troops; Frontier Forces Records; Minute Men Military Rolls; Republic of Texas Military Roll; Texas Ranger Muster Rolls; Texas Ranger Records
Woodhouse, M. P., Papers, 1837–42
Voter Registration
Texas Tech University, Lubbock
Southwest Collection/Special Collections Library, El Capote Ranch Records
Travis County, Austin, Tex.

County Clerk, Deeds; Deed Index; Marriages
District Clerk, Bar Docket; District Court Minutes
Troup County, LaGrange, Ga.
Probate Court, Marriages
University of Alabama, W. S. Hoole Special Collections Library, Tuscaloosa
Ely, William H., Letters
Warren County, Bowling Green, Ky.
County Clerk, Will Book; Deeds
Warren County, Vicksburg, Miss.
Circuit Clerk, Marriages
Washington County, Brenham, Tex.
County Clerk, Deeds; Marriages; Probate Records
Williamson County, Georgetown, Tex.
County Clerk, Deeds; Deed Index; Probate Records
District Clerk, District Court Minutes
Yale University, Beinecke Rare Book and Manuscript Library, New Haven, Conn.
Western Americana Collection, Luis Alberto Guajardo Collection of Músquiz [*sic*], México, Records; Luis Alberto Guajardo Papers on the History of Coahuila
Yell County, Dardanelle and Danville, Ark.
Circuit and County Clerk's Office, Marriages

GOVERNMENT DOCUMENTS

U.S. Congress. House. 22nd Cong., 1st sess., 1832. H. Doc. 269.
U.S. Congress. House. 32nd Cong., 2nd sess., 1852. H. Ex. Doc. 1, pt. 2.
U.S. Congress. House. 33rd Cong., 2nd sess., 1854. H. Ex. Doc. 15.
U.S. Congress. House. 34th Cong., 1st sess., 1855. H. Ex. Doc. 1, pt. 2.
U.S. Congress. House. 42nd Cong., 2nd sess., 1872. H. Ex. Doc. 277.
U.S. Congress. Senate. 30th Cong., 1st sess., 1849. S. Ex. Doc. 7.
U.S. Congress. Senate. 31st Cong., 1st sess., 1850. S. Ex. Doc. 44.
U.S. Congress. Senate. 40th Cong., 1st sess., 1867. S. Ex. Doc. 14.
U.S. Congress. Senate. 41st Cong., 3rd sess., 1871. S. Ex. Doc. 36.
U.S. Congress. Senate. 44th Cong., 2nd sess., 1877. S. Ex. Doc. 31.
U.S. Congress. Senate. 45th Cong., 2nd sess., 1878. S. Ex. Doc. 19.
U.S. Congress. Senate. 59th Cong., 1st sess., 1905–1906. S. Doc. 169.

U.S. CENSUS RECORDS

Census for 1820. Washington, D.C.: Gales & Seaton, 1821.
Return of the Whole Number of Persons within the Several Districts of the United States. Philadelphia: Childs & Swaine, 1791.
U.S. Census, 1790. RG 29, M637. NAB. S.C.
U.S. Census, 1800. RG 29, M32. NAB. S.C.
U.S. Census, 1810. RG 29, M252. NAB. S.C.
U.S. Census, 1820. RG 29, M33. NAB. Ga., S.C., Tenn.
U.S. Census, 1830. RG 29, M19. NAB. Ala., Ark., Ga., Miss.
U.S. Census, 1840. RG29, M704. NAB. Ala., Ark., Ga., S.C., Tenn.
U.S. Census, 1850. RG 29, M432. NAB. Ala., Ark., Ga., La., Miss., Mo., S.C. Tenn., Tex.; Slave Schedules: Tex.

U.S. Census, 1860. RG 29, M653. NAB. Ala., Ga., La., Mo., Tex.; Slave Schedules: Tex.

U.S. Census, 1870. RG 29, M653. NAB. Ala., Ark., Calif., Ga., Ky., La., Miss., Tenn., Tex.

U.S. Census, 1880. RG 29, T9. NAB. Ala., Ark., Ga., La., Miss., Tex.

U.S. Census, 1900. RG 29, T623. NAB. Ala., Ark., Indian territory, Tex.

U.S. Census, 1910. RG 29, T624. NAB. Ark., Tex.

U.S. Census, 1920. RG 29, T625. NAB. Tex.

U.S. Census. Nonpopulation Census Schedules, Texas. Agriculture, Manufacturing, Mortality, 1850–1880. RG 29, M1134. NAB.

BOOKS, ARTICLES, DISSERTATIONS

Abbett, Claire Elizabeth Stanley. "William Early Jones: Early Texan." Master's thesis, University of Texas, 1966.

Abbott, Patrick L., and C. M. Woodruff. *The Balcones Escarpment: Geology, Hydrology, Ecology*. San Antonio: Geological Society of America, 1986.

Abbott, T. S. *Carta general del Estado de Coahuila de Zaragoza, formada por disposición del gobierno del mismo estado.* New York: August R. Ohman, 1905. Special Collections and Archives, University of Texas–Pan American Library, Edinburg.

Abstract of the Returns of the Fifth Census. Washington, D.C.: Duff Green, 1839.

"Across the Isthmus." *Chamber's Journal of Popular Literature, Science, and Arts* 3 (1855): 250–53.

Acts of the Assembly of Georgia, in November and December 1857. Columbus, Ga.: Tennent Lomax, 1858.

Adjutant General's Office. *Official Army Register for January, 1873*. Washington, D.C.: Adjutant General's Office, 1873.

Aldridge, Franklin Rudolph. *Aldridge Records*. Nashville: Commercial Letter Shop, 1960.

Alley, Gene. *Alley Ancestors*. Wyandotte, Okla.: Gregath, 1994.

Althaus, Barbara Donalson. "Kyle, Claiborne." *Handbook of Texas Online*. http://www.tshaonline.org/handbook/online/articles/fky02. Accessed June 15, 2010.

Amberson, Mary Margaret McAllen, John A. McAllen, and Margaret H. McAllen. *I Would Rather Sleep in Texas: A History of the Lower Rio Grande Valley and the People of the Santa Anita Land Grant*. Austin: Texas State Historical Association, 2003.

Anderson, Gary Clayton. *The Conquest of Texas: Ethnic Cleansing in the Promised Land, 1820–1875*. Norman: University of Oklahoma Press, 2005.

Appendix to the Journals of the House of Representatives: Fifth Congress. [Austin, Tex.]: Gazette Office, [1841].

Austerman, Wayne R. *Sharps Rifles and Spanish Mules: The San Antonio–El Paso Mail, 1851–1881*. College Station: Texas A&M University Press, 1985.

Ayers, Charles H. "Lewis Ayers." *Quarterly of the Texas State Historical Association* 9 (1906): 269–81.

Bailey, Anne J. "Debray, Xavier Blanchard." *Handbook of Texas Online*. Accessed June 12, 2010. http://www.tshaonline.org/handbook/online/articles/fde02.

Baker, Brenda, Tosha Dupras, and Matthew Tocheri. *The Osteology of Infants and Children*. College Station: Texas A&M University Press.

Baker, D. W. C. *A Texas Scrap-Book*. Austin: Texas State Historical Association, 1991.

Barker, Eugene C. "Austin, Stephen Fuller." *Handbook of Texas Online*. Accessed June 9, 2010. http://www.tshaonline.org/handbook/online/articles/fau14.

———, ed. *The Austin Papers: October, 1834–January, 1837*. Austin: University of Texas Press, 1926.

Barnard, J. H. *Dr. J. H. Barnard's Journal*. Edited and annotated by Hobart Huson. Goliad Bicentennial Edition. Refugio, Tex.: Goliad Bicentennial, 1950.

Bartlett, John Russell. *Personal Narrative of the Explorations and Incidents in Texas, New Mexico, California, Sonora and Chihuahua*. 2 vols. New York: D. Appleton, 1854.

Baylor, George Wyeth. "Gen. Baylor Tells of Indian Fight." *Frontier Times* 21, no. 9 (1944): 359–62.

Beatie, Russel H. *Saddles*. Norman: University of Oklahoma Press, 1981.

Bell, James G. "A Log of the Texas–California Cattle Trail, 1854." Edited by J. Evetts Haley. *Southwestern Historical Quarterly* 35, no. 3 (1932): pt. 1, 208–37; 35, no. 4 (1932): pt. 2, 290–316; 36, no. 1 (1932): pt. 3, 47–66.

Bieber, Ralph B. *Southern Trails to California in 1849*. Porcupine Press, Philadelphia, 1974.

———. "The Southwestern Trails to California in 1849." *Mississippi Valley Historical Review* 12 (1925): 342–75.

Biesele, Rudolph L. "Early Times in New Braunfels and Comal County." *Southwestern Historical Quarterly* 50 (1946): 75–92.

———. *The History of the German Settlements in Texas*. San Marcos, Tex.: German-Texan Heritage Society, 1987.

Biographical Encyclopedia of Texas. New York: Southern Publishing, 1880.

Bishop, Curtis. *Lots of Land*. Austin: Steck, 1949.

Blanco County News. *Heritage of Blanco, Texas*. Dallas: Curtis Media, 1987.

Bliss, Zenas R. *The Reminiscences of Major General Zenas R. Bliss, 1854–1857*. Edited by Thomas T. Smith, Jerry D. Thompson, Robert Wooster, and Ben E. Pingenot. Austin: Texas State Historical Association, 2007.

Bollaert, William. *William Bollaert's Texas*. Edited by W. Eugene Hollon and Ruth Lapham Butler. Norman: University of Oklahoma Press, 1956.

Bonham, Dora Dieterich. *Merchant to the Republic*. San Antonio: Naylor, 1958.

Boswell, Angela. *Her Act and Deed: Women's Lives in a Rural Southern County, 1837–1873*. College Station: Texas A&M University Press, 2001.

Bowen, Eliza A. *The Story of Wilkes County, Georgia*. Edited by Louise Frederick Hays. Marietta, Ga: Clearfield, 1950.

Bowen, James L. *Massachusetts in the War*. Springfield, Mass.: Clark W. Bryan, 1889.

Brawner, Ann. *150 Years of Methodism in Seguin, 1841–1991*. Seguin, Tex.: First United Methodist Church, 1991.

Brazos. *The Life of Robert Hall*. Austin: State House Press, 1992.

Brice, Donaly E. *The Great Comanche Raid: Boldest Indian Attack of the Texas Republic*. Austin, Tex.: Eakin, 1987.

Brister, Louis E. "Adelsverein, *Handbook of Texas Online*, http://www.tshaonline.org/handbook/online/articles/ufa01. Accessed June 9, 2010. Modified on August 31, 2018. Published by the Texas State Historical Association.

Britten, Thomas A. *The Lipan Apache: People of Wind and Lightning*. Albuquerque: University of New Mexico Press, 2009.

———. "Treacherous, Deceitful, or Just Plain Smart? Lipan Apache Warfare in Spanish Texas." Paper presented at the 82nd Annual Meeting of the West Texas Historical Association, Alpine, Tex., Apr. 1–2, 2005.

Brooks, James F. "Served Well by Plunder: La Gran Ladronería and Producers of History Astride the Rio Grande." *American Quarterly* 52 (2000): 23–58.

Brooks, V. L. *History of the First Baptist Church*. Austin: First Baptist Church, 1923.

Brown, Gary. *Hesitant Martyr in the Texas Revolution: James Walker Fannin*. Plano: Republic of Texas Press, 2000.

Brown, John Henry. *History of Texas, from 1685 to 1892*. 2 vols. St. Louis: L. E. Daniell, 1892.

———. *Indian Wars and Pioneers of Texas*. Austin: L. E. Daniell, [1896]. Reprint, Austin: State House Press, 1988.

Brown, Thomas Elton. "Seminole Indian Agents, 1842–1874." *Chronicles of Oklahoma* 51 (1973): 59–83.

Bruhn, Richard. "Twin Sisters, TX." *Handbook of Texas Online*. Accessed June 15, 2010. http://www.tshaonline.org/handbook/online/articles/hnt40.

Brune, Gunnar. *Springs of Texas*. Vol. 1. College Station: Texas A&M University Press, 2002.

Bryan, J. L. "Rector, Claiborne." *Handbook of Texas Online*. Accessed June 15, 2010. https://tshaonline.org/handbook/online/articles/frebt.

Bryan, T. Conn. *Confederate Georgia*. Athens: University of Georgia Press, 1953.

Buder, John J. "Moore, Ike Henry." *Handbook of Texas Online*. Accessed June 15, 2010. http://www.tshaonline.org/handbook/online/articles/fmoas.

Bugbee, Lester G. "The Old Three Hundred: A List of Settlers in Austin's First Colony." *Quarterly of the Texas State Historical Association* 1 (1897): 108–17.

Burr, David H. *A New Universal Atlas*. New York: D. S. Stone, 1835.

Cadle, Ferris W. *Georgia Land Surveying: History and Law*. Athens: University of Georgia Press, 1991.

Callahan, Ben F. *Callahan, Being a Compilation of the Descendants of John Callahan (Deceased 1766, Rowan, Co., NC)*. Gold Hill, N.C.: self-published, 2010.

"Callahan's Body Taken to Austin." *Frontier Times* 8, no. 6 (1931): 247–48.

Campbell, Randolph B. "The District Judges of Texas in 1866–1867: An Episode in the Failure of Presidential Reconstruction." *Southwestern Historical Quarterly* 93 (1990): 357–77.

———. *An Empire for Slavery: The Peculiar Institution in Texas, 1821–1865*. Baton Rouge: Louisiana State University, 1989.

———. *Gone to Texas: A History of the Lone Star State*. New York: Oxford University Press, 2003.

———, ed. *The Laws of Slavery in Texas*. Compiled by William S. Pugsley and Marilyn P. Douglas. Austin: University of Texas Press, 2010.

———. "Slave Hiring in Texas." *American Historical Review* 93 (1988): 107–14.

Campbell, Randolph B., and Richard G. Lowe. *Wealth and Power in Antebellum Texas*. College Station: Texas A&M University Press, 1977.

Canales Santos, Alvaro. *Piedras Negras*. Saltillo, Coahuila, Mexico: El Dos, 2005.

Carey, Anthony Gene. *Parties, Slavery, and the Union in Antebellum Georgia*. Athens: University of Georgia Press, 1997.

Carlock, Marion Pomeroy. *History of the Carlock Family*. Los Angeles: Straube, 1929.

Carrier, Helen M. *One Zumwalt Family: Zumalt, Zeumalt, Zum Wald, Zumwault, Sommalt: Many Descendants of the Eleven Children of Andrew Zumwalt (1698–1765) and His Two Wives*. San Jose, Calif.: H. M. Carrier, 2000.

Carrington, Evelyn M., ed. *Women in Early Texas*. Austin: Jenkins, 1975.

Carroll, Mark M. *Homesteads Ungovernable: Families, Sex, Race, and the Law in Frontier Texas, 1823–1860*. Austin: University of Texas Press, 2001.

Cases Argued and Decided in the Supreme Court of the State of Texas during the Session of the Court Commencing the First Monday in December, 1872. Reported by Terrell and Walker. Vol. 38. Madison, Wis.: State Journal Printing, 1874. Reprint, St. Louis: Gilbert Book, 1882.

Casey, Bernice Brooks, and Robert Brooks Casey. *Brooks Family History*. Austin: Genealogical Information Systems, 2005.

Castañeda, C. E. *The Mexican Side of the Texan Revolution*. Austin: Graphic Ideas, 1970.

Cazneau, Jane McManus Storm [Cora Montgomery, pseud.]. *Eagle Pass; or, Life on the Border*. New York: George P. Putnam, 1852.

Central Georgia Genealogical Society. *First Hundred and Ten Years of Houston County, Georgia (1822–1932)*. Chelsea, Mich.: Bookcrafters, 1983.

Chambers, Richard J. *The Early History of Nicholson, Georgia*. Commerce, Ga: self-published, 1987.

Chebahtah, William, and Nancy McGown Minor. *Chevato*. Lincoln: University of Nebraska Press, 2007.

Christian, Carole E. "Washington-on-the-Brazos, TX." *Handbook of Texas Online*. Accessed June 15, 2010. http://www.tshaonline.org/handbook/online/articles/hvw10.

Chubb, Curtis. "Revisiting the Purpose of the 1855 Callahan Expedition: A Research Note." *Southwestern Historical Quarterly* 121 (2018): 417–30.

Clarke, A. B. *Travels in Mexico and California*. Edited by Anne M. Perry. College Station: Texas A&M University Press, 1988.

Clarke, Mary Whatley. *The Swenson Saga and the SMS Ranches*. Austin: Jenkins, 1976.

Clarkson, Kate Merritt. "Belle of the Sixties Recalls Dramatic Incidents." *Frontier Times* 5, no. 7 (1928): 272–77.

Clay, Comer, and Diana J. Kleiner. "Colorado River." *Handbook of Texas Online*. Accessed June 12, 2010. http://www.tshaonline.org/handbook/online/articles/rnc10.

Coalson, George O. "Alavez, Francita." *Handbook of Texas Online*. Accessed June 9, 2010. http://www.tshaonline.org/handbook/online/articles/fal53.

Coleman, Kenneth. *A History of Georgia*. 2nd ed. Athens: University of Georgia Press, 1991.

Collins, Michael L. *Texas Devils: Rangers and Regulars on the Lower Rio Grande, 1846–1861*. Norman: University of Oklahoma Press, 2008.

Coltharp, J. B. "A 'Hog-Killing Good Time.'" Notes and Documents. *Southwestern Historical Quarterly* 79 (1975): 182–88.

Comisión Pesquisidora de la Frontera del Norte. *Reports of the Committee of Investigation Sent in 1873 by the Mexican Government to the Frontier of Texas*. Translated from the official edition made in Mexico. New York: Baker & Goodwin, 1875.

The Constitution, as Amended, and Ordinances of the Convention of 1866 . . . and the General Laws of the Regular Session of the Eleventh Legislature of the State of Texas. Austin: Printed at Gazette office by Joseph Walker, 1866.

Cotham, Edward T., Jr. "'Nothing but Disaster': The Failure of Union Plans to Capture Texas." In *The Seventh Star of the Confederacy: Texas during the Civil War*, edited by Kenneth W. Howell. 130-48. Denton: University of North Texas Press, 2009.

Coulter, E. Merton. *Georgia: A Short History*. Chapel Hill: University of North Carolina Press, 1960.

Covington, Carolyn Callaway. "Runaway Scrape." *Handbook of Texas Online*. Accessed June 15, 2010. http://www.tshaonline.org/handbook/online/articles/pfr01.

Cox, S. S. "The Supreme Court of the Republic of Texas." *Texas Lodge of Research, A.F. & A.M., Transactions* 2 (1962–1964): 271–77.

Crenshaw, Ollinger. "The Knights of the Golden Circle: The Career of George Bickley." *Historical Review* 47 (1941) 23–50.

Crimm, Ana Carolina Castillo. *DeLeón: A Tejano Family History*. Austin: University of Texas Press, 2003.

———. "Fernando de León: Leadership Lost." In de la Teja, *Tejano Leadership*, 103–27.

Cummins, Bertie Lillian Beall. *Georgia Bealls and Their Kinfolks*. N.p.: self-published, 1964.

Cunningham, Bob, and Harry P. Hewitt. "A 'Lovely Land Full of Roses and Thorns': Emil Langberg and Mexico, 1835–1866." *Southwestern Historical Quarterly* 98 (1995): 387–425.

Cunningham, Robert E. "Somervell, Alexander." *Handbook of Texas Online*. Accessed June 15, 2010. http://www.tshaonline.org/handbook/online/articles/fs004.

Cuthbertson, Gilbert M. "Regulator-Moderator War." *Handbook of Texas Online*. http://www.tshaonline.org/handbook/online/articles/jcr01. Accessed June 15, 2010.

Cutrer, Thomas W. *Ben McCulloch and the Frontier Military Tradition*. Chapel Hill: University of North Carolina Press, 1993.

———. "Colquhoun, Ludovic," *Handbook of Texas Online*. Last modified August 14, 2015. http://www.tshaonline.org/handbook/online/articles/fc031.

———. "Handy, Robert Eden." *Handbook of Texas Online*. Accessed June 15, 2010. http://www.tshaonline.org/handbook/online/articles/fha49.

———. "Hemphill, John," *Handbook of Texas Online*. Accessed June 15, 2010. http://www.tshaonline.org/handbook/online/articles/fhe13.

———. "Jones, George Washington." *Handbook of Texas Online*. Accessed June 15, 2010. http://www.tshaonline.org/handbook/online/articles/fjo49.

———. "McLeod, Hugh." *Handbook of Texas Online*. Last modified Apr. 3, 2011. http://www.tshaonline.org/handbook/online/articles/fmc90.

———. "Oldham, Williamson Simpson." *Handbook of Texas Online*. Accessed June 15, 2010. http://www.tshaonline.org/handbook/online/articles/fol02.

———. "Pyron, Charles Lynn." *Handbook of Texas Online*. Last modified Mar. 28, 2012. http://www.tshaonline.org/handbook/online/articles/fpy01.

———. "Smith, Persifor Frazer." *Handbook of Texas Online*. Accessed June 15, 2010. http://www.tshaonline.org/handbook/online/articles/fsm36.

Dallam, James Wilmer. *Opinions of the Supreme Court of Texas from 1840 to 1844 Inclusive*. St. Louis: Gilbert Book, 1882.

Dary, David. *Cowboy Culture: A Saga of Five Centuries*. Lawrence: University of Kansas Press, 1989.

Davenport, Harbert. "The Men of Goliad." *Southwestern Historical Quarterly* 48 (1939): 1–41.

———. "Notes from an Unfinished Study of Fannin and His Men with Biographical Sketches." 1936. Edited by H. David Maxey, 2002. TSHA Online. http://www.tshaonline.org/supsites/fannin/hd_home.html.

Davis, Charles G. "Crystal Falls, TX." *Handbook of Texas Online*. Accessed June 12, 2010. http://www.tshaonline.org/handbook/online/articles/hncaq.

———. "Dawson, Nicholas Mosby." *Handbook of Texas Online*. Accessed June 12, 2010. http://www.tshaonline.org/handbook/online/articles/fda53.

Davis, Robert Scott, Jr. "Goliad and the Georgia Battalion: Georgia Participation in the Texas Revolution, 1835–1836." *Journal of Southwest Georgia History* 4 (1986): 25–55.

Day, James M. *Jacob De Cordova: Land Merchant of Texas*. Waco: Heritage Society of Waco, 1962.

DeBow, J. D. B. *The Seventh Census of the United States: 1850; An Appendix*. Washington, D.C.: Robert Armstrong, 1853.

———. *Statistical View of the United States, Embracing Its Territorial Population . . . Being a Compendium of the Seventh Census*. Washington, D.C.: Beverly Tucker, 1854.

De Cordova, Jacob. *Texas: Her Resources and Public Men*. Waco, Tex.: Texian, 1969.

Deems, Charles F. *Annals of Southern Methodism for 1855*. New York: J. A. Gray, 1856.

Delaney, Robert W. "Matamoros, Port for Texas during the Civil War." *Southwestern Historical Quarterly* 58, no. 4 (1955): 473–87.

de la Peña, José Enrique. *With Santa Anna in Texas: A Personal Narrative of the Revolution*. Edited and translated by Carmen Perry. College Station: Texas A&M University Press, 1975.

de la Portilla, Nicolás. *The Diary of Lt. Col. Nicolás de la Portilla, March 18th–April 23rd*. Edited and translated by Roger Borroet. East Chicago, Ind.: Villita, 1999.

de la Teja, Jesús F., ed. "Juan N. Seguín." In de la Teja, *Tejano Leadership*, 212-30.

———, ed. *A Revolution Remembered: The Memoirs of Juan N. Seguín*. Austin: State House Press, 1991.

———, ed. *Tejano Leadership in Mexican and Revolutionary Texas*. College Station: Texas A&M University Press, 2010.

de la Teja, Jesús F., Paula Marks, and Ron Tyler. *Texas: Crossroads of North America*. Belmont, Calif.: Cengage Learning, 2004.

D'Emilio, John, and Estelle B. Freedman. *Intimate Matters: A History of Sexuality*. Chicago: University of Chicago Press, 2012.

Denison, George Stanton. "Some Letters of George Stanton Denison, 1854–1866: Observations of a Yankee on the Conditions in Louisiana and Texas." Edited by James A. Padgett. *Louisiana Historical Quarterly* 23 (1940): 1133–169.

Denman, Clarence P. "The Office of Adjutant General of Texas, 1835–1881." *Southwestern Historical Quarterly* 28 (1924): 302–22.

DeVilbiss, John Wesley, Sr. *Reminiscences and Events in the Ministerial Life of Rev. John Wesley DeVilbiss*. Compiled by H. A Graves. Galveston: W. A. Shaw, 1886.

Deviney, Esther Gambrell. *A Link with the Past: First United Methodist Church, Prairie Lea, Texas, 1853–1980*. Prairie Lea, Tex.: self-published, 1980.

Dimmick, Gregg J., ed. *General Vicente Filisola's Analysis of José Urrea's Military Diary*. Translated by John R. Wheat. Austin: Texas State Historical Association, 2007.

Doherty, Frank J. *The Settlers of the Beekman Patent, Dutchess County, New York*. 13 vols. Orlando, Fla.: self-published, 1993.

Donecker, Frances. "San Antonio Express-News." *Handbook of Texas Online*. Accessed June 15, 2010. http://www.tshaonline.org/handbook/online/articles/ees03.

DuCoin, Candice. *Lawmen on the Texas Frontier: Rangers and Sheriffs*. Round Rock, Tex.: Riata Books, 2007.

Dunn, Roy Sylvan. "The KGC in Texas, 1860–1861." *Southwestern Historical Quarterly* 70 (1967): 543–73.

Dunn, William E. "The Founding of Nuestra Senora del Refugio, the Last Spanish Mission in Texas." *Southwestern Historical Quarterly* 25 (1922): 174–84.

Dunt, Detlef. *Journey to Texas, 1833*. Translated by Anders Saustrup; edited by James C. Kearney and Geir Bentzen. Austin: University of Texas Press, 2015.

Durivage, John E. "Through Mexico to California: Letters and Journal of John E. Durivage." In Bieber, *Southern Trails*, 157–256.

Eastman, Seth. *A Seth Eastman Sketchbook, 1848–1849*. Published for Marion Koogler McNay Art Institute. Austin: University of Texas Press, 1961.

Eccleston, Robert. *Overland to California on the Southwestern Trail, 1849: Diary of Robert Eccleston*. Edited by George P. Hammond and Edward H. Howes. Berkeley: University of California Press, 1950.

Eckel, Jennifer. "Evans, Onesimus." *Handbook of Texas Online*. Accessed Aug. 31, 2010. http://www.tshaonline.org/handbook/online/articles/fev31.

Edgar, Walter. *South Carolina: A History*. Columbia: University of South Carolina Press, 1998.

"1855 School Census, Hays County, Texas." *Hays County Historical and Genealogical Society Quarterly* 4, no. 2 (1970): 1–58.

Elliott, Claude. "Alabama and the Texas Revolution." *Southwestern Historical Quarterly* 50 (1947): 315–28.

———. "Georgia and the Texas Revolution." *Georgia Historical Quarterly* 28 (1944): 234–50.

———. "Ireland, John." *Handbook of Texas Online*. Last modified Feb. 24, 2016. http://www.tshaonline.org/handbook/online/articles/fir01.

Elrod, Frary. *Historical Notes on Jackson County, Georgia*. Jefferson, Ga.: Frary Elrod, 1967.

Ely, Herman. *Records of the Descendants of Nathaniel Ely*. Cleveland: Short and Foreman, 1885.

Emory, William H. *Report of the United States and Mexican Boundary Survey*. 3 vols. Washington, D.C.: Cornelius Wendell, 1857.

Engledow, Peggy White. "Record of Bills of Sale and Gifts of Deed of Slaves from Caldwell County, Texas: Deed Books." Unpublished monograph, 2005. Copy at Caldwell County Genealogical and Historical Society, Luling, Tex.

Enríquez Terrazas, Eduardo, and Martha Rodríguez García. *Coahuila: Textos de su historia*. Mexico City: Instituto de Investigaciones Dr. José María Luis Mora, 1989.

Erskine, Michael. *The Diary of Michael Erskine*. Edited by J. Evetts Haley. Midland, Tex.: Nita Stewart Haley Memorial Library, 1979.

Evans, C. E. *The Story of Texas Schools*. Austin: Steck, 1955.

Faulk, Odie B. "Bartlett, John Russell." *Handbook of Texas Online*. Accessed June 12, 2010. http://www.tshaonline.org/handbook/online/articles/fba93.

Fey, Everett Anthony. *New Braunfels: The First Founders; The History*. 2 vols. Austin: Eakin, 1995.

Filisola, Vicente. *Memoirs for the History of the War in Texas*. Translated by Wallace Woolsey. Austin: Eakin, 1987.

Fisher, O. C. *It Occurred in Kimble*. Houston: privately printed, 1937.

Fitzhugh, Lester N. "Saluria, Fort Esperanza, and Military Operations on the Texas Coast, 1861–1864." *Southwestern Historical Quarterly* 61 (1957): 76–98.

Flannery, Michael A. "The Early Botanical Medical Movement as a Reflection of Life, Liberty, and Literacy in Jacksonian America." *Journal of the Medical Library Association* 90 (2002): 442–54.

Foote, Henry Stuart. *Texas and the Texans; or, Advance of the Anglo-Americans to the South-West.* 2 vols. Philadelphia: Thomas, Cowperthwait, 1841.

Ford, John Salmon. "Callahan's Expedition: Indians and Mexicans Punished for Depredations." Extracted with additional information by Rosalie Roberts. *Plum Creek Almanac* 3 (1985): 3–11.

———. *Rip Ford's Texas.* Edited by Stephen B. Oates. Austin: University of Texas Press, 1987.

Ford, Lacy K. *Origins of Southern Radicalism: The South Carolina Upcountry, 1800–1860.* New York: Oxford University Press, 1988.

Franks, J. M. *Seventy Years in Texas.* Gatesville, Tex.: self-published, 1924.

Fretz, A. J. *A Brief History of John and Christian Fretz and a Complete Genealogical Family Register.* Milton, N.J.: Press of the Evergreen News, 1904.

"From Texas to the Gold Mines," 257–80. In Bieber, *Southern Trails.* Originally published as "Sketches from the Journal of a Traveler, Overland to California," in *The Texas Monument* (La Grange), Feb. 19, 26, Mar. 5, 12, 1851.

Gammel, H. P. N. *The Laws of Texas, 1822–1897.* 11 vols. Austin: Gammel Book, 1898.

———. *The Laws of Texas.* 16 vols. Austin: Gammel Book, 1902–31.

García, Luis Alberto. *Guerra y frontera: El Ejército del Norte, 1855 y 1858.* N. L., Mexico: Fondo Editorial de Nuevo Leon, Archivo General del Estado de Nuevo León, 2007.

Gard, Wayne. "Vigilantes and Vigilance Committees." *Handbook of Texas Online.* Accessed June 15, 2010. http://www.tshaonline.org/handbook/online/articles/jnv01.

Garrett, T. H. *A History of the Saluda Baptist Association.* Richmond, Va.: F. B. Johnson, 1896.

Garver, Lois A. "Benjamin Rush Milam." *Southwestern Historical Quarterly* 38 (1934): 79–121, 177–202.

Gelo, Daniel J. "'Comanche Land and Ever Has Been': A Native Geography of the Nineteenth-Century Comancheria." *Southwestern Historical Quarterly* 103 (2000): 273–307.

General Laws of the State of Texas Passed by the Forty-First Legislature at the Fifth Called Session. Austin: Baldwin & Son, 1930.

General Laws of the State of Texas Passed by the Thirty-Third Legislature. Austin: Von Boeckmann-Jones, 1913.

Gesick, E. John, Jr. "The 1855 Callahan Raid into Mexico: Pursuing Indians or Hunting Slaves?" *Journal of Big Bend Studies* 19 (2007): 47–64.

———. *Under the Live Oak Tree: A History of Seguin.* Seguin, Tex.: Tommy Brown, 1995.

———, and Seguin-Guadalupe County Heritage Museum. *Seguin and Guadalupe County.* Images of America series. Charleston, S.C.: Arcadia, 2010.

Geue, Chester W., and Ethel Hander Geue. *A New Land Beckoned: German Immigration to Texas, 1844–1847.* Waco, Tex.: Texian, 1966.

Gibson, Campbell, and Kay Jung. *Historical Census Statistics on Population Totals by Race, 1790 to 1990, and by Hispanic Origin, 1790 to 1990, for the United States, Regions, Divisions, and States.* Washington, D.C: Census Bureau, 2002.

Gilchrist, Gibb. "Kemp, Louis Wiltz." *Handbook of Texas Online.* Accessed June 15, 2010. http://www.tshaonline.org/handbook/online/articles/fke15.

Gillespie, Zelime Vance. "Tobin, William Gerard." *Handbook of Texas Online.* Accessed June 15, 2010. http://www.tshaonline.org/handbook/online/articles/fto04.

Gish, Theodore. *The Diary of Hermann Seele and Seele's Sketches from Texas: Pioneer, Civic and Cultural Leader, German-Texan Writer-Translator*. Austin: German-Texan Heritage Society, 1995.

Glenn, Frankie Davis. *Capt'n John: Story of a Texas Ranger*. Austin: Nortex, 1991.

Goar, J. C. "Bloody Times in Blanco County." *Frontier Times* 6, no. 11 (1929): 446–47.

Goetzmann, William H. *Army Exploration in the American West, 1803–1863*. Austin: Texas State Historical Association, 1991.

Gonzales County Historical Commission. *The History of Gonzales County, Texas*. Dallas: Curtis Media, 1986.

González Milea, Alejandro. "Entre Arcadia y planeación ideal (1848–1869): Poblamiento o colonización del norte mexicano." *Cultura Científica y Tecnológica* 43–44 (2011): 42–52.

———. "Las ideas de Emilio Langberg sobre colonias militares en el siglo XIX." *Meibró: Revista de Investigaciones Históricas* 5, no. 9 (2015): 127–41.

Gould, Lewis L. *Alexander Watkins Terrell*. Austin: University of Texas Press, 2004.

Gracy, Alice Duggan. "Pitts, John Drayton." *Handbook of Texas Online*. Accessed June 15, 2010. http://www.tshaonline.org/handbook/online/articles/fpi26.

Graham, Paul K. *Georgia Land Lottery Research*. Atlanta: Georgia Genealogical Society, 2010.

Gray, William Fairfax. *From Virginia to Texas, 1835, and a Second Journey to Texas in 1837*. Houston: Fletcher Young, 1965.

Green, Rena Maverick, ed., *Samuel Maverick, Texan: 1803–1870; A Collection of Letters, Journals and Memoirs*. San Antonio: Rena Maverick Green, 1952.

Greer, James Kimmins. *Colonel Jack Hays: Texas Frontier Leader and California Builder*. College Station: Texas A&M University Press, 1987.

Gregg, Josiah. *Diary and Letters of Josiah Gregg, Southwestern Enterprises, 1840–1847*. Edited by Maurice Garland Fulton. Norman: University of Oklahoma Press, 1941.

Gretchen, Mark. *Slave Transactions of Guadalupe County, Texas*. Santa Maria, Calif.: Janaway, 2009.

Griffin, Roger A. "Connecticut Yankee in Texas: A Biography of Elisha Marshall Pease." PhD diss., University of Texas, 1973.

Groneman, Bill. "Kimble, George C." *Handbook of Texas Online*. Accessed June 15, 2010. http://www.tshaonline.org/handbook/online/articles/fki10.

Guadalupe Regional Foundation. *Evolution of the Guadalupe Regional Medical Center*. Seguin, Tex.: Guadalupe Regional Medical Center, 2010.

Guerra, Michael. "Henry, William R." *Handbook of Texas Online*. Accessed June 15, 2010. http://www.tshaonline.org/handbook/online/articles/fhehg.

Gulick, Charles Adams, Katherine Elliot, Winnie Allen, and Harriet Smither, eds. *The Papers of Mirabeau Buonaparte Lamar*. 6 vols. Austin: A. C. Baldwin, 1921–27.

Guthrie, Keith. *Raw Frontier: Armed Conflict Along the Texas Coastal Bend*. 2 vols. Austin: Eakin, 2000.

Haas, Oscar. *History of New Braunfels and Comal County, Texas, 1844–1946*. Austin: Steck, 1968.

Hale, Duane K. "Ralph A. Smith: Gentleman, Educator, Scholar." *West Texas Historical Association Yearbook* 72 (1996): 177–92.

Haley, J. Evetts, ed. *The Diary of Michael Erskine, Describing His Cattle Drive from Texas to California Together with Correspondence from the Gold Fields, 1954–1859*. Midland, Tex.: Nita Stewart Haley Memorial Library, 1979.

Hall, Dovie Tschirhart. "Taylor, Creed." *Handbook of Texas Online*. Accessed June 15, 2010. http://www.tshaonline.org/handbook/online/articles/fta17.

Hallstein, Anna. "Bailey's Prairie, TX." *Handbook of Texas Online*. Accessed June 12, 2010. http://www.tshaonline.org/handbook/online/articles/hlb03.

———. "Brazoria, TX." *Handbook of Texas Online*. Last modified on May 1, 2019. http://www.tshaonline.org/handbook/online/articles/hgb10.

Hamilton, Lester. *Goliad Survivor: Isaac D. Hamilton*. San Antonio: Naylor, 1971.

Hanahan, Hardin Davant. *A Place in History: The Davant Family*. Columbia, S. C.: R. L. Bryan, 1972.

Handbook of Texas Online. "Burleson, Edward, Jr." Last modified on July 5, 2016. "http://www.tshaonline.org/handbook/online/articles/fbu41.

———. "Gaines Ferry." Accessed June 15, 2010. http://www.tshaonline.org/handbook/online/articles/rtg01.

Hardeman, Nicholas Perkins. *Wilderness Calling: The Hardeman Family in the American Westward Movement, 1850–1900*. Knoxville: University of Tennessee Press, 1977.

Hardeman County Historical Commission. *Hardeman County Historical Sketches*. Dallas: Taylor, 1979.

Hardin, Stephen L. "Plácido Benavides: Fighting Texas Federalist." In de la Teja, Tejano Leadership, 56-74.

———. "Texana, TX." *Handbook of Texas Online*. Accessed June 15, 2010. http://www.tshaonline.org/handbook/online/articles/hvt22.

Hardinge, Sarah Ann Lillie. *Views of Texas, 1852–1856: Watercolors by Sarah Ann Lillie Hardinge*. Introduction and captions by Ron Tyler. Fort Worth: Amon Carter Museum, 1988.

Hartley, Oliver C. *Reports of Cases Argued and Decided in the Supreme Court of the State of Texas*. Texas Reports, vols. 4, 5, 7, 9, 13. Houston: E. H. Cushing. Reprint, St. Louis: Gilbert Book, 1876, 1883.

Hartmann, Clinton P. "Fannin, James Walker, Jr." *Handbook of Texas Online*. Last modified June 30, 2016. http://www.tshaonline.org/handbook/online/articles/ffa02.

Hays, Louise M., comp. *Georgia Military Affairs*. 9 vols. Atlanta: Department of Archives and History, 1940.

Hazlewood, Claudia. "Fisher, George." *Handbook of Texas Online*. Accessed June 12, 2010. http://www.tshaonline.org/handbook/online/articles/ffi16.

———. "Troutman, Joanna." *Handbook of Texas Online*. Last modified Feb. 11, 2011. http://www.tshaonline.org/handbook/online/articles/ftr13.

Heitman, Francis B. *Historical Register and Dictionary of the United States Army, from Its Organization, September 29, 1789, to March 2, 1903*. 3 vols. Washington, D.C.: Government Printing Office, 1903.

Hendrix, Don. "Johnson, Francis White." *Handbook of Texas Online*. Last modified Mar. 23, 2016. https://tshaonline.org/handbook/online/articles/fjo10.

Henson, Margaret Swett. *Anglo-American Women in Texas, 1820–1850*. Boston: American Press, 1982.

Herring, Patricia Roche. *General José Cosme Urrea: His Life and Times, 1797–1849*. Spokane, Wash.: Arthur H. Clark, 1995.

Hill, Joseph J. *The History of Warner's Ranch and Its Environs*. Los Angeles: privately published, 1927.

Hines, Karen. *The Life of Eli Clemmons Hinds*. Converse, Tex.: self-published, 2009. Copy at Blanco County Library, Blanco, Tex.

"History of Prairie Lea." *Plum Creek Almanac* 4, no. 1 (1986) 47–48.

History of Texas, Together with a Biographical History of Tarrant and Parker Counties. Chicago: Lewis, 1895.

Hitz, Alex M. "Georgia Militia Districts." *Georgia Bar Journal* 18 (1956): 283–91.

Hogan, William Ransom. *The Texas Republic: A Social and Economic History*. Norman: University of Oklahoma Press, 1946.

Holley, Mary Austin. *Mary Austin Holley: The Texas Diary, 1835–1838*. Edited by James Perry Bryan. Austin: University of Texas Press, 1965.

———. *Texas*. Lexington, Ky.: J. Clarke, 1836. Reprint, Austin: Texas State Historical Association, 1990.

Hoover, Mildred Brooke, and Douglas E. Kyle. *Historic Spots in California*. Stanford, Calif.: Stanford University Press, 1990.

Horton, H. G. "Old Seguin Church." *Texas Methodist Historical Quarterly* 2 (1910): 165–66.

House Journal of the 10th Legislature Regular Session of the State of Texas. Edited by James M. Day. Waco, Tex.: Texian, 1965.

Houston, Thomas. *Thomas H. Crosby: A Soldier of Misfortune*. Dallas: self-published, 1988.

Hunter, J. Marvin. *Pioneer History of Bandera County*. Bandera, Tex.: Hunter's Printing House, 1922.

Huson, Hobart. "Norton, Milford Phillips." *Handbook of Texas Online*. Accessed June 15, 2010. http://www.tshaonline.org/handbook/online/articles/fno12.

———. *Refugio: A Comprehensive History of Refugio County from Aboriginal Times to 1953*. Woodsboro, Tex.: Rooke Foundation, 1953.

Huxford, Folks. *Pioneers of Wiregrass Georgia*. Adel, Ga.: Patton, 1951.

Isbell, George P. "Mitchell, Asa." *Handbook of Texas Online*. Accessed June 15, 2010. http://www.tshaonline.org/handbook/online/articles/fmi51.

Jackson, Jack, ed. *Almonte's Texas*. Austin: Texas State Historical Association, 2003.

———. *Los Mesteños: Spanish Ranching in Texas, 1721–1821*. College Station: Texas A&M University Press, 1986.

Jackson, Mattie. *The Rise and Setting of the Lone Star Republic*. San Antonio: self-published, 1926.

James, Vinton Lee. *Frontier and Pioneer Recollections of Early Days in San Antonio and West Texas*. San Antonio: Artes Graficas, 1938.

"James Hughes Callahan." Texas State Cemetery. http://www.cemetery.state.tx.us/pub/user_form.asp?pers_id=46.

Jarrett, T. W. "Reminiscence of T. W. Jarrett as Jefferson Was in the Early Sixties of the 19th Century." *Jefferson County Historical Society News* 9, no. 3 (2002): 1–8.

Jasinski, Laurie E. "Cooley, Albert O. [A.O.]" *Handbook of Texas Online*. Last modified Feb. 24, 2015.h ttp://www.tshaonline.org/handbook/online/articles/fcolu.

———. "Curry's Creek Settlement." *Handbook of Texas Online*. Accessed June 12, 2010. http://www.tshaonline.org/handbook/online/articles/hvcbh.

Jenkins, John H., and Kenneth Kesselus. *Edward Burleson: Texas Frontier Leader*. Austin: Eakin, 1990.

Jenkins, John H., ed. *The Papers of the Texas Revolution, 1835–1836*. 10 vols. Austin: Presidial, 1973.

Jenkins, John Holland. *Recollections of Early Texas: The Memoirs of John Holland Jenkins*. Edited by John Holmes Jenkins III. Austin: University of Texas Press, 1958.

Jennette, Elizabeth LeNoir, *Biographical Directory of the Texan Conventions and Congress, 1832–1845*. Austin: State of Texas, 1941.
Johnson, Frank W. *A History of Texas and Texans*. Edited by Eugene C. Barker. 5 vols. Chicago: American Historical Society, 1914.
Johnson, R. W. *A Soldier's Reminiscences in Peace and War.* Philadelphia: J. B. Lippincott, 1886.
Jonas, Donna Doring. *Kendalia: A History of the Settlement, 1847–1957*. 2 vols. Kendalia, Tex.: Kendalia Public Library, 2012.
Jones, Billy M. "Health Seekers in Early Anglo-American Texas." *Southwestern Historical Quarterly* 69 (1965): 287–99.
Jones, C. Allan. *Texas Roots: Agriculture and Rural Life before the Civil War*. College Station: Texas A&M University Press, 2005.
Jones, Fred Riley. "San Antonio Prisoners: the True Story of the Invasion of San Antonio and the Imprisonment of Its Citizens." *San Antonio Lawyer* (Mar.–Apr. 2008): 8–14.
Jordan, Terry G. "A Century and a Half of Ethnic Change in Texas." *Southwestern Historical Quarterly* 89 (1986): 385–422.
———. *German Seed in Texas Soil: Immigrant Farmers in Nineteenth-Century Texas*. Austin: University of Texas Press, 1966.
———. *Log Cabin Village: A History and Guide*. Austin: Texas State Historical Association, 1980.
———. *North American Cattle-Ranching Frontiers: Origins, Diffusion, and Differentiation*. Albuquerque: University of New Mexico Press, 1993.
———. "Pioneer Evaluation of Vegetation in Frontier Texas." *Southwestern Historical Quarterly* (1973): 233–54.
Jordan, Terry G., and Alyson L. Greiner, eds. "The Texas Travel Diary of Henry H. Field." *Southwestern Historical Quarterly* 99 (1996): 351–68.
Journal of the House of Representatives of the Second Legislature of the State of Texas. Houston: Telegraph Office, 1848.
Journal of the House of Representatives of the State of South Carolina. Columbia, S.C.: A. M. Pemberton, 1842, 1844.
Journal of the House of Representatives of the State of Texas: 5th Legislature. Austin: J. W. Hampton, 1853.
Journal of the House of Representatives of the State of Texas: 12th Legislature. Austin: J. G Tracy, 1871.
Journal of the Reconstruction Convention, Which Met at Austin, Texas, June 1, A.D. 1868. Austin: Tracy, Siemering, 1870.
Journal of the Senate of the State of South Carolina. Columbia: A. M. Pemberton, 1844.
Journal of the Senate of the State of Texas: 6th Legislature. Austin: Marshall & Oldham, 1855.
Journal of the Senate of Texas of the Second Called Session of the Thirty-third Legislature. Austin: Von Boeckmann-Jones, 1914.
Journals of the House of Representatives of the Republic of Texas: Fifth Congress, First Session, 1840–1841. Austin: Cruger and Wing, 1841.
Journals of the House of Representatives of the Seventh Congress of the Republic of Texas. Washington, Tex.: Thomas Johnson, 1843.
Journals of the Senate of the Seventh Congress of the Republic of Texas. Washington, Tex.: Thomas Johnson, 1843.

Kalteyer, Charles F. "Kalteyer, George Henry." *Handbook of Texas Online*. Accessed June 15, 2010. http://www.tshaonline.org/handbook/online/articles/fkamm.

Kayser, Grace A., comp. "King–Ranger Cemetery #85." Apr. 1999. TXGenWeb Project, Guadalupe County. http://www.txgenweb2.org/txguadalupe/cem/king/king2.html.

Keehn, David C. *Knights of the Golden Circle: Secret Empire, Southern Secession, Civil War*. Baton Rouge: Louisiana State University Press, 2013.

Kellar, Herbert A., ed. "A Journey Through the South in 1836: Diary of James D. Davidson." *Journal of Southern History* 1 (1935): 345–77.

Kemp, Louis W. "A Blanco County Tragedy." *Frontier Times* 11, no. 9 (1934): 412–16.

———. "Pettus, Edward Cratic." Herzstein Library, San Jacinto Museum. https://www.sanjacinto-museum.org/Library/Veteran_Bios/Bio_page/?id=665&army=Texian.

———. "Veteran Biographies," Herzstein Library, San Jacinto. https://www.sanjacinto-museum.org/Library/Veteran_Bios/.

Kennedy, Joseph C. G., comp. *Population of the United States of 1860; Compiled from the Original Returns of the Eighth Census*. Washington, D.C.: Government Printing Office, 1864.

———. *Preliminary Report on the Eighth Census, 1860*. Washington, D.C.: Government Printing

Kilpatrick, William H. "The Beginnings of the Public School System in Georgia." *Georgia Historical Quarterly* 5 (1921): 3–19.

King, C. Richard. *James Clinton Neill: The Shadow Commander of the Alamo*. Austin: Eakin, 2002.

"King Family Bible (transcript)." *Yesterdays* 17, no. 2 (1983): 46–49.

Kishbaugh, William G. "Henry B. King–Texas Ranger, 1818–1868." 2002. Sons of Dewitt Colony Texas. http://www.sonsofdewittcolony.org/kinghenryb.htm.

Klein, Rachel D. *Unification of a Slave State: The Rise of the Planter Class in the South Carolina Backcountry, 1760–1808*. Chapel Hill: University of North Carolina Press, 1990.

Koch, Mary Wilcox. "Sneed, Sebron Graham." *Handbook of Texas Online*. Accessed June 15, 2010. http://www.tshaonline.org/handbook/online/articles/fsn01.

Kohout, Martin Donell. "Magoffin, James Wiley." *Handbook of Texas Online*. Accessed June 15, 2010. http://www.tshaonline.org/handbook/online/articles/fma13.

Koury, Michael J. *Arms for Texas*. Fort Collins, Colo.: Old Army Press, 1973.

Lackman, Howard. "Howard, George Thomas." *Handbook of Texas Online*. Accessed June 15, 2010. http://www.tshaonline.org/handbook/online/articles/fho77.

Lambert, Alan. *History of Tuscaloosa County*. 2 vols. Centre, Ala.: Stewart University Press, 1977.

Landa, Harry. *As I Remember*. San Antonio: Carlton, 1945.

Lander, Ernest M., Jr. "General Waddy Thompson: A Friend of Mexico during the Mexican War." *South Carolina Historical Magazine* 78 (1977): 32–42.

Lane, Lydia Spencer. *I Married a Soldier*. Philadelphia: J. B. Lippincott, 1893.

Larson, Wendy Ann. "A History of Divorce in Texas." Master's thesis, Texas A&M University, 1986.

Lathrop, Barnes F. "Texas vs. Louisiana, 1849." Notes and Documents. *Southwestern Historical Quarterly* 50 (1949): 93–97.

La Vere, David. *The Texas Indians*. College Station: Texas A&M University Press, 2004.

Lee, Nelson. *Three Years Among the Camanches: The Narrative of Nelson Lee, the Texan Ranger*. Albany, N.Y.: Baker Taylor, 1859.

———. *Three Years Among the Comanches: The Narrative of Nelson Lee, the Texan Ranger.* Foreword by Gary Clayton Anderson. Norman: University of Oklahoma Press, 1991.

Leffler, John, revised by Brett J. Derbes. "English, Levi." *Handbook of Texas Online.* Last modified Mar. 20, 2018. http://www.tshaonline.org/handbook/online/articles/fen13.

———. "La Grange, TX." *Handbook of Texas Online.* Accessed June 15, 2010. http://www.tshaonline.org/handbook/online/articles/hgl02.

Lich, Glen E. "Sansom, John William." *Handbook of Texas Online.* Accessed June 15, 2010. http://www.tshaonline.org/handbook/online/articles/fsa28.

Linn, John J. *Fifty Years in Texas.* Austin: State House Press, 1986.

Lloyd, James T. *Lloyd's Steamboat Directory.* Cincinnati: James T. Lloyd, 1856.

Loflin, Brian, and Shirley Loflin. *Grasses of the Texas Hill Country.* College Station: Texas A&M University Press, 2006.

Long, Edith Harriette. "Tom, John Files." *Handbook of Texas Online.* Accessed June 15, 2010. http://www.tshaonline.org/handbook/online/articles/fto13.

———. "Tom, William." *Handbook of Texas Online.* Accessed June 15, 2010. http://www.tshaonline.org/handbook/online/articles/fto14.

Longnecker, Julia Ward. "A Road Divided: From Memphis to Little Rock through the Great Mississippi Swamp." *Arkansas Historical Quarterly* 44 (1985): 203–19.

Longstreet, A. B. *Georgia Scenes, Characters, Incidents, &c., in the First Half Century of the Republic.* New York: Sagamore, 1957.

Loomis, Noel M. *The Texan–Santa Fé Pioneers.* Norman: University of Oklahoma Press, 1958.

Los Angeles City Directory, 1887–8. N.p.: Smith & McPhee, 1887–88. Los Angeles Public Library. http://rescarta.lapl.org/ResCarta-Web/jsp/RcWebBrowse.jsp.

Lowe, Richard G., and Randolph B. Campbell. *Planters and Plain Folks: Agriculture in Antebellum Texas.* Dallas: Southern Methodist University Press, 1987.

Lowry, Robert, and William H. McCardle. *A History of Mississippi from the Discovery of the Great River.* Jackson, Miss.: R. H. Henry, 1891.

Lubbock, Francis Richard. *Six Decades in Texas; or, Memoirs of Francis Richard Lubbock.* Edited by C. W. Raines. Austin: Ben C. Jones, 1900.

Lukes, Edward A. "DeWitt, Green." *Handbook of Texas Online.* Accessed June 12, 2010. http://www.tshaonline.org/handbook/online/articles/fde55.

Lundy, Benjamin. *The Life, Travels and Opinions of Benjamin Lundy.* Philadelphia: William D. Parrish, 1847.

MacKinnon, William P., ed. *At Sword's Point, Part 2: A Documentary History of the Utah War, 1858–1859.* Kingdom in the West: The Mormons and the American Frontier series, vol. 11. Norman: University of Oklahoma Press, 2016.

Madray, I. C. *A History of Bee County with Some Brief Sketches about Men and Events in Adjoining Counties.* Beeville, Tex.: Bee-Picayune, 1939.

Malone, Ann Patton. *Women on the Texas Frontier: A Cross-Cultural Perspective.* El Paso: Texas Western Press, 1983.

Manning, William R., ed. *Diplomatic Correspondence of the United States, Inter-American Affairs, 1831–1860.* 12 vols. Washington, D.C.: Carnegie Endowment for International Peace, 1937.

Marmion, Bob. *A Texas Soldier & Marine during the Civil War, 1861–1865.* Melbourne, Australia: self-published, 1985.

Marrin, Richard B., and Lorna Geer Sheppard. *The Paradise of Texas: Clarksville and Red River County, 1846–1860*. Westminster, Md.: Heritage Books, 2007.

Marten, James A. "Hamilton, Andrew Jackson." *Handbook of Texas Online*. Accessed June 15, 2010. http://www.tshaonline.org/handbook/online/articles/fha33.

Martin, Mabelle Eppard, ed. "From Texas to California in 1849: Diary of C. C. Cox," *Southwestern Historical Quarterly* 29 (1925): 36–50, 128–46, 201–23.

Matovina, Timothy M. *Tejano Religion and Ethnicity: San Antonio, 1821–1860*. Austin: University of Texas Press, 1995.

Maverick, Mary A., and George Madison Maverick. *Memoirs of Mary A. Maverick*. Edited by Rena Maverick Green. Lincoln: University of Nebraska Press, 1989.

Maxey, H. David, comp. "Index to Military Rolls of the Republic of Texas, 1835–1845." TSHA Online. 2008. http://www.tshaonline.org/supsites/military/rep_cont.htm.

Maxson, Gayle. *Cottage Hill Cemetery, Collin County, Texas*. Decorah, Iowa: Anundsen, 2004.

May, Robert E. *Manifest Destiny's Underworld: Filibustering in Antebellum America*. Chapel Hill: University of North Carolina Press, 2002.

McCabe, Alice Smythe. *Gwinnett County, Georgia, Families, 1818–1968*. Atlanta: Cherokee Publishing, 1980.

McCaslin, Richard B. *Fighting Stock: John S. "Rip" Ford of Texas*, Fort Worth: Texas Christian University Press, 2011.

———. "Sutherland, John, Jr." *Handbook of Texas Online*. Accessed June 15, 2010. http://www.tshaonline.org/handbook/online/articles/fsu07.

McComb, David. *Galveston: A History*. Austin: University of Texas Press, 1986.

McCormick, Andrew Phelps. *Scotch-Irish in Ireland and in America*. N.p.: self-published, 1897. Microform at Texas Christian University, Fort Worth, Tex.

McCroskey, Vista K. "San Augustine, TX (San Augustine County)." *Handbook of Texas Online*. Accessed June 15, 2010. http://www.tshaonline.org/handbook/online/articles/hgs01.

McCutchan, Joseph D. *Mier Expedition Diary: A Texan Prisoner's Account*. Edited by Joseph Milton Nance. Austin: University of Texas Press, 1978.

McDonald, Archie P. "Nacogdoches, TX," *Handbook of Texas Online*. Accessed June 15, 2010. https://tshaonline.org/handbook/online/articles/hdn01.

McDonald, David. *José Antonio Navarro: In Search of the American Dream in Nineteenth Century Texas*. Denton: Texas State Historical Association, 2010.

McGowen, Stanley S. *Horse Sweat and Powder Smoke: The First Texas Cavalry in the Civil War*. College Station: Texas A&M University Press, 1999.

McGuire, James Patrick. *Iwonski in Texas: Painter and Citizen*. San Antonio: San Antonio Museum Association, 1976.

McKeehan, Wallace L., comp. "Tinney." Sons of DeWitt Colony. http://www.sonsofdewittcolony.org/dewittbios3.htm#tinney.

McKinney, Jack R. "Redfield, Henry Prentice." *Handbook of Texas Online*. Accessed June 15, 2010. http://www.tshaonline.org/handbook/online/articles/fre13.

McLean, Malcolm Dallas. *Papers Concerning Robertson's Colony in Texas*. 19 vols. Fort Worth: Texas Christian University Press; Arlington: UTA Press, 1974–1993.

McWhiney, Grady. *Cracker Culture: Celtic Ways in the Old South*. Tuscaloosa: University of Alabama Press, 1988.

Medical and Surgical Register of the United States. Chicago: R. L. Polk, 1890.

Medina González Dávila, José. "La Batalla de Rio Escondido." *La Revista Militar Armas* 73 (2013): 36–41.

———. "'¡Pero es tan sólo un río . . .!' Las implicaciones del Río Bravo como binacional para los Kikapús y Apaches." *Antropología: Boletín Oficial del Instituto Nacional de Antropología e Historia* 88 (2010): 56–70.

Medina Peña, Luis. *Los bárbaros del Norte: Guardia Nacional y política en Nuevo León, siglo XIX*. Mexico City: Fondo de Cultura Económica, 2014.

Memorial and Genealogical Record of Southwest Texas. 1984. Reprint, Greenville, S.C.: Southern Historical Press, 1994.

"Mexico, 1868; Convention between the United States of America and the Republic of Mexico for the Adjustment of Claims, July 4, 1868." In U.S. Department of State, *Treaties and Conventions*, 581–84. Compiled with notes by J. C. Bancroft Davis. Washington D.C.: Government Printing Office, 1871.

"Mexico, 1871; Convention between the United States of America and the Republic of Mexico for Extension of the Duration of the Joint Commission for Settlement of Claims, April 19, 1871." In U.S. Department of State, *Treaties and Conventions*, 586–87.Compiled with notes by J. C. Bancroft Davis. Washington D.C.: Government Printing Office, 1871.

Miller, Adam. "Hopefield (Crittenden County)." *Encyclopedia of Arkansas*. http://encyclopediaofarkansas.net/encyclopedia/entry-detail.aspx?entryID=5602.

Miller, Aragorn Storm. "McKee, James F." *Handbook of Texas Online*. Last modified Oct. 26, 2010. http://www.tshaonline.org/handbook/online/articles/fmchf.

Miller, Edward L. *New Orleans and the Texas Revolution*. College Station: Texas A&M University Press, 2004.

Miller, Katherine P. "Alsbury, Thomas." *Handbook of Texas Online*. Accessed June 9, 2010. http://www.tshaonline.org/handbook/online/articles/fal50.

Miller, Susan A. *Coacoochee's Bones*. Lawrence: University of Kansas Press, 2003.

Miller, Thomas Lloyd. *Bounty and Donation Land Grants, 1835–1888*. Austin: University of Texas Press, 1967.

———. "Fannin's Men: Some Additions to Earlier Rosters." *Southwestern Historical Quarterly* 61, no. 4 (1958): 522–32.

———. *The Public Lands of Texas*. Norman: University of Oklahoma Press, 1972.

Mills, Robert. *Statistics of South Carolina*. Charleston, S.C.: Hurlbut and Lloyd, 1826.

Minor, David. "Throckmorton, James Webb." *Handbook of Texas Online*. Accessed June 15, 2010. http://www.tshaonline.org/handbook/online/articles/fth36.

Minor, Nancy McGown. *Turning Adversity to Advantage: A History of the Lipan Apaches of Texas and Northern Mexico, 1700–1900*. New York: University Press of America, 2009.

Minton, John. "Leakey, Texas." *Handbook of Texas Online*. Accessed June 15, 2010. http://www.tshaonline.org/handbook/online/articles/hll27.

Mock, Shirley Boteler. *Dreaming with the Ancestors: Black Seminole Women in Texas and Mexico*. Norman: University of Oklahoma Press, 2010.

Moellering, Arwerd Max. "A History of Guadalupe County, Texas." Master's thesis, University of Texas, 1938.

Molbech, Oluf Christian. *General Langbergs Haendelser Fortalte I Breve Fra Ham Selv* [General Langberg's Events Told in Letters from Himself]. Copenhagen: Gyidendalske Boghandels Forlag, 1902.

Monday, Jane Clements, and Frances Brannen Vick. *Petra's Legacy: The South Texas Ranching Empire of Petra Vela and Mifflin Kenedy*. College Station: Texas A&M University Press, 2007.

Moneyhon, Carl H. "Davis, Edmund Jackson." *Handbook of Texas Online*. Accessed June 12, 2010. http://www.tshaonline.org/handbook/online/articles/fda37.

Moore, Ike, ed. *The Life and Diary of Reading W. Black*. Uvalde, Tex.: El Progresso Club, 1934.

Moore, Richard. "Swenson, Swante Magnus." *Handbook of Texas Online*. Accessed June 15, 2010. http://www.tshaonline.org/handbook/online/articles/fsw14.

Moore, Stephen L. *Savage Frontier, 1835–1845*. 4 vols. Denton: University of North Texas Press, 2002–2010.

Morgan, Cathy. "Ancestor Chart." *Plum Creek Almanac* 7 (1989): 139–40.

———, comp. "Family Tree of Jesse B. Green & his wife Sarah Ann Reed." In *Blanco County, Texas*. TXGenWeb Project. http://www.txgenwebcounties.org/blanco/jbgreen.htm.

Morgan, Paul. "Henry Bruemmer's Experience." *Frontier Times* 2, no. 7 (1925): 6–7.

Morrell, Zenos N. *Flower and Fruits in the Wilderness: Forty-Six Years in Texas and Two Winters in Honduras*. St. Louis: Commercial Printing, 1882.

Morris, Christopher. *Becoming Southern: The Evolution of a Way of Life, Warren County and Vicksburg, Mississippi, 1770–1860*. New York: Oxford University Press, 1995.

Moseley, Edward Holt. "The Public Career of Santiago Vidaurri, 1855–1858." PhD diss., University of Alabama, 1963.

Moursund, John Stribling. *Blanco County Families for One Hundred Years*. Burnet, Tex.: Nortex, 1981.

———. *Blanco County History*. Burnet, Tex.: Nortex, 1979.

Moursund, Mary Frances Stribling. *Stribling and Related Families*. Austin: Von Boeckmann-Jones, 1967.

Muckelroy, Duncan Glenn. "History of El Capote Ranch." *East Texas Historical Journal* 12 (1974): 3–21.

Muir, Andrew Forest. "State Cemetery." *Handbook of Texas Online*. Accessed June 15, 2010. http://www.tshaonline.org/handbook/online/articles/les02.

Mulroy, Kevin. *Freedom on the Border: The Seminole Maroons in Florida, the Indian Territory, Coahuila, and Texas*. Lubbock: Texas Tech University Press, 1993.

Muster Rolls of the Texas Revolution. Austin: Daughters of the Republic of Texas, 1986.

Nackman, Mark E. "The Making of the Texan Citizen Soldier." *Southwestern Historical Quarterly* 78 (1975): 231–53.

Nance, Joseph Milton. "Abel Morgan and His Account of the Battle of Goliad." *Southwestern Historical Quarterly* 100 (1996): 208–33.

———. *After San Jacinto: The Texas-Mexican Frontier, 1836–1842*. Austin: University of Texas Press, 1964.

———. *Attack and Counter-Attack: The Texas-Mexican Frontier, 1842*. Austin: University of Texas Press, 1964.

———. "Brigadier General Adrian Woll's Report of His Expedition into Texas in 1842." *Southwestern Historical Quarterly* 58 (1955): 523–52.

———. "Woll, Adrian." *Handbook of Texas Online*. Accessed June 15, 2010. http://www.tshaonline.org/handbook/online/articles/fwo03.

Neighbors, Kenneth F. "The Expedition of Major Robert S. Neighbors to El Paso in 1849." *Southwestern Historical Quarterly* 58 (1954): 33–59.

Neilson, George R. "Mathew Caldwell." *Southwestern Historical Quarterly* 64 (1960): 478–502.

News Items. *Southwestern Historical Quarterly* 16 (1913): 441.

Nichols, A. J. "From a Real Pioneer." *Frontier Times* 4, no. 9 (1925): 16.

Nichols, James David. *The Limits of Liberty: Mobility and the Making of the Eastern U.S.–Mexico Border*. Lincoln: University of Nebraska Press, 2018.

———. "The Line of Liberty: Runaway Slaves and Fugitive Peons in Texas-Mexico Borderlands." *Western Historical Quarterly* 44 (2013): 413–33.

Nichols, James Wilson. *Now You Hear My Horn*. Edited by Catherine M. McDowell. Austin: University of Texas Press, 1967.

Niemeyer, Stephanie P. "Benton, Nathaniel." *Handbook of Texas Online*. Accessed Mar. 17, 2011. http://www.tshaonline.org/handbook/online/articles/fbebu.

Nixon, Pat Ireland. "Field, Joseph E." *Handbook of Texas Online*. Accessed June 12, 2010. https://tshaonline.org/handbook/online/articles/ffi02

———. *The Medical Story of Early Texas*. San Antonio: Mollie Bennett Lupe Memorial Fund, 1946.

Norvell, James R. "The Reconstruction Courts of Texas, 1867–1873." *Southwestern Historical Quarterly* 62 (1958): 141–63.

Oberste, William H. *History of Refugio Mission*. Refugio, Tex.: Refugio Timely Remarks, 1942.

O'Connor, Kathryn Stoner. *The Presidio La Bahia del Espiritu Santo de Zuniga, 1721 to 1846*. Austin: Von Boeckmann-Jones, 1966.

Odintz, Mark. "Bullock, Uriah Irwin," *Handbook of Texas Online*. Accessed June 12, 2010. http://www.tshaonline.org/handbook/online/articles/fbupk.

———. "Patton, Samuel B." *Handbook of Texas Online*. Accessed June 15, 2010. http://www.tshaonline.org/handbook/online/articles/fpaea.

Olmsted, Frederick Law. *A Journey through Texas*. Austin: University of Texas Press, 1982.

150 Years Faith Celebration, 1851–2001: Sesquicentennial First Baptist Church. Seguin, Tex.: First Baptist Church, 2001.

Ornish, Natalie. *Ehrenberg: Goliad Survivor, Old West Explorer*. Dallas: Texas Heritage Press, 1997.

Owens, Elizabeth McAnulty. *Elizabeth McAnulty Owens: The Story of Her Life*. Whitefish, Mont.: Kessinger, 2010.

Owens, Loulie Latimer. *Taproot of the South Carolina Baptist Back Country: Fairforest Baptist Church*. Greenville, S.C.: A Press, 1980.

Parker, A. A. *Trip to the West and Texas*. Concord, N.H.: White and Fisher, 1835.

Parker, Nancy Boothe, ed. Notes and Documents. "Mirabeau B. Lamar's Texas Journal." *Southwestern Historical Quarterly* 84, no. 2 (1980): 197–220.

Patterson, Donald L., and Miranda "Nax'ce" Allen. *Tickanwa-tic: Informational Guide to the History and Culture of the Tonkawa Tribe*. Tonkawa Tribe of Oklahoma. http://www.tonkawatribe.com/Tonkawa%20Museum%20Booklet.pdf.

Paulsen, James W. "The Missing Cases of the Republic" *Texas Law Review* 65 (1986): 372–415.

———. "A Short History of the Supreme Court of the Republic of Texas." *Texas Law Review* 65 (1986): 237–303.

Pease, S. W. "Lacoste, Jean Batiste." *Handbook of Texas Online*. Accessed June 15, 2010. http://www.tshaonline.org/handbook/online/articles/fla10.

———. "Sweet, James R." *Handbook of Texas Online*. Accessed June 15, 2010. http://www.tshaonline.org/handbook/online/articles/fsw11.

Peterson, Dorothy Burns. *Daughters of the Republic of Texas Patriot Ancestor Index*. Paducah, Ky.: Turner, 1995.

Pharr, Henry Newton. *Pharrs and Farrs, with Other Descendants from Five Scottish-Irish Pioneers in America*. New Orleans: self-published, 1955.

Phelan, Macum. *A History of Early Methodism in Texas, 1817–1866*. Nashville: Cokesbury, 1924.

Pierce, Gerald Swetnam. *Texas Under Arms: The Camps, Posts, Forts, & Military Towns of the Republic of Texas, 1836–1846*. Austin: Encino, 1969.

Pingenot, Ben E. "Eagle Pass, TX." *Handbook of Texas Online*. Accessed June 12, 2010. http://www.tshaonline.org/handbook/online/articles/hee01.

———. "Paso del Águila." *Handbook of Texas Online*. Accessed June 15, 2010. http://www.tshaonline.org/handbook/online/articles/rkp21.

———. "The Piedras Negras Claims." TS, n.d.

———. "Sumpter, Jesse." *Handbook of Texas Online*. Accessed June 15, 2010. https://tshaonline.org/handbook/online/articles/fsu05.

Pitts, Alice Ellison, and Minnie Pitts Champ. *Collin County, Texas, Families*. 2 vols. Fort Worth: Landmark, 1998.

Poland, Charles Preston, Jr. *From Frontier to Suburbia: Loudoun County, Virginia*. Westminster, Md.: Heritage Books, 2005.

Porter, Kenneth Wiggins. *The Black Seminoles: History of a Freedom Seeking-People*. Edited by Alcione M. Amos and Thomas P. Senter. Gainesville: University Press of Florida, 1996.

———. "Lament for Wild Cat." *Phylon* 4 (1943): 39–48.

———. *The Negro on the American Frontier*. New York: Arno Press and New York Times, 1971.

———. "Seminole in Mexico, 1850–1861." *Chronicles of Oklahoma* 29 (1951): 153–68.

———. "The Seminole in Mexico, 1850–1861." *Hispanic American Historical Review* 31 (1951): 1–36.

Pruitt, Francelle LeNaee. "'But a Mournful Remedy': Divorce in Two Texas Counties, 1841–1880." Master's thesis, University of North Texas, 1999.

Ramos, Raúl A. *Beyond the Alamo: Forging Mexican Ethnicity in San Antonio, 1821–1861*. Chapel Hill: University of North Carolina Press, 2008.

Rather, Ethel Zivley. "DeWitt's Colony." *Quarterly of the Texas State Historical Association* 8 (1904): 95–192.

Reid, John Coleman. *Reid's Tramp; or, a Journal of the Incidents of Ten Months Travel Through Texas, New Mexico, Arizona, Sonora, and California*. Selma, Ala.: John Hardy & Son, 1858.

Reid, Stuart. *The Secret War for Texas*. College Station: Texas A&M University Press, 2007.

Representative Men and Old Families of Southern Massachusetts. 2 vols. Chicago: J. H. Beers, 1912.

Republic Claims. Archives and Manuscripts. Texas State Library and Archives Commission. https://www.tsl.state.tx.us/apps/arc/repclaims/.

Ribb, Richard H. "Colony of Kent." *Handbook of Texas Online*. Accessed June 12, 2010. http://www.tshaonline.org/handbook/online/articles/uecvj.

Riley, Glenda. *Building and Breaking Families in the American West*. Albuquerque: University of New Mexico Press, 1996.

Robinson, Charles M., III. *Bad Hand: A Biography of General Ranald S. Mackenzie*. Austin: State House Press, 1993.

Robinson, Duncan W. *Judge Robert McAlpin: Williamson, Texas' Three-Legged Willie*. Austin: Texas State Historical Association, 1948.

Rodríguez García, Martha. *La guerra entre bárbaros y civilizados: El exterminio del nómada en Coahuila, 1840–1880*. Saltillo, Coah., Mexico: Centro de Estudios Sociales y Humanísticos, 1998.

———. *Historias de resistencia y exterminio: Los indios de Coahuila durante el siglo XIX*. Mexico City: CIESAS, 1995.

Roell, Craig H. "De León, Martín." *Handbook of Texas Online*. Accessed June 12, 2010. http://www.tshaonline.org/handbook/online/articles/fde08.

———. "Shackelford, Jack." *Handbook of Texas Online*. Accessed June 15, 2010. http://www.tshaonline.org/handbook/online/articles/fsh01.

———. "Ward, William." *Handbook of Texas Online*. Last modified Feb. 22, 2019.http://www.tshaonline.org/handbook/online/articles/fwa53.

Roemer, Ferdinand. *Roemer's Texas, 1845 to 1847*. Translated by Oswald Mueller. Austin: Eakin, 1995.

Roller, John E. "Capt. John Sowers Brooks." *Quarterly of the Texas State Historical Association* 9 (1906): 157–209.

Ross, John R. "Lynching." *Handbook of Texas Online*. Accessed June 15, 2010. http://www.tshaonline.org/handbook/online/articles/jgl01.

Rounsavall, Mark S., and Brian E. Rounsavill. *Richard Rounsaveil and His Descendants*. 2 vols. Saline, Mich.: McNaughton & Gunn, 2002.

Russell, W. R. "The Murder of Captain Callahan." *Hunter's Magazine* 1, no. 7 (1911): 22.

Russell, Yancey L. "Devine, Thomas Jefferson." *Handbook of Texas Online*. Accessed June 12, 2010. http://www.tshaonline.org/handbook/online/articles/fde50.

Ruthven, A. S. *Proceedings of the Grand Lodge of Texas, 1837–1857*. 2 vols. Galveston, Tex.: Richardson, 1857.

Sager, Robin C. "States of Suffering: Marital Cruelty in Antebellum Virginia, Texas, and Wisconsin," PhD diss., Rice University, 2012.

Sansom, John W. "Thrilling Life Story of a Gallant Texas Ranger." *Hunter's Magazine* 1, no. 5 (Mar. 1911): 8–10; no. 6 (Apr. 1911): 4, 17; no. 7 (May 1911), 9–10.

Santa Anna, Antonio López. *Manifiesto que de sus operaciones en la compaña de Tejas*. Vera Cruz: Liberal á cargo de Antonio Maria Valdez, 1837.

Santos, Richard. *Santa Anna's Campaign Against Texas, 1835–1836*. Salisbury, N.C.: Documentary Publications, 1982.

Sartain, James Alfred. *History of Walker County, Georgia*. Dalton, Ga.: A. J. Showalter, 1932.

"Sauer Family Cemetery, Moore Ranch, Blanco, Blanco County, Texas." In *Blanco County, Texas: Cemeteries*. TXGenWeb Project. http://www.txgenwebcounties.org/blanco/Cemeteries/sauer.html.

Scarborough, Annie Cecil. *The Pass of the Eagle: The Chaparral Region of Texas*. Austin: San Felipe, 1968.

Scarborough, Jewel Davis. "The Georgia Battalion in the Texas Revolution: A Critical Study." *Southwestern Historical Quarterly* 63 (1960): 511–32.

Schoen, Harold. "The Free Negro in the Republic of Texas." *Southwestern Historical Quarterly* 40 (1936): 85–113.

Schwartz, Rosalie. *Across the Rio to Freedom*. El Paso: Texas Western Press, 1975.

Seele, Hermann. *The Cypress and Other Writings of a German Pioneer in Texas*. Translated by Edward C. Breitenkamp. Austin: University of Texas Press, 1979.

Seguin, Juan N. *Personal Memoirs of John N. Seguin, from the year 1834 to the Retreat of General Woll from the City of San Antonio in 1842*. San Antonio: Ledger Book and Job Office, 1858.

Shearer, Ernest C. "The Callahan Expedition, 1855." *Southwestern Historical Quarterly* 54 (1951): 431–51.

Sheehan, James J. *German Liberalism in the Nineteenth Century*. Chicago: University of Chicago Press, 1978.

Simpson, Harold B. *Cry Comanche: The 2nd U.S. Cavalry in Texas, 1855–1861*. Hillsboro, Tex.: Hill Junior College Press, 1979.

Smith, Craig W. "Early History of La Vernia." *Guadalupe Valley Trails* 11 (1995): 15–18.

Smith, Daniel Scott, and Michael S. Hindus. "Premarital Pregnancy in America, 1640–1870: An Overview and Interpretation." *Journal of Interdisciplinary History* 5 (1975): 537–70.

Smith, F. Todd. *From Dominance to Disappearance: The Indians of Texas and the Near Southwest, 1786–1859*. Lincoln: University of Nebraska Press, 2005.

Smith, George Gilman. *The History of Georgia Methodism from 1786 to 1866*. Atlanta: A. B. Caldwell, 1913.

Smith, Julia Cauble. "Camp Hudson." *Handbook of Texas Online*. Accessed June 12, 2010. http://www.tshaonline.org/handbook/online/articles/qbc16.

Smith, Ophia D. "A Trip to Texas in 1855." *Southwestern Historical Quarterly* 59 (1955): 24–39.

Smith, Ralph A. "The Mamelukes of West Texas and Mexico." *West Texas Historical Association Yearbook* 39 (1963): 65–88.

Smith, Thomas Tyree. *Fort Inge: Sharps, Spurs, and Sabers on the Texas Frontier, 1849–1869*. Austin: Eakin, 1993.

———. *The Old Army in Texas*. Austin: Texas State Historical Association, 2000.

———. *The U.S. Army and the Texas Frontier Economy*. College Station: Texas A&M University Press, 1999.

———. "U.S. Army Combat Operations in the Indian Wars of Texas, 1849–1881." *Southwestern Historical Quarterly* 99 (1996): 501–31.

Smither, Harriet. *Journals of the Sixth Congress of the Republic of Texas, 1841–1842*. 4 vols. Austin: Capitol Printing, 1945.

Smithwick, Noah. *The Evolution of a State; or, Recollections of Old Texas Days*. Austin: University of Texas Press, 1990.

Sofge, Virginia. "San Marcos River Valley Settlement and a Place Called Prairie Lea." *Plum Creek Almanac* 27 (2009): 13–24.

"The Soils of Texas." *Southwestern Historical Quarterly* 61 (1957): 168–69.

Solms-Braunfels, Carl. *Voyage to North America, 1844–45: Prince Carl of Solms' Texas Diary of People, Places, and Events*. Translated by Wolfram M. Von-Maszewski. Denton: German-Texan Heritage Society and University of North Texas Press, 2000.

Sons of the Republic of Texas. *The Sons of the Republic of Texas*. Paducah, Ky.: Turner, 2001.

Sowell, A. J. History of Fort Bend County, Houston: W. H. Coyle, 1904.

———. *Life of "Big Foot" Wallace.* Austin: State House Press, 1989.

———. *Rangers and Pioneers of Texas.* Austin: State House Press, 1991.

———. *Texas Indian Fighters.* Austin: State House Press, 1986. Originally published as *Early Settlers and Indian Fighters of Southwest Texas* (Austin: Ben C. Jones, 1900).

Speer, John W. *A History of Blanco County.* Edited by Henry C. Armbruster. Austin: Pemberton, 1965.

Speer, William S., and John Henry Brown. *The Encyclopedia of the New West.* Marshall, Tex.: United States Biographical Publishing, 1881.

Spellman, Paul N. *Forgotten Texas Leader: Hugh McLeod and the Texas Santa Fe Expedition.* College Station: Texas A&M University, 1999.

Spurlin, Charles D. *Texas Veterans in the Mexican War: Muster Rolls of Texas Military Units.* Victoria, Tex.: Charles D. Spurlin, 1984.

———. *Texas Volunteers in the Mexican War.* Austin: Eakin, 1998.

Statutes at Large, 18 vols. Boston: Little Brown, 1845–1878.

Statutes at Large, Vols. 19, 35, Washington, D.C.: Government Printing Office, 1877, 1909.

Steen, Ralph W. "Analysis of the Work of the General Council, Provisional Government of Texas, 1835–1836." Pts. 1, 3. *Southwestern Historical Quarterly* 40 (1937): 309–33; 41 (1938): 324–48.

Stillman, J. D. B. *Wanderings in the Southwest in 1855.* Edited by Ron Tyler. Spokane, Wash.: Arthur H. Clark, 1990.

Stock, Barbara. "Prairie Lea, TX." *Handbook of Texas Online.* Accessed June 15, 2010. http://www.tshaonline.org/handbook/online/articles/hlp50.

Stovall, Frances, et al. *Clear Springs and Limestone Edges: A History of Sam Marcos and Hays County.* San Marcos, Tex.: Hays County Historical Commission, 1986.

Strickland, Rebecca Carolyn. *Religion and the State in Georgia in the Eighteenth Century.* New York: AMS, 1967.

Strom, Ann Miller. "Kyle, TX." *Handbook of Texas Online.* Accessed June 15, 2010. https://tshaonline.org/handbook/online/articles/hjk08.

Stulting, Tommie. "A Pioneer Woman and Her Family." *Plum County Almanac* 8, no. 1 (1990): 5–20.

Stuntz, Jean A. *Hers, His, and Theirs: Community Property Law in Spain and Early Texas.* Lubbock: Texas Tech University Press, 2005.

Sumpter, Jesse. "Life of Jesse Sumpter: The Oldest Citizen of Eagle Pass." Edited by Harry Warren. 1902. Unpublished typescript. Copy at Texas Christian University Library, Fort Worth, Tex.

———. *Paso del Águila.* Austin: Encino, 1969.

Sverdlik, Alan. "*Augusta Chronicle.*" *New Georgia Encyclopedia.* Last modified June 8, 2018. http://www.georgiaencyclopedia.org/articles/arts-culture/augusta-chronicle.

Talbot, Zora M. *Stringtown.* Corpus Christi, Tex.: University of Corpus Christi Press, 1961.

Taylor, Lonn W. "Furniture." *Handbook of Texas Online.* Accessed June 12, 2010. http://www.tshaonline.org/handbook/online/articles/lpf01.

Texas Adjutant General Service Records, 1836–1935. Texas State Library and Archives Commission. https://www.tsl.state.tx.us/arc/service/.

Texas Almanac for 1860. Galveston, Tex.: Galveston News, 1860.

Texas General Land Office. Land Grant Search. Archives and Records. https://s3.glo.texas.gov/glo/history/archives/land-grants/index.cfm.

Texas Legal Directory. Austin: Democratic State Office, 1877.

Texas Runaway Slave Project. East Texas Research Center. Stephen F. Austin State University. http://digital.sfasu.edu/cdm/landingpage/collection/RSP.

Texas State Cemetery website. http://www.cemetery.state.tx.us/search.asp.

Thaxton, Donna, C. Stanton Thaxton, and Carlton J. Thaxton, eds. *Georgia Indian Depredation Claims*. Americus, Ga.: Thaxton, 1988.

Thompson, Richard A. *Fort Duncan, Texas: Rock of the Rio Grande Line of Defense*. Austin: Nortex, 2004.

Thonhoff, Robert. "Texas and the American Revolution." *Southwestern Historical Quarterly* 98 (1995): 511–17.

Thrall, Homer S. *History of Methodism in Texas*. Houston: E. H. Cushing, 1872. Reprint, 2018.

Thurman, Melburn. "Nelson Lee and the Green Corn Dance: Data Selection Problems with Wallace and Hoebel's Study of the Comanches." *Plains Anthropologist* 27 (1982): 239–43.

"Ticknor's Company, First Regiment, Alabama, Volunteers for Texas Revolution." *Alabama Historical Quarterly* 19 (1957) 413–14.

Tiling, Moritz. *History of the German Element in Texas from 1820–1850*. Houston: Moritz Tiling, 1913.

Tise, Sammy. *Texas County Sheriffs*. Albuquerque, N.M.: Oakwood, 1989.

Townes, John C. "Sketch of the Development of the Judicial System in Texas. I." *Quarterly of the Texas State Historical Association* 2, no. 1 (1898): 29–53; "Sketch of the Development of the Judicial System in Texas. II"; no. 2 (1898): 134–51.

Townsend, Stephen A. *The Yankee Invasion of Texas*. College Station: Texas A&M University Press, 2006.

A Twentieth Century History of Southwest Texas. 2 vols. Chicago: Lewis, 1907.

Tyler, Ronnie C. "The Age of Cotton: Santiago Vidaurri and the Confederacy, 1861–1864." PhD diss., Texas Christian University, 1968.

———. "Callahan Expedition." *Handbook of Texas Online*. Last modified July 5, 2016. http://www.tshaonline.org/handbook/online/articles/qyc01.

———. "The Callahan Expedition of 1855: Indians or Negroes?" *Southwestern Historical Quarterly* 70 (April 1967): 574–85.

———. "Cotton on the Border, 1861–1865." *Southwestern Historical Quarterly* 73 (1970): 456–77.

———. "Fugitive Slaves in Mexico." *Journal of Negro History* 57 (1972): 1–12.

———. *Santiago Vidaurri and the Southern* Confederacy. Austin: Texas State Historical Association, 1973.

———. "Slave Owners and Runaway Slaves in Texas." Master's thesis, Texas Christian University, 1966.

Underwood, Ammon. "Journal of Ammon Underwood, 1834–1838." *Southwestern Historical Quarterly* 32 (1928): 124–51.

U.S. Department of the Interior. Bureau of Land Management. General Land Office Records. https://glorecords.blm.gov/search/default.aspx.

Urwitz, Marie Bennet. "Valentine Bennet." *Quarterly of the Texas State Historical Association* (1906): 145–56.

Utley, Robert M. *Lone Star Justice: The First Century of the Texas Rangers*. New York: Oxford University Press, 2002.

Vaughn, Marshall M. *A History of Lebanon Baptist Church and Community (1815–1936).* Anderson, S.C.: Lebanon Baptist Church, 1987.

Vigness, David M. "Arista, Mariano." *Handbook of Texas Online.* Accessed June 9, 2010. http://www.tshaonline.org/handbook/online/articles/far04.

Vizcaya Canales, Isidro. *Incursiones de indios al noreste en el México independente, 1821–1855.* Serie Orgullosamente bárbarous N. 5. Monterrey: Archivos General del Estado Nuevo León, 1995.

———. *Tierra de guerra viva: Invasión de los indios bárbaros al noreste de México, 1821–1885.* Monterrey: Academia de Investigaciones, 2001.

Wall, James A. *History of Davie County in the Forks of the Yadkin.* Spartanburg, S.C.: Reprint Company, 1969.

The War of the Rebellion: A Compilation of the Official Records of the Union and Confederate Armies. Ser. 1, 53 vols.; ser. 2, 8 vols.; ser. 3, 5 vols.; ser. 4, 4 vols. Washington, D.C.: Government Printing Office, 1880–1901.

Watkins, Clara. *Kerr County, Texas, 1856–1976.* Revised, bicentennial ed. Kerrville, Tex.: Hill Country Preservation Society, 1975. [Original ed. by Bob Bennett published as *Kerr County, Texas, 1856–1956.* San Antonio: Naylor, 1956.]

Watson, Don. "The Callahan–Blassingame Incident (April 7–April 14, 1856)." In *Blanco County, Texas: (Family Links) Blanco County Families; Blassingame Incident.* TXGenWeb Project. http://www.txgenwebcounties.org/blanco/blass.htm.

Watson, Don, and Ray Phillips, comps. "Family Tree of James Hughes Callahan." In *Blanco County, Texas: (Family Links) Blanco County Families; Capt. James Hughes Callahan.* TXGenWeb Project. http://www.txgenwebcounties.org/blanco/callahan.htm.

Weaver, Bobby D. *Castro's Colony: Empresario Development in Texas, 1842–1865.* College Station: Texas A&M University Press, 1985.

Webb, James, and Thomas H. Duval. *Reports of Cases Argued and Decided in the Supreme Court of the State of Texas.* Texas Reports, vol. 1. 1848. Reprint, St. Louis: Gilbert Book, 1881; vol. 2. Galveston, Tex.: News Office, 1849; vol. 3. 1851. Reprint, St. Louis: Gilbert Book, 1881.

Weber, David J. *The Spanish Frontier in North America.* New Haven, Conn.: Yale University Press, 2009.

Weinert, Willie Mae. *An Authentic History of Guadalupe County.* Seguin, Tex.: Seguin Conservation Society, 1976.

———. *Methodism in Seguin, 1841–1951.* Seguin, Tex.: First Methodist Church of Seguin, 1951.

Weir, Merle. "Bailey, James Briton." *Handbook of Texas Online.* Accessed June 12, 2010. http://www.tshaonline.org/handbook/online/articles/fba08.

Weiss, Harold J., Jr. "Hays, John Coffee." *Handbook of Texas Online.* Accessed Aug. 31, 2010. http://www.tshaonline.org/handbook/online/articles/fhabq.

———. "The Texas Rangers Revisited: Old Themes and New Viewpoints." *Southwestern Historical Quarterly* 97 (1994): 621–40.

Westfall, Douglas. *Girl Across Panama: New York to San Francisco in 1854; The Memoirs of Mary Jane Arnold.* Orange, Calif.: Paragon Agency, 2013.

Wharton, Clarence R. *Remember Goliad.* Glorieta, N.M.: Rio Grande Press, 1968.

Wheeler, Frances Scoggins Wheeler. *John Sallis and His Descendants As I Know Them.* Okeechobee, Fla.: self-published, 1993.

White, Gifford, ed. *1830 Citizens of Texas.* Austin: Eakin, 1983.

———, ed. *Texas Scholastics, 1854–55*. Austin: self-published, 1979.

Wilbarger, J. W. *Indian Depredations in Texas*. Austin: Hutchings, 1889.

Wilder, John B., rev. by Brett J. Derbes. "Sneed, Thomas Eskridge." *Handbook of Texas Online*. Accessed June 15, 2010. Modified May 4, 2020. http://www.tshaonline.org/handbook/online/articles/fsn03.

Wilkins, Frederick. *Defending the Borders: The Texas Rangers, 1848–1861*. Austin: State House Press, 2001.

———. *The Legend Begins: The Texas Rangers, 1823–1845*. Austin: State House Press, 1996.

Williams, Elgin. *The Animating Pursuits of Speculation: Land Traffic in the Annexation of Texas*. London: Oxford University Press, 1949.

Wilson, Francis W., and Dorcas Baumgartner. "The Tennessee–Texas Land Company." *Plum Creek Almanac* 7, no. 2 (1989): 97–100.

Wilson, G. J. N. *The Early History of Jackson County, Georgia*. Edited by W. E. White. Atlanta: Foote & Davies, 1914.

Wilson, James E. "Kentucky Volunteers in the Texas Revolution." *Register of the Kentucky State Historical Society* 11 (1912): 17–28.

Winfrey, Dorman H., and James M. Day, eds. *The Indian Papers of Texas and the Southwest, 1825–1916*. 5 vols. Austin: Texas State Historical Association, 1995.

Winkler, E. W., ed. "The Bexar and Dawson Prisoners." *Quarterly of the Texas State Historical Association* 13, no. 4 (Apr. 1910): 292–394.

———. "Check List of Texas Imprints, 1846–1876." *Southwestern Historical Quarterly* 48 (1944): 217–37.

Woll, Adrián. *Expedicion hecho en Tejas*. Monterrey: Francisco Molina, 1842.

Woodall, Russell. "Callahan, James Hughes." *Handbook of Texas Online*. Accessed June 12, 2010. http://www.tshaonline.org/handbook/online/articles/fca16.

Woodhouse, S. W. *From Texas to San Diego in 1851*. Edited by Andrew Wallace and Richard H. Hevly. Lubbock: Texas Tech University Press, 2007.

Wooster, Robert. "West, Claiborne," *Handbook of Texas Online*. Accessed June 15, 2010. http://www.tshaonline.org/handbook/online/articles/fwe30.

Wright, Muriel H. "Wapanucka Academy, Chickasaw Nation." *Chronicles of Oklahoma* 12 (1934): 402–31.

Wright, William, and John Wright. *Recollections of Western Texas, 1852–1855*. Lubbock: Texas Tech University Press, 1995.

Wyatt, Frederica Burt. *Families of Kimble County*. Vol. 1. Junction, Tex.: Shelton, 1985.

Yeager, Marian, ed. "A Letter from Old Goliad." *Southwestern Historical Quarterly* 47 (1944): 325.

PRIVATELY HELD FAMILY HISTORIES AND MANUSCRIPTS

Babb Family Collection. Cindy H. Chase, Winston-Salem, N.C.

Beall, Elizabeth Rebecca, History, and Beall Family Papers. Steven Jennings Stuart, Greenville, S.C.

Berry, Rheney Lourahama, and Samuel Clinton Neill biographical information. Glenn McVey, Georgetown, Tex.

Brill, Mary, and Solomon Brill Family Records. Utah Rogers, Arlington, Tex.

Brooks, Daniel Baugh, to Robert Brooks. Letters. Hank Wenzler, Katy, Tex.

Callahan, Alzada, Bible. Yvonne Sageser, Seguin, Tex.

"Callahan–Blassingame Incident." Unpublished typescript. Don Watson, Martindale, Tex.
Callahan, James Sanford, Family Bible. Wayne Simpson, Tulsa, Okla.
Campbell, Isaac, Family Records. LoRetta Hughes, Saginaw, Tex.
"Committee of Twenty, Seguin, September 4th, 1854." Broadside. Ron Tyler. Fort Worth, Tex.
Day, Sarah, Prayer Journal. Unpublished. JoBeth Gerrard, Bulverde, Tex.
Descendants of Woodson Blassingame. Janelle Holmes, Dripping Springs, Tex.
Dikes, Mark Washington, Family History. Unpublished typescript. Lisa Lovic Hairston, Rogers, Tex.
"Erskines and Ehringhauses: Scottish and German Americans of North Carolina, Alabama, and Texas." 2009. Unpublished typescript. Chris Klasing, Simpsonville, S.C.
"Family of Erastus H. Harris and Adelaide Harriet McGaughy." Aug. 2013. Unpublished typescript. Wendy Pitre Roostan, Hampshire, England.
Gonzales, Michael, Papers on James Milford Day. Michael Gonzales, New Orleans.
Hankins, Eli, and Elizabeth Hankins Papers. JoBeth Gerrard, Bulverde, Tex.
Hicks, Fabian L., Family History. Prepared by daughter Hercilia Hicks Meadows. Original unpublished manuscript. Janet Graham Theberg, Fredericksburg, Tex.
Jarmon, Dorothy. "Old Ranger Station." Sept. 2012. Unpublished typescript. Dorothy Jarmon, Seguin, Tex.
Jones Family Papers. Candice DuCoin, Round Rock, Tex.
King Family Papers. William Kishbaugh, Winkelman, Ariz.
Lang, George, and Rosine Lang biographical information. Carol Denning, College Station, Tex.
Lawhon Family Papers. Linda Howard, Blanco, Tex.
Martin, James Claxton, Family History. Jackie Pattison, Lumberton, Tex.
McKee, Floyd, Papers and Photographs. (Great-great-great-great grandson of Sarah Hembree Day). Floyd McKee, Seguin, Tex.
McKee, Jody, and Floyd McKee. "The New McKee Family History." 2013. Unpublished manuscript. Floyd McKee, Seguin, Tex.
Medina González Dávila, José. Lipan interviews, field notes, 2009–2011, Coahuila, México. Copy in author's possession.
Mobbs, Naomi, Oral History. 1985. Unpublished typescript. Wayne Simpson, Tulsa, Okla.
Moore, Ike, Papers. Henry Moore, Hillsboro, Tex.
Nichols Family Papers, Billie Jo Nichols Bennett, Latexo, Tex.
Pate Family Bible. Ben Pruett, Orange, Calif.
Pharr, Augustus, and Meekness Amanda Day ancestry records. Katherine I. Mock, Mancos, Colo.
Phillips–Callahan Family History, 1955–1977. Otho Benjamin Phillips to Tommy McDonald, unpublished notes. In author's possession.
Smothers (Smithers) Family History. Unpublished typescript. Nena Smothers, Newport, Wash.
Speiser, Christian, biographical information. Kelly George, Austin.
Tanner Family biographical information. Julie Herald, Killeen, Tex.
"Wenona's Autobiography." Unpublished typescript. JoAnn Horne, San Antonio.
West, Bernice, Papers. (William Trainer's granddaughter). Bernice West, Blanco, Tex.
Wuppermann, Otto, Papers. Gerhard Vowinckel, Hanover, Germany.

Wuppermann Collection. Robert Lundy, Cannon Beach, Ore.
Vidaurri, Santiago, manuscripts. Catalina Roell and Patricia Roell, Monterrey, N.L., Mexico.
Zumwalt, David, and Mary Ann Zumwalt Family Papers. W. L. McKeehan, Houston.

NEWSPAPERS

Abilene (Tex.) Reporter
Alamo Star (San Antonio)
Albany (Tex.) News
Athenian (Athens, Ga.)
Augusta (Ga.) Chronicle
Austin City Gazette
Austin Daily Journal
Austin Republican
Baltimore Sun
Bastrop (Tex.) Advertiser
Blanco County News (Blanco, Tex.)
Blanco (Tex.) Courier
Boletín Oficial (Monterrey, Mexico)
Brazos Courier (Brazoria, Tex.)
Brownsville (Tex.) Herald,
California Farmer and Journal of Useful Sciences (San Francisco)
Charleston (S.C.) Courier
Clarksville (Tex.) Standard
Colorado Gazette and Advertiser (Matagorda, Tex.)
Columbus (Ga.) Enquirer
Comanche (Tex.) Chief
Commercial Advertiser (New York)
Commercial Bulletin (New Orleans)
Constitutional Advocate and Texas Public Advertiser (Brazoria, Tex.)
Daily Advocate (Baton Rouge, La.)
Daily Alta California (San Francisco)
Daily Bulletin (Austin)
Daily Ledger and Texan (San Antonio)
Daily Missouri Republican (St. Louis)
Daily Placer Times and Transcript (San Francisco)
Dallas Morning News
Dallas Weekly Herald
Democratic Telegraph and Texas Register (Houston)
Diario de la Marina (Havana)
El Bejareño (San Antonio)
El Monitor Republicano (Mexico City)
El Ómnibus (Mexico City)
El Restaurador de la Libertad (Monterrey, Mexico)
El Siglo Diez y Nueve (Mexico City)
Federal Union (Milledgeville, Ga.)
Flake's Bulletin (Galveston, Tex.)
Fort Worth (Tex.) Star-Telegram

Galveston (Tex.) Civilian and Gazette
Galveston (Tex.) (Daily, Tri-Weekly, Weekly) News
Galveston (Tex.) Journal
Georgia Citizen (Macon)
Georgia Journal (Milledgeville)
Georgia Telegraph (Macon)
Georgia Weekly Telegraph and Journal & Messenger (Macon)
Gonzales (Tex.) Inquirer
Hondo (Tex.) Anvil
Houston Daily Post
Houston (Daily, Tri-Weekly, Weekly) Telegraph
Huntsville (Tex.) Item
Indianola (Tex.) Bulletin
Kentucky Gazette (Lexington)
La Patria (Saltillo, Mexico)
La Sociedad (Mexico City)
Lockhart (Tex.) Register
Los Angeles Star
Macon (Ga.) Messenger
Macon (Ga.) Telegraph
Matagorda (Tex.) Bulletin
Milledgeville (Ga.) Intelligencer
Mobile (Ala.) Commercial Register and Patriot
Nacogdoches (Tex.) Chronicle
National Banner and Nashville (Tenn.) Whig
National Intelligencer (Washington, D.C.)
New Braunfels (Tex.) Herald-Zeitung
Neu Braunfelser Zeitung (New Braunfels, Tex.)
New Orleans Bee
New Orleans Daily Delta
New Orleans Picayune
New York Daily Tribune
New York Times
Niles Weekly Register (Baltimore)
North American and United States Gazette (Philadelphia, Pa.)
Nueces Valley (Corpus Christi, Tex.)
Pendleton (S.C.) Messenger
Reflector (Milledgeville, Ga.)
Sacramento (Calif.) Daily Union
San Antonio Daily Express
San Antonio Express
San Antonio Herald
San Antonio Ledger
San Antonio Ledger and Texan
San Antonio Light
San Antonio Sentinel
San Antonio Texan
San Antonio Zeitung

San Luis (Tex.) Advocate
Seguin (Tex.) Bulletin
Seguin (Tex.) Enterprise
Seguin (Tex.) Mercury
Southern Banner (Athens, Ga.)
Southern Confederacy (Atlanta)
Southern Intelligencer (Austin)
Southern Recorder (Milledgeville, Ga)
Southern Watchman (Athens, Ga.)
South-Western American (Austin)
Spectator (New York)
State Gazette (Augusta, Ga.)
State Gazette (Charleston, S.C.)
Telegraph and Texas Register (San Felipe, Tex.)
Texan Mercury (Seguin, Tex.)
Texas Christian Advocate (Austin)
Texas Democrat (Austin)
Texas Gazette (Austin)
Texas Gazette and Brazoria Commercial Advertiser
Texas National Register (Washington, Tex.)
Texas Planter (Brazoria)
Texas Presbyterian (Victoria)
Texas Ranger (Washington, Tex.)
Texas Republican (Brazoria)
Texas Sentinel (Austin)
Texas State Gazette (Austin)
Texas State Times (Austin)
Texas Sun (Richmond, Tex.)
Texian Advocate (Victoria, Tex.)
Trinity Advocate (Palestine, Tex.)
Tri-Weekly State Times (Austin)
Union (Galveston, Tex.)
Victoria (Tex.) (Daily) Advocate
Washington (Tex.) American
Weekly Citizen (Houston)
Weekly Journal (Galveston, Tex.)
Weekly State Gazette (Austin)
Weekly Statesman (Austin)
Western Texan (San Antonio)
Williamson County Sun (Georgetown, Tex.)

Index

The letter *f* indicates illustrations; the letter *t* indicates tables.